HB: Aspects of Havergal Brian

HB

Aspects of Havergal Brian

Edited from the Havergal Brian Newsletters
by Jürgen Schaarwächter

Foreword by David J. Brown

Ashgate
Aldershot • Brookfield USA
Singapore • Sydney

© Jürgen Schaarwächter and the contributors, 1997

All rights reserved. No part of this publication may be reproduced, stored in a retrieval system, or transmitted in any form or by any means, electronic, mechanical, photocopying, recording, or otherwise without the prior permission of the publisher.

Published by
Ashgate Publishing Limited
Gower House
Croft Road
Aldershot
Hants GU11 3HR
England

Ashgate Publishing Company
Old Post Road
Brookfield
Vermont 05036–9704
USA

The authors have asserted their moral right under the Copyright, Designs and Patents Act, 1988, to be identified as the authors of this work.

British Library Cataloguing in Publication Data

HB: Aspects of Havergal Brian
  1. Brian, Havergal, 1876–1972—Criticism and interpretation.
  I. Schaarwächter, Jürgen.
  780.9'2

ISBN 1-84014-238-3

Library of Congress Cataloging-in-Publication Data

HB: aspects of Havergal Brian/edited from the Havergal Brian newsletters by Jürgen Schaarwächter: foreword by David J. Brown.
    p. cm.
  'Catalogue of works by Havergal Brian': pp. 405–11.
  Includes bibliographical references and index.
  ISBN 1-84014-238-3 (hb)
  1. Brian, Havergal, 1876–1972. I. Schaarwächter, Jürgen.
  II. *Newsletter* (Havergal Brian Society).
  ML410.B8447H3   1997
  780'.92—dc21   97-39981
  [B]   CIP
                                                                MN

ISBN 1 84014 238 3

This book is printed on acid free paper

Printed in Great Britain by The Ipswich Book Company, Suffolk.

Contents

Foreword	vii
Preface	ix
List of books quoted	xiii

Life and personality

Harold Truscott: Havergal Brian - as *I* knew him	3
Bertram B. Walker: A voice from the past	33
Philip Scowcroft: Havergal Brian and Elgar	34
Malcolm MacDonald: "Dear Crusoe ... Always your Freitag": the Brian letters at McMaster University	37
Walter Allum: Friendship with Havergal Brian	53
Reginald Nettel: Aspects of Brian. With an excursus by Godfrey Berry and comments by Malcolm MacDonald, John Aldridge, Robert Timlin and Godfrey Berry	61
John Pickard: Havergal Brian's productive discontinuity. With a comment by Martyn Becker	93
Havergal Brian talking to Robert Simpson and Jeffrey Anderson	105

Symphonies

Malcolm MacDonald: Havergal Brian's letter to Herbert Thompson: some implications	127
Malcolm MacDonald: *The Gothic*: music and meaning. With a comment by Larry Alexander	130
Christopher J. Kettle: *The Gothic* revisited	148
Paul Rapoport: Beethoven's Ninth Symphony in relation to Brian's First	162
Robert Simpson in conversation with Stephen Johnson	167
Graham Saxby: Havergal Brian's Second Symphony	170
Martyn Becker: Brian's Third Symphony	193
Martin O'Leary: Havergal Brian's *Sinfonia Tragica*	198
Harold Truscott: Thoughts on Havergal Brian's Seventh Symphony	216
Martin O'Leary: Brian and Mahler: four symphonies in comparison	224
Tim Shuker: Havergal Brian's Thirteenth Symphony - not unlucky 13!	227
Rodney Stephen Newton: Havergal Brian's Fourteenth Symphony - an alternative view	233

Myer Fredman/Robert Simpson: Preparing Brian's scores for performance … 242
Barry Cronin: Arcadia v. Elysium: some thoughts on Symphony No. 27 … 244
Rodney Stephen Newton: Some thoughts on the 30th … 248
Harold Truscott: Havergal Brian and the single-movement symphony … 255

Miscellany

Neil Starling: Havergal Brian's large-scale choral works before 1914 - a preliminary investigation. With comments on Psalm 23 by Larry Alexander and Malcolm MacDonald … 267
Reginald Nettel: *Cleopatra*'s librettist … 311
Granville Bantock: Havergal Brian and *The Tigers* … 318
Malcolm MacDonald: Let the Roar of the *Tigers* be Heard in the Land ... … 333
Martyn Becker: Brian's impatient *Tigers* … 339
Mike Smith: Brian's word-setting … 342
Rodney Stephen Newton: Havergal Brian and the bare 5th. With a comment by Ted Heaton … 349
Harold Truscott/Peter Hill: Havergal Brian's solo piano music … 355
Rodney Stephen Newton: Havergal Brian and the percussion section: a broad survey … 381
Christopher J. Kettle: Brian, Mahler, Shostakovitch and Schoenberg: some idle thoughts. With comments by Larry Alexander and Malcolm MacDonald … 390
Robert Simpson: The Brian revival … 401

Catalogue of works by Havergal Brian … 405

Index … 413

Foreword

When Havergal Brian died, on 28 November 1972, he was ten months into his 97th year: a long life by any standards. He tends still to be regarded by newcomers to his life and work as a kind of *Guinness Book of Records* composer - the longest lived, the most prolific symphonist of the 20th century, the creator of the longest symphony ever written, the most neglected of composers. None of these actually is or was true, probably not even the last, though the fact that when he died not a note of his music had ever been commercially recorded silently signals the depth of his then obscurity. It is good that we can discard these spurious statistical extremes, because in doing so we are compelled back to Brian's music itself, and the ineluctable fact that only its intrinsic quality will dictate whether merely his name survives as a footnote curio in the future history of music, or whether the best of his work achieves a unique, honoured, and loved place in the experience of a broad range of listeners - as seems to be happening.

For more of his life than we might think now, Havergal Brian *was* intermittently known to small numbers of other musicians as a composer at least of interest, but not until it was almost too late did someone emerge who was able to bring about sufficient performances in a medium that reached enough listeners to begin generating a wider awareness. From 1954 until 1980 Robert Simpson, through his work as a radio producer for the BBC Third Programme, did this, and all who now enjoy Brian's music owe him a prime debt of gratitude. Through this realization generated by the broadcasts that Simpson organized of some Brian symphonies, above all *The Gothic*, and sidestepping the squirts of disdain that some professional commentators felt impelled to emit at what they regarded as special pleading, others began to notice, to take seriously, and to speak in praise of Brian's music. In the last decade of his life he became something of a celebrity, which he must have quietly enjoyed even as he claimed insulation from the world's praise or indifference. Contrary to custom, his death did not bring any sharp downturn of curiosity about his work, rather a growth in interest, and it was not a surprise when in 1974 two young enthusiasts named Martin Grossel and James Reid Baxter mooted, through the columns of music magazines, the establishment of a Havergal Brian Society.

The obvious prime purpose of any organization formed on the behalf of a composer is to promote his music: in Brian's case this was more difficult than almost any other one can think of. There was absolutely no performing tradition, in that no one of his works had ever achieved more than very isolated performance. Almost all of them were in manuscript, many still awaited their premières, and - most crucially - there was no part of his output, apart from some solo songs and part-songs, and a handful of piano pieces, which did not involve less than standard orchestral forces and often considerably more, and thus would not be highly expensive to perform. None of the solo songs had entered any soloist's personal repertoire, and the few piano works were formidably academic in title, if not altogether in nature, as well as difficult to play. A large body of chamber and instrumental works such as that which graced the output of Edmund Rubbra, or the kind of pieces tailored for non-professional performers that, say, Armstrong Gibbs wrote in large numbers, were simply not there.

The fledgling Havergal Brian Society thus had an immediate major problem in maintaining the interest of members, in that it was impossible to promote and supply a steady stream of small-scale performances and recordings while bigger projects gestated. When the original founders had to withdraw in 1975, I realized that though I had no knowledge whatever of running an organization, my professional experience in trade journalism would be useful to go on producing the *Newsletter* the Society obviously needed. With a membership too small and scattered to make frequent meetings possible, this type of regular contact was vital, and as any diary of events was going to be extremely short if not non-existent, the remainder of the publication had to be well worth reading!

Brian's work itself came to the rescue here. In short, there was a great deal to write about. His output - not vast as often erroneously assumed, but large enough - was not only unknown but largely undiscussed. That it is now reasonably well-ventilated is largely due to the existence of the Havergal Brian Society *Newsletter* and the expertise and insight that the authors represented in this volume brought - and most happily continue to bring - to bear. This in itself is of course a tribute to the range and depth of Havergal Brian himself. It has been a particular pleasure for me to read again so many of these contributions and to be struck all over again by their high quality: and not only as one would expect from those reasonably familiar in the world of British music like Malcolm (Calum) MacDonald, Harold Truscott, and Lewis Foreman, but also the rank-and-file members of the Society who have been impelled by their enthusiasm for Brian's music to share their thoughts and insights with the rest of us. Jürgen Schaarwächter has performed a signal service in bringing them back into the light; and what he has demonstrated in his devoted excavation and assemblage from our pages is not only how much can be said about Brian's music, but how many other avenues and areas within this inexhaustible composer these pioneer writings open up.

David J. Brown, Secretary/Editor, The Havergal Brian Society, 1975-1992

Preface

This book is closely connected with the Havergal Brian Society, and all the articles reprinted here first appeared in the Society's *Newsletters*, sometimes in as many as ten instalments published over a period of more than three years. The first five numbers of the *Newsletter* had been edited by Martin C. Grossel (and James Reid Baxter, Nos 1 and 2). With No. 6 (July 1976) the editorship was taken over by David J. Brown. (He has previously published without using his "J." initial, and is not to be confused with Professor David Brown of Southampton University, the music scholar and authority on Russian music. David *J.* Brown is undoubtedly among the authorities on Havergal Brian.) After *Newsletter* No. 100 Brown relinquished his functions as Editor (to Kevin Mandry) and as Secretary (to Dr Alan Marshall), so as to have more time for his own books. He subsequently became a Vice-President of the Havergal Brian Society and is now also its Chairman.

Introducing himself in *Newsletter* 6, David J. Brown wrote:

> This, my first Brian Society *Newsletter* as Secretary, has two purposes. It provides current news of Brian performances and publications, as I hope succeeding regular editions will continue to do, but also it is designed to function as an introduction to the Society for new members. Therefore, for the sake of the latter, I ask existing members to kindly bear with a brief reiteration of some facts about the Society which they will know already.

The Havergal Brian Society was founded by Martin Grossel and James Reid Baxter in 1974,[1] following the announcement of their in-

---

[1] Don Goodsell: *The time before this*, in *Newsletter* 8 (XI 1976), p. 4, tells us, in a different context: "You say 'The Havergal Brian Society was founded ...' but in truth this should read 'The second' or 'The New Havergal Brian Society' for a society of the same name and with the same aims was founded in the 1950s and operated until well into the 1960s. We had no regular newsletter, but we did, by bringing Brian's name before conductors and performers, pave the way to his wider acceptance. All record companies which had shown some sympathy towards modern music were approached, and though no commercial recording resulted directly from our efforts, we did have discs cut from recordings of performances for private use by our members. These were played to friends in our homes, and at gramophone societies, and by dint of the enthusiasm of members, spread as wide afield as Bavaria and South Africa, the name Havergal Brian was lifted from obscurity, at least for those more adventurous spirits who were not content to 'know what they liked and liked only what they knew'. Throughout the years that the 'first' society was active, Brian was always a helpful and agreeable correspondent, assisting us with the 'cataloguing' of his works - his letters always written in the same green ink. It is difficult, looking back, to assess how much the first (if indeed it was the first) society achieved. So much credit must go to those few who supported him at the BBC, and without whose efforts few if any of us would have come to know the name of Havergal Brian, let alone have the opportunity to hear his music played by orchestras of the top rank. Yet there is much that a society can achieve, however humble or young its members. Brian, like many of the greatest creative artists, was not a man to court mass popularity, but he was certainly not indifferent to the wave of support that followed the first performances of his Eighth and Ninth Symphonies. Might it be that the encouragement he

tention in letters to journals in the music and recording field. Later in the same year, a notice announcing the formation of the Society was circulated to interested persons, describing the Society's aims and objectives. These were as follows - and as far as I am concerned, substantially still stand:

> 'Our initial aim is to act as an information centre publicizing future performances of the music, answering queries about the composer, and to set up a library of tapes of the music together with a collection of the composer's letters (or copies of these). We will try to prepare a complete list of the missing scores and publicize this. We will assist people in obtaining material for performances and whenever possible try to arrange recitals of the smaller works like the piano pieces and the songs. In the longer term we hope to issue limited edition recordings of the smaller works ... .'[2]

It grew clear that there was (and still is) a great deal of research to be done, notwithstanding Malcolm MacDonald's highly important three-volume treatment of the symphonies and a few minor works. Although articles about Brian did of course appear in other journals, it was the *Newsletter* which became the prime forum for writing on Brian and his work.

As might be expected, it was going to need substantial financial resources to meet the declared objectives. The Society soon built up an enormous financial basis for sponsoring performances, recordings and the publication of books and printed music, and thus succeeded in "promoting" the music of an individual composer whose significance has never really been recognized in international music circles: in fact, Brian shows up as inferior the quality of many a so-called "first-rate" composer. It is of course clear that not all his compositions are of the same high quality, but whose are? It might have been better to pick out the best of his works, instead of getting Marco Polo to record all 32 symphonies, with not always first-rate results.

Brown's achievements as Secretary are enormous. He helped to create a Society with solid foundations, one which with the passage of time grew in effectiveness and, unlike the Bantock, Bridge and Boughton Societies, came ever closer to achieving its declared aims - akin to the Delius and Bax Societies and the Ralph Vaughan Williams Trust (although the Trust has aims of a different sort). Not only that, Brown made the *Newsletter* into the research forum which it is today, particularly in areas yet to be tackled by Malcolm MacDonald, and providing a platform for heterodox opinions.

The present volume reproduces from *Newsletters* 1-100 most of the articles of substantial interest, complemented by a considerable number of letters to the

---

received from so many quarters gave some of the stimulus for that great blossoming of creative output that filled the last 20 years of his remarkable life?"
[2] David J. Brown: Editorial. In *Newsletter* 6 (VII 1976), p. 1.

Editor (linked to the articles to which they relate).[3] Three major sequences of articles were nevertheless omitted: Malcolm MacDonald's work on Havergal Brian's journalism, to be replaced by the six projected volumes of *Havergal Brian on Music* (Volume 1, London: Toccata Press, 1986, Volumes 2-6 in preparation), Malcolm MacDonald's unfinished article on Brian and Variation Form,[4] and an unfinished article on the opera *The Tigers*, extracted from Adrian Ure's Ph.D. dissertation for the University of St Andrews. For the rest, I have omitted a couple of minor texts[5] and most of the reports and reviews of performances, recordings and publications, even though these in their own way reflect other aspects of the Society's objectives. The articles have been arranged in three main sections, clearly showing where there is still much need of research and where Brian research has been concentrated hitherto: namely on the symphonies (and chiefly on just a few of them), on the opera *The Tigers*, on the great choral works and on numerous minor questions. A great deal of research yet needs to be done if we are to have one day a worthy picture of that multi-faceted "Composer of the Year for 1971".[6]

Most of the authors still living (Martin J. Anderson, Martyn Becker, Godfrey Berry, David J. Brown, Barry Cronin, Brian Duke, Peter Hill, Christopher J. Kettle, Robert Keys, A. J. Luker, Malcolm MacDonald, Professor Vivian Moses, Rodney Stephen Newton, David Perrins, Graham Saxby, Philip L. Scowcroft, Tim Shuker, Robert Timlin, Owen Toller, Adrian Ure, David Yule and Jean Furnivall, Havergal Brian's daughter; from Australia Myer Fredman; from California Larry Alexander; from Ireland Martin O'Leary and Robert Simpson) have kindly given their consent to reprinting, as have Guy Rickards for the late Harold Truscott and Mrs V. M. Walker for Bertram B. Walker. Malcolm

---

[3] Two texts on one subject written (and published) independently which are but strongly linked are separated by three empty lines only.
[4] In *Newsletters* 19 (IX-X 1978), pp. 2-4, 20 (XI-XII 1978), pp. 3-5, 22 (III-IV 1979), pp. 1-3, and 25 (IX-X 1979), pp. 3-5.
[5] The following minor texts were omitted, due to reasons of extent of the book: Malcolm MacDonald: The first performance of the Concerto for Orchestra, in *Newsletter* 3 (V 1975), pp. 3-4; Graham Hatton: *Turandot, Prinzessin von China*, in *Newsletter* 7 (VIII 1976), p. 3; Reginald Nettel: *Ordeal of Music* and after, in *Newsletter* 7, pp. 5-6; Harold Truscott: British symphonies of European stature, in *Newsletter* 8 (XI 1976), p. 3; Malcolm MacDonald: Brian's fanfare from *The Grotesques*, in *Newsletter* 10 (III-IV 1977), pp. 2-3; Malcolm MacDonald: The importance of *Elegy*, in *Newsletter* 10, pp. 4-5; Malcolm MacDonald: English Suite No. 4, in *Newsletter* 12 (VII-VIII 1977), pp. 3-4; John Aldridge: How many masterpieces make a master?, in *Newsletter* 21 (I-II 1979), pp. 3-5, with a commenting letter to the editor by Bernard G. Counsell, in *Newsletter* 22 (III-IV 1979), p. 7; Martyn Becker: Havergal Brian - a personal odyssey, in *Newsletter* 52 (III-IV 1984), pp. 4-5; Christopher J. Kettle: Second thoughts on the Third Symphony, in *Newsletter* 78 (VII-VIII 1988), pp. 4-8; Adrian Ure: Some notes on Havergal Brian's work to 1907, in *Newsletter* 93 (I-II 1991), pp. 5-6; Paul R. Kettle: Second quality? [On the Second Symphony], in *Newsletter* 96 (VII-VIII 1991), pp. 5-6; and Symphony No. 30 introduced ... An interview with Calum MacDonald, in *Newsletter* 97 (IX-X 1991), pp. 3-4. For further omitted texts, giving more detailed information on the work-list, cf. p. 405 in the present book.
[6] The title of the Ralph Vaughan Williams' Award, given annually by the Composers Guild of Great Britain.

MacDonald, Martin O'Leary, Dr John Pickard and Professor Dr Paul Rapoport have revised and proof-read their articles, Lewis Foreman and Malcolm MacDonald the work-catalogue; Dr Alan Marshall has very kindly proof-read the whole book most thoroughly, giving lots of invaluable help and being rather more a co-editor than anything else; Gerd Hupperich has helped me typing the music examples and verifying index entries; and finally I am especially grateful to David J. Brown for contributing a foreword. The Havergal Brian music examples are reproduced by kind permission of the Havergal Brian Estate/United Music Publishers Ltd; further reproducing permission has been given by Stainer & Bell Ltd (Ralph Vaughan Williams, A *Sea* Symphony. Copyright 1926 by Stainer & Bell Ltd), Universal Edition (London) Ltd (Arnold Schoenberg, Chamber Symphony No. 1, Op. 9. Copyright 1922, 1950 by Universal Edition) and Chester Music Ltd (Jean Sibelius, Symphony No. 6, Op. 104. Copyright by Edition Wilhelm Hansen).

Jürgen Schaarwächter

List of books quoted

Reginald Nettel: *Ordeal by Music. The Strange Experience of Havergal Brian.* Oxford/London/Edinburgh/Glasgow/New York/Toronto/Melbourne/Capetown/Bombay/Calcutta/Madras: Oxford University Press, 1945.

Reginald Nettel: *Havergal Brian and his Music.* London: Dennis Dobson, 1976.

Reginald Nettel: *Music in the Five Towns 1840-1914. A Study of Social Influence of Music in an Industrial District.* Oxford/London/Edinburgh/Glasgow/New York/Toronto/Melbourne/Capetown/Bombay/Calcutta/Madras: Oxford University Press, 1944.

Lewis Foreman: *Havergal Brian and the Performance of his Orchestral Music. A History and Sourcebook.* London: Thames, 1976.

Malcolm MacDonald: *The Symphonies of Havergal Brian.* London/New York/White Plains: Kahn & Averill / Taplinger / Pro / Am Music Resources, 1974 (2nd edn 1983) (Volume 1), 1978 (2nd edn 1991) (Volume 2) and 1983 (Volume 3).

Malcolm MacDonald: *Havergal Brian - perspective on the music.* London: Triad, 1972.

Kenneth Eastaugh: *Havergal Brian - the making of a composer.* London: George G. Harrap, 1976.

Paul Rapoport: *Opus Est. Six Composers from Northern Europe.* London/New York: Kahn & Averill, 1978 (2nd edn 1985).

Harold Truscott/Paul Rapoport: *Havergal Brian's Gothic Symphony. Two Studies.* With Havergal Brian's article *How the "Gothic" Symphony came to be written* reprinted. Little Heath (Hertfordshire): Havergal Brian Society, 1978.

Life and personality

Harold Truscott: Havergal Brian - as *I* knew him[1]

That Havergal was a great composer - one of the two or three greatest in the history of British music - has been axiomatic for me since I first studied the *Gothic* Symphony and the vocal score of *The Tigers* during the mid-'30s. Further knowledge of his music has only confirmed that opinion. As a man, he was a truly human mixture, although personally I find it difficult to the point of impossibility to reconcile the man I knew as Havergal Brian with the more lurid revelations that have been made about him in recent years. He could be kind, generous, a very good friend, genuinely moved by one's successes or troubles, and, in the latter case, trying to help as much as he could, if only with real sympathy. Against this, he had a vivid verbal imagination, and would draw on this at times, almost as though he were compelled to do so, and depart from the truth in silly ways. I knew him in all these guises.

I would like to look at him, as I knew him indeed, and as I most want to remember him. I first met him in 1947 through my writing to the late Reginald Nettel. He passed my letter on to Brian and the latter then wrote to me. He said that he would like to meet me but it would have to be a little later on. He wrote again and arranged a meeting for a particular Sunday. He early adopted my wife and I; I was 33, my wife nearly 12 years younger, when we first met Brian. Here is a brief quotation from a letter of his dated 26 August 1949: "Dear Harold and Margaret" (he almost invariably linked us in this way - I have some letters addressed "Dear Harold" but more addressed to us both), "As you are both so young I feel like a father unto his children. All the same it was a delightful experience to have you both here and I hope you did not return too tired". I have other letters in which he describes us as "a son and a daughter". On 13 July 1950, when we were expecting our first baby, Brian wrote "Whatever else you lack - courage you do not lack. A baby, a symphony and trio - in a world falling to pieces. We do congratulate you both and are sure the expected will be a comfort to both of you". Later in the same letter he wrote: "I hope you will complete your symphony and when I am free I shall expect to see the *score*". In the same letter, referring to a chance of a broadcast of the overture *The Tinker's Wedding*, which seemed to have fallen through, he said: "As my father once remarked, 'In a world of liars - who tells the truth?'"; a significant quotation, for Brian, in some ways.

I shall keep autobiography out of these articles as much as possible, but a little there must be, to explain some of the quotations I shall make from Brian's letters. The baby referred to never materialized - alive. About this time my wife apparently developed a disease which was not diagnosed for some time; I say apparently, because whatever it was eventually went away, and it was certainly not

---

[1] From *Newsletters* 32 (XI-XII 1980), pp. 3-6, 33 (I-II 1981), pp. 5-8, 34 (III-IV 1981), pp. 6-7 and 36 (VII-VIII 1981), pp. 3-5.

what was diagnosed. What was diagnosed was disseminated sclerosis of the spine. The immediate point is Brian's reaction to this, shown in a large number of letters, of which I quote from two. The first is dated 22 March 1950: "I am really very sorry for you both in such a pack of trouble and you will have to fight to get out of it, for we live in a changing world in which nobody seems to care, things which do change sometimes have a fantastic appearance". Later in the same letter: "Poor Margaret, give her my love and if I can get into a mood which will propel this body to you, I will call and see her. But for heaven's sake take care and let me know what the specialist has to say about her". The second is dated 14 May 1950: "I am really very sorry about your doleful letter. I would have thought it was not beyond the skill of doctors to diagnose Margaret's complaint. If they cannot diagnose it how can they treat it? Do try to brace up your mind and overcome it - I know it is easy to give advice - but, *any* words are cold comfort".

What actually happened with regard to that first baby was this: the specialist Brian refers to put my wife, through our own doctor, on injections containing arsenic. But the first one laid her out for four hours, quite unconscious, and it was obvious that the injections would not do. Our doctor had it altered to a medicine containing a certain quantity of arsenic. Some months later our doctor gave up practice, virtually having had a breakdown, went away and his practice was taken over by a young doctor. When this one first saw my wife, he looked at her card - she was about seven months pregnant at this time - and said "Of course, this medicine that was prescribed was stopped?" She told him it had not been, and he was appalled. He had her in hospital that evening, and the baby was born - dead. It had, in fact, been dead from three months. Brian's reaction to this was: "My dear Harold, I am really distressed (so is Mrs Brian) by your letter and no words of mine can help, I fear - I should like to know what Margaret's reactions are, that is, in health; for I've no experience through life of anyone I have known giving birth to a *dead* baby. Under the circumstances you will both have less responsibility during your removal from St Aubyn's Rd. For heaven's sake, don't talk about the *Gothic* or any other symphony until your trouble has cleared".

This much autobiography was necessary to put into focus Brian's sympathetic reactions - and I cannot put into words how much his letters meant to us both at this time. The reference to *The Gothic* concerns an analysis of this work Brian asked me to do. I had already studied the mighty work for a considerable period long before I met its composer, and the idea of an analysis had been in my mind for quite a long time. I had so far done nothing about it in writing, however. Brian's suggestion sparked it off. But I felt that I needed another session with the score, and it was through his trying to get one for me from Cranz that he eventually discovered that the firm had moved to 8 Denmark St, W.C. And this is where difficulties came in. He was annoyed, to begin with, because they had made this move and had not informed him; on top of that, he could get no satisfaction from Cranz. On 11 October 1949, he wrote: "About the Cranz matter there is silence and I am somewhat surprised that *nobody* is surprised about it.

Cranz of Brussels has not written - although I pointed out to him that when the London firm published the opera I handed to them hundreds of orchestral band parts of the dances and variations which cost me over £100 for the copying. Apart from intervals of lying fallow I've never ceased to write and, apart from the *Gothic*, no attempt has been made to produce any of the symphonies. Perhaps the Cranz revelation of the loathsome underground operation may deter further large works". I am not sure just what Brian meant by "loathsome underground operation"; certainly by this time he seems to have got it into his head that there was a plot to withhold scores of his music from him, and it may be that his final words "may deter further large works" partly explain - although they cannot be the whole reason - why from that time on there were no more symphonies on anything like the scale of the first four. Why there should have been any such plot I cannot think, and this may have been simply a phobia on Brian's part; but, for whatever reason, Cranz certainly were behaving peculiarly.

I have no idea to what attempted performance of *The Gothic* Brian refers; I did ask him once in a letter, but to this query he never gave an answer. It could hardly be a reference to Goossens in Cincinnati, for that never got off the ground; but what else?

To pursue for the moment the question of an analysis of *The Gothic*; in another part of the letter of 26 August 1949, from which I have already quoted, Brian wrote: "Two people, Nettel and Dagg [Norman V. Dagg, editor of *Modern Mystic*], attempted an analysis of it and like most swimmers who attempt the Channel, gave it up. When I asked Bantock what he intended to do next, after his analysis of *The Tigers*, he replied - 'The *Gothic* Symphony: I have already started on it'. Pity he did not live to complete it - for he was *en rapport* with it".

I did eventually manage to borrow a score of the *Gothic* Symphony from Dr Greenhouse Alt, then Principal of the Trinity College of Music, through a note that Brian wrote to him and which I presented. He lent it willingly, and when I asked him how long I might keep it he replied "As long as you like, within reason; if we want it back we will let you know". I had it, in fact, for about three and a half years, when at last there did come a note intimating that the College would like it to be returned. But long before that I had gone through a fairly gruelling examination on the work, maintained over a number of visits, by Brian himself. He did it in the form of talk and questions, supplemented by my playing longish stretches of it, mostly from the first three movements but with some from the *Te Deum*, on the piano; this delighted him, for they were from memory. He told me at this time of Tovey playing it through at sight, from the score, which Brian held on the piano stand for him. But, well before this examination was over, Brian wrote to me, on 25 May 1950, partly about some programme notes of mine that he had read "I like the programme notes - they are of splendid unconventional quality. I once had a similar enthusiasm as you evince for these 18th century composers, Johann Christian Bach, etc., but I failed to find anyone else who even had the slightest knowledge of or interest in his music. You seem well supported with *your* 18th century composers. I should imagine that you know all about the *Gothic* by now and it is a pity that you continue to be hindered from writing your analysis of it". Later in the same letter he referred to Bantock and his analysis of *The Tigers*, which, when finished, "Made a small book with twenty-six music examples - which was the reason it was refused by *Musical Times* - its length. Bantock worked at that opera as long as you have worked at the *Gothic* and I don't know what happened to his writings. I felt sorry for him when he showed me the letter of refusal. I certainly knew where *I* stood and was not surprised". I am not surprised, either, but not for Brian's reason. I am at a loss to understand how either Brian or Bantock ever expected a magazine such as *Musical Times* to accept for publication "a small book"; it was quite the wrong venue. I mentioned this to Brian the next time I saw him, and he shot a look at me, very penetrating, as though he was trying to size up exactly why I said this, and then said, very abruptly, "You're right, of course; Bantock didn't use his brains over that". I could never find out, however, why no more sensible outlet was tried, or if it was. Perhaps there is something about this in the Bantock letters.[2]

I did eventually write my analysis of *The Gothic*, with which Brian expressed himself as very pleased indeed; but I have not got it today, for he never returned it to me. He promised to on various occasions, but when I visited him he said he could not find it, and even intimated that he had already returned it - which he had not. I often wondered what eventually happened to it. However, the best of it is now in the one contained in *Two Studies*; and I wonder sometimes what he would have thought of that. There is another ironic coda. On 17 February 1958, Brian wrote to me, as part of a longer letter: "I wonder you never wrote that essay on the *Gothic* [! - well, he was 82 and his memory was failing]. Had *you* written the *Gothic* I should have spread myself on the *Te Deum* and particularly on the climax of the whole symphony in that vast processional line 'Judex crederis esse venturus'. I don't think I have surpassed that climax, when the procession is halted by 4 distant trumpets and a long wail in the high register of a distant soprano. Sometimes I wonder who was that voice. I cannot recall any singer who would suggest it as I heard it. And that 'Judex', with its immense orchestra and four distant choirs - crying 'Judex crederis' - is my tribute to Hans Richter. I think my old schoolmaster and Hans Richter taught me all I know".

Obviously, the "disappearance" of the full score of *The Tigers* dates from that removal of Cranz from Langham St to Denmark St in 1949; and its reappearance recently at those same premises, 8 Denmark St, now occupied by Southern Music, seems to indicate that it was there all the time when Cranz could not find it! On a postcard dated 17 September 1949, Brian wrote:

> I don't like the appearance of the Cranz matter. Apparently their depot at Denmark St has been handed to *Agents* at 8, Denmark St. When I rang up the other day the people at Denmark St said they were all at sixes and sevens and Miss Pursey of Cranz was ill and 'never comes now to town'. When the contracts with Cranz were

---

[2] Bantock's analysis of *The Tigers* is reprinted below - without, however, any music examples (pp. 318-333).

made *originally* I wrote to a then well known composer and told him of what appeared to me to be a piece of luck. I remember his reply - 'Surely - you are not trying to make a friend of your enemy - Impossible!'

Referring back to the question of programme notes and analyses, only two days later, on 19 September 1949, Brian wrote to me: "Thanks for letter and MS. This promises to be interesting and what you say in your letter about the manner of approach to it - is, for me, *the only way*. Composition cannot be taught, in spite of so many official opinions to the contrary". The manuscript referred to was a study of *Schubert's Forms*, which I had written during the War, and in the accompanying letter I had outlined my own idea on this subject: that you cannot teach anyone to compose, you can only induce, develop and to some extent guide the vital spark in someone who already has it. That spark, if absent, cannot be put there, but if it is there and is sufficiently strong there are no extraneous rules it *must* obey, it can only go its own way, impose its own rules on itself, which is what happened with Schubert - and, of course, Brian.

Now, the subject of *The Tigers*. Here I come up against that side of Brian which, for whatever reason, would insist on departing from the truth. I had from him, altogether, three verbal accounts of how that opera came into being, and one other, in a letter, which I shall reproduce, for I believe it to be nearer the truth than anything else. Like all artists, Brian needed an audience. As we know, for long enough, as a composer, he was denied one. How much this affected him as a man it is difficult to say, or whether, if the recognition he had begun to have accorded him in the early years of this century had continued and grown, he would have been the same man or developed differently. In the absence of such recognition one can only take him as he was, and assume that that experience of supreme neglect must have left a very big mark upon him. Naturally, he affected not to care, but that not only did not deceive his listener, it was easy to see that it did not deceive him. No composer goes on writing, producing, as he did, for so long, purely as a reaction to inner creative prompting, and with no thought, hope or care for performance of what he writes. He may not get it, as Brian did not for so many years - nor is he the only one - but it would be foolish in the extreme to suppose that he does not want it, and his attempted pretence of not caring is natural but not designed to deceive anyone, least of all himself.

But Brian needed an audience in a different way. At times he was, it seems, driven rather as Berlioz was, and compulsively told stories because they were, or seemed to be, good stories. These were always very convincingly told; only as contradictions crept in on later occasions - sometimes straight denials - did one begin to realize that he was often romancing, and at times did not even remember his previous romance on the same subject. Such things may well have been part of his shield against the buffetings he had received over the years. The case of Brian, *The Tigers*, and I is an example. His first account to me of the writing of that opera ran in this way: about 1916 Beecham began to press Brian to write an opera for his British National Opera Co., and for a time Brian, being occupied with other things, put Beecham off. At last Beecham cornered him - on the steps

8   *Life and personality*

of Birmingham Town Hall - and would take no answer but "Yes". Brian gave in, put aside what he had been doing, wrote his libretto, on a subject that had long interested him, and wrote the music, after numerous sketches. Brian did not say how long all this took. When the score was complete he packed it up and sent it to Beecham in London. Two years or so later he had heard nothing from Beecham, not even an acknowledgement of the receipt of the score. He had to go to London on business, so decided to visit Beecham and find out what had happened to the score. When he arrived Beecham was not there, but someone from the Official Receiver's office was, going through Beecham's flat - the conductor having one of his periodical bankruptcies. Brian said what he had come for, whereupon the man fished around in a stack of items and came up with a huge parcel and handed it to Brian asking him if that was what he wanted. It was - unopened, exactly as Brian had sent it. Beecham had not even looked at it. The O. R. told Brian that in going through Beecham's things he had found over 2,000 unopened letters stacked away in a cupboard. Now this is what Brian told me on that first occasion: except that I have put it into the third person it is practically word for word as he told it to me.

Some months after this, Brian started again on the theme of *The Tigers*; he began to tell the same story, including the steps of Birmingham Town Hall, and I was on the point of reminding him that he had already told me about it; but something stopped me. It may have been that I sensed that he would not like being interrupted. Anyway, I was glad I let him run on, for what followed was a different story. He grumbled because he had allowed Beecham to persuade him, only to find when he was in the middle of writing the opera that the B. N. O. C. had broken up for lack of funds. "So I was left with it on my hands", he growled. "Having got so far, I had to finish it. But there was no performance, and no chance of any". "You never sent it to him?" I asked him. His reply was a facer. "Of course not; what was the use?" I just goggled at him. "But you told me before ..." I said, and went on through the earlier version of the story. He listened to me quite calmly, and did not bat an eyelid. He simply denied that he had ever told me anything like it, and said that I had a marvellous imagination, but he wished I would not use it on him. I was deflated, and left it at that; I was not looking for an argument with him, still less a quarrel, and that, I am sure, is what it would have meant if I had persisted. That was version No. 2.

No. 3 came a few months later again, when he returned to the subject of *The Tigers*. At this period he seemed, so far as I could see, compelled to talk about the work, and I believe that, on each of these occasions following the first one, he had quite forgotten that he had spoken to me about it before, or what he had said. He had also forgotten a letter he wrote to me on the same subject. With No. 3 I wondered what was coming, and even thought for a moment that he might be going to repeat No. 1. However, although it started, like the other two, with Beecham, Brian did this time complete it and sent it to Beecham, who returned it later saying that he wished he could do it, for it was the most original opera he had encountered; but it would be almost impossible to stage, and there were no funds available, etc. That was the last of *The Tigers*, in Brian's conversations with me. He maintained, at the same time, that he had discussed the opera with people well versed in stage technique and production (no names mentioned), and they had agreed that, although difficult, it was possible to produce *The Tigers*, with the right sort of stage - and of these there were not many; only Covent Garden and Drury Lane, in fact, in this country.

On the occasion of version No. 2 Brian asked me if I would write to Sir John Anderson at Covent Garden about the opera. Brian said, rightly, that if he himself wrote it would have no effect, for naturally he would be biased; but that if I, a member of the public, wrote about it persuasively enough, adding a list of other signatures - Vaughan Williams, Benjamin Britten and Lennox Berkeley were among the names he suggested - it might at least get the work looked at. I agreed, but my letters to VW and the others were never answered. I duly wrote to Sir John Anderson without the benefit of their signatures, pointing out, with detail, the great originality of the opera, and the fact that if it had been performed at the right time, we should not now be naming *Peter Grimes* as the *first* great modern English opera. I cannot now remember how I put it, but this is what it came to. Obviously, if I had been sending a letter which had Benjamin Britten's name appended to it, I should have omitted the reference to *Peter Grimes*. But since Britten was not interested I saw no reason why I should not state my real belief, even in a mild form; for I really believed (and still do) that *The Tigers* far surpasses *Grimes* in sheer artistic merit and stature. Needless to say, my letter to Sir John Anderson remained unanswered.

Finally, on the subject of *The Tigers*, here is the letter to which I have twice referred. It is dated 24 July 1949, and came between the first two verbal versions. Except for a few lines in the middle which did not concern music I quote it complete. It will be noted that there is already a suggestion of my writing to Sir John Anderson, a suggestion he expanded when he launched into verbal version No. 2 a few weeks later:

> Dear Harold,
>
> Thank you for your letter, which pleases me. I also am fond of *The Tigers*! It was written in the evenings as an escape from desultory war work and without a piano. When the sketches were complete I hired a piano and I played it for hours and loved every note of it. It met with many vicissitudes due to my selling my place as it stood at the close of the *first* war under the impression that things would naturally fall into place again. But they didn't.
>
> Eventually vocal and orchestral scores were completed (about 11 years after the sketches were finished) and Cranz took it up. He felt he had another *Die Meistersinger* and was sure it would go the round of the opera houses in Germany which possessed a stage large enough for it. He sent a copy to Fairbairn the opera producer, whose report was so enthusiastic that Cranz offered to have it produced at Drury Lane at a cost of £12,000. He offered to put down £6,000 if I could find someone who would put down the other £6,000. I sent both

Fairbairn's and Cranz's letters to the late Samuel Courtauld and asked him to think it over. He did. At the end of a week he returned both letters and said 'No'.

In the days of the Thames Wharf BBC Studio Bantock broadcast with the BBC Orchestra three of the dances from *The Tigers*, and Adrian Boult also did the same set a few years later[3]. D. Godfrey at Bournemouth produced the 'Kelly' Variations from *The Tigers* and afterwards wrote to me and said that it had caused more excitement with his audience than any work he had ever played at his Symphony Concerts. Those are facts, and all I can tell you about the work. I say it without conceit that to me *The Tigers* is the happiest large scale work in British music. Performances of such works need some manoeuvring - and I'm no diplomat. The creative side of music has always *dominated* me - the productive side hardly at all. Also - Cranz the publisher did not stick to his guns. After spending £2,000 on the full score of my *Gothic* Symphony and the vocal score of *The Tigers* - he gave up and broke all his contracts and I haven't seen him since 1932. If he had put his back into it *The Tigers* would have been produced ere this. But - he just funked! He may be dead for all I know ... Mind you - as you like that work so much - it might result in something happening if you wrote a letter to Sir John Anderson - who is the presiding spirit at Covent Garden - and got others to add their signature to your letter, drawing attention to the work, and ask him to recommend its production. It is *not* for me to do this and there are only two stages in England capable of putting on *The Tigers* - Covent Garden and Drury Lane. Actually, the work was written for Sir Thomas Beecham - he was the inspirer of it - for he was always urging me to it and when I left him at Birmingham Town Hall in 1916. I told him I *should* do it. But I haven't seen him since 1916.

Yours sincerely,
Havergal Brian

This is a fascinating letter; part of its fascination for me is that, although Brian writes "Those are facts, and all I can tell you about the work", there is no reference to the "facts" he had already given me, or did again after this letter, nor is there in his reference to Beecham, except that he was "the inspirer of it". No further comment is necessary - but I have often wondered what is the truth about the inception of *The Tigers*; I think the letter I have quoted is as near the truth as we shall get. In actual conversation the temptation to romance was often too strong. As to whether Beecham, who is at least constant as the force that pushed

---

[3] The Radio Symphony Orchestra of Luxembourg recorded in 1981 the Symphonic Dances and Symphonic Variations from *The Tigers*, conducted by Leopold Hager (Forlane 3 LP set UM 3529/31, reissued on 2 CDs as UCD 16724/25).

Brian into writing *The Tigers*, ever saw the work, I do not think so, because I do not think Brian ever sent it to him.

One last point on the subject of this opera. Supposing that VW and the others had agreed to support a letter to Sir John Anderson, and the latter had actually agreed eventually to mount the opera, what would Brian have used for a score? By that time, it was, presumably, for all practical purposes, lost. Or was there more than one? Brian writes of Cranz sending Fairbairn a copy - but a copy of what? The score? Or a vocal score? The more one goes into this business the more the mysteries pile up.

It occurs to me that to those who read that first article it might appear, in the quotation from a letter dated 11 October 1949 - "... apart from the *Gothic*, no attempt has been made to produce any of the symphonies" - that Brian was merely referring to Cranz's having published the score of that symphony. Of course, in part he was, and that thought crossed my mind when I first read the letter. But subsequent conversations, and one remark in particular, led me to believe that he had in mind an actual projected performance of the work. The particular remark was made when I referred to this part of the letter. Brian said "Oh, that, too" - meaning the publication - "but Cranz did go some way towards a performance. It never materialized, of course; he went at it the wrong way. But so often one's hopes are fruitlessly raised - mine are, at any rate".

Exactly what Cranz had done that was "the wrong way" I never found out, for I could not get Brian to be more explicit: he liked the tale as he told it: but I did get an impression of him sitting there in judgement on those who were making some effort to promote a performance of a work they believed in - and a work that was not easy to get performed. There is a passage which supports this view in the long letter I quoted at the end of the first article, in which he writes: "Performances of such works need some manoeuvring - and I'm no diplomat. The creative side of music has always *dominated* me - the productive side hardly at all". And there is no doubt that he could, and did, take this attitude: he had done his part, in writing the music; it was for others to secure performances. Up to a point this is fair enough, but I think that at times he went beyond that point, and this may, to some extent, explain some of the neglect he suffered, for he could be bitterly ungrateful for efforts made on his behalf; at least, at this time he could, and I gathered that it was so earlier. For instance, the first work of Brian I heard was *Doctor Merryheart*, in a concert broadcast in 1934 by the Bournemouth Municipal Orchestra, conducted by Sir Dan Godfrey, a brilliant man who virtually made this orchestra from a reasonable seaside band into the force it has become as the Bournemouth Symphony Orchestra. On the occasion of my first meeting with Brian, I mentioned this performance and the importance it had for me. All he said was: "Oh, yes; I remember that. I was there. It needs three harps and there was only one. I told him so, too". He said this in a very grim, hard tone, almost as though he were remembering something that had taken place only the day before. He also added a remark I cannot remember clearly enough to quote it *verbatim*, to the effect that he listened to *Merryheart* from the broadcasting control room. I was disconcerted by his tone and attitude. Even if what Brian said were true, surely Godfrey's effort merited a better memory than this? This was all Brian said of it, nonetheless, and then turned the conversation to a totally different channel. Godfrey had already performed the English Suite No. 3, *Fantastic Variations* (twice) and *Symphonic Variations* from *The Tigers* (twice) - a total of five performances. Whether he would have performed more Brian after this one cannot tell, for he retired the following year, 1935, and died in 1939. He was 71.

But the question now arises: did Godfrey actually conduct that performance? For, in the list of performances included in Lewis Foreman's book *Havergal Brian and the Performance of his Orchestral Music*, he gives Brian as the conductor of this 1934 Bournemouth performance of *Doctor Merryheart*, which is a complete surprise to me, for I have remembered ever since I heard it that Godfrey conducted it; I feel sure that I should have noticed if it had been conducted by its composer - I was already too interested in the activities of Havergal Brian, having bought the vocal score of *The Tigers* the year before. Also, when I mentioned this performance to Brian I spoke of Godfrey as conducting it and Brian did not correct me. (It is possible, of course, that it suited him to let me think that Godfrey had conducted it, but I do not think this was the case.) As I have already written, he merely said "I was there", adding the remark about hearing it from the control room. Some confusion here. At any rate, it seems certain that part - by no means all, of course - of the neglect of Brian's music is due to himself, and his own recalcitrant and, at times, curmudgeonly attitude.

The Godfrey episode had a sequel many years later. It was a long time after that first meeting with Brian that I first saw a score of *Doctor Merryheart*. When I did, I was flabbergasted, for it calls for only *one* harp! So what was behind the nonsense Brian spoke to me in 1947? It was said, too, so determinedly, as though he really nursed a grudge over this matter. And I think that this really hits a spot in the nature of this extraordinary and many-sided man. I believe that he did really like, at times, to nurse grudges over events that had taken place many years before. I believe, further, that in some cases he imagined a grievance where in fact there was not one. I think that this was part of the defence wall he set up against the fact that he *had* been neglected as a composer for so long. There was not the slightest doubt in his mind as to his musical worth, and neglect triggered off these recitals of grudges, some of them real, if exaggerated, some of them fantasies, but real, at the time, to him. And in the end, I believe that he often did not know which was true and which was not.

There were certainly times, I am convinced, when Brian said what had occurred to him at the moment, and always most persuasively, whether or not it was the truth. Nor were such occasions confined to the matter of possible grudges. Maybe, at the moment he said it it was the truth, to him, even if it really was not true. An instance occurs to me concerning Reger. One day when I arrived Brian was playing the piano - the Busoni transcription of Bach's C major organ Toccata - and playing it superbly. He stopped as soon as I went into the room, and seemed somewhat annoyed that I had heard him playing, which I could scarcely have avoided. After a moment he said "I don't mind you so much, but I don't like snoopers". I will quote from a letter on this same subject a little later. For the moment, he went to the music stool, opened it and put away the Bach. As we talked I spoke of his own *Double Fugue* for piano, which I had lately been studying and playing, and said that its themes and some of its textures and layout reminded me of Reger, although the sound of the music did not. Quick as a flash he said "Don't know a note of Reger", and he said it triumphantly, almost as if inviting me to pick the bones out of that. I did not follow it up, but his remark connected in my mind with something I thought I had seen as he slipped the Bach into the stool. Later he left the room to get some tea ready and I took the opportunity to look into the stool. I had not been mistaken. Under the Bach was Reger's Op. 99, six Preludes and Fugues for piano, in two books; both books were there, and showed some use. Under that, a little way down the pile, I came across Reger's Symphonic Fantasy and Fugue for organ, Op. 57, as well as miniature scores of the D minor and E♭ String Quartets. Something else, I was pleased to note, was there too, a work already a favourite of mine, the *Weihnachtsmysterium* of Philipp Wolfrum. I said nothing more about Reger to Brian on this occasion.

On a later visit, obviously having forgotten the episode I have just recounted, he said "You're keen on Reger, aren't you?" This was out of the blue, *à propos* of nothing we had been talking about. I admitted that I was, and he went on "I was, at one time. Still am, for that matter, only I don't get around to it these days. I used to play the organ Symphonic Fantasy a lot at one time - on the piano, mostly". I said that he must have a marvellous technique, and he answered that Reger was good for the fingers. "You know", he went on, "Reger's music always looked as if it could do with having half the notes removed. Some people have said so. But they're wrong. I know, I've tried. What an ear that man had; he'd heard everything he wrote - and every note's essential". This was so exactly my own opinion of Reger that I could have kissed Brian. I didn't, of course, but merely said that that was the opinion I had come too. And I told him of a friend of mine who maintained that some pruning - he actually said a lot of pruning - would improve Reger's music. I invited him to try; I left him alone with the slow movement of the C minor Piano Quintet, Op. 64, the piece which had produced this remark. After half an hour he was all but climbing up the wall. No matter how he tried, the absence of the note or notes was obvious to the ear. He came to the conclusion that the piece actually needed all the notes Reger had given it! Brian laughed at this, and said he sympathized; he had been there. He laughed still more when I said that my friend's conclusion reminded me of Weingartner's orchestrating Beethoven's Op. 106 Piano Sonata, in order to reveal its greatness as the piano could never do, and, having done this and performed his orchestration, admitting that Beethoven had been right - the piano *was* the proper medium, and all the striving was necessary to the music, while the orchestra removed it all. There is indeed a further story, which did not occur to me when I was with Brian, which also illustrates the foolishness of some people. Tovey recounts it in his essay on Chopin's E minor Piano Concerto in Volume III of

Essays in Musical Analysis, and I have seen the edition concerned. Karl Klindworth, editing the Chopin Piano Concertos, decided that the orchestration of the E minor Concerto could be improved to make the whole work more exciting. He set about doing so, and then found that he had to re-write the piano part to fit. He added a footnote to his edition to the effect that those who wished to use Chopin's original piano part would, of course, need to use also his original orchestration, which seems to me a long way round to prove that Chopin knew what he was doing in the first place.

On that occasion, too, Brian said that Reger must have been writing the Symphonic Fantasy and Fugue about the time that he, Brian, was writing *Doctor Merryheart* (1911). I shook my head to this, and said that Reger's Op. 57 had been written and published in 1901. This shook Brian. "1901? Why, he was barely 28 then". I said yes, he was, but it was the truth nonetheless. Reger started very early. "He must have", he growled. "In fact", I added, "in 1911 he had already started conducting the Meiningen orchestra and helping to ruin his health thereby, and was on the final spurt of composition. He was only 43 when he died". Brian seemed stunned. "I had no idea he was so young", was his final comment.

To return for a moment to Brian's piano playing. I quote from a letter dated 25 February 1958:

> Thirty years ago I commenced playing piano arrangements of pre-Bach composers: Buxtehude, Georg Böhm, etc., each morning before leaving home for the office of *Musical Opinion*. I followed these with Busoni's editions of the Bach 48, the chorale preludes, the Prelude and Fugue in D (which I got H. J. Wood to do at a Prom in Respighi's orchestral arrangement) and the two big Weimar Toccatas in C major and D minor. The two Toccatas were exciting, particularly the D minor, and took time to master.
>
> We then lived in a place, a large house made into two maisonettes. We lived in one and a young married couple in the other. One day the lady from the maisonette (2) stopped my wife and said:- 'I was at a Courtauld-Sargent concert at Queen's Hall the other night and I listened to Horowitz playing the Bach Toccata in D minor - I must say I enjoy your husband's performance of the Toccata far more than the Horowitz'. That was a surprise. I do not like snoops - so my piano playing ceased, and today I don't even listen to a piano - no matter where. We have no radio here - only the TV and that is Mrs B's possession.

It is noticeable that in spite of his writing "my piano playing ceased", it obviously did not do so entirely, or I could not have heard him.

I make no apology now for referring to and quoting from letters concerned with some of my own activities, both as writer and composer. First I quote from a letter written on 4 September 1969, a few days after John Ogdon had broadcast two of my piano sonatas, one of which was No. 7: "Dear Harold, How pleased we were to learn so much of your musical activities from Bennett Tarshish a few days ago, and my appreciation for your dedication to me of your Seventh Sonata. Ever since you played that sonata to me at Harrow I've talked of the impression it made on me when I had an opportunity to talk to anybody about". He continues, in this same letter, about the article I had written about him for the then new Pelican book, *The Symphony*: "Your analysis of the symphonies in the Pelican - wonderful penetration and wonderful to read and think about. We missed your broadcast because we have not a radio. Very sorry about missing such an opportunity".

When I first met Brian he asked me, in the course of conversation which ranged widely, if I composed. I think, while he may not have lost interest if a musician did not compose, it certainly increased his interest if one did. I replied that I did, piano music mostly, but some chamber and orchestral music. His comment was not encouraging. "Ah, yes, piano music; so many young people today sprawling about on the piano because they think it's easy and anyone can do it. Believe me, it is not easy. No composition is easy - *if* it's composition. But writing creditably for an orchestra is easier than writing well-conceived and controlled piano music". (I wondered, later, when I thought about it, how, without a radio, he kept abreast of what was going on.) By this time I was feeling a bit flattened. He finished: "Anyway, let me see some. Bring something with you next time". In some trepidation I took a piano sonata with me next time - my Third, in G♯ minor. As it happened, the evening so went that my wife and I were on the point of leaving for home before he mentioned it, and I was in some hope that he would not ask for it. However, he did, right in the middle of talking to my wife quite enthusiastically about gardening, in which she is interested, and so was he. I fetched the score and put it on the table in front of him. He glanced at the cover, but went on talking to my wife; as he did so, he opened the score, glancing apparently idly at the first page, still talking. Then he closed it. A few minutes later we left, and he said "I'll have a look at that sonata tomorrow, and see what you've been up to". A few days later he wrote to me, a letter from which I cannot quote with verbatim accuracy, as I have in other cases, since it is mislaid; no doubt it will come to light, probably when I am looking for something else, which is the way I find most things that go missing. He began by saying that he put my manuscript away very carefully before going to bed that night, and that next morning he woke up with a theme running around in his head, which he could not place; he knew it was nothing of his. It recurred at various intervals during the day. That evening he took out my sonata to read it and at the very beginning was confronted by the theme that had haunted him during the day. His idle glance had taken it in very quickly, so that it was there uppermost in the morning. He went through the work in a most approving analysis, discussing my handling of various passages, and finishing by saying that this was real piano music, he had not encountered anything like this work before, and I should concentrate on piano sonata, for I had obviously a great gift in this direction, with something new to say. To say that I was pleased gets nowhere near what I felt. If I'd ever wanted reassurance that I could do what I thought I could do - and I *had* needed it - I had it and this was something no one could take away from me. Brian also offered a suggestion which I was pleased to adopt. There was a passage where I had rapidly repeated chords in the left hand, with a sustained version of the same chord in the right. He suggested that the upper chord should repeat, as well - and he was absolutely right. The alteration was made.

Returning to the letter dated 25 February 1958, from which I have already quoted, there is a further passage concerning my piano sonatas, which is one of my best memories of Brian. The letter followed an occasion on which I played to him my Fifth Sonata, in B minor (written in memory of Nikolay Medtner, who died in 1951), and the Seventh, in C, a single-movement work. It was on this occasion that he described the Seventh as a *tour de force*, and this caused me to dedicate the work to him. It was a description he repeated in the letter. He wrote: "These sonatas of yours somehow remind me of Bach and Brahms idiom, a healthy sign. The music is after my own heart, impulsive and unhesitatingly fluid. I offer no criticism for - 'it is easier to be critical than to be exact'. I admire the smooth skill of the inverted melodies - no folking. You seem most attached to the C major. I have spent some time on the B minor with its thunderous first movement. Do you think - at foot of p. 17 the passage to the Poco Allegretto is abrupt? I suggest inserting a bar of *rallentando* to liberate the mind. Middle of p. 23 - third section, reminds me of Brahms (I think it is slow movement of No. 3). On p. 28, Poco Allargando - does that bass figure lose effect by its repetition? I put a pencil suggestion and also on p. 29. A four note figure is often made more emphatic by the elision of first or fourth note. This movement is big stuff. Of the 11/4 - I should mark it *pp* throughout, like a closed swell on the organ, and only gradually open the shutters to mf at the middle of p. 32, and closing to *pp* before entry to the finale. I appreciate the dedication of the C major - but - I am not a lucky person. What I have written about the influential idioms and manipulation of your technique applies to this extension in one movement. It is a *tour de force*. Did you offer to play them to the BBC auditors? Why not send them to a publisher, Oxford Press, Augener, Lengnick, Schott, *and offer to play them*?"

In making the remark about the passage from the bottom of p. 17 of the first movement of the B minor sonata to the Poco Allegretto over the page, Brian had not noticed that the end of p. 17 had a double bar line after it; he thought it was meant to go straight into the next page without a break, and he had obviously forgotten that when I played the sonata to him I had made a break at this point. The end of p. 17 was also the end of the first movement - a rather startling end, but the end, nonetheless. I wrote and pointed this out and he understood straight away; he said he was relieved that there was a break between the two.

The matter of the four note figure with the first or fourth note omitted, and the pencilled notes on pp. 28 and 29, made a little mystery that was never cleared up. I understood well enough what he meant, the point of rhythmic relief and subtlety of which he wrote, but it did not apply in either place he had mentioned. At both these points the bass had a *three*-note figure which was repeated for a number of bars. I wrote and pointed this out, but when he wrote next he did not mention the matter. However, when I visited him next I took the score with me, and showed him the two places. He studied them for a few minutes, then said "I'm getting old; I just don't know what I had in mind. I was being too clever". Well, he *was* over 80 years old at the time.

I followed his advice with regard to the publishers, but none were interested in either seeing or hearing the two sonatas. As to the BBC, I had already submitted the same two to the panel of the New Music programme, and had them returned with a polite little note to the effect that they could not see their way to broadcasting them. After Brian's letter I wrote to Dr Robert Simpson and asked him if I could re-submit them, offering to play them. Apparently I could, for he arranged that I should go and play them to Eric Warr. I played them, went out of the room, and after a few minutes Dr Simpson came out and said that Eric Warr was not interested in them. He did not put it like that, but that is what it came to. As Brian put it in a letter I quoted in my first article, "I knew where *I* stood" - and my music. Thirteen years later, in 1969, the Seventh Sonata was one of two, the other the Tenth, which were broadcast by John Ogdon. But Warr had departed by that time, though whether peace reigned in his stead is debatable.

However, it was like a breath of fresh air to have Brian so solidly at the back of me. That he could do nothing practical towards performances for me did not matter. His support did. I was more concerned at that time with performances of *his* music.

In March 1958, I contributed an article to *The Listener* on Brian's music, in preparation for the broadcast of the Ninth Symphony on 22 March in that year. I told Brian I was doing this, and he sent me the score. Later he sent a second package, and a postcard dated 11 January 1958. (This was an error on his part, as the card is postmarked 11 *February*.) "Dear H. T., I sent you a second reg. packet last Wed. (5th inst.) containing sketches and Nettel's book *Ordeal by Music*. You will see from the sketches I now have to ink them in before I can use them. I can no longer see pencil sketches on my stand. I thought Nettel's book would give you some information, as regards your fancies and certain things. [I already had a copy, which Brian knew, but had forgotten.] Before publication the *Tigers* was known as *The Grotesques*! When I listened to Boult's broadcast of 'The Wild Horsemen' I fancied I heard bagpipe tunes, Chevalier's 'Laugh, laugh, I thought I should have died' and his 'Knock 'em in the Old Kent Road', but it could only have been fancy. The Seventh Symphony to be exact - consists of *three* movements and an Epilogue (a long movement) called 'Once upon a time'. I told Clarence Raybould it needed lots of rehearsals and he could have it for his student orchestra. He said he could not make head nor tail of it".

The reference to the Seventh Symphony, which seems to come from nowhere in the postcard, was in answer to a remark I had made about it in a previous letter. I always had a great respect and admiration for Raybould as a conductor and musician generally, and I was surprised to learn of his reaction to Brian's Seventh, which I have always regarded as one of the clearest to understand of all Brian's symphonies. Pursuing Raybould for a moment, I have a letter from him which I value. He was a great champion of Dvořák, at a time when that composer was represented in our programmes largely by a small handful of works, the *New World* Symphony, less frequently the G major, then known as No. 4, the *Dumky* Piano Trio, the *American* Quartet, then known as the *Nigger* and the *Carnival* Overture; that just about covered it. But Raybould gave us all sorts of other Dvořák. In 1946 he broadcast a concert which included Alexander Mackenzie's Piano Concerto and Dvořák's early D minor symphony, the real No. 4. Even the later D minor, No. 7, was rarely played, the earlier one never. None of the early four symphonies had then been published in miniature score, but Simrock's had published two of them, the D minor and the E♭, in a piano duet version, and these I had. The soloist in the Mackenzie concerto was a young Scottish girl. When I wrote, having thanked whoever was concerned for giving us the Dvořák symphony, I went on: "Unfortunately, I must partly qualify my gratitude. It was a great pity to spoil this fine work on one of its very rare appearances with three ugly cuts. The one partly excusable cut was that of the final appearance of the second theme in the finale. This may in a way have tautened Dvořák's scheme, but it is still regrettable. The other two are quite inexcusable. To excise the beautiful third variation from the slow movement was to impair not only the beauty of the music, but the balance of one of Dvořák's finest slow movements. And the omission of the shortened recapitulation of the scherzo, with the result that the movement simply passed from the trio to a coda based on the trio, simply obliterated Dvořák's very real musical design, and made the coda meaningless. This is a real musical crime, and Mr Raybould should be heartily ashamed of himself". Which was really ramming it home; oh, I felt in fine fettle after that little outburst. Raybould's answer calmed me down, and I did not feel quite so clever. He wrote:

Dear Sir,

Thank you very much for your unexpected, but interesting, remarks about my recent performance with the BBC Northern Orchestra of the early D minor Symphony of Dvořák. I offer no excuse for the cuts which were made - there can be no excusing such vandalism on musical grounds - but when you have learned an explanation of the reasons which led up to this necessity perhaps you may feel inclined to curtail the amount of shame you wished me to feel!

As far as I could make out there had never been a previous broadcast of this work, consequently when I wished to include it in my programme there was no record of its duration. I therefore had to give an estimated timing by reading it through. It was not until I came to rehearse it that I discovered that two of the orchestral parts were missing and the harp part was actually being copied while I was rehearsing the Mackenzie concerto. When we had played through the complete programme I found, to my consternation, that I had undertimed the symphony and I had therefore to choose between cutting one or the other of the pieces. As this occasion was the first appearance of the young scottish pianist with the Northern Orchestra, my old-fashioned sense of chivalry prompted me to give the lady the opportunity of performing the concerto in full, and I therefore had to sacrifice my own feelings in the matter of the symphony. I must admit that I had never expected any listener to be able to put his finger on the three cuts which I was obliged to make, between the rehearsal and transmission.

I entirely agree with your criticism and am glad to know that someone else shares my opinion of the beautiful slow movement. I shall naturally seek an opportunity of playing the work in full.

Which he did.

Before I sent the article to *The Listener* I sent a copy to Brian for him to approve or otherwise. He wrote, on 17 February, "Thanks for the script, a splendid thoughtful piece of writing. I think you should mention the *date* of performance of the Ninth - 22nd March. That is the only suggestion I can think of". I had not included the date in the article because *The Listener* always gave the date of the broadcast concerned at the head of the article, and it did on this occasion.

Brian had already, on 1 February 1958, written to tell me he was sending a full score of the Ninth. In the same letter he wrote: "You know a lot about my work - the *Gothic*, *The Tigers* and the fugues, etc. - so you are in a position of authority. If you spread yourself in *The Listener* - please do not forget to mention my music dramas: *The Tigers*, *Faust* (in German), *Turandot* (in German), *The Cenci* (in English), *Agamemnon* (a one act tragedy from Aeschylus in English)". I did not have room to spread myself in the article, but I did mention all he wanted me to, as well as some other works, apart from the symphonies - up to No. 12, which was as far as he had reached at that time.

Of the Ninth Symphony he wrote in the same letter: "What caused the 9th I don't know. Most of my symphonies are a growth from poetry or the drama - but I cannot recall anything about the dramatic qualities of the 9th - except that they are there". They certainly are: but, although, like Berlioz, Brian seems more often than not to have drawn initial inspiration from outside sources - usually, as he says, poetry or drama, as with the Eighth Symphony, which found its origin in Goethe's *Die Braut von Corinth* - his music seems always, to me, to run away from the thing that sparked it off; in other words, it is, as far as music can be, absolute music. No music can be without the human element, unless it is designed as an abstraction, and even that probably has some such thing in it somewhere, but Brian's music left obvious programme far behind, and became universal.

One of Havergal Brian's strangest peculiarities was a tendency to expect to be visited by burglars, however ridiculous the idea might be in the particular circumstances. In his book on Brian, Reginald Nettel refers to an incident concerning Walter Allum: "For the first time, too, he [Allum] realized that Brian was an unnecessarily nervous man, who often answered the door at night with a poker in his hand. On one occasion he told Allum that someone had broken into his bedroom through the window, and had left footprints. (It was snowing at the time.) But Allum could see no footprints". I can confirm this nervousness, and the tendency to delude himself, for I had a similar experience with him. During one of Mrs Brian's absences, visiting a married daughter in South Africa, I think, he wrote to me that he had been out shopping and when he returned he sensed as soon as he entered the house that someone had been there while he was away. He even thought they might still be there, and went round the house with a poker in his hand. He found no one, but was certain that some objects had been moved from where they were. However, he searched and could not discover that anything had been taken. But later, either that evening or the next day, he went to a drawer in a cabinet, in which he kept some manuscripts, sketches mainly, and discovered that the sketches for the Tenth Symphony were missing. He was convinced that whoever had broken into the house had taken them - in other words, they had been burgled. The situation as Brian saw it seemed laughable to me; why should anyone break into the house merely to steal the sketches of his Tenth Symphony? Not even those of the Ninth and Eleventh as well, which, I gathered, were in the same drawer, but just those for the Tenth. It was so ridiculous that I forgot myself and wrote to Brian somewhat in this strain. His answer came back rather like an explosion. (I have to rely on my memory here, for the letters concerned, and one from Nettel on this subject, which was put with the Brian letters, are part of a little group that at present are mislaid. I can say positively, however, that they have not been burgled.) It was the only angry letter I ever had from him. He was incensed that I should thus doubt what he had said. I wrote a quiet answer, which had the effect I hoped for. When he wrote next he was back to normal, and no reference was made again to the missing sketches. So, however it had come about, I accepted the fact that the sketches for the Tenth Symphony *were* missing. As a fact, not perhaps of great importance, it remained at the back of my mind.

When I read the first volume of Malcolm MacDonald's work on Brian's symphonies and came to the Tenth, I stared in astonishment. For there, reproduced, was the beginning of the first pencil sketch of the "storm" from that symphony. Obviously, MacDonald must have had access to those "lost" sketches. I wrote, not to MacDonald, whom I did not know at this time, but Nettel, telling him the whole story and the reason for my puzzlement, and this is, almost word for word, what he replied (from the letter I have already referred to):

> What you say about the Tenth sketches going missing does not surprise me. Such fictions seem to have been a necessity for Brian. There is no doubt, however, about his fear of burglars; he would behave as though he had the rarest possessions in the house. Rare, indeed, we know they are, but not of any concern for a burglar. But I can imagine what happened to the sketches. Mrs Brian and Havergal did not always get on so well together, and she seemed to resent his preoccupation with music. She also had a rather peculiar sense of humour - peculiar in a quite different way from Brian's - and from time to time she would hide things, MSS. usually, that she thought he would want. Often she would put them in a box and lock it away for a time. When this happened Brian always had to account for it to

himself in a way that satisfied *him*. He was annoyed with you because you did not play this game with him.

Of course, there might well be another answer, or other factors involved, but Nettel's explanation could be the true one - he knew Hilda Brian far better than I did.[4]

---

[4] Jean Furnivall, Brian's daughter, wrote in a letter to the Editor in *Newsletter* 35 (V-VI 1981), p. 2: "I felt I must write to you after receiving *Newsletter* 34, in which Mr Truscott quotes an extract from one of Mr Nettel's letters regarding the missing sketches of Symphony No. 10. I found the latter's remarks quite appalling and completely untrue. My mother at no time hid any of my father's manuscripts and I do not think the idea ever entered her head. She certainly had a very keen sense of humour but in no way 'peculiar' or malicious, and I do sincerely wish to put the record straight on this score. We as a family were quite aware that from time to time my father had these somewhat paranoid ideas regarding his music, and they were most in evidence when he was writing a new work. In fact he kept his manuscripts under lock and key most of the time. He certainly had no physical fear of burglars - only regarding interference with his manuscripts. Since my father died I have been surprised at the lack of loyalty and affection on the part of some of the people he regarded as his friends. He was a very emotional man and it was during these emotional states that he wrote so many of his letters. He did have an obsession with writing letters but I do not think he ever anticipated for one moment that at some later date these letters or extracts would be put into print." More information on Hilda Brian is given by Robert Simpson in his Obituary ("an appreciation") in *Newsletter* 31 (X 1980), p. 1: "To be the wife of Havergal Brian required fortitude of an order normally saluted with medals; even in his later and mellower years he was not an easy man to live with - before that most of his companions and even his best friends found him at times impossible. Through a great many of these difficult years, Hilda remained a stead-fast and deeply loved mother to his family. To them, even at her advanced age, she must have been a severe loss. Anyone who has been a family friend for 25 years or so cannot have failed to discover a deep affection for this remarkable and humane woman, so free of respect for personages, so gifted with sardonic humour, so full of instant sympathy when it was deserved, so quick to see justice or injustice, yet never dogmatic or self-righteous. She was a person of natural simplicity, not unreasonably chary of intellectuals but often quick to see the point of an argument; she never pretended to understand what passed over her head, and looked at things in the most direct human way. Her sense of humour and her uncomplicated ability to see through pretensions often saved her the necessity of using sophisticated means of expressing her opinion. She never affected to understand her husband's purpose in life, or his work as such; circumstances often rendered her scepticism not at all surprising; she was not reared in artistic circles and at the beginning cannot have had more than the usual romantic ideas about what life with an artist must be like. She soon became disabused of any such illusions: 'I must have been mad', she said. Mad or not, she set about giving her children the securest possible emotional base in the face of their father's unpredictabilities, coping with daunting financial as well as psychological difficulties. That is why the family never ceased to adore her, and why she was always regarded as a haven of sanity in a sometimes crazily incomprehensible world. If anyone was mad, it was never Hilda Brian! It was sometimes wryly amusing to hear the two old companions and adversaries being short with each other - a long-established habit, no doubt - yet Havergal was never at rest when Hilda was away or even out of the house. When I first visited him in the 1950s she was in Zambia visiting her daughter Freda, and he greeted me at the front door with a brightly coloured pinafore across his middle, full of apologies that I would have to put up with a meal cooked by him. It turned out a very good meal, but he kept returning to the absence of his wife - I wondered what she must be like and innocently imagined that this must be one of those long, mythically perfect relationships one reads about in Victorian biographies. Yet even after the facts were all clear to me I could still be struck by the way he would sometimes stand at the gate waiting for her to come back from

Life and personality

In November 1958 the Brians moved from North Harrow to Shoreham-by-Sea on the Sussex coast. But that move was very nearly never made. In 1954 I went from individual piano and harmony teaching (which was very poorly paid) to school teaching at Sandwich Secondary Modern school. But I had no recognized teaching certificate and so, after two years at Sandwich, Kent Education persuaded me to do a course at a teachers' training college. Purely to get a certificate I spent a year at Bretton Hall, which was a miserable waste of time for me and a nightmare for my wife; but I got the certificate and, as it happened, never needed to use it for, towards the end of the year, I got a post as lecturer in the Music Department of Huddersfield Technical College. This went through a period as a College of Technology and in 1970 became a Polytechnic. From there I retired as Principal Lecturer 18 months ago. When I knew that I was going to Huddersfield, naturally I wanted to make arrangements to sell my house at Deal. Equally naturally, I told Brian of my plans. He was delighted for me and

---

shopping, impatiently and as if half afraid some life-line was under threat. He was a self-centred man, and we could suppose that his own security lay behind his concern; but who can say what goes on in a man's mind - in so strange a mind? We must account for those unexpected touches of human tenderness in his music, often occurring at the very moment when we have begun to get used to the bull in the china shop. He was used to Hilda, and she was inured to him. Of the two, he seemed the harder, but only because he was the less considerate, the less imaginative when it came to other people's feelings; yet if Hilda had died first he would have been the less able to survive calmly, the less able to remain a stable part of his own family. Hilda's natural independence and her quick awareness of others' needs made her reluctant to become dependent on the children, but she was quietly part of the family in a way the old man would have found impossible. Towards the end she seems to have suffered some depression, but this can have been only due to ill-health; to the last she was surrounded by love, which was no more than she richly deserved." - Malcolm MacDonald likewise touches on the question of missing sketches in a letter to the Editor, also in *Newsletter* 35, p. 2: "First of all it is important to understand that Brian's 'sketches' are continuous short score drafts of an entire work, on anything from two to seven staves. Drafts of this kind survive for nearly all the symphonies, and I was able to examine them at Shoreham shortly after Brian's death, thanks to the generosity of Hilda Brian and Jean Furnivall. The second point is that well into his 80s - when he eventually made do with a single such draft - Brian's normal practice was to make *two* short scores before progressing to the full-score stage: a preliminary, rather basic pencil one, and a more fully developed and elaborated version in ink. This is certainly the case with the symphonies of the late 1940s and early 1950s. Only a few pages survive of the pencil drafts of Nos 7 and 9, but their complete ink drafts are extant; and two complete drafts, both pencil and ink, survive for Nos 8, 11, 12 and *Elegy*. The odd one out in this pattern is No. 10. There was a complete pencil short score of this work at Shoreham (a little of it reproduced in facsimile on p. 174 of my Vol. 1), but no sign at all of an ink draft - and that feels wrong. The pencil short score is precisely analogous to those of Nos 8 and 11 - that is to say, a long way from the full score, and apparently requiring an intermediate stage of realization of the kind represented by the ink drafts of Nos 8 and 11. (It is true that No. 6, the *Sinfonia Tragica*, is also represented only by a single pencil short score - but that is a very different document, highly detailed, neatly written, and much nearer the state of the eventual full score; it could be, of course that the sketches for *Deirdre of the Sorrows* which Brian presumably destroyed, constituted the 'first draft' in this case.) On the face of it, there ought to have been an ink draft - which Brian would have called 'sketches' - of No. 10. While there is no direct proof, I believe it existed. But it isn't at Shoreham. Though the notion that someone stole it from Brian is hardly credible, I would like to put it on record that there does seem to be some underlying basis of fact - an unaccountably missing score - to his 'paranoia' in this case."

interested for himself and Mrs Brian. They wanted to move either to the sea or near it, and they both expressed interest in seeing the house and Deal as a town. So it was arranged that they should come down for a day; this they did and they were both enchanted (this was the word that Mrs Brian used) with Deal and very taken with the house, which was kept in good repair and which we had improved considerably since we bought it in 1954. They went away to think about it, and about a week later Brian wrote that they felt fairly sure that they would like to make the move, but that they would like to see the house again. So again they came down, for a weekend, Saturday to Sunday evening. This time they both seemed even more impressed, and I feel convinced that Brian was, and that he had set his heart now, as he told me, on moving to Deal. In the meantime, of course, my house was on several agents' books for sale. There was no rush of buyers, and it seemed that the Brians would have a clear field. However, they never moved to Deal, as is fairly obvious. On 17 April 1958, just after they spent the weekend with us, Brian wrote to me: "Dear Harold, I fear you and Margaret will be disappointed - we are already so: for the removal from here to Deal is impracticable. No thought had been given to the costs - I had a vague idea that Deal was not far along the coast from Brighton. Yesterday we started to calculate costs of fares and removal. A return to Deal from here is 32/6 [railway fares have increased a little since 1958] and the cost of only *one* van load of goods is extortionate - we should have to pay for an empty return, as they call it. So we must reluctantly give up your very kind offer. At the same time it has brought to mind - your number of removes and the money you have had to find for them. There is only one source of income here - pension - and it just manages to stretch over the quarter - and leaves no margin at the end of it". So Deal's loss was Shoreham's gain.

Only a matter of weeks later we were very glad that the Brians had *not* bought the house at Deal. The West Yorkshire climate - or that around Huddersfield - proved mostly inhospitable to our children, and to one in particular. We had two girls and, the youngest, a boy. The elder girl was the least affected, and the boy, who was then two and a half, was coping, though neither were happy. However, if that had been all, no doubt we would have stuck it out and hoped that they would become acclimatized. But there was no doubt about Veronica, the younger girl. Huddersfield brought out alarmingly a dormant asthma, to such an extent that she had bouts during which she was beside herself, and could bear no one, including her mother, to touch her. She would simply scream, and was obviously in a very bad way. At last, our doctor told me that she must go south again; and south she went, with her sister and brother, and her mother, back into the house at Deal which had never been sold, and where my wife and I live to this day. Although the Brians *not* coming to Deal was a great disappointment at the time, it proved to be a godsend to us.

From time to time Brian and I discussed composers. He had moods about this. Sometimes it was obvious that he just did not want to discuss music at all, and any attempt to do so was blocked immediately. At times he would insist on talking gardening, which was all right if my wife was present, and all wrong if she wasn't. He knew it was a subject that did not interest me, and I feel sure he got a somewhat malicious pleasure from continuing to talk about it to me. Once I set out to get a little of my own back. I have an inordinate love for silent films, and I knew from various things he had said that he had little or no interest in films at all. So, before he could start on gardening, or some other subject that bored me, I started talking about silent films; he had once said that he thought Chaplin was the best of them all - not that he had seen much even of him, but it was the thing to say. Anyway, he stood this for longer than I expected, and after about half an hour, he suddenly said "You've an amazing memory - and you're very vivid, even if you do seem to have spent half your life watching films. I could almost see what you were describing". I was taken aback, and before I could say anything he went on: "I only once remember seeing a film that really made me laugh, and I can't remember what it was or who was in it. It wasn't Chaplin. I do remember that it was short, and it had to do with someone putting together a prefabricated house, and at one point the house revolved in a gale. I nearly collapsed at this chap's attempts to get into the revolving house". He laughed as he spoke. I identified the film straight away - in fact, nowadays I have a copy of it. He'd picked the greatest comedian of the lot - Buster Keaton. It was a film called *One Week*, and was made in 1920; it certainly did concern Keaton's attempts to build a house from prefabricated parts, with his wife's "help", and the disadvantage of a disappointed suitor for his wife who messed things up by altering the numbers on the parts. The house, when finished, was a rather peculiar shape. Like most of Keaton's silent films in the '20s, it was simply one of the funniest films ever made. The attempts by Keaton to get into the moving house included, as it first started to move, his trying to open a door which wasn't there each time it had moved as he got to it - and then, when it was going full pelt, his succesful attempt to get on to a verandah which ran the full length of the house, and because of his speed and the contrary direction of the house, whizzing along the verandah to find himself off the other end.

And this film had made its impression on Brian. He told me eventually that shortly after he saw it he began to plan an overture which sprang into his mind directly from his reaction to this film, but that he never finished it, and that what he had written went into other things. I wonder what other things - and when. He would never tell me. It seems that we nearly had virtually a Buster Keaton Overture from Brian (it would have been actually his second comedy overture, and those to *The Tinker's Wedding* and *The Jolly Miller* the third and fourth) - but what sort of music that would have drawn from him it is impossible to say. What can be said is that comedy of the order of an artist such as Keaton projects all sorts of things beyond and around itself. I have often wondered what became of the original of Brian's unfinished overture. Probably it did not get beyond the sketch stage, but it should still exist somewhere, unless it is another of the "lost" works, or it was hidden away and never recovered.

Some years ago I mentioned this to Reginald Nettel. He was genuinely surprised. He said that on only two occasions, so far as he could remember, had films been mentioned in conversation, and each time it was he who mentioned them. Each time Brian's reaction was abrupt, and he made it clear that films as such had no interest for him. What quite bewildered Nettel was my speaking of the partly worked overture inspired by Keaton's *One Week*. In all their conversations over the years about Brian's work the latter had never so much as referred to it. I could see that he felt hurt. But, as he said, that was so like the man; he had had so many exasperating experiences with Brian, from the time he first began to plan *Ordeal by Music*. By the time I spoke to Nettel about this his newer book on Brian was complete and he was having a great deal of exasperating trouble with Dobson's over it; it was too late for any mention of the Keaton overture to go in.

I have referred elsewhere to my disappointment at the fact that Brian wrote so little piano music, and that in his later years he did not write any large scale work, such as a sonata, for it. I once suggested to him that he should, and here is his answer, in a letter dated 27 October 1949: "I am sorry that your suggestion of a Piano Sonata makes no more appeal to me than if you asked me to write a concerto for that damnable crossbreed - Saxophone. I *have* used Pianos in my third and fourth [now second and third] Symphonies - only for the dramatic amplification of the orchestra and to impart a tone colour of which the orchestra itself is incapable - not because I wanted to see 3 women sitting at the piano with their elbows crooked". So that was that; I was amused at his assuming that the pianists in the symphonies would automatically be women rather as Belloc in his essays and novels would sometimes refer with gentle sarcasm to his reader (singular), who was always female. In the same letter, on quite a different subject: "When Adrian Boult suggested that I should write my reminiscences - I told him they were better unwritten for if they *were* written nobody would believe them".

Coming back to the piano, I quote from another letter dated a little earlier, 4 September 1949: "Thanks for your letter - I am pleased to hear how much the D minor and major Prelude and Fugue appeal to you. I also was somewhat surprised when I unearthed it for I don't remember attaching much importance to it". Before I continue the quotation I must refer the reader to what I have written concerning Reger, and Brian's reaction. It should be remembered that (a) Brian did not know a note of Reger, (b) I discovered works by Reger in his music stool, (c) Brian referred to playing the Symphonic Fantasia and Fugue, Op. 57, in earlier days, and remarked that Reger must have written this about the time he (Brian) was writing *Doctor Merryheart* (1912); also, my correction of this, and Brian's stunned reaction when I told him that Reger was only 43 when he died. All this, it is true, took place after I had received the letter I am quoting. In this letter Brian went on: "Your reference to Reger is interesting - for up to now I have not seen nor heard a note of Reger's music. I threw up my organ work at 26 [that is, in 1902] and parted with my library at the same time. *I shouldn't think anything of Reger's had been published then*". Of course, by 1902 a good half of Reger's total output had been published. Later, I told him that the Op. 57 Fantasy and Fugue was written and published in 1901, which shook him. For the moment I did not answer the letter, leaving what had to be said until I saw him again, with results of which I have already written above. Continuing the letter: "At that time I had not reached the plane necessary to 'understand' J. S. B. -

although I did play a number of the shorter fugues. 'Understanding' J. S. B. came through my study of the B minor Mass and hearing a performance of *St Matthew Passion* under Hans Richter. It is strange, though, that there *should* appear a Reger mannerism. When the two last Fugues were issued a lady wrote to me, after seeing them, and said she thought I was much influenced by Berlioz, and Keys, to whom the first fugue is inscribed, said he thought Mussorgsky might have written the third fugue in C minor. So there we are."[5]

Yes, there we are. Brian was proud of his memory, but there were times, I think, when it was definitely cloudy, either intentionally or genuinely. So where are we? So far as the lady and Robert Keys are concerned, I must say that, for my part, neither Berlioz nor Mussorgsky have ever suggested themselves to me in connection with the piano Preludes and Fugues. The Reger mannerism, of course, is in the *Double Fugue* for piano - a type of writing which is similar to some of Reger's, although the sound is not. But, unique though Brian is, there is one earlier composer I have encountered who at times, and in one work especially, did get some of the sound that we find in *The Gothic*. That work was written in the mid-'80s, when Brian was about ten years old. I realize, too, that some way back I began to write of discussions Brian and I had about other composers, and I got sidetracked.

It is evident that the letter from Reginald Nettel, which I quoted in connection with the lost sketches of Brian's Symphony No. 10, caused distress to members of Brian's family. I quoted it in good faith, although it was perhaps thoughtless of me. But Nettel was not a malicious man, and he would not have invented what he wrote to me; he could, of course, have mistaken the import of what he thought he knew. However, I deeply regret that anything in that article should have caused hurt to any member of Brian's family.

From time to time Havergal Brian and I discussed composers. Sometimes he would speak quite freely, sometimes he would not discuss any composer but himself, and there were times when he would not indulge himself even that far, unless I asked a direct question. Then he would answer it, briefly, and that was all. We did discuss literature, but I found that his tastes and mine did not run in quite the same direction, and one such discussion got me a black mark. This concerned Goethe, who for Brian was almost a god, whereas although I appreciated what I had read (in English, not German, which was one way Brian had the advantage) I much preferred, and still prefer, Jean Paul Friedrich Richter. When I first mentioned Richter's name Brian grimaced. Asked for an explanation, he said "A little goes a long way". To this I quoted Ford Madox Ford, one of the greatest and most neglected of 20th century writers, who had written in a wonderful book, *The March of Literature*, "We may say of him [Richter], as we said of Gib-

---

[5] Robert Keys writes in a letter to the Editor in *Newsletter* 36 (VII-VIII 1981), p. 6: "Mr Truscott's mention of Brian quoting me as remarking on a similarity in the C minor Fugue to Mussorgsky came as something of a surprise! I fancy that I saw at that time a resemblance in the 'block' writing for piano to parts of the *Pictures at an Exhibition*; but that was 30 years and more ago and I don't imagine I would say that now!"

bon, that a man is hardly a complete man until he has read a great deal of Jean Paul". I added that it was not because of Ford's sentence that I liked Richter; I had already taken to him before I read Ford's book; but I fully agreed with him. Brian laughed and said "Obviously, I am not a complete man". I replied, quite gravely, "I think Ford would have made an exception in your case". Brian laughed again and abruptly changed the subject. He asked "Why do you dislike Goethe?" I pointed out that I had not said that I disliked him, but that I preferred Richter. "Well, why do you prefer an inferior writer?" he retorted, to which I answered that I did not think Richter inferior to anything of Goethe's that I had read, remembering that I had read all of this literature only in English, and that Richter had, for me, one great advantage over Goethe. "And what's that?" Brian asked quietly. There was something ominous about his tone, as though he might explode any moment. This put my back up. I said "He has a wonderful sense of humour, which is essential to any artist, so far as I am concerned, and I have not found the slightest trace of humour in anything of Goethe's I have read". "And what have you read?" His tone was still ominously quiet. "A lot of the short poems, *Faust, Werther, Wilhelm Meister, Novels and Tales, Conversations with Eckermann* - and if I had been Eckermann I should have been bored stiff". I *was* piling it on a bit, mainly because of Brian's attitude, but nonetheless what I said reflected a good deal of what I felt - and still feel.

Instead of exploding, he gave up Goethe, no doubt thinking that I was beyond redemption in this respect. Honours, I thought, were about even so far. "Anyway", he said, evidently not content to leave Jean Paul where he was, "the trouble with Richter is that he was sickly sentimental". "Not in anything I have read", I retorted, "and if you want sickly sentimentality, I think *Werther* can supply that admirably". And before he could interrupt, I went on hurriedly, "Richter wrote a pastoral short novel, *The Life and Death of Quintus Fixlein*, which is always quoted as though it is terribly sentimental, typical of his work and a major production in his output. It is *not* sentimental, although there is sentiment in it, it is not typical of his work as a whole and I would not call it a major work. But there is something to attract one in the mere titles of his books: *Greenland Lawsuits, The Devil's Papers, The Invisible Lodge, Jottings under the Cranium of a Giantess*; not only is his humour prodigious, so is his satire. I have the greatest affection and admiration for a novelist who can write a preface which begins: 'It has often been a source of much annoyance to me that every preface I write I am obliged to append a book - like the endorsement on a bill of exchange - or an appendix to letters A to Z. Many a man who dabbles in authorship by way of amusement has his books sent to him all ready written and complete, straight from the cradle; so that all he has to do is to attach his gold frontlets of prefaces to their foreheads - which is nothing but painting the *corona* about the sun. As yet, however, not a single author has applied to me for a preamble to a book, although for several years I have had a considerable number of prefaces by me (all ready beforehand, and going at great bargains), in which I extol to the best of my ability works which have not as yet come into being'".

I rolled this out from memory (as I have even now written it from memory), and while I did so Brian was gazing at me fascinated, as though he were a rabbit and I a snake. When I paused, and he saw that I was preparing to continue, he said quickly "All right, all right, that's enough of that". Then he added, rather sourly, "Thanks for the lecture". I smiled. He looked at me very keenly. "It's nonsense, you know that?" I shook my head. "If it is, it's meaningful nonsense - the kind we need a lot of in this life". He made one more attempt against my obstinacy. "But you can't put him against Goethe". "Why not? This is an old argument. I can enjoy both, but I prefer Richter. After all, I love Hugh Walpole's books, but he was completely puzzled because Hilaire Belloc once wrote that P. G. Wodehouse was the greatest living master of English. And he was probably right". Brian shrugged his shoulders as though once more he gave me up as hopeless. Tea interrupted us, and literature was shelved, much to my relief.

We did have other, more agreeable, conversations about literature, but if I go on with them I shall never get to composers. And, in fact, I think that generally speaking it is the matters on which we did not altogether agree that are the more interesting. Not that we disagreed so much - at least, not on composers. Bruckner was an object of admiration for us both. Interestingly, it was in connection with Bruckner that I first encountered Brian's name, a short while before I read Holbrooke's book *Contemporary British Composers*. In my early teens I used sometimes - when a local newsagent happened to have one left on his hands, which was only at intervals - to buy *Musical Opinion*. In the issue for November 1928 - a copy I still have - there was an article on Bruckner's Fourth Symphony by Brian. It was short, but obviously the work of a man who had a profound admiration for this, at the time, new composer to me. Shortly afterwards I obtained, with great difficulty, for my finances were severely abbreviated and I had to save for it - also, it was an imported record and took a long time to come - Horenstein's magnificent recording in the late '20s (1928 was it?) with the Berlin Philharmonic Orchestra of Bruckner's Seventh Symphony. From the first time I heard *that* there was no question about Bruckner's position; he was on the list of supremely great composers for me. I had only a portable gramophone with steel needles and I all but wore out that recording. It remained with me, however, through a variety of removals from one place to another, over long distances, for many years, but at last some of it succumbed and finished up broken. Now, I have the transfer to LP of this performance and it seems as great as ever. I started collecting miniature scores (the long dead William Reeves of Charing Cross Road was a goldmine here, even if he was rather expensive) and piano arrangements; the Fourth and Seventh, beautifully done by Cyrill Hynais, the First, Second, Fifth and Eighth, the last abominably arranged by August Stradal (but useful since there was no other way of getting to know them), and the Ninth, with the *Te Deum*, arranged reasonably by Ferdinand Löwe, who so horribly rescored parts of the Ninth and, in one instance, dared to alter a climax chord in the Adagio. The scores, of course, were of "revised" versions - Robert Haas' originals did not begin to penetrate until 1936 and after.

So Brian and I had a lot in common here, although he looked aghast at me when I mentioned how I had got to know most of these symphonies by playing them on the piano. "Good God! What determination!" was his comment. I told him that I had always, leaving aside these particular works, found that playing orchestral and chamber works on the piano - that is, docked of the colour imparted by their scoring, which can lead one astray until one knows the works - was by far the best way of getting to know them. He agreed, after a short discussion, in principle, but said that I was the only person he had encountered who had actually put this into practice and obviously enjoyed it. "What do you do when there is no arrangement available?" he asked me. "Make my own" I retorted. He shrugged his shoulders and grinned. "You'll never die of want of enthusiasm" was his comment. I explained further that, since when I was growing up there was no radio, and we had no gramophone until I was about 16, and no one took me to concerts, if I had not played piano arrangements I would have known nothing of the orchestral or chamber music repertoire, other than by reading scores, which I could do pretty well; but I liked to feel the music under my fingers, too. I told him that until I was about 16 the only way I had heard any orchestral music other than on the piano was through a military band at Dover, where I heard by this means Beethoven's *Egmont* Overture, the finale, only, of the Fifth Symphony, and Schubert's B minor. The picture I had painted seemed to appal Brian, but I was quite happy about it. "After all", I said, to finish, "if I hadn't had this experience there's an awful lot of music I would never have known as well as I do know it - or as early. I can't be unhappy about that".

Concerning Bruckner there arose one of the very few occasions when religion was mentioned between us. He spoke of it; I have never been in the habit of initiating religious discussions with anyone. If others start, then I will follow. He wandered to the piano and played the opening bars of Bruckner's Fourth Symphony. Then he sat down again and gave me a very straight stare. "Faith!" he burst out. "That's what those symphonies are made of - sublime, unquestioning faith". I said something under my breath, and he took me up quickly. "What's that?" I said it louder: "Christ said to Doubting Thomas 'Because thou hast seen thou hast believed. Blessed are they who have not seen and have believed'". He nodded. "Don't I know it. I wish to God that I had such a faith. If I had a faith like that, I would not be crippled. As it is, I haven't any". I forebore to remark that he had just evoked the God he did not believe in. And then he said something that I have heard often, in one way or another, from people who profess atheism. He said "You're all right, though. You're a Catholic, too". So far as I could get him to talk on this subject - which *he* had chosen - his impression seemed to be that, because I am a Catholic, there is a God for me to meet when I die, but that for unbelievers such as himself, there is nothing. It is a delightfully naïve idea which, as I have said, I have met in other people, that God exists if you believe in Him, but not if you don't.

I was reminded, too, by this conversation, of something Sibelius once wrote on the same subject, in the autumn of 1911, according to Karl Ekman's biography. In a letter written after a performance of Bruckner's Fifth Symphony,

Sibelius wrote: "Yesterday I heard Bruckner's B (flat) major symphony and it moved me to tears. For a long time afterwards I was completely enraptured. What a strangely profound spirit, formed by religiousness. And this profound religiousness we have abolished in our own country, as something no longer in harmony with our time".

Richard Strauss was an object of overwhelming admiration for Brian, an admiration which I discovered gradually was particularly concentrated on certain of the operas: notably *Elektra* and *Rosenkavalier*. Obviously, there were other works he greatly admired, one of the rare non-stage works being *Eine Deutsche Motette*, Strauss' Op. 62, written in 1913, for 16 voices and four soloists; technically a sort of earlier *Metamorphosen* for voices. This has been described as the most difficult work in the whole German choral repertory, although Reger's almost finished 12-part setting of *Vater Unser* runs it close, as also, in English choral music, does Bax's magnificent *Mater Ora Filium*. I think this work of Strauss may have had a very positive influence on Brian's writing, especially in some of the unaccompanied choral writing in *The Gothic*. Of Strauss' orchestral music, obviously Brian knew and greatly admired the tone poems, which themselves show some influence in his own earlier orchestral music in various ways, without detracting from Brian's own personality, already very strong. But he made the surprising remark to me that he would, nonetheless, have given all the tone poems for more operas of the stature of *Elektra* and *Rosenkavalier*. I asked him what he thought of the latter work. "What can one say?" was his reply. "It's just a colossal masterpiece". Which, of course, musically it is.

Of *Elektra*, however, he had much to say. In spite of his comprehensive praise of *Der Rosenkavalier* in that one sentence, I think there is no doubt that the economical and very pointed one-act masterpiece was closest to him. Nettel tells us that *Agamemnon* was conceived as a prelude to Strauss' *Elektra*, and I am sure that nothing would have given Brian more pleasure than for *Agamemnon* to have been performed as the first part of a double-bill with Strauss' opera. In fact, we spoke of this coupling once and he was ecstatic about it. "If it could only be so", he said, very feelingly. I further suggested his Twelfth Symphony as a prelude to the two operas and he nodded his head vigorously. (Nettel, too, writes of this possibility, but this conversation took place long before Nettel wrote his book.)

There was an occasion fairly early in our friendship when he talked for nearly an hour about *Elektra*. I have often wished I had been able to record what he said. He spoke of performances he had seen, their shortcomings - especially of these. Only one did he speak of as being just about right, and I never found out - or do not remember - who was concerned or where it was given. But he thought *Elektra* the most difficult of Strauss' operas to produce and perform; although others gave the impression of being more difficult, it was an illusion. They came a part of the way to meet one, whereas *Elektra* did not. It was vigorously uncompromising, and he left no doubt that this was for him one of its great merits. One thing he said was that, in their efforts to be as uncompromising as the work, and as terse, singers often became shrill rather than intense; to judge the absolutely right line was one of the great difficulties of the opera: to be able to relax without letting the result become flabby. He doubted if there would ever be an ideal performance. He talked at length of the structure, the careful building of scene upon scene to produce the suggestion of effortless and relentless onward movement, the proportion of scene to scene, and the musical placing of individual scenes in the work as a whole.

On one of these visits, after talking of Strauss, we gravitated to Pfitzner. At least, I did. I do not think we would have done so so far as Brian was concerned; he seemed singularly uninformed about this great contemporary of Strauss. I noticed at various times that where his interest was already engaged, as with Strauss, no detail was too little to interest him. But with a composer he did not know, or knew very superficially, arousing his interest could be difficult. At first he gave vent to an opinion I had heard from other people, who also knew little or nothing of Pfitzner, that he was a sort of pale copy of Strauss. I asked him how he first got to know any of Strauss' work. He stared. "I heard performances, studied scores", he answered. "How else would I?" "Exactly", I said. "You heard performances. If you'd heard performances of Pfitzner as well, perhaps you would have got to know him, too. But while Strauss was performed here, Pfitzner was not. It goes like that with some composers. Even foreigners have their own ideas of what will suit the English and what will not". I told him of an occasion when Harry Newstone, after a quartet recital, asked Adolf Busch why his quartet, great champions of Reger on the Continent, did not play any Reger quartets in England. Busch raised his eyebrows and said simply "Reger? - in England?" And yet if the Busch Quartet had played here a work like Reger's great E♭ Quartet, Reger might have become a partially known composer to sympathetic audiences in this country in the '30s, instead of being a closed book whom everybody "knew" - and dismissed, on their lack of knowledge and, sometimes, their inability to read (which means "hear", mentally) music accurately.

Brian digested this and nodded. "Fair enough", he said. "So what about Pfitzner?" "I'll show you some", I said. On my next visit I took three works with me, a score of Pfitzner's *Käthchen von Heilbronn* Overture, the three *Palestrina* Preludes and the Piano Quintet. He read the Overture and was very interested. "Strange technique", he remarked, "but it works". Then he began on the Preludes. The first one took him by storm. "Good God, what an imagination". That was enough for me. "Straussian?" I queried. He grinned. "Don't rub it in. No, this chap's certainly a quite different proposition - and a genius!" Then he put his finger on what had struck me about that first Prelude. "How does he do it? The style's a 20th century romantic one, utterly personal, and yet he manages to bring the whole 16th century to one's mind". There was no obvious answer to how Pfitzner did it; it was a question that had often puzzled me, but there is no doubt about the result.

Later, after a rather more cursory look at the Quintet - chamber music was never very much Brian's cup of tea - he asked me how I summed up Strauss and Pfitzner, since I obviously knew a lot of both. I told him that to me Strauss was a magnificent genius, and that, in spite of certain exceptions, his music struck me as being very earthy, very much planted on this planet. Brian nodded and said "Yes,

I'd agree with that. It's one of the things I like about him". Pfitzner, on the other hand, always gives me the impression of a man who was in the world, but very much against his will. I could develop this theme here, although I did not at the time, but I think I have said enough. It would take in music, too, which Brian never knew, and which most of my readers probably will not know, either. Brian thought this an interesting point of view, about Pfitzner being unwillingly in the world, and added "Perhaps that's why I would always prefer Strauss. But", pointing to the *Palestrina* Prelude, "that chap disturbs one, and I'm not sure I want to be disturbed". An odd remark, perhaps, from a composer who has written more disturbing music than most; but I think the manner in which Pfitzner disturbed him was different, and worried him. At any rate, I was satisfied; at least, I'd shown Brian that Pfitzner was very far from being a copy of Strauss, pale or otherwise.

Strangely, apart from one or two side remarks, we never talked about Elgar. Bantock we did discuss, and Brian's admiration was tremendous. He considered that there was no-one who could excel Bantock as an orchestral composer (I am not sure how large a field this was meant to cover). "Great stuff!" he said.

He did not go into detail about any of Bantock's works, but he did mention the *Pagan* Symphony as a masterpiece of design and orchestration (which it is), as well as the vocal "orchestration" of Bantock's second choral symphony, for unaccompanied choir, *Vanity of Vanities*, which flowed, he said, with the ease of water. The only other comment he made was that mastery was the most obvious quality in Bantock's music.

These remarks were occasioned by Brian's telling me that Lady Bantock had written to him that she wanted a biography and study of her husband's music written, and asking him if he knew of anyone who could do it and would be interested. Brian said "You're just the man for it. Would you be interested?" I said I would, most decidedly, so he gave me Lady Bantock's address and suggested that I write to her. I did so, and she replied that she was most grateful for my interest, and enclosed a fair amount of interesting and useful data. She added that I should not begin until she wrote to tell me she had a publisher who was willing to publish the book. Over a year later she wrote again to say, sadly, that she had tried them all and none was interested. So I never started that book. There is a sort of sequel to this, but it has nothing to do with Brian, therefore this is not the place for it.

The only other English composer of whom Brian spoke was Holbrooke. Here he was quite definite that Holbrooke's greatest talent was his quick concern about English music and musicians, and the tremendous energy he expended in trying to secure performances of other composers' works, and in putting them on himself (which also involved the expenditure of considerable amounts of money). As a composer, Brian thought that Holbrooke was like the boy in the poem: when he was good he was very, very good, and when he was bad he was horrid. But he thought that there was far more very, very good than bad, and that agreed with my own opinion.

Of more recent composers he professed very little knowledge, pointing out that he had no radio, and did not want one.

Bertram B. Walker: A voice from the past[1]

As a small boy I can remember my father saying to me "You are as bad as Billy Brian", a remark which at that time conveyed nothing to me. It was subsequently explained that "Billy Brian" was an old pupil, who spent most of his time asking questions: "Why only five lines?", "Why only A to G?", "Why Treble and Bass clef?", etc.

I cannot recollect any further conversation concerning "Billy's" musical progress, but as I got older I can recall snatches of conversation within my family relating not specifically to Billy, but to his wife Isobel and his sister Martha - who was married to Leonard Graham, a friend of my mother's family. The next I heard of Billy was that he had "gone away" - where, when or why I was not told. It is only in later life that one learns that such matters were "not discussed in front of the children".

It was not until I had left the Potteries for the West Country that I heard from one of my late brothers that he had read that Havergal Brian had been taught the rudiments of music by Bertram B.Walker. I had always understood it to be so, but had never read of it in print - neither was I aware that Brian had become a composer of some standing. It was only when I got sight of the article *Another clue in search* in the *Staffordshire Evening Sentinel* dated 10 May 1983 that I really became interested.

Having obtained copies of two excellent books on Brian, I was surprised to find that the only reference to my father was that he had given Brian organ lessons. In Kenneth Eastaugh's book (p. 24) surprise is expressed that Brian did not go to Elijah Waine for lessons. This, I imagine, is explained by the fact that young Billy, with his parents, had lived all his life within 100 yards or so of my father, and obviously on good terms, until he removed from Longton to Stoke. Furthermore, one would not be expected to tackle a three-manual organ without a good knowledge of music, and why change tutors? - music was my father's profession.

Returning to the *Sentinel* article of 10 May 1983, as the result of an interview with Wilfrid Chadwick it was ascertained that it was not a manuscript that had been given to my father but an inscribed book (a copy of *The Organist's Handbook*, by E. F. Rimbault).[2] I now have added interest in revisiting the Potteries to try to find out what happened to the missing manuscripts.

The following may also be of interest - I think that my mother was a colleague of Martha Brian (Billy's sister) as a decorator of pottery, before marriage (I am seeking confirmation of this). Leonard Graham, who married

---

[1] Letter to the Editor from *Newsletter* 51 (I-II 1984), p. 9.
[2] This is reproduced from *Newsletter* 50 (XI-XII 1983), p. 5.

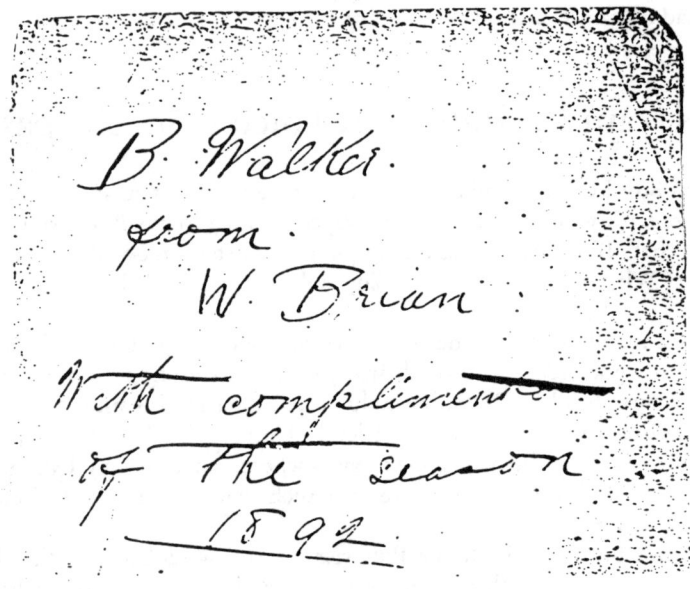

Martha, was a great friend of my mother's family, and was, I imagine, instrumental in getting the Duke of Sutherland to commission my grandfather (J. Allen) to paint a picture of some rare orchids which were flowering in his hothouse at Trentham (colour photography was not yet thought of). My grandfather made a copy of the picture which I have in my possession. I also have the violin which my father lent to Frank Hughes for a few days whilst his own was repaired. He taught Brian to play the violin.

When Brian left Longton to go to Stoke (shortly after his marriage to Isobel) I should not be in the least surprised to discover that my father introduced him to Dr Hemmings (or Dr Challinor), both of whom were friends of my father. It had happened in other cases.

Philip Scowcroft: Havergal Brian and Elgar[1]

A comparison between Elgar and Havergal Brian may at first sight seem strong to the casual observer, for the former is recognized as one of the greatest, if not the greatest, of all British composers and was widely regarded as such during his lifetime, while the latter, despite a long life and a prolific output, has always been

---

[1] From *Newsletter* 12 (VII-VIII 1977), pp. 4-5.

an obscure figure and even now his music is known to relatively few concert-goers.

Yet there are several striking parallels. Both came from the Midlands, which have contributed at least their fair share to the sum of creative music-making in this country. Both were largely self-taught (Elgar, being virtually born into a music shop, had perhaps the better opportunities). Both had a long struggle to have their music recognized and both, though each composed widely in other mediums and in fact began their careers as church organists, lived for the orchestra. Furthermore, the two men knew each other quite well for a time and, as we shall see, their acquaintance was of mutual benefit.

Brian first became aware of Elgar's music at the première of the latter's *King Olaf* at Hanley on 13 October 1896; this work, notably in its orchestral writing, had a great effect on him and much later he wrote "I still believe there is no music so instantly arresting as those opening bars of *King Olaf*." Shortly afterwards Brian, who at the time held an organist's post at Odd Rode Church in Cheshire (it is curious, by the way, that no organ music by him is extant), sent an anthem of his own composition to Elgar for comment and received the encouraging observation that it was original, if involved, and that he should keep on composing. Brian had enquired about how to obtain tuition in composition. Elgar replied "I have had to get on without it, but I am afraid this will be cold comfort to you." Far from being this, however, it was an inspiration to the younger man (he was just 20); what Elgar had done, surely he could do?

From that time Brian eagerly followed Elgar's music. He bought the score of *The Dream of Gerontius* and immediately recognized its genius. He played the Prelude one Sunday morning as an organ voluntary and then prevailed on his friend Arthur Bailey (who had heard him) to use his influence with the North Staffordshire District Choral Society to perform the oratorio. This was a daring undertaking as the work at this time (1902-3) was still deep in the shadow cast by its disastrous first airing at the Birmingham Festival of 1900, but the choir took up the challenge. At the final rehearsal Elgar said to them "You must be angels for you sing like angels". After the performance he placed them "in the highest rank", describing their singing as "almost flawless", and asked them to perform *The Dream* in London which they subsequently did, triumphantly. This was the first time it had been heard in the metropolis.

It is well known that Elgar thought highly of the Northern choral festivals - he had them in mind when he said in his Birmingham University lectures that "the living centre of music in Great Britain is not London but somewhere farther north" - and he wrote many part-songs as test pieces for these occasions. Brian too was attracted to them, describing them collectively as "the most remarkable movement in English music for several centuries". His works include some half-dozen choral songs written in the first decade of this century for competitive Festivals at Blackpool, Morecambe and Barrow. The first of them, set to Shakespeare's words "Shall I compare thee to a Summer's Day", was written soon after the first London performance of *Gerontius* mentioned above and sent to Elgar for comment. The other man was interested, so interested that he recommended the song to the Morecambe Festival organizers who adopted it as the principal choral test piece in the next Festival. Elgar for his part continued to like the piece, asking for it to be encored when it was sung in a private concert at his home. Soon afterwards he invited Brian to the Worcester Three Choirs Festival (1905).

Havergal Brian benefited, along with a number of other younger British composers, from the short-lived Musical League, of which Elgar was President. The first Festival promoted by the League in 1909 included Brian's choral work *By the Waters of Babylon* which had been written some six years previously; Sir Edward personally expressed his warm appreciation of this to the composer after the performance.

Brian's admiration of Elgar's music was such that he was greatly incensed by a performance he heard in Hanley in October 1909 of the First Symphony, conducted by Beecham, admittedly never a sympathetic Elgar interpreter. He wrote indignantly to the *Musical Times*: "The first movement was cut down one half; part of the development was cut out and some minutes sacrificed in the succeeding movements ... an insult to the composer and also those responsible for the concert. This is surely not the use to which so exceedingly fine an orchestra should be put, to say nothing of the misuse of the genius with which nature has endowed Mr Beecham".

Curiously, Elgar did not take kindly to this advocacy - he was always, of course, on the side of the performer, however misguided, rather than that of the critic, however favourable, and we should also remember the severely cut versions of some of his major works he himself conducted on early gramophone records. The two men, indeed, gradually drifted apart after this incident, though this was also due, as Reginald Nettel has pointed out, to Elgar turning from oratorio to orchestral music and moving as a consequence from the Midlands to London which had most of the best orchestras, and also perhaps to Brian's own development as a composer which was inevitably causing him to write music of greater modernity than Elgar's own. In any event the acquaintance had never been intimate and, furthermore, Sir Edward's moodiness and abruptness in several of his personal relationships are well documented; Brian, too, was never the easiest of men to get on with.

Elgar's musical influence on Brian is a topic which deserves a fuller study than space allows here. Naturally enough, this is strongest in the works the younger man wrote in his "first period", up to the First World War. *By the Waters of Babylon*, which as we have seen was admired by Elgar, shows the latter's influence in harmony. The breezy scoring of the First English Suite may recall Elgar to some; the 'March of Heroes' section of the Comedy Overture *Doctor Merryheart* (really a set of symphonic variations rather than an overture) owes much to Elgar; and *In Memoriam* has been compared to the elegiac slow movement of the older man's Second Symphony. Even in later life Brian's tunes often have an Elgarian feel about them, for example in a symphony as late as No. 21; the writer recalls being attracted to Brian's music years ago on admiring in a broadcast performance of the Ninth Symphony, especially in its superb final climax, a breadth and imagination which seemed Elgarian. Comparisons should not be pushed too far; no composer, of course, works in a stylistic vacuum but Brian's mature music owes less to earlier example than most composers. It could be argued in any case that Bantock, Richard Strauss and Mahler, to name but three, had an effect as great, if not considerably greater than Elgar. Certainly Brian's later orchestral technique, at least, seems little influenced by him, though admittedly both men share in this respect an admirable professionalism and a love of orchestral colour for its own sake, in particular in their bold, often flamboyant, writing for brass instruments.

Although Elgar and Brian moved apart after the first decade of the century, the latter retained his admiration of the former. He said to an American visitor only five years before his death: "There once was a great man in this country. His name was Edward Elgar. And Elgar was great, not because he belonged to a 'modern' school, but because he was not afraid to be himself musically. That is why he started a whole musical tradition and why his music is not only national but international in its appeal". This tribute reflects Brian's love of Elgar's music, so vital to his initial musical development, and much of it is true of himself, though it still remains to be seen whether his music will ever enjoy as "international" an appeal as Elgar's.

Malcolm MacDonald: "Dear Crusoe ... Always your Freitag": The Brian letters at McMaster University[1]

From 12 December to 2 January I was fortunate in being able to visit McMaster University, Hamilton, Ontario and (through the good offices of Paul Rapoport) to spend a considerable time in the University's Mills Memorial Library reading the collection of Havergal Brian's letters to Granville Bantock which the University purchased at Sotheby's in 1978. It was an enthralling experience. Many extracts from this important body of correspondence have already been published, as most members will know, in Reginald Nettel's books and, especially, Kenneth Eastaugh's *Havergal Brian: the Making of a Composer*. Other passages have been quoted by Trevor Bray in an unpublished article written some years ago, of which he kindly sent me a copy. But no amount of extracts can give the full flavour of this extraordinarily rich, provoking, sometimes baffling, often very funny, and frequently moving record of 30 years in the life of a struggling composer. It is no exaggeration to say that there is hardly a scrap of this correspondence that is without interest - human, historical, musical, factual or anecdotal. There is plenty of food for thought for the student of Brian's musical development: this was my chief reason for wanting to read the letters, and the results of my thoughts will appear in due course, I hope, in Volume 3 of my book on the

---

[1] From *Newsletters* 28 (V-VI 1980), pp. 3-5 and 35 (V-VI 1981), pp. 7-10.

symphonies. There are, too, very many letters which must surely one day appear in any anthology of Brian's correspondence. (The publication of such a volume is, I believe, one of the Society's long-term objectives.) Brian was, in his own way, as entertaining and idiosyncratic a letterwriter as Elgar, and in full confidence of his close friendship with Bantock he ran the gamut of epistolary pyrotechnics.

These letters demand, and in time will surely receive, years of close study to clear up ambiguities, elucidate obscurities, and relate them to Brian's day-to-day life and the development of his music; for they are without doubt a major and priceless source of information about his thoughts and feelings, opinions and activities. This is not the time or place even to begin such an attempt. What I want to do here is to make a few comments on the arrangement of the collection as it now stands; to indicate its limitations as well as its contributions to our knowledge and to examine briefly the fidelity, or otherwise, of the versions of certain passages which have already appeared in print.

The collection is housed in the Research Area of the Mills Memorial Library, near to their famous Bertrand Russell Room (which contains the largest collection of Russelliana in the world). It is catalogued simply as "Havergal Brian Letters" and is kept in two large box-files, clearly sorted into years, months, and chronologically arranged within those divisions. The Director of Research Collections, Charlotte Stewart, who performed the initial sorting when the collection arrived at McMaster, has prepared a 19-page Guide to the letters which is made available to students wishing to study them. The Guide lists the letters chronologically, indicates whether they are autograph or (in a few cases) typescript; whether actual letters, letter-cards, postcards or telegrams; whether an envelope or enclosure is attached, and the date on which they were written.

Considering the vast amount of material that had to be disentangled, and the fact that Ms Stewart herself had no prior knowledge of Brian, she did an excellent job. Nevertheless, there are some inaccuracies in the Guide as it stands at present. Mostly these concern letters which lack a year-date, which have been conjecturally arranged according to their position in the collection on its arrival at McMaster. Usually internal evidence (addresses, etc.) suggested to me that their placement was wrong, and in most cases I was able to suggest a more likely chronological position. Occasionally a date has been mis-read, or a letter incorrectly described. In two cases Brian's astonishing repertoire of humorous aliases had foiled the cataloguer, and the letters had been placed at the end of the collection among "Correspondence addressed to Granville Bantock, *not* from Havergal Brian". I made a note of all such anomalies that came to light as I read through the collection, and I hope that my notes will lead eventually to a revised ordering of the collection and an improved Guide.

The collection consists of one signed photograph and 636 letters from Brian to Bantock; five letters from Brian to Bantock's secretary and biographer H[oward] O[rsmond] Anderton; one letter from Brian to Lady Helen Bantock; one letter from Brian to Josef Holbrooke; one letter from Brian to the secretary of the Birmingham City Orchestra, and seven letters (all dating from 1969) from Brian to Raymond Bantock (Sir Granville's son). There are also a dozen letters to

Brian from various correspondents such as his patron H. M. Robinson, Josef Holbrooke and various publishers (some of these are contained as enclosures in letters to Bantock, while others are filed separately at the end of the collection); two letters to Bantock from other correspondents, relating to Brian; and one, unidentified, telegram which is probably to Hilda Brian from an employer.

Altogether, then, the collection represents an enormous documentary cache. But it is not, and should not be expected to be, the one all-sufficient source of knowledge on Brian for the years that it spans. It does have several inherent limitations which require that it should be used with care and discrimination.

First, the collection is only half of a correspondence. Though it is certain that Brian was much the more active correspondent, nothing of Bantock's side is included. We are left to infer the spirit in which he responded to the younger composer's varied and sometimes ceaseless sallies; but the simple fact that he continued throughout his life to be the recipient and preserver of such an amazing range of missives indicates that the friendship and regard in which Bantock was held by Brian were sentiments which he warmly and actively reciprocated.

Second, the collection now residing at McMaster cannot, by any stretch of the imagination, be the complete letters which Brian wrote to Bantock. They became friends in (apparently) 1906; they remained so until Bantock's death in 1946. With one possible exception, no letter in the collection predates 1912: the last dates from 1943; and several of the intervening years are represented by no letters at all. Yet there is every reason to believe that the correspondence continued fairly constantly, at varying rates no doubt, but built on a strong sense of continuity. There were quite clearly more letters than the 636. Quite often, in the McMaster collection, one finds Brian referring to a subject he had mentioned "in my last letter" - but the "last letter" is not there. It is instructive to make a break-down of the letters by totals for each year as follows:

1907 - one signed photograph;
one letter with the spoof date of "June 6, 1819" which is possibly earlier than 1912 and not later than 1914;

1912 - 44 letters;	1913 - 20 letters;	1914 - 133 letters;
1915 - 67;	1916 - 83;	1917 - 22;
1918 - 21;	1919 - 39;	1920 - 15;
1921 - 24;	1922 - 17;	1923 - 20;
1924 - 26;	1925 - 8;	1926 - 6;
1927 - 9;	1928 - 2;	1929 - none;
1930 - none;	1931 - 14;	1932 - 5;
1933 - 4;	1934 - 18;	1935 - 2;
1936 - 1;	1937 - none;	1938 - 4;
1939 - 4;	1940 - 3;	1941 - 3;
1942 - 13;	1943 - 8.	

(A few of these totals might need minor adjustment owing to the ambiguous dating of a couple of letters, and I have included in the 1921 total one undated letter which could have been written any time between October 1920 and the summer of 1922.)

It is obvious that 1914 was an extraordinary year, and it is probable that the volume of correspondence did gradually taper away during the 1920s and '30s, as these figures suggest. But we are not yet in a position to understand the erratic fluctuations in apparent volume. From the "feel" of the letters themselves, the very low figures for certain years are far too low; and the three letterless years are frankly unbelievable. Perhaps more Brian letters remain still with Raymond Bantock? Some supporting evidence for this comes from the fact that on p. 277 of his book Kenneth Eastaugh quotes a letter of 6 July 1931 - which is not to be found at McMaster. On p. 221 he quotes a letter of 20 December 1916 concerning Brian's proposed "Symphonic Drama" *Razamoff* and goes on to quote from a "synopsis" of the work's action which he says is attached. The letter is at McMaster, all right; but there is no sign of the synopsis. It is slightly worrying, too, that Charlotte Stewart's Guide lists a one-page letter of 20 April 1920: but I failed to find this item in the collection itself.

Partly because of these gaps and fluctuations in volume of letters, there are large gaps also in the information they can provide us with about Brian. The practically day-to-day commentary of 1914 is of course exceptional; but often in the following years the letters will give out for a space of several months and resume with Brian in a totally different situation with different concerns - a whole network of biographical and musical threads are left hanging loose.

Third, although Brian may have been franker with Bantock than almost any other friend about a whole range of subjects, especially in the period 1913-16, there is no reason to suppose that he was invariably so, and there is some evidence that in later years at least he was cautious about letting Bantock know of the progress of his larger works and deeper musical thoughts - fearing perhaps that the older composer would try to reduce the scale of his cherished conceptions. Thus for instance, *The Gothic* is not discussed exhaustively: Brian presents the completion of its constituent parts to Bantock more as a *fait accompli*. On the knotty problem of dating *The Gothic*, the letters supply little evidence in addition to that already set out by Kenneth Eastaugh on pp. 251-3 of his book,[2] on which Paul Rapoport's verdict (*Opus Est*, p. 88) still stands: "He may be right, but the evidence for these conclusions is not presented convincingly ... a close examination of what Eastaugh reveals of the Bantock correspondence does not in

---

[2] Bernard G. Counsell writes in a letter to the Editor in *Newsletter* 22 (III-IV 1977), p. 7: "I wonder if I am in a minority in appreciating the value of this book, which I used to borrow from the library and have now purchased for myself? I do not think the aim of our society is to canonize Brian the man (or indeed the musician!); Brian's experiences of life tended to make him a sort of Super-Everyman and there are bits of Brian in all of us somewhere. His grand passion would seem to be with the Spirit of Music - a love unrequited in life. He was not one to 'Write the vision ... that he may run that readeth it' - unless by 'run' we mean 'run away'! If ever there was a need to read, mark, learn and inwardly digest, it is with Brian's works, and I can only agree with the idea that one has to force oneself to listen time after time to something that on first hearing sounds unpalatable (like a mixed metaphor?). But generally there is something to make one feel in sympathy with or attuned to Brian and it is worth searching for. But as in battles, crime detection and espionage, it is helpful to know the man concerned; it is useful to understand the foibles as well as the strengths of a composer, the better to understand his works."

fact rule out the *possibility* that both parts of the symphony were completed in all but final form long before the winter of 1924-5. Most importantly, he gives insufficient substantiation for November 1924 as the completion date of Part I". There is in fact no such substantiation in the letters: they only establish that it was completed in full score at some point between 12 November 1924 and 5 January 1925. There is likewise no precise completion date for Part II - Eastaugh, p. 251, quotes the letter of 27 June 1926 in which Brian states that "the sketches are complete"; but he has misread Brian's handwriting at one important point - the composer wrote, not "This is most written" but "This is now written".

A passage in a letter of 24 November 1921 may however shed a little more light. Bantock has written to Brian pointing out some misprints in the printed copies of the *Four Miniatures* for piano, and after thanking him Brian continues: "Your letter has confirmed my resolution to write everything in the open key [he means without key-signature]. It does away with all risk ... In the orchestral scores I am doing now - when I get the chance - I am writing in the open key - transposing instruments treated in the same manner."

It is perhaps relevant to note here that the first movement of *The Gothic* begins in the key-signature of D minor, and continues to use various signatures until the middle of the development at bar 148; thereafter key-signatures disappear. This *may* mean that the first half of the first movement, at least, had been written in full score before the date of the letter. Brian's reference to "scores" in the plural could also include English Suite No. 3, completed a couple of months earlier: its last three movements are without key-signatures, and in the last two movements this applies to transposing instruments as well.

To read these letters is to realize how closely *Havergal Brian: the Making of a Composer* depended on them for its material and narrative structure. Gaps in Eastaugh's tale, or comparatively skimpy sections, almost invariably reflect gaps in the letters and make clear that much more research needs to be done. Eastaugh has (quite legitimately, and effectively) skimmed the "cream" from the letters. There are no major revelations, personal or artistic, still lying open on the surface of the texts. But there are masses of material he did not use in his book. A true appreciation of the letters will require close study of details, of tone, and the many "leads" they provide as to who Brian was in contact with, where he was on particular days, what books he happened to be reading, what thinking about, and so on. Their flavour will only be appreciated through the publication of a large number of them, uncut, with a minimum of moralizing commentary. And the individual letters can only be seen in perspective against the balance of the whole collection - and indeed, Brian's letters to other people. Brian must be allowed to speak for himself, and we must be allowed to make up our own minds as to whether in any particular instance he is being unreasonable, or hysterical, or "whining", or any of the other loaded descriptions Mr Eastaugh so liberally employed. Passages quoted in his book often take on a quite different aspect when restored to their original context.

Certainly Brian was a man of extreme moods, and in those years where the letters are frequent enough to provide an emotional barometer, he goes up and down like a yo-yo. He contradicts himself many times, starts every new ploy with brave words and as often as not ends up cursing, makes firm resolutions and immediately breaks them (imagine my feelings when I found Brian vowing to write *no more letters* - it was 18 June 1914 and I had another 450 to read - the next written the following day!). But many things remain constant: the drive to write great music, to do something of lasting worth; the admiration of great music by others; the love of nature, of gardening, of the simple things in life; the wonderment at a mad world; his affection for and loyalty to Bantock; and the amazing resilience of the man, his ability to bounce back with a joke from the blackest of situations.

Whether or not all his problems were self-made - and in part they surely were - 1914-15 was a period of disaster for Brian as much as for the world at large. His big works - *Kevlaar* and English Suite No. 2 - and the ones he hoped would be popular successes - *Red May* and the children's operetta now known to have been entitled *The Maiden and the Flower Garden* - get thought about and their progress reported on to Bantock, are written, completed, sent to publishers and conductors - and just *disappear* from the correspondence as literally as the scores themselves seem to have vanished into thin air. He moved to Birmingham in January 1916, to be nearer Bantock and in search of both employment and inspiration, but it was mostly a fallow year, tinkering with ideas for books and articles, until October. Then began a slow upturn of his creative if not his material fortunes. Reading all the letters in sequence, the crucial psychological reversal seems to be contained in the one written on 9 October (Eastaugh, p. 218, gives a couple of phrases from it, but not the whole passage); the underlining is Brian's:

> On Wednesday last I had one of those extraordinary moods of ecstasy which used to come often in the old days. I went into the country round here and the autumn perfume, the leaves & swaying branches were all in harmony. I felt etherealized and I knew then - what I have often wondered - that I *was not dried up*.

The Tigers and *The Gothic* lay ahead. The former emerges, ever more clearly, as a work of fantasized autobiography: not only in the general correlation between the anarchic eponymous infantry regiment and Brian's own experiences in the Honourable Artillery Company (whose base at Mount Felix must be echoed in the opera's "Mount Duresco") but in all kinds of details. Why, for instance, should Sir John Stout be visited (Act II Scene I) by the "apparition of a Red Indian"? Perhaps because while working in the records office of the Canadian Contingent, Brian met an Indian Lieutenant, as he reported to Bantock on 24 August 1915. Why all the business with church bells in the last act? Was it sparked off by the out-of-tune bells Brian heard on the night of 25 June 1916, and commented on to Bantock, complete with a music example? There is a gap in the letters between 29 July and 11 August 1914 - but one begins to wonder: what was Brian doing on 4 August, when war was declared? Was he, perhaps, at a carnival on Hampstead Heath?

Another salutary effect of the letters is that one is continually brought up against Brian's sense of humour. With someone he trusted as closely as he trusted Bantock, Brian was able to drop the pose of solemnity at a moment's notice, and laugh at the world and himself. In a similar fashion does wit peek forth slyly round the corners of his most imposing symphonic structures, or give itself up to belly laughs from English Suite No. 1 onwards. The sheer range of Brian's epistolary humour is amazing, and can hardly be demonstrated without 20 pages of quotations. To take just one fairly obvious aspect, his store of funny names for himself and Bantock seems to have been inexhaustible. Many examples are given in Eastaugh, p. 71 - but Brian also signed himself, on occasion, "Horrie", "Granville Ransome Elgar", "Pietro", "Josquin", "Burglars", "Pabrun" (this was also his alias when submitting *The Vision of Cleopatra* to the Norwich Festival Committee), "Toot Toot", "William Blick", "Marie", "Loo C. Long", "William Wallace" (a joke on Bantock's Scottish enthusiasms - and against the eponymous composer), "Zarathustra", "Euripy" (writing to "Pericles"), "Alfred" (Lord Tennyson writing to "Vic"(toria)) - and even copying his patron's invariable mode of signing off "yours truly, H. M. Robinson"!!!

The letters from "Friday" (or, as often, whenever Brian was feeling in a pro-German mood, "Freitag"[3]) to "Crusoe" are scattered throughout the collection, and form almost a separate series in themselves. They are amongst the funniest, the fullest-stuffed with private jokes and the warmest in Brian's expression of feeling for Bantock. They also tend to take off into pure fantasy - a fantasy of desert isles, exotic birds and fishes, and an idyll of honest servitude with Bantock as his master.

Sometimes Brian's whimsicality can lead the unwary astray. Kenneth Eastaugh (pp. 186-7) makes much of Brian's supposed joining of the French Foreign Legion as yet another instance of his erratic behaviour. But Brian, in the letter quoted on those pages, says nothing about the *French* Foreign Legion - it's more likely that this was his joking way of referring to the British Expeditionary Force. Again Eastaugh (p. 263) implies that Brian shows callous unconcern in announcing the birth of his daughter Jean to Bantock *after* announcing his acquisition of a typewriter, an unconcern compounded by spelling her name wrongly. What he seems to have failed to note is that the whole letter (19 February 1923) is a virtuoso performance built on the comic premise of "here is a silly ass using a typewriter for the first time" - the entire text is riddled with intentionally amusing typing errors. In the passage he quotes, Mr Eastaugh has silently corrected them all, apart from the mis-spelling of Jean's name! The letter is signed "Haptygal".

Finally here is Brian telling Bantock, I think (!), that he is too busy to come and see him, in a postcard of 19 February 1918. I quote the text entire:

---

[3] The name "Freitag" occurs throughout the collection, from the later years of the Great War onward, and is not, as Eastaugh on p. 282 would seem to suggest, confined to the correspondence of the early 1930s.

Will try to see you when I am fixing up various things as did not control out of centre in brush did when newmatics all bust, flour sent hospital in bag, suffocated bursting, bad eye and Arlekin no trousers too.

Jim

In his book *Opus Est*, Paul Rapoport had some trenchant things to say about how it appeared authors had used, or misused, Havergal Brian's letters to Sir Granville Bantock as a source:

> Comparing supposedly identical quotations in Nettel's and Eastaugh's books reveals important discrepancies. Words are omitted, inserted, substituted, and rearranged without marking or comment. Authors ought to know better. Of course, without the original documents in hand, little more can be said about these authors' faithfulness to the sources. However, in his book, Eastaugh misreads words in a letter from Brian's patron Herbert Robinson to Brian which is given in facsimile among the illustrations. Eastaugh's transcription of it is on pp. 213-14. He is forced to add punctuation to the original to get quasi-grammatical sense out of his misreadings. Such things do not inspire confidence in the author's ability to handle his sources. (*Opus Est*, p. 87)

This was a timely note of warning. Now that the originals of the Brian letters to Bantock are available for study (albeit on the far side of the Atlantic, in McMaster University's Mills Memorial Library), it emerges that the inaccuracies which Rapoport noted in Kenneth Eastaugh's transcription of Herbert Robinson's letter extend very widely to his transcriptions of Brian's own letters - and, more generally, that both Reginald Nettel's *Havergal Brian and his Music* and Eastaugh's *Havergal Brian: The Making of a Composer* should be used with caution when they quote from these sources.

The greater caution is required with Eastaugh, both in proportion as he has made much more extensive use of the letters, but also because his shortcomings in their transmission frequently extend further than the simple inaccuracies enumerated above. Misreading of words is not uncommon, and the result is often the loss of some comic or ironic nuance. On p. 280 of his book, for example, Eastaugh has Brian addressing Bantock as "Dear Darling" - but this salutation is less blush-making when the original discloses Brian to have been in one of his Irish humours, and writing "Dear Darlint". Eastaugh is often capricious about dating his quotations - in general I think he dates them far too rarely, especially when he is using passages written long after the event to cast some light on an earlier period in Brian's career - but even when he gives dates in full he is not always accurate: the letter from Josef Holbrooke quoted on p. 247 should be dated 1 January, not 11 January, for instance. Sometimes his vagueness in dating creates a misleading impression: a case in point is the quotation given on pp. 198-9 (Brian's encounter with four seriously wounded soldiers on Christmas Eve,

1914). Eastaugh's preamble implies that it was written in or after February 1915, following Brian's move to 62 Rosendale Road; but the letter is in fact dated 26 December 1914 - only two days after the incident recounted. Sometimes his avoidance of precise dating leads Eastaugh into error: e.g. his editorial interpolation into the letter quoted on pp. 145-6, explaining that the "new work" Brian mentions therein is "probably" the re-writing of the Violin Concerto. If he had mentioned that the date of the letter was 29 April 1934, someone could have pointed out to him that the *original* Violin Concerto is much more likely to be meant: it wasn't completed (in short score) until 7 June, and its loss on a train, referred to by Eastaugh in the same note, occurred on the following day.

Mr Eastaugh quotes lavishly from the letters, but in very many cases he quotes several times from the same letter in different parts of his book. There is no particular reason why he should make this clear on every occasion that he does it, but the result is to increase the impression that Brian's letters to Bantock are largely made up of complaints, self-justifications, hysterical outbursts, and the like. All these things are there, but they are only a moderate proportion of the whole - and Mr Eastaugh, in his zeal to correct what he sees as an over-simplified and sanctified picture of the composer, rather lets them stand for the whole.

His policy with excisions and compression of material is difficult to fathom. Sometimes whole sentences and paragraphs are omitted with no editorial dots to mark their passing. On the other hand, his quotation on p. 262 contains two sets of three dots, indicating excisions - yet the first set is redundant: the two sentences separated by them run on one after the other in Brian's original! Where real excisions have occurred, they are sometimes puzzling, for the material is often interesting. Of course, it is not always germane to the picture of Brian that the author is constructing, but one sometimes wonders if he rejected it because of the limitations of his knowledge of the period of the "English Musical Renaissance". Some of Brian's professional acquaintances thus drop out of the story altogether, making him appear even more isolated than he was in fact. It is noticeable, for instance, that from the quoted portions of the letters written during Brian's sojourn in Birmingham (January 1916-mid-1919), Eastaugh has deleted all mentions of the name *Fenney*. William J. Fenney (1891-1957) may be forgotten now, but he was considered a talented composer then, perhaps with reason;[4] he was obviously someone with whom Brian was in fairly frequent con-

---

[4] I possess only two works by Fenney, a pleasant early piano suite *In Early Spring* (Chester, 1915) and a photocopy of the manuscript of a later, more characteristic *Rhapsody* for cello and piano (not, apparently, the same work as the *Rhapsody* mentioned by Josef Holbrooke in his *Contemporary British Composers*, London 1925, p. 266). He seems a rather tragic figure. A Birmingham man, at first self-taught and later a pupil of Bantock, Fenney wrote mainly songs, piano pieces, and chamber music, though I have read somewhere that Ernest Newman reviewed a performance of one of his few orchestral works with an astonishing eulogy to the effect - I cannot remember the exact words, but this was the sense of them - that Fenney was "clearly the natural successor to Elgar". A quiet and retiring personality ("as aloof as Delius" - Brian to Bantock, 2 December 1915), he seems to have fallen silent musically after the Great War, feeling out of sympathy with the times or otherwise unable to compose. However, he lived out a reclusive existence in Epsom, to die in the deepest obscurity. *Everyman's Dictionary of Music* gives

tact at this time, and for whom he had a very high regard (expressed not only in the letters to Bantock but also in one of his early letters to Walter Allum). Maybe the name simply meant nothing to Mr Eastaugh.

There are several instances of rather larger violence being done to Brian's texts. On p. 147, in the large quotation introduced by the words "He wrote in 1919" (the date is actually 1 March 1919), Mr Eastaugh, for no very obvious reason, has reversed the order of some of the sentences. On p. 203, he gives a short quotation in which Brian is comparing Tchaikovsky with Franck. It consists of two sentences, linked by three editorial dots. The dots in fact span a period of four days - the sentences are from two different letters. A larger variation on this device will be found on pp. 81-2: a sizeable quotation of reminiscences introduced by the words "Writing to Bantock thirty-five years later ..." (my editorial dots indicate the suppression of the remainder of Eastaugh's introductory sentence). The quotation consists of three paragraphs. The first paragraph ends with the words "Do you remember the head waiter George who always brought you the Stilton?", and the next one begins "Do you remember that night when we were larking ...?". Quite a nice literary effect, the repetition of the phrase "Do you remember". Unfortunately, it isn't Brian's, and this isn't taken from one letter, but fabricated from two. The first paragraph occurs in a letter of 25 June 1942 (which is, indeed, 35 years after the events recounted in Eastaugh's text); but the last two, beginning with the artful iteration of "Do you remember", are taken from a letter written on 10 November 1939.

Perhaps the oddest violation of the lot is to be found on p. 184 of Eastaugh's book, which "reproduces" the following, from a letter which the author does not date:

> My wife left on the 10.24 for Saxmundham and she refuses to return until I can give proof that I am in possession of a salary which will maintain us without interference. The whole thing is the most horrible botch I've ever known inside - or outside, of fiction.

Careful examination of the letters failed to disclose the passage in question: yet there *is* a letter which begins with exactly the same 15 words. It is dated 2 May 1914, which accords well with Eastaugh's narrative context, and there is no hint in any other letter of this period that Hilda made a habit of jaunting off to Saxmundham, still less by identical trains. What Mr Eastaugh *should* have transcribed, therefore, is this:

> My wife left on the 10.24 for Saxmundham and she refuses to return until I complete up to the first episode I sent you. Just now Blake is leading - I set his *Chimney Sweeper* yesterday!

A slightly discrepant version. It is more interesting than Eastaugh's rendering, and as such in need of some slight commentary - which may have been his reason for suppressing it. "The first episode I sent you" is a reference to Brian's second

---

the date of death as "*c.* VII. 1957" - perhaps a reflection of the story, apparently genuine, that the body was discovered in an unknown period of time, but certainly a matter of days, after his death.

attempt of this year to write a quasi-autobiographical novel: he had recently sent Bantock some drafts of chapters dealing with his childhood. The second sentence is of course a priceless piece of information, dating one of his finest William Blake settings for children. In fact, all other contents apart, in letters for the first half of 1914 Brian chronicles his creative, compositional progress in a way that he had never done before and was seldom to do again - and one is staggered by his capacity for hard work when the need drove him. All his shows of bravado and self-congratulation aside, the figures speak for themselves: between the last days of December 1913 and the end of July 1914, Brian completed the full score (for the largest orchestra he had yet employed) and wrote the vocal score of his large-scale choral work *Pilgrimage to Kevlaar*;[5] wrote a short orchestral work (*Red May*); composed a half-hour operetta for children's voices and piano, and scored some dances from it for orchestra; composed at the most conservative estimate 33, and possibly over 40, songs and part-songs; and still had energy enough to draft parts of novels and - it goes without saying - maintain a lively and voluminous correspondence of which the Bantock letters are only one part.

I mention only one short orchestral work from early 1914, and not two, because I think the putative second - the English Rhapsody included by Mr Eastaugh in the list of works on p. 320 of his book - is a chimera, and a careful reading of the letters seems to support this view. The title appears only once (21 March 1914) in a list of future projects: "I have about 20 poems I'm going to set in various ways - do an orchestral English Rhapsody & then your brass band piece". After this we hear no more of it. The "brass band piece" became *Red May*, written early in May 1914: "*Your* march! ... It will make a fine orchestra or brass band titbit", wrote Brian at 4 a.m. on the night of 7-8 May in the last of the *five* letters he wrote to Bantock on the 7th: he was then hard at work sketching it. But it was for orchestra that he scored it, and it was clearly this, and not the phantom English Rhapsody, which he sent unsuccessfully to Henry Wood later in the month (cf. Eastaugh, p. 169), and compared favourably to *Finlandia*. *Red May* seems never to have been given a brass band guise - and where is it now?

Reginald Nettel, as we would expect, takes far fewer and slighter liberties with Brian's text, but he is not always 100% accurate. Such an important psychological document as the letter reproduced on pp. 95-7 of his book (the "Drunk on a dead peacock" dream) is transmitted with many minor textual errors. Like many others, they will probably have to wait until a proper edition of Brian's letters for correction. Moreover, this letter was not written, as Nettel states, "while Brian was working on *The Tigers*": it is dated 9 June 1916, and thus comes in the middle of the long fallow period before the opera was begun.

When he came to write *Havergal Brian and his Music* Mr Nettel sometimes expanded the quotations from letters which he had used in his original book on

---

[5] This appears to be the correct title of this work, as contained in Novello's letter of rejection of it for publication on 24 April 1914 (which forms part of the McMaster collection). Brian usually referred to it just as *Kevlaar* or, occasionally, *Die Wallfahrt nach Kevlaar* - but it was a setting of an English translation. - Editor's note: A cantata *Die Wallfahrt nach Kevlaar* has also been written, for example, by Engelbert Humperdinck.

Brian, *Ordeal by Music*, in 1945 - at least to the extent of naming individuals whose identities he had previously thought it advisable to suppress. On pp. 116-18 of *Ordeal by Music*, for instance, he had reproduced part of a letter in which Brian gives an account of his experiences as a music copyist ("this hideous form of slavery"), and the low rates he is forced to work to by a fellow-composer. Nettel dated this letter "March 8th, 1924", and identified the composer only as "H_____". The date has in fact been misread: it should be 18 March. In his later book (pp. 105-6), however, Nettel allowed the erroneous date to stand; but he restored the full name of the composer (Holbrooke). He did not, however, correct a further suppression which he made in 1945 (presumably because the original texts of the letters were no longer available to him). Now that we know that it was Holbrooke who was paying Brian 6d. a page, there is hardly any point in concealing the fact that Brian did not vaguely write that he was drawing string parts from "his opera score": the work in question was *Bronwen*, and he said so.

Many of the simple misreadings in Nettel and Eastaugh - and even some of Eastaugh's grosser errors - probably resulted from insufficiently accurate transcription in the worknotes which they presumably took (as I did) while reading the letters, frantically trying to assimilate as much relevant information as possible from this enormous correspondence which ideally would require months, if not years, of attentive sifting. To some extent the same reason may lie behind the alteration of Brian's punctuation - but so wholesale is this practice in both authors that much of it must have been deliberate. It is doubtful if they saw this as any kind of sin, and from their viewpoint they were probably right: they were writing books for popular consumption, and therefore easy readability - which they may have seen as requiring them to "improve" Brian's punctuation to avoid grammatical obscurity, without at the same time disturbing the reader with too obvious an imposition of the editorial hand.

I tend to feel, however, that a writer's punctuation, or lack of it, is part and parcel of his personal literary style. To silently "correct" Brian is to lose something of his own inimitable flavour, and I suggest that any future editions of the letters should let the texts stand as Brian wrote them - except where haste, excitement, or exhaustion have taken such toll of his syntax, punctuation, or handwriting as to render his meaning totally obscure. Such occasions are rare. Certainly Brian did not bother to punctuate his letters as carefully or as fully as his published articles and musical journalism; but the punctuation he does apply, if not always that of Standard English, is usually consistent in its own terms. Like the poetess Emily Dickinson, he often made very expressive use of the dash where we might expect a comma or colon - but care is necessary - for when he wrote at speed - his commas (and occasionally his ampersands) had a tendency to turn into short horizontal strokes that the unwary could interpret as dashes - which accounts for the jerky feeling - rather like this - which we find in some of the published extracts from his letters. Careful scrutiny will be necessary in the preparation of any future edition. "Proper" punctuation is not, in any case, as necessary to the sense of a sentence as the clarity of thought behind that sense - and in this respect Brian's letters sometimes remind me of the defiantly unshackled prose of the Northamptonshire "peasant poet" John Clare, whose cogent and expressive qualities manage triumphantly without punctuation of any kind.

My comments in this article are not intended as nit-picking criticisms of minutiae, nor of the often valiant efforts of Nettel and Eastaugh to pick their way through the tangles and contradictions of Brian's cornucopic correspondence. The 650-odd letters now reposing at the Mills Memorial Library (to whose staff, especially the Director of Research Collections, Charlotte Stewart, I am grateful for their courteous helpfulness - as I am to Paul Rapoport for the opportunity to visit McMaster) are obviously one of the prime sources for an understanding of Brian's development, both as man and artist. But the two most easily available biographical accounts of Brian's life can hardly be said to have fully assimilated them, and their renderings of the texts should be consulted with caution. There are contradictions and mysteries enough in Brian's writings without fathering any more on him.

To conclude this necessarily brief discussion of selected aspects of the Brian-Bantock letters, and to provide a prelude to my resumption, in the next *Newsletter*, of my series examining Brian's works in variation form, I shall chronicle the appearances in the correspondence of just one work, the Comedy Overture *Doctor Merryheart*.

The letters in general have little to tell us directly about Brian's inner creative intentions in writing particular works, and in the case of *Merryheart* they tell us nothing of the circumstances of its composition either - for the letters in McMaster really only begin after the completion of the full score in January 1912. However, the work does figure prominently in the earliest stages of the correspondence in connection with the twin topics of performance and publication. In July 1912 Brian, with H. M. Robinson's co-operation, decided to try to get a representative selection of his orchestral works printed and published; several firms were approached for estimates of engraving and printing costs, and the score of *Doctor Merryheart* was sent to both Novello's and Breitkopf & Härtel for this purpose.

It was apparently still away from Brian's hands when, on 5 November, he received a letter from the second Musical League Festival accepting a work of his for performance the following January: not *Merryheart*, but *Festal Dance*. Brian immediately wrote to Bantock: "Does this selection meet with your approval or would you prefer my 'Comedy Overture'?" Whatever Bantock's response may have been, Brian decided to substitute the larger and more recent *Merryheart*, and from now on preparation of performing materials took priority over publication. A few days later parts were being copied by Goodwin & Tabb, and on 21 November Brian heard from Julius Harrison that he had been invited to conduct the première of *Merryheart* at the Festival. The copying went slowly - or at least slowly enough to arouse Brian's anxiety that the work would not be ready in time. "Any other work I should not mind being withdrawn", he wrote to Bantock on 1 December, "but there is too much fun in *Merryheart* for us to miss its production". In another letter of the same date he laments his inability to

50   *Life and personality*

check the few parts so far received: "I shall have to await the arrival complete wind & score for I have no sketches whatever" (had he destroyed them?). By 18 December, with the performance only a fortnight away, Brian had still not received the bulk of the parts and was making contingency plans to substitute *For Valour* - he would take the score and parts to the Festival, conduct it himself, "& make it go like the devil".

Meanwhile the issue of publication was still being pursued. On 6 December Robinson and Brian had agreed that Breitkopf & Härtel would publish "some scores". Though never actually stated in the letters, it is clear that *Merryheart* was to be the first to go to press, both because of the publicity of the approaching première and because Brian had hopes of securing other performances, especially from Henry Wood. On 23 December Brian met Julius Harrison to discuss the conducting of *Merryheart*, and the remaining parts must have arrived by then, as there are no more mentions of them in the letters.

Doctor Merryheart was heard for the first time, under Harrison's baton, in Birmingham on 3 January 1913, as part of the final concert of the second - and last - Musical League Festival. It was at least moderately successful, to judge by the reviews. The letters do not contain Brian's reactions to the event, for the obvious reason that, since he was staying with Bantock at Broadmeadow for the Festival, he would have had plenty of opportunity to make his feelings known verbally. But he soon turned his attention to Henry Wood, in hopes of securing a second performance: the two men met to discuss this on 11 January, and Wood, hearing that *Merryheart* was to be published, asked to see a set of first proofs. The score must have gone back to Breitkopf immediately for engraving to begin, for before the end of the month they sent a revised estimate for printing, which as it was higher than expected caused Brian some worry. But a letter of 5 February informs Bantock that Robinson and he are going ahead with Breitkopf & Härtel as previously resolved. Presumably Wood got his proofs: Brian received his acceptance of *Merryheart* for performance on 19 April, and also his own set of proofs for correction. At this rate of progress it is perfectly possible that the full score of *Merryheart* was published and on sale in time for the second performance, by Wood and the Queen's Hall Orchestra, at a Promenade Concert on 7 October.

We lack Brian's immediate reaction to this performance as well, as there is a gap in the letters between 21 July and 22 December 1913 - and by the latter date Brian had moved to London and had many other things on his mind. But in retrospect he seems to have preferred Harrison's interpretation to Wood's. Writing to Bantock at midnight on 22 February 1914, he recalled:

> When I lunched with Wood in October his wife remarked 'Henry can only read one book - *Kipps* - and you know he keeps reading it'. I think that is the solution of everything W conducts - he paints with the brush very decently and looks at everything from a *pictorial* aspect. But doesn't it seem a narrow life not to wish to read the finest & best in literature? He didn't over-impress me with his grip of *Merryheart*...[6]

---

[6] Mr Eastaugh reproduces this passage, and more, on p. 122 of his book. Readers wishing to

Later he talks of having told Otto Kling, who had overseen *Merryheart*'s publication, that Harrison had done the piece far finer than Wood.

Brian's initial pride and confidence in the Comedy Overture is reflected in his eagerness to secure performances soon after its completion, whereas *Festal Dance*, *Fantastic Variations*, and *In Memoriam* had to wait much longer. But later his attitude to *Merryheart* was ambivalent, and he periodically had doubts about the work as it stood. On 20 October 1915 he wrote: "With regard to *Merryheart* it remains one of my jobs to prune it. There is nothing in the way of design wanting alteration, but I think I might underline some of the undergrowth and make it more *straightforward*. It was all very well writing *how* I liked at Trentham, but the experiences at B'ham and London have taught me that I was much to blame for not giving Harrison and Wood a fair chance. I may say I've already stuck the blue pencil into it."

This reference to "the blue pencil" may help to explain the existence, among the material at Shoreham which I examined after Brian's death, of a heavily-annotated copy of the printed score of *Doctor Merryheart*, which looks as if it might have been intended to serve as the basis for a "revised edition" - there are many deletions, as well as a few additions, in blue pencil, with a general trend towards decomplication of the textures. But since Brian's opinions changed again, he seems to have made no move to implement these revisions further. Instead, on 20 March 1920 we find him writing: "I often talked with you about *Merryheart* & I condemned it from various points. Whilst I have been in the grip of the 'flue' I've been looking it over: I always felt after the London show in 1913 that the final dance was too short. I didn't think that when it was done in Birmingham. I don't think that now! I think for what it is & pretends to be it is the best thing I've done apart from the opera and is all you said & thought about it in 1911. I shall not alter a note of it. There is a 'success' in it when it gets a free & easy light-footed performance & the brass doesn't blaze away like the Salvation Army."[7]

This reference to 1911 may indicate that Bantock discussed the work with Brian during its composition - perhaps even had a hand in the development of its programmatic content; or, given Brian's habit of misremembering dates one year too low, he may mean 1912, after the work's completion. In any case he seems to have felt this work was a particular favourite of Bantock's - though the older man never conducted it - and according to a letter of 28 March 1922 he had intended to dedicate it to him: "You know I placed your name on Merryheart when it went to B & H to be engraved & it came back without it and the sectioning altered too."

---

compare the texts will find that even in the sentences above, Eastaugh deviates from the original in over a dozen places (most, but not all, minor). By not dating his quotation, and suppressing the words "in October", he creates the impression that the letter was written in 1913, prior to the break-up of Brian's first marriage.

[7] Part of this quotation is in Eastaugh, p. 123, and part of his main text on that page is founded on a precis of the rest of it. The aforementioned annotated copy of *Merryheart* includes, in the final "Dance of Merryheart" variation, an insert mark, indicating that new material was to be introduced just before the end.

The printed score of *Doctor Merryheart* is indeed without dedication: but there is no dedication on the manuscript either (Brian could, however, have been speaking figuratively, and have issued instructions for the dedication by letter; or he could have marked it on the proofs). His comment about the "sectioning" is not immediately clear to me, and must await a comparison of manuscript and printed score for explanation.

Merryheart had to wait 20 years for its third performance, if we discount vague references (cf. Foreman, p. 51) to a performance in Scotland under Landon Ronald - this has not been traced and may well be a confusion with Ronald's well-documented performance of *In Memoriam*. The Bantock letters do not, however, add any information about the mysterious Hamburg performance of 1933 - indeed they pass over it in silence: 1933 is in any case a sparse year, with no letters in the final quarter at all. However, in January 1934 the work had its fourth performance - and Brian his first BBC broadcast - and this seems to have set the seal of conviction on his belief in its musical worth. Lewis Foreman (pp. 51 and 101) gives the conductor of this performance - live from the Winter Gardens, Bournemouth by the Bournemouth Municipal Orchestra - as Brian himself, apparently on the strength of information given in Radio Times for 17 January 1934. Harold Truscott (see above) has cast grave doubts on this, and he is vindicated by the letters, which make quite clear that the conductor was Sir Dan Godfrey, one of Brian's most consistent champions. Mr Truscott has also recalled the apparent grudge which Brian nursed against this performance in later years - a grudge which is reflected neither in his many published writings about Godfrey, all of which are warmly admiring, nor in the letters he wrote at the time. There are two to Bantock about the performance; the first, written on 14 January when the work was still under rehearsal, simply includes the sentence "Godfrey is wild with delight about *Merryheart* - which he says only yielded itself *after an hour's rehearsal*". The second, of 17 January, was written immediately after the broadcast (and incidentally seems to contradict Brian's statement to Mr Truscott that "he was there" for the performance. In spirit, perhaps, but it seems he listened on the radio[8]):

> I thought of you this afternoon - for I had my first broadcast - *Dr. Merryheart* from Bournemouth. Godfrey did it wonderfully well - some of the variations - 'Smiles & Storms' for instance came out with surprising effect. Of course I was somewhat mystified not having heard the work for 20 years - it is a better score than I thought it though I always had a sentimental regard for it - but, except for releasing a couple of tied notes in the horns and cancelling accents I find not the slightest suggestion of alteration. I am inclined to think

---

[8] Truscott notes later, in *Newsletter* 36 (VII-VIII 1981), p. 6: "Brian's listening to *Doctor Merryheart* in 1934 on the radio: of course, if Brian's remark to me indicating that he listened in the radio control room at Bournemouth was true, he would still have been listening 'on the radio'."

that *Dr. Merryheart* will have a future after the first 'virtuoso' performance has taken place ...

The only hint of coolness is in the last sentence. Fine as Godfrey's performance was, it was evidently not the "virtuoso" performance of Brian's dreams. One may, indeed, doubt whether any single performance could have met his exacting standards. But he had no doubts about *Merryheart* from now on. The gaps in the letters for most of 1936, the whole of 1937, and early 1939 rob us of any comments on the various performances by Clarence Raybould, a pupil of Bantock and an old friend of Brian's - and these were the last which Brian heard before Bantock's death.

Walter Allum: Friendship with Havergal Brian[1]

The dark clouds of the 1914-18 war were obscuring the skies when I first met Havergal Brian at Mrs Valentine's house, known as *Naerodal*, at 73 Gravelly Hill North, Erdington, Birmingham, where I had lodgings. Brian was given Mrs Valentine's address by the Dunlop Company, by whom he was employed at that time. I personally have no record of the exact date of this meeting, and the evidence relating to it is indeterminate. In a letter to me dated 14 February 1968, Brian writes:

> Thank you for your letter and also for your generous gift [bottle of Bristol Cream Sherry] which appropriately enough arrived this morning - Valentine's Day, for it was at Mrs Valentine's house that we met years ago at Erdington. 50 years is a long time ...

This dates the meeting as having taken place in February 1918, which date is recorded by Reginald Nettel in *Havergal Brian and his Music*. It was from Mrs Valentine's house that Brian moved to 97 Edwards Rd, Erdington, where I visited him on several occasions. Contrary statements made elsewhere relating to this move are incorrect. Brian again refers to the date of our meeting in a letter written from West Dulwich dated May 1939. This letter indicates 1917 as the year in question. He writes: "I've often thought of you and wondered what you were doing. But letter writing has become a bore and I never write unless compelled." (The letter covers nine closely written pages - quarto size!) "Those months we spent together under the same roof are vividly recalled in your book *Music on the Wing: a Pilgrimage*. I've no criticism to offer ... I've no wish to alter anything you have said about me. I think it is just as it should be." Since the elusive date is of no importance, one can perhaps more readily adopt Brian's philosophic motto "Nothing matters" - a sentiment echoed by Ernest Newman when he concluded one of his letters to me with the phrase "Culture in England is dead anyhow, so what does it all matter?"

---

[1] From *Newsletter* 10 (March 1977), pp. 6-9.

But what of Brian at this time? This question I will answer by quoting an abridged extract from *Music on the Wing* which I wrote in 1936:

> From being a musical waif hugging about me the tattered remnants of my musical compositions I now began to feel the beneficial effects of a friendship which enriched my musical thought and by so doing stimulated my desire to compose. It was a kindly fate which directed Brian to Mrs Valentine's house where I lodged, for this man was none other than the composer Havergal Brian, described by Gerald Cumberland as a fire-eating genius from the Potteries in his book *Set down in Malice*.
>
> I have to dispute this description since I found Brian to be not so much a fire-eater as a fire-worshipper, especially on wintry nights when 'icicles hang by the wall'. Nor did I find in him a fiery dragon of a man such as Cumberland's appellation might have led one to expect. Instead I found a keen musical intelligence allied to a homely wit and a refreshing outlook. At all times Brian would gaze into the future through the eyes of an idealist - a dreamer of dreams. It can be said at once that Brian owed little to convention, either in personal affairs or in his musical work, which at one time was said to compare with Erik Satie when in mischievous mood. It may be remarked however in passing that Brian refrained from associating himself with Satie's notes in red ink and staves without bar-lines, even in such a freakishly droll trifle published under the title *Three Illuminations*, in which I feel Brian's sense of humour placed a lamentable strain upon his musicianship.
>
> But it is in large-scale works that Brian comes into his own and at the time of which I write he had already produced his (First) English Suite (1904); *By the Waters of Babylon* (1905); *The Vision of Cleopatra* (1907); *In Memoriam* (1910); also the contrasting Comedy Overture *Doctor Merryheart* (1912) and the (Second) English Suite (1915) and several other works.
>
> Brian's mind revels in the complexities of orchestral scoring, characteristically abounding in adventurous harmonics and unorthodox transitions vitalized by intricate cross-rhythms. When Brian played the piano in embracing his Muse, nothing less than full orchestral tone was demanded in his *crescendos* - a fact confirmed by Gerald Cumberland - whilst the *tutti* passages were something to be feared! ... yet in Brian's music tender moments are by no means uncommon. Many instances bearing witness to this tenderness are to be found in his songs and no less in the most passionate utterances where they steal into his orchestral music.
>
> As I write I have in mind one such theme, laden it would seem with haunting sorrow. It stirs into life in Brian's Sixth, the *Sinfonia Tragica*, the passage being marked Lento espress. solenne. Of this, Malcolm MacDonald writes as follows (Volume 1, p. 125):

... the long theme that now unfolds on muted violins - infinitely sad yet instinct with a nobility and tenderness of feeling that no words can convey - could only be the work of a melodist of the first rank and can surely stand comparison with the finest inspirations of Elgar or Vaughan Williams.

I well recall an amusing incident when on one occasion Brian took advantage of Mrs Valentine's absence to try something out on the piano (he would only do so if he were alone in the house) and Mrs Valentine returned earlier than had been expected. Brian was "banging away" as usual, with vocal *obbligato*, when a startled face appeared in the doorway. It was that of our landlady anxiously enquiring "Whatever is the matter?" Fortunately I was able to motion her to beat a hasty retreat and Brian played on - blissfully unaware of the intrusion.

My book of reminiscences was never published, largely owing to difficulties arising from the Second World War and a waning interest on my part - but Brian thought well of it (as did Dr Ernest Walker) and had the book gone to press it would have included an introduction by him in which he had proposed tracing a line from medieval music to the present day, advancing the theory that music is not so young an art as the official historians state and that it did not begin in the 16th century. In a letter he writes: "I am not sure whether I don't derive as much pleasure from *reading* the works of a great Flemish monk - Josquin des Prés (1445-1521) for instance, as I do in listening to a Beethoven symphony ..." But I digress.

When Mrs Valentine informed me that a man was coming from the Dunlop Company to occupy the annex (used as a surgery during Mr Valentine's lifetime) and that his name was Havergal Brian, the news was not without interest, for as a reader of musical journals the name was not unknown to me. But the prospect of the person of whom I had read coming to *Naerodal* seemed so improbable that I dismissed the possibility from my thought - regarding the duplication of names as coincidental. The expected lodger duly arrived, and since his bedroom was adjacent to my own it was inevitable that we should meet and exchange nods, if nothing more. But the day arrived when Brian remarked that he had heard me playing the piano, adding that he assumed that I had been playing "my own stuff". I conceded this, saying that it had to be "my own stuff" since I could not play anything else - or words to that effect. This was perhaps a slight over-statement, I having worked for some years to acquire a reasonable technique, helped along in this matter by Clarinda Mallol - a gifted pupil of Arthur de Greef, the Belgian pianist and close friend of Grieg. But the fact that I was playing "my own stuff" evidently aroused Brian's interest, for he suggested that we should meet and have a talk - a proposal to which I readily agreed. In the abridged extract from *Music on the Wing* already quoted, I have very briefly recorded my impression of Brian at that time, but I can add that his general demeanour was quiet but by no means subdued. He appeared to be temperate in his habits, an inveterate pipesmoker, and one seemingly not discontented with life. I judged that he normally elected to retreat behind a defensive barrier, but when the defences fell, one's heart warmed to him in friendship.

Looking back on those far-off days it is now known of course that at the time under review Brian was involved in prolonged marital problems and financial difficulties, and it is to his credit that he refrained from wearing these troubles on his sleeve. He seemed to be motivated by the sole desire to help me with my musical work and poetry. At his suggestion the poems were read to him aloud. Happily none of these poems have survived the test of time. If Brian was bored (as I fear he must have been on occasion) he gave no indication of it, and invariably urged me to "go on writing". The same advice was given with regard to composition - "go on composing" at least a little every day, this being necessary in his opinion to further the development of musical fluency. Chopin was cited as a model of fluent writing, it being maintained that any of his parts (treble, alto, etc.) could sing. But let it be remembered that Chopin, as a perfectionist, paid dearly in terms of emotional stress when engaged in composition - even when his creations were initially spontaneous. George Sand recounts how he would sometimes isolate himself for days, weeping in torment and on occasion taking weeks over a single page, subjecting his ideas to endless revision, yet liable to return when all was spent to the original version! Truly this was genius in travail. In later years Brian wrote that his three fugues were not composed for the piano, although they were published by Augener as such - they were written to develop flexibility in technique for writing the *Te Deum* forming part of the *Gothic* Symphony.

In conversation with Brian it was immediately apparent that he intended to follow the star of destiny which indicated that he should devote his life, as far as possible, to music and literature. By comparison, my own aspirations were positively mundane. My star was nearer to Mother Earth - although I too had my dreams and visions, loving the arts, music, poetry, painting - embracing these pleasures, being well content to share them with my friends in leisure hours. Brian was familar with all that was best in these various fields, with particular emphasis on Bach (whom he venerated), Elgar (his one-time talisman), Strauss, Schubert and Dowland. In a letter dated May 1923 Brian wrote: "Do you know the work of Malipiero, Goossens or Bliss? There is a great deal of fine work in all these men. Goossens is in my opinion the most promising young figure in contemporary music today. Some of his work contains long sustained flights in continuous thinking and his language is not that of any other man than Goossens - and as modern as either Stravinsky or Malipiero". Brian also studied the scores of Berlioz and Wagner, whilst in the field of poetry he held in high esteem Shakespeare, Shelley, Blake, Yeats, Goethe, Heine and the early English poets such as Herrick and Donne. By no means least he was greatly attracted by the writers of Greek tragedy - in letters, Euripides and Aristophanes are mentioned, whilst it will be remembered that *Agamemnon*, Brian's opera in one act, was based on the tragedy by Aeschylus.

In discussing music of the future one was left in no doubt that Brian had no great liking for the 12 note chromatic scale although he was well aware of current developments. If some of his early works tend to reflect the influence of "modern" idioms - that of Schoenberg for instance, whom paradoxically he greatly admired - his later works usually identify with a firm, if shifting, tonal base. It is not surprising, therefore, that he held definite views on the subject of Temperament, writing: "... all these fads are of no use to me. Bach settled the matter for all time when he adopted Equal Temperament." And mention must also be made of his regard for Bantock's music. Writing in December 1946 - (I quote from *Musical Opinion*) - "As a master of the orchestra, Bantock has no superior. Not only in *Omar [Khayyam]* but in the song cycle *Ferishta's Fancies* and *The Great God Pan*, Bantock's orchestral *métier* has a seductive, sensual quality, with an effortless improvisatory style of melodic invention, unusual in English music and unlike that of any other composer."

Brian seldom spoke of his own music but there was one notable exception, and this relates to his setting of Psalm 137 *By the Waters of Babylon*. At our first meeting he produced the vocal score, explaining the general lay-out and how certain passages had been treated and developed. This was my first confrontation with Brian's music, and as he took me through the work I became acutely aware of the unorthodox melodic line and harmonic modulations which in pianistic terms (beyond the horizons of which I had not journeyed) would, I felt, be uncomfortably discordant. It was not sufficiently appreciated that a combination of timbres from different groups of instruments - strings, woodwind and brass - could render discords less abrasive than when produced on a piano, which after all is a percussion instrument. It is my belief that Brian's heartstrings had been deeply touched by the poetic imagery and dramatic savagery of this Psalm, which presented a huge canvas against which, from his musical palette, a composer could fling his most resplendent colour in riotous array with shattering effect.

It may well be that *By the Waters of Babylon* also had special significance in Brian's mind owing to Elgar's reaction to the work upon hearing it performed at the Music League Festival in 1909. Recalling this occasion in later years Brian wrote:

> ... After the first performance of my Psalm 137 I came out of the box and a short distance away Elgar arose from his box. He came to us and putting his hand on my wife's shoulder said 'Half this success is yours'. Turning to me he said 'Brian I never heard anything in my life like your music - you must come to us at Hereford and we will go for long walks together and throw pebbles in the Wye.' He did not write ... and when he went to the Festival platform he forgot to tell the audience what he had told me. I never met him again after Liverpool though I never lost an opportunity of listening to first performances of his works whenever I could get to them.

Elgar's kindly gesture to Isobel (Brian's first wife) lends credence to the belief that behind every man there stands a woman (sometimes alas several women!) but here Elgar's Lady Alice comes readily to mind, as does Schumann's Clara, and a salute to Hilda (Brian's second wife) may not be out of place. Yet could these two men have for long enjoyed each other's company? The question is very much in doubt as will be obvious from a letter written by Brian dated Feb. 1937. It reads:

... But he [Elgar] became very friendly when a few years afterwards he recognised I meant it - and if we drifted and relations became less cordial, well, it was my fault. I'm no clairvoyant - he had a genius for social life, and I loathe it. I'm happiest when I'm alone. My greatest craving in these later years - is for silence, and how little I can get of it. There is so much of farcical or grotesque nonchalance. I wonder the whole system of life doesn't come to a standstill.

Brian again declares his love of silence in a letter dated 7 February 1969. He writes: "My last Symphony No. 32 was completed some time in June. It is the last I do believe, for I've had no thought of music since and have enjoyed, and shall enjoy silence." In this aspiration he was attuned to the Bard of Avon who says "Silence is the perfectest herald of joy" (*Much Ado about Nothing*). The character-revealing phrase "I'm happiest when I'm alone" may suggest the warped mind of an introvert, but at no time was there evidence of this. He spoke quite freely and apparently without reserve on cultural issues. I attribute this amicable relationship in part to the fact that my interest in music was not professional.

I recall with nostalgia our all-too-infrequent escapades at the piano when Brian would teasingly test my ability to improvise on groups of notes at his dictation - the notes having no particular key relationship. These diversions included fugal subjects! He was kind enough to say that I had an inborn flair for the piano and composition so that I derive some pleasure from the thought that the enjoyment resulting from these meetings was mutual.

Brian spoke of Beecham's suggestion that he should write a comic opera and I am under the impression that he tried out some preliminary sketch work at *Naerodal*. He sang and played excerpts which were dramatically lively - these may well have been from *The Tigers* in embryo. When later I visited Brian at Edwards Road he was usually at the piano engaged in song-writing. The preliminary sketches would be written away from the piano, for he did not look to the instrument for inspiration. Indeed it may be felt that he did not write gratefully for the piano - I confess it to be a view which I share. His flair, remarkable in a man who was largely self-taught, was for orchestral scoring, and where the respective claims of piano versus orchestra arise, it seems that "never the twain shall meet". There are nevertheless exceptions where composers of note have successfully wooed at the trysting gate to our delight.

I profited greatly from Brian in my approach to song-writing for this was at a time when he was particularly active and successful with settings of Blake and the early English poets. It was a field of music-making to which he never returned. It would seem that he had outgrown this medium which was to be carried away on the gathering stream of his later works - a torrent sweeping all before it when in full spate.

When visiting Brian in the months following his departure from *Naerodal* I could not fail to observe signs of irrational behaviour - the suspicion that somebody was entering the house whilst he was absent, interfering with papers and defacing manuscripts. Nettel, with rare insight concerning the reactions of a man such as Brian, summarizes the situation (*Havergal Brian*, p. 101): "Truly there were two sides to Brian: he evidently compensated in his daring music for a certain nervousness in his thinking: his extreme sensitivity no doubt induced both responses." Of course, the phenomenon is not new, for it is on record that whilst in Majorca, Chopin was sometimes terrified by a phantom - a figment of his own imagination whilst engaged in composition.

This sensitivity manifested itself another way. Writing from Upper Norwood in January 1937 Brian comments on the environmental conditions: "... Someday I shall compose again and then I'll set some of your poems to music. But not in this house. I loathe it!" On a more pleasant note Brian writes: "... Being in the Cotswolds you are in touch with wonderful English scenery which is now expanding into Spring growth ... I listened to the nightingale for forty minutes on the borders of Hertfordshire and Middlesex. I've never forgotten it. A countryman I used to meet and chat with told me much of the habits of nightingales and their nests built in nettles." These brief extracts are indicative of the composer's love of the countryside, as with Beethoven before him.

But Brian in common with many composers of note, also suffered from periods of deep depression - a malaise which not infrequently follows as a reaction from the exhilaration of creative achievement. Rakhmaninov, for instance, was the personification of melancholia. Tchaikovsky was unstable and a neurotic, confessing that but for music he would have gone mad. In our time that most prolific composer Benjamin Britten spoke of the agony of choosing the right note truly expressive of his emotion. Elgar, whilst subject to moods and despondency, would on occasion cheerfully indicate that he was "on the boil" when composition was going well.

The shadow of tragedy darkened the Shoreham home in the last year of Brian's life, and he was grief-stricken by the untimely death of his beloved daughter Elfreda, resident in Rhodesia. I quote briefly from his letter dated 27 April 1972: "... We have had a shock which seems it will never leave us. Our departed daughter was unique in many ways, as musician (in early years) and as a landscape gardener. She had the magic touch." I feel that the grief reflected in this letter contributed in no small measure to Brian's failing health at this time. The last letter I received is dated 10 August 1972. It tells its own unhappy story, although the Spirit still flickers.

> Very pleased to have your letter sometime ago. I wondered about you and your wife and that you can indulge in your loved music creations and send some to me.
>
> Sorry I cannot respond this time. I have been ill with jaundice for some weeks and am slowly recovering - but it is slow and I have many things on my table waiting for attention and hoping that I can attend to them.
>
> So, Walter, please understand and sometime later you can let me know how your creations move and I will have a look. But not yet. Wish it would clear up so that I could feel myself.

Within the space of a few months Brian himself had passed away - the lifelong struggle for fame and fortune was over. But happily not before he had known the tide to be on the turn - many of his major works having been performed and broadcast by the BBC, largely through the advocacy of Dr Robert Simpson, himself a composer of distinction. Before this resurgence of interest in his music down long years tangled with poverty and deprivation, Brian had, however, continued to write large-scale works without the stimulus which would have derived from the prospect of performance. In this he was obeying the dictates of the Spirit which activates all human endeavour - be it as musician, poet, painter, sculptor or the mountaineer who deliberately attempts a climb fraught with danger just because the mountain is there. Brian had indeed followed his Star unfailingly to journey's end and by so doing proved himself no idle dreamer of dreams.

There is but little to add. If my notes have contributed, even in small measure, to a better understanding of the composer then my purpose will have been served.

Brian frequently suffered from the "slings and arrows of outrageous fortune", some of which may have been of his own fashioning, giving rise to tensions and irrational behaviour, torn as he was between the conflicting claims of compulsive composition and the need to support his family. Fortunately none of this spilled over into our friendship, proving beyond doubt that if on occasion Brian seemed to appear, in naïve folly, in the unenviable guise of an "awkward cuss" or as a man "difficult to get on with" - well, there was another side to his character wherein the flame of loyalty and affection burned brightly. I feel greatly privileged that some of the light from this source should have fallen on me.

Shakespeare tells us: "All the world's a stage, and all the men and women merely players". On this stage Havergal Brian played many parts, but the role in which he should be fittingly remembered is that of a musician of rare distinction and achievement. He has in his music - symphonies, operas, choral and other large-scale works - left a uniquely rich legacy to this country and to countries beyond the seas. It now remains that this music should be increasingly brought to life in performance whereby all lovers of that which is best in music may enjoy the fruits of his labours.

Reginald Nettel: Aspects of Brian. With an excursus by Godfrey Berry and comments by Malcolm MacDonald, John Aldridge, Robert Timlin and Godfrey Berry[1]

A PILGRIMAGE TO ODD RODE

Last year found me driving northwards along the old London to Manchester road A34, and as I came opposite to that fake castle perched on the hill at Mow Cop between Kidsgrove and Congleton, I saw a signpost directing me to a little lane on my left and marked "Rode Heath", at the village which goes by the name of "Scholar Green". Turn down this lane and you will quickly come to a small church, nearly opposite to the gates of a private park. It is a bit of still-unspoilt Cheshire, peaceful and calmly beautiful. I parked and went into the church.

It is not an old church, being in fact one of the happier creations of Giles Gilbert Scott, but it has a well-proportioned interior, good carved reredos and a good organ. This is the instrument on which Havergal Brian played when organist here at All Saints', Odd Rode, from 1896 to 1906. Every Sunday morning his choirmaster, Arthur Bailey, met him at Harecastle Station with a horse and trap and drove him to Odd Rode. Morning service over, Brian was free until the evening service, and could spend his time composing, or walking alone in the quiet lanes, collecting his thoughts, or, in the 'nineties, paying court for a time to a Miss Major, whose father was factor to the Wilbrahams - owners since 1669 of the Rode estate. The courtship came to nothing, but Brian looked back in later life to his Sundays at Odd Rode as the happiest days of his life.

On this organ Brian played the Prelude to Elgar's *Dream of Gerontius* and persuaded Arthur Bailey that its calamitous first performance at Birmingham was a slur on British choristers, and Bailey's choral society set out to put this right. On this organ, at morning service, Brian liked to improvise on a theme from the Prince Consort's *Te Deum*, which he had admired since he was ten and had taken part in its performance in Lichfield Cathedral at the Golden Jubilee of Queen Victoria. Among some old papers in the Church House here the present choirmaster, Mr P. Stanley Briggs, came upon a copy of Brian's *By the Waters of*

---

[1] Reginald Nettel's text was first published in *Newsletters* 3 (V 1975), pp. 4-5 (introductory section), 21 (I-II 1979), pp. 2-3, 22 (III-IV 1979), pp. 3-5 and 24 (VII-VIII 1979), pp. 2-3. Malcolm MacDonald's letter to the Editor in *Newsletter* 23 (V-VI 1979), pp. 7-8 is entitled *Brian and the Psychologists*. John Aldridge's reply from *Newsletter* 29 (VI-VII 1980), pp. 7-8 is entitled *The Importance of Illogical Thinking*. Robert Timlin's letter to the Editor was published in *Newsletter* 24, p. 4, and Godfrey Berry's articles from *Newsletter* 48 (VII-VIII 1983), pp. 4-5 and *Newsletter* 31 (X-XI 1980), pp. 10-11 are entitled *Havergal Brian: a case of hyper-intelligence?* and *Havergal Brian's Musical Personality - a personal view*. Berry's excursus was published, under the title *The Influence of Brian's Social Environment on his Musical Style: Some Thoughts*, in *Newsletter* 38 (XI-XII 1981), pp. 2-3.

Babylon, which Brian composed while organist at Odd Rode, and which he may have tried out on this very organ; and of course Mr Briggs is determined to get a performance of this work in All Saints as soon as he can purchase the copies of the new edition for choir and organ now being prepared by Musica Viva.

When he does so I shall be there, and I hope it will be in summer, with the church decorated with flowers, a refreshment tent in the field opposite and parking space sufficient for all those who want to come from Manchester, Stockport, Newcastle-under-Lyme and Stoke, Congleton, Macclesfield - all within easy distance, and whose inhabitants as likely as not have no idea that beauty and peace can be so near to a busy main road.

The beauty and peace was there in Brian's day too, when he earned his living as a timber-merchant's representative, travelling about Cheshire and Shropshire buying and selling timber, often on foot, calling on farmers. From these days come the ideas for the English Suites and the Comedy Overtures - rural England with a sense of humour - and the great settings of Psalms 23 and 137, and an early version of Psalm 68, now lost, but possibly a precursor of the tremendous Fourth Symphony.

These Psalm settings are not in the same class as the rurally-inspired suites, but were derived from the Psalms themselves. For Brian was a great interpreter of great literature. The intense hatred of the exiled Jews was not within Brian's experience in his Odd Rode days, but he made a bold approach to the Psalms, not trying to soften them as so many other composers had done. There is no setting of *By the Waters of Babylon* as downright as Brian's (of 1903) until we come to Walton's *Belshazzar's Feast* of 1931, and that is nowhere near so intense as Brian's setting of Psalm 68 in *Das Siegeslied* (Symphony No. 4 of 1933). Until well on in his long life, Brian took some great literary theme for his starting point in any tragic work. He drew on his subconscious mind for the matter of his symphonies, but the mood came to him from the Psalms, from Blake, Goethe or Shelley; Shakespeare was a great influence in his songs - greater perhaps than any poet other than Blake - and remember that he never had these poets crammed into him for examinations - he sought them out because they appealed to him, and, I like to think, because they were a topic of conversation with the clergy with whom he came into contact in his work as a parish church organist.

1. "THE JOKER"

When Elgar stood up to conduct the first performance of *King Olaf* in the Victoria Hall, Hanley, on 13 October 1896, there were two people in the audience as yet unknown to him and unknown to each other; one of them was a young organist named Havergal Brian, and the other was a schoolgirl, the daughter of the Vicar of Christ Church, Tunstall - the Rev. Alfred Penny. Dora Penny was later to be honoured as the "Dorabella" of the *Enigma* Variations, and Brian was to be honoured by advice from Elgar regarding his compositions, and some practical help in getting them performed.

The Rev. Alfred Penny had recently returned from the Melanesian Mission, but previous to that he had been a curate at Stoke Church, under the eye of the

Rector, Sir Lovelace Stamer, who had had for his first organist there a pupil of Sir Frederick Gore Ouseley of Christ Church, Oxford. Stamer and his organist disagreed about the music in the church, and the organist - named Theophilus Hemmings - built a private school in the town and established himself as a teacher of boys up to academic standards, and of musicians up to doctorate level. (Hemmings himself was a B.Mus., but very proficient as a teacher.) It was to Hemmings that Brian went for lessons in harmony, counterpoint and keyboard playing - piano and organ. Hemmings was very well equipped, with a good organ and grand piano in his house. Thus we may see that although people may be unknown to each other they are nevertheless to be related by invisible links.

Rev. Alfred Penny lost his wife, married a lady who was a friend of Elgar's wife, and so Dora became friendly with the Elgars. Elgar liked her. She was young, and a change from the serious business of life, which to him was musical composition. He took Dora to see Wolverhampton Wanderers play, and they laughed together over the press report which described how a player "Banged the leather for goal". Elgar set it to music. She quizzed him about the secret theme incorporated in the *Enigma* Variations. Elgar played up beautifully: "Why, you, of all people, ought to know", he said, but he never told.

Dorabella was very kind to me when I was writing my first book about Brian, and I have no great opinion of those who tried to discredit her book, *Memories of a Variation*. She knew Elgar in a way which cut through judgements arrived at by ratiocination, in the same way that I can tell when someone has missed the point in his estimation of Brian. It cannot always be proved on the spot, but meditated upon it comes into the focus of thought and something clicks. One knows it is right. If you will admit this sort of psychological discernment as valuable we shall be able to agree, but don't try to tie me down to whichever doctrine you hold; we shall never get to the root of Brian's character that way, for Brian had a sense of humour which gave him pleasure in pricking the bubbles of the doctrinaire.

It was a valuable asset, of course, for one living among people who did not understand what he was driving at; it enabled him to keep his end up. When Brian conceived his Comedy Overture *Doctor Merryheart* he actually wrote a set of symphonic variations on two lines of music, which are cleverly transformed in the work and given titles in the score, just as Richard Strauss would have done - "Merryheart Kills a Dragon", "Merryheart leads a Procession of Heroes", "Asleep in the Arms of Venus", "Merryheart as a Chivalrous Knight chases Bluebeard". Was this Brian aping Strauss, and if so, for what reason? Was he enamoured of Strauss or was he poking fun at him? I get the most fun out of *Merryheart* when I am looking for the satire, but it is good-humoured satire - not in any way objectionable. Remember that all humour has its positive side and its negative side. One side comes out on top and the other is laughed at. *Merryheart*'s heroism is comical when it is "taking the mickey" out of chivalry, just as Strauss' *Don Quixote* did; but Strauss and Brian were at one in principle in another feature, for both made their compositions acceptable as abstract music if the listeners wanted to take them that way. Both *Merryheart* and *Quixote* are symphonic variations.

Similarly Elgar and Dorabella were allies in poking fun at the Wolverhampton journalist's style. But she was on the negative side and Elgar was on the positive side when he came to write the "Dorabella" interlude in the *Enigma* Variations. (He put her little stutter into the beginning of the theme.) As Elgar does it, it is attractive - even lovable - and in good taste. There is a world of difference between this and the belly-laugh of the red-nosed comedian, but both are related.

If you can't see the joke it may be anything but funny; it may be nasty. In his *Fantastic Symphony* Brian made variations on *Three Blind Mice* the subject of his first movement, and for the third movement gave us a *Dance of the Farmer's Wife*. If you are a strict moralist you will deplore her sadism, but the more fool you, for the whole thing is fiction and nobody can take it seriously without ignoring its true quality as an original mental quirk; you are then on the negative side and are to be laughed at. Brian comes out on top.

These examples depend on a play between the music and a literary parallel. They are programme music. Strictly within the music the humour may not be so easy to point. But Brian took from Strauss the trick of making muted trumpets laughable. Strauss did it in *Don Quixote* as the windmills turn into a flock of sheep, and Brian did it in the First English Suite when he made Punch and Judy sing *God Save the King*. And again, if you are unsympathetic (say, a dyed-in-the-wool Royalist) you will take offence, and you will be accused of not seeing a joke. But consider the muted trumpets further. The earlier jazzmen used these for comic effect, but as time went on, and the trick was made common, the effect became absorbed in a tradition and to be regarded as essential to the jazz style. In the end jazz acquired learning and grew abstract, at which point the comedians deserted the show and up popped Pop in music just as Pop Art came in reaction to Abstract Expressionism.

Humour can be trivial or it can be great, but there are very few great comedians - far less than there are great tragedians. But in *The Tigers* Brian achieved his measure of greatness. His libretto is his own, and is fiction, but the fiction can always be seen as being a reversal of the expected. The wooden horses of the roundabout turn at first to a trivial tune, but as the movement goes on they acquire a touch of Wagnerian pomposity and end by thinking themselves the horses of the Valkyries. We laugh at the horses, but we feel pleased with ourselves that we recognize Wagner too. But is Brian taking the mickey out of Wagner or not? All we can be sure of is that Brian has made a piece of great music out of a triviality. He is on the positive side in two ways - in making a joke of the horses and in making us listen willy-nilly to a fine orchestral interlude.

Similarly in *The Tigers* he plays on a relationship between the plot and his musical quotations. All men from seven to 70 are being called up for military service, and the police are looking for a man named Kelly. They show his photo to the passers-by while the orchestra brings in the tune of the popular song *Has anybody here seen Kelly?* There are snatches of other tunes too; a suggestion of *cherchez la femme* with a phrase of *Alice, where art Thou?* and a hint at *Bobby Shaftoe's gone to Sea*. All this is part of the jocular trick of bringing two contrary themes together so that a previously unthought-of related idea suddenly explodes, but Brian's artistry is further shown by the fact that, while the audience is being made to think of cheap tunes, that of *Kelly* is being built up into a fine set of symphonic variations. Brian has brought the music-hall and the opera-house together; what was the province of the red-nosed comedian and his stooge is sneaked into the realm of art, and the joke is sparked off. And all the time we can imagine Brian laughing up his sleeve at us.

> Life's a jest, and all things show it. I thought so once and now I know it.

That is in the same category, but on John Gay's tomb in Westminster Abbey. Gay, too, it will be recalled, brought common tunes into an "opera". But there are better places than Westminster Abbey for epitaphs in this vein. Carved in wood above the village stocks at Crantock in Cornwall you may read:

> I paid my price for finding out, But never grudged the price I paid;
> I sat in clink without my boots, Admiring how the world was made.

They didn't put Brian in clink; they just cold-shouldered him; but how he would have admired the word "admiring" in that context!

The man in the stocks was a sailor - a working-class type and therefore vulnerable, and in that situation funny to those who came to mock him; but he countered their mockery with his humour. So, in spite of his disgrace, he kept his end up. Such is the effect of humour. It is a gateway to success which many working-class lads and lasses have gone through - Gracie Fields, Charlie Chaplin, and so on. Anyone with a local accent is funny to those who have a different one; his difficulty is in making people believe him when he is serious. For this purpose he must have education.

Brian got the education he needed in music, and he found its serious purpose in the Church ritual. This will be discussed more fully in the next article. Here it is enough to point out that Brian uses his critical faculty to look down on the simpler people. He exaggerates. In *The Tigers* he even makes the crowd illiterate. Late in life he made fun of a village band in *The Tinker's Wedding* on much the same lines as Beethoven had done in the *Pastoral* Symphony. But Brian went further; in some of his symphonies he actually makes jokes in abstract music - without reference to any human character. Beethoven did this too in his Eighth Symphony, and Brian's method is basically like Beethoven's - he brings in a feature which makes the listener sit up and fear a musical *faux pas*, only to realize almost immediately that he has been deceived - that the composer has taken the mickey out of him for being so clever.

We are getting ourselves involved now in a conflict of psychology and aesthetics, and that can take up volumes without a solution ever being found. For as soon as a joke is explained it vanishes like the Cheshire Cat. A joke has to be irrational. I want to point out in a future article that all art is essentially irrational - that only the technicalities of its presentation can be explained.

These were what Brian got from his teacher, but the magic in Brian's music - the part which came from his own imagination - was inexplicable in the terms used by his teacher. The secret of its appeal lay in something that emerged from the subconscious which, left alone, would come, but which he found he could bring out more readily by meditation or came in his dreams. His trick - which he had to teach himself - was to amplify these emerging motifs (which came each with its ambivalent partner) until they were clearly known to him as themes, then it was a matter of using all his technical expertise to fashion them into the composition which they ultimately became.

At first he needed a non-musical spur - either the verses for a song, or a story, or a flash of opposites which would often be comical but as time went on he found extra-musical ideas unnecessary and the later music became quite abstract. In this Brian was not unique. All great thinkers become more abstract as they develop their thought.

2. "THE CREATOR"

When Billy Brian applied for a job as office-boy at a small colliery the manager asked: "What do you do in your spare time?" The boy replied "I play the organ in church." He got the job. No doubt the manager had had enough of boys who didn't want to go down the pit or work in an office, but here was a lad trying to better himself.

In spite of that, was young Brian so different from other boys; those, for instance, who wanted to be engine-drivers? And were they different from boys today? Then it was the Steam Age; now it is the Space Age, with Superman for its hero. But is Superman any more heroic than the lad imagining himself with his hand on the throttle-lever of a monster able to command thousands of horse-power at a push; to drive his thundering steed into the teeth of the wind while his sweating underling shovels coal into the gaping maw of the fire-box? With a shriek of the whistle his throbbing monster tears into the vulva of the tunnel, even though Sigmund Freud had not yet published *The Interpretation of Dreams*.

But Billy Brian did not want to be an engine-driver. Despite all that Freud says, I don't think he ever dreamed about it. He had a practical substitute. Every Sunday he could command hundreds of whistles with the touch of his fingers. His sweating underling was the organ-blower. "Praise to the holiest in the height", screamed the scrannel-pipes; "And in the depths be praise" boomed the bourdons. Later, Parson would have his say, and people would try to keep awake; but let the organ start up again and Brian was in charge - once more the boss. It gave a lad a great sense of power. Engine-driving was a dream; this was reality.

And it wasn't going to stop at this. Brian had heard the City Organist at Liverpool, A. L. Pearce, and he was determined to make himself a great solo organist, able to play *The Storm* until the organ-blower collapsed. There was plenty of time. Stick at it. He changed his teacher and got into trouble for it. Then he had a stroke of luck when the organist of a neighbouring church took a fancy to a churchwarden's wife and, since they couldn't do justice to themselves in the respectable company they kept, they fled to Canada. Brian got the organist's post and £12 a year, with which he could afford to have lessons from a reliable man. Billy dressed respectably and called himself "Havergal".[2]

Under the tuition of this man, Brian's fingers were so trained that he could play difficult passages without having to think digitally, and his mind soon acquired a store of harmonic and contrapuntal clichés which would have got him through a stiff examination. Theophilus Hemmings had done his duty. Brian could "take his letters" and secure an organist's post worth having. But the young fool wanted to be a composer. On this they broke off their association; we must ask ourselves why.

During his studentship under Hemmings, Brian changed his mind. He now no longer wanted to appeal to a popular audience. He wanted to create worthwhile music. He was warned. He was stubborn. A psychological change had taken place. On the one hand he was now taking an interest in girls, and on the other was looking more into himself. As time went on he became more and more introversive, but that was a lifetime's development. In his younger days he simply found that what satisfied others did not satisfy him. Even the girls had to be a bit above the common. His special love was for a young schoolteacher - intelligent and very pretty. Nature took its course before they were prepared for it, and they had to marry or be shunned by all their respectable friends. So started Brian's difficulties. They had to go and live with Brian's parents in an overcrowded house.

Had Brian still been set on a public career as a performer it would not have been so bad. Performers are extroverts, up to a point. All-round musicians like Bach, Handel, Haydn and Mozart had written and performed their own works as a matter of course. But the profession of all-round musician needs two separate environments - a private one while composition is taking place, and a public one

---

[2] Brian Duke tells us in a letter to the Editor in *Newsletter* 44 (XI-XII 1982), p. 9: "There is in the *English Hymnal* a sweet, soothing and innocuous tune called 'Franconia' (No. 370 in the *English Hymnal*; no doubt in other hymnals too) to which are set the words of John Keble:
> Blest are the pure in heart,
> For they shall see our God,
> The secret of the Lord is theirs,
> Their soul is Christ's abode.

and three more verses in the same style.

In view of Brian's early activities on the organist's bench, he would likely have known the tune, for the composer, W. H. Havergal, lived from 1793 to 1870; the tune he adapted from a melody by J. B. König, who lived a century earlier. He was a country parson, and attended Merchant Taylors' School when it was in Suffolk Lane in the City of London. Apparently all his music was Church music, according to Grove."

when the work is brought to performance. Mahler was a great conductor as well a great composer. So was Benjamin Britten - and a great organizer. The money is made by public appearances; the creative work is done in isolation. By rejecting his chances as a performer Brian laid himself open to economic stresses. Hemmings had warned him.

At first it didn't matter. Brian was earning enough to live on, and his composition could take place in the evenings. It got difficult when the children arrived, and the father was torn between the love of his wife and children and his need for silence. Under these circumstances he won, however, the approval of Elgar, found outlets for the performance of his songs, part-songs and some early orchestral works, and gained the financial support of a director of the famous pottery firm of Minton, with artistic taste and a generous disposition.

Meanwhile, Brian's social standards had been undergoing development. In the same way that he had been choosy about girls in his earlier days, he gradually became more choosy about musical associates. The peck-order he favoured was (a) audiences at the base, (b) performers in the middle and (c) composers at the top. He had now climbed this pyramid and took his stand with his composer friends. It was a special aspect of mankind, based on artistic achievement and neither on money (which Brian almost despised) nor on heredity. He seems to have thought that this classification was fixed, but in fact it is fluid.

We may illustrate the situation by imagining that Brian, instead of concentrating on music, had found his joy in chess. (It might have been, for he had a chess-player's mind.) Supposing he had done so, he would have sought men similarly disposed, and could no doubt have joined a club. Such a club would not have judged him by his income or his family, but by his ability to give them a good game, and Brian would have climbed the ladder of approval by his skill. In the chess club there would be players of various grades and, supposing Brian had shown himself skilful, he would seek out better and better players, and they would seek him, and all those of his standard would find themselves bored if they had to take on an opponent unworthy of their own standard. So it was with Brian and his music. He gradually left behind his early associates as he reached the higher levels of taste, and it follows from this that his associates would become fewer. Loneliness is the lot of genius.

There are antidotes to this. One is in the social activity of music, by performing his own works or by lecturing on them and his musical friends. This the introvert Brian had rejected. Another antidote to boredom is humour, and here Brian was lucky. He could turn his wit on to the follies of lesser men and give original expression to them. Another antidote - and this I believe to be all-important - was what we may call creative evolution of the material at his command. The best example of this is the way in which he took the Anglican Church anthem and enlarged it into the settings of Psalms 23 and 137 while he was still a church organist.[3]

---

[3] There was also a *Requiem* made on passages from the Prayerbook and verses from *Hymns Ancient and Modern*. Since this is lost we cannot comment on it, except to say that it must have

Through it all we must not regard Brian as one who thought himself underprivileged. On the contrary, he was sure he was specially gifted. He was proving it as he moved higher and higher up the difficult mountain of aesthetic and intellectual values. There was nobody who could help him. His composer friends could show their approval, and conductors would occasionally choose one of his works for performance, but he had only himself to rely on for his musical ideas.

But where did those ideas come from? There was much mystery and even self-contradiction. Elgar said once that music was in the air: you just stretched out and took what you wanted. But at other times he complained that people had no idea how fatiguing the process of composition could be. Long concentration on a complex problem is exhausting. Brian spoke as if music came unwanted, like children in Samuel Butler's *Erewhon*, and pestered him to give them birth, but, having been born, he had to do his best for them. Both Brian and Elgar were speaking in riddles; neither of them could give a rational explanation.

Yet they were speaking of the act of creation as it seemed to them. Music welled up from somewhere unplumbable. But how did it get there? How about our analogy with the chess-player? He had learnt the moves by long practice and stored them in his memory-bank, from whence he could retrieve them as he needed them. So had Elgar and Brian learnt and stored the moves of music. Turn their minds to some form of composition and in due course the memory-bank would be opened. It only *seemed* as if the music came out of the air; in fact they had put it in there before they began to take it out again transformed.

This explanation would no doubt have satisfied Theophilus Hemmings whose pupils could, when required for an examination, rake up a fugue in a matter of 20 minutes. But would that fugue have satisfied Brian or Elgar? Would it have satisfied an audience? Of course not. We cannot thus explain why a Bach fugue or a Brahms quartet holds our attention long after the facts of construction are known to us. There is a magic in music which defies all theories; it almost ignores heredity (for Mozart's magic is not that of his father) and completely ignores Darwin's theory of natural selection. These were the theories most discussed in Brian's youth. The old fashioned belief that creation was of God had had more to recommend it. But Brian had lost his early belief in God! Where was he?

Well - we know something at least. Since Brian would have nothing to do with God, or with any sort of philosophy, and he wasn't a scientist, he was left standing alone. He became obsessed with silly superstitions, and a belief that some evil person was trying to steal his scores. He pretended he didn't care, but in fact he went on frightening himself with these notions, at the same time rejecting any rational explanation. All theories were to him absurd - Darwin, Wagner, Marx, Freud, Nietzsche, Shaw, as well as the religious leaders. Leave them alone and they contradicted each other. All he knew was that the music came from within himself. He had to be self-reliant.

---

been on the theme of death and the hereafter - one of the most basic of all psychological problems.

This was it; the principle by which Brian guided his main object in life - musical composition. He had to get it from deep down in his mind, and what came up was his alone. Nothing annoyed him more than the criticism that someone else had had the same musical idea. Library ideas were a different matter. They were not his, but they could turn his thoughts toward original music. His earliest passion was for songs, and a song is not music alone; it is a marriage between music and poetry, and there is a magic in the poetry which must be matched in the music. How often, as he sat on his organ-bench, must he have known that the tune being used for a hymn was not a match for the verses? Such tunes were journeyman's work. They would not suit Havergal Brian.

So it began; but purely instrumental compositions also had their literary counterparts, as we have seen when discussing his humorous pieces, and they continued in later life even after he turned to symphonies. He said that his *Gothic* Symphony was partly inspired by Goethe's *Faust*, and his Second Symphony by Goethe's *Götz von Berlichingen*, giving hints of the nature of each movement with reference to the character of Götz. Later he denied this, but kept to the title of his "Battle" symphony. Like many another composer Brian was shaky in his attitude to programme music; he felt that a programme was disturbing to those trying to concentrate on the music as such, but he nevertheless wanted to give them some guidance to the mood he had intended. His second thought about his Second Symphony, that it revealed man's essential loneliness, is much more valuable psychologically than the earlier thoughts about *Götz von Berlichingen*.

Even more to the point is the quotation on the title-page of the score of *The Gothic*. "He who strives continually to the uttermost can be saved." The union between the striving mind and the conflicting resources of the symphony is apt. Here he has brought the literary motto and the musical thought into a truly abstract context. There is no attempt at picturing any scene from *Faust* in the symphony; strife is an abstract concept just as the music is; you would think the first part of that symphony would be enough. But we know that it wasn't. The second part - the *Te Deum* - had to follow and, since it has done so, do we still believe that the *Gothic* Symphony would have been better without it?

Here is the mystery that must arise when we encounter a great composition. The fascination with the striving can be explained in terms which apply to the chess-player, but God cannot be so explained, especially in a man who claimed to be an atheist. It must have come from a source deep in Brian, which he had rationally rejected, but which was aroused again with the memory of that childhood scene in the first Gothic cathedral he saw, and where he sang the *Te Deum*. Back (as the Viennese psychologists are always reminding us) to first causes.

But was it impressionism or expressionism? Was it an attempt at describing what appeared to him from outside, or was it something forced out from his inner being? I believe it was the latter. This is not the striver so much as the willer. Not the chess-player but the engine-driver with terrific forces under his command. You can give it any name you like, according to your choice - the *libido* of Freud, the *élan vital* of Bergson, the *life-force* of George Bernard Shaw -

and still you will not have grasped the nature of it unless you realize that it is, like the humour and the striving, two-pronged. All emotions are ambivalent.

The psychologists have told us this, but did they tell Brian? He could hardly have cared less what they wrote, for he went not to them but to their forerunners. Freud was still unpublished when Oscar Wilde wrote his *Ballad of Reading Gaol* with its telling line - "For each man kills the thing he loves", and the psychologists to a man took their illustrations mainly from Greek myths, which they allied to modern observations among their patients. Brian went to the Greeks, too, for their dramas told him what his subconscious self revealed; man was not a pretty notion, but a compound of egoities which society knew as evil.

Time and period have to be considered. Brian saw the Greek concept of Prometheus reinterpreted by Shelley, and gave it a further drive onwards in 20th century music. The magical element was the same but the means of interpretation had undergone change. The two aspects - psychological origin and medium of expression - have to come together to create a work of art, and the first of these is always with us while the latter is part of the life we live in society. The life-force needs to be expressed by the means to hand, and these are related to our education (by which I mean our opportunities for learning - not necessarily formal education). We put two and two together and make four, if we are practical people, but if we are like Brian we make them five. This is the way I look at the creative process. Brian, of working-class origin, got the education he needed partly from his early training in the Church of England, then by his own will-power, through which he earned enough to pay for specialist musical training, then by his study of scores and attendance at concerts; but all the time by reason of his love of literature, which led him to relate great literary themes to music. He did not have it handed to him on a plate - he had to fight for it, and it did him good as an artist.

I will end with a silly story. You can call it folklore if you like. It was told to me 50 years ago in the Staffordshire Potteries and my memory is not what it was; but here is the tale as I remember it:

> A certain Bishop of Lichfield was on his visitation to Stoke-on-Trent, and expressed a desire to see some of their industrial life. They took him to the great steel-works at Shelton Bar. In the offices they asked him if he had any special interest which they could satisfy, and he said: "Yes. I should like to see, in addition to your industry, any man who is specially gifted. For example, have you anyone here who can write music or poetry?" They had nobody in the offices, but they had heard of a man in the works who wrote poetry, so they made sure that the Bishop met him. Unfortunately it was at an inconvenient moment, for the man was a puddler and they were drawing a furnace. The man was grimy, half-naked, sweating and red-eyed with the heat, but the Bishop didn't mind. He offered the man a theme to work on - to put into his own words - and the theme was:
>
> "By the waters of Babylon we sat down and wept,
> when we remembered thee, O Sion ....

> For they that led us away captive required of us a song.
> 'Sing us one of the songs of Sion.'
> How can we sing the Lord's song in a strange land?"

An hour later the Bishop returned, and the puddler was now free, had his shirt on and his poem ready:

> "Bi th'wayters o' Babylon us sat dyne an' blarted."

So it started, but like most ancient folksingers I have forgotten the middle bit. However, it ended like this:

> "But 'ow can us sing o' th' land as us loves in a bloody 'ot 'ole like this 'ere?"

The story ends here, with the confusion of the Bishop. But not my story. There, but for his early musical experience in the Church of England, might have gone Havergal Brian. The puddler's poem was the result of the psalm, his having been asked to reinterpret it at the furnace, his wish to please the Bishop and his lack of education. By his own determination Havergal Brian raised himself out of the Slough of Despond in which that man had wallowed. The Bishop missed a good point.

3. "INFLUENCES"

"When did you first hear *Die Frau ohne Schatten*?" asked an American, and Brian laughed. The American could not be expected to know that that particular opera of Strauss had not been performed in England at that time.

But Brian was on less firm ground when he said (as he did to me) that he had not heard that Holbrooke had written a set of variations on *Three Blind Mice*, or that he had never seen Elgar's setting of *Stars of the Summer Night*. Both these works were well-known to those taking an interest in British music in the Edwardian period. Brian had of course written variations on the same rhyme in his *Fantastic Symphony* and an eight-part setting of the same words which Elgar had used. Brian was fending off any suggestion that he was copying. He need not have done so. Brian's settings are better than the others' but that is not how the mind works; disgust at facile criticism blocks the path of reason and the "victim" tells a lie.

Yet no man is an island. Anyone who moves in a cultural circle will be affected by aspects of that culture, and those composers were Brian's contemporaries. All of them were under the wider influence of German 19th century music. This in turn was part of the political drive which was taking place at that time. When I see the word "Kulturkampf" I do not myself think of Bismarck's use of this word (to describe his weapon against Roman Catholic influence) but of the battle between *Les Beaux Arts* and *die Kultur*, both of which are very obvious to me.

("There is no French music", said the great conductor Hans Richter, and he then conducted Debussy with his fists. The path of reason had again been blocked and somebody was lying.)

Some of you may think that Brian was an underprivileged member of the proletariat. Forget it. Had Brian thought like that he could have joined the Longton branch of the Social Democratic Federation and led a brass band followed by banners and a procession, but he did not; Brian thought himself privileged, for he could get away to Manchester on a day excursion and hear the Hallé Orchestra conducted by Hans Richter. Others didn't do so, but that was their own fault; if he could manage it they could. They were inferior.

German influence was therefore predominant in Brian's musical education. Arnold Bennett tried to bring in an interest in *Les Beaux Arts* but Brian responded very feebly to it, and, as Richter left Manchester in 1911 Thomas Beecham was bringing into London, with the help of Diaghilev, a strong Franco-Russian influence, and Brian noted this; but it was the German language that Brian learnt, not French.

This was brought home to me in the early '20s, when I became friendly with a Dr Fletcher (whose views on music were advanced along the same lines as Brian's), and Fletcher's mistress at that time, who was a refined lady of French extraction. In her house I heard modern French, German and British music, and learned the nature of their inter-relations. By this time Brian was far away and writing letters to the deposed Kaiser Wilhelm II, and *die Kultur* had moved on to Expressionism, but Brian was apparently not aware that he had gone with it.

As a result of the War, most British composers were trying to eliminate from their thinking the influence of Wagner, and those who attracted my attention most at that time were the humorists - Lord Berners and Eugene Goossens (whom you will have heard of as a conductor but may not know as a promising composer in the '20s, worshipped in the courts of Oxbridge). I now see how the conflict of the two cultures, and the shame of our dependence for so long on them, brought about a national resolution which showed us a way out through Vaughan Williams' pseudo-modal nostalgia. This was the creative process operating at a national level.

It is always so. Two themes, ambivalent, inspire a third theme which is sufficiently original to enable a new line of progress to be followed. We have seen in *The Joker* how the two ideas clash, throw up an absurdity and bring a release of energy in a laugh. Read Ted Heaton's article on *The Physics of the Bare 5th* [pp. 353-354 in the present book] and you will see how the two frequencies of a musical 5th generate a third note an octave below the lower note of the 5th. Brian would know this as an organist, from the nature of the Quint, which Ted Heaton describes. This is a physical demonstration of two factors generating a third. The mind does it too.

Note that there is nothing schizophrenic about this. Schizophrenia is when two personalities in one mind become separated. Normally the mind works like a sonata, with two themes ambivalently suggesting a new dimension which we recognize as a single whole, and greater in its significance than the sum of its parts. There is in fact a "magic" in it. It looks at first sight as if we are trying to discredit the formula *Ex nihilo nihil fit*, but we are in fact proving it.

I do not believe that all our ideas are predetermined by the nature of our subconscious. I have shown how our minds cheat us when we try to reason out things that are being blocked, but I have, when writing about Brian's organ playing in *The Creator*, mentioned how by practice a musician develops a digital skill which frees his mind to concentrate on interpretation. The fingers seem to be playing without guidance though in fact they are not. The subconscious takes over after training, just as it does after we have learnt to swim or to ride a bicycle. It is an addition to the part of our being which controls all the most important functions of our body, such as breathing, heartbeat and digestion. The rational mind is really a minor mind.

I contend that Brian knew how to "use" his subconscious to facilitate the creation of his music. This may be a bit difficult to grasp. Malcolm MacDonald, [in his comment], mentioned Jung's attempt to psychoanalyse himself. Freud also tried to do this, to the amusement of Jung, who recalled that Freud had said nobody could do it. Yet here are these two men, experts at the game and playing on their own ground, both attempting what by their own theory was impossible. But why not? It is part of the dissatisfaction which men need in order to keep mentally alive. We must, however, try to recall how Brian learnt the trick of stimulating his subconscious and bringing forth the results.

It is not so uncommon as it may seem. Many of you will have seen a choirmaster training his choir, stopping them to make some comment on the work, then starting them again without any introductory chord. You would think that the pitch had been forgotten during the long speech, but in fact it lay there all the time, to be brought out again without the singers giving conscious thought to the matter.

"We learn to swim in winter and to skate in summer", I was told when a young man. Ice skating rinks and heated swimming pools were rare in those days. What was being drilled into me was the theory that we try to learn a new activity, have to leave off, but when we come to it again after a long break we find we can do it much better. A related incident is when we are worried about something, go to sleep on it, and next day the solution is so obvious that we wonder why we ever worried the day before. Dreams are not all repressed instincts finding a devious way out; many of them are made of thoughts arising from what we were thinking about the day before. At the moment of awaking from a dream we can sometimes relate it to actuality, although transformed and often ridiculous.

Brian could meditate on a musical theme, find himself in a mood that fitted it, forget it, and in time it would emerge much more certain and he could get to work on it, write it down, forget it again, bring it up again, and so on. In time the work would be complete to his satisfaction. I do not know how any creative work can be produced other than in this way. It cannot be produced from a process of ratiocination.

Most composers have been professional musicians, doing practical work like conducting or performing on an instrument. In so doing they are required to perform the works of other composers, which they do conscientiously. While this is happening their own creations have to be forgotten, but they come to them again - during holidays from conducting, say, as Mahler did - and their own thoughts have in the meantime consolidated themselves.

Brian was not a professional musician to this extent. He did musical journalism and in earlier days worked as a clerk. There was always a temptation while he was earning his living to take time off for his composition, but he rarely succeeded. During his periods of useful toil his creative thought lay fallow, but fallow ground is not dead - the process of fertilization goes on underground. That will serve as a reminder of the creative process in musical composition. Brian had to adapt himself to these conditions of useful toil for half the time and dreaming and composing the other half. It was a long process, and all the more so because Brian produced such long works, but it explains what I mean when I say that Brian learned to use his subconscious. It was just as much the use of a faculty as was the application of his knowledge of harmony, counterpoint and orchestration to bring the composition to fulfilment.

In this way was Brian's distinctive style evolved. What came out of his subconscious he set down, but back it went, and in this way he was feeding his subconscious; his music did not entirely come unwanted, like a bastard child, although he spoke at times as if this were so, and all he could do was to make the best of it; he had started the process; it was his fate to have to nurture the thing once he had brought it to life.

You can say that Brian's difficulty in adapting himself to society forced him to think differently from other people, but there is nevertheless the strange relevance of the German Expressionists, with their obsession for *die Angst unserer Zeit*. Brian denied he was an Expressionist, for he disliked being labelled, but *Angst* is the only proper word to explain the strife which permeates his major works, and even creeps into the minor ones. Brian said he was not an Expressionist because he did not follow the path of Schoenberg, but that missed the point. Not every Expressionist composer followed him, although many did. The 20th century *Zeitgeist* materialized in Vienna, with Freud, Schoenberg and - yes - Adolf Hitler involved in the seance. There is a style of a period just as much as there is of a man, and all interlock. Twentieth century thinking was transformed by the Viennese when politically their country was in the last stages of decline. Former thinkers had looked into themselves to find ideas; they (the Viennese) looked into themselves and found the subconscious. All major subjects - medicine, education, criminology, sociology, science and the arts - have been transformed in this 20th century. I say nothing about morality.

The British were the last to succumb in music, as might, perhaps, be expected, and Brian is significant because he was regarded as unBritish, and therefore out of favour. Does the revival of interest in his music mean that chauvinism is now on the decline in this country? Do you know - I think I've got something there!

Malcolm MacDonald comments:

I've derived a great deal of interest and profit from Reginald Nettel's two articles on *Aspects of Brian*. I believe it has always been one of his chief aims to provide a framework for understanding the psychological basis from which Brian's music sprang. We are all in his debt for the various steps he has taken towards this, most recently in *Aspects of Brian*: as we are for his clear-sighted recognition that perhaps the main issue requiring exploration, before any final evaluation of Brian can be attempted, is the mystery of Brian's mind - or, more prosaically, the relationship of Brian's conscious intellect to the creative forces of his unconscious.

(For example: in my studies of the symphonies, I am forever blithely pointing out developments, derivations, metamorphoses, correspondences and allusions in the motivic working, and perhaps I give too much of an impression that all these details were consciously calculated. I'm damn sure that a significantly large proportion of them were; I'm equally sure that many of them arose spontaneously, with no conscious worry on Brian's part as to how they fitted as pieces in the puzzle. This isn't to suggest that at some times he "knew what he was doing", and at others didn't: rather, that he "knew" in both cases, but that we have to widen our definition of "knowing". Brian's approach was creative, not analytical. We have no means of distinguishing whether any particular motivic allusion, apart from the immediately obvious ones, is conscious or unconscious: I simply see it as my duty to point out what is *there* in the scores, and how it seems to function in an overall process.)

I would, however, have liked to see Mr Nettel further develop a subject which he just touches on at the end of *The Joker*, and hints at obliquely elsewhere in the articles - though I have heard him state it directly in conversation: that Brian's great creative secret was that he had learned to *make use of* his unconscious mind: that he could summon up his music, or at least the driving conceptions behind it, through meditation, often with a work of literature as catalyst. His role as an artist was to respond to, but also capture and channel, these outpourings from the psyche.

I can't help feeling - though it's a dangerous area, where I wallow in ignorance - that the second-hand post-Freudianism which serves, at least in this country, as the dominant psychiatric orthodoxy, is not going to be a great help to us in understanding Brian (apart, perhaps, from elucidating some of his obsessional neuroses). Freud, if I understand correctly, thought the unconscious was a nasty dark hole into which we repressed everything that gave us the horrors. He didn't have much idea of it as a fundamentally *creative* persona, in its instinctual fashion perhaps "wiser" than our conscious intellect - whether because it may be in touch with all the inherited knowledge of our forebears, or because it simply remembers everything that our conscious minds have forgotten. Mr Nettel describes how composers imbibe knowledge of multitudinous musical techniques and the great music of the past, and store it up in their "memory-bank", but their resources of inspiration may go deeper yet - they may emanate on occasion from the Collective Unconscious.

And it wasn't Freud, the "father of psychoanalysis", who coined *that* familiar phrase. It was the man Freud stigmatized as his "errant son" - who as a result is still intellectually distrusted, little-read, and whose thinking is, in any case, much more difficult to grasp: because, unlike Freud, he propounded no dogma, passed fewer moral judgements, and spent his life *exploring* the contents of the unconscious which Freud believed himself to have adequately catalogued already: Carl Gustav Jung.

Now, if my grasp of Freud is sketchy, my understanding of Jung is probably even slighter, but I do know the following:

(1) That while Freud evolved his psychology in the treatment of hysteria and obsessional neuroses (as Reginald Nettel points out, Brian was something of a prey to the latter), Jung's insights into the unconscious stemmed from his work with schizophrenics (and while cautiously agreeing with Harold Truscott's conclusion, in his essay on *The Gothic*, that Brian's music contains a "schizoid" element - using the term loosely and unclinically - I think I would go further and hazard the opinion that certain aspects of Brian himself, his obliqueness, deviousness and secretiveness especially, may amount to clinically identifiable symptoms of a schizoid personality. I do *not* suggest that Brian was therefore "a schizophrenic" - I think that, like Jung, he possessed a strong enough ego to withstand a total mental collapse, and was able instead to capitalize on the experience in his creative work).

(2) That Jung was specifically interested in the creative aspects of the unconscious mind.

(3) That Jung developed what seems, on the face of it, a far more sensible, pragmatic and informative method of dream-analysis than that practised by Freud. (I would be fascinated to see a really high-powered Jungian analysis of some of those dreams which Brian wrote down and which obviously meant a lot to him - especially the "Nuremberg" dream he recounts in *How the "Gothic" Symphony came to be written*: as Reginald Nettel points out, he needed no psychiatrist to tell him these were important communications from his unconsciousness. I'm not equipped to interpret the "Nuremberg" dream, but it seems numinous in the extreme.)

(4) That whereas Freud's one-sided emphasis on sexuality (itself the result, Jung thought, of Freud's own obsessional neurosis) makes his psychology especially relevant to people in the first three or four decades of their lives, Jung was more concerned with the continuing intellectual development and self-realization of people in middle and old age - the period in which Brian produced his most important works. Among contemporary psychologists, Anthony Storr - in no sense a blind follower of Jung - has come to the conclusion that Jung's ideas are intrinsically more useful than Freud's for the understanding of the forces at work in a creative artist.

I don't want to give the impression that I am trying to stir up some kind of academic contest between "Freudian" and "Jungian" interpretations of Brian and his music. I daresay that most people would find such a debate bewilderingly far from their experience of the works themselves. Mr Nettel is quite right, too, to warn us away from any "doctrinaire" approach to Brian's psychology. But insofar as I understand anything about Jung, he doesn't seem to have laid down any fixed doctrine or dogma (indeed, he once said that he wanted there to be no school of "Jungians" to petrify his work), but to have developed a means of holding a dialogue with the contents of an individual's unconscious, and of exploring the relationship, in that individual, between the conscious and unconscious minds. I think this could, ultimately, prove relevant to our understanding of Brian's creative achievement.

But I have a different reason for invoking the name of Jung: namely a hunch that it may be possible to arrive at an overall conception of Brian's work by a direct comparison between his career and that of the Swiss psychologist. During the years 1917-19, Jung himself went through a period of acute mental stress, with marked schizophrenic characteristics. His psychological disturbance seems to have had several different causes - a "mid-life crisis", the violent break with the father-figure Freud, guilt about this and about the complications of his marital life; also, he felt, the influence of the apocalyptic *Zeitgeist* which presently broke forth throughout Europe in the shape of the Great War. Recognizing his own danger, he decided to psychoanalyze himself, to seek a "confrontation with the unconscious", to "probe the depths of his own psyche". (Some readers may remember a rather bad and barely-comprehensible dramatized documentary about this episode which was shown on BBC Television a couple of years back.) Through this long and painful process he arrived at the insights which he spent the rest of his long life refining and exploring in a vast body of writings, many of them of daunting density and allusiveness.

I have a strong conviction (guardedly expressed in my article on *The Gothic* in *Newsletter* 16 [pp. 130-135 in the present book]) that Brian, at a slightly later date, went through a very similar experience. He seems to be telling us so, in language as plain as his habitual obliquity will allow, in *How the "Gothic" Symphony came to be written* - a document of even greater *psychological* importance than musical or biographical. There are striking parallels, both in the possible sources and actual circumstances of his disturbance, too numerous to outline here. Of course, he did not psychoanalyze himself - he wrote music instead. His music of 1916-27 tends to support this interpretation - perhaps from as early as 1915, if the lost English Suite No. 2 was really a set of "Night Portraits", exploring a world of darkness, complete with a "Witch Dance", as Kenneth Eastaugh suggests. The ballet-sequences in *The Tigers*, with their strange symbolic figures, strongly suggest a deeper, metaphysical reality breaking through to the surface, and the whole opera can be understood as a funny but disturbing dream. Several of the songs written at or just after the end of the War, such as *Defiled Sanctuary*, seem to spring from a real agony of mind. And *The Gothic*, the work about which Brian felt he had to "discover a solution to all its mysteries", seems to mark a seven-years' "confrontation with the unconscious", at the other side of which Brian emerged as a different kind of composer from what he had been before. Doesn't the *Te Deum* sometimes seem to have ripped the lid off the Collective Unconscious of Western Music, which pours forth clamouring and demanding an expression and a shape that the composer is hardly able to command?

What I'm trying to say here, I think - and it's a view I've been gradually moving towards over several years - is that *The Gothic* cannot be evaluated purely as a musical phenomenon, without a recognition that it constitutes a psychic one as well. (And maybe even a psychotherapeutic one. One of the means by which Jung eventually came to terms with his mental turmoil was to paint mandalas -

circular quasi-abstract drawings symbolic of his inner state, whose shapes usually resolve into four quarters. Though the mandala seems to be ultimately Oriental in origin, Jung points out that it has been well-known in European art for millennia, and that it has a more familiar Western counterpart, the cross. Could it be that we have arrived, by a very different route, at Paul Rapoport's famous cruciform diagram (as described in his *Opus est*, pp. 91-95)??? I sympathize with anyone who thinks that I have at last gone off the deep end in mere fanciful speculation - but I find the notion of *The Gothic* as a gigantic mandala so picturesque that I can't resist airing it just this once.) It is both more and less than a self-sufficient, self-consistent work of art - unlike the symphonies which followed. As I shall attempt to show in Volume 3 of my book, Brian's entire symphonic canon is suggested, *in potentia*, by the contents of *The Gothic*; the later works refine, extend and develop separate aspects of its encyclopaedic totality, with a greater degree of artistic control.

The motto from *Faust* on *The Gothic*'s title-page gives further cause for thought. Goethe, and his *Faust* in particular, exercised a life-long fascination on Brian. On Jung also. It was Jung's contention that Goethe, in his heroic adaptation of the Faust legend, had created a potent symbolic drama of the struggle of the artist (Faust) with the ungovernable forces of the unconscious (Mephistopheles). In the "On the Other Hand" column of the March 1939 issue of *Musical Opinion*, Brian, writing as "La Main Gauche", published a short article about Goethe's *Faust* which in general parallels Jung's conclusions. Much more striking is the fact that some of Brian's comments on *Faust* duplicate the phraseology he had used about himself in *How the "Gothic" Symphony came to be written* (published four months previously): for instance, Faust is "seeking a solution to the mysteries of the unknown".[4]

Perhaps this can extend our insight into the relationship between *Faust* and *The Gothic*; and possibly between Brian's symphonies and literary sources of inspiration generally. I think I would take issue with Mr Nettel when he says that "as time went on [Brian] found extra-musical ideas unnecessary and the later ideas became quite abstract". In some ways I believe Brian's music may have become more, not less, programmatic. But the programmatic element became more profound, more absorbed into the drama of the symphonic structure itself; less concerned with pictorial illustration, more a matter of drawing universals from particulars. The metamorphosis of Symphony No. 2's *Götz von Berlichingen* programme into "Man [=Brian] in his cosmic loneliness" provides a useful metaphor for Brian's own creative processes. Faust, Götz, the young Goethe (Symphony No. 7), Agamemnon (No. 12), Oedipus (No. 30) - and who knows

---

[4] Editorial note: The artist's idea of identifying himself with Faust has an extensive tradition which includes the opera by Busoni, the *Scenen aus Göthe's Faust* by Schumann, Thomas Mann's novel *Doktor Faustus* (1947), Mahler's Eighth Symphony as well as Marlowe's play. Not all the adaptations are based on Goethe's version, but use instead the older version of the 15th century. See the series of publications on treatments of the Faust subject in music. Moreover, many artists liked to identify themselves with Goethe, whom they considered a hero comparable to Beethoven.

what other literary figures stand behind the intervening symphonies? - were, so to speak, lenses through which he could look into his own unconscious, and find out what of them lay within himself, and could be shared with others. In other words he was aware of them as Archetypes - and it was Jung, of course, who coined that term, too.

Though many of Brian's techniques of allusion and cross-cutting are precisely reminiscent of the "stream of consciousness" to which I used to compare his mature music, I now find that phrase too slipshod and novelistic. The structural, form-giving, symbol-creating power is too active in Brian's symphonies. It may be more accurate to say that Brian eventually found himself writing programme-music of the psyche. And so do all composers, one way or another, it might be argued. Perhaps - there are certainly other striking cases (such as Schoenberg, who also capitalized in his music on a psychological crisis for much of his life, and who in his last years wrote that classic example of "psychological programme-music", the String Trio) - but few have seen their role, as I think Brian may have done, to be that of cultivating exactly that uncharted field and expressing it in such fluid forms, their unexpectednesses in themselves suggestive of the functioning of the unconscious. Whence, perhaps, proceeds his music's extraordinary potency, its capacity to shock, outrage or move its hearers.

John Aldridge replies:

I was very interested in the articles in recent *Newsletters* concerning the workings of the creative mind in the field of the arts. Rightly or wrongly, I decided that the implication of Malcolm MacDonald's thesis concerning Brian's modes of thought was that "the medium is not actually the message" but that "the medium, process or method considerably affects the form and content of the message". Malcolm MacDonald also contended that Brian, and some other composers such as Schoenberg, actively charted in music the workings and conflicts within their own minds. In other words, they were writing symphonic poems about psychic states.

Reginald Nettel said that Havergal Brian developed the use of the subconscious mind rather more than most artists. He implied that Brian may have used ideas sparked off by non-rational processes but explored them and subjected them to further development subconsciously but in a reasonably orderly and logical manner.

He also said that (deliberate?) use of the subconscious is more common than we think and that most artists and composers get their inspiration this way. This leaves a half impression that Brian's thought processes were generally similar to those of many other artists. Again, I may be wrong in making this inference.

However, Mr Nettel did also refer to the confrontation of two ideas with the interaction producing a third but apparently unrelated or unpredictable idea. In other words, not A plus B equals C, but perhaps something surprising such as A over B equals Z.

Were these two writers actually saying the same thing? I believe so, but I can't be certain. Maybe Havergal Brian was the first composer to use systematically what the psychologist and popular writer Edward De Bono calls "lateral thinking". It seems that Malcolm MacDonald himself has also come to the same conclusion. Since first drafting this article I have heard him use exactly this phrase about Brian (during the Introduction to the Society's *Gothic* Symposium on 25 May last). This encouraged me to submit my manuscript to the Editor.

(Most people must have heard of lateral thinking by now, but in case someone hasn't, De Bono defined it as a kind of free association of ideas or leap in the dark, as opposed to normal "vertical" thinking, that is, logical steps leading carefully from one to the next. He does equate lateral thinking with some types of creativity.)

The following list is a classification of synonymous, or at least related, pairs of opposites:

(1) Lateral versus vertical
(2) Associative versus sequential (or logical)
(3) Creative (synthetic) versus analytical

A classification of ways of thinking into just two mutually exclusive categories must be a gross over-simplification, but may sometimes be a useful way of looking at things.

Personally I regard lateral thinking as the natural basis of Goonish humour.

Goonery Mk. 1
"Eccles, why have you got three legs?"
"Oh, 'cos the other one fell off!"

Goonery Mk. 2
"So you're emigrating to Canada eh; what's your profession?"
"I'm a professional idiot."
"So why are you leaving England?"
"There's just too much competition here!"

Goonery Mk. 3
"He disappeared from under her very nose."
"What was he doing there?"
"It was raining, I believe."

Lateral thinking has its serious aspects too. Most inventors are supposed to have developed it to a high degree, otherwise they would not be able to break out of the strait-jacket of existing laws and practices to invent something entirely new.

For example, if you wished to travel across water with a conventional land-based vehicle you would have to put it on a car ferry or train ferry. So what would you do if you wanted to take a large boat to the top of a steep hill without dismantling it? You might have to invent a giant lifting cradle supported by 50 hoverpads or 5,000 helium balloons, or perhaps a dry dock on big roller skates, or even an "inside-out train ferry".

The last alternative isn't as crazy as it sounds. Such a machine actually exists on a canal in Southern Belgium, or rather between two parts of the canal at different levels. It consists of a huge water tank with a sloping bottom mounted on wheels running on rail tracks up a steep incline and cable hauled by large electric motors. The tank on wheels accommodates full scale barges which enter by watertight gates at each end - that is, when it is docked onto the canal sections at the top and bottom of the incline. The acceleration and deceleration of the tank are carefully controlled to avoid "slopping the bath water". This particular installation was designed to replace a flight of 27 locks. The same components are present as in a train ferry - water, boat and rail vehicle - *but they are now assembled in a different order.*

I'm sure this idea of turning conventional practical or even abstract concepts upside down or inside out is an example of lateral thinking as defined by De Bono. I read his first book about 10 years ago and in it he suggests training oneself to deliberately invert normal concepts and modes of thought in order to think "laterally". However, I do not believe that in the long term many people can improve their natural aptitude for this significantly - they either use it instinctively or hardly at all, depending on how they are made.

My use of practical or humorous examples does not imply that I am attempting to trivialize the works of artists or composers, but that I have tried to find related concepts from other spheres of activity. In the case of Brian I do not think that the Goon joke analogy is too unfair in certain instances. On first hearing, some of Brian's abrupt transitions (or endings) have exactly the same level of unexpectedness or even shock. In the case of transitions, the following development often represents a change of viewpoint or change of direction, as in the jokes.

For instance:

(1) In Symphony No. 9 the second half of the short violin solo (in the middle of the slow movement) seems to be a (distorted?) mirror image of the first half. For me, this makes the music step backwards instead of moving on. It is like a billiard ball rolling up a slope, coming to stop and then rolling back down again.

(2) Again in Symphony No. 9, in the last few bars there is an outburst of bells/glockenspiel which does not seem to fit the rest of the symphony (strayed from *1812* perhaps?). It gave me a rather uncomfortable feeling for the first few hearings.

(3) Symphony No. 14 feels as though it ends on the wrong chord, not the one I would have expected from the sequence leading up to it. Being unable to read music, I can't properly appreciate the explanation given by Malcolm MacDonald in his Volume 2. I can only repeat that "it doesn't feel right".

(4) No. 14 also has a massive outburst in the middle of the slow section which has a great air of finality about it. When I first heard it, I really thought it was the end of the symphony and was most surprised when the music continued.

(5) Still on the subject of endings, Symphony No. 21 finishes with drumbeats: the final expected orchestral chord is missing. This makes the drumbeats ultimately far more important than one would initially expect.

(6) Another type of Brian shock or surprise occurs with certain themes which start out by being reminiscent of some popular tune (sometimes only in rhythm or colour) and rapidly develop into something different. One example is the trumpet theme at the end of the plaintive violin solo in the last movement of

Symphony No. 20. When I first heard it, I thought it was going to be something like *Jingle Bells* but of course it isn't. It quickly becomes a kind of fanfare which soon involves the whole orchestra. There are two or three other symphonies with themes which remind me of something trivial but maybe these are purely personal associations.

Brian did sometimes use simple popular tunes deliberately (*Three Blind Mice* and *The Jolly Miller* for instance) and I wonder if at other times he used them subconsciously as a starting point for something much more elaborate. Also, in the early symphonies there are one or two "Wagner near-misses" which stand out from their background, for example the "Siegfried's Funeral March" theme in the last movement of Symphony No. 2. I cannot recall any instances of either type of near-miss occurring after Symphony No. 20.

I am not suggesting that Brian's symphonies consist mainly of shocks, jumps or twists. It is obvious, even to a non-score reader, that they are extremely complex and that many of them exhibit great compression, both vertically and in the time dimension. The reaction to my six examples may be that they represent somewhat superficial aspects of these complex structures. This is true, but given that Brian's symphonies require many hearings to appreciate them, it is the more bizarre characteristics which catch one's attention on the first or second hearing.

Personally I shall carry on listening to them as the opportunity arises. It has just occurred to me that it will be a long time before many of us have heard them all at least seven times - the equivalent to a total listening duration of about 97 hours!

Robert Timlin comments:

It was with considerable interest that I read Malcolm MacDonald's letter in which he emplyed Jungian terminology to discuss the nature of Brian's creativity, and I would like to add my support to Mr MacDonald's thesis. Such an approach is particularly illuminating as an aid to understanding many writers, artists and composers, Brian being no exception. In fact, one could go on to state that the quality of the insights gained through this method of analysis (provided that the application is neither fussy nor doctrinaire) invariably produces effective criteria for assessing greatness.

By greatness, I am not referring to subjective matters of taste, where one person's works are simply preferred to those of another, but to something far more fundamental, something not in the least subjective (actually the opposite); the decidedly numinous nature of certain works of art - in Brian's case, what Mr MacDonald calls the "music's extraordinary potency, its capacity to shock, outrage, or move its hearers".

To designate the deeper strata of the unconscious psyche as the Collective Unconscious in the way that he did, Jung was anxious to stress that he was speaking of a phenomenon which he regarded as essentially objective. The creative artist's ability to exploit and express in appropriate artistic form this area of the unconscious, containing impulses and images common to all mankind, indicates the scope and profundity of his genius.⁵ That contact with this part of the psyche requires not only enormous courage but also mental powers of a unique kind, is amply illustrated from Jung's own "dark night of the soul".

Returning to Brian, and bearing in mind Mr MacDonald's letter, I think the word which, more than any other, describes Brian's art is "objectivity", a sense that the works have somehow evolved independently of any individual consciousness, as organic and finely wrought as anything in nature. The fact that in his music Brian never aimed at popular appeal by opting for the obvious solution was the result of neither cussedness nor a deliberate desire to be obscure; it arose from a great mind's integrity and ability to remain true to his vision. For this reason, our response to Brian is unlikely to be the easy comfort of the wiped away tear, but, rather, the disturbance of an apocalypse.

One final point; it is curious that two such erudite students of Brian's music, Malcolm MacDonald and Rodney Stephen Newton, should be unable to agree upon the relative merits of Symphony No. 14. Is this merely a matter of musical aesthetics? Maybe we should hearken to the words of Stephen Dedalus in *Ulysses*: "A man of genius makes no mistakes. His errors are volitional and are the portals of discovery." Strangely enough, the work on which both commentators share doubt, Symphony No. 13, I find a compelling and moving experience.

Godfrey Berry comments:

At first sight both Havergal Brian's art and his personal character present us with a paradox. It is clear that he lacked neither intelligence nor imagination. Yet it is equally clear that his conduct towards others could be insensitive to the point of folly, and that he was almost wilfully blind to certain practical difficulties in his music - difficulties which he could have avoided, and which have worked against the wider performance and appreciation of his works. This apparent contradiction has been the cause of much puzzlement, but it seems to me that it may, in reality, be quite easy to explain.

To my mind the key lies in a wealth of evidence indicating that Brian was not merely intelligent, but abnormally so. Many members will already be familiar with Malcolm MacDonald's view - deriving largely from a long and detailed study of Brian's works - that Brian was possessed of a remarkably powerful intellect capable of solving triumphantly almost any problem he chose to find interesting. Harold Truscott has testified even more directly, in his reminiscences of the composer, to insights on Brian's part which can only have resulted from deep and penetrating thought. If we add to such testimony what we ourselves can deduce from Brian's writings, and from his remarkable track record as a self-educator (composition, several musical instruments, two languages, etc.), one conclusion seems inescapable. Whatever other endowments he may or may not have brought into the world, Brian was clearly born with a quite exceptional IQ.

---

⁵ Editorial note: This sentence had to be restructured because the original sentence contained a serious anacoluthon. The original sentence was: "It is this area of the unconscious, containing impulses and images common to all mankind, which the creative artist's capability to exploit and express in appropriate artistic form indicates the scope and profundity of his genius."

Going one step further, it seems possible to hazard that he was, or very nearly, what we should nowadays call a case of hyper-intelligence.

To a young child - especially one born into the rather narrow world which faced the infant Brian - such a super-abundance of intellect would hardly have been an unmixed blessing. At the very best he would have found himself singled out as a bit odd, first by his family and then by other children. At school he would almost certainly have displayed a tendency to develop at a different pace or in a different direction from his classmates, something which Victorian teachers, in line with contemporary ideas on child discipline, would have regarded as an unwelcome sign of independence: at best a nuisance to be discouraged; at worst a deliberate contrariness to be punished. The childish custom of ganging up on anyone who stands apart and preoccupies himself with matters beyond the awareness of the common herd has persisted even into this supposedly enlightened age (and sadly not only amongst children, who at least have the excuse of immaturity). One can imagine only too readily that a markedly individual child, such as the young Brian must have been, would have attracted more than his fair share of this kind of playground bullying accompanied by its traditional taunts of stupidity and madness. Is it too fanciful to suggest that Brian must have become used, almost from the cradle, to fighting an uphill battle against parents (or at least a mother) who found him alarmingly precocious, teachers who regarded him as "difficult", and playmates who were only too ready to believe him a little mad?

The feeling of being misunderstood can be deeply wounding, especially if there is some suspicion that the obtuseness of others may be partly malicious. There are at least two ways in which a sensitive person can respond. The first is to exploit the image which other people seem determined to wish upon one. If one's every effort to shine is going to be seen as nothing more than further evidence of one's "awkwardness", why not enjoy the benefits of actually being awkward? The trouble is that an assumed characteristic acted out with sufficient conviction eventually becomes a part of one's "real" personality. The second, not mutually exclusive, stratagem is to retire more and more into one's own private world. If those around one do not understand and cannot satisfy one's intellectual and imaginative needs, what other course is there but to rely increasingly on one's inner resources? Dreams at least cannot be held back by the inadequacies of other minds.

An abnormally intelligent child from a working class background, isolated in the small world of a 19th century industrial village, would have few, if any, chances of meeting living minds the equal of his own. Anyone much above the prevailing average in intelligence in any community knows the mortification of watching a cherished idea or aspiration founder, not because it lacks merit, but because no-one else seems able to understand it, or even appreciate its worth intuitively. It can be scarcely less galling to see others laboriously arguing themselves round to some obvious conclusion, blissfully unaware that this was the point of view one put forward at the outset. It would be surprising if a child of Brian's intellectual ability, growing up in an environment devoid both of rivals and similarly endowed friends, had not had many such experiences during his formative years - enough, at least, to convince him of the general worthlessness of other people's insights and advice. In a middle-class child, such a view of the world, and the over-reliance on one's own unaided intellect and intuition, to which it would lead, would normally be corrected by exposure to competition from peers in the sixth form or at university. For obvious reasons these were influences which the young Brian missed.

If we add all this up we arrive at a picture of Brian in early maturity which, I would suggest, goes a long way towards explaining his conduct in later life. We see an imaginative and highly intelligent young man of the kind who would, in any event, tend to be much absorbed in his own inner world, and in this case one whose early experience would have done much to encourage and little to counteract this tendency. That he would, even then, have been unusually self-centred seems beyond doubt. One can be fairly sure that, up to this point in his life, Brian would have encountered very few people sympathetic to his aspirations, and even fewer who understood them clearly enough to be capable of making any constructive contribution (even if they wanted to). He would already feel isolated from all but a few, very special, kindred spirits.

It would be asking a lot of a young man, especially one so totally lacking in suitable mentors, not to conclude from such a sense of isolation that he must somehow be one of the elect: an individual picked out for some pre-ordained task. Even though he was a professed agnostic, and by definition quite intelligent enough to be able to recognize its inherent absurdities, Brian would have been hard put to it to prevent the insidious growth of such a notion in his subconscious. To be aware of the danger and counteract it effectively would have asked of him a degree of worldly wisdom seldom, if ever, possessed by young men, especially ones deeply absorbed in themselves. In the circumstances, the early, and apparently opportune, arrival of a generous patron can only have seemed to confirm Brian's special status, or at any rate that of his mission. By his early '20s, at the latest, Brian would have had a rooted conviction that it was his right, if not actually his duty, to sacrifice himself, and if necessary anyone else, to the accomplishment of his life's work. This attitude is not necessarily arrogant - it can easily be adopted in a spirit of genuine humility - but this makes it no less difficult for others to deal with.

In Brian's case we should not lose sight of the fact that abnormally intelligent and gifted people are also abnormally sensitive to slights, real or imagined, and especially to criticism. As a child, Brian may well have had a tendency to attract wounding comments, many of them sufficiently misconceived to leave a lingering sense of injustice. This would undoubtedly have exacerbated any initial sensitivity to criticism and left him in later life with a tendency to see any criticism of himself or his works as destructively intended. Add this to a sense of mission, and memories of a childhood spent out-thinking one's elders and supposed betters, and one surely begins to understand Brian's apparent reluctance to profit from the good advice even of respected colleagues. Brian would long have conditioned himself to believe that his only impartial and consistently reliable guide was his own intuition. To take advice, even well-intentioned, was to risk compromising one's vision, and watering down one's message.

Defensive attitudes engendered, at least initially, by a painful sensitivity to criticism may well explain some of the inconsistencies and contradictions apparent in Brian's professed opinions and attitudes both on music and on some other aspects of life. He who wishes to escape wounding comments can do worse than hide behind a verbal smokescreen. Those intent on inflicting pain start at something of a disadvantage if they do not know what really matters to their proposed victims. In old age Brian may really have come to believe in his own stoicism, but some unguarded comments, and most of his music, say that at least at the outset matters were quite otherwise.

Doubtless not all the problems surrounding Havergal Brian and his life's work can be explained by reference to his abnormal intelligence, and the impact which this must have had on his early development. But these surely exercised a powerful influence on his later attitudes and actions, and one which it would be foolish of us to ignore. Things might well have turned out differently if Brian had been born a middle class child, or if he had somehow managed to go to a university or music college. But in taming the man, might not such institutions also have tamed the music? It is a tantalizing question, the answer to which we shall never know.

The recent correspondence and articles in the *Newsletter* about the workings of Havergal Brian's creative mind have been very interesting. They highlight one of the most puzzling features of Brian for many newcomers to his music - the fact that, in spite of its apparent heavy reliance on the traditional basic materials of music, it is very far from being as conventional as this might seem to indicate. The writers have usually attempted to explain the nature and meaning of Brian's brand of unconventionality in terms of one or two clearly defined peculiarities in his personality.

Could it be that the truth of the matter is more complex, and that each of them has illuminated one part of a much broader canvas? Are not the initially baffling aspects of Brian's musical personality attributable less to one or two particular quirks in his creative make-up than to a coming together of several unusual traits - none of them, perhaps, unprecedented but each comparatively rare in a composer?

One such trait is Brian's predilection for what might be called "progressive musical argument". Traditionally, composers have been concerned with producing something which has the inbuilt symmetry of a mathematical equation. Form is simply an elegant proof of one's initial proposition. This can be seen most clearly in strict sonata form where the development frequently leads to little more than an unvaried restatement of the opening material. Brian's treatment of his material is very often much more like a genuine voyage of discovery. A proposition is stated, subjected to a wide-ranging process of development, variation and dissection and a new or radically modified proposition derived to take the place of the original. The relationship between this and traditional formal procedures is perhaps analogous to that between a scientific experiment and the "mathematical equation" referred to above. Of widely known symphonic composers, Sibelius is possibly the one who comes closest to Brian in this particular respect.[6]

---

[6] Harold Truscott writes in a letter to the Editor (*The nature of musical forms*) in Newsletter 32 (XII 1980), p. 8: "I agree with what he says in that paragraph about Brian; indeed, I will add to it, and say that the classical composer who most resembles Brian in his treatment of what is usually called a recapitulation (and in no other way) is Haydn, who, more often than not, replaces the recapitulation in his symphonic first movements with further developmental exploration. But Mr Berry's other remarks in that paragraph are in the nature of rather thoughtless generalizations and, whether or not this is the case, he writes as one who sees music rather than hears it. 'Traditionally, composers (which?) have been concerned with producing something which has the inbuilt symmetry of a mathematical equation'. *If* such symmetry is there it can only be appreciated *visually* - if it is there. But, in fact, to produce even visual symmetry the recapitulation would have to be back to front - to form, with the exposition, a palindrome; by which time the aural relationship of the recapitulation to the exposition would be non-existent. So much for symmetry. Mr Berry is not the first to have the illusion that such a thing can exist in music. It cannot. Palpable symmetry is a visual thing. 'Form is simply an elegant proof of one's initial proposition'. It sounds well, but let us examine it. First of all, in which composers? Mr Berry should tell us; otherwise, his statement is all too vague - an Aunt Sally put up to be knocked down. Is this view of form true of, for instance Beethoven's recapitulations? - or of Schubert's? or Brahms'? or even Mozart's? Mozart comes closest of the great composers to a superficial likeness to Mr Berry's argument. It certainly is not true of Clementi, or of Dussek. Are we, then, considering the lesser fry, the imitators? Who makes up tradition? And form: where, outside of the textbook, and those manufacturers of music who follow the dictates of the textbook, will one find form indulged in on the basis described by Mr Berry? He is not talking about living form, which is all the greatest composers know about, but about formula, which is a very different thing. And this connects with the next point: 'Strict sonata form': where does one find this, outside, again, the textbook? Certainly not in any of the composers I have mentioned. In living music, there is no such thing. There are principles, as there must be in anything organic, and there is an infinity of ways of dealing with them. 'The development frequently leads to little more than unvaried restatement of the opening material'. Very seldom in the composers I have listed, who, in any case, think the recapitulation from the basis of the exposition and development; Mr Berry, it would appear, does not listen on these lines. And - if the result was, on occasion, what Mr Berry describes, there is more to listening to music than calculating what repeats what. For instance, if one has really listened to the first movement of a Beethoven sonata or symphony, the whole of what has happened, including the development, following the music as a language, it is impossible to hear the recapitulation, even if nearly exact (absolutely exact is not possible, except under very unusual circumstances), as a repetition of the exposition. Music has impact; one's eyes do not take this in. Only one's ears, in conjunction with one's brain, do, coupled with a familiarity with the language of music, without reference to anything external to music, at least on a level with the knowledge of English necessary to read Conrad or James novel and understand it. Lastly, I am a little puzzled to imagine why Mr Berry is concerned with this aspect of sonata style in considering the habits of a composer who scarcely ever used that style, and who, when he did, did so in such a way that his use of it was either in the nature of a parody, or a visual resemblance without an aural one, or a deliberate attempt, so far as the music is concerned, whatever was in the composer's mind, to destroy the sonata structure." Godfrey Berry replies (*ibid.*): "It is flattering that a Brian scholar of Harold Truscott's distinction should have taken my humble efforts so seriously. However, I should have been even more flattered had he not misunderstood such a large slice of my argument so fundamentally. Not only do I accept that 'sonata form' has very little to do with Brian: this is precisely the point I was trying (perhaps a little clumsily) to make. Had I been developing a learned thesis on symphonic structures I

Another very unusual trait is what John Aldridge characterizes, by analogy, as Brian's "lateral thinking". In essence it consists of the ability to cast off the blinkers imposed by logical reasoning of the type first codified by Aristotle, and to perceive intuitively possibilities and relationships of a kind which such reasoning does not readily suggest. It is an essential element in any kind of truly original creative or scientific endeavour. Brian's individuality lies less in the possession of such a faculty than in his all-pervading use of it. His scores are full of unusual relationships and startling juxtapositions - one of the most persistent features, for example, being his predilection for putting the really important musical material at the bottom of the texture, instead of its usual place at the top. From the ordinary listener's point of view this device should present no special difficulty other than the original shock of unfamiliarity. The bottom line is scarcely more difficult intrinsically to perceive than the top: it simply gives a different angle of view on the rest of the music.

John Aldridge's analogy with *Goon Show* humour is very appealing and also, up to a point, very illuminating. It is worth recalling that when the *Goon Show* first began it ran into considerable disapproval, and even opposition, from those with a traditionalist attitude to humour, and that even in its heyday there were many who never understood it. Consider, for example, the shockingly irreverent treatment of English grammar in the following:

Bluebottle: Do not trifle with me! I have two O levels and a budgerigar!

One can quite imagine some elderly English professor frothing at the mouth with indignation at the inept use of the conjunction - two disparate objects in unholy grammatical wedlock. Of course if one understands the basis of *Goon Show* humour one understands that, in Bluebottle's mind, both O levels and budgerigar are status symbols. He sees no incongruity in yoking the two together, and it is precisely because he sees no incongruity that the line is irresistibly funny. It encapsulates very neatly the comic sadness of the Bluebottle character. On an altogether more serious level Brian's music is full of "lines" which function in very much the same way. Their seeming awkwardness or incongruity is very much part of the message, a part which is inevitably lost if they are taken over-literally. More than with most composers the incidents in Brian's scores can be understood properly only in and by their context.

---

might well have made many of the points which Mr Truscott makes, but my sole concern was to draw a distinction between those composers whose approach to symphonic structure is conditioned by the general concept of sonata form and one like Brian who favours an altogether more 'open-ended' approach. For brevity I presented my argument in a somewhat simplistic, black and white form but I am as aware as Mr Truscott that, in real life, things are mostly different shades of grey. Mr Truscott has lived with Brian's music longer than almost anyone, and he may find it hard to believe that anyone could be so naïve as to believe that Brian's symphonies should conform to the sonata model. There are many people, however, who have been brought up to believe that any real symphony *must* contain most of the elements of sonata form, and many of these find their first acquaintance with Brian's radically different approach disconcerting (to say the least). My concern was simply to pinpoint the rest of the difficulty - not only for those who are struggling to get to grips with Brian, but for those of us who have taken it upon ourselves to explain him to the unconvinced."

A third unusual trait in Brian's musical personality - at least unusual in someone thought of primarily as a symphonist - is his leaning towards the role of musical dramatist. Some of Brian's symphonic works, it seems to me, are structured in a manner very similar to Shakespeare's better chronicle plays. For instance, in *Henry V* the style varies from lofty heroics to low comedy - sometimes within the space of a single scene - but all in the service of single central thesis concerning the English nation and the English ideal of kingship. The diverse strands are eventually brought together in the epic achievement of Agincourt. They both explain how it was possible, and provide it with a human context which makes it all the more impressive. To my mind the *Gothic* Symphony represents an achievement of almost exactly the same kind and scale in musical terms as *Henry V* does in the dramatic field.

None of these traits represents anything radically beyond the understanding of ordinary mortals: indeed to varying degrees we all possess them. However it must be admitted that to the newcomer to Brian - especially the newcomer schooled in traditional musical practice - they can offer points of real difficulty. The trained listener finds himself entering a musical territory where many of the landmarks and mileposts look familiar, but stubbornly refuse to conform to the system his training has conditioned him to recognize. If he persists in trying to relate them to that system he will simply go more and more thoroughly astray. Those who have, or are prepared to, rely solely on their basic musical instincts will almost always fare much better, at least initially, although how quickly they learn to find their way around Brian's musical landscape will depend to some extent on the degree to which they share his particular mental characteristics.

That Brian is widely misunderstood - even by some of his professed admirers - cannot be doubted. Many a smart young critic, observing Brian's adherence to the traditional basic materials of music, has made the mistake of believing that here is a would-be conventional composer. Starting from this one false premise it is easy enough to find all the evidence one could desire of chaos, confusion and over-inflated ambition in the music. Start from an appreciation of what the music is really trying to say and the impression is immediately different. Relationships begin to emerge between apparently unrelated passages, and the music's seeming incongruities become telling flashes of revelation. If pomposity is sometimes present so too is the banana skin, and one may be sure that Brian is illustrating something pertinent with both. His approach to music was, in reality, no less original and deeply thought out than that of the acknowledged early 20th century radicals such as Schoenberg and Webern. The difference, as I see it, was that Brian was much less interested in the development of musical language as an end in itself, and much more interested in opening up new areas of meaning and experience, whether or not these could be expressed within existing musical formulae. He was willing enough to explore but only if the new territory seemed to hold immediate promise for him. (My own view is that subconsciously Schoenberg and Webern were not really revolutionaries at all but arch-conservatives looking for an esoteric new language to bolster the elitist tradition in German art music. Brian was the real iconoclast bent on creating music which truly reflected the 20th century - the somewhat confused "age of the common man".)

All this may explain why, with one or two honourable exceptions, the music critics have been even slower than the rest of us to appreciate Brian's true worth. To many, both critics and public, the whole basis of the profession appears to be a claim to be an élite in the interpretation of matters musical. Even if newspaper deadlines did not tend to demand an instant opinion, what self-conscious member of an élite would feel like risking his professional reputation by grappling publicly with kind of interpretative problems presented by Brian - much better to fall back on the usual (but irrelevant) stock of professional reflexes. Those who would understand Brian need the time and space to pause and reflect, and this is precisely what the professional critic so seldom has.

EXCURSUS: THE INFLUENCE OF BRIAN'S SOCIAL ENVIRONMENT ON HIS MUSICAL STYLE

Discussions and analyses of Brian's creative personality have tended to concentrate mainly on the peculiarities of his individual emotional and intellectual make-up. Yet any creative artist, however original and independent of influences he may seem, must to some extent be conditioned by his experiences of the world in which he operates and the social environment from which he came. Impressions received in childhood and adolescence are particularly important since it is rarely possible to throw them off entirely, even when subsequent experience shows them to be wrong or even dangerous. Rationally I ought not to find it any more difficult to trust a German than a human being of any other nationality. In practice I have to fight a prejudice left over from a childhood in which war against Germany was the "normal" state of affairs. (Peace seemed very strange and unnatural when it came!)

Some time ago a colleague on the Havergal Brian Society Committee took strenuous exception to someone describing Brian as a "working-class composer".[7] He has a point. The term "working-class composer" is almost a contradiction in terms. Composing music, especially "serious" music, is not a characteristically working-class activity. Even the liveried composers at 18th century courts generally enjoyed sufficient status to lift them above the working-class category attached to most domestic servants. Certainly, according to most conventional systems of socio-economic classification, Brian, whether as a freelance composer or as a journalist, would have been regarded as "middle-class", not "working-class". However, the real point is surely not that Brian was working-class but that he came from a working-class background. The influences working on him

---

[7] The question arose from Ronald Stevenson's article *A late harvest*, published in *Newsletter* 11 (V-VI 1977), pp. 2-3 and first published in *Books and Bookmen* in December 1976, as a review of the books by Nettel, Eastaugh and Foreman published in 1976. David J. Brown's comment was published, with Stevenson's reply, in *Newsletter* 11 (V-VI 1977), pp. 3-4. Don Goodsell's comment, to which is referred here, was a letter to the Editor in *Newsletter* 12 (VII-VIII 1977), pp. 5-6, Stevenson's reply was published on p. 6.

during his formative years thus differed significantly from those working on a middle-class child.

Even in a society where class is as strong as it was in 19th and early 20th century England, differences in attitudes and behaviour between the classes are seldom black and white absolutes. They are more matters of emphasis and degree, and within any class there will always be many individuals who espouse attitudes or patterns of behaviour commonly thought of as belonging to some quite different class. Any reference to the influence of an individual's class background must be understood as a reference to the insidious influence of a vaguely-defined and changing ethos, rather than of a closely-defined set of received values. We create our own values from the materials available to us, and our social background provides only some very raw materials. That said, certain broad differences between the classes and their likely influence on an artistically sensitive youngster's development can be discerned.

One such difference is in aesthetic attitudes. The dominant tendency in the middle class has been to value a work of art for its elegance, clarity, economy of means and "sophistication". Many middle-class youngsters are methodically educated to believe that adherence to these criteria is synonymous with "good taste", and that anything which is not in good taste is, *ipso facto*, an appeal to man's baser instincts (and therefore not serious art: yes, we have heard of someone who enjoys Brian's music but "doubts its value"!). The working-class tendency, in contrast, has been to value solid substance, richness of texture and "good workmanship". Almost anyone with working-class relatives will testify that, at least among the older generation, one of the highest terms of approbation is "look at the work that went into that!"

If Brian was indeed surrounded by such attitudes as a child, need we be surprised that solidity is such a marked feature of his characteristic musical expression? Superficial critics may tend to dismiss the resultant rich textures as mere turgidity, but in fact Brian is doing what any honest and truly sensitive creative artist does, embodying in his work the values of the society which helped to create him. This aspect of his style is as much part of his creative birthright as a "middle-class" reticence and spareness is of Benjamin Britten's.

It would obviously be wrong to suggest that the only aspect of Brian's youthful environment which influenced his creative development was his social class. There were, for example, peculiarities about the social role accorded to music in the time and place of Brian's childhood and adolescence. In an area such as North Staffordshire during the latter half of the 19th century a very large proportion of all musical activity would have been associated with religion or some form of competition. Both in moral and practical terms music would appear as a deadly serious business connected with the pursuit of excellence. Real excellence would be rewarded with spiritual salvation or, better still, a gold cup! Brian often appears to take it for granted in his scores that any real musician will welcome technical difficulties as a challenge, rather than regard them as an insuperable obstacle to performance. Could his apparent disregard for the practicalities of performance have something to do with being brought up in an atmosphere where *the* major preoccupation of many fine musicians was to go that little bit further than the next man? Certainly aspects of the *Gothic* Symphony seem partly explicable in these terms.

One could go on - for example, to explore the difference between "provincial" and "metropolitan" attitudes to the arts - and doubtless one would find many other factors which might have influenced one or other of the strands in Brian's musical personality. However, that would amount to a major research project, and go far beyond both my abilities and the scope of a *Newsletter* article. If I have succeeded in drawing attention to one or two avenues which need to be explored, that will do for now.

John Pickard: Havergal Brian's productive discontinuity. With a comment by Martyn Becker[1]

With the recent release on disc of Brian's Seventh and 31st Symphonies,[2] it seems that the critical debate as to the value or otherwise of this composer's music has reared its head once again. As usual, there are passionate defenders, hostile detractors and, somewhere in the middle, those who, like the reviewer in *Gramophone*, ultimately hoist the white flag in some bewilderment. And, as ever, it is one stylistic trait in particular which remains highest on the critical agenda: Brian's seemingly curious predilection for jumping abruptly from one musical idea to another without apparent regard for continuity of thought. Readers of the *Newsletter* will be aware of the kind of criticisms I am talking about:

> ... a self-defeating succession of gear-changes and non sequiturs (Hugh Ottaway)
> ... ellipsis to the point of incomprehensibility (Andrew Porter)
> ... breaking off in a sort of nervous exasperation (Desmond Shawe-Taylor)
> ... peculiarly dislocated phraseology (Anthony Payne)
> ... no shape, no coherence (Stanley Sadie)

This apparent eccentricity often constitutes a major stumbling block for even the most ardent Brian enthusiast and it consequently requires detailed consideration by those who believe him to be one of the most powerfully original composers of the 20th century.

This article is not intended to be a comprehensive survey of what I defensively term Brian's "Productive Discontinuity": a thesis could be written on the subject. Nor is it an apology to the hostile criticism which would have one believe that this characteristic is a symptom of incompetence. Such a defence is

---

[1] From *Newsletter* 79 (IX-X 1988), pp. 5-7. Martyn Becker's comment was first published in *Newsletter* 84 (VII-VIII 1989), pp. 2-3, entitled *Brianus ellipsis*.
[2] With the Royal Liverpool Philharmonic Orchestra, conducted by Sir Charles Mackerras, EMI CDC 749 558 2, now CDM 764 717 2.

no longer necessary since the final volume of Malcolm MacDonald's mighty survey of the symphonies appeared and systematically clobbered many a critical misapprehension concerning Brian's competence. Indeed, *so* masterly is MacDonald's vindication of the music that one hesitates to add anything that might detract from the force of the argument.

Naturally, MacDonald does provide several convincing explanations of the discontinuities in Brian's music (particularly Volume 3, pp. 198-202). One explanation given is that Brian wants to jolt the listener into active thought about what is being heard, rather than just let it wash over him. This is true enough but, on its own, it does not constitute a valid artistic aim. As a child, I used to chop up Classical Sonatinas for piano into individual bars, then paste them back together in random order (the title always came out as "Snotiana"). The exercise, intended for fun, did teach me something about the nature of continuity and it certainly got me listening more carefully to what I played. But I must concede now (if not then!) that the works were rather better in their original order. The serious and relevant point here is that, as music is more than a mere intellectual exercise, this explanation of Brian's discontinuities is worthless if we ultimately fail instinctively to feel their rightness.

I shall now examine various types of discontinuity in Brian's music: firstly, the most straightforward - discontinuity for dramatic purposes. This type of treatment is already apparent in relatively early works. For example, the opening of *In Memoriam* juxtaposes six bars of loud ceremonial introduction with quiet, intimate music which opens the "First Scene" and which consists of three "verses" of increasing intensity, each of which abruptly ceases and is answered by a "refrain". Ex. 1 shows the first appearance of the "refrain".

Ex. 1

The pattern of verse and refrain is used to regulate the emotional temperature of this First Scene: the first two statements of the refrain are points of repose, so that the third refrain, which this time extends the powerful climax generated by the third verse, comes as a surprise, for it actually breaks a pattern of discontinuity established by the first two verses and refrains. This type of contrast is again used impressively, though less systematically, in the Second Scene to steer the music through what is basically an *accelerando* until the tensions of the whole work are discharged in a massive climax which disintegrates with remarkable rapidity (ex. 2).

Ex. 2

It is instructive to compare this passage with the very different way in which Elgar dismantles the main climax of the slow movement of his Second Symphony - music not a million miles removed from the spirit and technique of *In Memoriam*. The Elgar will be seen to be far less abrupt in expression - the edges are softer. So we can already see Brian using extreme contrast as a structural basis of his music in 1911, and this gives *In Memoriam*, despite the strong influence of Elgar, a distinctive and individual musical voice.

In Memoriam is one of many funeral marches to be found in Brian's output. The finale of Symphony No. 2 is another powerful (and I think under-rated) example. Again, the music proceeds by a process of dramatic contrast. The opening recitative-like figure forms a constant interruption to the development of the movement's early stages (ex. 3).

Ex. 3

This recitative recurs (in slightly varied forms) 12 times in all and, on each appearance, no attempt is made to integrate it with the massive funeral march whose progress it dogs. The result is that when the music does eventually shake off the inhibiting influence of the recitative, it is at last able to stride purposefully

96 *Life and personality*

to the climax of the entire symphony. But, in the bleak coda, the recitative returns and the work ends darkly.

In this case, the breaking up of continuity by the insertion of recitatives objectifies the whole, curbing the excesses of the music's emotional progress and thereby strengthening, rather than undermining, the overall structure. It must be remembered that the apparent Romanticism which some commentators ascribe to Brian's music is illusory, or at most a stylistic impurity which, with the instinct of the born Classicist, he successfully excised in his later music. In this case, discontinuity is used to distance and objectify the musical drama. This procedure continually recurs in Brian's other works: for example in Symphony No. 8 where a huge climax, achieved after a long preparation, is suddenly cut off just as its romantic ardour threatens to bring the music to a grinding halt (ex. 4).

Ex. 4

However, continuity is not entirely broken up in this passage. First of all, the *type* of harmony used in these two bars is quite similar: all are "added note" chords - the first, an E major triad with added 6th *and* 7th; the second, basically a dominant 7th in E but with the 5th of the triad (i.e. the second degree of the E major scale) flattened. The Neapolitan implication is further strengthened by the fact that the chord is presented in 2nd inversion so that the flattened 2nd is the root. This will inevitably tilt the music towards F (E♯ being the enharmonic equivalent of F), so that the appearance of the flute figure in the next bar over a dominant 9th in F is nothing like such a drastic tonal shift as it might at first appear. This is not the only means by which continuity is subtly achieved. What cannot be seen in the given example is that the flute and glockenspiel figure shown here has, in fact, been clearly anticipated some seven bars earlier. So the connections are motivic as well as harmonic. What really makes for discontinuity in this passage is the sudden and radical change in orchestral texture.

Brian's characteristic use of enormously contrasting dynamics and types of orchestration is, of course, guaranteed to impair our perception of any underlying continuity in the music, but, as has already been shown, this is not to say that the continuity is not there at a deeper level if one listens attentively. Here, Robert Simpson's advice that it is often helpful to listen to Brian's music from the bass upwards is apposite (it is advice validated by the example just given -

look at the simple stepwise movement in the bass: E, E♭, G, F). If one listens to the descending scales (piano, then tuba, then piano and harp) near the beginning of Symphony No. 8, and notices their inversion (i.e. *ascending*) a couple of bars later, it is then easy to perceive the astonishing extent to which the whole piece is built on descending/ascending scale patterns (among other things!) and to follow one level of continuity in the musical thought of the whole symphony. In this way, superficial listening is easily overcome and many of the music's supposed "difficulties" evaporate.

So, why the sudden changes in orchestration? One reason lies in Brian's concern with *balance*. In later life he described "balance of form" as his greatest concern when writing music. It goes much deeper than just the desire to contrast loud and soft, *tutti* and solo, but this is undoubtedly one of the manifestations of his Classicist's concern for contrast of extremes (for a well-known Classical equivalent consider the opening bars of Mozart's *Jupiter* Symphony).

In Brian's case, the desire for contrast can be traced even further back - to Baroque models. Strong contrast is, of course, the basis of the Concerto Grosso, but it also manifests itself in many other Baroque forms. For example, the opening of Bach's great Fantasia and Fugue in G minor for organ contrasts loud *tutti* (block chords) with soft solo writing (polyphonic), as shown in ex. 5. Harmonically, the continuity is unbroken, but the sense of contrast suggested by the change in texture and implied change in registration is often emphasized in performance by the necessity for a brief pause while a change in registration is made.

Ex. 5

Bruckner has often been accused of writing organ music transcribed for orchestra. This is, of course, utter nonsense - Bruckner's symphonies, like Brian's, are brilliantly conceived in orchestral terms. However, the fact that both composers were organists is not, I feel, without significance. If a composer is an accomplished instrumentalist (the vast majority are), the instrument he plays will have an effect - perhaps not so much on the way he writes, but on the way he *listens*. Music, however original, is the result of a practical experience of music - there is no shame in this. Brian's musical life began as a choirboy and continued as a church organist. His formative musical experiences were in the context of the church - although, unlike Bruckner, he did not pursue a career as an organist. Nevertheless, the two composers share two important characteristics in their orchestral writing which I am sure reflect this common aspect of their musical backgrounds. Firstly, they tend to build up orchestral textures in much the same way that an organist is often forced to build up a texture. The uses of the Swell pedal being restricted, it is often necessary to achieve a *crescendo* by gradually increasing the registration (i.e. adding more stops) and the resulting effect is of the gradual addition of *layers* of sound, rather than the smooth increase in the intensity of a single timbre. Many examples of the orchestral implications of this technique are to be found in Bruckner's symphonies (e.g. the coda of the finale of No. 8, or the long build-up to the climax of No. 7's slow movement) and a similar process is often to be seen in Brian's music. A most striking example is provided by the second movement of *The Gothic*. In both cases, the procedure, though quite valid and effective in purely orchestral terms, has its roots in lessons learnt as an organist.

The second similarity is something not so much learnt as absorbed instinctively, and it concerns resonance. An organist must constantly adapt the way he plays to the particular acoustical conditions of the building in which he happens to be playing, otherwise a harmonic mush may result in a particularly resonant acoustic. This is particularly the case when playing fast music or music which alternates loud and soft dynamics and it often necessitates short, unmeasured pauses in the music to give the sound time to clear. To do this requires skill and instinct because what one hears from the organ loft is unlikely to correspond to the sound filling the rest of the building. Malcolm MacDonald points out that the abrupt breaks between loud and soft, common to both Bruckner and Brian are achieved by measured and unmeasured pauses respectively (Volume 3, p. 141) - Brian writes a "breath mark" like two large inverted commas or two diagonal parallel lines. Were either procedure to be encountered in organ music, no one would give it a second thought - it is a convention one expects and, if a composer did not allow for it, the chances are that the organist would have to put it in at some point anyway. Of course, these pauses are not silent: the resonance is still clearing and the change of texture, dynamic or whatever is nothing like as abrupt as it would be if it were heard in a dry acoustic. Anyone fortunate enough to have heard a Bruckner symphony in the vast spaces of a great cathedral will know that the effect is far removed from that of a performance in, say, the Festival Hall. In fact, the Bruckner symphonies would be in their true home if they were to be played in cathedrals. I believe that the same is true of Brian's symphonies and that to perform them in the hermetically sealed and lifeless acoustic of a modern recording studio does them a disservice. If proof of this theory be needed, consider almost any passage in the *Gothic* Symphony: for example, the last five bars of the fourth movement and the alternation of a grinding *fortissimo* with a delicate *pianissimo*. This sounds fine in a resonant building, the *pianissimo* emerging magically from the massive resonance of the *tutti*. Now (briefly, and with a shudder of dread) imagine that same passage in a dead acoustic ... fortunately, given the size of building required to accommodate the forces, such an eventuality seems unlikely.

One of the most remarkable qualities of Brian's later symphonies is the way in which they suggest enormous size and scale while often playing for less *actual* time than many a longwinded overture. The relationship between "real" time and the "subjective" time which music can create on its own terms is a fascinating one and the reasons why two pieces of equal length can feel vastly different in duration deserve closer and more detailed study. Solutions concerning the relative boredom threshold of different listeners can, on the whole, be discounted because if one performs tests on unsuspecting, but musically sensitive, friends and colleagues the response to the relationship between structural balance and time seems to be pretty consistent. Viewed in purely abstract terms, the idea of attempting to balance, say, a 25-minute slow movement with a very fast one of under five minutes would seem ludicrous. Yet this is precisely what Shostakovich does in the first two movements of his Symphony No. 10, with impressive results, the scherzo proving the perfect foil to the epic scale of the first movement. The reason for this is that each movement creates its own kind of momentum, to which the attentive listener will respond, irrespective of the passing of "real" time, and this in turn is the result of the speed at which musical events occur (particularly changes of harmony). The fact that the first movement is cast as a single-span arch, in which the material gradually unfolds, results in a compensatory slowing down in the rate of the listener's expectations. The fact that the scherzo is much more episodic in character, moving between ideas with greater abruptness, gives the impression of great distance travelled in a far shorter time. The fundamental principle common to both movements is the control of the rate of activity.

By switching abruptly from one musical event to another in a relatively short space of time, Brian is concentrating, rather than diffusing, the musical action (always provided the material is distinguished enough!), and thereby creating his own epic scale within a severely restricted time-span. This is effected in a variety of ways, but two particularly important ones stand out: those in which the contrasting material can be audibly related to what has just preceded it and those in which it cannot, and is thereby justified (or not) by some other means.

The example of the former is taken from Symphony No. 16 and it involves a contrast between a massive *tutti* and just the strings (without double-basses). The crashing of gears is mighty indeed, but continuity of thought is nevertheless maintained by the very clear motivic connection between the two sections (ex. 6).

Ex. 6

100 Life and personality

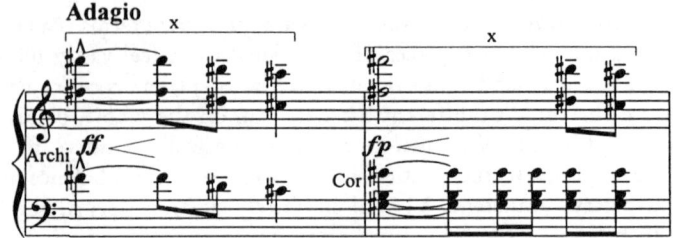

The Adagio then unfolds into a magnificently serene passage which, as Malcolm MacDonald says, seems to contain the hidden heart of the work. For this to be the case (not forgetting that it occurs very late on in the symphony), the passage could not have been arrived at in any other way. Strong contrast of texture throws it into relief, though the deeper continuity of thought remains intact and could in no way be considered "non sequitur" as Hugh Ottaway would have presumably argued - it is certainly the opposite of "self-defeating".

Ex. 7

The second example - that of a productive juxtaposition of unconnected passages - comes from Symphony No. 17 (a fascinating and, I think, worthy successor to No. 16) (ex. 7). The connection between the rather noble first five bars of this example and fig. 43 at the end of it is apparent - indeed, it would be possible to cut out the intervening five bars without any loss of continuity. It is precisely *such* continuity which Brian is here deliberately avoiding by placing, in the middle of the passage, material which is in complete textural, tonal, harmonic, melodic and emotional contrast. The result, as with the example from Symphony No. 16, is to throw the passage into relief. Heard in terms of the music which appears just before the given example begins, the apparently inconsequential flute solo at fig. 42 turns out to be a derivation of earlier material, the whole passage giving the impression not so much of "verses and refrains" as "refrains and commentaries" and, again, forming the still point at the heart of the symphony. There is about this technique far more of parenthesis than non sequitur.

The procedure outlined above must not be misunderstood in terms of a juxtaposition of "blocks" favoured by so many composers since Brian (for example Birtwistle, Messiaen and later Tippett). The essence of that kind of technique is the recurrence of contrasted and self-contained types of material in different combinations. It is basically non-developmental, static and gestural. This is a perfectly valid approach to composing but it does not explain the nature of Brian's symphonism. In his music, material is rarely recapitulated in a literal way. Everything is in a constant state of transformation and, as any living process will often yield surprising results at unexpected times, so Brian's music never does precisely what one might expect it to do - to the delight of the Brian enthusiast and, one supposes, the irritation of the hostile critics.

My defence of what many consider to be the most problematic and insoluble aspect of Brian's music is, to a certain extent, superfluous: either the finished result convinces on its own terms or it does not and no amount of justification or special pleading will make it otherwise. That said, I believe that the number of instances where Brian's "productive discontinuity" cannot, on reflection, be shown to be justified is extremely small and that this highly individual approach to symphonic structure may come to be regarded as the most revolutionary aspect of his art. It certainly has the most far-reaching consequences.

Martyn Becker comments:

The various and fascinating comments on Brian, his technique, his musical background, and his sound-world contained brought home strongly to me why Brian's "productive discontinuities" (as John Pickard called them) have never to any great extent surprised or worried me as much as they obviously do the correspondents Messrs Taylor and Toller, who mentioned this aspect of Brian in their letters. My curious lack of worry (if I can term it so) has in fact much to do with what John Pickard's admirable article highlighted in terms of the similarities of orchestral layering operated by Havergal Brian and Anton Bruckner.

It is interesting to note that reaction to both these composers is usually of the extreme variety: love or hate. There appears to be very little middle ground -

very little "pleasant indifference", if you like - and it seems to me that the reasoning behind this all boils down to one thing: patience, and how much of it the listener is prepared to spend in getting to know a composer and his traits. Getting to know a composer can be relatively easy, or relatively difficult, according to the particular composer's mode of expression, and his public eye. Tchaikovsky, for example, is easily amenable to most music lovers, but that does not diminish his great melodic and orchestrative genius.

If Tchaikovsky makes it relatively easy to come to terms with his style, Brian and Bruckner do not. Stylistically, Bruckner is long-breathed and architectural; Brian, terse and monolithic. Both composers, however, require a different kind of patience from their listeners: Bruckner in the sheer timescale required for his symphonic logic, Brian in the rapid changes of direction in the compact later symphonies. Taking all this into account, it still seems to me that if you love Bruckner, then Brian becomes less of a hard nut to crack.

Having thus framed Bruckner with Brian in this way, there in fact appear to be even more relevant aspects to their musical relationship than John Pickard brings out in his article, although I appreciate that his were self-confessed introductory thoughts. There are certain similarities between the two composers, the hiatuses and the registration effects in the orchestration to name but two. Their developments in terms of symphonic language, though, are entirely different. Whereas Bruckner's cycle of 11 symphonies displays organic growth, and an increasing sense of maturity and confidence from post-Mendelssohnian delicacy to pre-Schoenbergian paranoia, Brian's cycle is tonally eclectic, and not as fundamentally developmental from work to work as Bruckner's. Brian's is more of a metamorphosis; from the large, multi-layered, extended early symphonies to the massive, condensed later ones; the moving from the longhand writing of a schoolboy to the more direct, enforced shorthand of a student working against time to get the lecture notes down on the page.

Then there is the question of the sonority of Brian's orchestra, and its relationship to that of Bruckner. The hiatuses in Brian's more mature symphonies would indeed provide an impressively long decay time in a resonant acoustic, as may be heard in the Brian Centenary Alexandra Palace performances of the mid-'70s.[3] The early symphonies appear to me to be a different matter entirely, though. Would the tortuous chromatic choral lines of the *Gothic* Symphony *really* sound that good in the cavernous spaces of a cathedral acoustic, or would they just mush together into unintelligible noise? The notorious Royal Albert Hall "sound" is perhaps not the ideal venue for decision-making on the acoustic requirements of *The Gothic*; much less so than for Mahler's Eighth, say, which is less complex, musically, spatially, and structurally.

Staying on the theme of Brian's sonority for a moment, the recent performance of the Third Symphony at Maida Vale No. 1 (a studio most kindly de-

---

[3] The four Brian Centenary concerts took place, as reported by Lewis Foreman (*Newsletter* 4, I 1976, pp. 2-3), Malcolm MacDonald (*Newsletter* 7, VIII 1976, pp. 6-7) and David J. Brown (*Newsletter* 8, XI 1976, pp. 1-2), in September and October 1976.

scribed as "acoustically damped"!) was actually enhanced by the lack of reverberation, because it was possible to hear clearly the internal workings of Brian's orchestration. Without doubt, the performance of a Bruckner symphony in a cathedral is a spectacular and uplifting experience. With Brian, it is much more "horses for courses" as far as this acoustic aspect is concerned. As such, this facet of Brian's symphonism may indeed have been something of a miscalculation on the composer's part, perhaps due to the lack of performance of his music and therefore the lack of opportunity to "fine-tune" the orchestration as Mahler frequently did, or revise on a major scale, as Bruckner was prompted into. Having said that, I hope it does not come across as sheer effrontery on the part of a layman such as myself to question the workings of a major musical mind! Perhaps it must be admitted, as Messrs Taylor and Toller rightly point out, that Brian was not perfect after all. He was, however, a good deal *more* perfect than a large number of lesser composers.

John Pickard mentions two distinct types of "productive discontinuities" (what a lovely phrase!) in Brian's music - the related and the unrelated: the former is based on an apparently pointless insertion of contrasting material into a musical paragraph, and the latter is an abrupt change of direction and texture. Having compared Bruckner's sonority with Brian's it is interesting to note that there are similar discontinuities to be found in Bruckner's music also. Pickard's example in Brian's 17th Symphony of a flute interpolation within a passage containing related musical material finds a parallel in the *Adagio* of Bruckner's Eighth (Haas edition) where an interpolated quiet passage (coincidentally containing a prominent part for the flute) separates two *tutti* passages, and therefore throws the musical argument into relief. Fascinatingly (and again coincidentally), this happens to be the very same passage excised from this movement by Leopold Nowak in his edition of the Eighth Symphony. Similar discontinuous logic may be found within the finale of Bruckner's Third in its 1877 version.

The above comparison with Bruckner is instructive for two fundamental reasons. Firstly, the remarkable similarities and obvious differences between the music of the two composers stand out starkly. Secondly, that Bruckner, together with Beethoven and Sibelius, was among the select band of composers who were most influential on the development of symphonic form in the 190 years since the turn of the 19th century. Bearing in mind the first reason, the implications of the second reason are there for all to see.

Lastly, in terms of Brian's connection with Bruckner comes the vexed question of "crackjaw platitudes". Robert Simpson uses the phrase in his book *The Essence of Bruckner* regarding a theme within the second subject group of the finale of Bruckner's Fourth. Simpson's reaction to this particular theme appears to be embarrassment, which is of course a valid reaction. Whether you agree or disagree with Simpson's point in the context of the book is neither here nor there (for the record, I don't!), but the concept is easily applicable to Brian, as well as it is to many other composers. By dint of strange coincidence, there is to my mind an example of this in the music of Havergal Brian currently staring us in the face. Even after countless playings of the EMI recording of the Seventh and 31st

Symphonies, I still cannot *quite* listen to the first ten seconds of No. 31 without a slight wince at the plain, almost banal, throwaway beginning. The remainder grips me more each time I hear it, although as a performance I marginally prefer Mackerras' 1979 reading for the BBC; but oh, that beginning!

I also agree with Mr Taylor in respect of Brian's unevenness - but then name one major composer who is not guilty of this in some measure. It is all a matter of degree, and not one of the great composers is immune to it. Beethoven's *Eroica* is balanced by the hardly-inspired *Rage Over a Lost Penny* - the *Emperor* Concerto by the *Choral* Fantasia. Tchaikovsky's *Romeo and Juliet* Fantasy Overture is balanced by his workaday symphonic poem *Fatum*; and so the list could go on. Thus while I agree with Mr Taylor *in principle*, the extent to which I agree differs. Yes, the 32 symphonies contain chaff among the wheat, but I would venture that perhaps there is not so much there as may be thought.

Looking at Brian's symphonic oeuvre, the unique *Gothic* has to be set aside as a special case, as Malcolm MacDonald says in his third volume on the symphonies. Indeed, who would *dare* to cast aspersions on such a work as that, even if the aspersions could be justified? Not me, certainly: I would gladly chicken out of that one. Personally I would expand Mr Taylor's ranks of quality Brian symphonies from the four of the group 6 to 9 to the group 3 to 11 of the earlier works (with 3, 4 and 11 being major pieces), 15 to 19 in the middle, and the odd-numbered 25, 27, 29 and 31 (even with that beginning!) as fine examples of Brian's late style, with the trilogy of Nos 22-24 tagging along behind. This amounts to approximately two thirds of Brian's symphonic output. The remainder may be curate's eggs, but what David J. Brown said in his Editorial to *Newsletter* 79 can certainly be applied to them. The single performances to which some of his symphonies have been treated can be confusing in any appraisal of them, to say the least of it. Nos 28 and 30 still escape me, due maybe to Stokowski's and Newstone's readings respectively - and despite Malcolm MacDonald's advocacy of the latter work - and they still await good performances.

There is more good Brian by far than there is mediocre or bad Brian (even if there are the odd mediocre patches in the good works!) - a sign of quality in the music of this major composer. For "uniformly eulogistic" as Mr Taylor refers to the *Newsletter*, I would use the word "enthusiastic", because no member of the Society is going to regale the pages of its *Newsletter* with destructive criticism - I hope. As a Wagner Society would not publicly dwell on the derivations and extent of, say, his well-known anti-semitism, then our Society should be aware of Brian's shortcomings, which of course do exist, but which should be discussed *constructively*. Constructive criticism is of course the essence, and certainly does not undermine what the Society is attempting to do; namely bring the name of Havergal Brian before a wider musical public.

Havergal Brian talking to Robert Simpson and Jeffrey Anderson[1]

R.S. Now tell me, there's a thing I've always been wondering, Havergal, and that is that in the last, how long is it now? - since you were 80 - that's the last 13 years or so - you've written, I think, 20 symphonies ...

H.B. Probably.

R.S. ... and a Concerto for Orchestra and a Cello Concerto. It's phenomenal. I mean, I've never heard of anybody of your age doing such a thing. It would be astonishing even if the music was bad, but the music isn't bad. Can you tell me whether this sudden acceleration in last years is due to the fact that you heard suddenly a lot of your music after a long time? Did this make you get going again?

H.B. I wouldn't say so, but I can assure you that after I heard Bryan Fairfax's performance of *The Gothic*, for a long time I couldn't get *The Gothic* out of my head. It might have been by Wolf or some other composer, and it simply soaked in my system. It was a long time before I could get rid of it.

R.S. Almost as if it were by somebody else?

H.B. Yes, yes.

R.S. Because it was a long time between the time when you wrote it and the time when you actually heard it?

H.B. That's right; that's right.

R.S. I've often wondered whether in fact this was a sudden great stimulus which suddenly made you accelerate. Can you account for the fact that you've written at such a greater rate in your 80s than you did, say, in your 60s or even your 50s?

H.B. Well, I wouldn't say that I did because - what's the date of the operas - the *Faust* and *Turandot*?

R.S. All about 1940s I suppose, are they?

H.B. Well, those works followed in succession ... I think *The Cenci* was the first - *Turandot* followed immediately afterwards; *Faust* followed after the *Turandot*. I don't know how many years I was working on those.[2]

R.S. That was when you had a patch of writing operas, dramatic works, and then later on you turned back to symphonies.

H.B. That's right.

---

[1] In early 1969 Havergal Brian was interviewed in his home by Robert Simpson, together with Jeffrey Anderson of CBC. Here the entire unedited interview is given; the tape lasts something in the order of 75 minutes; it was broadcast only in part. As a kind of appendix another interview is reprinted here. It was taken in November 1966 and is carrying the title *Composer's Portrait*. The interviews were published in *Newsletters* 56 (XI-XII 1984), pp. 2-5, 57 (I-II 1985), pp. 3-4, 58 (III-IV 1985), pp. 4-6 and 59 (V-VI 1985), pp. 2-4 and 54 (VII-VIII 1984), pp. 1-3. Both interviews were transcribed by Philip Edwards, slightly revised by Malcolm MacDonald.

[2] Brian's memory is at fault here. The dates are *Turandot*, 1950-51; *The Cenci*, 1952; *Faust*, 1955-56.

106   Life and personality

R.S. Was there any special reason, do you think, why you switched back to symphonies?

H.B. I think it was ... Schotts had *Turandot* and it went to Mainz I believe, and was read there. I think it was Mr Strecker[3] said how difficult it would be for an English composer to get even a work in German performed in Germany. I think something ... I wouldn't say a damper, but I found that there were difficulties in the way. Probably that is the reason[4] but don't forget also that, in between those symphonies, didn't I write *Agamemnon* which you have?

R.S. Yes, indeed, and of course some of the symphonies like the Twelfth are closely connected with it.

H.B. That's right. They were written about the same time.

R.S. But it also interests me this remark you make about being perhaps discouraged by the thought that it was difficult to get operas performed.

H.B. Oh no, no.

R.S. You weren't really discouraged by that - obviously not.

H.B. Actually, discouragement has never troubled me. Not a bit, oh No. The only ambition I've had is to create, create, and as I've often told you, when I finish a work I forget it. Over the Fourteenth ... until I got the score, you see, I didn't know what you were talking about. But the moment I saw the front page the whole thing was there.[5]

R.S. It came back, yes.

H.B. The whole symphony was there. The same with 21. You talked about 21; well, until I got the score and all those parts, I'd forgotten all about 21, d'you see? But the moment I open the pages it's all there again.

R.S. When you compose - I mean all these years you've been neglected and the music's not been played except in recent years - a few works have been done and they've created quite a considerable impression. But before that you went on and on and on without the slightest degree of encouragement. Did you think about performance or about any particular kind of audience when you composed? I mean, did it bother you whether they were performed or not?

H.B. No, I don't think so, no.

R.S. No, but you're pleased enough when they are done, presumably.

H.B. I remember when I was working on the *Götz von Berlichingen*.[6] Newman saw the slow movement. He thought something very wonderful about the

---

[3] "Mr Strecker" is Willy Strecker (1884-1958), son of Ludwig Strecker who inherited the firm of Schott from its family founders. As Managing Director he was responsible for the firm's association with Stravinsky, Hindemith, Schoenberg, Orff, Weill, Hartmann, and Markevitch, to name but a few. Brian must have been in fairly frequent contact with him - not only because Schott took several of his works on a hire basis for a period in the 1940s and 50s, but because Strecker took over the firm of Augener, for which Brian wrote a large number of songs and part-songs, as early as 1910. (Malcolm MacDonald in a letter to the Editor in *Newsletter* 57, pp. 2-3.)

[4] *Turandot* is in German, *The Cenci* in English, whilst *Faust* is again in German.

[5] The Fourteenth and 21st Symphonies had been recorded for broadcast in January 1969 by Edward Downes and the London Symphony Orchestra.

[6] Symphony No. 2 (1930-31). Havergal Brian told Reginald Nettel, when he was researching his pioneering biography, *Ordeal by Music* in the early 1940s, that it was inspired by Goethe's hero.

slow movement. At that time I was working on the scherzo, with all those pianos and the 16 horns.

R.S. Yes, in the Second Symphony ... what is now ...

H.B. I said to him, of the finale, "It's a rather imposing finale and the end of the life of Götz." I said to him "By the way this is a new idea; this is a slow rondo." He says, "Well, why not make it fast?"!

R.S. Take up less time, obviously.

H.B. That was like Newman, wasn't it? "Why not make it fast?"

J.A. Apart from your colossal *Gothic* Symphony, which is becoming better known to the public at large through the two performances that have been given of it, what other symphony in your number of symphonies that you have written do you feel most satisfied with - one that you set yourself certain symphonic problems to solve and you feel that you accomplished those?

H.B. No. 5; well, you call it No. 4 now, don't you?

R.S. The *Siegeslied*.

H.B. It's a choral symphony, the *Siegeslied*. That's Psalm 68.

J.A. Is it an all-choral symphony?

H.B. Two big choral divisions and a soprano solo in the middle of them. It's a big work; well, you know ... We can talk about that ...

J.A. It's not as big as the *Gothic* Symphony, though?

H.B. Well in a way it's bigger. Do you think so?

R.S. It's not the same length of course. It's a very large orchestra and a very large chorus.

H.B. It lasts about 50 minutes, but it's scored for a very large orchestra, isn't it?

R.S. Very impressive, I think.

H.B. It's a different type, you see ... Psalm 68 is a ferocious thing in a way. It was sung by Cromwell and his Ironsides before the Battle of Dunbar. It's so different from the *Te Deum* which makes *The Gothic*. That's all praise and it's wonderful and so on: there's no denunciation, no fury, and Psalm 68 is full of it.

R.S. Yes - real savagery.

J.A. Did you not write a large-scale cantata or oratorio called *The Vision of Cleopatra*?

H.B. That's right, yes.

J.A. Could you tell us something about that?

H.B. Oh yes. That was produced at the Southport Triennial Musical Festival in 1909, and recalling that reminds me of the sitting that we had at the studio a week last Tuesday, the Fourteenth and so on, because *Cleopatra* was for a choir, a very large orchestra, four soloists: a tenor, two contraltos and two girl sopranos and Landon Ronald was the conductor. The interesting thing about it is that when I arrived at Southport the day before the Festival, I met him in Lord Street, limping. So I said, "This is not a good sign if you're going to conduct *Cleopatra*", because he had been specially engaged for it. He said, "I think I shall be alright

---

In his last years, he referred to it as "Man in his cosmic loneliness". His passing reference to the original subject here, at the age of 93, is interesting.

but if I can't get an extra orchestra rehearsal, I won't conduct it." So I went up and saw the chorusmaster and he said, "Oh, don't worry about that, we shall arrange it." So they did have the orchestra rehearsal on Monday with the Hallé Orchestra alone, and the following morning the orchestra was rehearsed again, and late in the morning with all the chorus and the principals. Coates was the tenor.

J.A. John Coates, was it?

H.B. John Coates, one of the best men we ever had.

J.A. Best tenor, yes.

H.B. I saw him and he was pulling his coat off. He says, "Brian, it's a muck o'nettles this time!" A Yorkshireman, you see!

J.A. Did it have any further performances, *The Vision of Cleopatra*?

H.B. No, I didn't expect it.

J.A. Just one performance. What kind of text was used for that work?

H.B. It came out through a competition. The Norwich Festival advertised for a libretto for a choral work. Curiously enough, a Manchester friend of mine won the prize. It was on Cleopatra, and *Cleopatra* was then offered to British composers in a competition of which I think the first prize was £50... oh, there was only one prize, that's it: £50. So I took this work up. At that time Bantock was conducting orchestral works of mine in Liverpool. I didn't know much about him, but he was one of the adjudicators in this competition for the setting of *Cleopatra*. By the way, 70 English composers dared to set it to music! He gave me a hint: he said, "I've spotted your handwriting. You can go home and lie in bed; it's yours." I said, "Really?" He says "Yes". So I was disappointed when the result came out, because a few weeks ... after I'd seen Bantock in Liverpool I saw in *The Times* or the *Telegraph* that he'd withdrawn from the list of adjudicators and his position had been taken by Ernest Walker of Oxford. So that the adjudicators were Coleridge-Taylor, Ernest Walker and Fred Delius. The funny thing was that they gave the first prize to Bantock's pupil Julius Harrison with a high recommendation for Havergal Brian. A day or two after the announcement in the Press I got a letter from the Norwich Festival saying that they felt it was due to me that they should send this, although there wasn't a second prize. They sent a cheque and they said "Our conductor, Mr Henry J. Wood, has been a very generous subscriber to this cheque."

J.A. Oh, I see. So in fact you got a prize?

H.B. Yes. Now then, the trouble was, with all these works; you see, there were 70 of them. Now Julius Harrison's work was sure because he got the prize, which was a Norwich Festival production. Well, what about the others? So, when I heard that Southport were considering my setting, you see, we'd got to get permission from the people who'd published Harrison's work, and permission from Harrison, too - because it was the same libretto, d'you see? What I heard afterwards of the adjudication was that Delius was the opponent over this, the two, the Harrison and the Brian works. Delius went for Harrison, they didn't want Brian. The funny thing was, arising from this - this was all in 1907 - in 1911 there were Empire symphony concerts; it was the Coronation year of George V, and Coleridge-Taylor was to conduct the South African concert, and they put my *For Valour* in the South African programme. I was very proud about this because I'd always had a hunch for South Africa although I'd never been there. I met Taylor at Cramer's in Oxford Street I think. The first thing he said to me - now he was one of the adjudicators of the *Cleopatra Vision* - he said, "Do you know, Brian, I never understood why you didn't get the *Cleopatra* prize."

J.A. There must have been some funny work!

H.B. I shall never forget Taylor, he was a very nice fellow.

J.A. He died very young didn't he?

H.B. I was just going to tell you. I went to the rehearsals. It was the Queen's Hall. I shall never forget Taylor, at the end of the rehearsal. He was doing this, you know, all the time.

J.A. Mopping his brow.

H.B. And whilst he was doing this he said, "For God's sake, Brian, go to America. Take this work, they'll worship you there, they'll never have it here. If you'll only go, I'll get the Coleridge-Taylor Society in America to help you." The last time I saw Coleridge-Taylor was after that rehearsal and he was running for a bus at Oxford Circus, and a few months after it I heard of his death. I didn't attend the performance, I only attended the rehearsal.

J.A. He'd been a pupil of Stanford's hadn't he, Coleridge-Taylor, and had of course this great success with *Hiawatha*.

H.B. Oh yes. He was very popular. In fact he was more popular than any composer I've ever known. Elgar never had the popularity that Coleridge-Taylor had. Oh No. Jaeger, a great friend of Elgar - helped Elgar - he also helped Coleridge-Taylor. I think it was over the very first part of *Hiawatha* that Jaeger wrote a long article, bringing the young composer along, in *The Musical Times* and he finished with Schumann's quotation on meeting Brahms: "Hats off, gentlemen, here's a genius." Now, the year that Jaeger died, 1908, I saw him and I said "By the way, were you ever disappointed that Coleridge-Taylor didn't get up to the size that you thought he would?" He said "No, I don't think so but, you know, nigger blood comes to maturity at about 20." That was his answer!

J.A. That was an extraordinary thing to say.

R.S. Yes, typical of the times, really, I think. I remember reading only a few weeks ago, a very fine Clarinet Quintet by Coleridge-Taylor, written when he was 19: a very fine piece, very promising indeed.

H.B. Oh, he was, and he was very brilliant as a conductor. Do you know that a friend of mine had a small choral society. I said to him one day, "What are you thinking of doing?" He said "We're thinking of doing *Meg Blane*." That was Coleridge-Taylor. "If we do", he said "we shall try to get Coleridge-Taylor to come down to conduct it." Well, time went on and this work was prepared and the Hallé, 70 members of the Hallé were engaged. Now this is cute on the part of Taylor: he'd got a chorus there of about 50 and an orchestra of 70, and he just opened the score and said, "Gentlemen, half marks please". Wasn't it clever? Fitting in his 70 orchestra with the voices of 50.[7]

---

[7] Compare these reminiscences, 35 years on, with Brian's item on Coleridge-Taylor in *Musical Opinion*, September 1934, reproduced in Malcolm MacDonald (ed.), *Havergal Brian on Music*, Vol. 1, London 1986, pp. 244-6.

R.S. Tell me, a story I'm interested to hear about - I remember someone telling me that Tovey sight-read the *Gothic* Symphony at the piano. Did you hear him doing this?

H.B. Yes. That was at Bantock's flat. I went down there one Sunday morning and Tovey was there. He was very unassuming; the only thing was he talked very fast. I remember it was an upright piano, and I turned the pages over for him. But he played through the manuscript of *The Gothic*.

R.S. The *manuscript*?

H.B. Oh yes - it wasn't published.

R.S. How did he get to see it? Did you take it there specially to show it to him?

H.B. Oh, that was the arrangement: Bantock asked me to. He said that Tovey was calling on Sunday morning, he'd like me to meet him. That's what brought this about. It was his idea. He just put *The Gothic* on the piano and started to play it. There was no pre-arrangement that *The Gothic* was going to be discussed. The thing was, he was the man who took it to Vienna, to the International Jury.

R.S. That was the Schubert Centenary, wasn't it, in 1928?

H.B. That's right, 1928.

R.S. Wasn't it disqualified because it had a choral finale?

H.B. That's right, it was put out - wasn't even considered in the competition. They only considered the three orchestral movements.

R.S. I remember hearing that Tovey was very enthusiastic about it and fought very hard for it. What did he say, actually, when he played it?

H.B. I can't remember what he had to say, but what I remember him saying, that I'd lost the prize through one vote: that was Glazunov. Glazunov had a casting vote and he gave it favour of a Swede - was he a Swede?

R.S. Atterberg. Kurt Atterberg.

H.B. But you talking about the Schubert prize: I ought to have won it because of what I did for Schubert years ago. Yes, at a time when I conducted the Stoke-on-Trent Orchestral Society, we practically lived on Schubert's music. I remember we had his *Tragic* Symphony, the *Unfinished Symphony*, *Fierrabras* Overture, *Alfonso und Estrella* Overture, *Rosamunde* Overture, and I think the only other things we were rehearsing were two overtures by Sullivan, *Di Ballo* and *In Memoriam*. But the Schubert was going for months.

R.S. I was fascinated to see, actually, not long ago, that on that Schubert Centenary jury was Carl Nielsen.

H.B. Yes.

R.S. And I'm fascinated to think of him looking at the *Gothic* Symphony and wondering what he thought of it. I wonder which way his vote went?

H.B. I don't know, but that is what I heard from Tovey, that Glazunov gave his casting vote in favour of the Swede, Atterberg.

J.A. After initial successes that you had with your orchestral music and some of your choral music, then came years of neglect and oblivion, but I understand that in one point in time, just prior to the First World War, there was a gentleman who did help you out, so to speak, financially for a short period of time.

H.B. Oh, that was long before the First War.

J.A. What date was that?

H.B. It was 1907. It lasted until 1913. That's a, what shall we call it? ... a free understanding: I mean I could draw what I wanted from him, but in 1913 it came to a stop ... just an Allowance of £6 a month.

J.A. And you managed to devote most of your energies to composition as a result of this?

H.B. All sorts of things. I was very lucky. By the way, before these orchestral works began to get performances, I had a long series of successes with choral works.

J.A. Part-songs were they?

H.B. Part-songs - for four voices, six voices, eight voices, or for female voices only - never male voices only - and they were done at all the festivals on the Lancashire coast and Barrow-in-Furness. Some of the works were written specially for the festival committees. These things were performed year after year from the end of the 19th century to the early years of the 20th and they continued until the First War when the whole thing stopped and it's never been renewed. The choirs disappeared. I suppose they went in the army, the men d'you see?, and it came to an end. It was a great movement.

J.A. Choral?

H.B. Yes - it only affected the Midlands.

J.A. Some of Elgar's part songs and Bantock's part songs were done ...

H.B. Elgar was heart and soul in it - so was Bantock. Oh, some of the things have been extraordinary. The experience of listening to some of these choirs - they were quite as efficient as a professional string quartet. And they were choirs of 60 to 70 voices. To hear these people sing songs of Brahms or Cornelius or things for male voice like [Friedrich] Hegar - he's a Swiss composer. His *Phantom Host* would make your hair stand straight. If you ever heard the Manchester Orpheus, about 80 voices, sing that *Phantom Host* you'd never forget it, you know. The Manchester Orpheus doesn't exist. I don't suppose Manchester people living today know anything about Manchester Orpheus but it did. It did this marvellous thing, and in the particular work of Cornelius *O Tod, du bist die erklarte Nacht - O Death Thou art the tranquil Night*[8] - I've seen these folks in judges' box wiping their eyes with their handkerchiefs. You would get probably half a dozen choirs singing that in succession. It was a marvellous experience, you know.

R.S. They were competitive festivals, I suppose?

H.B. Oh yes. It was more the honour than anything, you know, because the prizes were never of any high value - money value. It was the honour.

J.A. But the tradition of competitive festivals has carried over to countries like Canada and Australia, where we used to have, still do, troops of British adjudicators coming out each year mainly to judge the choral entries. Where I come from in Winnipeg in Manitoba we have apparently, and have for some time, the largest choral festival in the Commonwealth.

---

[8] Brian probably means Cornelius' choral work *Der Tod, das ist die kühle Nacht* Op. 11/1 (poem by Heine, composed in 1871) which has to be translated *Death, that is the cool night*.

H.B. Oh yes, and do you know Toronto? Did you know the Mendelssohn Choir?

J.A. Yes indeed.

H.B. Well, Fricker performed my first orchestral work in Leeds.

R.S. Really? I had no idea about that. Which work was that?

H.B. The English Suite [No. 1], which we'd had such a success with. Oh yes, that was an event. And it wouldn't have happened but what led to it was ... there was a revival of the old *Musical World* in Manchester, and I wrote to the *Musical World* asking if I could do anything for them where I was living, in the Potteries. I heard nothing about this until I got a telegram: could I meet the editor? The same morning I got the telegram I'd received a letter from Elgar, a very long letter about the full score of my *Babylon*: a most enthusiastic letter. I went to Manchester and I took one or two things that I'd already written in a local paper. I showed this to him and he says, "Well, you can write". So I took Elgar's letter out and I said, "I can also write music". He says "Well, if you take it on you can have this special criticism of the Thursday Hallé concert. I will be very glad to have you." That's how I got to Manchester.

R.S. How long did you live in Manchester?

H.B. Two years. I didn't live there. I used to go down every Thursday morning or if there was any special rehearsal of the Hallé on a Tuesday in - I forget the name of the hall - Museum I think they called it ... I used to go down on Tuesday too. Oh, it was a great experience.

J.A. Did you know Langford or Neville Cardus?

H.B. Oh yes, Neville Cardus was a youngster in those days. He hadn't started writing for the *Manchester Guardian*. Ernest Newman was on the Manchester ... oh no, Alfred Johnston was the critic when I went there, then Johnston died and he was succeeded by Ernest Newman. Oh yes, I often had little chats with Richter, I remember going down at the end of a Tuesday rehearsal. They'd just finished rehearsing a work of Smetana, I forget now which. I said, "This is the only score I can't get, will you lend it to me?" He said, "No, you don't need it, you'll understand the first time you hear it".

R.S. Your relationship with Manchester has now been finally cemented by the University there giving you an honorary doctorate recently.

J.A. When did they give him an honorary doctorate?

R.S. Was it two years ago?

H.B. Yes, May 1967. I'll tell you, this is rather interesting of Richter because he's probably had more influence on my music than any other personality. It was a day something like this - pouring! - and I was going down Deansgate and I bumped into a man: it was Richter. He'd got an umbrella. He turned round and he saw me and took the umbrella down. He'd brought a young boy. He said, "My son". He was a nice lad. He says, "By the way, your paper tells awful things". I said, "What about?" He said, "Bayreuth. You say the soprano slapped the necks of the contraltos ... your paper did". He said, "We don't want that kind of thing in our beautiful Manchester". And it was pouring like this! By the way, that was one of two boys and they were both injured in the First War. I think one was killed. Richter's son-in-law told me the other one was given something to do in the box office at Bayreuth.

J.A. They would be in the German army I guess?

H.B. Oh yes. By the way, you know that when he resigned Manchester, he resigned in 1913 ... he was living in Bayreuth. When war broke out the German boys used to go and throw stones at his door and shout "Der Engländer, der Engländer". Oh yes, Richter's son-in-law told me this, it must be true you know.

J.A. The other day I was in a music shop and picked up a score of Vaughan Williams' oratorio *The Holy City*, and noticed that you did the piano reduction for it.

H.B. I did a lot of work for him.

J.A. For Vaughan Williams? Were you employed by him or by Curwens, the publishers?

H.B. Oh no. I did it for him personally. I made him a copy of ... what is that opera of his ...?

J.A. ... *Hugh the Drover*?

H.B. That's the one. I made a copy of that for him - the full score. His full score, when I came to open it, it was smothered with tobacco and smudges - in one place a pot of ink must have been knocked over it.

J.A. His scores were pretty scratchy! Was this a means to earn a living?

H.B. Oh yes. I was working for a firm of ... Goodwin & Tabb. I had an arrangement with them. That was soon after the close of the First War. My arrangement was that I undertook to do anything in the way of arranging or copying for £5 a week. I was very happy to do it. I had a lot of interesting work. I don't know whether that was how I met Vaughan Williams ...

R.S. Were you at all influenced by the music when you copied it?

H.B. No.

R.S. Not at all?

H.B. No.

R.S. I haven't felt any influence at all in your works.

H.B. The music I liked most was Vaughan Williams, Holst - and when I got hold of the First Symphony of Arnold Bax, I wrote to Bax and I said I'd like to write an article on this. He said, "I wish you would", and I wrote a long analysis of his First Symphony, with musical illustrations. *Musical Opinion* did it very well - nice copying of the extracts from the score. Now here's another funny thing: I wrote to Bax after I'd finished this article and it had appeared. I said, "By the way, whilst I was doing the copying of the parts of his symphony, I was also working on my *Gothic* Symphony". I said "Now, I would like to make an arrangement with you. As I have written an article on your First Symphony, if ever *The Gothic* is published, will you do an article on that?" And he wrote back and said he would. Well, I never thought *The Gothic* would ever be published, you see. I mean to say I don't think I was very serious when we were writing that. So when it was published I sent him a copy of the score and reminded him of this pact that we had made, and he didn't reply.

R.S. Too stupefied I should think!

H.B. Then I wrote and said, "If you're finding it difficult to get along with, will you return the score?" No reply, so in the end - he had a brother named Clifford Bax, a dramatist - I wrote to Clifford. I said, "Will you ask your brother Arnold if he would wake up and send me the full score of *The Gothic* that I had sent to him." And so he did, with a letter: "I'm very, very sorry. I wouldn't dare to write an article on this work unless I could hear it".

R.S. Can you tell us a bit about your early acquaintance with Elgar and the early performances of *Gerontius*? For instance, I remember you telling us some time ago about how you got a performance of *Gerontius* going once.

H.B. Well, what led to it was: I set a sonnet of Shakespeare's to music, for voices unaccompanied, and this was taken up by a young conductor and we got it lithographed, and he performed it with this choir. I sent a copy of this lithographed production to Elgar. His wife wrote back to say that he was astonished and in love with it and that he'd taken the liberty of forwarding it to the Morecambe Festival Committee as their principal test piece in what they called the Shield Competition; and that was the first work of mine to be published. ... then I had a letter from Elgar. He was coming down to conduct. I didn't meet him at the time of that famous performance of *Gerontius*, and I don't think he ever knew that I had a hand in it. I never said anything to him - I never referred to it.

R.S. Tell us how it happened - this performance.

H.B. *Gerontius*? Well, I was friends with the choirmaster, the church where I was organist, and I went to his house with a copy of *Gerontius*, played through the work, sang the solos, fired his enthusiasm and the following day he went off to influence members of the committee of this choir, and the following week they went down to see Elgar at his place in Malvern to obtain a promise from him that if they took up the work, would he conduct it, and he did. For that performance this choir - which had won its reputation by always winning first prizes - 250, an orchestra of 100, Coates was the tenor, Muriel Foster the contralto, Ffrangcon-Davies the bass, and Elgar conducted. The performance made such an impression on him that - the people in connection with the music in Westminster Cathedral also wanted to perform *Gerontius* - and Elgar recommended this same choir, which he referred to as a choir of angels, and they went and sang it for him at Westminster Cathedral. At that time I hadn't met him, but he wrote to me asking me to meet him and bring some of my work for him to look at when he came down to conduct a performance of his *Apostles* with the same choir. I met him at breakfast with his wife and immediately after breakfast he got hold of the full score of my setting of the 23rd Psalm and fixed it up on the back of a chair and studied the score and turned it over and he jumped up. He said, "Lovely, I see that you write for the horns in the modern manner, good, good! Now" he said "wait". He had just at that present time been giving some lectures as Professor of Music at Birmingham University, so he said "You wait, we're going to make Birmingham an English Leipzig. We're going to have a permanent orchestra of 100, and you shall have your work performed as you would like it to be". But of course that never came off because he resigned from Birmingham and an "English Leipzig" went too.

R.S. It would take a Superman to make Birmingham into an English Leipzig I should think! Did Elgar's music influence you very much?

H.B. Oh, I think so, yes. He was a great influence. I was very much in love with his very first work *King Olaf*. I thought it was a lovely thing, and also the work which preceded it, *The Light of Life*. As a matter of fact the moment I saw the Prelude to *The Light of Life* I thought, well, no other English composer writes like this, and at that time I was very much in love with Dvořák's *Spectre's Bride*. I'd heard quite a number of performances of it and always enjoyed listening to this work, but I thought when Elgar came with his *King Olaf* it was a newer note ... something about his writing that I hadn't found in Dvořák.

R.S. And of course you and Elgar were both very much admirers of Strauss.

H.B. Very much, yes.

R.S. And yet, when I hear the *Gothic* Symphony, which is your first very large work, I can feel no influence really of Strauss.

H.B. You don't find any Elgar and you don't find any Strauss - no, no, that's right.

R.S. No, it seems to me completely individual. In fact, that's what seems to strike most people.

H.B. Bantock always said that the *Te Deum* was a miracle. After listening to it last Sunday, I thought it was a marvel!

R.S. Well, I think this work ought to be recorded on gramophone records. I hope one day it will because one of the strange things that I've found is that since it's been broadcast in this country, there are lots of illicit tapes floating about.

H.B. Yes, there are, and I get letters from America.

R.S. Yes, they've got to America. People are sending them around and I myself, too, I've lots of letters from people asking me about it.

H.B. A young fellow from Los Angeles came to us last summer. He'd got a tape of *The Gothic* and he said that he'd been to - André Perrin, is it? Henry Perrin?

R.S. Previn, yes, the conductor.

H.B. Yes, telling him all about this wonderful thing.

R.S. Yes, there's a sort of underground movement going on, apparently - we must feed it as much as we can.

J.A. Mr Brian, the contemporary British composers of today, do you take any interest in them? I'm thinking of people of, say Walton, Britten, Tippett, that age group.

H.B. The only work of Walton's that I've heard, and that must have been on the wireless, I think, is the Concerto for Viola. I haven't heard the First Symphony yet. No, I haven't heard *Belshazzar's Feast* yet.

J.A. But they're actually sort of keystones.

H.B. But I remember the originality of his Viola Concerto.

R.S. Do you know any of Tippett's music - Michael Tippett?

H.B. Wait a minute ...

R.S. Because there's an incredible passage in the *Gothic* Symphony that looks forward to Tippett, whether you realize it or not.

H.B. No - I remember reading of Sargent's performance of - was it his First Symphony in Liverpool? I wanted to hear that but I've not heard it ... and I've not heard his second one.

J.A. Yes, that's a very good piece.

H.B. And I've not heard any of his choral pieces.

R.S. How about Edmund Rubbra? Do you know any of his symphonies? Have you heard any?

H.B. No, I've heard Vaughan Williams: I love his *Sea* Symphony and - is there one in F minor?

J.A. No. 4. yes.

H.B. Yes, I've heard that.

R.S. What about contemporary music in general? What do you think, for instance, about the 12-note school?

H.B. As I said just before you came in, I've always enjoyed Schoenberg's music. I studied his *Pierrot Lunaire* years ago - 30 years ago! And his *Das Buch der Hängenden Gärten* - they're Stefan George's poems, aren't they? And then, of course, we had a full-scale performance of the *Gurrelieder* years ago just when Boult I think became conductor of the first BBC orchestra. I attended all the rehearsals of that. I think it was going on for about a week. Of course, the prime mover there was a pupil of Schoenberg who was at the BBC, Edward Clark.

J.A. Did it have an influence on you, the 12-note method of composing?

H.B. Not a bit. No, I regard myself as a diatonic composer ... I think you'll find that in the Finale of *The Gothic*, the *Te Deum* ... I think it's a great surge in diatonic and chromatic harmony - quite apart from its contrapuntal work.

R.S. Did you find yourself, with Schoenberg for instance, interested rather than in sympathy with it, or did you actually find the music sympathetic?

H.B. Oh, quite sympathetic. Yes, I've always enjoyed Schoenberg's music. I've always enjoyed Mahler and Bruckner. As I say, I heard that wonderful performance of the *Romantic* Symphony of Bruckner with Furtwängler and the Vienna Philharmonic, but I also heard other works of Bruckner. I don't know which symphonies I heard, but they were conducted by Karl Böhm, I think, on German gramophone records during the war. That was where I heard Mahler's Fourth and I think it was the Sixth. The Fifth I heard on the wireless conducted by Rudolf Schwarz.

R.S. Your later symphonies seem to have a sort of concentration a feeling of condensation which in some ways reminds me of Sibelius. Have you ever been impressed by Sibelius?

H.B. Very much so, yes. I've not heard, but I know his Violin Concerto and ... funnily enough, as a score I know more about his First Symphony than any of the others but I've never heard it! But I've heard the Second: I heard the first performance of the Second with Richter and the Hallé. I've heard the Third, and I heard the Fifth under Harty. Oh yes, I'm a great admirer of Sibelius.

R.S. In late years I remember you telling me you've enjoyed Nielsen's symphonies, too, very much.

H.B. Oh yes, very much so. Yes, I've heard the one - is it the one with the timpani?

R.S. The side drum?

H.B. The side drum, that's right. Which one is that?

R.S. The Fifth.

H B Yes, I heard that.

R.S. Very dramatic!

H.B. And I think also the Third - I think it was the Third.

J.A. *Espansiva*.

H.B. That's right, yes.

R.S. Well, it seems to me that your later symphonies have more in common with Sibelius or Nielsen than they have with the more expansive, Romantic composers like Mahler of even Strauss, who obviously you admire very much. But there's this concentration which is quite different for instance from the enormous canvas of the *Gothic* Symphony of the earlier years. You've been very conscious of this, have you?

H.B. Oh quite, quite. It's difficult to know how these things happen, but unfortunately when I've written a work I'm inclined to forget it.

R.S. Yes. When you start a work do you start with a sort of germ idea and gradually develop it?

H.B. Yes, I regard my process as the growth of a plant and its flowering. What I'm always anxious to do and strive to do, is to make a perfect balance.

R.S. When you start a symphony, do you start with some small germ of a thematic idea? Do you have a general plan of the whole symphony in mind, or how does it work?

H.B. It develops, it expands. The moment I set down to work it's matter of continuity. But over the last symphony that I sent you - No. 32 - it was written in a style or a manner that I've never done such a thing before. I did the slow movement first, the scherzo second, the first movement next, the last movement next. Now, will you make that out?

R.S. Yes, well, that doesn't surprise me. I think that sort of thing happens quite often.

H.B. I've never done such a thing before. I always work straightforward, always.

R.S. Do you have an idea where it's going, I mean before you start, you know the plan of the whole symphony?

H.B. Oh yes, the plan is in my imagination, or in my mind.

R.S. In other words you don't just improvise on paper, it's a question of getting the whole and then sorting out the details.

H.B. That's right. And I can assure you that very often sketching is the thing which becomes difficult. I work with a pencil and rubber, and how many times a thing is rubbed out before I pass it, I couldn't tell you, but very often it may be a whole page you see.

R.S. The rubber's more important than the pencil, really.

H.B. That's right, yes.

R.S. You do a lot of sketching?

H.B. Very much so, yes.

R.S. And you sketch it in short score?

H.B. Sketch it in three or four staves and in pencil, yes, and if I do a good - what I call a good pencil sketch, I ink it in, over the lead, d'you see, to save my writing out another one.

R.S. Your works are still very tonal - I mean they're in definite keys, or sometimes they start in one key and end in another. Now do you, when you plan the whole symphony, do you have an idea of what tonalities you're going to traverse during the course of the work?

H.B. No, I hear them as I'm going along.

R.S. You find this happens as the thing develops?

H.B. Yes.

R.S. So if the symphony ends in a key different from the one it started in, this is the result of a continuous process?

H.B. Well, it's psychological - it just happens. It's what I call natural, you see. I know the old idea was they said you should finish in the key you started in, but by the time you've reached the end of the symphony, you've forgotten all the keys haven't you?

R.S. Well, of course nobody really expects that nowadays, do they?

H.B. For instance, *The Gothic* begins in D major and ends in E major.

R.S. Yes. But the interesting thing about that which I noticed, and which Deryck Cooke also noticed was the fact that by the time E major comes at the end of the *Te Deum*, it's a kind of natural development which has been happening all through the symphony. One can see this sort of di-polarity between D and E and it gradually grows and E takes over. When you worked out the whole symphony you must have been conscious, surely, of a process like that going on in your head?

H.B. Oh, I should say rather unconscious than conscious.

R.S. You feel it just happened?

H.B. It just happens as you go along.

R.S. This is rather similar to what Nielsen said about his own symphonies because he developed this progressive tonality. He did it in such a way that it all happens wonderfully subtly all through the piece. But he said himself that it was rather a natural, almost unconscious process.

H.B. Yes. Mind you, very often an idea which may happen whilst you're working may suggest something which you probably didn't hear when you started, and it happens in the course of the work.

R.S. And of course changes the course of the work.

H.B. Yes. I've always tried to keep - in the case where the movements are divided - I always keep, what shall I say? - a relationship between what follows, and what ... closed before the following.

R.S. Are you conscious of trying to preserve the thematic connections between the work, between the whole thing, the fabric, so that one theme grows into another?

H.B. Always, yes ... the thing that I strive for, always hope to achieve in writing is balance of form - a complete picture.

R.S. Well, I must say, I felt particularly in No. 21, the last one that we heard, I felt that was magnificently achieved - wonderfully coherent.

H.B. By the way, I had a letter from Edward Johnson, talking about the "impassioned slow movement".

R.S. Yes, well it is!

H.B. I said to you, didn't I, I said this is lovely orchestral playing; you said, yes, it's lovely music!

R.S. Tell me, why do you always use such large orchestras? It's obviously an impractical thing to do when people are short of money, but you usually use a very large orchestra.

H.B. Oh, I don't know. I write as I feel. It isn't to do with any desire to expand or do something out of the ordinary. Oh no, it just happens.

R.S. What part of the orchestra ... where do you feel you need most extras, over and above the normal classical orchestra?

H.B. I think the cor anglais and the bass clarinet.

R.S. How about the brass?

H.B. Always the tuba, which I regard mostly as the bass of the horns rather than the bass of the trombones. I never regard ... I never associate the tone of the tuba with the trombones.

R.S. No, it doesn't blend with them.

H.B. I'll tell you ... Harry Barlow, who was in Richter's opinion the finest tuba player in Europe. Well, he played in *Doctor Merryheart*, and after the performance of *Merryheart* he sent me a postcard: He says "Thank God you understand the genius of the tuba, I'm fed up with doubling the G trombone".

R.S. Yes, well, I can imagine his pleasure because I think you write marvellously for the tuba.

H.B. I think that's innate because as a boy I'd follow a brass band on the march until I was tired of it.

R.S. But you use a lot of percussion too. What strikes me about that is that it's not something stuck onto the orchestra, it's part of it.

H.B. Yes. By the way, you talking about percussion - the conflagration at the end of *The Gothic* ... [omission on the tape here] Bryan Fairfax - the other one, you know. It was due to the placing of the drums at the Albert Hall, because there's something of the eye in the Central Hall. There were six over there and six over there. Do you remember that girl that played over there? Did you ever see such a drummer? She played like mad, didn't she?

R.S. Of course there is one thing about that you have to remember and that is that the Albert Hall is so much bigger.

H.B. Oh yes, yes.

R.S. The sound doesn't make the same impact there as it did in the Central Hall.

H.B. I thought it was due to the placing of the drums: I couldn't make out where they were in the Albert Hall.

R.S. I think they were spread out on either side. - You don't seem to have written any chamber music, or very little.

H.B. No. It's a very odd thing because I played cello in a string quartet, an amateur string quartet - in which we played Mozart, the early quartets of Beethoven - but I've never had any inclination to write a quartet, oh, not since I was a youngster.

R.S. I think you ought to write a few "late quartets" now. Now you've just finished your middle period, you should write some late quartets.

H.B. Yes well, we'll see, we'll see. I shall never hope to attain that supremacy in late quartets that Beethoven did in his last quartets.

R.S. No, well, who could?

H.B. I used to go down to the Royal Academy and listen to the string quartets when they were playing the last quartets of Beethoven.

R.S. But it didn't inspire you to write.

H.B. Oh, not a bit! All that I could marvel at was the music and the man that had done it.

J.A. Does that also apply to your music dramas - you call them music dramas as opposed to operas, don't you?

H.B. Yes, I would rather have the word "drama". I hate the word "opera" because, you see, you've got all sorts of things under the name of opera which are flimsy and shallow, and there's nothing of that kind about these things. Besides, my works, you call them operas but they're written symphonically. The music is as symphonic as the symphonies I've written. They actually are great long symphonies.

R.S. Of all the works which you have never heard, which would you like most to hear?

H.B. *Faust.*

J.A. Is that a three-act music drama? Is it a large music drama?

H.B. Yes. I've taken the libretto from the *Faust* of Goethe. There are operas that have been drawn from that: of course they are real travesties of the actual thing.

J.A. Gounod's *Faust.*

H.B. Gounod's - awful stuff, d'you see. But it's popular and other people have done popular operas on that same subject, but I've been guided by the intellectual side of it. I have a scene between Mephistopheles and the undergrad. Well, it's very funny, you know. There's nothing so comic as the Mephistopheles stuff, because the boy calls to see Doctor Faust, but Doctor Faust is out. But Mephistopheles always quick on the uptake, you see, he puts on Doctor Faust's cap and gown and receives this student, and what goes on - it's very funny, it's really very funny!

J.A. Who wrote the books for your music dramas?

H.B. I did.

J.A. You wrote your own books?

H.B. Oh yes, I drew it from the original. It's very funny because the course of the ... when he dismisses this student, you see, he says remember, "Leben ist grün, Theorie ist grau".[9] Those are his last words to the student.

R.S. "Life is green, theory is grey". I've often noticed in your music ... or what's struck me, is a sardonic streak sometimes. One place where I've noticed it very much is *The Tigers.*

H.B. Oh yes.

---

[9] In the original: "Grau, teurer Freund, ist alle Theorie,/Und grün des Lebens goldner Baum." - "Grey, dear friend, is every theory, and green the golden tree of life."

R.S. There is something sardonic in that, you know, and I think you have a great flair for this. I've noticed it even in late music. I felt it in the 21st Symphony, in the last movement where there's a sort of almost Elgarian tune ... comes out on the violins, and then immediately after that there's some rather sort of wispy passages in the orchestra as much as to say "well, where the hell has all this grandeur ..."

H.B. That's in the third movement, no, the second ...

R.S. In the last movement.

H.B. Oh, is that the last?

R.S. Yes. It's almost as if to say, well, where the hell has all this splendiferousness gone - you know, it's all gone now, it doesn't mean anything anymore. Is that reasonable? It was purely my impression.

H.B. Well, it's one side of your character, isn't it? *The Tigers* shows that there is something in the humorous side of things, yes.

R.S. How did you come to be a musician in the first place?

H.B. Oh, it goes back to childhood, because the sounds of the organ in the church where I was attending at the age of three, or the distant beat of a drum, would set my mind going, and I think those are about the earliest impressions I have. The first music that made any impression upon me was a brass band contest in which the three crack Yorkshire bands were in competition - Black Dyke, Besses o' the Barn, Kingston Mills - and the test piece was a selection from Berlioz's *Faust*. As a child I was electrified by that.

R.S. How old were you then?

H.B. I was 11 and I'd just had my first lessons in music, which were singing and reading staff notation. About that time I commenced to learn the violin and worked at it for some time, probably a couple of years. The first instrument, I should have said, was an American organ. The teacher that I was taken to - he was the organist of the Roman Catholic Church in Longton - he said, "You won't do any good with an organ, you'll need a piano for the keyboard technique". So the organ was changed for a piano, and then organ pedals had to be attached to the piano. To get these organ pedals I went with my father to Whitchurch, to a Mr Rogers who had the pedals for sale.

R.S. Had you by this time decided to be a musician?

H.B. Well, I never wanted to be anything else! But such a thing was impossible. The first thing that I had to do was to get out into the world and begin to earn money.

R.S. How did you do that? What sort of jobs did you have?

H.B. The first job that I had was on the railway as a clerk, for which I got ten shillings a month. After that I went into an architect's office, and from there I moved into a colliery office. Incidentally, I may tell you that I only got the job in the colliery office because the proprietor was a staunch churchman, and when he was hesitating about giving me the job I happened to say that I was already a church organist, and he said, "Oh well then, the job's yours". Somewhere about 16, I suppose, I was appointed organist of a church very hurriedly, because the organist of the church had run away to America with somebody else's wife! With the salary of this appointment I took lessons from a professional.

R.S. Yes, I remember you telling me about him. He was a bit of an arch-conservative wasn't he?

H.B. Yes, very much so, very much the conservative. He said "Well, what are you wanting to do?" He suggested that I should study for examination. I said "I don't want examinations, I want to be a composer". He said "Well, composers are not wanted. They killed Mozart and they'll kill you, and you're not a Mozart."

R.S. Well, they haven't managed to do it.

H.B. No, they haven't done it yet.

R.S. Tell me about these piano works that we're going to hear. First of all there's *John Dowland's Fancy*. How did that come about?

H.B. *John Dowland's Fancy* was the result of a promise I made to Granville Bantock to write a suite of four pieces for Trinity College, London. I'd always had great admiration for Dowland's airs and what music of his I'd been able to get hold of. It came to my mind to write a suite called *John Dowland's Fancy*. But I stopped after I'd written the Prelude.

R.S. Do you still like the piece after all these years?

H.B. Oh yes. I'll tell you why, because I don't know whether it is true, but it always seems to me, when I used to play it it always sounds as though the piano was out of tune.

(In the broadcast, a performance by John Lill of this piece was included at this point.)

R.S. What other interests have you had in your life apart from music?

H.B. Oh, literature, the theatre, opera. I've done a great deal of reading, always. I must have been reading, I should think, at the age of six or five. At that time there were various books in the house, the most of which attracted me was "Chambers Miscellany" with all sorts of stories about the Mutiny on the Bounty, why the sea is salt, and so on. Later I became very much interested in all the novelists of that time: Scott and the English novelists - Hardy, Meredith, Gissing, Arnold Bennett.

R.S. You knew Arnold Bennett, didn't you?

H.B. Yes, at that time he lived in Paris. He was very much interested in what I was doing. He offered me a libretto on *Antony and Cleopatra* which he'd arranged from Shakespeare.

R.S. He must have been an entertaining chap to talk to.

H.B. Yes, he was, but he also had a slight impediment; he stammered a little. Bennett was very much interested in all that was going on in music at that time in this country: Elgar, Bantock, Delius and so on. He had a great admiration for Newman, the critic, and one of the things he requested to me was to introduce him to Bantock and Ernest Newman, which I did one morning at the National Liberal Club.

R.S. Of course Bantock was a friend of yours too wasn't he?

H.B. Oh, Bantock was a great friend of mine. He was a great stimulant in a way. He was so worldly in his outlook. From his earliest days Bantock had a great urge to help English composers. Later, when he went to New Brighton ... actually he was to conduct a brass band at the opening of the New Brighton Tower. Bantock very quickly transformed his brass band into an orchestra and used to give Sunday symphony concerts with an orchestra of a 100 in the Tower at Brighton. In those concerts he used to give whole programmes to ... one would be Elgar, another would be William Wallace, or Cowen, Holbrooke. They all had a share of his programmes when he was at New Brighton.

R.S. He did some of your works too, didn't he?

H.B. No, not until later. I didn't know Bantock personally in those days. I didn't know Bantock actually until 1905 or -6, and it was through a work of mine, a choral work; a setting of a Shakespearian Sonnet, which he admired very much, and wrote to me about it. But after then Bantock did ... also when he was in Birmingham he was also conductor of the Liverpool Orchestral Society, a society founded by Rodewald, an amateur; a stockholder on the Cotton Exchange in Liverpool. When Rodewald died Bantock took it over and it was there that Bantock performed my works and also gave the first performance of Delius' *Brigg Fair*.

R.S. Do you ever worry about not hearing your works?

H.B. Never. That's never been a trouble with me.

R.S. What about the other pieces? How did the fugal works come to be written?

H.B. The fugues were written at a time when I'd got so far with *The Gothic* and I always had an idea that it must be a choral finale and I started to work at writing fugues and canons. I wrote many of them. Some of them were published. The fugues, and also the *Double Fugue*, were actually written to give fluency in technique in writing the finale of *The Gothic*. Afterwards I wrote preludes to the two single fugues, but the *Double Fugue* always seemed to me about the length of piano sonata.

R.S. Yes, it's quite a massive piece, isn't it?

H.B. Yes, it is.

R.S. I think it'll interest listeners to know that in fact it is connected with the *Gothic* Symphony, which of course they were able to hear quite recently. Now, what about the *Gothic* Symphony itself? This enormous work - did you ever expect to hear it?

H.B. No, No. I just wrote it to gratify my own - ambition, if you like. Actually, the size of the orchestra stems from conversations I had with Henry Wood many years ago when he had a popular success with a work of mine. He suggested that I should write a suite for him which would incorporate all the old instruments in complete families. In the oboes there was to be the oboe da caccia, the oboe d'amore, and so on. And the same with the pedals. I remember him mentioning the pedal clarinet. I said "I've never heard of one; do you think there is one?" He said "Well, I only know of one, it's in the British Army".

R.S. How did you feel when you actually heard the *Gothic* Symphony after all these years? Did you remember it?

H.B. Yes, it was just as I had imagined it, when I heard Bryan Fairfax rehearsing it. Yes, I think that there are instruments that I used there that ought to be incorporated in the ordinary specifications of the orchestra of today, like the oboe d'amore. I think it's a marvellous instrument, a wonderful instrument.

R.S. Yes, it's surprising that these instruments got dropped. What are you composing now?

H.B. I'm writing my 27th Symphony.

R.S. What's it like? Can you tell me anything about it?

H.B. Well, it's lively. I think, if you speak of the dramatis personae of a play, I think somehow the flute may be considered the principal character, because it opens the work and closes it.

R.S. Is it different in any way from the symphonies you've written in the past few years?

H.B. I think they're all different. It's a three-movement work and I think it's much longer than the 26th. It has these features. In the finale it opens very briskly and tapers down to a slow movement. Then the quick movement follows and it ends almost similar to the slow *Andante* movement, with the flute closing it. It doesn't finish with a big clash from the orchestra. Its finish is very quiet.

R.S. You seem to be writing symphonies at such a rate that we can't keep up with you.

H.B. Well, you see, I've got nothing else to do, and nothing else to think about.

(A performance by John Lill of the Double Fugue ended the broadcast.)

Symphonies

Malcolm MacDonald: Havergal Brian's letter to Herbert Thompson: some implications[1]

The letter Brian wrote on 9 July 1909 to the critic of the *Yorkshire Post*, Herbert Thompson - which surfaces for the first time in Lewis Foreman's *From Parry to Britten: British Music in Letters 1900-1945* (London 1987, pp. 39-41) - is a salutary reminder that we have a great deal still to learn about our composer, and that whole works (and stages in the genesis of works) have vanished from our ken without leaving any trace on the published literary record. After informing Thompson - an influential figure, connected to the committee of the Leeds Festival - of the forthcoming performance of *The Vision of Cleopatra* in Southport, Brian goes on to speak of two more recent compositions:

> I have recently perpetrated a long satirical orchestral work, *Humorous Legend on "Three Blind Mice"*. *My* version differs from most others in that I introduce a policeman and the Farmer's wife to carry on the dramatic idea. It is in three movements & lasts 45 minutes.
>
> 1st movement
> A   *The blind mice*
> B   *The Chase by the farmer's wife*
> C   *Enter the policeman* who
> D   *Makes Love to Farmer's Wife* (all Caruso)
> E   *Chase resumed*
> F   *Capture*
> G   *March to the Scaffold, execution. Apotheosis*
> II   Scherzo - "The Bogey Man"
> III   Finale - "Dance of the Farmer s Wife"
>
> I've also completed a setting of a poem by Scott for chorus and orchestra. It is in four movements, but *without* break and this lasts forty minutes.

Foreman has presented us here with three priceless pieces of information, though in his commentary on the letter he neglects to mention one of them (Brian's "programme" for the first movement of his *Humorous Legend* - which is of course the *Fantastic Variations on an Old Rhyme*, or a form of it); and of the other two revelations the note only mentions that "it is impossible to identify Brian's Scott setting", and that "the orchestral work Brian describes ... was ultimately named *Fantastic Symphony*, but after the outer movements had been published separately ... the middle one was lost". To take that second point first, I am not sure that Foreman's interpretation really integrates this letter with what we knew already. What I think we have here is evidence of an *intermediate* form of the work that Brian *originally* called *A Fantastic Symphony*, before it was finally split up.

---

[1] From *Newsletter* 75 (I-II 1988), pp. 3-5.

Against this new letter we should immediately set one that Brian wrote to Granville Bantock on 17 March 1921 (partially quoted in Kenneth Eastaugh's *Havergal Brian: The Making of a Composer*, p. 107), at a time when Lyell Tayler and Julius Harrison were showing interest in conducting the *Fantastic Variations* and *Festal Dance* respectively (I give here rather more of the text than Eastaugh, without his "tidying-up" of Brian's syntax and punctuation!):

> ... You have a right to be proud of it [*Festal Dance*, which Bantock had performed in 1919] & I wish you would do the other portion of the work to which it originally belonged.
>
> Do you remember those days at Broadmeadow & the Institute? The time when you sat at the piano & pulled the thing to pieces & how I cut the thing down and rewrote it?
>
> I wonder where the scherzo & the slow movement are - I suppose with *Carmilhan*, *The Lord is my Shepherd*, the *Soldier's Dream* &c &c &c do you remember those early things?

I too wonder where the slow movement is, especially as it isn't mentioned in Brian's letter to Thompson. There have long been two conflicting ideas about the original form of the *Fantastic Symphony* (which was composed, going by the dates on the MSS. of the extant movements, between mid-1907 and mid-1908): one, that it was a four-movement work with a scherzo and slow movement; the other, that it was a three-movement work with a central scherzo. This latter was what Brian told Reginald Nettel, who reported in *Ordeal by Music* (p. 69) that the second of the three movements was "a *pizzicato* scherzo in which the souls of the little creatures were to be imagined flitting away to a mousy paradise". Brian must have said this in 1944; yet in 1921 he had recollected the existence of a slow movement which somehow hadn't been part of his scheme in 1909.

I tentatively advance the following hypothesis: Brian wrote a four-movement work he called *Fantastic Symphony* in 1907-08. Bantock, it is fairly clear, vigorously criticized it - among other things, for being over-long. Brian "cut the thing down and re-wrote it". The result was a "new" three-movement orchestral work: *Humorous Legend on "Three Blind Mice"*, whose first and last movements corresponded to the first and last movements of the symphony. I advance even more tentatively the possibility that the scherzo might actually have been new: it depends whether anything that might be evoked by the gnomic title "The Bogeyman" can be reconciled with the description of the "*pizzicato* scherzo" reported by Nettel. Finally, when he began to prepare his orchestral works for printing by Breitkopf & Härtel in late 1912, Brian dropped this scherzo, "purged the variations on 'mice' of its worst crudities" (as he put it in a letter to Bantock, 21 November 1912), and allowed the first and last movements to be published as separate works. This may not really be what happened, but as an interpretation of the so-far available facts, it seems to fit.

Brian's "programme" for the first movement is fascinating. It is for a form of the *Fantastic Variations* that pre-dates the 1912 revision, of course, but it may help us to gauge the extent of that revision. In fact, the programme seems to apply pretty well to the work as we now have it:

"The blind mice" - from the opening to fig. 3 in the score;
"The Chase by the farmer's wife" - from one bar after fig. 3 (first appearance of the "feminine element" theme) to four bars after fig. 7;
"Enter the Policeman" - (what trauma of Brian's youth lay behind his perennially disrespectful treatment of the noble embodiments of Law and Order? To the sizeable force of reprobate policemen represented by the third *Illumination* and *The Tigers*, we now have to add this specimen!) - the ponderous fanfare at *Lento*, five bars after fig. 7, to two bars before fig. 9;
"Makes Love to Farmer's Wife" - *Con moto e espressione,* one bar before fig. 9, to six bars after fig. 13. The comment "(all Caruso)" - is this the original Singing Policeman? The one in the *Illumination* was an opera-fancier too - helps to explain the floridly vocal quintuplet gruppetti in this section;
"Chase resumed" - seventh bar after fig. 13, all the way to fig. 23;
"Capture" - the fateful bars from fig. 23 to one before fig. 25;
"March to the Scaffold, execution. Apotheosis" ...

There is no "March to the Scaffold" that I can see in the work we now have; in fact the *Fantastic Variations* is rather remarkable for *not* containing one of the march-forms of which its composer was so fond. The music proceeds by means of a brief timpani link to something that Brian calls a "Chorale Finale", which probably corresponds to the "Apotheosis" of his programme - with a curious *ad lib.* organ part, mostly cued into the woodwind, that might have been fuller and more integral to the original conception. It looks as if the March and "execution" were among the "crudities" that he "purged" in 1912. Otherwise nothing else is obviously missing, although the rather foreshortened proportions of the early part of the work lead me to suspect that he did some cutting in that region, most likely in the fairly short-winded first "Chase".

Turning now briefly to the "setting of a poem by Scott for chorus and orchestra" - this certainly is the only known reference to such a work, making it a major addition to the Brian canon, even if only to that frustrating canon of lost works. At first I wasn't sure that this was the only reference; I thought that it might be the mysterious *Soldier's Dream*, mentioned in the 1921 letter I've quoted above, and for which I had hitherto failed to come up with a plausible text.

However, after a long hunt through Sir Walter Scott's *Complete Poetical Works*, I drew a blank: he wrote no poem entitled *The Soldier's Dream*, and the only promising candidate (the song "Soldier, rest! thy warfare o'er ... Dream of battled fields no more" from *The Lady of the Lake*) would have furnished neither a four-movement structure nor anything approaching a 40-minute duration. Then, almost by chance, I happened upon a poem that really was titled *The Soldier's Dream* - not by Scott but by a close contemporary of his, Thomas Campbell (1777-1844), author of the once-famous ballads *Hohenlinden, Lord Ullin's Daughter,* and *Ye Mariners of England*. Moreover, I was able to establish that Campbell's *The Soldier's Dream* - the kind of swinging warsong for which he was celebrated in his own day - was perennially included in the various editions of *Palgrave's Golden Treasury*, one of Brian's primary sources for many of his song-texts (it's still in the current edition).

130 Symphonies

It seems overwhelmingly likely that the work Brian mentioned to Bantock in his 1921 letter was a choral-and-orchestral setting of Thomas Campbell's poem; and thus the Scott setting is something different again. Presuming a roughly similar rate of word-setting to Brian's other cantata-like works of the period, *The Soldier's Dream* was probably about the size of Psalm 23. The Scott setting was clearly a bigger conception altogether - although Brian's "40 minutes" is probably an over-estimate (note that he times the *Humorous Legend* at 45 minutes, which is plainly impossible unless the scherzo was truly gigantic). As yet there is no way of identifying the text, although Brian's specification of a single poem which has furnished him with a four-movement structure (which might not be immediately apparent in the poem, of course) is a useful lead. It rules out the famous short lyrics, and also, presumably, selected passages from the long poems like *The Lay of the Last Minstrel* and *The Lord of the Isles*; but that leaves a rather large middle ground in an author as dauntingly prolific as Brian was himself!

From one point of view this is all rather satisfactory. The period 1908-late 1910 (from the completion of *Festal Dance* to that of *In Memoriam*) has until now looked a rather empty patch in Brian's creativity, and was the basis for Kenneth Eastaugh's assertion that under the patronage of H. M. Robinson, Brian became indolent and produced little. Suddenly, into those years we have to fit two largish-scale choral works (the Scott setting and *The Soldier's Dream* - which is almost certainly later than the letter to Thompson, otherwise Brian would surely have mentioned it), along with a possibly quite major revision of the *Fantastic Symphony*. The image of continual toil and creative fecundity rings truer to the composer as we know him.

Malcolm MacDonald: *The Gothic*: music and meaning. With a comment by Larry Alexander[1]

"The search for the unknown is the ambition of every composer of genius."
Havergal Brian

Havergal Brian's Symphony *The Gothic* (1919-27) is that strangest and most infrequently-encountered kind of masterpiece: a work which sets out to be one thing but which turns, against its creator's will, into something very different in the process of creation.

---

[1] The first part is from *Newsletter* 16 (III-IV 1978), pp. 3-4. The second part is a revised version of the lecture Malcolm MacDonald gave at the Havergal Brian Society/British Music Society "*Gothic* Day" at the London Penta Hotel on 25 May, under the title *What is "Gothic" about The Gothic and what is Faustian about The Gothic?* While it hardly deals directly with the music of *The Gothic* at all, it is of a piece with his other rather "speculative" writings round and about the work, exploring the attitudes of mind, both conscious and unconscious, out of which *The Gothic* may have sprung. The present article develops certain themes from both the previous ones, and therefore at a couple of points uses almost the same wording; MacDonald apologizes to all who find this irritating. It was first published in *Newsletter* 30 (VIII-IX 1980), pp. 3-7, entitled *Brian as Faust*; Larry Alexander's comment is a letter to the Editor in *Newsletter* 31 (X-XI 1980), p. 8.

I do not mean here its implicit subject-matter and structure: no "one thing" could sum up those properties. This gigantic, labyrinthine symphony is an inexhaustible store of musical riches which must surely possess a different significance for every listener; and the better one comes to know it, the more layers of meaning one recognizes at work in it. It is an evocation of a whole epoch in the human mind; a purely musical parallel to parts of Goethe's *Faust*: a compendium of musical history from mediaeval times to the early 20th century; a huge experiment in new kinds of style and form, reaching out to the future; a celebration of architectural splendours so vivid that (as Paul Rapoport has shown in *Opus Est*) the symphony's form can be viewed as a musical equivalent to the cruciform plan of a Gothic cathedral; a response at several different psychological levels to the experience of World War I; one man's personal venture into the unknown; and much else besides. No, I want tentatively to isolate here the gap between intention and achievement - what was Brian trying to *do* when he set out to write *The Gothic*, and what has he actually *done* in the finished work that confronts us today? Since his own statements on the matter were seldom particularly revealing, the comments which follow are partly personal speculation - but speculation that arises directly from the nature of the music itself.

I believe Brian was trying - single-handed, by an almost superhuman feat of compositional power - to proclaim the dawn of a new Gothic age of expansion of the human psyche; but that, faced with the reality of the 1920s and his own bitter personal experience, he could not maintain the integrity of that vision, and found himself wrestling instead with uncontrollable forces which almost, but not quite, reduced him to final despair. In this general sense *The Gothic* is indeed a "Faustian" work - a lived drama of ambition,[2] self-knowledge and (perhaps) salvation on a mighty scale - and thus a work very much of and for our own times. From this stems its enduring fascination and capacity to move us.

Why "Gothic"? Perhaps a few dictionary definitions of the word provide clues:

> Of, pertaining to, or characteristic of, the Middle Ages; esp. Gothic architecture, which spread throughout Europe approx. 1160-1530; mediaeval; Germanic; romantic as opposed to classical - thus lack of classical simplicity or unity; combination of sublime and grotesque.[3]

All of these phrases touch on aspects of Brian's symphony; taken together they hint at a certain grand inclusiveness, impatient of stylistic niceties, that is certainly one of the work's cardinal features. But why, then, *The Gothic*? That isn't so much an indication that the piece has "Gothic" characteristics as a way of saying that it is *itself* an embodiment of the Gothic Age in all its richness - an enormous

---

[2] Brian's occasional rueful comments that he wrote *The Gothic* "to satisfy my own - ambition, if you like" (BBC Radio Three "Composer's Portrait", February 1967) are on this interpretation very much more than conventional platitudes. (The complete interview is reprinted below, pp. 121-124.)

[3] This "quote" is not a single genuine entry but a miscellany culled from various dictionaries, principally the *Concise Oxford* and *Webster's New International* (1934).

continuum of artistic, intellectual and spiritual growth, a homage to the past in the language of the present.

To write such a symphony in the immediate aftermath of the Great War - which in the minds of so many had slashed right across the orderly progress of history, opening a great rift in the traditional values, which had to be abandoned for something more makeshift and cynical - now seems an almost symbolic act of faith. The work's basic stylistic premises, as set out in the purely orchestral movements of Part I, are a demonstration of artistic continuity, a logical development from the achievements of Wagner, Bruckner, Strauss, Elgar, Mahler and early Schoenberg: and by implication the symphony is the latest link in an unbroken chain of succession reaching back to the wellsprings of "serious" music in Western culture - the church music of the Gothic Age. The cultural rift *can* be healed, Brian seems to be saying, if we have sufficient largeness of vision, if we can accept and integrate all that is valuable in the previous tradition, and not shut ourselves up in little cells of Neo-Classicism, satirical triviality, Ballets Russes chic, or English Nationalism.[4] To quote the motto from Goethe's *Faust* that stands at the head of the score, "Whoever strives with all his might, That man we can redeem". And so Part II of the symphony, the incredible *Te Deum*, seems to ransack the whole history of Western music in search of a way forward.[5] Mediaeval organum, modality and free verbal accentuation; spatial disposition of forces resembling that of the Venetian masters (and also the *Te Deum* of Berlioz); long, florid, melismatic lines that recall pre-Reformation Tudor composers such as Taverner; multiple polyphony on the scale of Tallis' *Spem in Alium*; chromatic freedom of harmony that rivals Gesualdo; echoes of the great Choral Festivals of the 1900s, of Wagner's *Tristan* and Bach's Passions; ceremonial fanfares; popular marching-songs - all this, and much more than was ever dreamt by any previous composer, goes into the melting-pot. With breadth of vision goes a daring modernity, as for instance in the choral "cluster" chords at the start of the

---

[4] Let us also remember that during the Great War some of the greatest composers of the Austro-German tradition - even Beethoven! - had been anathema to many English musicians for "patriotic" reasons, and performance of German music generally had fallen off sharply. One might almost say that there had been a conscious attempt to sever British music from the mainstream of the European tradition. To begin a *Gothic* (that is, by one definition, Germanic) Symphony in 1919 was no small act of defiance. Brian's own attitude to the promotion of Englishness in music, at the time of writing *The Gothic*, may be gathered from his highly important article *The British Spirit* (in *The Sackbut*, Vol. IV, No. 8, March 1924; Reprint in Malcolm MacDonald: *Havergal Brian on Music*, Vol. 1, London 1986, pp. 202-208), which includes a spirited defence of the pre-War generation's reliance on Germanic models, as well as bold proposals for a national approach to the development of excellence, rather than "Englishness", in new British music - which would still bear looking at today.

[5] David Lambourn writes in a letter to the Editor in *Newsletter* 66 (VII-VIII 1986), p. 7: "Bruckner's Ninth Symphony was given its British première in Manchester by the Hallé Orchestra in November 1912, using the *Te Deum* as finale, in accordance with the composer's wishes (see Michael Kennedy, *The Hallé Tradition*, p. 183). Could this subconsciously have provided a model for Brian's *Gothic* Symphony so many years later?"

"Judex" and the shattering Varèse-like[6] outburst that makes the "Non confundar" such an agonized appeal.

The Gothic is, in fact, the most extreme example of what Sir Michael Tippett has called - apropos of his own relatively unambitious Third Symphony - "the famous hybrid work": of which the prime example is of course Beethoven's Ninth. And Brian seems, like Beethoven, to be proclaiming a message of universal brotherhood, by reminding his audience of their possession of a common cultural heritage. The intention, therefore, seems to have been to provide a new "Ninth" for the times. There could be few higher ambitions.

The symphony took eight years to complete, and we still know little of the reasons that prompted Brian to shift its final emphasis away from Faust (the archetypal Gothic Age man and seeker after knowledge). In 1938 Brian wrote in *How the "Gothic" Symphony came to be written* that he had planned to set a large part of Goethe's *Faust* Part II for his finale, but instead the *Te Deum* text (traditionally held to be the joint composition of St Ambrose and St Augustine in the late fourth century, and in use in the Christian liturgy ever since) "pushed itself forward as the only possible finale for a *Gothic* Symphony". This although he was, by that stage of his life, no kind of Christian, and had never had much knowledge of Latin. The choice of that text, however, leads us back to the Gothic Cathedrals; to the music that was sung in them; to mediaeval Christianity and the Latin language as the great international civilizing forces of an entire epoch. Also, as a "great poem" at once archaic, impersonal and universal (in contrast to the highly subjective paradisal vision at the end of *Faust*), it admits of very personal interpretation by the various composers (Berlioz and Verdi, to give only two examples) who have made settings of it. Thus it was more of a unifying force than *Faust* would have been, whilst it made the extent of Brian's individual statement more immediately recognizable.

But the unequivocal affirmation which Brian seems to have intended to express in his *Te Deum* somehow fails to materialize. It opens, indeed, with a sense of almost cosmic rejoicing; but its progress is increasingly disturbed by harsh, violent elements and mysterious tensions; by the arrival of the line "Judex crederis esse venturus" ("We believe Thou shalt come to be our Judge"), which gets an astonishing 20-minute movement to itself, we (and Brian) are in deep water indeed. There is a revealing remark in Brian's *Modern Mystic* article. After referring to various strange psychological phenomena he experienced during the composition of the *Te Deum*, he says: "such happenings must drive others off their mental balance. I have always felt that I, being the only person interested in my work, would discover a solution to all the mysteries about it".

---

[6] I persist in suspecting that the experience of extracting the percussion parts for the first performance of *Amériques* had a profound impact on Brian, and that the "Non confundar" cataclysm is a direct reflection of it. If true, it detracts not at all from Brian's originality - there was probably no other composer alive capable of making the same imaginative leap. His comments on Varèse many years later (*Musical Opinion*, October 1939) are of great interest: "that score of *Amériques* still convinces me that something unusual happened when the music it represents was given to the world ... Varèse has attempted to express the age in which we live ... I think of *Amériques* as the expression of a distorted age or as a fierce denunciation of it".

In probing the "mysteries" he was discovering areas of his own unconscious mind. In *The Gothic* he had invoked a conjunction of ideas so powerful it could lead anywhere. In seeking to defend European culture from the undermining effects of the Great War on the European consciousness he had himself to experience that undermining: to recall perhaps his work as an Army clerk, listing the personal effects of men killed in the trenches, and later as a clerk in a munitions factory; maybe also those horrific newspaper pictures of the invasion of Belgium, with Ypres Cathedral a gaunt shell-blasted ruin; certainly, in a work that represented the summation of all that he had known and learned in his first 50 years, he would have to come to terms with his own personal weakness and fallibility, and the impotence of his present obscure position as a hack music-copyist and occasional critic. It would be surprising indeed if he did not, at crucial moments, suffer pangs of self-doubt.

"For almost ten years" after 1918, he wrote in the preface to his earlier anti-war work, the opera *The Tigers*, "I continued to hear the tramp of an army"; that is, throughout the period he was writing *The Gothic*. Inevitably, the "army" in his mind invaded the music. War-visions are a continually-evolving element in *The Gothic*, a dark counterpoint to its grand cultural theme. Warfare is implicit in the wilder sections of the first movement and in the funereal tread of the great Lento (which, to my ears, seems profoundly influenced both in general orchestral style and actual motivic content, by another English masterpiece about the War - Elgar's *For the Fallen*). Battle breaks out nakedly in the middle of the Vivace, with thudding timpani like an artillery barrage, bugle-calls in the brass, and fantastic orchestration - and culminates, at the movement's climax, in a "battle-scene" of tremendous power. However, all these disruptive elements are, in Part I, firmly integrated into the musical argument. In the *Te Deum*, which deliberately abandons conventional structural controls in favour of a freely-evolving, much more "spontaneous" exploration into the unknown, they begin to acquire a malevolent life of their own. Brian's grappling with such a huge range of material brings him literally to the edge of chaos.

The *Te Deum's* first movement, while generally jubilant, accumulates several warlike features, and its very proliferation of detail begins to breed a sense of doubt in the listener ("Things fall apart, the centre cannot hold ..."). The "Judex" movement sways tensely between light and darkness, especially the latter. The last and longest movement, "Te ergo quaesumus", tries to restore the balance with a sustained sweep of beautiful and joyous music, despite the *a capella* tensions of "Salvum fac populum tuum". The victory of light over darkness seems complete with the downright roof raising jollity of "Et laudamus nomen tuum" - a brilliant passage for the full forces, enclosed by two statements of a jaunty march on nine clarinets and percussion. But this march is a strangely ambiguous invention, not least because of the astonishingly close resemblance it bears to a well-known marching-song of the *Second* World War - the US Air Force march *Off we go into the wide blue yonder*. I have not yet discovered whether the tune of *Off we go ...* already existed, and had military associations, during World War I.[7] Even if it

---

[7] Bernard G. Counsell notes, similarly, in a letter to the Editor in *Newsletter* 53 (V-VI 1984), p. 6: "In *The Gothic* I have always been taken a bit aback by the lively little dance melody which

didn't, Brian's march-theme would be a remarkable instance of creative foreknowledge, conjuring into being a popular tune well in advance of the popular consciousness. At any rate, after the march has receded, the final stages of *The Gothic* are no longer optimistic, but see the emergence of a vulnerable individual consciousness - until the veil of Heaven is rent by the penultimate brass-and-percussion cataclysm, bringing all-enveloping darkness; except for the final subdued glow of the *a capella* "Non confundar" in E major - which, like the last high cello note of an imaginary composer's imaginary last work (in Thomas Mann's *Doktor Faustus*) "abides as a light in the night". That light shines throughout all Brian's subsequent work.

Havergal Brian's music *invites* speculation - as to his intentions, as to his sources of inspiration, as to (contentious word) his work's *meaning*. The key to the mysteries of Brian's music is the mystery of Brian's mind - and *The Gothic* is undoubtedly one of the crucial demonstrations of the scope and power of that mind. The composer's unassuming, impassive, seemingly naïve exterior must not deceive us into thinking that it mirrored an ordinary or conventional or undeveloped intellect. This was a mind of unusual power; and also of unusual lines of thought. That is one of the main sources of confusion for critics of his music. They look for logical connections, when the connections are often spiritual, imaginative, creatively catalytic. As far as going off on inspired tangents is concerned, Brian has us all beaten hollow before we start.

Consider for a moment his 1938 article, called *How the "Gothic" Symphony came to be written*. Most of it isn't explicitly about *The Gothic* at all. Instead it's a very selective piece of autobiography: musical impressions of his youth, men who helped him, things and historical personalities which fascinated him, a strange dream he had in about 1909, and so on. The only passage in which he explicitly connects something with *The Gothic* is when he is discussing what he calls the "mental stimulation" afforded by the scenery of the South Downs:

> I can think of nothing more mentally invigorating than gazing at miles of freshly made ploughed furrows, uniform and symmetrical, glistening purple red in the autumn morning light, unbroken by a

---

suddenly appears in Part II amidst other rather solemn music, which makes the intrusion rather ... could I say almost frightening? Often I have looked at *The Gothic* as a sort of choreographers' delight and I often wondered how I would cope with this particular music. I have recently been reading *Musical Box* by Sidney Harrison and I quote: 'The fact is, the association of ideas between music and some external circumstance is largely a matter of history and tradition. A single example will serve to illustrate the point. The medieval church composers wrote slow melodies in free, vague rhythms. In the course of centuries they established a tradition of a "sacred" style. The tradition was highly artificial for, according to a much older and longer tradition, religious music should be wildly exciting and full of dance rhythms. Nevertheless they did establish it, and, despite Hallelujahs and march-like hymns and syncopated negro spirituals we accept the general idea that devotional music is slow in tempo and not strongly rhythmical.'" And A. J. Luker notes in a letter to the Editor in *Newsletter* 100 (III-IV 1992), p. 2: "That odd march tune in the last movement of Brian's *Gothic* is a little bit like the fugue subject in Marcel Dupré's Prelude & Fugue in G minor for organ, written about 1913. Has anyone noticed?"

single hedge, over the vast rolling downs. This I have always felt to be the pivot of the *Gothic* Symphony.

"Pivot of the *Gothic* Symphony"? Freshly ploughed *fields*? You can't get much more tangential than that. But because it's tangential it's not meaningless, even if I'm not too sure what he means; nor are the other things he mentions in this essay. His selection of them is very deliberate - and they all, in some way, have a bearing on *The Gothic*. It's just that he leaves us to make the connections for ourselves. Brian, in short, was one of the earliest practitioners of what is nowadays often called "lateral thinking" - quite the opposite of the scholastic logic and Enlightenment rationalism which has exercised such domination - even though its influence may now be waning - over the last four centuries of Western habits of thought. It was the Age of the Enlightenment which invented the term "Gothic", to denote an Age which was barbarous, uncouth, irrational, and everything the modern age was not. That is still one of the residual meanings of the word "Gothic", and no doubt Brian was aware of it, when he came to write his symphony.

To the 18th century, also, the "Gothic" age was one of horror, hag-ridden by superstition, an age of dark supernatural deeds - the period described in novels of "Gothick" romance. This too may have been a distant shade of meaning which the word possessed for Brian. (Not too distant, maybe - for the author of the seminal work of English "Gothick" fiction, "Monk" Lewis, had been British attaché in Weimar, had known Goethe, and had modelled the protagonist of his grisly *The Monk* (1796) on Goethe's *Faust*. But Brian had his own means of approach to Faust, of which more later.)

However, among the many areas of meaning covered by this ambiguous word "Gothic" - some of them quite contradictory, and encroaching on many areas of human thought and achievement - I think we can agree that two were of especial importance for Havergal Brian. One is architecture, specifically the architecture of mediaeval cathedrals; the other is the idea of the "Gothic" age as an opening-up of the resources of the human mind and spirit. It is worth remarking that these two aspects are not synchronous in time. Gothic architecture, though still being practised in parts of Europe as late as the mid-16th century, really had its heyday in the 13th and 14th centuries; and the great age of the cathedrals was also a great age of faith, with a comparative degree of Christian unity. Its intellectual achievements were primarily in the realm of codification and neo-Aristotelian systematization, above all in the work of Thomas Aquinas. The great leap forwards and outwards, the spiritual and intellectual ferment, belongs more correctly to the 15th and 16th centuries, to the later Middle Ages and Renaissance. "Gothic" somehow bestrides the two periods. The spiritual force is amassed in the first, and put to work in the second. One could do worse than the previous sentence for a thumbnail characterization of the two parts of Brian's *Gothic* Symphony.

Take architecture first. In that essay, *How the "Gothic" Symphony came to be written*, Brian recounts one of the crucial musical experiences of his childhood - how, as a chorister, he took part in the performance of a setting of the *Te Deum*, in a Gothic cathedral, during Queen Victoria's Golden Jubilee celebrations. Admittedly it was Prince Albert's *Te Deum*, and Lichfield Cathedral is by no means the most impressive Gothic pile in Europe, but it would be foolish not to accept that this childhood experience finds a gigantic echo in Brian's symphony, with its huge *Te Deum* setting. "I retained", wrote Brian, "an impression of something on a vast scale"; and indeed the sheer scale and magnificence of Gothic cathedral architecture was one of its chief attractions for Brian, throughout his life.

One of the most significant effects of that 1887 experience may have been that in it, the emotional effects of music and architecture seem to have become indissolubly linked in his mind. Few people would deny the massive architectural quality of much of Brian's music; it seems to be a quality he consciously strove for, perhaps in the *Gothic* Symphony above all. In his book *Opus Est*, Paul Rapoport has written a speculative analysis showing that *The Gothic* can be heard, in its tonal and durational aspects as well as in many details, as a musical equivalent of the cruciform ground-plan of a Gothic cathedral. Without going that far, one can simply say that Brian seems to have had an acute awareness of the spiritual affinity of the two arts. For instance, he wrote in the July 1935 *Musical Opinion* that one of the "indisputable facts in the history of music" was that "music is an expression in sound of the same principles of all the great schools of architecture: that certain fundamental principles govern the whole, though in parts they differ, as we see in Gothic and Norman architecture".

Brian was very likely aware of the Renaissance Neo-Platonist conception of architecture as an art whose structures were patterned after the principles and proportions of cosmic harmony - a view which goes back to Pythagoras' "music of the spheres" and has naturally attracted many composers, down to its contemporary (and rather crude) reflection in many of the recent works of Stockhausen. As an avid reader of Goethe, Brian doubtless also knew and approved the German poet's dictum in the *Conversations with Eckermann* that architecture is "eine erstarrte Musik" - a frozen (or solidified) music; he might aptly have reversed the comparison and called his music liquified architecture. What both terms recognize is the fact that neither a cathedral nor a symphony is a static object: they are both processes, whether it be of harmonic tension and release, or the stress and counter-stress of great blocks of masonry.

Gothic cathedrals are a paradox in stone. The pillars soar, lifting the ceilings high on bays and arches that curve gracefully and launch out into space as if with no effort at all; the rose windows let in dazzling light; they are visionary places of space and air. But everything is achieved by mass and gravity and tremendous weight; the points of those arches meet under incredible pressure, with an awesome authority and finality. Cathedrals are also the embodiments of spiritual power and terror; Robert Simpson has told me that Brian once told him this was one of the aspects he had wanted to express in *The Gothic*. This paradoxical aspect of Gothic architecture is brilliantly expressed in a poem by the great Russian poet Osip Mandelstam, written in 1912, and called *Notre Dame*:

> In the place where a Roman judge judged an alien people there stands
> a basilica, and the light groined arch - joyful and first, as Adam once
> was - plays with its muscles as it spreads out its nerves.

But the secret plan is revealed from without: here the strength of the saddle-girth arches has taken care that the ponderous mass not crush the wall, and the battering-ram of the bold vault is idle.

An elemental labyrinth, an inscrutable forest, the Gothic soul's rational abyss, Egyptian might and Christian modesty: next to a reed - an oak, and everywhere plumb is king.

But the more attentively, O stronghold Notre Dame, I studied thy monstrous ribs, the more frequently I thought: some day I too will create beauty from cruel weight.

(Prose translation by Clarence Brown, from *Mandelstam*, Cambridge University Press, 1973)

"Beauty from cruel weight". Brian would have loved that line. The sense of *weight*, of mass, in Brian's music is something quite unique, as far as I know. It's often confused by hostile critics with thickness or heaviness of scoring - which of course are not among the neo-classical Enlightenment virtues - but in fact it seems to me that Brian's instrumentation has the precise expressive purpose of giving the music an overwhelming physical presence. "Everywhere plumb is king" - Brian makes you feel the granitic reality of those mighty Gothic pillars.

Mandelstam's poem aptly introduces the second meaning which Brian seems to have understood by the term "Gothic" - the spiritual and speculative quest for understanding: what Mandelstam calls "the Gothic soul's rational abyss". To the late mediaeval intellect a cathedral was not simply a place of worship: it was also, by virtue of its cruciform plan, a symbolic representation of the human body - the body of Christ, the Second Adam. And to the "hermetic" philosophers and physicians and alchemists at the turn of the 15th and 16th centuries, the human frame was the bridge between the microcosm and macrocosm, the physical and the higher reality. Theoretically there was no great divide between microcosm and macrocosm - everything was part of a continuous chain of being, and the higher world was mirrored in the lower. The great pillars of a cathedral could be seen as if they were as much a part of nature as human ribs, or the tree-trunks in a forest - "an inscrutable forest", as Mandelstam's poem says. Havergal Brian had something of that cast of thought. There's a passage in an article written in 1924 where he compares the experience of being in a forest with a blazing sun above the trees, to that of being in the interior of a weird cathedral. Perhaps, when he talked of those ploughed fields as the "pivot" of *The Gothic*, he was seeing a connection between the geometrical regularity of the furrows and the symmetrical placement of pillars either side of a cathedral nave. Pure speculation: but it would be a very *Gothic* mental process.

Cathedrals are first and foremost places of Christian worship, and the *Te Deum* is a deeply Christian text. But by the time Brian came to write his great symphony he was no recognizable form of Christian, and what attracted him about the Gothic Age, apart from its architecture, was not its mediaeval piety. One has to conclude that it was the reverse of that piety, the proud probing for unknown or forbidden knowledge which, towards the end of the Gothic Age, put Man in the centre of the spiritual stage in a new and revolutionary way.

"Man the great miracle" is the resounding theme of the *Aesculapius*, an occult text attributed to "Hermes Trismegistus", who was supposedly an Egyptian priest who lived before the time of Moses. It was this work, long known to the Middle Ages, which, when combined with the other so-called "hermetic" texts first translated into Latin in 1463, provided the motive force behind the tremendous upsurge of interest in magic, and especially alchemy, that characterizes the late Gothic spiritual quest.[8]

Even today, "alchemy" and "magic" are highly-charged and suspect terms from which the "Enlightened" modern mind flinches. However, properly pursued, they were anything but superstitious occult mumbo-jumbo. The great analytical psychologist Carl Gustav Jung devoted many books to expounding the fact that alchemy had a serious psychological aspect: that the transformation of lead into gold, and other sensational claims, whether or not they had any basis in fact, were only the outward symbols of the *important* transformations, which took place in the practitioner's own psyche - the development of personality through opening up the mind to new spiritual influences.[9] And in the last 30 years the historian Frances Yates has fully chronicled the process by which hermetic philosophy, alchemy, astrology and other "magical" practices formed a vital transition stage to the de-occultized scientific materialism of the 17th century.[10] She has shown that "maguses" like Marsilio Ficino, Pico della Mirandola, Paracelsus, Giordano Bruno, and John Dee hold a very significant position in the history of Western thought, and especially in the way that Man has seen himself in relation to "life, the universe and everything". They were the first to suggest that Man could control the elemental forces underlying his existence, and led on to a practical, scientific attitude to the physical world (Paracelsus, indeed, was a great physician in his own right, and Dee a great mathematician and pioneer in the science of navigation). It can be shown that such diverse figures as Copernicus, Galileo, Kepler, Francis Bacon, Shakespeare, Inigo Jones - even Sir Isaac Newton were deeply imbued with the influence of these men's ideas; it can be argued that we cannot properly understand the rationalism of Erasmus, Mon-

---

[8] The *Corpus Hermeticum* derived much of its authority from its supposed fabulous antiquity: it was believed to contain "pure" Egyptian learning which the Judaeo-Christian world had lost. In the mid-17th century Isaac Casaubon proved the texts to be "forgeries" of the second and third centuries AD. His very effective debunking was the deathknell of Renaissance hermeticism, but he also prevented a rational evaluation of the genuine intellectual content of these interesting and influential writings which are, in fact, deeply imbued with Gnostic philosophical ideas, along with Platonism, Stoicism, and Jewish and possibly Persian influences. As Frances Yates has remarked (*Giordano Bruno*, p. 431), they might even, for all anybody knows, contain some genuine Egyptian learning. I hold no brief for Immanuel Velikovsky's recent and highly controversial "alternative chronology" for the ancient world, but its re-dating of Egyptian history 600 years closer to the Christian era would make this more possible (see, especially, his *Peoples of the Sea* [1977]).
[9] Most of Jung's writings on the subject will be found in Vol. 12 (*Psychology and Alchemy*), Vol. 13 (*Alchemical Studies*) and Vol. 14 (*Mysterium Coniunctionis*) of his *Collected Works*.
[10] *Giordano Bruno and the Hermetic Tradition* is the central book; but practically all her others map various areas of the same general field.

taigne or Descartes until it is realized that they were engaged in bitter argument with these same ideas. To a certain extent the "maguses" formed a kind of free-thinking intellectual opposition to the established forms of Christian belief; because their magic - for want of a better word - was not only their art, but their religion.

Brian wrote *The Gothic* before Jung's alchemical studies began to appear, and long before the first of Frances Yates' books. But this new view of Gothic Age magic is one which, on the face of it, might have appealed to him. Moreover Brian was, in his own fashion, prodigiously widely-read; he might even have got there by himself.[11] So it was with a certain feeling of satisfaction that, while going through Brian's letters to Bantock last December, I came upon a reference, in a letter of February 1942, to the fact that, many years before, Brian had possessed "mystical books ... by Jacob Böhm, Swedenborg, Paracelsus", (and possibly several others), as part of the extensive library he abandoned in Stoke in 1913. Swedenborg is of course a later mystic, and Brian's interest in him might be adequately explained by his passion for William Blake, who was greatly influenced by Swedenborg. But Paracelsus and Böhm are Renaissance alchemists, central figures in this era of magic I've been describing.[12]

Which brings us, very logically indeed, to Doktor Johannes Faustus of Württemberg. As far as we know, this "magus" never lived, but his story is located firmly in the historical context I've been sketching; and it was current in chap-book form and puppet-plays when there still lived men who claimed to be able to conjure angels and devils.[13] The Faust legend is one of those archetypal "matters" which has generated, and continues to generate, an entire literature. Goethe's *Faust* is one of its classic expositions, and it was a book which fascinated Havergal Brian all his life. For him, Faust must have seemed the ideal Gothic Age figure, summing up the bold, exploratory tendencies of the period.

In his article *How the "Gothic" Symphony came to be written*, Brian writes that the first part of the work - the three orchestral movements - was "largely coloured by Goethe's *Faust* (Part I)", and that his original idea was to write a choral finale setting a large part of the last act of *Faust* (Part II). He didn't do that, as it turned out: instead the *Te Deum* "pushed itself forward as the only possible

---

[11] As is strongly suggested by a passage on Strauss' opera *Die Frau ohne Schatten* (*Musical Opinion*, October 1931, p. 18), where Brian comments that in the later operas of Wagner "we move in a world of magic or in the subconscious mind of the creative artist". His "or" is ambiguous, but he seems to imply an identification between these two "worlds".
[12] I have traced only one other instance of Brian mentioning their names - a previously nonplussing reference, in the September 1924 *Musical Opinion* (p. 1194), where Paracelsus and Böhm bring up the rear of a list of "philosophers and divinities" that also includes Marcus Aurelius, St Francis of Assisi, and Jesus Christ!
[13] Marlowe, in his *The Tragicall History of Dr. Faustus*, may have been hitting at his contemporary, Dr John Dee (who made precisely this claim). Shakespeare, who created the "magus" Prospero in *The Tempest* (a play Havergal Brian almost turned into an opera a few years before beginning *The Gothic*!), may, as a young man, have known Dee and have had the use of Dee's great library at Mortlake (cf. Frances Yates' *Theatre of the World* and *Shakespeare's Last Plays: a New Approach*).

finale for a *Gothic* Symphony". But on the title-page of the *Te Deum* - and though it appears also on the title-page of the printed score of the whole symphony, it seems it was meant to be attached only to the *Te Deum* in the original two-volume edition of the work - he placed two lines from the final scene of Goethe's *Faust*, Part II: "Wer immer strebend sich bemüht, den können wir erlösen". These words are sung by a chorus of angels bearing Faust's immortal soul towards heaven: approximately translated, they run: "He who strives with all his might, that man we can redeem".

Brian makes no reference to this line in his article about writing the *Gothic* Symphony, but in talking at one point about his view of inspiration, he does give vent to a homelier version of it. "It has been argued", he says, "that inspiration and prayer are the same. Though I am convinced that great work of any kind is impossible without inspiration, I no less hold the belief that the only practical prayer is that of the inner voice and urge such as in the old fable of Hercules and the Wagoner, who, when his wagon got stuck in the mud, prayed to Hercules to come to his aid. The voice replied, 'Man help thyself'."

"Man help thyself" - "Wer immer strebend sich bemüht" - both quotations would seem to agree, at any rate, that Brian believed it was up to him to work out his own salvation, whether religious, artistic or philosophical. Now of course this is hardly an uncommon view among composers - we need to look no further than Beethoven for a classic parallel - but philosophically speaking this view descends from the hermetic philosophers of the late 15th and early 16th centuries, who theorized that a man inspired by the right influences could attain knowledge, and therefore power, without any of the aids of conventional religion. It was precisely this view which gave rise to the legend of Faust, and it is still active in Goethe's play,[14] where Faust does not repent, and what is accounted to him for righteousness is the fact that he has never ceased seeking and striving after new experiences.

So: what is Faustian about *The Gothic*? It seems to me that what is Faustian about it is Havergal Brian. On some level he appears to have identified with Goethe's hero. In March 1939, in *Musical Opinion*, he published a short article on *The Legend of "Faust"* which makes it clear that what he found most compelling was the idea of Faust the searcher and striver after illumination: in Brian's words, Faust is "seeking a solution to the mysteries of the unknown". In his essay on *How the "Gothic" Symphony came to be written* he employs virtually the same phrase about himself while composing *The Gothic*: "I have always felt that I, being the only person interested in my work, would discover a solution to all the mysteries about it".

I suggest that through his many years' absorption in Goethe's *Faust* Brian saw his own life-experience, his experience as a composer, as Faustian. Remember that though he had a good basic musical education, he had no academic training

---

[14] On p. 104 of her *Shakespeare's Last Plays: a New Approach* (1975), Frances Yates has tentatively suggested possible routes whereby hermetic philosophical ideals could have been transmitted to Goethe himself and the German Romantic movement generally, via the German Rosicrucian movement of the early 17th century.

in composition; he was no composer's pupil and he had to make his own way from the beginning, grappling with the mysteries of making music out of his own inborn gifts. At the period when he was writing *The Gothic*, and for several years previously, it was his practice to do most of his composing "in the deep silences of the night, long after the family had retired to bed, usually between 11 p.m. and 2 and 3 a.m.", with a shaded table-lamp which kept all the rest of the room away from his desk shrouded in thick darkness. Would he not have seen the parallel between himself and Faust, conjuring in solitude in his dark chambers? Brian even recounts seeing before him the figures of Bach, Goethe, Berlioz, as if present to him in the spirit. He's fairly sceptical in the way he talks about these "visions", which may have been tricks of his unconscious brought on by exhaustion, but surely he thought of Faust conjuring up Mephistopheles? Of course, Brian was no magician: he was a composer. But like an alchemist he was wrestling with the mysteries of the universe by means of his personal art; and we should remember that many of the Renaissance alchemists and hermeticists considered music itself to be one of the magical arts and a powerful aid in invoking beneficent influences of various kinds. (Such an idea was the basis for Jean-Antoine de Baïf's "Academy of Poetry and Music" in Paris in the late 16th century. The chief composer of "incantatory" music there was the gifted Huguenot Claude Le Jeune, several of whose works have survived.)

If Brian saw him*self* as a Faustian figure, perhaps in *The Gothic* he was trying to do something Faustian: something that could be described as a piece of conjuring.

In his talk, Paul Rapoport demonstrated in some detail that Brian's *Gothic* may take Beethoven's Ninth Symphony as a partial model. In more general terms, I would certainly say that Beethoven's Ninth is the most powerful archetype of the genre to which *The Gothic* belongs: that of the great choral-orchestral "world-renewing" symphony. After all, Beethoven's Ninth isn't simply providing a pretty frame for some less than first-rate poetry - Beethoven surely meant it to have some kind of moral force, and Schiller's words are a symbol of a state of human existence which seemed to him desirable, even if unattainable in this life.

Brian's even vaster symphony can be no less of a statement of belief: belief in the desirability of a *new* Gothic Age, a new epoch of the opening-up of the human spirit and receptiveness to fresh experience; a new "Ninth" for the times and since those times were the immediate aftermath of the Great War, his conscious or unconscious impulse may have been to produce this vast "Gothic" symbol to point the way forward for a rather tired and weary Western civilization, in which the Age of Enlightenment had clearly come to the end of its tether.

Brian wrote comparatively little - and that little, as we have seen, tantalizingly oblique - about his own music and his creative intentions. But he wrote copiously about the music of others: and his articles on the works of composers he admired, as well as suggesting by implication the qualities which he himself strove for, contain many fascinating and suggestive digressions which help to illuminate Brian's own view of himself. An extremely important example occurs in the first part of his large-scale study of Delius, which appeared in several successive numbers of *Musical Opinion* throughout 1924. After some remarks on the evolution of musical forms, and the composer's individual role in this process, he suddenly instances the Faust legend as a parallel example of "something persisting and refusing to die, yet slowly evolving into something definite" - in this case, through Goethe's treatment of it. Brian continues:

> Was Goethe conscious in his lifetime that he had revitalised the literature of a whole continent and recreated the literature of Germany, as Shakespeare did for England several centuries previously? Probably not. When Goethe was slowly evolving the Faust legend into the stature of a cathedral - a process which occupied him a lifetime - he was not conscious that he was bringing to a close a centuries-old myth. His mind was occupied and troubled with the destiny of humanity, and it was his brooding upon it which gave us the wonderful philosophy and poetry which remains enshrined in that gorgeous tragedy. We have instances of the same kind happening in music ...
> (*The Art of Frederick Delius*, Musical Opinion, March 1924, p. 598)

Note there the extraordinary identification of Faust and the cathedral! But more important, this passage is the prelude to a discussion of the present evolutionary stage of music, and especially the symphony as a form. Brian claims Delius as "the last Romantic of the Chopin-Grieg line; but he also sees Richard Strauss as a parallel contrasting figure who has brought to an end the tradition of "the romantic symphony as it was left by Liszt and Berlioz".

The date is extremely important. However we argue over the precise dating of *The Gothic*, there can be little doubt that Brian was deeply involved with it in early 1924. And here he is implying that "the romantic symphony" has run its course, while invoking comparisons with the undying persistence of the Faust legend. This *may* give us grounds for thinking that Brian, through his own post-war "brooding upon ... the destiny of humanity" (in which both cathedrals and the Faust archetype would surely have had a part), was being driven to write what he considered a *new* kind of symphony. We may even tentatively guess where this "newness" lay. In the discussion of musical evolution just referred to, Brian singles out Bach, Beethoven, Wagner, Strauss and Delius as composers who have brought a particular branch of the art of music to its highest expression; in each case, he views the process as one of "gathering all the threads" of their predecessors together, and giving a "definite" and final shape to their chosen musical field. He implies that an intense understanding of tradition and the ability to transform the achievements of the past into "a living art" is an absolute necessity for a great composer. It may be (though an article on Delius was obviously not the place to say it) that Brian saw the symphony which he was writing as a culmination, not just of the "symphonic" tradition, but of the whole art of music, uniting the various traditions of vocal and instrumental music, fugal polyphony, lyric tone-painting, the symphony, and opera. Such, at least, would be a logical conclusion to his argument: naturally withheld to make way instead for a discussion of *The Art of Frederick Delius*.

The composition of such an all-embracing work as a sign to post-Great War Man echoes the wider, socially committed, purposes of some of the hermetic maguses. The noblest kind of late-mediaeval and Renaissance magical practices were those which sought to bring about a spiritual cleansing of the state by concentrating beneficent astrological and spiritual influences through the use of the arts - especially drama, painting, dance and music. This could be done in symbolic pageants and concerts; or alternatively a single magus, it was believed, could draw these influences into himself and thus possess the power to do great good works.

Consider *The Gothic*: it invokes parallels, not only with Beethoven's Ninth, but with mediaeval music, with Renaissance polyphony, Palestrina, Byrd, Schütz, Bach, Handel, Berlioz, Wagner, Strauss, Elgar, Bruckner; it uses ideas from Goethe and a great Christian text; and we know from many things that Brian said about it, that it embodied a whole host of personal associations: as he wrote once to Bantock: "This work has been inside my heart for a lifetime & naturally there is inside it all those who have been very dear to me - who helped & moulded me." We can guess that all the people he mentions in *How the "Gothic" Symphony came to be written* are in some sense "inside" the symphony. It is, of all his works, perhaps the one which is most *charged* with personal and musical influences, as if he felt he needed the support of all his friends and the great composers of the past, inside his imagination at least, to help him succeed in his mammoth task.

All of which is very natural. But a Renaissance alchemist would recognize what Brian was doing: he would say that Brian was performing a piece of conjuring - that *The Gothic* is a vast incantatory spell to capture and channel beneficent influences, to put them to work in a contemporary situation.[15] In such a view, the hoary old musicological chestnut of the "influences" on a composer becomes a very trivial matter indeed.

In *Newsletter* 23 [pp. 75-80 in the present book], discussing the idea that Brian had "learned to make use of the powers of his unconscious mind", I suggested that one way in which he may have done this was through self-identification with powerful archetypal figures from literature. Perhaps I have now made an approach to understanding how this process might actually have worked, when he used his identification with Faust, a most potent archetype, to unlock the full powers of his creative imagination.

But it is also characteristic of Faust, the over-reaching magus, that he attempts too much; in his pride, he believes himself capable of performing Godlike acts; but, as Jung[16] once wrote, Faust is eventually overwhelmed by the weight of his own knowledge - he cannot hope to control the powers of the universe single-handed. *The Gothic* perhaps shows us this aspect of the Faustian experience in Brian as well. I love *The Gothic*; but I feel, as I know many others do, that

---

[15] In his 25 May talk, Paul Rapoport pointed out how Beethoven isolates and therefore intensifies Schiller's idea that humanity must go out and seek God among the stars, and that Brian seems, in the "Judex" of the *Te Deum*, to reverse this process and draw God in. Perhaps it isn't entirely irrelevant that one of the central texts of late mediaeval alchemy, one which deeply influenced Paracelsus, whom we know Brian had read, is a book by Marsilio Ficino called *De Vita Coelius Comparanda*: on the drawing-down of life from the stars.

[16] *Faust and Alchemy*, recently reprinted in Vol. 18 (*The Symbolic Life*) of Jung's *Collected Works*.

something happens to it, during the *Te Deum*, that it is blown off course and ends in a quite different way from that which Brian intended. I feel he meant it to be gigantically affirmative, in the spirit of the *Te Deum*'s opening, a great positive statement for the post-War world. But he seems to have been unable to sustain this joyous vision; something like despair eventually sets in, and the choral cries of "Non confundar in aeternum" seem like agonized prayers for succour and sustenance, as if Brian has found he has taken on just too much of the spiritual burden of Western Man for his single soul to carry.

Or perhaps I'm wrong, and Brian intended it this way from the beginning. In which case we would need to consider *The Gothic* in closer relation to its text - as a religious choral work. It is surely insufficient to say that Brian chose to set the *Te Deum laudamus* because he considered it great poetry. Why *this* piece of great poetry, so central to Christian traditions, and why did he choose to set it in the way that he did? What, or Who, is being celebrated, when the paeans of praise eventually disclose the "Judex", a baleful prophecy of judgement; and at the work's end an apocalyptic enactment of it? Why should Brian's other major choral work on a religious text, the Fourth Symphony, set Psalm 68 with another, more clearly deliberate, counterpointing of triumphant celebration and barbaric violence? Why should he, at the age of 85, have contemplated a setting of "Dixit insipiens": "The fool hath said in his heart, there is no God"?

Brian's religious beliefs remain, at present, an enigma: he clearly rejected conventional churchgoing Christianity, and on occasion proclaimed himself an out-and-out atheist. No doubt his convictions fluctuated over the years, as they did on many other subjects. But if, as it seems, Brian sometimes entertained a concept of a god, or force, that could punish transgressions (his own included),[17] he would be likely to approach an apparently bright and optimistic religious text with an awareness of a shadow-side. His treatment of Christian texts would then, perhaps, reveal a Faustian cosmology dominated by a spirit both light and dark, a god of opposites, creator and destroyer, "love and love's murder, the saint and his betrayer, the brightest light of day and the darkest night of madness".[18]

I advance this view very tentatively indeed, unsure whether I have exceeded the permissible limits of speculation: in some ways it is more comfortable to believe that Brian simply miscalculated his effects, or "got blown off course". But he *does* seize on the text's one line about judgement, and inflates it musically to

---

[17] For example cf. his letter to Granville Bantock of 16 December 1915: "I have no sympathy at all with religion in the churches, but I've always believed in the God of Shelley. A god everywhere and one who punishes through the god in ourselves". On 30 September 1916, he affirmed a belief in "natural laws, which consist of every sin ... bringing its own punishment".

[18] As Jung says poetically of the spirit he names the supreme god, Abraxas, in his *VII Sermones ad Mortuos*. Written in 1917, the *Sermones* were the first thing Jung wrote after his own schizoid upheaval to which I alluded in *Newsletter* 23 [p. 77 in the present book]; they are quite unlike the rest of his output, approaching as near as anything in this century to a Blakeian "prophetic book". Brian's ideas of God are likely to have been influenced by Blake as well as Shelley, and he might well have been fascinated by the *Sermones*, which were published in an English translation in 1925, when he was deeply involved with the *Te Deum*. It is, however, unlikely that he had an opportunity to read them, as it was a severely limited edition.

gigantic proportions, apparently in contradiction to the joyousness of the *Te Deum*'s entire opening movement; and he *does* eventually cast the cosmic merry-making of "et laudamus nomen tuum" onto the jagged rocks of the "Non confundar" outbursts. If this is not to be understood, as Harold Truscott understands it in his portion of the Brian Society *Gothic* book, as an instance of what he sees as Brian's music's tendency to "self-destruction", then perhaps it is some kind of objective statement, both musical and, in the widest sense, religious. A belief in irreconcilable dualities and oppositions in the universe would certainly go a long way to providing a larger philosophical context for many features of Brian's musical language. For instance (merely to touch on a potentially enormous subject), it might have a bearing on the close connection he clearly felt between relative major and minor keys - the relative minor being, as it were, the "shadow" of the major key whose same pitches it employs. Throughout the *Te Deum*, E major is menaced by its relative minor, C♯; and though *The Gothic* does eventually close in the former key, it does so only by a hairsbreadth. Until that final, mysterious choral murmur, C♯ minor seems inevitable.

Perhaps, however, Brian had yet another intention in mind. Perhaps, as Paul Rapoport hinted, the *Te Deum* is a deliberate inversion of Beethoven's *Ode to Joy*.

But that hint reminds me that the classic 20th century formulation of the Faust legend is, precisely, Faust as composer. Thomas Mann's novel *Doktor Faustus* is that classic formulation, and in that novel the composer-protagonist, Adrian Leverkühn, does write a work, called the *Lamentation of Dr. Faustus*, which is a deliberate spiritual inversion of the finale of Beethoven's Ninth. Mann's novel was published exactly 20 years *after* Brian completed his symphony. But life doesn't imitate art too literally. In Mann's novel, the *Lamentation of Dr. Faustus* is the composer's last work. *The Gothic* is Brian's first symphony - throughout no less than 31 others, he continued to work out many of the implications of *The Gothic*. Though he often, in later years, said that his philosophy of life was "nothing matters", his great series of symphonies would seem to suggest rather that he remained true to the end to the Faustian ideal of salvation through unremitting personal effort and refusal to abandon hope:

> He who strives with all his might, that man we can redeem.

"Man is a great miracle", says Hermes Trismegistus, or whoever it was who wrote the *Aesculapius*. In his own way, Havergal Brian is a most impressive proof of the truth of that statement.

Larry Alexander comments:
By odd coincidence, I happened to have read Thomas Mann's *Doktor Faustus* for the first time not a week or so before departing for England this past May. You can imagine how my ears perked up when Malcolm MacDonald used the reference in his presentation at the Penta. But I'm not sure that I can agree with his juxtapositions (Brian as Faust), at least not as Mann *subsequently* expressed them in his book. Unless I'm mistaken, Mann's model(s) were more along the Mahler-Schoenberg line, but even the fact that he couldn't have known much if anything

about Brian isn't the real point. Adrian Leverkühn's deal with the devil brought him Mahleresque success (speaking of the composer as the world-famous conductor) and Schoenberg-like notoriety, hardly Brian's lot in either case. The price extracted by the devil for the deal was the death of the child ... as Mahler's daughter died, so does the child in *Doktor Faustus*. Certainly Brian could have thought of himself as Faust and yet somehow I just don't buy the notion that the dealmaking part of the legend would have entered into the composer's concept. After all, if Brian did make such a deal, he sure got the short end of the stick, both in the fame and the notoriety departments, for an awfully long time. And if appreciation comes late in life, better late than never. No, to paraphrase Flip Wilson, the devil did not make him do it. A fascination with a legend, absolutely.

Another point. MacDonald feels ("as many others do") that something happens to *The Gothic*, that it gets "blown off course and ends in a quite different way than Brian intended". Of course, one can never really *know* when it comes to intentions, a fact which is true even were Brian to have said precisely the opposite. I for one never trust creative people's recollections of their intentions. They are always out to protect the final work. And whatever - whatever!! - they have to say they will say, even if it is an outright falsehood. After all: who is really to know, especially when the kind of composing Brian did was intensely personal and solitary. No one was looking over his shoulder. There was no "mind machine" illustrating his thought processes from A to Z. So whether the end of *The Gothic* was "meant to be gigantically affirmative" can only be a subject for speculation. I further suggest, as a creative person myself, that critics in general (and in this instance in specific) have a tendency - good or not - to expound philosophical theories for the creators they write about; to, in other words, put ideas in their now-dead heads. These ideas might very well be 100% accurate ... but they might not. And they almost universally ignore the other part of "creativity" - the nuts and bolts part. The craft of it. Inspiration and influence are one thing, but the working out of the piece is where the time is spent. There are authors and composers who, I am sure, through-compose in the sense that they begin at the beginning with only a vague impression of where they are going to end up when they get there. Most creative people, however (at least most of those in my experience), write only after they have the piece down in their heads *as a whole*: they outline their intentions up front, or at least work toward a goal previously determined, even if only in theory. And my money says that those who through-compose only through-compose for first draft - after which they rewrite and revise, knowing now where they want to get. In all the years it took Brian to complete *The Gothic* I cannot believe that he could not have brought the symphony to the triumphant, affirmative conclusion Malcolm seems to want. All it would take was technique - and no one can tell me that Brian in the 1920s lacked that. No, the fact (and I truly believe it *is* a fact) is that *The Gothic* was always intended to reach that great outcry of terror and its inevitable aftermath, the hushed prayer. This cannot be because Brian found he took on "just too much of the spiritual burden of Western Man for his single soul to carry". It can only be because this is the way Brian "heard" the music, even before he wrote a note of it - the appropriate "sound" for the words he was setting; the appropriate *progression* of sounds. I'd back this up with a discussion of the key shift to that final E major, but I don't think it's necessary. What we are involved in here is overall concept, and I think it is a trap to suggest that the piece isn't a unity. Beethoven *wanted* to end his Fifth and Ninth as they now end - had he wanted to end "down" he would have done so. Sibelius' Fourth to me arbitrarily ends "down", the composer "going wrong" half-way through what is well on its way to being a celebration of heaven-storming proportions. But to say that Sibelius couldn't have written a celebration of that kind is to put Sibelius down as a composer. Surely Malcolm wouldn't do that with Brian, a composer he professes to love - a composer he has devoted a large part of his own life to supporting!?

Christopher J. Kettle: *The Gothic* revisited[1]

Yet more about *The Gothic*? It is several years now since Malcolm MacDonald warned us against the dangers of being mesmerized by it, to the exclusion of the rest of the symphonies; and now that the excitement surrounding the Schmidt performance[2] has receded it is perhaps right that our attention should be turned elsewhere - particularly, of course, to *The Tigers*. Gone are the days when the *Guinness Book of Records* was the only readily available source of information about the symphony; the Society and the *Newsletter* have especially done the work proud, and I would be no more than a fool to rush onto ground already trodden to such effect. But the great service which those who have already shared their knowledge of, and enthusiasm for, *The Gothic* have done has been in making the work clearer and more accessible to those of us who sense its greatness, even though our grasp of it is limited by our sketchy understanding of musical theory (I, for example, find the details of Prof. Rapoport's published study very hard to follow, even with a score). Our chief debt, of course, is to those who have given us the opportunity to hear Brian's music - especially the tireless Dr Simpson; but we owe an enormous debt as well to those who have enriched our experience of it - particularly, in the case of *The Gothic*, Messrs Truscott, Rapoport, MacDonald, and, most recently, Dr Lionel Pike.[3]

I am lucky enough, I am aware, to have heard the work at all; Boult's performance, heard furtively over the radio during my last term at school, was my

---

[1] From *Newsletters* 43 (IX-X 1982), pp. 6-8, 44 (XI-XII 1982), pp. 3-5 and 46 (III-IV 1983), p. 9 (Postscript).
[2] Ole Schmidt conducted a performance of the *Gothic* Symphony at the Royal Albert Hall on 25 May 1980, and in consequence became a vice-president of the Havergal Brian Society. In connection with this performance the "*Gothic* Day" was held at the Penta Hotel the same day where the texts by MacDonald, Rapoport and Truscott were read (in this book pp. 135-146, 162-166 and 255-264).
[3] Lionel J. Pike: *Havergal Brian's Testament?* Originally published (entitled *The Tonal Structure of Brian's Gothic Symphony*) in *Tempo* 138 (London, September 1981), republished in *Newsletter* 37 (IX-X 1981), pp. 3-6.

first encounter with Brian - I had to miss most of the *Te Deum*, but I well remember the impact Part I made on me. I wasn't able to go to the Schmidt performance, but I went to Stoke on that memorable night in 1978, well summed up by the Editor in the course of his Schmidt review.[4]

All this must not be allowed to become the prelude to decent burial. Surely, one sensed in the attitude of critical hardliners after the Schmidt performance, those Brian maniacs must be satisfied now? Well, I'm not - it cannot be laid to rest so easily. Its impact reminds me of that of Mahler's Third on Bruno Walter, returning to Hamburg after a summer with Mahler at Steinbach am Attersee during which the symphony had been completed and played over on the piano: "I carried the music of the Third with me and it was long before its exciting presence had turned into a soothed possession." Like Mahler's Third for me, I don't think *The Gothic* ever will. Even if this vast and many-sided work is not Brian's greatest, even if it is not a complete artistic success, it demands a response. I am aware that my own attempt to define a response is of little or no objective value - my debts to others are obvious and much of the rest is probably wrongheaded; but it is an attempt which I have had to make before trying to come to terms with the symphonic torrent which followed it. So here it is - please stop reading when you begin to feel irritated!

Many metaphors have been used to describe *The Gothic*. The one which I seem to be stuck with at the moment is that of a vast arch, intricately wrought, but seizing the attention chiefly by its power and mass - its "cruel weight", in Malcolm MacDonald's apt borrowing from Mandelstam. Its scale is such that its dimensions and its detail cannot be apprehended together: the massiveness of its design predominates, but from close up the eye is overpowered too by the staggering vividness and variety of the detail with which the design is fleshed out. Its formidable beauty is, indeed, so hypnotic that it is easy to overlook its significance as an entrance; it stands not only as self-sufficient artifact but as gateway to one of the most unfamiliar and extraordinary territories in the whole of music.

I shall pension off the now-creaking metaphor before it lures me into arranging the later symphonies into a ludicrous landscape; but I cannot think of them without *The Gothic*, and I can no longer conceive of that work on its own. It opens out onto them; in all its urgency and expansiveness it introduces us to Brian's sound-world, and the processes which are later to be tautened until they achieve the tension which creates weight, power and scale by economy, controlled energy, concentration and release. *The Gothic* not only offers us a perspective on this process, leading through the massive conciseness of the Twelfth to its explosive culmination in that utterly characteristic masterpiece, the 30th; it actually sets it in motion - a huge initial impulse which powers Brian's symphonic growth and almost, it seems with hindsight, determines its direction. Its

---

[4] David J. Brown: Editorial in *Newsletter* 29 (VI-VII 1980), pp. 1-2. The *Gothic* performance on 21 May 1978 in Victoria Hall, Hanley, Stoke-on-Trent, was conducted by Sir Adrian Boult, patron of the Havergal Brian Society.

relationship with the later symphonies is living and organic; it feeds them, bursting with energies which demand to be harnessed and so make further symphonies essential and inevitable.

These energies are fully generated in Part I. If we expect the Allegro-Lento-Vivace scheme to lead us onto reasonably familiar ground, it is immediately blown from under our feet by the very opening. Each of the movements accumulates an intensity too great to be contained in an orthodox three-movement plan - these forces need a bigger field for the conflict to be fully fought out. Small wonder that Felix Aprahamian, hearing the music at Stoke after his car had boiled over on the way, described it as "overheated".

At the 1974 Proms, Pierre Boulez framed a performance of Stockhausen's *Gruppen* with works by Wagner and Berg, placing the Stockhausen at the end of the German Romantic large-scale orchestral tradition. Relating *Gruppen* to this tradition in his pre-Prom talk, Boulez described it as "an apotheosis; at the same time a destruction". I think something of the sort could be said of Part I of *The Gothic*. In each movement the music seems to stretch its traditional frame to the limit, threatening to burst it; and in the scherzo, it does just that. Brian is not merely left, as others have been, with a "finale problem"; his wine has burst the old wineskins. Later he was to perfect his own, many of them of startlingly original design; for the moment he needs the vast vat of the *Te Deum* to hold the heady flood.

The sudden loss of momentum in the first movement - an early marking-out of extremes - does sound odd to me; rather as though Mahler had put the brakes on the headlong opening bars of his Eighth Symphony and floated in the Mater Gloriosa melody, awash with harp and harmonium, instead of "Imple superna gratia". There's no context for it to make sense, nothing to qualify our response to the disconcertingly expressive gesture, nothing to help us "place" it; here, at the outset of Brian's symphonic career, we are unused to such sudden transitions. It sounds like an unsuccessful attempt to bring off the kind of contrast achieved in the opening movement of Mahler's Second Symphony, where the grim funeral march relaxes into a rapt melody on the violins, singing like Hardy's "Darkling Thrush" of "some blessed Hope", as yet unattained, barely conceivable. Of course, Brian probably intended nothing of the kind. In any case, both the sound of a lone violin and the sudden unexpected conjunction of two utterly different worlds are to become Brian fingerprints; and the brief, high music for piccolo and flutes which accompanies the violin soon after its appearance reminds me of those cool, remote sounds into which the most strenuous orchestral activity in the later symphonies can suddenly and unnervingly evaporate. Compare, for example, the central section of *Das Siegeslied* - where the surrounding savagery qualifies our response to the soprano's lyricism - especially when the voice returns after the barbaric orchestral centrepiece (likened by Malcolm MacDonald to the fall of Milton's angels), apparently unaffected by it.

Boulez's description of *Gruppen* applies more clearly to the other two movements. In their contrasting moods of elegy and energy they hark back to the corresponding movements of the first great Romantic symphony, which opened out the physical scale and emotional scope of the form - Beethoven's *Eroica*. They are like final statements of two different modes of Romantic expression, invested with both the accumulated weight of tradition and a consciousness that it is going to have to be sloughed off; neither is adequate to the things that Brian is trying to articulate.

Thus the Lento, described by David Rudkin as "one of the great symphonic movements of all time", recalls in sound an identifiable tradition - its huge edifice carries echoes of Schumann's awe in Cologne Cathedral, Bruckner's chaste grandeur, Elgar's stately sorrow - in which intense personal feeling is expressed through the formal gestures of ceremonial; passion is clothed in dignity and restraint, and outward ritual is informed and animated by feeling which is thereby made communal and universal. But Brian's music strains this marriage of form and feeling to breaking point; as the movement gains momentum and tension it threatens to shatter, and the magnificent climax brings us to the brink of a new world.

Boulez, in his *Rituel* in memory of Bruno Maderna, seems to be doing something similar. His work looks back over another clearly recognizable, and closely related, tradition - that of ritual severity, moving sharply away from Romantic "feeling" in formalized expressions of worship or grief. The pioneering masterpiece of this tradition is probably Stravinsky's *Symphony of Psalms*, completed three years after *The Gothic*. Characteristics of the tradition are large-scale conception, often in terms of vast, resonant (or open) spaces, and an austerity of sound marked by the dominance of wind and percussion. Boulez seems to be thinking particularly of the gong-laden mixture of the hieratic and the exotic in his teacher Messiaen's commemoration of the dead of two world wars, *Et Expecto Resurrectionem Mortuorum*. The two works were paired at last year's Proms; one critic wrote of the extraordinary impact of "their monumental ritualizations of sound and rhythm echoing from one to the other in the listener's memory".

Boulez wrote a prose poem to accompany *Rituel*, translated by Stephen Plaistow as follows:

> In perpetual alternation, as it were verses and responses, for an imaginary ceremony.
> Ceremony of remembrance: whence the many returns over the same formulae, while outlines and perspectives change.
> Ceremony of extinction: ritual of disappearance and survival.
> Thus are the images imprinted on musical memory - present, absent, in uncertainty.

"Ceremony of remembrance ... Ceremony of extinction". This is what the Lento, and perhaps the whole of *The Gothic*, seems to enact.

The transition to the Vivace is masterly: the bass clarinet, slithering down between the flagstones at our feet, quietly prising them up to reveal what lies underneath, creates a sensation similar to Auden's nasty vision which begins:

> When the green field comes off like a lid,
> Revealing what was much better hid,
> Unpleasant ...

It is as though the cathedral of the Lento has crumbled, by a Wagnerian "dissolve", into Mervyn Peake's Tower of Flints, which "arose like a mutilated finger from among the fists of knuckled masonry and pointed blasphemously at heaven". But the diabolical energy of the third movement is very much more than an exercise in Gothick horrors, for all the nightmare clarity of its images swarming upon the imagination like the corrupt infestation of Gormenghast. The music is essentially modern - a response not merely to the forces which shaped themselves into demon-driven Wild Hunts in the Romantic imagination (though we may well imagine Faust and Mephistopheles, or Waldemar and his vassals, being sucked into the heat of Brian's furnace as the rout races on to destruction), but to the fact of war. The forces which are here brought to the surface cannot be placated or dismissed as an exercise in the picturesque. This movement is not just a violent episode; it is a statement from which there can be no turning back, and which the *Te Deum* will have to deal with. As it approaches its climax it reminds me powerfully of Matthew Arnold's prophetic vision in *Dover Beach*:

> The world, which seems
> To lie before us like a land of dreams,
> So various, so beautiful, so new,
> Hath really neither joy, nor love, nor light,
> Nor certitude, nor peace, nor help for pain;
> And we are here as on a darkling plain
> Swept with confused alarms of struggle and flight,
> Where ignorant armies clash by night.

Such a statement cannot be swept aside by hearty optimism; it is a Rubicon, and since Brian is a composer of integrity his music must be written from the far side of it.

Initially the movement seems to engage Brucknerian gear - a telling touch after the resonant splendours of the Lento - but this ostinato could not be less like Bruckner. It is a coup as effective as Mahler's use of the Brucknerian *tremolo* to open his Second Symphony, its character transformed by a *fortissimo* and *diminuendo* which invest it with Mahlerian nervousness, turning it into a shudder, a severing from the certainties with which Bruckner dealt. To be fair, despite its superficial resemblance to the ostinato which powers the scherzo of Bruckner's Eighth Symphony, Brian's opening is more closely related to that of Bruckner's Ninth Symphony, by turns sinister, savage and disturbing; but then that far-ranging, exploratory work shares something of *The Gothic*'s character anyway. It would be hard to find two composers less temperamentally alike, despite the odd parallels - both were provincial organists who, like Brahms, only emerged as symphonists in their 40s - yet Bruckner, in the face of death, wrote a work in which all his certainties seem to be shaken, eventually reaching a crisis as shattering as that in *The Gothic* from which he emerged into serenity on the other side, and dedicated it "dem lieben Gott" with a faith which was beyond Brian's reach. He intended, of course, to write the kind of mighty Finale with which he had crowned his Fifth and Eighth Symphonies; it is a curious coincidence that when he realized that he wouldn't live to complete it, he suggested that the three finished movements could be followed by a performance of his *Te Deum*. They are musically unconnected, and I have not heard it done; but when Bernard Haitink prefaced the symphony with the *Te Deum* in a concert performance broadcast early last year, I found it a moving and in some ways a Gothic-like experience, with the purely orchestral and choral-and-orchestral sections reversed, but the proportions preserved. It left me with an impression of Bruckner, after the vigorous affirmation of the *Te Deum*, leaving his lifelong rock to set sail, like Tennyson's Ulysses, on the uncharted waters of the symphony - a voyage which is to make his boat seem very frail before the harbour is reached. Fanciful, no doubt; but I think that Brian, at the threshold of his symphonic career, is undertaking a voyage of a similar nature, though he is very differently equipped for it, and the harbour proves no more than an inaccessible "light in the night". It is worth noting in passing that Tennyson's Ulysses, using the same image of an arch, exactly defines *The Gothic*'s Janus-like character as the embodiment of a tradition and the threshold of a new adventure:

> I am a part of all that I have met;
> Yet all experience is an arch wherethrough
> Gleams that untravelled world, whose margin fades
> For ever and ever when I move.

Before going on to the *Te Deum*, I want to consider one further detail of the third movement (from which I seem to have strayed a long way): the repeated horn-call which alone offsets the movement's sense of anarchy, expressive overloading and impending catastrophe. It is an inevitably suggestive device, with inescapably Romantic associations; Brian is to use it again, and we may think of other scherzo movements by other composers - the *Eroica* again, or the romantic interludes in Mahler's Fifth Symphony. Curiously, I am reminded most powerfully of the Allegretto of Shostakovitch's Tenth Symphony, where the repeated call assumes a structural importance similar to Brian's, acting not only as evocative contrast to the main material but eventually, and imperiously, as a brake when the waltz tune becomes possessed by the explosive, pent-up fury of the preceding movement, which is far from being spent and which threatens to drive the music to a catastrophe. Shostakovitch's horn-call effectually dams up the music's headlong rush, restoring a provisional calm which colours the Finale's high spirits and makes its final tense triumph so memorably insecure. Brian's call is heard at important points, but it is detached from the frightening acceleration of intensity which runs unchecked to its crisis, in whose very explosion we sense Brian's victory in the search for his own voice. Anarchic it may seem - "Things fall apart, the centre cannot hold" - yet in fact everything is being poured into a crucible in which (Yeats again) "all (is) changed, changed utterly: a terrible beauty is born".

There is no question of applying a brake to this elemental energy; but when it is all over the horn-call is still there, and the calm ascent to the D major chord which launches the *Te Deum* takes us onto a new level which, it seems, has been waiting while Brian fought out his battle with a dying tradition, simultaneously freeing himself of it and coming into his inheritance.

Brian's choice of the *Te Deum* as text - or rather his handling of it after it had "pushed itself forward as the only possible finale" - has been much discussed. Art has long been autonomous, secularized, independent of its function as an element of worship; Romantic composers (and others) have tended to differ from their great predecessors in their treatment of religious texts, using them less for liturgical, devotional purposes, more as familiar documents from our cultural tradition, convenient contexts in which to depict human fears and aspirations. The theological content of the texts may be exploited in various ways, or even explicitly negated. Berlioz and Verdi responded to the dramatic possibilities of the Requiem Mass, whereas Fauré's "Dies Irae" scarcely troubles his *Requiem*'s gentle spirit. Janáček admitted dealing with what he called a "legend" of the Crucifixion[5] in the course of his *Glagolitic* Mass (in the great orchestral interlude in the "Credo"); but after the first performance, in the year *The Gothic* was completed, he answered the charge that he was "an old, believing man" by explaining that his intentions were humanistic: "I wanted to capture here the faith in the security of the people on a basis not religious but ethical, strong ..." and pantheistic: "And high is this cathedral, reaching to the vaults of heaven. And candles are burning there, these are the tall fir-trees and there are scintillating stars at their tops. And the bells of the cathedral are those hanging from the necks of a flock of sheep. And my work deals with this cathedral."

Beethoven chose a secular text for the *Choral* Symphony; Tippett in our own time has followed his example in his Third Symphony, providing his own texts, explicitly rejecting the supernatural, regarding religion (as Blake did) as joyless, life-denying and repressive, modifying Schiller's optimism in the face of a century which has seen the world turn on its dark side, yet maintaining a passionately idealistic belief in man's own power to establish the peaceable kingdom: "What though the dream crack! We shall remake it." But Beethoven also wrote the *Missa Solemnis*, a work of very different character and direction from the Ninth Symphony, to which I shall briefly return.

Mahler, too, emulated Beethoven in his own Second Symphony, extending Klopstock's *Resurrection* Ode to embrace his own vision - "Behold, there is no judgement; there are no sinners, no just" - and concluding with an affirmation of the Faustian gospel: "Was du geschlagen, Zu Gott wird es dich tragen" - "What you have beaten will carry you to God". In his Eighth Symphony, he yoked together a Christian hymn and the final scene of Part II of Goethe's *Faust* - the closest apparent parallel to Brian, who originally intended to set the same scene. *Faust* is the acknowledged inspiration for Part I of *The Gothic*; it is followed by a Christian hymn and preceded by a motto from *Faust* which is totally at odds with the *Te Deum*, promising a divine endorsement of human endeavour. Brian's setting in fact turns out to be a Vision of Judgement for which neither confidence in man nor confidence in God is sufficient.

---

[5] Original: Crucifiction.

The Gothic resembles Mahler's Eighth only in its proportions (apart from one curiously Brian-like orchestral passage in Part I, soon blown away by the "Accende"); if Brian had intended to write a heaven-storming ending like Mahler's, the *Te Deum* provided the perfect battle-ground for such optimism in the face of "the war to end all wars" and Brian's own experience and convictions. The struggle is as doomed as it is necessary to the formation of his artistic personality - a "tendency to destruction" indeed, but vitally creative too. Brian never returned to this ground - unlike Mahler, who could no more shake off the desire for religious certainty than he could maintain such certainty in the face of his experience; for Brian there was to be no turning back - from the ensuing consideration of "man in his cosmic loneliness" (a destruction, as it were, of Psalm 8 - no creating, sustaining, caring "Governor", just a vast emptiness into which human life, loves and battles vanish) he pursued his path with dogged consistency.

Brian's setting of the *Te Deum* has some affinities with Berlioz's, of which David Cairns has written: "The rites are quickened into urgent life: the symbolic community takes on a visionary reality, the formalized terrors become personal; 'humanity' is you and me and everyone who fears extinction, God an idea willed into being by man out of the extremity of his need ... over and above this [quality of ritual grandeur] there is another feeling running through it, an immense feeling, haunting though partly indefinable, of a past stretching back to the Middle Ages and beyond, an antiquity 'old as man's weariness'." We may also detect in *The Gothic* most of the features seen by Cairns as common to the Berlioz *Te Deum* and its "brother", the *Requiem*: "their monumental, deliberately slow-moving style, their blend of austerity and brilliance, their systematic use of boldly juxtaposed texture, volumes and densities, their concentration on two main ideas in the text, the majesty of God and the littleness of man, the occasional altering of the liturgy for dramatic reasons, and the use of space as an element of composition - the concept of music as the 'soul' of a great church, filling and animating the body".

Brian's handling of his Latin text has been called irresponsible, and certainly goes beyond Berlioz's "occasional altering of the liturgy for dramatic reasons". There are some curious consequences of the *Te Deum* "pushing itself forward" on a man heavily under Teutonic influence. No greater contrast could be imagined than with the fastidious Stravinsky, writing *Oedipus Rex* at the same time (it was first performed, like the *Glagolitic* Mass, in 1927); he had Cocteau's French version of Sophocles turned into Latin because it gave him "a medium that was not dead but turned to stone". For some tastes, Brian's treatment of this "stone" may rival Alaric's Sack of Rome as an act of Gothic vandalism. Interestingly, when Brian next came to a religious text he actually reversed Stravinsky's process, using Luther's German version of Psalm 68 for his ironclad *Das Siegeslied* - a medium as marvellously suited to his purposes as was Stravinsky's in *Oedipus Rex*. The awkwardnesses in *The Gothic* are not the result of an uneasy truce: the conflict between medium and message produces a dislocation entirely apposite to and characteristic of a work in which the "message" of the text is gradually undermined, eventually overpowered and all but negated.

The gentle opening and close of the first section seem to bring us within its orbit and then return us to earth: unaccompanied voices emerge, and eventually recede with a quiet halo of high woodwind, organ and strings. In between, "the symbolic community takes on a visionary reality" indeed: Brian provides the most marvellous setting of a hymn of praise which abolishes the dimensions of time and space, temporality and eternity, uniting all the earth, all angels, the Heavens, the Church throughout history and throughout the world, and its predecessors, the Prophets.

The unaccompanied opening of the central "Judex" movement is utterly different in character. There is a sense of awe, tentativeness, rudderlessness, of humanity adrift in a vast space without bearings. The voices sound as if they are practising nervously a formula which is going to be useless anyway. The Prodigal Son rehearsed his speech of penitence on the way home; here, we sense, there will be no father waiting to run and meet his errant son with a robe and a ring, but rather a tyrannical authority-figure - Blake's Nobodaddy. The disembodied soprano which answers them out of the vast emptiness is coldly impersonal, indifferent, like Mahler's Bird of Death crowing out in the silences as the Last Trump is sounded. The harsh trumpets which follow are not mysteriously remote like Mahler's off-stage brass, but terrifyingly immediate; so too, is the ensuing march, heralding the approach not of the "Judge enthroned in splendour" but of a victorious dictator - *Das Siegeslied* with the jackboot on the other foot. The imagery strikes me as being similar; and when the four choirs enter successively with their prepared acclamations I think less of Donne's "round earth's imagin'd corners" than of a captive populace herded into groups along the triumphal route, compelled to acclaim the conqueror from whom they can expect no mercy, prompted by his troops behind them (timpani and brass). The undertow of unspoken feeling is perhaps suggested in the subdued plangency of the bars separating the choral cries. As the tempo quickens, the people are driven to judgement, or execution, as graphically as in Berlioz's "Lacrymosa"; the millions are not embraced, but enchained. We hear them cry wordlessly in awe or terror; and finally, after six massively deliberate chords, the ground seems to open up and engulf them, their voices drowned by three more slamming chords like earth on a mass grave.

Fanciful again - but the music really does seem to interpret the theme of judgement through the now-familiar imagery of war, atrocity, physical destruction. We do not forget the theme; the foreground realism banishes its remoteness and lends it a chilling immediacy. Our century has too often confirmed Brian's vision.

What can follow such a vision? Unsurprisingly, a complete contrast: the oboe d'amore which opens the final section (echoed by cor anglais a little later) is faintly reminiscent of the pastoral cor anglais which establishes *Ein Heldenleben*'s final mood of autumnal serenity - the only incident in the whole work which reminds me of Richard Strauss, the symphony's dedicatee. But for all the radiant beauty of Brian's portrayal of the "saints in glory everlasting", we cannot forget the Judge who stands between us and them: if the mood of the first section is here recalled, that of the "Judex" cannot be far behind.

But before that comes the extraordinary passage which Dr Lionel Pike designates "musica mundana", framed by the clarinet march - sly, enigmatic, unrelated to the foregoing music, reminiscent for me not only of the Turkish March in the last movement of Beethoven's *Choral* Symphony (which it perhaps treacherously parodies) but also, in its atmosphere, of the third movement of Beethoven's Fifth Symphony as Helen Schlegel experiences it in a famous passage from *Howard's End*: "the music started with a goblin walking quietly over the universe from end to end. Others followed him. They were not aggressive creatures: it was that that made them so terrible to Helen. They merely observed in passing that there was no such thing as splendour or heroism in the world."

Forster's description exactly catches what I hear as the inscrutably malign character of Brian's march. It slithers and sways like a snake; the chorus, beguiled by its apparent jauntiness, begins to join in imitatively, wordlessly - lured off, perhaps, "into the wide blue yonder" (cf. MacDonald, *Perspective*, pp. 130-135). On this is constructed the huge edifice of "Et laudamus nomen tuum in saeculum saeculi". After the vast climax Forster's "flaming ramparts of the world" do not merely fall - the whole edifice vanishes, the monumental rejoicing blotted out in a moment as if it had never been, like the baseless fabric of Prospero's vision, or like the Limbo of Vanity in *Paradise Lost*, the Paradise of Fools described in Book III after the celestial celebrations of the Father and the Son. The march is audible again, almost as if it had been playing all the time, like the strings in Ives' *The Unanswered Question* - uninvolved, unaffected, indifferent to the vanished tumult, as chillingly efficient in its quiet negation as the apocalyptic thunder which is soon to follow it. The prospect of dissolution, as in Prospero's prophecy, strikes in like a cold wind:

> ... the great globe itself,
> Yea, all which it inherit, shall dissolve,
> And, like this insubstantial pageant faded,
> Leave not a rack behind.

Hearty optimism is played out, and the mood darkens. The whole of the "Et laudamus" has been neutralized, placed in brackets, by the clarinet march; its triumph proved hollow, founded on sand, on the vanity of human wishes. Bruckner's *Te Deum*, grounded on the rock of faith, builds on the last line to blazing triumph; after the bass solo, Brian's "In te, Domine, speravi" is a beautiful but forlorn prayer of exhausted and almost extinguished hope.

The final section returns to the imagery of war - the grim reality which awaited the men who marched away. As the timpani thunder, I am reminded less of their massed roar in the Berlioz *Requiem* than of the "vast malison" of the "long black arm" in Owen's sonnet about the "Great gun towering toward heaven, about to curse", set by Britten in the *War Requiem*. Indeed, the mood of Brian's final pages seems to me best expressed in another sonnet of Owen's, also set in the *War Requiem*, starkly expressive of the effect of the war in which Owen died - "the undone years, the hopelessness" - appropriately called *The End*. Even the imagery of Owen's vision recalls Brian's:

> After the blast of lightning from the East,
> The flourish of loud clouds, the Chariot Throne,
> After the drums of Time have rolled and ceased,
> And by the bronze west long retreat is blown,
>
> Shall life renew these bodies? Of a truth
> All death will He annul, all tears assuage?
> Fill the void veins of Life again with youth,
> And wash, with an immortal water, Age?

Owen gives an answer; and despite the consoling beauty of the final unaccompanied bars, it is the answer towards which *The Gothic*'s energies have been driving it, and which the oboes and cellos have effectively conceded:

> When I do ask white Age he saith not so:
> 'My head hangs weighed with snow.'
> And when I hearken to the Earth, she saith:
> 'My fiery heart shrinks, aching. It is death.
> Mine ancient scars shall not be glorified,
> Nor my titanic tears, the sea, be dried.'

1922, the year in which Brian completed his sketches for *The Gothic*, saw the publication of what many would regard as the greatest novel and poem written in English this century (though neither of them by an Englishman): *Ulysses* and *The Waste Land*. An interesting conjunction - though the symphony is less obviously radical, and obviously less influential than they, suffering the fate feared for Adrian Leverkühn's music by the narrator of *Doktor Faustus*, that "it would be forgotten, would miss its own age and only in later one receive historic honour".

I propose to pursue the comparison with Eliot a little, since the "*Gothic*" years were also crucial to him; it would be idle to imagine any significant connection between the famous and much-imitated poet of the post-War decade and the unknown composer struggling to realize an immense private vision in imagined sound, but at times they speak with a strangely similar voice.

Writing *Dover Beach* in the mid-19th century, Arnold had mourned the ebbing of the Sea of Faith, hearing:

> Its melancholy, long, withdrawing roar,
> Retreating ... down the vast edges drear
> And naked shingles of the world.

Eliot is the poet of the age Arnold prophesied, and *The Waste Land* is the classic statement of the dryness and aridity, the spiritual bankruptcy of the post-War era - a portrait of a culture in decay, cut off from its roots - ending, like *The Gothic*, in disintegration and only the faintest possibility of hope for the future. Two important poems of this period flank *The Waste Land* - *Gerontion* (1920) and *The Hollow Men* (1925).

Gerontion is "an old man in a dry month ... waiting for rain" an ageing Prufrock looking back on a life of lost opportunity, obscurely aware that "the cunning passages of history" have involved him in a betrayal: a sign has been given, the infant Christ, but He has been ignored, the Word deflected, diluted, corrupted:

> I that was near your heart was removed therefrom
> To lose beauty in terror, terror in inquisition.

He is committed now to decay and death, waiting for "the Gulf" to take him, afraid of judgement, afraid of confrontation with "Christ the tiger", who may spring and devour him: "After such knowledge, what forgiveness?"

It was Blake who provided the archetypes of the Tyger and the Lamb for the apparently contradictory forces manifested in creation and in the nature of God. Tippett, like Brian a great admirer of Blake, wrote in his note on his Third Symphony: "To his period's belief in natural law Blake asked: What true law of equity can be found in a nature that has produced both the Tyger and the Lamb? Again, to those who still held to the Christian creed, he said: How can you believe both in Nobodaddy-Jehovah who demanded 1,000 Amalekite foreskins as a sacrifice, and an all-forgiving Jesus? The answer in our own day is that we cannot. It is better for us to accept the Tyger and the Lamb, Jehovah and Jesus, as enduring states of our common humanity, now one, now the other in the ascendant." (Blake's passionate mythology underlies *A Child of Our Time* too, in which Tippett responds to the Second World War with a determination to come to terms with the contrariness in human nature: "I would know my shadow and my light, so shall I at last be whole". Tippett sought Eliot's collaboration on the text, and took as the work's motto words from *Murder in the Cathedral* which in context have a specifically Christian significance: "The darkness declares the glory of light".)

Eliot and (on the evidence of *The Gothic*) Brian found it less easy to dismiss the Christian doctrines of sin, judgement and redemption in the search for equity and wholeness. Tippett's model for the Third Symphony was Beethoven's Ninth, which he quotes directly - a work whose relevance to *The Gothic* Prof. Paul Rapoport in particular has shown. Yet *The Gothic*'s ending brings to my mind rather the closing section of Beethoven's *Missa Solemnis*: trumpets and drums - "rumours of war", unmistakably military-sounding trouble, an explicit prayer for mercy addressed to the Lamb of God; with the aid of that dubious faculty, hindsight, they sound like distant pre-echoes of the naked violence which engulfs *The Gothic* - a hint of the Tyger.

The plight of the Hollow Men, in Eliot's darkest poem, is more clearly illustrative of the end of *The Gothic*. Darkness is falling over the Waste Land; there is a sense of time running out, of an impending "final meeting" which the Hollow Men would like to avoid, but they are no longer capable of any action. Fear has paralysed them:

> Between the idea
> And the Reality
> Between the motion
> And the act
> Falls the Shadow

The fourth section evokes the conclusion of *The Gothic* with particular clarity, though the vision - a gathering darkness in which hope of redemption is reduced to the faintest glimmer - is here conceived in Dante-esque terms:

> The eyes are not here
> There are no eyes here
> In this valley of dying stars
> In this hollow valley
> This broken jaw of our lost kingdoms
>
> In this last of meeting places
> We grope together
> And avoid speech
> Gathered on the beach of the tumid river
>
> Sightless, unless
> The eyes reappear
> As the perpetual star
> Multifoliate rose
> Of death's twilight kingdom
> The hope only
> Of empty men.

Eliot's famous ending, "This is the way the world ends Not with a bang but a whimper", also recalls Brian's; contrast Mahler in his Second and Eighth Symphonies, building from an unaccompanied choral whisper to a bang, a strenuously-willed triumph in which decibels temporarily drown out doubt. In *The Gothic*, the Mahlerian drive towards apotheosis is broken up: the final choral murmur, whimper almost, is all there is breath for - "The hope only of empty men."

For Eliot, the eyes did reappear; the Sea of Faith came in again. In 1927 he announced his conversion to Anglo-Catholicism, and in his work darkness and desert dryness began to give way to new images: images and rhythms of water permeate *Marina*, the loveliest of his "Ariel poems" written at that time, with its sense of imminent landfall, of fog hiding the scent of pine and the sound of birdsong, and the promise of "new ships". His work became a personal quest, through the penitential *Ash Wednesday* and the *Four Quartets*, for "the point of intersection of the timeless with time"; Auden, whose first well-known and characteristic poem, *The Watershed*, was also written in 1927, replaced him as the popular voice.

Brian's voice, of course, continued to be completely unheard. After *The Gothic* he became perhaps less like Eliot than Beckett, in Hugh Kenner's phrase "not a dreamer of rose gardens but a cultivator of what will grow in the waste land". And of course he was like nobody but himself; and *The Gothic* is like no other work. I look forward eagerly to Malcolm MacDonald's reassessment in his forthcoming third volume of *The Symphonies of Havergal Brian*; but I still sense the truth of the words with which he ended his chapter on the symphony in his first volume: "one cannot help feeling that it is one of the handful of creative achievements by which posterity will seek to judge our century, and know us". Let us hope that it has the opportunity to do so.

Having made much (perhaps too much) of the merging of the idea of Judgement with the imagery of war - the one finding expression through the other - at the two great dramatic peaks of the *Te Deum* (the central "Judex" movement and the final cataclysm), I omitted to mention that it is possible to see this association already in the pivotal passage of the Vivace, which signals the acceleration of intensity towards the work's other great peak, the end of Part I. This passage, 12 bars of ponderous chords on horns and bassoons, supported by tubas, contra-bassoon, cellos and basses, anticipates what is to become the dominant idea of the *Te Deum* by initially recalling the *Dies Irae* plainsong tune, much used by other composers. It is framed by two statements of the recurring horncall and followed by a rapid *crescendo* on a bass drum roll - and war breaks out: the music, in Malcolm MacDonald's words, "becomes a little wild".

The passage bears some resemblance to the solemn appearance of the *Dies Irae* as a chorale on low brass and contra-bassoon in the Finale of Mahler's Second Symphony (fig. 10). This occupies a pivotal place in a process moving in the opposite direction: Mahler's Finale begins "a little wild" (it is actually marked "bursting out wildly"), driven by a furious wooden-sticked tattoo on two sets of timpani, similar to Brian's "timpani like gunfire" (MacDonald); then it settles down through the first appearances of several important themes to an expectant silence out of which the chorale emerges, leading directly into the Resurrection theme and opening out via a percussion *crescendo* into a grandiose paragraph which anticipates the work's final orderly triumph. This concludes the series of "pictures" which together make up the first panel of Mahler's huge triptych; there is another silence (rather Brianish in its suggestion of a vast abyss occupied only by deep harp notes and bass *pizzicati*) from which emerges the famous percussion *crescendo* which launches the movement's central conflict.

Brian's passage perhaps similarly prefigures the very different direction of his symphony, establishing the work's intensely-imagined association - identification, almost - of the idea of Judgement with images of war. Mahler's music belongs to an epoch which was swept away by the "war to end all wars"; Brian's took shape in its shadow, and is seared and scarred by the vast desolation in the wake of which it was written. It is no more merely illustrative than, for example, the "storm" in his Tenth Symphony, which is both "a psychological storm" (Truscott) and "more vivid than that in Strauss' *Alpensinfonie*" (Nettel); it is a wholly successful fusion, "a mighty metaphor of an interior, psychological upheaval, expressed in the imagery of nature" (MacDonald - it is hard to resist the temptation to quote the rest of his description!). The second half of the Vivace of *The Gothic* is music of a very different order from the rather mechanical "battle music" with which Mahler keeps the pot boiling at the centre of his imagined drama of Judgement; and though it would be misguided to see Brian's work primarily as a conscious homage to those who were led to the slaughter - the strident laughter of *The Tigers* had provided the direct utterance for his anger at the futility of war - part of its lasting power lies in its uncompromising effectiveness as a memorial to a generation which Brian had been singularly well-placed to watch, painfully and unheroically, being sacrificed and lost.

Paul Rapoport: Beethoven's Ninth Symphony in relation to Brian's First[1]

When it was mentioned to Brahms that the main theme of the last movement of his First Symphony bore a close resemblance to the equivalent theme of the last movement of Beethoven's Ninth, Brahms is reported to have replied something like: "Any ass can hear that." So too will anyone notice certain resemblances between Beethoven's Ninth and Brian's *Gothic*: both are long works nominally in D minor and in four movements (if Brian's Part II of *The Gothic* may be considered one "movement"), with a choral finale using four vocal soloists. My aim in this short essay is merely to point out a few further correspondences between the two works, some simple and some more complicated. Some of the points mean rather little by themselves, but when considered with others or in the contexts of the music, may lead somewhere. Yet even if conclusions about the significance of these correspondences prove possible, it will certainly not be possible to claim that Brian "copied" Beethoven or was trying to comment on or rewrite Beethoven's Ninth. We must ultimately realize that the relationship between the two works can be very complex, at times as difficult to grasp as the workings of the creative process in general. The oversimplification in what you will read below does not do justice to what was unquestionably Brian's ongoing creative response to Beethoven's Ninth, the rest of Beethoven's music, and for that matter, the rest of Western music history.

My discussion will proceed mainly movement by movement; the correspondences will be both similarities and differences-arising-from-similarities. (That last term will explain itself!)

Brian's and Beethoven's first movements

1. Brian's movement relates to a sonata design in D minor, as does Beethoven's. In Brian's case the design is stretched to the breaking point partly because of a *lack* of relationship between the two main themes: note their peculiar alternation in the coda, where this lack is as clear and forceful as it is much earlier. In Beethoven's coda there is also an alternation, certainly less peculiar and sudden, of two theme types, the second of which may derive from the second theme of the movement.

---

[1] From *Newsletter* 32 (XII 1980), pp. 6-8. This is a slightly revised version of the talk given at the Havergal Brian Society/British Music Society "*Gothic* Day" meeting held at the London Penta Hotel on 25 May 1980.

2. The second tonal area of *The Gothic* is B♭ minor/D♭ major; the second tonal area in the Ninth is B♭ (major). Despite this similarity, *The Gothic* as a whole has no important relationship between the keys of B♭ and D, whereas in my view it would be no exaggeration to state that the whole tonal procedure of Beethoven's Ninth centres around the many possible connections between B♭ and D (as significant an idea as anything in this symphony, and one which has received rather little attention).

3. The very beginning of *The Gothic* announces D minor; after the first string and bassoon sounds present the notes D and F, the horns confirm D minor with their open 5ths. The beginning of the Ninth is the other way around: the horns' open 5ths, equally prominent, come first, but only later is the key of D minor confirmed.

4. The main theme of Brian's movement is built on a rising arpeggio; the main theme of Beethoven's is built on a falling arpeggio.

Points 3 and 4 separately mean very little, but together they may have a larger significance which will be touched on later. The question of the arpeggio will also return very shortly.

Brian's third movement and Beethoven's second

Here we must compare the two "scherzos", which of course occupy different locations in their respective symphonies.

1. Brian's scherzo is an eerie, grotesque movement with a "trio"-like refrain in F major and D minor and dominated by the horns. Beethoven's scherzo is nearly as grotesque, but perhaps wittily so. It too has a trio, in D major and with prominent horn parts.

2. Brian's opening theme is marked by ♩♩♪ (later also ♩♪♪) Beethoven's is full of ♩♩♩ as well.

3. The opening and closing of the scherzo in *The Gothic* are built on the same rising arpeggio as is found in the main theme of movement I. The opening and closing of the scherzo in the Ninth are built on the same falling arpeggio as was mentioned for the main theme of its movement I.

There is more to the arpeggio comparison than this. Consider the very last gestures of the two symphonies' last movements: Brian's rising 3rd from tonic to mediant (to be sure, in E major), Beethoven's falling 5th (A to D). Both copy their respective symphonies' beginnings, and as fragments or representatives of fuller arpeggios maintain the difference in direction pointed out for the first and scherzo movements' main themes.

4. Brian's "trio" theme is a simple one. It relaxes the tension, it is always repetitious, its basic melodic motion goes through a rising perfect 5th, it always has a moving line accompanying it (with an F or D pedal). Beethoven's trio theme is also very simple. It too is a foil for the excitement preceding it, it is repetitious, its basic melodic motion does the same thing as Brian's, and it always has a moving line as accompaniment (as a reminder of the sonata part of the scherzo), with a D or A pedal.

5. Consider the "noise" that Brian builds by the sinister ostinatos and the wild xylophone solo leading to the movement's climax. Notes are added to the osti-

nato until 10 of the 12 different pitches are present, and they are added as single notes or groups of *3rds* a *3rd below* the bottom of the existing ostinato chord or chords (a process much easier to grasp from the score than to describe!). The last note added (G) is not part of the ostinato, but it is the 11th different note in the passage and is a third below the B♭ added a short time before.

The Beethoven parallel is remarkably close, although in a different part of his movement and with a dose of deliberately clumsy humour which is not to be found at the climax of Brian's scherzo. Going into the development section, Beethoven treats his main ♩♪♩ rhythm to a sequence of *falling 3ds* in the bass as follows: C A F D B♭ G E♭ C A♭ F D♭ B♭ G♭ E♭ C♭ A♭(=G♯) E C♯ A. This extraordinary sequence also sounds 11 different pitches. As in Brian's case, the 12th note is reserved for the goal of the passage.

6. Some years ago I pointed out the importance of the descending bass pattern B♭-A-A♭-G, which sounds eight times in Brian's third movement, regardless of the key of the music. (See my contribution to the *Two Studies*, p. 65.) This four-note fragment is remarkably persistent and carries a different musical "meaning" on each sounding, whether it belongs to the harmony conveyed by the lines occurring with it or whether it doesn't and seems to be an intruder. Equally unusual and persistent in Beethoven's second movement is the timpani note F. It is the only note the timpani play, and it is not the tonic or dominant of the key of the movement (D minor), but its mediant. In the sonata part of the movement it too sounds on eight occasions, and each time carries a different harmonic function. It too may fit the prevailing harmony or may act to disturb the proceedings when it comes in.

Brian's second movement and Beethoven's third

These are of course the two "slow movements".

1. Brian's movement is on the flat side (G♭ major/E♭ minor), with D minor lurking here and there. It is a complex set of double variations. Beethoven's movement is on the flat side (B♭ major); D (major) is important but unstable. This movement is also a set of double variations.

2. The *Gothic* movement is its most chromatic one; V-I progressions are rare. Its harmonies are rich, its melodies stark. The slow movement of the Ninth is its most diatonic one; V-I and I-V progressions saturate the movement, and there are some enormous dominant pedals. The music is rich in melodic ornamentation and has much less harmonic interest.

3. The prominent opening interval in the Brian is a rising perfect 4th. This interval later distorts to a minor 6th, major 3rd, diminished 4th, and (especially) tritone. The *falling* perfect 4th is prominent in Beethoven's opening theme. On its returns, this 4th may be highly decorated, but it never disappears entirely.

Brian's and Beethoven's fourth movements

It is a little odd to call Part II of *The Gothic* its fourth movement, but I shall do so for the sake of continuing the comparison.

1. Brian sets a sacred text but often gives it a secular musical treatment. Beethoven sets a secular text with some religious ideas in it, and gives it some sacred musical treatment.

2. Formally, Brian's movement is very free, perhaps because of the large number of styles of music in it. Beethoven's is free too, but as Robert Simpson and others have shown, it contains a number of formal procedures based on well-known patterns: sonata, rondo, variations, fugue, concerto.

3. Brian's movement is also operatic: note especially the tenor and bass solos expressing prayers near the end. Beethoven's is operatic in different ways, but note its baritone and tenor solos near the beginning and middle expressing joy.

4. *The Gothic*'s "Salvum fac" section uses a male chorus with much unison and homophony. The Ninth's "Seid umschlungen" section begins the same way.

5. *The Gothic*'s fourth movement is famous for its "old" music - the old instruments used, the music derived from plainchant and from renaissance polyphony. The Ninth has its "old" style too, especially in the "Seid umschlungen" section with its doubling trombones, G dorian, and long-note counterpoint - all references to pretonal music.

6. The clarinet march in *The Gothic* returns to provide a frame for the greatest joy the symphony expresses. The "Turkish" march in the Ninth does not return intact, but its distinctive percussion returns in the coda.

Throughout this list of points from all four movements, you will have noticed a number of differences between the two works which, partly because they arise from aspects of similarity, seem so striking as to preclude mere coincidence. Once grasped, these differences, even opposites, are not likely to be ignored. Many may be found in a comparison of the fourth movements, and there are many more than I've mentioned. The conclusion to me is inescapable. *The Gothic*, especially in its *Te Deum* finale, is a reversal, both musical and philosophical, of Beethoven's Ninth and its *Ode to Joy* finale. I can't prove this; all I can do is add a little more evidence.

Beethoven's finale *starts* with a noisy assault: that famous gesture is heard twice, the second time when the movement "starts over". The equivalent in Brian's finale is the pair of massive assaults near the *end*; the second one is harmonically very close to Beethoven's second "assault" chord, although Brian's is scored very differently.

Beethoven's cello recitatives occur near the *beginning* of the finale; Brian's is again near the end. In the Beethoven, they are closely tied to the rejection of the darkness, grotesquerie, and melancholy of the earlier movements, and the development towards joy and universal love. The progression in the Brian is the opposite: the joyful praise at the beginning of the fourth movement gives way ultimately to doubt if not outright despair. The beginning of Beethoven's finale rejects previous melodic shapes (of the first three movements); the beginning of Brian's exults in them. *The Gothic* ultimately rejects them or at least hides them, and finally, to return to those two massive assaults, seems to reject as well two *keys* representing two earlier movements. The first outburst lands on C♯ (p. 255 of the published score), but the chorus twists that beyond recognition. The second outburst lands on D♯ (or E♭), and the chorus destroys that too. The C♯ may well represent things in the first movement (especially the second theme); the D♯ may refer to the second movement. D, which might better represent the first movement as a whole and much of the third, has long since been put away and cannot, for both philosophical and musical reasons, come back here.

One final point on the possibility of Brian's fourth movement being a reversal of Beethoven's. The heart of *The Gothic*'s finale seems to me to be the "Judex" section: it is marked as such in many ways in Brian's treatment of it. And I think that Beethoven marks the "Seid umschlungen" portion of his finale to hold a similar weight. Certainly in Schiller's text as Beethoven used it, these words (down to and including "Über Sternen muss er wohnen") contain the only real commands and the most specific advice to humanity. And here we have something really interesting. Beethoven (through Schiller) advises us to "go out", to seek the creator beyond the realm of the stars. Brian (through the *Te Deum*) doesn't use the "creator", but the "judge" - the opposite end of the religious time-span - and he doesn't have us going out to his world, but him coming into ours: "Judex crederis esse venturus". Beethoven's is a clear plea for action; Brian's is a disguised plea for help.

I know of no methodology for comparing works like these. I've merely mentioned a few correspondences and hinted at what I think is the significance of some of them. There are many other relationships to be discussed, including some applying across movements. If you accept some or many of the parallels, does this mean that Brian's originality has decreased? No. Brian believed firmly that the role of the artist was to build on and extend the riches of the past, and in light of this, we should get rid of, once and for all, the idiotic notion that a composer's resemblance to another composer proves weakness and lack of originality. In a most superficial sense, Brian's *Gothic* Symphony is rather unoriginal. But in the most profound ways, his use and transformation of the past, including Beethoven's Ninth Symphony, constitute one of the greatest and most original creative acts of the 20th century. *The Gothic* surely belongs in the mainstream of Western musical thought, by which I mean not that it must become a repertory work, but that it is affected by *and affects* our understanding of the rest of the Western tradition. Beethoven's Ninth Symphony affects the way we hear *The Gothic*, but the reverse is just as true: anyone who knows the *Gothic* Symphony must surely hear Beethoven's Ninth in a new, more meaningful, way. Only the greatest works of art have this power, to transform the past and our relationship to it, and not just once but continually.

If I have discovered anything about *The Gothic* in the past ten years, it's that it is an infinitely renewable resource, irresistible and indestructible, whose ability to reinterpret and be reinterpreted has no limit.

Robert Simpson in conversation with Stephen Johnson[1]

... On a line from Ireland, where he now lives, Robert Simpson spoke to Stephen Johnson who began by asking him whether *The Gothic* really justifies its length and enormous resources.

R.S. I think it does. I really think it does, and I think it for instance justifies it more than Mahler's Eighth Symphony, which I find a rather uneven work. Well, the *Gothic* Symphony is also uneven in certain ways, but I think the Mahler Eighth falls off in concentration and power and originality, whereas the *Gothic* Symphony increases its energy and its creative imagination so that it gets more and more astonishing as it goes on.

S.J. One criticism there has been of Brian, one recurring criticism, is that he composes interesting gestures but doesn't always work them out very compellingly, and sometimes in some pieces I can see the point. Is that true here?

R.S. No, I think it's not. It may be slightly true in the first movement, but not in the rest. I think the rest, as I said before, it gains in concentration and real momentum as it goes on. I think we must remember, when we listen to the *Te Deum*, that it is really three movements, not one continuous choral finale, it is three movements - it is a six-movement symphony, the last three of which are choral, and I think it is important to realize that in order to understand, you know, what's happening.

S.J. Yes, several people seem to have had problems with the first movement of *The Gothic*.

R.S. It is probably the weakest movement of it, it doesn't really have the momentum that it should have for being the first movement of a huge symphony. It's also, I think, a little bit too "English", if you see what I mean. That disappears as the work goes on. It becomes more and more comprehensive and non-national, in fact there are passages in the *Te Deum* which sound almost Middle Eastern in character.

S.J. Yes, it's quite extraordinary isn't it? There are passages that people have gleefully pointed out, sounding like Bruckner, Mahler, and composers more recently perhaps, even Schoenberg, and there's one critic who even mentioned Varèse.

R.S. He was interested in Schoenberg, he met him and found him rather a congenial character. He told me he liked him, and found his music interesting. He was also very much in advance of most of the critics of his time. When he was writing in the *Musical Opinion* he was one of the people who advocated Berlioz when nobody would look at him, and Bruckner and Mahler who were, you know, non-persons in England at that time. He was very much influenced, I

---

[1] From *Newsletter* 96 (VII-VIII 1991), pp. 4-5. The broadcast of the Slovak recording of the *Gothic* Symphony (Marco Polo 8.223 280-281, released in 1990) was preceded by this telephone interview which was transcribed by Alan Marshall.

think, by Berlioz, and particularly his instrumentation of course, and a great influence on him in those early days was Strauss.

S.J. I'm just thinking of one other problem that some people have said they have with Brian actually, which is that it's not just the working out, sometimes even the melodic lines; they seem to follow fairly recognizable lines for a bar and a half or so, and then suddenly veer off in some strange direction. It's ... the unpredictability is on the small scale as well as on the large scale.

R.S. Yes. I think you have to get used to that. I think another thing you have to get used to with Brian very often, particularly in the later symphonies, is that he thinks from the bottom upwards, not from the top down, and most people seem to listen from the top down, don't they? They hear the top line, and what goes on underneath is maybe exciting and all that, but it's not the most important thing. But in the case of Brian the bass is immensely important, and in fact that is what one sees in his scoring: the way he writes for the tuba, for instance, is quite unique. The bass instruments of the orchestra are really an absolute fascination to him, and he thinks the music upwards, rather than downwards. And of course, very often it's very difficult to perform. I mean the *Gothic* Symphony is particularly murderously difficult, especially for the choirs; and it's up to the performance, of course, to make these things clear, and it doesn't always come off.

S.J. Yes, I mean that is one way in which listening to a recording like this may be an immense advantage over a concert performance; there isn't the same danger of everybody just getting too tired out by the middle of the fifth movement.

R.S. Well, there is of course that, it's very exhausting. I think it's astonishing what they've done in the Slovak recording. The choral singing there really makes the imagination boggle; I don't know how they managed it.

S.J. The other thing that struck me is that the orchestra - the playing may have problems in one or two places - but that they do seem to have found their way into Brian's lines expressively.

R.S. Yes. I think also that may be due to the fact that in Czechoslovakia the standard of string playing is quite out of this world. I remember one of my symphonies they played there, and the string playing just left me gasping. And so that makes a basic difference to the orchestra's approach to the music, because most of the time the strings are still the nucleus of the orchestra. It's astonishing, really, what they managed to do; marvellous, it's the best performance it's had, certainly.

S.J. Some of the writing, particularly for the brass, is quite terrifying.

R.S. Yes, yes. But I remember Bill Overton, who was then principal trumpet of the BBC Symphony Orchestra when Boult did it, said to me afterwards, he said "I looked at that trumpet part" and he said "I thought, this is not playable". But he said "Much to my amazement, I found it was". The old chap knew what he was doing, you know; he knew a hell of a lot about orchestration. I used to show him my scores and he used to give me all sorts of nice tips.

S.J. Because this symphony has the official number "No. 1" a lot of people have the idea that it was a kind of early effort, but it wasn't anything of the kind, was it?

R.S. No, it was originally called No. 2 because there had been a previous one which got broken up into separate pieces, and then *The Gothic* became No. 1. It was actually I who suggested to him to change the numbering, but by that time in the 1920s - I mean 1927 when he finished *The Gothic* - he was in his 50s, you see. It was later in his life, say, than Brahms' First Symphony, and he'd written a lot of music, particularly choral music, and that got quite well-known; it was performed quite a bit. He used to do a bit of conducting, too. He was very much a practical musician - he played the organ, he was regarded as one of the coming lights in English music, and somehow it all went wrong. Nobody really quite knows why; he wasn't the most tactful person, of course, and he tended to upset people.

S.J. Now, the title. In what sense is this work "gothic"?

R.S. Well - in a very large sense, I think, it's not just based on the idea of Gothic architecture, although it is in many ways; it's based on a feeling for the Gothic period, with all its superstitions and wildness and violence too. You'll find there's lots of gargoyles in the *Gothic* Symphony, things like that.

S.J. At the time he began to write *The Gothic*, which is - what after the War?

R.S. 1919, I think; yes, yes ...

S.J. I wonder, you know there do seem to have been many composers who went through a kind of crisis or a change after the end of the War; Elgar virtually stopped composing [Yes], Bridge suddenly toughened up and started writing in completely new directions [Yes] and this looks almost like a kind of gesture of defiance, in a way.

R.S. Yes, I think it was - in a way - although ... he just felt he had to do it. He wasn't a complicated person in the sense that he had complicated psychological reactions to what was going on; he just was very direct and straightforward and, if he couldn't sleep, he'd get up and write some music. One of his last things he said to me was - he was 95, 96 nearly then - he said to me "You know, nothing matters"; and he said that was his real philosophy.

S.J. It seems an extraordinary thing for someone to say who'd gone to the enormous trouble of writing down a work like this!

R.S. Yes, well, he didn't know whether it mattered or not, but that's what he had to do!

S.J. Do you think, when he wrote this piece, that he had any conception that it would one day be performed?

R.S. Well, I think he may have, because it was Henry Wood who suggested to him the idea of writing a work which contained all the known instruments, obsolete and current, and this sort of occupied his mind for quite a long time. He was very interested in the idea, and finally he did it, and then other people showed a great deal of interest in it - Eugene Goossens, for instance, wanted to do it in America; Harty, Beecham, Henry Wood of course wanted to do it, but it was always a question of finance, and I think Brian at that time really did have some hopes that somebody would pull it off.

S.J. Brian heard this symphony, didn't he? He was able to hear it - I think he heard it twice, is that right?

R.S. Yes, he heard it in a performance that Bryan Fairfax conducted in 1961, I think it was, which was mainly an amateur performance; that was the first shot at it. And then he heard it when Adrian Boult did it in the Albert Hall in '66, and that was the first professional performance of it.

S.J. How did he react to hearing this extraordinary work?

R.S. Oh, he was thrilled to bits, obviously, but the comic thing was that, at the Boult performance, I was sitting with him in the stalls, and the audience just erupted at the end, it was an enormous reception, I mean everyone stood, there must have been six or seven thousand people in the Hall, and the din was colossal, and I bellowed in his ear, I said "Come on, you've got to come round the back and get you on the platform". So he got up, we went round the back, and as soon as the door closed behind us we could hear each other speak, and he said to me "Cor" he said "it's good to get up on your feet after sitting there all that long time", he said, "it gets you behind the knees". That was his first reaction! And then when I got him onto the platform, I sort of gave him a little push, and he sort of walked on, he didn't know what to do with himself; there was all this terrific row going on, fantastic applause, and he just stood there and scratched his head. And then Adrian came across and put his arm round him and took him in hand, you know, and practically tilted him over to make a bow, and everybody went wild - it was the most moving occasion: he was 90 then.

S.J. He wrote 31 more symphonies after this, that's over a space of 40 years. [Yes] What did he think of this piece, at the end of it all?

R.S. Well, right at the end I said to him "What do you think's the best thing you've ever done?"; he said "*The Gothic*". No hesitation, not a moment's thought - "*The Gothic*" ...

Graham Saxby: Havergal Brian's Second Symphony[1]

In spite of broadcast performances of his works over the past few years, and a good deal of publicity from some fairly influential musical figures, it is probably true to say that, for most of the public (and a good many music critics), Havergal Brian's sole claim to fame is a symphony that lasts longer, and requires more performers, than any other symphony (neither of which may be, nor can be proven to be, true). To those whose interest in music goes beyond the *Guinness Book of Records* he is a man who, with very little of his music played in public between the ages of 40 and 80, went on after that age to complete 20 symphonies and two operas amongst other music - an achievement that dwarfs even Janáček's Indian Summer - and lived to be nearly 97. But Brian's music cannot be judged in terms

---

[1] From *Newsletters* 33 (I-II 1981), pp. 4-5, 34 (III-IV 1981), pp. 4-6, 35 (V-VI 1981), pp. 3-5 and 36 (VII-VIII 1981), p. 3. The title of the *Newsletter* 36 article is *Götz von Berlichingen and Brian's Second Symphony*. The article began life as the main Project in an Open University Course "The Rise of Modernism in Music 1895-1935" which the author was studying in his final year for an honours degree with the Open University.

of its seeming prolixity any more than his approach to the symphonic concept can be deduced from an examination of the structure and orchestration of the *Gothic* Symphony, useful though that may be in understanding *The Gothic* itself. In fact, every one of his 32 symphonies is quite different from all the others; and yet, paradoxically, the hand of the composer can readily be recognized in a few bars taken at random from any one of them. Like Charles Ives, Brian was a rugged individualist in his music, and gave the impression of not being particularly interested in whether anyone wanted to perform it, once the act of creation was over. Again, as with Ives, recognition was late in coming to Brian, though at least he lived long enough to hear *The Gothic* and several of his other works performed in public, and to be acknowledged by a number of discerning critics and musicologists as one of the major symphonists of the century.

Though he may in some respects have resembled Ives, Brian's character was very much unlike Ives'. He was an indifferent businessman and for most of his life was very poor. He was outspoken and lacking in tact, and his imperceptiveness seems to have lost him the friendship of several valuable allies, including Elgar and Arnold Bennett. He was also the victim of a number of misfortunes not of his own making. He refused to compromise his ideals, whether musical, political or social, and to make any concessions to current tastes. This led him eventually to be dubbed (not without affection) "the original Awkward Cuss".

Let us begin by examining Brian's general approach to the symphony. It was his declared wish to continue along the traditional path of the European Romantic school, though in the event he travelled much further along it than any of his predecessors, and altogether in his own way. As Malcolm MacDonald has put it in the introduction of his first volume on the symphonies, stylistically his symphonic music stands midway between the poles of Mahler, for whom a symphony needed to express the whole world, and Sibelius, for whom it had to create a profound inner logic by stylistic unity and severity of form. That Brian succeeded to large extent in reconciling these two ideals is already evident in his Second Symphony.

Much as he admired the late German Romantic idiom typified by the work of composers like Richard Strauss, Brian was concerned that his music should be thoroughly English. Moreover, he was determined to achieve this by purely symphonic means, and not to produce an artificial flavour by incorporating folk elements as so many of his contemporaries were doing. In this respect he followed Elgar's lead: the spirit of Elgar permeates the Second Symphony. Nettel (*Havergal Brian*, p. 367) points out that Brian's early working-class environment in the Potteries must have given him little chance to hear any genuine folk-music; and there is certainly no folk-element in any of his symphonies. However, like Elgar and Mahler, Brian grew up with the sound of splendid brass bands in his ears; and in his music, as in theirs, the spirit of the military march, with its compelling imagery, is never far away. His writing for brass is, indeed, so powerful as to form one of the cornerstones of his symphonic style, and can arguably be said to be at the heart of his very personal and original idiom. Brian tends to deploy his orchestral forces in a way that is the antithesis of the traditional

Romantic style: instead of the main material being carried by the string body, with the brass used to highlight it, Brian structures his orchestration around the brass, so that the strings become the complement. This is to some extent an oversimplification, for Brian's orchestration is too subtle to be pigeonholed in this manner, but it is broadly true. Time and again the brass body is at the heart of the music, and in reading the score the eyes are continually drawn to it. Elgar, too, sometimes used these methods, though on nothing like so consistent a scale. It is this practice that appears to have offered Brian the opportunity to draw such unusual timbres and unexpected textures from his orchestra. There are some striking examples of these to be found in the Second Symphony, as we shall see.

It must emphatically not be assumed that because Brian was self-taught there is anything crude about his orchestration, or that his strange timbres were the result of ignorance or an untrained ear. The truth is that he had a flair for orchestration that far outshone that of his contemporaries such as Bantock or Holbrooke. From the start his orchestration was original and brilliant; and there is, too, little doubt that the difficulties in performance that such scoring raised, as well as the unfamiliar sounds it produced, contributed to the neglect of the music. Brian was an excellent reader of scores; and though his favourite instrument was, and remained, the organ, he had at an early age learnt to play many of the orchestral instruments. From his study of the organ he learned a great deal about sonorities, in particular the generation of sum and difference tones by mixture stops. Dr Ted Heaton has shown (pp. 353-354 in the present book), for example, that the bare 5th with which Brian so often ends his orchestral works generates a powerful difference-tone an octave below the fundamental. In fact, the same combination also generates a sum-tone an 18th above the fundamental, that is, an octave and a major 3rd above it in just intonation. This sum-tone is real and audible (piano tuners make use of it); and with an appropriate mixture of instrumental timbre it can be clearly heard. Indeed, it *is* heard in those symphonies where a "major" tonality seems to be indicated by the final notes. Such felicities do not occur by accident.

The structures of Brian's symphonies are also highly original. Leaving aside *The Gothic*, which can really only be discussed within its own frame of reference, we find in the symphonies, disparate though they are, a number of common characteristics. Brian distrusted conventional sonata forms, and had an extreme dislike of exact repetition - in both respects a parallel to Debussy. And, like Debussy, he found his answer in a structure which developed by internal growth and thematic metamorphosis: the achievement of unity by thematic rather than formal structural means. His thematic treatment is highly personal. Though he was capable of writing splendid chorale-like material (and often did so), his thematic developments tend to be highly contrapuntal, the lines so independent as to be heterophonic[2] in a way reminiscent of Schoenberg's *Pierrot Lunaire*. Another trait seen particularly in Brian's later symphonies, but already evident in

---

[2] This is a term coined by Rudi Blesh in *Shining Trumpets* (1947) to describe an idiom in which contrapuntal lines have become totally independent of one another.

the Second, is his tendency to juxtapose material so as to produce abrupt changes in mood, often at climaxes. This is a habit which can at times be disconcerting, though a careful study will usually show a good reason for the change. Another individual characteristic is the way the endings of his symphonies show a tendency to disintegrate rather than integrate, producing what Harold Truscott has called an "anti-symphony" rather than a "symphony" (Harold Truscott in *Two Studies*, p. 11).³ This is, of course, not unprecedented: Tchaikovsky's *Pathétique*

---

³ Owen Toller writes in his article *Preconceptions and the Anti-Symphony* in Newsletter 87 (I-II 1990), pp. 5-6, a reply to a number of letters to the Editor by P. J. Taylor and David Hornby in Newsletters 79 and 80: "Mr Hornby took exception to my use of the term 'anti-symphonic' as if it were a synonym for 'unsymphonic'. In fact, Mr Hornby's comment 'I cannot understand how anyone can describe Brian's music as "anti-symphonic"' illustrates unconsciously exactly the point I was trying to make. We who are enthusiasts for Brian's music are distressed when 'neutral' critics react negatively to favourite works (such as Malcolm MacDonald's review of the Third Symphony in *Gramophone*). I suggest that what we should do is not jump back to aggressively dogmatic positions in the manner of Mr Hornby but to consider coolly why Brian's music sometimes provokes negative responses in the uncommitted, and what we can do to help overcome them. By 'anti-symphonic' I mean such elements in Brian's style as the 'productive discontinuity' and the unorthodox use of key, both of which contradict standard and Classical procedure. Where a Classical symphony makes a point of establishing two different keys and bringing them into opposition, ending with the triumph of one of them, Brian makes rapid switches into new keys without either dispelling the old key or providing clear motivation for the establishing of the new one. I am thinking of the final transfer to E from D in *The Gothic*, the refusal of the first movement of the Second Symphony to get very far away from E (not the same phenomenon, but an equally anti-Classical procedure), or the strange relationships between C and A in the Seventh. I wish someone could persuade Robert Simpson to give us a commentary on some of these works; his exposition of the difficult tonal processes in Bruckner and, particularly, Nielsen is so illuminating that I feel he could explain the logic behind these things which even Malcolm MacDonald does not explain but describe. The use of foreign keys is of course a defining characteristic of late-Romantic and post-Romantic music. You have only to think of Strauss' harmonic side-steps or Reger's use of distant keys as local harmonic colour to hear how central to their style is the use of tonality. But these composers do not overthrow the basic axioms. It seems to me that Brian uses keys in the examples I have quoted, not for local colour, but in order to make a statement about Classical procedures, to negate them and to suggest their irrelevance in terms of his own day. The result has all the productive dynamism and tension of more orthodox symphonism and I would never call it unsymphonic. But making a sort of destructive critique of received assumptions is certainly both disturbing and tending to place a hurdle in front of easy acceptance. In any case it is very difficult to convey negatives in music. Parody is often attempted but it is exceedingly unusual for it to be successful as music in its own right (it is stimulating to make up one's mind as to whether movements such as the finales of Mahler's Seventh or Liszt's *Faust* Symphony are really 'good music'), and I think the same is true for other self-conscious attempts to deny the established order. The third main element of Brian's style that I find disconcerting, after the 'productive discontinuity' (so stimulatingly discussed by John Pickard and Martyn Becker) and use of tonality, is orchestration. This element seems to have received relatively little comment in the Havergal Brian Society recently, although a reader of *Gramophone* wrote a couple of years ago complaining of Havergal Brian's 'gritty orchestral style'. The problems seem to stem from complexity of texture, awkward balances leading to shrill tuttis, and the use of percussion. Texture is another of a composer's fingerprints and complex textures are hardly bad orchestration *per se*, but the similarly complex music of Franz Schmidt generally sounds much more smooth and lucid while retaining clarity. It is perhaps over-simplistic to criticise Brian's orchestral balances as the result of lack of opportunity to hear

the music, and I should like to read the views of a conductor experienced in Brian on whether a good tonal blend can be achieved. But turning to the use of side-drums and cymbals, we must accept this as a central part of Brian's expressive texture, whether we like it or not. Now the real difficulty for the 'neutral' listener is that all these three elements of Brian's style break the 'rules' of composition, either as taught explicitly or as observed from experience in the Classical masters. The first thing a tyro composer has to learn is how to achieve a sense of continuity, in accordance with Wagner's famous dictum that the art of composition is the art of transition. Brian does not eschew transition entirely but it is often bypassed, to say nothing of the frequent breaks and 'pauses for effect'. They are more common than in Bruckner and I understand the feelings of those who suggest, especially in the late symphonies, that they are overdone. The Classical use of tonality is so firmly ingrained in most people to whom it matters at all that it is hard to discard its axioms, except in thinking of Robert Simpson's dictum: 'Any muddle-headed dabbler can end in a key other than the one he started in'. As for orchestration, all students are supposed to assume that a well-balanced overall tone is the unquestioned aim, and 'don't over-use the percussion' is a standard injunction. In other words, Havergal Brian's music breaks a lot of beginners' rules. Nor does it help that, like Ives but not Schoenberg, there is little 'early' Brian that shows that he could obey the rules if he wanted to. And if mention of 'rules' makes me seem rather Beckmesserish, I would like to emphasize that, whatever the *text* of *Die Meistersinger* might imply, the *music* demonstrates that the only fruitful way of developing a new style is in growth from within the established traditions. Hans Pfitzner says the same thing in *Palestrina*, despite the obscurantist nature of his theoretical writings; in practice Wagner the revolutionary and Pfitzner the conservative are agreed. We are in effect faced with two choices: either Brian is an incompetent blunderer or his music cannot be judged by 'normal' standards. Rejecting *ex hypothesis* the former alternative, we are left with the problem of what standards if any to apply to him. And at this point I should like to ask two questions: (1) Can you name a bad piece of music? (2) Why is it bad? I really don't think that there's an answer to the second question. Most plausible attempts ('It's tasteless', 'It's technically incompetent') reduce to such statements as 'I dislike it' or 'It doesn't do what most pieces do', or can be challenged with the question 'How do you know that you have understood the composer's intention?' Even in the face of a work that manifestly fails to achieve the aims it sets itself, that is not enough *per se* to make it a bad piece of music. (Does the *Ring* completely fulfil all its aims?) The trouble is that the uncommitted find it easy to fall Assyrian-like on unconventionalities to 'explain' their own lack of positive response, and all music that refuses to 'obey the rules' has suffered from related penny-in-the-slot criticisms from Beethoven's Ninth onwards. It's too easy to say that a piece of music is 'bad', or to accept *ex cathedra* judgements of this sort by critics; I think one should take every opportunity to expose the shallowness of such statements. It's not hard to maintain that there are no such things as absolute standards, but no one wants to think that all music is equally good, that Beethoven Seven is no better (nor worse) a piece than Beethoven One. Surely what matters, regardless of what the analysts say, is the *individualness* of a work of art, the way in which it creates an atmosphere and an existence unlike that of anything else. Undoubtedly, as far as I am concerned, Brian achieves this, and we need to find ways of persuading those listeners who have not yet experienced it that it does exist, that perseverance will be rewarded. Talking to intelligent music-lovers I am well aware that preconceptions regarding Havergal Brian continue to exist. We need to find ways of dispelling the still widely-held myth that Brian is merely a composer of excessively long and impractical works; at least one can hope that the recording of *The Gothic* will bring it down from the mythological clouds. We have at all costs to dispel the overtones of crankiness which can still adhere to the Havergal Brian enthusiast in the way that they used to adhere to the Greens. (Even I was cautious about whether enthusiasm for Havergal Brian was merely crankish before I made the acquaintance of Havergal Brian's music, and I apologise to the shade of Havergal Brian and to the Society for my unspoken doubts.) And we must bear in mind that at present more unfamiliar music is coming more rapidly to public attention than at any time in history, thanks to the success of CD. We are, if you like, competing in a very full market.

and Mahler's Ninth are obvious parallels; and so, in a rather different way, is Ravel's *La Valse*. Both of these characteristics are the direct antitheses of the methods of composers such as Sibelius who, in MacDonald's words, "reconciles extremes by imperceptible transitions from one to the other, [whereas] Brian brings them into direct confrontation" (Volume 1, p. 12). Although these elements are already discernible in the Second Symphony, in his later symphonies Brian was to take the practices a good deal further.[4]

In this connection one should bear in mind that the Second Symphony was not an early work. Brian was 55 when he completed it, and had already composed two symphonies (*The Gothic* and an earlier one which he had dismantled and used in other works) as well as a full-scale opera, several orchestral suites and a large number of songs.

In view of the excellent analysis of the Second Symphony carried out by MacDonald (Volume 1, pp. 56-71), it would be presumptuous as well as pointless to attempt to repeat the process; and in the discussion which follows I have tried as far as possible to avoid anything resembling a paraphrase of MacDonald's work, though in order to provide an adequate discussion of the symphony's qualities it is, of course, necessary to use a certain amount of formal analysis.

The symphony had a literary origin. Brian was inspired to write it after reading Goethe's drama *Götz von Berlichingen*, and the four movements were associated respectively with Götz's ambitions, loves, battles and death. It is not programmatic in the way Strauss' *Ein Heldenleben* is, but is, rather, suggestive or evocative, as is, for example, Mahler's Second Symphony. Later, Brian withdrew the literary allusions, and claimed instead that the symphony represented "Man in his cosmic loneliness"; its overall tragic atmosphere certainly gives this impression. Throughout his life, however, he referred to it as his "Battle Symphony", the tumultuous scherzo suggesting the title. However, one should beware of attaching too much to a nickname, even one bestowed by the composer.

Superficially, the symphony appears to be fairly orthodox in overall structure. There is a first movement in sonata form, a slow movement, a scherzo, and a finale cast in a form that resembles a sonata-rondo. But when we look more closely we find that such a description is grossly oversimplified. To begin with, the first movement does not have the weight that one might expect of a traditional first movement: it is more of a curtain-raiser, setting the scene both thematically and in terms of orchestration for the rest of the symphony. Its most important thematic material is to appear again, most notably at the climax of the finale, and

---

If the music speaks for itself, the problems don't matter, as Martyn Becker said. It's rather like the problem of delay in *Hamlet*; looked at coldly, there are huge difficulties to overcome; but when the play is done at all adequately doubts are overcome. We will do ourselves no good at all by pretending that other people shouldn't have problems with music that we feel we know and understand, and I think we have to tread a narrow path to combine enthusiasm with realism."

[4] Christopher J. Kettle, in his article *Second thoughts on the Third Symphony* in *Newsletter* 78 (VII-VIII 1988) comments (p. 8): "Brian, already older than either Tchaikovsky or Mahler lived to be, but working on the first fully successful symphony of a long career, chooses another way: picking up the threads with the flowing second theme, he builds the music in a series of waves which gradually amass tidal force, at which point the Coda bursts in."

on a very much grander scale. The orchestration of the first movement begins traditionally, but its recapitulation has a completely transformed texture, one which foreshadows the extraordinary orchestral effects of the finale. As to the other three movements, a closer examination shows that they, too, have formats that are far from traditional. However, in dealing with the special qualities of each movement it is important not to lose sight of the unity of the entire symphony, a characteristic which, while often elusive, is crucial to Brian's symphonic thought.

Since I completed the draft of this article, Malcolm MacDonald has suggested in conversation that the symphony falls into two parts: the agitated first movement leading directly into the expansive second, with its glittering climax and final disintegration, mirrored by the obsessive dance of the third which leads directly into the fourth, with its parallel effect of brilliant climax and similar disintegration. The short first movement and much more expansive second are matched by the even shorter third movement and even more expansive finale. The durations of the two halves are the same: indeed, in the performance in May 1979 by the BBC Symphony Orchestra under Sir Charles Mackerras, there were only five seconds in it. This two-part structure appears in several of Brian's early symphonies, most notably of course in *The Gothic*; but he seems to have abandoned it in his later symphonies.

The symphony is written for a large orchestra including quadruple woodwind, four trumpets, four trombones including parts for bass and contrabass, two bass tubas, and a number of horns which ranges from six in the first two movements to 16 in the scherzo. The final two movements also require two pianos and organ. There is a large array of percussion, with parts for three timpanists, and 1-3 side-drums (from Symphony No. 6 onwards Brian invariably specified three side-drums, to be played *sempre a 3*, and later suggested that this should also apply to his earlier works).

The opening of the symphony is dramatic. Against a *pianissimo* timpani roll on a bare 5th chord, the lower strings, *pizzicato*, play a slow chromatic theme consisting of a 3-note motif (ex. 1 a), and a number of further motifs which are clearly derived from it. The motif and its metamorphoses are very important: they will eventually dominate the finale; and before then they reappear more than once in different guises. The motif spans a tritone; this interval is destined to play an increasingly important part as the symphony progresses.

Ex. 1

Adagio solenne

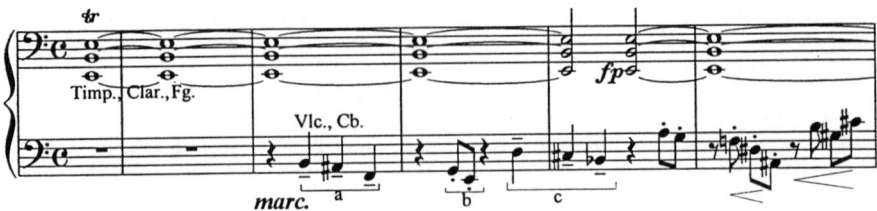

Each of the two main subjects has three themes. The first is highly chromatic and lacks a definite key centre, beginning in what appears to be A minor, but contradicted by the bass instruments in something like a Dorian F♯ minor. The theme itself is in 3rds, rapid and impassioned, and in a way reminiscent of the later Elgar.

Ex. 2

The brief second theme on woodwind merges into the third, a chromatically-inclined canon at the 5th, with each repeat of the motif raised by a semitone, so that the imitation actually sounds at the tritone.

Ex. 3

After a brief but fierce climax the sound abruptly collapses (a gesture typical of the composer) into the second subject, which begins with a theme on strings that is even more redolent of Elgar.

Ex. 4

However, its elaborated repetition, varied and with contrapuntal accompaniment, is nearer to the world of Mahler's Ninth Symphony (there is no evidence as to whether Brian had heard Mahler's Ninth at this time, though he may well have seen the score). The second and third themes have a yearning quality that suggests the Romanticism of early Schoenberg. However, this does not dominate for long. A strange rustling on strings, *con sordini*, and slow-moving woodwind chords (ex. 5) carry us into the development.

Ex. 5

The development itself is short and very complex, mainly contrapuntal, with the themes greatly metamorphosed and the contrapuntal lines in several keys at once. But at bar 143 the sound abruptly fades to nothing, as when a radio is switched off, and we hear, in a dreamlike state, the notes of the introductory theme on flute, oboe, glockenspiel and harp, while the violas play a languishing chromatically descending motif, and quietly stalking arpeggios in strange tonalities are heard from cellos and basses.

Ex. 6

It is as if the unconscious were suddenly exposed. Episodes of this type occur often in Brian's symphonies, where the external clangour suddenly disappears and the mood turns, as it were, to one of inner contemplation. Here, in the shadows, we hear ex. 1, quiet but firm, with a hint of menace. It is still there, and will return.

Just as suddenly, we are plunged back into the development, this time of the second subject group. The recapitulation, when it comes, seems fairly orthodox, though the themes are presented in rich new orchestrations that are entirely Brian's own. But at the conclusion of the final theme comes, not the expected coda, but a passionate outburst (ex. 7) in which the first two motifs of ex. 1, the second modified by a passing-note, ring out *fortissimo*, like the sudden materializing of some dark power. As the sound fades, the bass instruments mutter a widely-spaced mutation of ex. 1 a, and the movement closes with a sombre reiteration of the opening timpani chord.

Ex. 7

In this first movement the themes are orthodox enough: even the first, passionate theme, with its wide span and violins in 3rds, belongs to a world not far from that of Elgar's Second Symphony; and the orchestration of the exposition is fairly traditional, though Brian produces some interesting timbres - for example the pairing of muted cellos and clarinet at the octave at bar 108, ushering in the mutterings on strings (ex. 5) that grow and erupt into the development. The texture of the development is far from orthodox, however, abounding in a highly individual kind of polytonal counterpoint that Brian made his own. The eerie effect of the "other-world" episode in the development is achieved largely by the unusual timbre of the instrumental combination, with its stealthy bass accompaniment. And when the recapitulation arrives, its orchestration is entirely novel: it has, so to speak, been Brian-ized. For the most part the brass body carries the burden, seen strikingly in the score between bar 212 and 220. In this section, not only are trumpets, horns and tenor trombones carrying the burden, but the bass trombones and the tubas each have powerful counterthemes (ex. 8). This type of orchestration was to become one of the hallmarks of Brian's instrumental style, as was his use of timpani as a melody instrument (a practice he had adopted earlier in *The Gothic* and in his comic opera *The Tigers*).

Ex. 8

The second movement follows immediately. Its structure is one of continous development by thematic metamorphosis, with the introduction of new and contrasting material at two points. The movement could, very loosely, be described as being in the form A-B-A'-C-A"-coda. However, the steady metamorphosis of the initial theme means that it is never actually repeated: only the atmosphere of the theme is present. The theme itself (ex. 9), on solo cor anglais, is first cousin to the flute theme which opens Debussy's *Gigues*.

Ex. 9
Andante sostenuto e molto espressivo

Indeed, Brian's approach to structure in this movement is similar to that of Debussy's: growth from within, by continuous thematic development and metamorphosis. Other composers such as Strauss and Schoenberg also used this approach, and no doubt influenced him in this respect, though Brian's orchestral textures are in a different world from those of any of these. The theme is repeated on oboe, accompanied by a doleful chromatic counterpoint on second oboe, two cors anglais, two clarinets, two bass clarinets and muted cellos and violas *divisi*, an extraordinary and haunting sound. The atmosphere of this theme never leaves the music, though it is never heard again in the same form. Sometimes the intervals are changed; sometimes only the rhythm remains; sometimes even this is distorted. The theme appears in many guises: as a canon at varied intervals from bar 301 (ex. 10); as a powerful melody in the cellos from bar 320; and, greatly transformed, in the string accompaniment from bar 335. It makes its final appearance, fragmented but still recognizable, in the disintegration which occurs from bar 420 to the end of the movement; and its elements are present in the final valediction in the strings.

Ex. 10

There are many original strokes in this movement, both thematic, harmonic and textural. One example is the interruption of the steady progress of the metamorphosis of ex. 9, at bar 295, by a heavy-footed processional on upper woodwind, stopped horns and timpani in what is clearly a foretaste of the mood of the funeral march that forms the finale.

Ex. 11

This is swept away after only two bars, but it has made its ominous mark, like the sudden appearance and disappearance of a spectre. The first main episode breaks in at bar 314. It is a violent chromatic outburst, with thick chords in parallel movement (ex. 12) marked "Sempre Pesante Possib[i]le (Each note hard and heavy)".

Ex. 12

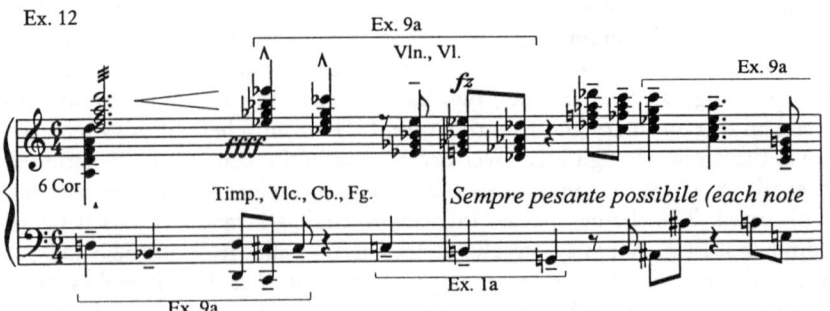

fz
hard and heavy)
etc.

But despite the change in melodic line, rhythm, speed, texture and dynamics, the spirit of ex. 9 is still palpably present. This mysterious ability to retain thematic unity throughout such thoroughgoing transformations of the material was something Brian possessed to a remarkable degree. Another interpolated episode occurs at bar 353, a jagged chordal theme on all the bass instruments.

Ex. 13

Ex. 7a inverted

On examination this turns out to contain none other than ex. 7 a in inversion: the introductory motifs from the first movement have once again emerged from the shadows, this time in disguise. (As the second movement of the symphony was composed before the first, I may be wrong about this. Nevertheless the resemblance is strong enough to seem more than coincidental.) As before, the episode ends abruptly, and a further development, marked *ppp teneramente* follows at bar 356. Cellos and basses play a wide-ranging melody to a glittering accompaniment of celesta and flutter-tongue flutes and harp arpeggios. There is another reminder of ex. 1 (bearing in mind the above proviso concerning the order of composition of the movements), but the tranquil mood continues; and though there is yet another interpolation by the brass, this time of ex. 9 a in thick harmony, the mood is set. A cadenza-like passage for solo violin ushers in a langorous, chromatically-falling motif (ex. 14 a) in the tenor instruments, surrounded by an evocative, shimmering accompaniment which dominates the remainder of the movement. From bar 404 the motif appears against a background of downward-rushing arpeggios from harps and woodwinds. Now the music begins to die away and disintegrate. The cor anglais dolefully picks up the fragments of its theme, and the strings (*divisi*) consign the movement regretfully to oblivion.

Ex. 14

The third movement is the so-called "Battle" scherzo. However, in spite of its literary origins the movement seems to suggest a wild whirling dance rather than a battle. It requires four groups of four horns each, playing concertante, and in addition two pianos and organ (mainly pedals). This powerful *moto perpetuo* in 6/8 time is the very apotheosis of the ostinato.

Basically the plan of the movement is simple. The horn groups play in antiphony, each group having its own spatial position, motivic material and timbre at the outset. The interplay between the groups becomes more complex, and more and more ostinati are added to the accompaniment. The music works up to a final climax, then draws to a close.

The movement begins quietly with repetitive figures on harps, which are joined by muted violas and violins playing the first of the ostinato figures:

Ex. 15

Next the two pianos enter, playing bare chords of ambiguous tonality in parallel movement in trochaic rhythm; then come the three timpanists. The first group of horns, in the distance, announce their long repetitive theme which is in a tetratonic scale that could belong to C major or C minor - or perhaps to neither?

Ex. 16

In contrast, the timpani ostinato seems to be in D minor - but again we cannot be sure, for there are notes missing. The first horn theme is answered by a snarling echo from the second group, stopped, with a "theme" restricted to two notes. The third group enters, closer, with its theme an ostinato figure; and the fourth group also has an ostinato figure which, however, moves up a semitone at each repetition. The first-group theme is treated in canon, and new ostinati are added. The antiphonal horn parts become steadily more virtuosic, and further ostinati enter in new tonalities and rhythms, until the accompaniment is both heterophonic and heterorhythmic, a veritable hell's kitchen in music. The frenzied dance mounts in tension until it reaches a veritable climax: four massive chords from the full brass and organ are answered by four hammer-blows from pianos, woodwind and *pizzicato* strings. The music subsides as if exhausted at last. A solo horn bids farewell to ex. 16, and on a strange, plangent chord from the woodwind the movement ends.

This is highly original music. Unique it certainly is (though there is a clear precedent in the "scherzo" of *The Gothic*) in the respect that no other extant symphonic movement contains so obsessive a use of ostinato. Thematic interest is minimal: the interest lies in the polytonal and heterorhythmic effects of the concertante groups set against simultaneous ostinati of different types. The rhythmic tension can be seen in almost any bar from the score, for example in bar 608, where we have the simultaneous rhythms:

Ex. 17

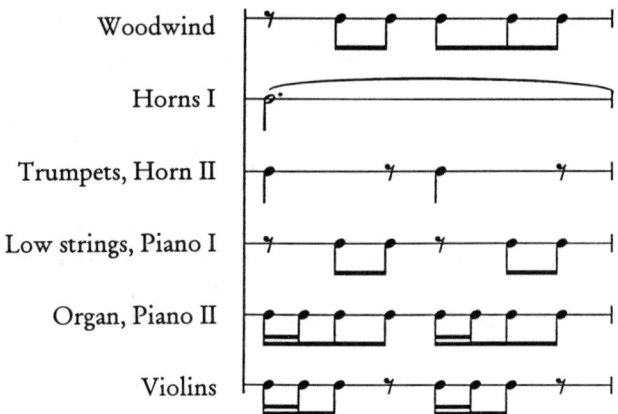

Notice that Brian achieves all his effects within the 6/8 tempo: there are no 2-against-3 or similar polyrhythms.

The tension in this movement is not only rhythmic. It is largely generated by the pull between different tonalities, both successive and simultaneous. At the very beginning we have an ambiguous C major in the horn theme against an ambiguous D minor in the accompaniment (though, as we shall see, it is wise to be cautious about accepting anything in this music at its face value). As further ostinati enter, each with its own tonal centre, the music becomes more firmly bitonal, then polytonal: at the height of the movement there are so many independent ostinati that the music becomes truly heterophonic, and we can choose to listen to any of the ostinato lines (or rhythms) and hear it independently of the others. Listening thus becomes a matter of active choice: one can *deliberately* hear the work differently on different occasions.

If the scales used by the horns are oddly restricted, those used in the orchestral ostinati are odd in a different way. They are, it is true, diatonic scales (almost everything in the scherzo is diatonic): the climactic ostinato which enters at bar 587 (ex. 18) is simply the scales of F and A♭ juxtaposed:

Ex. 18

To the ear, though, it sounds like some strange new scale. The figure is set against ex. 16 played in canon at the unison by the first two groups of horns; and while these remain stubbornly in the same tonality the ostinato motifs swing wildly from one tonality to another. And just as Brian can achieve what seem to be complex polyrhythmic effects without leaving the strict 6/8 framework, so he produces what appear to be equally complex polytonal effects wholly within the limits of the diatonic, and indeed often pentatonic, scale. At the climax of the movement the four shattering chords, marked $ff<$, consist simply of D♭ major on the trumpets and F minor on the trombones and tubas, both reinforced by the organ. This bitonal chord is contradicted four times by a D major chord on woodwind, pianos and *pizzicato* strings, marked *fff*. As the music subsides it moves to a kind of pentatonic C tonality, and at last seems to agree with the solo horn as it sounds ex. 16, far away, for the last time. But Brian still has a trick up his sleeve: the last note of the horn solo is not C but D. At last we perceive what the tonality of ex. 16 really is: it is the Dorian mode on D. So we see that at the beginning there was no clash of keys between horns and timpani: the D minor Dorian and the C major scale use the same notes. If we now think of ex. 16 as a Dorian D-centred tonality, the rationale of the opening bars becomes clear.

Brian had made use of modes in the *Gothic* Symphony, and was to do so many times more; but his use of modes is neither that of Bartók and the European composers in the folk idiom, nor the bucolic pentatonicism of the early symphonies of Vaughan Williams. It harks back to early English music, to Tallis and before, when modes as well as hexatonic and pentatonic scales were part of the standard musical language, and when melodic lines for the different voices were written "horizontally", without regard for the "vertical" sound; and the listener received no sense of discord because the voice lines were heard as separate (though simultaneous) entities. Only with the coming of the Baroque era did the "vertical" element become important, so that such things as consecutive 5ths became musical solecisms. It is to the older tradition that Brian looks in his approach to tonality and counterpoint.

There is one last surprise to come. The final chord is spelt out from the top downwards by oboes, cors anglais, clarinets and bassoons; and a strange chord it is:

Ex. 19

Not a bitonal chord, and not a note-cluster, this chord is indescribable in formal terms; and its sound is strange indeed, almost mocking. A bare 5th flicker from the violins; and as the strange sound fades, the final movement begins.

The first impression of this movement is of a vast time-scale (it actually should last about 17 minutes), a broad sweep of vision and an intensity of emotion that at times borders on the apocalyptic. Although, as already noted, this movement has some of the appearances of formal construction, with episodes and returning thematic material which give it some of the character of a Mahler sonata-rondo, this is a very general and somewhat misleading description. It is a strongly unified movement, though much of its thematic material is plainly drawn from other movements, particularly the first. Although there are numerous changes in tempo and rhythm, the overall impression is of a gigantic funeral march, complete with appropriate triplet figures and other motivic material which proclaim its kinship with its distinguished predecessors in the

Eroica Symphony and *Götterdämmerung*. One should, of course, beware of attaching too much literal meaning to the thematic material, and of talking glibly of "nobility" or "grief". Equally, though, one need not go to the other extreme and assert, as did Stravinsky, that music is essentially powerless to express anything. It seems to me that since this music is clearly "about" death (in much the same way as is the finale of Mahler's Sixth Symphony), it serves no useful purpose to deliberately ignore the fact.

The opening phrase (ex. 20) occurs a great many times during the movement. The ascending scale which forms its second part is sometimes a simple major scale and sometimes minor, and occasionally a kind of quasi-diatonic scale that is neither, as for example in bar 721 (ex. 20 a). It presents us with something of an enigma. It appears before each new episode, but it appears in many other places too. MacDonald suggests that it is a punctuation mark and also a heightener of tension; but for either purpose the phrase seems curiously unsatisfactory. Its banality contrasts oddly with the nobility of the music it so frequently interrupts. But perhaps that is the effect the composer had in mind: he was capable of being an "awkward cuss" in his music just as in his life. Be that as it may, the frequent repetition of this fussy little phrase serves not so much to increase tension as to provoke irritation. It seems to have been one of Brian's rare miscalculations.

Ex. 20

The opening bars of the funeral march

Ex. 21

are almost exactly the same as ex. 7, and are clearly derived from ex. 1. The theme is first played on clarinets, to a bleak accompaniment in bare 5ths by harp and *pizzicato* strings. The theme ends with a series of falling tritones, and a solo horn adds a codetta (ex. 22) like a sad reminiscence of ex. 15 a of the scherzo, in funeral march rhythm.

Ex. 22

A new theme in the brass is cut off by ex. 20, and an upward-striving variant of ex. 21 leads to the *Götterdämmerung* passage, where reiterated chords, *fortissimo* alternate with ex. 20. At bar 726 an episode marked *grandioso* breaks in: it is none other than ex. 7 transformed, combined with inversions and imitations, and with a glittering semiquaver accompaniment on flutes, cors anglais and strings *divisi*.

Ex. 23

These four bars are another example of the astonishing orchestral effects Brian was capable of creating. The funeral march continues with ex. 21 again metamorphosed, leading into a new episode. On cellos and basses, divided into no fewer than seven voices, arises a grave and beautiful elegy that is utterly English in character. This noble passage looks back to Elgar, and at the same time forwards to Tippett. The violas join in, then the violins, and with exultant upward runs marked *con passione* lead to a further climax - but we hear once again the ominous ex. 7, this time framed in steely glitterings which turn downwards to despair. The final section continues the metamorphosis of ex. 21, with further climaxes. At bar 837 the final climax begins *pianissimo* with *tremolandi sul ponticello* on strings, closely harmonized brass chords and echoing

Ex. 24

horn calls. Three times the *Götterdämmerung* motif is hammered out by the full orchestra; then at bar 844 ex. 23 espisodes like the dazzling setpiece that culminates a firework display, in the most scintillating orchestration yet. But the most lavish of setpieces must burn out, leaving only empty shells. The music begins to disintegrate. The themes break into fragments, caught by small groups of instruments. The clarinet's tritonal descent is heard again, and quietly turned into a perfect 5th by the lower strings; and as they mutter ex. 20 for the last time the few remaining instruments, including timpani, confirm the bare 5th E minor with which the symphony began.

What does the score tell us of Brian the symphonist at this point in his life? As with other composers who have extended an existing tradition, Brian had, like Newton, stood on the shoulders of giants. In Brian's case the giants were the composers in the late 19th century Romantic tradition such as Elgar and Richard Strauss: echoes of these, as well as Wagner and Mahler, can clearly be heard in the themes of the Second Symphony. But as we have seen, his roots go back much farther in time, to the contrapuntal lines and the modes of Tallis and his predecessors. At the same time his treatment of symphonic form is already breaking with tradition, looking for a unity through thematic development rather than formal structure based on classical symphonic forms. He was well aware of the new music, of the innovations of Debussy, Bartók, Schoenberg and Stravinsky, and he knew and admired their music, as is clear from his own writings. But, looking at this comparatively early symphony, it is equally clear that Brian's individualism, and his extraordinary musical imagination, left little room for adopting other composers' methods, however admirable they might be. He had too much to say himself, in his own musical language. Showing as it does its Romantic origins, this symphony often looks back over its shoulder; but it also looks forward, in a highly original way. It shows us how a formal sonata movement can be transformed without losing its essential nature - as Bartók and Hindemith were also showing, in their own way. It shows how counterpoint can be extended in concept to become so free and independent as to be truly heterophonic, without losing its basic musicality - as Ives and Schoenberg were showing, also in their own way. It shows us the path Brian was following towards new ways of treating diatonicism, in which even a scale of C major can be made to sound strange and disturbing, as Sibelius and Vaughan Williams were also doing in their rather more traditional way; and it goes further, showing us that new and exciting music can be written with scales that are not merely diatonic but restricted to a few notes. It shows how a knowledge of the effects of mixing different timbres and pitches, combined with an extraordinary ability to construct an edifice of sound in the head and write it down with precision, can enable a composer to widen the limits of timbre and texture in orchestral music to an unprecedented extent. It shows, too, that it is possible to write funeral music that is utterly English, containing no concessions to Teutonic idiom, yet of a grandeur that fits it to stand alongside that of the German masters. But, perhaps most important of all, it shows that a composer of sufficient talent and doggedness can thumb his nose at the rest of the musical world and write a symphony of genius without any expectation of public performance. That the music was, indeed, not performed until 41 years after its composition was our loss, not Brian's.

Before beginning work on his Second Symphony Brian had been reading Goethe's play *Götz von Berlichingen*, and had been much impressed by it. He intended to model the four movements respectively on Götz's ambitions, loves, battles and death. After the symphony was completed, however, he denied that it was in any sense programmatic, and later discounted its literary origins entirely. At the time I was preparing my study of the Second Symphony. I was not well acquainted with the play which inspired the symphony, and felt - as I still do - that a symphony should stand or fall in terms of music alone. However, I have recently had the opportunity to study *Götz von Berlichingen* to some depth, both in the original and in the excellent translation by Charles Passage, and it now seems to me to be worthwhile looking for any light the character of Götz can throw on the symphony, particularly the problematical final movement.

In contrast to the real Götz, an archetypal robber-baron who, after a lifetime of pillage, died peacefully in his bed, Goethe's depiction of him (drawn from Goethe's imagination and Götz's own memoirs) is something like a conflation of Sir Lancelot and Robin Hood. In the play, Götz's ambition is to overthrow the corrupt princelings and clergy and to re-establish the rule of law and justice, the barons to be directly responsible to the Emperor for keeping the land peaceful. There is, of course, no obvious attempt at a direct portrayal of this, though Götz's impetuous nature may be reflected in the first main group of themes (ex. 2). A very similar type of writing is to be found in the more boisterous sections of Elgar's *Falstaff*, a frankly programmatic work. Again, it is possible that the passionate outburst (ex. 7) near the end of the movement has something to do with Götz's rage and despair at the frustration of his noble aspirations, particularly in view of the way it reappears in subsequent movements.

The connections with the music of the second movement are more tenuous. As Götz (in the play) is a happily married man, the term "loves" must imply, in addition to his wife, his sister Maria, his two closest friends Selbitz and Sickingen, his squire Georg, and the false friend Weislingen. Perhaps the glittering climax (ex. 14) has something to do with Götz's elation at the loyalty of Sickingen, who, when Götz is on trial before the corrupt Imperial Councillors, marches in with his forces and rescues him; but the lonely atmosphere which characterizes the opening theme, and is never far away, perhaps symbolizes Götz's certainty that sooner or later all these passionate friendships will be lost to him. Indeed, by the end of the play all of his dearest friends are either imprisoned or dead; his world is disintegrating, and the news of the death of Georg finally kills him. The desolate end of the movement may well be connected with this.

There are several battles in the play, the most dramatically important being that in Act III, between Götz and the Imperial forces sent on Weislingen's instructions to capture him. In the many scenes that comprise this, Goethe (no doubt influenced by Shakespeare) switches us from place to place in rapid succession in a way that almost anticipates the editing techniques of action films. Likewise, in the music we switch rapidly between the four spatially-separated groups of horns, which are gradually brought together as the tumultuous climax approaches. On the other hand, apart from the use of horns themselves, there is in no sense any explicit musical battle (as, for example, there is in Strauss' *Ein Heldenleben*), rather a headlong whirling dance; indeed, in the play no fighting actually takes place on stage - just a whirl of scenes, some of which are of a few lines only.

In the play, Götz dies in captivity. The oppressed peasants have revolted, and in order to stop the looting and sacking that is going on, he agrees to take command of them. But he has been tricked; he is unable to control them, and is made the scapegoat for their crimes. The Emperor's troops are called out, and he is wounded and imprisoned for treason. Twice betrayed by his childhood friend, judged a traitor by the Emperor he has served all his life, this noble and generous knight dies of a broken heart. It seems to me that the two concepts of nobility and betrayal are the key to the thematic construction of the final movement of the symphony. The nobility is manifest in the funeral music; indeed, it twice becomes explicit with the quotation of the two *ff* chords from Siegfried's funeral music from *Götterdämmerung*: the "noblest hero of them all", too, was betrayed by a false friend, tricked into breaking an oath, and slaughtered for it. Betrayal is represented by the sinuous unison figure (ex. 20) which continually interrupts and mocks the noble music of the funeral. In the end, for both Götz and the symphony it is the betrayal that triumphs. Perhaps the clue to the whole outlook of the enigmatic finale is to be found in the two final lines of the play, spoken after Götz's death (and considerably more elegant in the original German) by Maria and Lerse respectively: "Noble man! Woe to the age that rejected you." "Woe to the posterity that fails to appreciate you!"

In spite of Brian's discounting of the literary origins of the symphony, I feel that the knowledge of the aspirations of the protagonist, and of their frustration, genuinely helps towards a full appreciation of this final movement, and helps to justify its waywardness when considered in purely musical terms. As "pure" music I still find the movement less than completely satisfactory. David J. Brown, in a private communication, disagrees, considering the movement's musical and dramatic content indissoluble, and goes on to point out that far from ex. 20's being a musically unsatisfactory phrase, it was precisely what was required from a structural point of view. Also, Brian even made musical capital out of this sinuous motif by never repeating it exactly. I cannot deny that Brian clearly knew precisely what he was doing. Indeed, I think that this symphony is fully the equal of Elgar's Second, which in so many ways it resembles; and I wish it could be recorded commercially with the questions of balance, and the sheer technical difficulty of playing the symphony right through in one take no longer a problem. How about that for a project, once we have got *The Tigers* under our belt?

Martyn Becker: Brian's Third Symphony[1]

What makes a great symphony great? If the answer to that was known, then it would be the most valuable commodity in the entire world of orchestral music, and we would be in the enviable position of having countless masterpieces to try to cram into concert programmes and record catalogues. That there *are* masterpieces to be heard by such composers who have that extra "something" is a testament to the indefinable quality that we call genius, and its comparative rarity makes it all the more valuable. Would we hold Mozart in such high esteem if the 18th century had produced scores (*sic*) of such comparably gifted men? No, of course not. "Genius" is not a word to be bandied about lightly, and we are fortunate that in the realm of British music we have our fair share, past and present.

It would be invidious to name names at this juncture, but as far as Havergal Brian is concerned, genius surfaces time and time again throughout his life's work, and at no time with greater intensity than with the creation of his Third Symphony. Indeed, it is instructive to view this work alongside another great epic symphony of the 1930s - the First of Sir William Walton, as the contrasts stand out starkly. Walton, with his perhaps more orthodox tonality, builds a grim, forbidding edifice which dissolves via heartrending melancholy into grand triumph. Brian, similar in format and length, couldn't be more different in device and treatment, giving us a sight of a mythical, never-never land where many nameless things flit across the vast scenic canvas that Brian paints. In the grim reality of the pre-War years, the reactions of these two hugely different composers to surrounding stimuli is nothing short of stunning.

Brian's Third occupies a special place in his oeuvre of 32 symphonies for several reasons. Because of its dimensions and layout it is easily approachable by

---

[1] From *Newsletter* 60 (VII-VIII 1985), pp. 4-5.

all who appreciate the symphonic diversities of many composers between the times of Schubert and Shostakovitch. The Third is tuneful in the Romantic sense to a degree rarely found in Brian's other symphonies. It is meticulously crafted in its overall design, and as Brian's longest symphony after *The Gothic* it has an aura of bigness which is very impressive on first encounter.

The word "Altarus", semi-erased on the cover page of the manuscript, has provoked much thought amongst various commentators. What significance the title had for Brian can only be guessed at, as reference books and encyclopaedias have no entries to help elucidate the matter. Indeed, the word appears to have no place in standard Latin grammar, three words coming close with only one letter different: ALTARIS - "from the high altar": ALTARUM - "from on high"; ALTURUS - "about to cherish". Whether or not Brian intended to use one of these but mis-spelt it is a matter for considerable speculation, as is "Altarus" being a mythological or astronomical name buried in the realms of obscurity. Whatever the source, it is likely to remain obscure unless further evidence comes to light.[2]

---

[2] David Yule writes in a letter to the Editor in *Newsletter* 70 (III-IV 1987), p. 2: "In *The Symphonies of Havergal Brian*, Vol. 3, Malcolm MacDonald points out that Altarus is the latin form of Altair - the name of the brightest star in the constellation Aquila. However, later in the volume he seems to have missed the possible significance of this. To quote p. 251: 'Although Symphony No. 3's suppressed title Altarus has proved to have an astronomical derivation, a double meaning might still be lurking in it, with the Alt-root suggesting height, 'reaching for the sky', the symphony progressing "per ardua ad astra".' I would suggest that the derivation of the title is not astronomical but mythological. Altair belongs to the constellation Aquila - in English, 'the eagle' - and as with most constellations there is an associated legend. In Greek mythology Aquila represents the eagle which carried the youth Ganymede from Earth up to Mount Olympus to become the cupbearer to Zeus. This progression from Earth to heaven would certainly agree with MacDonald's description of the symphony (on which incidentally, I must rely since I have never heard the work, nor can I read music), and considering Brian's interest in classical drama and the ancient Greeks I feel that this explanation must at least be a possibility." Christopher J. Kettle in his article Second thoughts on the Third Symphony, in *Newsletter* 78 (VII-VIII 1988), p. 7 goes still further and points to "the epigraph of Varèse's *Arcana* (a Brianically brief, dense and pugnacious work, and a title he might well have used - 'hidden things', 'mysteries'; alchemically, 'elixirs'). The quotation begins 'One star exists higher than all the rest', and ends - five stars later - 'Beside these there is still another star, imagination, which begets a new star and a new heaven'. This comes from Paracelsus' Hermetic *Astronomy* (one of Varèse's connections with Brian is his interest in these matters), and it intrigued me enough to look him up in Colin Wilson's book *The Occult*, where I learned much. This is not the space to expand on such things; but at the risk of distortion, here is a very edited version of Wilson's explanation of 'the inner core of truth in Paracelsus', which caught my attention: 'Again and again there is this insistence on the power of imagination ... Man is a small model of the universe, but seen as if in a mirror. Vast spaces stretch inside him - the 'inner firmament' - and he identifies imagination with this inner firmament. In a state of imaginative inspiration, these inner spaces seem to open up, giving rise to a sense of freedom, of other realities ... Imagination is the explosive flare that lights up the inner spaces, revealing meaning.' I mustn't labour this comparison, arrived at by accident; but it chimes closely with my own imaginative response to the slow movement as an opening-up of inner spaces, almost a kind of self-disclosure: a rare privilege, if so, for listeners to this enigmatic composer. The 'meaning' eventually revealed is sombre; but the quest for it is a uniquely beautiful and moving one. (As for Paracelsus himself - unconventional, prickly, obstinate, unfortunate, rejected by patrons, dying at exactly half Brian's age - he seems to have been

As a listener, it is not my intention to present a critical dissection of the music *per se*, or a series of signposts by which to follow the music, but rather a range of impressions left by listening to the only performance thus far of this monumental symphony. Regardless of what the title may have been meant to convey, there is a tremendous sense of powerful doggedness in this music, a great sense of purpose which can be felt directly from the outset. It is a symphony of many moods: of grim determination, struggle, joy, exhilaration and ultimate frustration during which the orchestra is asked to produce some daringly original sounds. The peculiar bleakness which is so often part of the tonal palette of so many English composers (Brian included) is absent from this work, and right from the word go throughout the first two movements, the originality of the orchestration cascading about our ears is almost bewildering in its brilliance.

The feeling of purpose with which the first movement begins is immediately impressive, and it is easy to be carried along by the stateliness of the thing without realizing what the underlying rhythm is doing. Woven into the gravity of the introduction by a Brian that I can only imagine with a smirk on his face at the time, is nothing short of a *habañera, à la* Bizet! Perhaps it is the very familiarity of this rhythm allied with the originality of the scoring that gives the feeling of "other worldliness" that is so integral to these first two movements. The music, as it progresses into the first movement, is highly evocative, and highly surprising at every turn. The concertante pianos impart a fantastic quality to the overall texture which constantly cause the little hairs on the back of one's neck to tingle with anticipation. Delicately scored sections are juxtaposed with martial music, and in one case with upward-swirling piano and string figurations that are simply dazzling in their effect. The whole structure is almost deliberately anti-Romantic; except that Brian slips in the occasional phrase that almost lifts you out of your seat. There are a couple of lush bars for strings just before the onset of the movement's development which almost echo any of the great Romantic masters.

Yet underlying all this fascinating music is a striving that gradually becomes more insistent until one is suddenly presented with a cadenza for the two pianos and the timpani which throws all that has gone before it into stark relief. Angular and jagged, the great piano chords thrust through the fabric of the movement like exposed ribs and remind us that maybe all is not as clear-cut as it may seem. The ascent to the movement's final climax crystallizes the striving into a sense of disquiet as the final chords pound out derivative of the *habañera* rhythm in the minor.

The second movement is the most pictorially evocative of the four, depicting a very weird pastoral scene indeed. The first thing we hear is the vague pottering of - what? It sounds elephantine, but that seems a little incongruous. Mammoth? Brontosaurus, even. The landscape still isn't "real" in a sense that we can recognize. Solo violin and woodwinds evoke images of insects and birds; the music ex-

---

something of a kindred spirit. He adopted his name for effect (as Brian did 'Havergal'); one of his real ones, Bombast, might be considered by some not inappropriate to Brian himself.)"

pands melodiously in a shimmer of tropical heat when suddenly a change in harmony and texture brings an invading chill borne in the rattlings of a xylophone. A subdued, ponderous march initiates in the bass instruments and soon begins to incorporate the tonal coloration of the string and woodwind flutterings, allied to distant, fragmentary trumpet fanfares. The potterings continue in the bass and all the while the sense of unrest is still there, though not so overtly as previously. The movement climaxes in a full-throated pseudo-Romantic haze reminiscent of Part I of *The Gothic* before the music brings itself to a halt in much the same mood as it began. In a way, this movement has a sort of "day in the life" feel about it, as if we're on the outside looking in on a scenario that it is impossible to alter: a dream that one can't influence in any way. It must run its course in its own way, in its own time. The music here is unmistakably English, and unerringly, poignantly beautiful.

Brian, as was his wont so often, has lulled us into a sense of false security and expectancy. All the disquiet that the music has engendered up to now is swept aside by a quicksilver scherzo that is as robustly English as anything that Elgar put into a *Pomp and Circumstance* March. The concertante pianos, an essential tone-colouring up to this point, are now silent, and the orchestration for the initial exposition slightly reduced. The good-natured bustle that one encounters here is hardly characteristic of the mature Brian of the later symphonies; indeed, some of the woodwind writing is reminiscent of *The Tigers* in the feel of its harmony, and its almost comic, fantastic quality is characteristic of the opera itself: or at least it is until we come across the trio. From a most unorthodox man writing a most unorthodox, powerful work, one realizes that here is a classic scherzo-and-trio in the mould of Schubert or Bruckner: one of the last things we expect from Brian! From the scherzo's ebullient, carefree soundworld we are dropped into the half-light of what for all the world could be a backstreet club in the depths of murky Vienna: dinginess and unease; maybe the haze of cigar smoke. This very evocative music brings to mind the *Rosenkavalier* waltzes of Richard Strauss, or perhaps the subtle harmonic shifting of Franz Schmidt, and the delicacy with which it is scored is an absolute delight to the ear. We realize that Brian has done it again. In the first two movements we were being so fascinated with the masterly use of all the orchestral colour that the underlying unease crept up almost unnoticed, like a viper in the grass. Now Brian, having elevated the spirits in a different direction with the robust Englishness of the scherzo's march, slips us into this honey-sweet waltz with barely a hiccup. The trio is capped finally with some of the drive and energy of the main scherzo's rhythm and percussion, and it becomes obvious how marvellous Brian's invention really is as waltz and march elements begin to mesh before the reprise of the scherzo proper. When it does reappear, it is with the full orchestra but still minus pianos. It is now a riot of sound and the end comes with much fanfaring and final chords that don't really end where one expects them to.

The Finale instantly returns us to graver matters. A mournful, dropping bass clarinet line gradually leads to an unfolding of a noble, almost elegiac tune which will reappear in various guises in the course of the movement as it develops towards the ultimate climactic pinnacle of the whole work. The finely-spun polyphony introduces a gradual climax, after which Brian makes us catch our breath yet again. Over a shimmering chord in the strings, a distant trumpet calls out a ghostly fanfare; time stands still and an answer is demanded. The shimmering chord rises a semitone, a solo horn echoes from a similar distance, and the effect is magical. Romantic allusions have flickered in and out of this symphony like wraiths, and this one, the most effective of all, betrays Brian's compositional roots in the late 19th and early 20th centuries. It doesn't last long though, and soon we are back in the mainstream of the music, an energetic development making it plain that the unsettled tension of the earlier movements is still there, and waiting to make itself felt. The pianos glitter in the orchestration like jewels, and their presence heightens the feeling of expectancy when restive figures in the bass instruments act as the tiny pebbles which, tumbling down a mountainside, cause the landslide which is the almost catastrophic climax to the movement, and the work. There is a feeling of inevitability about the progression to the climax: the tension in the music dictates that it must come; that it must break free, like a great whale smashing through the surface of the sea. There is more than a trace of that imagery present, for when the organ-augmented final bars do come, they are crushing, decisive, and sweep away all that has gone before peremptorily, but there is no victory, or even resolution. As the frustrated tumult dies, there is the image of a shackled leviathan silenced - for the moment.

It is a matter for great sadness that there is no performing tradition associated with any of Havergal Brian's works: indeed, this great symphony and many others have been performed only once. It is surely one of the injustices of the 20th century that Brian's Third has not only not become a concert repertoire item, but indeed had to wait for over 40 years for a first performance, and we must be grateful that Stanley Pope conducted that performance in 1974. Valuable though it is, though, it has faults: given that Brian's multi-divided textures are very difficult to bring off, and rehearsal times are notoriously short, ensemble is untidy, noticeably so in the first movement. Perhaps lack of rehearsal time would have accounted for this, but not for the scrappy playing in parts of the scherzo. This may not be totally the players' fault - the music is very tricky here, and Pope takes the scherzo too fast for comfort, robbing the music of a sense of swagger; of fun. In the Finale, too, there is a moment in one of the build-up passages before the great climax where the horns swoop in a great tuneful arch over a rhythmic pulse in the rest of the orchestra; but Pope doesn't induce the New Philharmonia horns to sing out as they should. There are many fine moments to balance these out, though, not least the ending which is truly magnificent.

How this work has submerged again after its solitary performance defeats the imagination. There is invention in it to rival the best that Elgar could offer in his two symphonies, and worthy to stand alongside those of Vaughan Williams. Walton's First has a fitting partner here in the representation of the best of Thirties' British symphonism, and we can only hope that Brian's Third is rediscovered, and performed regularly to the acclaim with which it deserves to be greeted.

Martin O'Leary: Havergal Brian's *Sinfonia Tragica*[1]

Symphony or Operatic Prelude?

Havergal Brian wrote his Sixth Symphony, subtitled *Sinfonia Tragica*, in January and February of 1948, at the age of 72. It was the first work he had written in over three years, since he had completed a setting of Parts I and II of Shelley's *Prometheus Unbound*, lasting around four hours, which he considered a crowning achievement of his creative life. Work on that mammoth composition had gone on for seven years, and while it is true that Brian would have needed a long rest after finishing it, he also seems to have felt that he would write nothing more. *Prometheus* certainly constitutes a major punctuation point in his output, just as the twin opposites of the *Gothic* Symphony and the opera *The Tigers* had done almost 30 years earlier. The return of his creative powers came as a surprise to him ("a very strange circumstance", as he wrote to the conductor Eric Warr), and he worked on two pieces simultaneously, both very different from each other, although both inspired by plays by John Millington Synge. As well as the *Sinfonia Tragica*, Brian was sketching at the time a Comedy Overture on Synge's *The Tinker's Wedding*. The *Tragica* was originally intended to form an Operatic Prelude to a setting of *Deirdre of the Sorrows*, but when Brian applied for permission to set the then copyright text, he was refused, at the request of the Arts Council of Great Britain, who had commissioned an opera on that very subject from the Musical Director of Covent Garden, Karl Rankl.[2]

The refusal of permission to set *Deirdre* must have come as a cruel blow to Brian; especially so considering his own view that the best of his music was to be found in his operas, rather than his symphonies; but, undaunted, he finished the *Sinfonia* and, when re-numbering his symphonies in the 1960s, added the *Tragica* to the canon as No. 6. (An early *Fantastic Symphony* had been broken down into individual pieces, and *The Gothic*, formerly No. 2, became No. 1, and so on.) The decision to include it as a symphony raises the interesting question of what Brian considered a symphony (and what he didn't). There are two other works, neither of them registered as symphonies, but produced at a time when his output consisted largely of works in the genre, which may illuminate his thoughts on this matter. Between his Eleventh Symphony and the opera *Faust*, Brian wrote a piece titled *A Song of Sorrow*, which he described as a symphonic poem. However, he wrote to Robert Simpson about it in 1962, and after a reference to the as-yet unnumbered *Sinfonia Tragica*, he mentioned the *Song of Sorrow*, describing

---

[1] This edited reprint of Martin O'Leary's Master's thesis was first published in *Newsletters* 82 (III-IV 1989), pp. 4-6, 83 (V-VI 1989), pp. 6-9, 84 (VII-VIII 1989), pp. 5-6, 88 (III-IV 1990), pp. 5-8 and 91 (IX-X 1990), pp. 4-7. The extensive analyses of bars 1-15 and 132-159 have been omitted.

[2] Editorial note: Another work on the same subject and with the same fate was written, in 1926-7, by Rutland Boughton. First planned as a ballet, it was later transformed into his Symphony No. 2.

it as another symphony without a number. In 1970, he wrote to Graham Hatton of Musica Viva, who were preparing facsimile editions of some of the scores, that he now preferred the title *Elegy* for what he called "that movement". Since it was not added to the symphonic canon, he seems to have changed his mind about it being a "symphony without a number". If nothing else, this episode shows that Brian's conception of what constituted a symphony changed with time (and perhaps changed as the style of his own symphonies changed).

Brian described the *Song of Sorrow* or *Elegy* as a symphonic poem, although no programme is provided. The title fits, however, if one considers that the finished work is both symphonic and poetic; it is not a tone-poem, which would imply a more literal depiction of programmatic events, but rather a poem written in symphonic language. The title points to the emotional content of the music, and in particular the opening melody, which returns before the coda, framing and defining the music that takes place in between. The work is in six sections, and is a succession of events without dramatic interpenetration, but motivically united by a consistent use of major and minor 3rds to form melodic and thematic ideas. One element crucial to Brian's most typical symphonic manner is entirely absent from this work: juxtaposition of disparate strands of the musical argument does not take place, although one section may stop abruptly to be succeeded by another. As a result of this, the sections retain a greater degree of independence than is the case with the *Tragica*, and it may be for this reason that Brian decided against including the work as one of his numbered symphonies. The music is slow at crucial points, namely the beginning, middle and end, and although the quicker, louder music makes its impact, the balance leans towards a slower, calmer style, lending the work a certain stillness. The quicker sections, therefore, are not so much developmental, as depictive of separate emotional states outside of the main concerns of the work, and they enlarge upon, rather than eat away at, the calm at the centre of the music. *Elegy* is more poetic, or contemplative, than dramatic or dynamic; for this reason too, perhaps, Brian decided on the subtitle "Symphonic Poem".

The second case where Brian chose a different title was for his Concerto for Orchestra, written between his 21st and 22nd Symphonies, two very different works, and just after his Cello Concerto. It is not without significance that Brian sketched and destroyed a "Symphonic Movement" just before beginning work on No. 22, which marks a new departure and great change of style from the preceding symphony. Again, the line between a "symphony" and a non-symphony seems to have occupied his thoughts. The Concerto certainly follows on from Symphonies Nos 18-21, and is no less closely argued than any of those works. It is, in fact, a good deal shorter than Symphony No. 21; both these works end in E♭ major, but the latter, in contrast to the former, is less firmly rooted in E♭ for much of its course. The Concerto is continuous, unlike the symphonies, there being two "transitions" of eight bars each, between the first section and the slower middle span, and between the latter and the short finale. The principle of a three-movement work in which the slow movement lasts longest is also apparent in No. 19, with which the Concerto also shares a skittish mood in the finale. The tautly argued first movement also shares a certain harshnass of tone with the first movement of No. 18.

The Concerto exhibits a tendency towards a concertino-like treatment of small instrumental groupings, and this is not found to the same extent in any of the symphonies of that time. It may well be that this slight shift in emphasis within the fabric of the work led Brian to decide on the title Concerto for Orchestra rather than Symphony. The music is just as closely argued otherwise, and therefore as "symphonic" as any of the preceding works, but the soloistic treatment of some instrumental colours (however brief) *does* represent a new departure in this work. Brian does not use the title as Bartók, Lutosławski, or Tippett have done, but rather more *à la* Petrassi or Hindemith. It is closer to a concerto grosso than to a display piece for full orchestra. On his own terms, the shift in emphasis justifies the change of title. The reasons for his choice of title as in the case of *Elegy* are not of primary importance; the incidents show, however, that the octogenarian composer was not writing for orchestra in a headlong manner and dubbing the finished work, whatever its shape, size, or form, a symphony. Despite the speed at which he was writing (22 symphonies between the ages of 80 and 92), he was careful in his choice of titles, and for him, the word "symphony" implied a certain type of musical work, and certain compositional principles. Just what those were should become clearer from a close examination of the Sixth Symphony and its construction.

Brian's symphonism

To counter any charge that Brian changed his mind with each new work as to what a symphony should be, there are overriding concerns in each symphony, which can be summarized here, and dealt with in more detail in relation to the particular case of Symphony No. 6. Those concerns are, in no particular order, since his emphasis is on a different aspect in diverse works:

(1) tight motivic argument;
(2) contrapuntal elaboration;
(3) the interchanging and superimposition of diatonicism (i.e. major and minor keys) with other types of harmony: whole-tone, intense chromaticism, parallel movement of chords, and modality;
(4) the use of harmonically ambiguous chords (i.e. with false relations or dissonant intervals) to sidestep harmonic tension;
(5) the complete avoidance of the "dominant" and the sharpened *leading-note* moving to tonic. Where there is a tonic (as in the scherzo of Symphony No. 3) it is approached in a variety of ways other than by the dominant;
(6) the bare 5th as a neutral consonance;
(7) discontinuity - abrupt stops and changes of direction, again to divert tension (therefore alleviating the tension temporarily but storing it up);

(8) giving his music a sense of spacing: off-stage trumpets in No. 6, 16 horns grouped in fours in No. 2, etc. - also by sudden changes of direction, dynamics and orchestration (finale section of No. 6);
(9) very little modulation.

Brian is a "harmonic" composer; not tonal, atonal, bitonal, modal, whole-tone, but a combination; his idiom utilizes major and minor chords as primary consonances, but it allows of harmonies that can defuse tension by having a lower level of dissonance than the preceding music, but still some tension so that the thread of the musical argument is sustained. Brian's strongest consonances are 3rds and 6ths; he also uses major 2nds, minor 7ths, and perfect 4ths and 5ths as consonances of a secondary nature, capable of temporarily defusing tension but not closing off a piece. His ending on a bare 5th is therefore, on his terms, an ambiguity, neither major nor minor: beyond both. His dissonances are the tritone, minor 2nds and major 7ths. The degree of dissonance depends to a large extent on the scoring and registral placing. One can see this clearly in the first chord of the Sixth Symphony (i.e. bar 10). This use of consonance and dissonance is a unifying factor in his music, which can, as a result, include many different harmonic configurations. The resultant danger of inconsistency can be averted by orchestration, dovetailing of harmonic areas, and clear voice-leading. The moments when this harmony is expressed vertically are few and far between, and therefore both striking and significant. Long stretches of his music are conceived contrapuntally, or as he would have termed it, "horizontally" (i.e. the line determines the vertical sound, rather than the other way round). Once an intervallic content is consistent, this is not a weakness, and, as shown below, Brian is as clear-headed in this area as he is in many others.

One can now suggest strong reasons for Brian's use of discontinuity: (1) his avoidance of modulation, and its general unsuitability for his style, given the cross-currents in it; (2) his liking for shifts of harmony (i.e. up or down a minor or major 2nd). These can become tedious and dangerously lower the tension, as the music would tend to divide into blocks, rather than accumulate a sense of direction or intensification. Abrupt stops, if judiciously used, can increase tension and accomplish these changes of harmonic orbit. The role of orchestration is important here; if the stops are orchestrated in a like manner their effect in the long run will be cumulative, and constructive, rather than destructive, adding to the work's sense of structure rather than taking from it. Brian's use of melody is also striking; his choice, and placing, of melodies is often masterly; for instance the terse and highly contrapuntal first movement of Symphony No. 22 culminates in a broad-spanned melody which represents both the culmination, and the most stable point of the movement. No. 6 centres on two different harmonizations of the same long melody: how they differ is of fundamental importance to the work and represents the still centre of the music, contrasting with the fragmentary and abrupt music which precedes and follows it. This contrast is central to the tensions of the symphony.

Contrast, then, whether of harmonic areas, orchestration, melody and motif, or dynamics, is a central concern in Brian's symphonism, which is natural and common to all symphonies, because without contrast one cannot have tension, or, for that matter, resolution. This contrast, in turn, results in, and necessitates, a sense of direction; one cannot endlessly change abruptly from one type of texture to another; there must be a building towards a culmination-point, as distinct from an ending. This overall sense of direction gives the work a sense of oneness, of unity; each element, each strand of argument, however divergent, is of necessity a contributing factor towards this unity. Unity achieved by the drawing together of contrasting types of music is central to Brian's conception of what a symphony should be.

Listening to the symphony: overview

Before a consideration of the individual sections of the *Sinfonia Tragica*, an overview of its shape is necessary to explain the subdivisions used later. Malcolm MacDonald treats the symphony as a three-part design, a judgement which I would support, albeit with two slight modifications, to be explained in due course. I would call each unit of the symphony (as discussed in sequence) a "section", not a movement for the reason that "movement" implies a greater degree of independence between parts of the work than is the case here. As will be stated later, there are significant factors at work in the sections of this piece, matters beyond the occurrence of themes from one section in a later one, which create the necessity for the work to be heard as a whole if its full impact is to assert itself. To clarify this distinction, one need only compare Brian's symphony with any Beethoven work in four movements, for example the Fourth Symphony. Each Beethoven movement is presented as a unit, and while the symphony should always be heard as a whole, there are four separate blocks, each of which concentrates on different strands of the musical argument, and each of which is clearly marked off from the others by a double bar-line. The effect is akin to that of chapters of a novel, or, if you will, single novels within a tetralogy.

Brian's Sixth Symphony, however, not only presents itself as complete from beginning to end, but each section is not as singular in its concentration on separate strands of the musical argument, with the possible exception of the opening which I regard as a Prologue, slightly distanced from the symphony's main events. The sections are clearly marked off by cadential gestures, but Brian does not allow the music to stop; each section is linked, either "attacca" or by a sustained note, to the next. To consider the symphony's build from another angle: just as it is, I believe, erroneous to speak of the *Tragica* as a three-movement work (but not a three-section work), it is equally so to regard it as a one-movement symphony. Again, I find fault with the term used: the *Tragica* is most certainly a single-*arch* symphony (in that it should be heard as the sum of its parts (or sections) for its full significance to emerge); it is hardly alone in that; virtually every symphony is viewed by its composer as an indivisible unit. One can recall Mahler's gall at having to settle for performances of the second movements of his Second and Third Symphonies as better than no performances at all, but doubtless these helped to generate a public which could then be led to digest the works as a whole, having had its appetite whetted. An exception to this indivisibility is the *Sea* Symphony of Vaughan Williams [or Holst's *First* Choral Symphony], where the composer states in the score that each movement *may* be performed separately, although this is rarely done in present-day performances.

Brian's Sixth Symphony, then, is an indivisible unit, but it is not a single-movement symphony. There are, indeed, very few so-called one-movement symphonies which do not subdivide into sections, whether those sections are interlinked or *attacca*. Sibelius' Seventh Symphony is a good example of this type of work, consisting as it does of dovetailings between sections to provide a continuous, and a continuously-changing, sound-world. Other single-span works, such as the Chamber Symphony No. 1 of Schoenberg, and the Fourth Symphony of Franz Schmidt, clearly subdivide into different movements. It is not without significance that both these works exhibit many tendencies towards a cyclic nature, and the lack of divisions between movements helps to ensure a continuity which complements the single-mindedness of their thematic workings. Brian's symphony falls somewhere between the two extremes represented by the Beethoven Fourth Symphony and Schoenberg's First Chamber Symphony; it cannot be subdivided in performance, as each section follows on from the previous one without a break, and yet these sections are, to a certain superficial degree, independent of one another. But since Brian's musical grammar is unusual enough, and disjointed in its initial effect, it is my opinion that a substantial break between, say, sections I and II of the *Tragica* would greatly weaken the work's unified aspect by imposing a period of relaxation on the listener. This has already been catered for in the music by the way the events of the work are presented.

To return to the division between sections I and II, the first is transparently easy to follow, and there is no need to pause before proceeding to the next stage of the musical argument. It also makes musical sense to go straight on because of the way the note E♭ is highlighted in the harp part, then excluded to maximize its re-entry at the very beginning of the next section; a substantial gap would cancel this clearly audible pitch-link between the two sections. One can contrast this need for continuity with Mahler's recommendations, in the cases of his Second and Third Symphonies, that there should be substantial breaks between the huge first movements and the succeeding ones (the second movement in each case is planned on a much more intimate scale, and Mahler rightly felt the first movements would dwarf their successors were there not a sufficient amount of breathing space between them). To give a further example, the fourth movement of Tchaikovsky's *Pathétique* should follow hard on the heels of the third movement's thundering March; the contrast is made all the more effective by its direct juxtaposition. Brian seems, in his Sixth Symphony, and in particular in the direct run into section II from section I, to have "written in" the gaps, so to speak. His use of spacing, both orchestral and temporal, is masterly, and bears comparison with the very different use of those features in "Summer Marches In", the first movement of Mahler's Third Symphony. The effect is rather cinematic; the "editing" complements, if not dictates, the pacing of the music.

Two further instances will suffice to illustrate Brian's technique of interchanging ideas without transition, which is what I mean by his "editing". The first case is that of the way the chords at bar 10 and bar 33 are preceded by rests; the music gets louder as the tuba's motive moves upwards registrally and contracts rhythmically, and after the rest, the chord is marked *fpp*, which in both cases represents, if not an anticlimax, certainly a very quickly deflated peak. The rest creates a sense of distance between the build-up to the chord and its presentation, and by distancing the two events, "edits" one from the other. The second case is the last section of the symphony, where, as will be discussed, there are rapid changes of pace, direction and timbre, to great cumulative effect; again, there is no transition and one gets the impression that the music, with its various march rhythms, is approaching from all sides. As a result of this lack of transition, music is often left hanging (the bare 5th at bar 92 is a case in point: even though the same notes resume, the extreme change in dynamics separates one very clearly from the other), only to be taken up again later, or approached from a different angle. It is this fragmentation which actually creates a stronger sense of unity between the sections than would at first appear to be the case, and this explains my reluctance to confer the title "movement" on each of those sections.

The ensuing discussion of the *Tragica*, then, divides the work up into the following sections:

(1) bars 1-56: section I: Prologue;
(2) bars 57-92: section II (a);
(3) bars 93-210: section II (b);
(4) bars 211-288: section III (a);
(5) bars 289-end: section III (b): Epilogue.

Section II is divided into two parts for the following reasons:
(a) the major break in texture across bars 92-93;
(b) between bars 93-210 there are no disruptions of the slow pace, as was the case between bars 57-92;
(c) bars 93-210 are centred on the two presentations of the long melody; this marks off the character of the music from bars 57-92.

Section III is divided into two for the following reasons:
(a) the music moves towards its final cadence from bar 289 to the end;
(b) the lightning changes and violence of the music from bars 211-288 are past, which is why I call the last section an "Epilogue".

Section I: Prologue: bars 1-56

There are three main factors which contribute to the unity of this section of the symphony, and mark it off as distinct from the rest of the work. The first is the frequency of semiquavers in the music; indeed, they contribute greatly to its sound-world and are rarely absent. The second factor is the way in which the music is organized, in that there are three chordal points in the section, each of which divides up the music into three compartments; the second chord is an expanded re-scoring of the first one, a semitone lower, whereas the last presentation hints at a triadic resolution of the harmonic tensions of the music, before returning to a more ambiguous harmony at bar 56. These three events stand out all the more clearly in relief from the predominant semiquaver motion preceding them. The third unifying factor is perhaps the strongest of all. Brian's treatment of the orchestra is very tightly organized; melodic lines are almost always given to low instruments (as in the tuba idea starting at bar 5), an exception being where the glockenspiel, at bars 36-37, and later at bars 40-43 with *pizzicato* first violins, plays a series of crotchets whose intent, indeed, is more the outlining of a scale than a "cantabile" melody. The strings play mostly semiquavers, the woodwinds and brass, chords, with a few departures. These associations help to present the musical materials as clearly as possible, and one could use Brian's terminology in describing their roles: the strings mostly "horizontal", the winds "vertical". Of note also is the contrast between the glockenspiel and harp, one well exploited by the composer in this section. The former is associated with strings (as well as flutes and piccolo at the beginning, and at bars 17-18 and 19-20, where the appearance of the woodwinds is on account of their sustaining ability, thus adorning the glockenspiel's percussive sound); the latter with woodwind and brass chords.

The music is narrative rather than dramatic, in that it is concerned with a sense of flow, a continuous onward movement, rather than being built as a series of juxtapositions of disparate textures creating conflict. The chords do not interrupt the semiquavers; rather, they are the outcome of the build-up (whether dynamic or registral) before their arrival. They are the three cumulative points of the section, but in this sense the music promises more than it delivers, in that the first two climaxes are quickly deflated (being marked *fpp*). The third chordal event is concerned less with climax than resolution but, as has been noted, it doesn't fully deliver on that level either. These are considerations which override the sectional divisions, and one can say that the true climaxes do not come until the first part of section III. Another element which suggests future events is the appearance, on two successive occasions, of a trumpet fanfare (marked "in the distance, remote" in the second copy of the full score), suggestive of a human element otherwise absent from section I of the symphony. The melodic or motivic content of this first section is certainly not "vocal"; in this sense, again with the exception of the associations suggested by the fanfares, this Prologue is instrumental music of great purity.

Despite this purity, or perhaps as a consequence of its coexistence with the fanfare, the music does "suggest" something; it is not "music about music", although if one disregards the military associations of the fanfare and considers it merely as an interesting rhythmic motive, it *can* be regarded as such. Because of the consistency of the scoring, and allied with the registral spacing of the music (the sparse opening, for example), there is a suggestion of atmosphere, a setting. It is a music suggestive of place rather than character, a consideration supported by the dynamic comings and goings. The associations of the trumpet fanfare, in the distance, add mystery to the atmosphere, and if one wishes, one can "interpret" the high octave As as piercing bird-calls, the timpani rolls as portents of a future storm, the harp arpeggios as ripples on the surface of a lake (caused by the rising wind, in semiquavers). Doubtless the music would suggest different associations to different listeners. To this listener, the spacing in the music (the rests before chords, the *crescendi* and *diminuendi*, and the fanfare, as well as the sheer distance between top and bottom at the beginning) is suggestive of geographic as well as temporal distance, and the cold landscape of the semiquaver-dominated music contrasts very strongly with the warmer, chordal sounds in which those "cold" passages culminate. What is important is that although the chords are the audible outcome of the preceeding music, the change in orchestral timbre is startling, and contributes greatly to the mysterious, atmospheric effect of the section.

Bearing in mind this sense of mystery in the music, it is of relevance that the symphony was originally conceived as an operatic prelude, although the question of how much of this music was written, or reshaped when the project fell through, is an unanswerable one. However, even though the work as it stands today does not rely on association with *Deirdre* for its full import to be felt, Brian did decide, once the copyright had been refused and he had written a self-sufficient orchestral work instead, to give the title *Sinfonia Tragica* to it. The result is that before the listener has heard a note of music, its general character (as opposed to the particular relevance of the music as an operatic prelude to the story and the predicament of Deirdre) is implicit in the title. Perhaps it is against this foreknowledge of imminent catastrophe that the shadows, contrasting colours and distances of what I have called the "Prologue" can be said to operate. Brian's Eighth Symphony, for example, could be called a "Tragic" work, although he chose not to attach a subtitle to that particular symphony, perhaps for the reason that its jarring juxtapositions and funereal opening mark it out very clearly, from the outset, as a tragic work. On the other hand, it is unlikely that one would correctly associate the Wagner Overture with the particular legend of the Flying Dutchman, although its stormy character is unmistakable, were one not told the title of the work before listening to it. Brian's use of the subtitle clearly plants a preconception in the listener's mind, and this, in combination with the fanfare, the long "vocal" melody which stands, on its two appearances, as the twin centre of the piece, and the battle sounds of the first part of section III, gives the work its character. It is a tragic work, but the tragedy is general, or universal, rather than particular or personal. The "imaginary landscape" of section I is impersonal, but not totally so (on account of the fanfare), and even though it hints at the violence to come, its singular character and atmosphere separate it from the main body of the symphony, and this justifies the appelation "Prologue".

Section II: part one: bars 57-92

This is music which is unified by its use of sharp contrasts. There are three upheavals in the section, each of which pushes the music to extremes, whether of register, dynamics or thematic intensification. The first occurs at bars 64-65, and in its extreme violence rids the music of all the flats and moves the harmonic plane over to the sharp side. Although it effects harmonic change, it is not transitional, but abrupt and dismissive. Its crudity makes the strongest possible contrast with the music on either side of it. The second and third upheavals are less abrupt, and are closely related to one another. The second, at bars 74-75, pushes the top and bottom register far apart and intensifies the rhythm of the preceeding music in both areas, accompanied by an increase in dynamics. It provokes the reappearance of material from the Prologue: firstly semiquavers plus high notes, leading to the return of the tuba motive at bar 84. The third upheaval stretches from bars 84-92 and is concerned with an intensified, two-part treatment of the tuba motive, at first a semitone apart (+ octave transposition), later in canon at the 4th. The canonic passage leads to a cadential opening out onto the perfect (and very bare) 5th, E-B, again pushing the dynamics and register to extremes, but augmenting the rhythm to prepare for the cadence. These three climaxes continue the thread from the first section (along with the thematic recurrence mentioned above) by leading the listener closer still to the climactic eruptions of section III, part one. The music just about stops short (at bar 92) of completely delivering what it has promised; the violence has come very clearly into focus, but has not (as yet) reached its peak. Brian doubtless pulled the reins back at this point because he considered it too soon for the work to reach its climax, and by introducing breathing-spaces, and thematic and emotional contrast and respite, succeeds in enlarging the expressive scope of the symphony and prevents it from sounding too compressed. He uses temporal spacing to increase the comprehensibility of the symphony, and by so doing allows the cumulative section III "battle" sequence to assume its maximum power.

The cor anglais melody which begins the section, being the first melodic idea presented by a woodwind instrument, introduces a new, more human expression to the symphony. Its repeated, tolling E♭s and the downward melodic turn at the end express sorrow, prompting one to make the connection, if one wishes, between this idea and Deirdre herself. The descending minor scale and the ensuing unisons for cor anglais and two flutes confirm this mood. The idea for cor anglais and two flutes is particularly expressive, using four notes and stepwise motion, with the exception of two upward leaps to B♭ (a perfect 5th the first time, a perfect 4th the second), as well as rests between the halting phrases, to enlarge upon the sorrowful mood presented at the opening of the section by the cor anglais. This simplicity of presentation is rudely interrupted by the first upheaval, after which the bass clarinet reprises the cor anglais idea, against a fanfare-like idea on solo french horn. This dual presentation represents a development of both ideas, in that the two parts remain distinct, despite their simultaneity. One can speculate that this "represents" the martial and the human in direct conflict, but what is important is that the perfect 4th on which it ends (and on which the cor anglais and two flutes lament had ended as well) leads to an intensified treatment of the cor anglais idea, eventually pushing the registers apart and culminating in the return of the "landscape" music of the Prologue. The music, by this time impersonal, becomes harsh with the semitonal clashes of the entries of the tuba motive from section I at bar 84. Of note at this point is the first entry of the three side-drums, further adding to the harsh tone of the music and providing another sound with military associations (again, one can, if one chooses, regard the side-drums' entry as an interesting addition purely in terms of timbre). The bare 5th at the end is very harshly scored and is an "open" sound on account of the registral disposition (mostly high and low, very little in between) and the fact that the highest note is the 5th (B) rather than the root (E).

This is music about themes, and about how those themes are developed; it is not suggestive of place, but rather of drama and of conflict. It is interesting to note how Brian's writing for percussion in this section affects the tone of his music. It has already been remarked how the entry of the side-drums affects the passage from bar 84 onwards; his use of the bass drum at the opening of the section is also noteworthy, its rumble underlining (and undermining) the sorrowful lament between bars 61 and 63 (where it stops after the first beat and thereby makes its absence strongly felt), before the thud at bar 64 sets off the upheaval that immediately follows at that point. That upheaval is made all the more violent by the presence of a cymbal clash at its climax, which is then allowed to reverberate. The cymbal also returns at bar 84 to enhance the semitonal clash implied in the entry of the oboes and trumpets at that point (and later at bar 86). To this listener, its subsequent absence until bar 92 (and that of the side-drums) is very effective, in that one expects it to come crashing in at the highpoint (a fact which ensures the passage cannot register as the true climax of the work). Indeed, it does not return until the beginning of the "Battle" section.

This section constitutes not so much a succession of events (which could be said of the first section) as a succession of juxtapositions, of a very violent nature (particularly the first upheaval). It is made all the more abrupt by the complete absence of transition. It is line which is more important than harmony (indeed, in one sequence - bars 70-75 - moving chords become moving parts), and this sense of line gives the music its strong sense of direction and onward movement. As a result of this single-mindedness and direct (not to say abrupt or crude) presentation, the music, in strong contrast to section I, does not have any sense of mystery; it is clearly music of conflict, and it creates the need for breathing space in the next section on account of its harsh, violent expression.

Section II: part two: bars 93-210

The music of this subsection is presented in a processional manner; it consists of a succession of distinct and distinctive units marked off from one another orchestrally, yet linked as a chain of related, though diverse, events by subtle connections of register, dynamics and general musical character. Although the music stands clearly as a succession of events, it is also developmental. Ideas (both musical and philosophical) from the earlier parts of the symphony are moved forward and presented in new guises, so that while the music may well be considered as an extended interlude from the tragic drama of both earlier and later parts of the work (thus the "breathing space" referred to above), it also develops the purely musical argument, albeit in a subtle and low-key manner. It begins by looking back, both in terms of pitch (starting with the bare 5th (E-B) which brought the last section to a halt), as well as musical character (a fanfare followed by bird-like calls on solo flute, which together with the spacing of the bare 5th evoke once again a sense of landscape, a sense similar to that evoked in the Prologue). This changes the tone of the symphony, moving away from the harshness of the preceding music towards the more impersonal mode of expression found at earlier points of the work (the Prologue in particular).

The slow march (or procession) which ensues presents two distinctive instrumental colours which look back to earlier events, as well as one which is to be a strong link in the chain uniting the various strands of this subsection. The use of three solo flutes ("unis but Solo" is the direction in the score at this point), as well as the melodic character, harks back to the two flutes and cor anglais idea in section II, part one (bars 61-63); to this listener, the absence of the cor anglais makes the flute-only sound a colder timbre, less of a personal lament than an inhuman, objective processional. The use of three side-drums and bass drum as markers of the slow march complements this effect, as well as providing a subtle link with the use of these instruments in the previous part of section II (and hinting, in subdued fashion, at their explosive use in part one of section III). Incidentally, Brian maximizes their re-entry in the later section by silencing them until then, a choice which greatly enhances the calmer motion of the music under discussion. The forward-looking instrumental colour again underlines the processional aspect of the music and, indeed, acts as a rhythmic marker in a percussive way, thus subtly compensating for the absence of the three side-drums and bass drum. The use of harp, violas, cellos and basses in crotchet rhythm and parallel motion acts as a link with the first harmonization of the long melody that occupies a twin central position in this symphony. It is, again, a rather cold, impersonal sound; it is in this manner that Brian keeps his "military" or "martial" thread alive; it switches, for the duration of this span, from violent foreground to unobtrusive yet distinctive background, and strongly colours the character of the music as a consequence.

As a preparation for the presentation of the long central melody of the work, Brian uses two devices conspicuous by their absence from the music up to this point. By so doing, he very effectively frames the melody and makes its entry both striking and immediately apparent for the important event which it is. Firstly, there is a transition; a one-bar change repeated, but a transition nonetheless. This is followed by a cadence onto E♭ major, confirming the change in harmonic area from the sharp side back to the flat side. If the music is not to stop dead at this juncture, something must happen, and the "something" which happens is the first presentation, underpinned initially by the harp and low strings' crotchets in parallel motion, heard just before (bars 102-107), of the central melody of the symphony (starting at bar 111).

Brian's two presentations of the long melody contrast strongly, while at the same time offering some interesting points of comparison. The accompaniment to the first version starts out as a processional, and moving in parallel motion, only to switch (at bar 120) to alternating brass and woodwind support, both joining together at bar 128, before three bassoons accompany the entry of a solo French horn at bar 129. These changes in instrumental accompaniment not only provide variety, but rather more significantly substitute a more chordal support for the martial accompaniment above which the melody had started. The chords at the end are offering harmonic background, in sharp contrast to the greater independence of the parallel chords in harp and low strings; the effect is of moving closer to a triadic harmony for the melody, which is where the second version of it clearly starts out. If one can refer to the first version of the melody as being "on" E♭, whether major or not (the hint of major is there, especially in bar 115 in violins, where the triad is presented horizontally in the melody), the second version is, at its opening particularly, "in" E major. The lower part-writing (another stage in the growth of the accompaniment) is supporting the melody, rather than shadowing it or merely taking place at the same time; melody and accompaniment are interdependent. This changes before the end; from bars 174 to 178 the melody repeats the same rhythmic pattern, highlighting the high E, and below this the chords of the accompaniment move downwards in parallel motion, as they had earlier moved in parallel motion under the E♭ version of the melody.

The music between these twin versions of the melody, at the heart of this symphony, is transitional in intent and effect, but it is a transition achieved in blocks rather than by degrees. By treating ideas found earlier in the work in a new way, it moves the musical argument forward by developing those ideas. The music from bars 133 to 152 is concerned with canonic entries of different versions of the cor anglais melody first heard at the beginning of section II. The first series of entries occurs on solo woodwinds over a bass line moving in steady crotchets, harking back to the steady crotchets which accompanied the three "unis but solo" flutes heard earlier. Changed though the melody is (the first note repeated five times instead of 10; a leap upwards of a perfect 4th instead of the earlier minor 3rd), it is clearly recognizable, and acts as a strong tie with the earlier music on this account. The string passage which follows features two more versions of the melody, each treated canonically, but the music is chordal and more static, rather than contrapuntal and processional. This in turn is followed by another short passage using the flute (this time solo) over a bass, moving, once again, in crotchets. The oboe plays an E as a central pedal-point, preparing the way for the clear E major treatment of the long melody to come.

After the second presentation of the long melody, which constitutes the lyrical high-point of the symphony, Brian leads, via a bass line moving upwards in crotchets underneath high, static woodwind parts, to a section which gives the impression of marking time, albeit in an uneasy fashion (caused by the high writing for piccolo, oboe and bassoon, as well as the static nature of their individual parts). The tension is temporarily abated by string chords moving downwards (in crotchets), but this leads to the recall of the high As (this time on flutes only) heard at the very beginning of the symphony, again underpinned by crotchets in the bass, but the *più animato* marking pushes the music forward. This thematic recall serves to forge a link forward as well as backward, because it hints at the return, not only of impersonal, but harsh music, such as has not been heard since the high notes were last heard (at bar 75, as Gs). However, the closing bars of this section are given to a new, long and lyrical cello melody which eventually lands on a perfect 5th on D (bar 208), linking back to the end of the first part of this section (bar 92), followed by a harp arpeggio which spells out D minor with a prominent E, culminating in a *pizzicato* D minor chord on violins over a sustained D pedal in cellos. This return to more impersonal music at the end (the cello melody becomes a bass line at the end, moving from the personal to the impersonal, or from the vocal to the instrumental) means that the silence above the cellos' D is an uneasy one. The E in the harp's pattern also contributes to this atmosphere of unease. The presence of the harp also makes a strong link with the Prologue, where it figured prominently.

This succession of events is remarkably easy to follow, but what should not go unnoticed is the way in which Brian shapes the music around the two appearances of the main melody, as well as preparing for the events of part one of section III. The music is not disruptive, but represents a progression as well as a succession, which by itself would imply static blocks of material. Each appearance of the melody is prefaced by impersonal and processional music (featuring the flute on both occasions) and succeeded by objective, contrapuntal part-writing. The string passage from bars 141 to 152 represents a further stage of transition between the two melody versions, balancing as it does strict counterpoint with expressive harmony. The music as a whole can be said to continue the philosophical thread of earlier parts of the symphony, but in strong contrast to part one of section II it presents the human and the impersonal, not in direct juxtaposition, but as a series of carefully judged and subtly interlinked subsections. By means of the links, he avoids becoming too discursive, a danger always inherent in what is the most expansive part of the symphony (in terms of overall pacing as well as melody). This section is not a slow movement, although it does contain the slowest music in the symphony; its thematic relation to the rest of the symphony ensures that as well as providing "breathing space" it carries and maintains the momentum of the work, albeit at a lower level, and paves the way for the climactic section to follow.

Section III: Part one: bars 211-288

Brian returns to the manner of the first part of section II for this climactic sequence of the music, but with the difference that the juxtapositions here are of musics of like character, as opposed to the strong contrasts which typified the earlier section. The music gains a great sense of momentum out of these juxtapositions, in which rhythm and melody alternate, and finally clash. The overall pattern, then, is geared towards the elimination of the human element of melody in the symphony by the two impersonal forces which have been consistent features of the work up to this point, namely fanfare-like rhythms and continuous semiquaver motion. Thematic development is not achieved in a large span (or a "development section"), but in short, successive spurts in which the "battle" between melody on the one hand, and rhythm and semiquaver motion on the other, is carried stage by stage to its culmination. The effect to this listener is extremely cinematic, and the music is again suggestive of place, namely a large, multi-sided battle area, from all sides of which the "military" and "vocal" music seem to emanate. The multi-dimensionality is achieved by the cuts from one type of fanfare to another, as the intervening melodies are gradually drowned out and then transformed into the very patterns against which they were originally in conflict. The process could be described as one of dehumanization, which complements the warlike imagery of the music.

The section begins with a small-scale presentation of the conflict which generates the music of this sequence. Over a pedal D, the violas play the cor anglais melody from the beginning of section II, with a new, dissonant three-part harmonic support from three trombones; this is immediately followed by an outburst from the percussion section which, as has been noted above, has had nothing to play since the beginning of the previous section in a slow march. Timpani play three rapid descending triplet semiquavers, E-C-G; there is a roll on three side-drums, and a thud from the bass drum. The latter accompanies the return of the tuba motive in the brass, at bar 214, in a slightly changed form, using the first four notes in a new rhythmic shape. The sequence is marked by two changes of tempo in as many bars, firstly to Allegro Vivace at bar 213, then to Adagio at bar 214, as well as the use of a long pause. The effect, one of violent juxtaposition, is expanded upon in the ensuing music. At the end of the section, Brian uses similar gestures to close it off (bar 285), although by that stage the cor anglais melody has been reduced to three As at the top of the three brass chords. The timpani figure in bars 285 and 286 bears a very strong resemblance, nonetheless, to the gesture referred to above. It is also noteworthy, and of significance as a musical signpost, that the top and bottom of the chord are the same; A above middle C and D below the bass clef respectively, although the notes in between differ strongly. This similarity binds the two gestures together and unites, by implication, the music that comes in between.

The "Battle" proper begins with a rendition of the cor anglais idea, accompanied by *cuivré* horns and battering timpani (at bar 286); already the "human" melody (which, as has been mentioned earlier, could be taken to represent Deirdre) has acquired a violent tone through the combative, tense nature of the accompaniment. On a purely musical level, the melody, last heard at bar 211, has been placed on top of a timpani pattern not unlike that of bars 218-222; the musical argument has been carried forward by a certain type of development of the material, namely superimposition. The next melodic presentation does not take place until bar 246 with the return of the tuba motive. The intervening music has been dominated by various rhythmic patternings, and the melody here is preceded by triplet semiquavers on three trumpets and three side drums; once again the warlike tone is patently clear. The tuba melody, now on all low brass, woodwinds and all the strings, rises in register as it had done on its two appearances in the Prologue, but has to compete with the continued triplet semiquavers, which contract into demisemiquavers on side drums as the melody reaches its apex. The gesture as a whole is an intensified restatement of bars 5-9, but it is followed, not by a chord, but by a new long melody in horns, violas and cellos, which in turn has to fight its way through an increasingly strongly profiled rhythmic accompaniment (bars 255-260 in particular). The next part of the section returns purely to rhythmic devices and rapid-note patternings, but just before the climactic version of the tuba motive, there is a brief, minimal melodic fragment on oboe (bars 272-275) using just three notes (D, E, F) and having only one true vocal idea, the last two quavers of bar 274 and first crotchet of 275 constituting a tiny melodic curve. As has been said, the tuba melody, in this its cumulative appearance, loses its melodic and rhythmic profile, and by bar 284 has become a descending scale fragment of four semiquavers, rapidly falling from piccolo down to contrabassoon in the course of that bar. These melodic presentations act as a brief, and increasingly short-lived, contrast to the succession of military rhythms which dominate and overwhelm other elements in this section of the symphony, in league with the rapid-note patterns as a dehumanizing force in the music.

Brian begins his rhythmic assault at bar 213, with the return of the untuned percussion, as well as the triplet semiquavers on timpani, which return at bar 218 in a changing rhythmic configuration consisting of semiquavers, quavers and semiquaver rests. The five-bar unit is marked by a *poco crescendo*, suggesting that the drumbeats are approaching from a distance; their arrival is signalled by a thrice-repeated chord in semiquavers from the woodwinds. The ensuing music for strings is related both in terms of rhythm and timbre, being percussive in effect. Thereafter the primarily rhythmic profile of the music is accentuated by the use of bar-long patterns which are repeated (at bars 231-3 in 5/4; bar 234 in 3/4; bars 239-240 in 3/4; bars 270 and 271 also in 3/4), or a pattern extending over a few bars, such as occurs at bars 261-268. Beyond these passages, where there is no competing melodic interest, there are strongly profiled rhythmic accompaniments to the melodic sections when they occur (the triplet semiquavers which precede and underline the return of the tuba motive at bar 245; the entire accompaniment to the new melody at bar 251, from bar 254 especially, as the rhythm grips the entire orchestral complement to the cor anglais, French horn, violas and cellos). Brian's resourcefulness is remarkable, as he manages to sustain variety and tension in the music by a careful choice of rhythm, whether using two semiquavers plus a quaver, or triplet semiquavers, as well as by well-judged and articulated changes of time signature. The momentum is sustained, but the pacing or rhythmic profile never becomes predictable, and the volatile surface activity is a major factor in binding the sequence together as a cumulative unit, rather than a miscellany of fanfare-like gestures.

The section as a whole, then, represents a true climactic point of the symphony, and not only in terms of noise. After the restraint of the previous section, this is virtuoso music for conductor, for orchestra and, not least, for composer. The thematic and dramatic preoccupations of the earlier sections of the work are brought together in fittingly violent clashes, as the tensions inherent in the very first build-up of the tuba motive, as well as the music from bars 84 to 92, are driven to their ultimate points. It is very striking, however, how Brian uses silence at the climactic moment to enhance the harsh and brutal nature of the music at that point; the pauses over rests from the beginning of the section return, and rather than have the full orchestra play a climactic chord or gesture, he reverts to the crude manner found in earlier points of the symphony. The result is starkly effective; all sense of mystery is banished, and chords are used again as the culmination of a massive orchestral build-up, matching up in tone, if not in register. This represents a subtle reversal of the way in which the chords in the Prologue fitted registrally, but did not represent a true culmination of the previous build-up in terms of tone. The orchestration of the whole section is masterly, as the orchestral body is augmented by the addition of tambourine and castanets to the very active and prominent percussion section, although Brian reserves the *coup de grâce* for the climactic moment of bar 288; he recalls the tam-tam, not heard since its dual appearance with bass drum in the Prologue, and its sound, combined with cymbal clash and timpani quavers, again using the notes C, E and G, all add immensely to the impact of the climactic chord in the brass. The chord is, in fact nothing more dissonant than C major, but its context, as well as tone, contributes very importantly to its shattering, and fittingly climactic impact; the brass approach their notes by use of parallel tritones. This has the effect of wrenching the music onto C major, rather than a cadence in, or modulation to, that key. Brian's refusal to use modulation as a major element of his musical style has borne very striking fruit; the culmination-point is not only effectively climactic, but consistent.

Section III: Part two, Epilogue: bars 289 to end

Brian begins his final summing-up by reverting to the slow march used at earlier points of the work (bars 102-107 in particular) and by recalling the solo cor anglais to add an elegiac tone. The march divides into four distinct units, each characterized by a different rhythm. Over the first three-bar unit, the cor anglais plays two minor 3rds, and then a major one; the first interval and the choice of instruments form a tentative link with bars 57-58, perhaps reducing that idea to its essentials. The next unit (bars 292-294) reintroduces the crotchet bass in harp and low strings, also from bars 102-107, as well as the first version of the central melody of the symphony. The cor anglais hints at that melody in the first three notes here, but the rhythmic presentation is different: three quavers as opposed to a quaver and two crotchets. The cor anglais ties this subsection with the next one by continuing its melody and reaching a dynamic highpoint; the semibreves in bars 295 and 296 are underpinned by another march rhythm in trombones and tuba, while the tam-tam is heard again. The final unit is scored entirely for percussion, bass drum and side drums marking the bar and half-bar respectively underneath a rhythm in timpani which succeeds in changing the note expected at the beginning of the next bar from E to A. Even in this short span of music, which because of its links with earlier events of the symphony sounds akin to a subdued summary of the course of those events, Brian's rhythmic resourcefulness and mastery of the percussion section, as well as his thorough understanding of the march, is most noteworthy; the addition of cor anglais succeeds in binding the units together. March and elegiac melody are combined rather than contrasted, to produce a very effective lament, which expands the expressive range of the work in a new way after the climax of the previous section, and paves the way for the peroration and tonal resolution to come.

The peroration is preceded by a one-bar flourish, a further link with earlier events; the way in which the notes accelerate as they rise in register is akin to bars 80-83, 230 and 234-235. The timpani roll on A which underpins it accentuates its upbeat nature, and the end of the bar leaves both top and bottom hanging in the air in the pause which follows, akin in some degree to what had happened in bar 75 and bar 92. Brian's answer to the silence is to purge the music of the minor scale in both directions, starting from the middle register and using a rhythmic pattern close to that of the tuba motive from bar 5 of the Prologue. The inner part complements this effect, moving increasingly in parallel 4ths, and this three-part harmonic counterpoint prepares for the resolution at bar 304 onto D major instead of D minor. The harmonic tensions of the music find their ultimate resolution in the consonance of this D major chord, which fills the entire register. Brian had featured a march rhythm in the passage from bars 300 to 303 in side drums and trumpets, underpinned by bass drum (on beat 1) and cymbal (on beat 4); the feeling of slow march is retained, albeit at a subdued level, in order to allow the harmonic events to occupy a central position. The final *coup de grâce* is typical; as the D major chord continues, the violas play the cor anglais melody from bar 57 one last time, contributing a harmonic ambiguity by means of the melodic turn, this time using C and B♭s in the D major chord, so the ambiguity is one of scale rather than one of a direct clash between two contradictory semitones. The final scale D-E-F♯-G-A-B♭-C combines both major and minor in a way which is harmonically consistent with the rest of the symphony. One can say, if one so wishes, that harmony is major and melody is minor, but one does not separate one from the other. In combination with this final appearance of melody in the symphony, march rhythm returns to a more forward position in timpani (augmenting and complementing the rhythm already present in trumpets and side-drums). As the chord fades, or perhaps more aptly recedes, the symphony closes with two dismissive sounds on percussion; the tam-tam is struck, and allowed to vibrate, and on the last beat of the last bar the bass drum closes the work with a subdued stroke.

Harold Truscott: Thoughts on Havergal Brian's Seventh Symphony[1]

This is not intended as an analysis of Brian's Seventh Symphony, but as some thoughts about a work that especially fascinates me.

My first aural hearing, as distinct from various mental hearings on reading the score, goes back I think to 1968 or thereabouts, when Harry Newstone, with the Royal Philharmonic Orchestra, broadcast its first performance. Coming, as it did, as the final work in a concert that had already included Berlioz's *Béatrice et Bénédict* Overture, Mozart's Piano Concerto No. 16 in D major, K. 451, and a News Summary, the effect of the symphony was electric. Naturally, I taped it. Harry Newstone has always been one of my favourite conductors, who gets his results without toil and trouble or fuss and bubble, and he has never, it seems to me, received the acknowledgement that is his due. Largely as a result of restricted rehearsal time, there are some faults in this performance, but it still ranks as one of the most exciting and truthful I have ever heard. There have been many other much-lauded performances of Brian which do not reach their objective as this one does. But my mind goes back further, to a time when Brian was no more than a name to most musicians, as that of the peculiar composer who had written the largest symphony in the history of music, although no one had ever heard it, and Harry Newstone broadcast the Eleventh Symphony and that most chilling work, the Twelfth as well as the *Doctor Merryheart* Overture. We have much to thank Harry for, with regard to Brian alone.

However this article is not about Harry Newstone (although one should be devoted to his work in a variety of types of music, not least on unfamiliar Haydn symphonies at a time when Robbins Landon was not even a name to us), but about Brian's Seventh. At that time, Brian had already renumbered certain symphonies (not all of them, as is sometimes implied in broadcast statements, for this was not necessary), up to No. 7, by cutting out the already-dismembered First and bringing in the *Sinfonia Tragica*, hitherto unnumbered, as No. 6. What the announcer read on that occasion in 1968 was wrong, however, referring to No. 7 as No. 6.

Malcolm MacDonald, in writing of this symphony in Volume 1 of his *The Symphonies of Havergal Brian*, has said that it is "Brian's last really large-scale symphony, with a playing-time of over 40 minutes". This is true - up to a point. But I think the work, in part, is also in character the second in type of his shorter symphonies, following up the start made in this direction by the slightly earlier No. 6. It seems to me to be a transforming work, in which the older type of Brian symphony, very much there in some respects, gives way to the newer, already adumbrated in No. 6, and which went ahead without let or hindrance from No. 8 onwards.

---

[1] From *Newsletter* 61 (IX-X 1985), pp. 2-5.

This is not, in the case of No. 7, a matter of length, nor does it concern the whole work; it is a matter of material and its treatment. In fact, it is even a matter of the dichotomy between the material and its clipped treatment, and the length of the individual movements. This kind of opposition often crops up in Brian, although not always with the same elements, but by some alchemy that was his secret, he fashions a complete work of art each time. Such opposition, the arguing of two opposing sides, was I think deep in Brian's nature, and it would have been strange if it had not surfaced in his music.

In such cases, including No. 7, the edginess, the roughnesses, even the failure of the work to jell that one might expect from the rubbing together of two elements that are in such opposition (note, not as an argument in the sense of a sonata conflict), are just not there. It is one of the mysteries of Brian's nature that such things produce works of art in which the elements, in their opposition, provide in a peculiar way, the unity on which the work stands or falls. He has been said to have been cantankerous, a difficult individual to get on with, with points sticking up like the quills of a porcupine (rather like William Cobbett who even called himself at one stage of his career, "Peter Porcupine") - an ornery cuss, the Americans would say, and I know from personal experience that he could be all of these things, although this is far from being the whole man. But such things, when they appeared, were the breath of life to his composition. They brought it to vivid life, and the music leaps and runs like a world-class athlete.

I do not want to take this too far, but No. 7 is an ideal example of this dichotomy, which has a special place in his music since it was responsible to a considerable extent for his work as a symphonist increasing, at the age of 73, from the seven he had written so far to the amazing production of the remaining 25 in 20 years. So much solid achievement came from the recalcitrant elements present and so beautifully handled in No. 7. At the end of it he was a different composer from the one who began it.

The trumpet sounds with which the symphony begins, after two bars of quiet percussion, certainly act as a sort of introduction. But, apart from being one of the most thrilling beginnings to any work that I know, it is far more. Its spirit (and rhythm) underlies a good deal of the symphony. It is part of Brian's musical make-up to make apparently unrelated passages related, but in a very subtle way that only gradually seeps through, with growing knowledge and experience of the music, and it is more than possible that often he was not consciously aware of these workings of his musical creativity. What that trumpet opening leads to is one of the few sounds in Brian's work that can make me think of another composer; the bracketed figure in Brian's theme (ex. 1) always brings to my mind a fragment of Sibelius' Sixth Symphony (ex. 2). The likeness (not complete in every way) is only momentary, and the two ideas are quite different in their meaning, as are the two works as a whole; and Brian's is only the beginning of an idea. But such things are not subject to reason. The two continue to remind me of each other. There is an echo of ex. 2 also in Sibelius' Seventh Symphony, which is simply a matter of Sibelius using a similar idea in two succeeding works - but associated with the same key.

Ex. 1

Ex. 2

In itself this is of no importance, and I would not have mentioned it if the connection in my mind was the only thing about it. But there may be something psychological beneath this. It may be that the likeness I hear in these two quotations has been pointing the way to something bigger that I have only gradually come to realize, which is that, dissimilar in most ways though Sibelius and Brian were as composers, there is I believe a link between them in one particular way. Both developed a way, different in each composer, of stating ideas that are different from each other, often breaking off one to start another that sounds almost like a contradiction, but where gradually wholeness of conception makes itself felt. I state this simply as something that has impressed itself on me. Others may disagree.

I find little suggestion or even echo of sonata style in this first movement. What we seem to have is a march composed of a first main idea, ex. 1 (or ideas), from which variations on this material are drawn almost continuously, sometimes with ordered harmonies that follow naturally from each other, sometimes with a sudden break in an unexpected direction.

All of what I may call the opening group, consisting of continual extensions, not so much of the material of that initial theme as of its mood and key, which it asserts over many bars (as Brian seldom does) is genial, again to an extent rare in later Brian. It is riddled with the rhythm shown bracketed in ex. 3 in various placings, always as part of a larger thematic figure, but without any attempt to use ex. 1 as it stands, so that the theme seems to exist firstly to initiate an optimistic march-like style in the music, and secondly to provide this basic rhythm (second bar of ex. 1).

Ex. 3

Ex. 4

As a theme rather than a rhythmic figure, such as ex. 1 yields, there is another which crops up far more than ex. 1; or rather its beginning does (ex. 4). This first appears just after ex. 1 and is followed by new thematic matter, the point of which is twofold: it is built on the ex. 3 rhythm and it is the perfect answer to ex. 4. It comes again almost immediately, extended upward by the ex. 3 rhythm, and yet again with an extension which first of all moves from a suggestion of F to that of E in the course of two bars, and then harmonically dithers between F, A minor and C major and continues in this way, C major by far the most prominent. But the next few bars tail off to a fairly long tune which has suggestions of the English folksong composers' love of the pentatonic scale about it. It starts obliquely on D, on bass clarinet and bassoons, cellos and basses, its first two notes emphasized by upper strings, stressing their connection with the first two notes of ex. 3. This emphasis, not on the same notes, occurs several times more in the course of this lengthy melodic line. It is its length without deviation that draws attention to the kind of phrasing we have been hearing, which is mainly of two bars' duration at a time, sometimes extended to four; short-breathed phrases but with so strong a connecting line in development from phrase to phrase that there is no suggestion anywhere of the music being short-breathed. But the lengthy melodic line makes this stand out. This, apart from the emphasis placed on its two opening rising notes, seems to me to be its main function (apart from its value in itself), even more so than the contrast in mood it offers to what precedes it. It never appears again, so to regard it as a second subject is being over-optimistic. It has served its purpose.

On one point concerning this tune I must differ from Malcolm MacDonald. He states that it is in D minor. I cannot hear it that way. Allowing for the pentatonic nature of the line, everything combines to emphasize F as its tonic. What is more, above it is a flute counterpoint which also strongly stresses F as the central note. Certainly it comes to four strong half-bar chords of D minor, with trumpets and trombone busily suggesting the influence of the trumpet opening of the work (an effect prepared here by a side-drum reminiscence of that introduction), reinforced a few bars later by the horns, which stress the root and octave drop on the 5th of the scale that is prominent in the introduction to this movement.

For the moment, what happens is a quite unexpected plunge on to C♯, which, since the previous bar ends on a strong dominant of C, has an effect similar in music to that in Buster Keaton's film *Sherlock Junior*, where he constantly finds himself in one situation only for it to change completely as he prepares to deal with it; poised to dive into the sea, for instance, the scene becomes a desert and he lands on his head in the sand.

What balances the constant opening up of this material, carried mainly by short phrases which now and again become larger, is a quiet, thematically unrelated passage which comes roughly half way through the movement. Like so many things in Brian's music, it can be deceptive in the impression it makes. Before I discuss this, however, there is another feature to be mentioned. Twelve bars before this section appears, and following a quite large climax of syncopated wind chords with double basses, Brian changes his time signature from steady 4/4 with which the movement has so far moved, to 2/2, with a minim now the same value as the previous crotchet. Just why he did this it is difficult to see. He may have thought it made things clearer, but so far as I can see it simply makes a mystery. He could just as well have continued with his 4/4. If he wanted more frequent accents, one added on each half bar would have produced the same effect as the change of time. After the 12 bars he immediately reverts to 4/4, each crotchet equaling a preceding minim. To the ear there has been no change.

At any rate, that brings us to this middle section, which certainly has a complete change of mood. The martial character has completely vanished, and the music is meditative, almost as though taking a rest in the middle of explosive action. So strongly is this change conveyed that one can have the impression that one is listening to a slow section in the middle of a fairly fast movement. In fact, that would be a misconception. Although the mood is so different, the tempo of the music is precisely the same - the same four beats at the same tempo as before. It is true that after nine bars of this he writes "slower", but the sense of the music shows that this cannot be very marked. And this it is, I think - the fact that the tempo for this quiet, contemplative section *is* the same as for the rest - that more than anything else imparts such unity to the movement as a whole.

Seldom does any thematic idea come twice exactly as it was originally, and Brian's resumption of the martial strain stresses a version of ex. 1 which spreads over two bars around C minor to E♭, then goes on through D♭, F minor, to A minor, which stays more or less for a few bars - scarcely long enough to make it an effective opposition to C major, which itself has been in abeyance for some time. The music soon marches through harmonies remote from A minor or C major, to come almost immediately to an undoubted C major, with a theme that reminds us of ex. 3 without being that theme. From here variants of this theme pass from horns to trumpets, to woodwind and strings. Constantly we are given the vague impression of hearing themes we have heard before, although, in fact, we have not - in the form in which they now come. We have only heard something like them.

More and more the rhythm of semiquavers in the woodwind and brass shows that the trumpet introduction exerts its sway, too. The last reference to ex. 1 (again by no means exact, but with a sufficient likeness) strides across the final bars to make an end.

One of the tonal peculiarities of this first movement is that, following the most unusual clinging to C major with which the movement begins, the music continually dives off through quite remote harmonies, and now and again resumes C major, sometimes as though it had never been away, or as though it had suddenly remembered that its key is supposed to be C major.

The second movement, a scherzo of sorts, makes its first joke with the first theme to be heard. Brian's time signature here is 5/2, but he begins with what sounds like a figure of three beats, which actually proves to be 2, 3 and 4 of a four-beat figure, for what follows is a plain four-beat group, no matter how his accents are faithfully reproduced. So that this regularity of the four is, in fact, an irregularity against the five. He has begun as he intends to go on (ex. 5). This theme, with its repeating figure, underlies a good deal of the rest of the movement, sometimes breeding other themes related to it but not the same. But, of course, as we might expect from Brian, ex. 5 is rarely precisely the same on its various appearances. Once again the rapid repeated notes of the symphony's trumpet introduction are in evidence, and this use is considerably extended as the movement progresses.

Ex. 5

In spite of the irregularity of the rhythmic stress in ex. 5, it is but a small part of the greater rhythmic irregularity that grows as this incomparable movement proceeds. The whole conception is unique, as is the complete symphony. There is no category into which it will comfortably fit. As in the first movement, Brian seems to be intent, as one of his objectives, on obtaining the maximum mood contrast, with this second movement's extreme reaction to ex. 5 in a country dance, and the later devastating development of this, as also of orchestral sonorities, while preserving the overall beat rhythm - so that his changes from Allegro maestoso ma moderato to Allegretto or Allegretto grazioso, and from 5/2 to 6/4, with an *animato* and *più animato* intervening, are not tempo changes at all, but mood changes. Always the basic beat remains the same. I stress this rather than the change of material because this is the focal point of the piece. It dominates the overall impression that comes from the music.

This handling of the same beat rhythm through changes of mood remains a main feature of the symphony as a whole to an extent I have not found in any other symphonic work of Brian. It dominates the third movement also, and perhaps to an even greater effect, in spite of the composer's indications of ♩ = 60 for the opening Adagio and ♩ = 80 for the scherzo music. The music is so written that the two, ostensibly one slightly faster than the other, can scarcely suggest anything other than the same beat rhythm governing both.

The movement is a disturbing one. The music is itself disturbed, and one of the prime causes is exactly this dominating sameness, or similarity, of beat rhythm; where in the second movement it has a liberating rather than an inhibiting effect, here it provokes something almost mesmeric; as of someone unwillingly in a trance - that is, until the real Adagio arrives; although even that, as it turns out, consolatory though it is to a great extent, has not thrown off all its fears.

I used to think of all the scherzo part of this movement as a sort of Brianesque *Midsummer Night's Dream* music; but I have changed my mind. The antics of the fairies in Shakespeare's play, even the jokes of Puck, while obviously nonhuman and mischievous, are goodhumoured and are not inimical to the human characters. Brian's music is; it is more like a "Midsummer Nightmare". Malcolm MacDonald has written of this: "It is a scherzo that gets nowhere - a scherzo that runs on the spot". Well, it does get somewhere, eventually; it gets to the Adagio, and it has managed, in the course of its twistings and turnings, to dredge up a theme that at last grows into an extended Adagio melodic line.

Ex. 6

This is its first appearance. Only the first four notes (fig. a) are concerned, but it will be noticed that the phrase as a whole, having started on B♭, leans to E major at its end. And it is on E major that it appears for the second time. However, I understand what MacDonald means by his "running on the spot". It *is* like that, except that I find something rather more sinister in this scherzo than he appears to.

Another point is that the G♭ on which the movement starts, the harmony of E major, and various other harmonies on which the music settles momentarily, are all transient. The E major of ex. 6's second appearance does not remain. When the Adagio proper begins, it is on E♭ that it does so; but this, too, is transient; it does reappear, but it is blown away by a *vivo agitato* which has scant regard for any particular harmony, although all the time fig. a is strengthening, digging in, as it were, being tested in a variety of characters, with various continuations, and the piece does at last manage to end on a firm E♭. The movement as a whole, however, is as nearly atonal as Brian could ever be and remain Brian.

If we accept, as I do, the nightmarish quality of so much of the third movement, or perhaps, view it as an interpretation of one of the grimmest of Grimm's fairy tales, and leaving aside Brian's own association of the finale with Goethe and Strassburg, which we can scarcely experience for ourselves, "Once upon a time" becomes apt for the finale of this symphony - especially since its mood more often than not outdoes the Grimm aspect of the third movement, even at its grimmest. But this is no nightmare. It has become reality.

It begins at a moderate pace, *on* A minor; I put it this way because although it also ends, suddenly, on A, it would be a gross exaggeration to say that the tonal aspect of the movement suggests that it is *in* A, minor or major. Following the five-bar opening, with the horn rhythm (notice again the repeated semiquavers,

Ex. 7

which have featured so much in previous movements and really go back to the trumpet opening of the work), there is an attempt to get a melody going on woodwind, but this peters out in the strings, and from this a string cadence arises like a phoenix from the ashes, eight bars of melodic writing, moving in crotchets which suddenly become minim beats until it reaches a climax on what would be a chord of A major if it were not for an F replacing E. But, although ostensibly the lengthy passage starts around A minor and ends on this perversion of A major, its harmonies mostly stress C major as the tonic. After the climax a similar continuation, back with 4/4, lasts for five bars, and accelerates in 6/4 as the harmonies stride right out of range of A minor or C major. This reaches a much bigger climax which sounds like all the devils of hell let loose, with a rising dotted rhythm figure in the bass, occupying each bar and descending in pitch with each bar. Brian is being Brian again, but with an unleashed malevolence that is chilling and gripping at the same time.

There is a switch to what appears at first to be C minor, but establishes itself after a few bars as E♭. And with this the march element is back. With occasional slidings into and out of 3/4, the march proceeds, mainly fairly genial, although with here and there rather menacing mutterings. From one 3/4 intrusion it slides back through the subdominant of E♭, and momentarily produces almost a touch of Vaughan Williams in his folksong mood, although Brian's tune is no folksong. After more 3/4 and martial interruptions, peace descends on the music for a time with some of Brian's loveliest writing, eventually reducing the music to solo violin, solo viola and solo cello. They are concerned with descending mordents, the rising dotted rhythm figure which went with the devils from hell quite transformed, and the ex. 7 figure.

Ex. 8

All this coalesces to an E♭ for *tutti* violas followed by what is, I think, one of the most beautiful single moments in all Brian (ex. 8). Based, as this is, on the horn rhythm of ex. 7, it illustrates the range of Brian's thinking in terms of sound, for the opening of the movement, quiet though it is, could never have predicted this lovely passage. Ex. 8 inaugurates a period of quiet contemplation, based, in various ways, on that ex. 7 rhythm; it leads to a sudden *forte* outburst, which has an intimidating effect, not merely because of its sudden appearance after the quietude, but even more because the C of the immediately previous bars is rudely contradicted and thrust out of the way by a blaring C♯, to some extent a reminder of a similar loud contradiction of C major by C♯ in the first movement. More than that, for the first time in the work the repeated semiquaver rhythm is changed. It has a dip of one step down on the last note of the four, exactly as at the opening of the *Gothic* Symphony.

224 Symphonies

Ex. 9
Trb., Tb., Arch.

With this outburst, the march becomes menacing, fierce thrusts marking the beginning of two of the bars. The drum beats out ex. 7, the harmony moves through C minor to E♭, and the whole passage is like a Brianesque *March to the Scaffold*. But, as so often with Brian, in a moment everything clears, like a mist before the sun, and we reach calm waters with C major, a harp gently climbing. A solo violin quietly sings to itself. For the last time a shadow comes over the music, a last outburst shakes it, but sinks impotently to the final four-bar statement of ex. 7 and the closing A major chord with the Strassburg bell - surely the deepest and most surprising ending in all Brian's symphonies.

What a curious man Brian was. Such a conglomeration this symphony is, taken element by element, and yet ... Could anyone else have made of it the unique work of art it undoubtedly is? I wonder.

Martin O'Leary: Brian and Mahler: four symphonies in comparison[1]

The best way of comparing and contrasting the symphonic writing of Mahler and Brian is to see how each went about composing works with an overall factor in common: in the first instance, a general mood of tragedy; in the second, a progression from minor to major. The individuality of both composers emerges clearly. Although they differ greatly, something can be learned from the manner in which they differ. As representatives of "tragic symphonies", I choose Mahler's Sixth and Brian's Eighth, and as minor-to-major works Brian's Ninth and Mahler's Seventh.[2]

The "tragic symphonies"

Although both symphonies are taut and tightly argued pieces, Mahler's Sixth is more than three times the length of Brian's Eighth; Brian's time-scale in general differs greatly from Mahler's. The former work represents a long journey towards a tragic conclusion, whereas the latter is a static work, firmly rooted in tragic soil. Grim and lyrical music alternate in it, and as it unfolds, the gulf

---

[1] From *Newsletter* 38 (XI-XII 1981), pp. 3-4.
[2] Brian's Eighth and Ninth Symphonies were recorded by the Royal Liverpool Philharmonic Orchestra under Sir Charles Groves, released on compact disc in 1989 (CDM 769 890 2, now deleted).

widens between these two moods. We end, however, where we began, as the symphony confirms its tragic standpoint. Both composers highlight the tragedy of their works differently. Mahler ends his first movement joyfully, but eclipses that joy by the gloom of the end of the final movement, whereas Brian follows exultant music directly with the gloomiest possible contrast. It should be added that each procedure is as effective as the other, although Brian's might seem initially more problematical.

Mahler's main stretches of slow music are the central episode of the first movement, and later the full flowering of the E♭ Andante Moderato movement. The overall motion of Brian's symphony is slow, but his lyricism expands and grows more intense as his single-movement structure unfolds, culminating in the beautiful G major melody on muted violins.

There is also what might be called the different role of "Fate" in each work: in Brian, it is a negative force which ignores, rather than struggles with, lyricism, whereas in Mahler it struggles through the course of the work until it emerges triumphantly negative at its end.

Unity is achieved in different ways by each composer. Mahler uses a dotted rhythm and familiar melodic lines to construct his world, and a remarkable example of his skill in making new themes out of old thematic material is demonstrated in the finale. After each stoppage in the movement, new material appears as the struggle recommences. Brian unites his lyrical themes by giving each an abundantly filled first bar, and by re-introducing old themes at crucial points in the work's architecture. Despite the diversity of thematic material the single movement form hangs together excellently, and there are no loose ends.

Both composers have a place in their works for fantastic music, Mahler in the scherzo, Brian in his first Passacaglia. Also, at the very nadir of tragedy, both use the canon in a murky, gloomy passage on low instruments. Brian's comes on bassoons in the centre of his work, Mahler's on trombones and tuba at the end of the final movement.

In the final analysis, these two tragic symphonies differ considerably in the impression they leave, at least on this listener. To me, Mahler is uplifting in defeat, whereas Brian leaves mystery in the air, his enigma unsolved.

Major-to-minor works

Mahler's Seventh Symphony and Brian's Ninth both have a large, tonally ambiguous first movement, slow movements with a particular orchestral colouring (oriental and nocturnal) and rondo finales with a barnstorming show of optimism at the outset, neither of which, I feel, is fully convincing in the end. Both first movements have slow introductions, though on different time-scales - each containing a "false start". Mahler introduces his main theme before it receives its full treatment, whereas Brian has a D minor theme separate from the main theme of the movement. Whilst Brian, for once, keeps fairly rigidly to a sonata structure, Mahler's recapitulation differs widely from his exposition. There is a lyrical interlude at the heart of both movements: in Brian a C major horn theme; in Mahler an expansive episode in B major in his most lyrical vein. Brian, however, resumes his development, whereas Mahler begins his recapitulation with the theme of his slow introduction. But whereas Brian relaxes into his interlude, Mahler stops his *allegro* with a high B and trumpet fanfare calls.

Their slow movements differ greatly, serving different purposes in each work. Brian's is an integral part of the struggle taking place in the symphony, but Mahler's movements are two interludes, complementing by contrast the outer movements. Brian uses cor anglais and gong, and Mahler guitar, mandolin and cowbells to achieve the colour of each movement.

The finale of each work starts with a massive display of optimism. Brian then relaxes into an interlude of drifting reserved music tinged with sadness, but Mahler pours out theme and counter-theme which culminate in the recall of the main theme of the first movement. Both repeat their themes at the end, Brian again sticking to his original closer than Mahler. At the very end, each composer binds his outer movements together. Brian reiterates A and D major chords, reminding the listener that the work set off in A minor, and Mahler, in an exultant B major passage, recalls the key of the main body of the first movement. Again, a surprise is sprung by both at the end, when Brian seems to be about to end on an A major chord until the final D major one, whilst Mahler lets an augmented chord hang tantalizingly in the air before bringing the curtain down with his final C major.

Listened to in isolation, these codas are convincingly optimistic, but the music that precedes them in both cases clouds the proceedings and darkens the mood. Brian's slow middle section lingers in the memory, as does the harmonic wildness and piercing, almost frantic progress of the last pages of Mahler's development before the recalling of his themes.

It is interesting to note that both composers refer to their previous symphonies in the ones just discussed. Brian's Ninth uses the typical Brianian rhythm heard at the beginning of his Eighth Symphony. Mahler uses the major-to-minor chord sequence which is so essential to the Sixth Symphony, and also uses the cowbells, although to different effect. Whereas Brian's use of the rhythm in the slow movement of No. 9 provokes a climax, Mahler uses his chord sequence at climaxes, as though the progress of the music led inevitably to its recall.

Both composers have suffered from the application of oversimplifying "labels" by others. While Brian has been dubbed "difficult" due to his reliance on lower instruments to carry the main melodic burden, Mahler has been labelled "neurotic" because of his high soaring melodies. Neither appellation fits: both aim at, and achieve by varying means, clarity. They were both masters of orchestration.

It has been said that both owe the origins of their symphonic writing to Beethoven's *Choral* Symphony. Mahler followed a path whose roots were clearly in Beethoven, whereas Brian went further and further away after *The Gothic*. Perhaps their debt to Beethoven is their main point in common: there could hardly be found two more diverse successors to Beethoven than Havergal Brian and Gustav Mahler.

Tim Shuker: Havergal Brian's Thirteenth Symphony - not unlucky 13![1]

The two full scores of Brian's Symphony No. 13 are dated "Nov-Dec 1959". This means that it was the first orchestral work he had completed for two years since the Twelfth Symphony was finished in February 1957. The latter was written in the shadow of his one act opera *Agamemnon*, and is a highly compressed work in which the conventional four movements are deftly welded together to make a one-movement structure of great power and panache. It is one of his shortest symphonies, all of 11-12 minutes long, but bearing in mind that, as Arnold Schoenberg once said, compression is equal to expansion, the Symphony No. 12 has all the emotional impact of a work three or four times its size, and is a masterly display of inevitability. Having achieved extreme symphonic compression in this work and similar operatic compression in *Agamemnon*, the logical conclusion of Brian's tendencies at this time would have been, unlike Anton Webern's direction toward ultimate silence, a kind of musical "Cosmic Big Crunch", with all the music happening at once. This had to be avoided and so Symphony No. 13 is both an expansion of form and an emotional relaxation.

It can be split, broadly, into seven sections as follows:

1. Slow introduction (figs 1-5)

The honours in this symphony are given to the timpani. They open *pp* with exactly the same rhythm that began the Fourth Symphony in 1933 (exx. 1 a and 1 b).

Ex. 1 a

Ex. 1 b

The context in this case, however, is vastly different. In the earlier work, this was both a rhythmic and melodic figure and was the prelude to a great triumphal

---

[1] From *Newsletter* 92 (XI-XII 1990), pp. 3-5.

march. Here, the suggestion is neither marchlike nor triumphal; rather, it is uncertain, as if feeling its way. The difference is so great that one does not really notice the conjunction of rhythm, even when listening to the two symphonies back-to-back. This is one of the marks of a great composer: economy of means, variety of expression. In bar 2 the three tenor and the bass trombone join in holding down a *sostenuto* chord of A minor. In bar 3 the tuba enters, uttering in bar 5 ex. 2,

Ex. 2

a variation on a motif to be used in many varying guises throughout the symphony. By bar 7, there is a tonic chord of C major, altering in bar 8 to the subdominant of C minor, changing again in bar 9 to the first inversion of the tonic chord of B♭ minor. The section grows in power and menace, horns joining in and oboes making lamenting cries above the held-down brass chords. Finally the dynamics rapidly increase as the side-drums join in the rhythmic tattoo (ex. 3),

Ex. 3

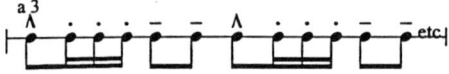

to a first climax, *mf*, for brass and percussion on chord of A♭. The dynamics drop again to *mp* and the lamenting oboes return, accompanied by trombones. This only lasts for two bars and then the fuller brass forces of horns, euphonium and tuba return to prepare the way for the transition to the "first movement", reaching temporary home in a loud chord of B♭. There follows a connecting passage of four bars where the strings hold down a quiet bare 5th on A, above which sounds twice a distant trumpet call which alternates with timpani in the same rhythm - again a variant of the symphony's opening figure (ex. 1 a). After the second statement of the rhythmic figure by timpani alone, there is an expectant and very short pause and suddenly we are jolted into a "first movement".

2. *"First movement"*: Andante Moderato ma Marcato (fig. 5 to double bar after fig. 17)

Ex. 4

The figure (ex. 4) stated at the outset of this "movement" is extremely important, and could be said to be the "germ cell" of the entire work, as this basic rhythm appears in many varied guises throughout. Those who know their Brian will also be aware that it is virtually the same, at least in rhythmic terms, as the figure which opened Symphony No. 8 (ex. 5).

Ex. 5

It also appears as the rhythm of the second, "funeral march", section of Symphony No. 12 (ex. 5 a).

Ex. 5 a

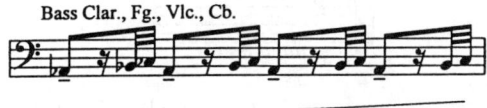

Variety being the spice of life, however, as with the figure at the very start of No. 13 its resemblance to earlier incarnations is virtually unrecognizable. The rhythm is taken up by the oboes four bars after fig. 6 *poco movimento e semplice* in canon with a bassoon. At two bars before fig. 8 the key has reached D major and the "germ cell" motif is being split up into separate quavers and dual semiquaver groups. The bass figure here (ex. 6) is the reverse of the original "germ cell". The cellos repeat the

Ex. 6

original figure from fig. 9 to one bar before fig. 10, where it is then taken up in derived form by a solo violin. A derived form of ex. 3 is used by the entire orchestra from fig. 11 to fig. 12. At two bars before the latter, ex. 3 is used by the side-drums as a rhythmic base (ex. 7).

Ex. 7

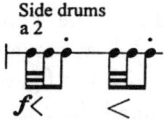

There is a hint that this figure has been discussed enough for the moment in the four-crotchet motif played by the upper woodwind and all other instruments apart from the tuba, horns, and side-drums one bar before fig. 12. At fig. 12, the "germ cell" is replaced by a chromatic four-note crotchet figure which focusses to ex. 8 at two bars before fig. 13.

Ex. 8

This comes to dominate in canon, played first by flutes, harp 1 and glockenspiel, and then trombones, harp 2, and basses. In reverse form this is very similar to the second theme of Symphony No. 22 of six years later (ex. 9).

Ex. 9

At fig. 13 there is a *diminuendo*, then, three bars before fig. 14, a flute sings an extended melody, another variant of the symphony's opening figure. This is taken up and discussed by the violins in the ensuing passage. At fig. 15, the descending figure returns, this time in quaver form on flutes, clarinets, and first violins, while a two-note ascending figure, the reverse of the descending one played two bars before fig. 9, appears on most of the other instruments. At three bars before fig. 16, a semiquaver variant of ex. 3 on a side-drum means that a fragment of the original figure insinuates itself into the melodic discussion. Originally two notes, it now extends to four and grows through the whole orchestra like a disease. The volume rises to an angry *ff* with all instruments apart from brass and percussion rattling out the four-note figure. At fig. 17 a quiet *molto ritard.* bar brings the "first movement" to an inconclusive close. The attempted melodic flight in its central section is still being held down by the symphony's all-pervasive opening figure.

3. "Second movement": Andante Moderato ma Marcato (Adagio) (Double bar after fig. 17 to fig. 30)

The beginning brings a more lyrical version of the symphony's opening idea (ex. 4), scored for muted strings alone. The whole passage (fig. 17 to double bar after fig. 18) is reminiscent of the "slow movement" of Symphony No. 12. A discussion of this opening ensues, with the figure appearing in various guises. A lyrical version is presented three bars before fig. 19 by solo violin, then a terser version as a split quaver/semiquaver is played by the strings, joined with a discussion of the descending motif from the "first movement" in quaver form on clarinets and violins two bars after fig. 20. This debate reaches an angry climax at fig. 21 with a rhythmic tattoo idea on the horns (ex. 10).

Ex. 10

A short section headed *misterioso* follows a one-bar *ritard.*, relaxing the overall tempo, before returning to it in the very next bar. In this section of the "movement", an opening rhythmic idea is compressed in time-scale until, *molto crescendo* at three bars after fig. 22, we are back with the side-drum's four-semiquaver tattoo from the "first movement", played on flutes and clarinets. Variants of the symphony's opening figure appear on bass instruments throughout the orchestra and the previous descending figure becomes a rising quaver motif which helps achieve a kind of shrill, brash release led by the horns and trumpets three bars after fig. 24. At the double bar (two bars after fig. 25) the tempo slows to Adagio and the preparation begins for the climax of the "movement", which comes from figs. 28-30. Following alternating string and horn chords - a kind of question and answer - the strings and flutes are finally allowed to make a full melodic statement incorporating elements of ex. 4, and one bar before fig. 30 also incorporate the descending idea from the "first movement" now reversed into a rising figure. This provides a kind of answer to the symphony's problem: the descending melodic idea, turned on its head to form a rising figure, and the opening idea make music together in peaceful coexistence, not pulling in opposite directions as they were in the "first movement". Nevertheless, there is still more to be said, so the climax is not allowed to reach fruition and the final chord before fig. 30 is of G major, the dominant of the ostensible key of the symphony. This is a premonition of the final solution. Someone hearing this work for the first time, and with no previous knowledge of Brian's music, remarked that the climax of this "movement" from figs. 28-30 was very reminiscent of Bruckner, whose music Brian admitted had a draw for him. Now, we also need a Brucknerian pause for thought and this is precisely what Brian provides in:

4. Interlude: Recit. a Piacere/Adagio Solenne (figs. 30-33)

This consists of two recitatives: the first, from figs. 30-31, is for solo clarinet and its music seems, emotionally at least, a comment albeit a wistful one on what has gone before in the previous two "movements". It contains another related mention of ex. 3 and sinks down in a series of waves from a high B (3rd of G) to a low E, finally fading away on a low G at fig. 31. This is followed by the violin's accompanied recitative, a comment akin to the clarinet's, but from an altogether different and emotionally more hopeful angle. It is first accompanied *pp* by the basses alone from figs. 31 to 32; these are joined by muted horns at fig. 32 holding down a minor 2nd chord. The violin comes to rest, like the clarinet, on a G,

232   Symphonies

while the horns play a bare 5th on the dominant of G. As the horns and violin come to rest, we are ready for:

5. *"Third movement"*: *Più Movimento ma Sostenuto - Recit. - Adagio* (figs. 33-42)

This really begins two bars before fig. 37 with the Adagio section. It is, however, prefaced by two linking passages, the first initially for wind instruments, in an abrupt two-rising figure, joined two bars before fig. 35 by loud chords in the strings. This is another recitative-type passage, but of an altogether more imperious nature. This changes abruptly at fig. 36 for a recitative identical in type to that for the violin at fig. 32, played this time by the flute. This fades at fig. 37 into the Adagio, the "third movement" proper.

In this, there is a distinct sense of everything beginning to expand, and there is a reappearance of the four-note crotchet figure, the melodic idea so summarily stifled in the first movement. This time it is allowed full rein, the music rising in pitch and dynamic in great waves until it is abruptly halted one bar after fig. 40 (distinctly recalling ex. 3), first for trumpets and then for full forces minus woodwind, with side-drum and cymbals adding extra weight. This halts suddenly at fig. 41 and the woodwind hold down a long chord which again suggests G major; to be followed by skittering semiquaver figuration on, successively, clarinet, horn, bassoon and tuba. There is a pause mark and then the strings hold a quiet chord of $G\flat$ ($=F\sharp$ - the leading-note of G major, dominant of C major - the stated key on the title-page of the symphony). The $G\flat$ becomes a $G\natural$ in the final note played by cellos and basses before fig. 42. This quiet dominant preparation, which can now be seen to have been going on since the melodic flowering at the end of the "second movement", launches us into:

6. *"Fourth movement"*: **Allegro Vivo** (fig. 42 to two bars before fig. 62)

This is basically a very quiet, light-hearted scherzo in 12/8 time, the skittish opening figure being discussed over and over by all sections of the orchestra, the main interest being in the way Brian throws his ideas from one, generally small, section of instruments to another, always with dazzling speed. This gives the lie to the charge levelled by some critics that Brian's orchestration is always woefully opaque or his melodic lines ponderous and heavy-footed. Abruptly, this scherzo comes to an end with a quiet *Ritard. ed Dim.* two bars before fig. 62, the strings modulating through five bars until at fig. 63 we are into:

7. *Coda: Moderato* slowing into *Adagio* in the final bars (fig. 63 to the end)

The melodic idea which has been gradually allowed to gain ascendancy throughout the symphony here speaks out for the final time in its fullest expression, the dynamics expanding from *mf* at the beginning to *fff* in the final bars. Interestingly, the melodic idea and the rhythmic figure which opened the work can be seen working together to increase the power of the climax, the melody generally in the woodwind, while the rhythmic idea is in the brass, bass instruments and percussion. It is from these regions that the conclusion of the work comes: first, the original descending melodic idea from the first movement becomes a rising figure for strings and harps, then brass and percussion thunder out a variant of the rhythm of ex. 4, the chord here being G major - the dominant of C. Finally there are two mighty chords for full forces establishing the destination unshakeably as C major.

Thus it can be seen that the whole work has been one of progressions - from indeterminate tonality to G major and finally to C major. Thus, C can be seen as the key to which the symphony aspires rather than that in which it is written. Also, there is a progression from rhythmic and melodic ideas which pulled initially in opposite directions, eventually working together to provide the final solution to the symphony's problems. Ideas flow smoothly from one section to another suggesting a work written at great speed. To me, it is clearly inspired throughout and, like a good novel or any great work of literature or music, holds the attention from arresting beginning to inevitable end. The "hidden programme" sensed by some listeners is rather their sensing of the very real unity of thought and idea at work in this symphony, which I believe to be one of Brian's very best works.

Rodney Stephen Newton: Havergal Brian's Fourteenth Symphony - an alternative view[1]

In discussing the music of Havergal Brian with fellow musicians, reading music critics' opinions of concerts and broadcasts of Brian's music and reading analytical studies of Brian's works by the various musicologists expert in his music, it becomes very clear that all of us listen to Brian in different ways. What for one listener might be a stunning experience may for another be half an hour or so of total boredom - and this is as it should be. We all have our own personalities, our own tastes in food, art and literature, our own preferences in styles of dress and our own perfect right to state our beliefs. Thus, it is not unusual for differences of opinion to occur concerning the merits of individual works of art. What is sometimes surprising is to find that one is in opposition over one particular work with a person with whom one usually agrees. Such an instance is the opposing views taken by Malcolm MacDonald and myself over Brian's Symphony No. 14 in F minor. I have long been greatly impressed by this work, even before the opportunity arose to study it with a score, and was therefore somewhat dismayed to find that Malcolm (with whom I am normally in agreement in matters concerning Brian) gives the work a considerable hammering in the second volume of his study of the symphonies. Even more surprising was the fact that the Sympho-

---

[1] From *Newsletter* 23 (V-VI 1979), pp. 4-6.

ny No. 13, which I personally consider to be a crude patchwork of ideas (despite the impressive opening and glorious lyrical outburst around fig. 30) concluded by what must surely be one of Brian's most banal codas, received comparatively lenient treatment. In a letter answering a criticism by David J. Brown, Malcolm MacDonald (cf. David J. Brown's review of MacDonald's Volume 2 in *Newsletter* 18, pp. 7-8) assures us that opinions set out in his studies of the Brian symphonies are purely personal ones, and not to be taken as "holy writ". Therefore I feel fully justified in offering my own view of the much-maligned Fourteenth Symphony in the hope that people will be persuaded to give it another chance.

In any study of the Brian symphonies I have always considered it helpful to compare a work under discussion with the symphonies immediately "fore and aft", so to speak. I have already indicated my somewhat unflattering opinion of No. 13 - my own candidate for Brian's "one true failure" - and, although I consider the Fifteenth Symphony to be an attractive work, one soon comes to realize that Brian is here taking leave of his cosmic struggles and writing a comparatively relaxed work for immediate enjoyment. Not so the Fourteenth Symphony! Here we have a work redolent of the grim power of No. 12. The orchestra is large with six horns, as in the Twelfth, and includes an organ. Although nominally in one movement, the work seems to be divided into two main sections, the division delineated by a departure from the previous inexorable 5/4 time - each section containing within itself a number of sub-divisions. The official key signature is F minor, but the work spends a good deal of its time in the related keys of D♭, A♭ and also in G♭. The tension generated by alternating between keys a semitone apart - a favourite device of Brian's - is a distinctive feature of the symphony, the struggle being kept up to the final bars. Brian's musical "language" may be remarked upon at this point. In the Symphonies Nos 13 and 15 we have Brian displaying - to my ears at least - distinctly "English" gestures. The lyricism of fig. 30 in No. 13 is reminiscent of Elgar, and the jolly *Rule Britannia* rhetoric of No. 15 brings to mind the rustic world of Brian's English Suite No. 5. The Fourteenth Symphony, however, is free from passages of either kind - indeed, were the work to be played on Dr Simpson's "Innocent Ear" programme, I should imagine the average listener would have the utmost difficulty in deciding the nationality of the composer, let alone his identity. The overall impression, however, is distinctly European - the opening bars sounding not unlike Mahler's *Der Einsame im Herbst* from *Das Lied von der Erde*. Over a wandering cello accompaniment a cor anglais sings a sad melody (ex. 1). Notice that already in the fourth bar the tonality tilts upwards from F to G♭, then sinks back again by the sixth bar.

Ex. 1

The tension between these two keys is generated at the very outset of the work. At fig. 2, Sibelian horns shed a faint gleam of light over the surrounding darkness before being extinguished by bassoons and cellos - the chromatic meandering of the latter being abruptly terminated. A rumble of distant thunder from a low timpani E leads us to a five-bar Moderato bridge passage which acts as an introduction to a more extended passage at fig. 4 marked Allegro Moderato (ex. 2). Notice how, in the bridge passage, the opening cor anglais theme appears as the bass line.

Ex. 2

At fig. 4 itself the upper parts of the preceding bridge passage are freely distributed about the orchestra and the battle commences. The cor anglais theme is now transformed into a descending scale which appears in various rhythmic disguises throughout the symphony, assuming increasing importance towards the end of the whole work. Apart from one bar in 2/4 time (third bar of fig. 4) the time signature is exclusively 5/4 to the end of the first half of the symphony.

The mood for the most part of this section is bright and heroic, but a brief episode marked Lento between figs 8 and 9 re-introduces the cor anglais theme, this time glowering at us from the depths of the contra-bassoon. Flute and cor anglais hint uneasily at the previous "heroic" material whilst the timpani lend the air of a bizarre ritual dance (ex. 3).

Ex. 3

The Allegro Moderato returns, however, three bars before fig. 10 and leads into a more relaxed section around figs 11 and 12. The foregoing material is transferred from urgent upthrusting quavers to flowing crotches and minims. Three bars before fig. 13 oboe and clarinet hint at something like the opening cor anglais melody:

Ex. 4

The urgent music returns once more before being cut off suddenly on a great *crescendo*. A short bridge passage, carrying a faint trace of the convoluted cello music of the symphony's opening, leads us into an Adagio section. The mood is dark and searching with occasional glimmers of light, all seemingly governed by a brief phrase which leads into a descending scale:

Ex. 5

At fig. 21 a yearning phrase from the violins sets up a sympathetic response from the rest of the orchestra and the music swells, ever seeking some hidden goal. Fragments of earlier material are now treated to variation and, although Brian has dispensed with key signature, the semitone G♭ to F tension is still in evidence:

Ex. 6

The music passes, with *pizzicato* strings, to a descending episode for violas and cellos - the effect of which is something like a heavy, velvet drape being lowered across the scene. We have now arrived at the crossroads of the symphony. The opening cor anglais theme sounds dolefully from bass clarinet, bassoons, euphonium, tuba and double basses against a dreamlike backcloth of rolling percussion and glittering harps:

Ex. 7

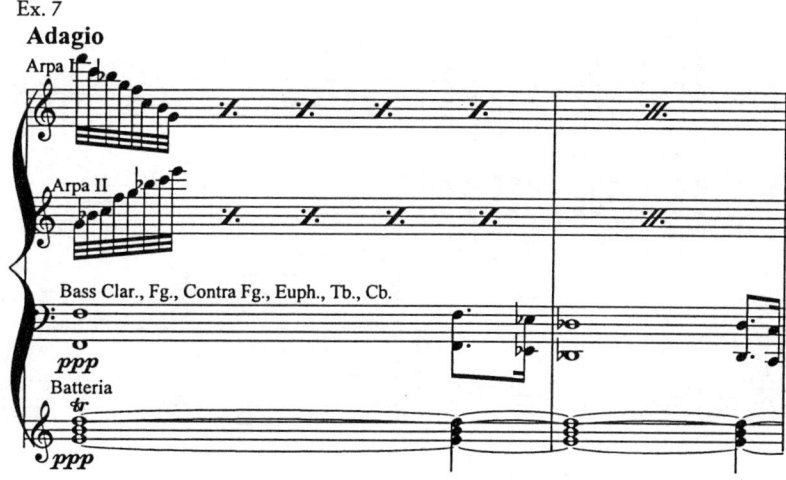

The second half of the symphony begins with a Tempo Grazioso announced by the fourth horn in 6/4.

The mood at first is somewhat solemn and muted, but suddenly light dawns and a warm *crescendo* ensues. The horn phrase passes to a flute over a pedal D and A in the strings, finally to be taken up by the whole orchestra. The excitement mounts. The theme is stated strongly, backed up by the side-drums, and a passionate outburst leads to a further quickening of the pace, the organ making its first appearance in the symphony at this point. Breathless flutes urge the music onwards, but a change has now occurred. The warmth of the previous material has given way to a tense, strained atmosphere. The fury finally breaks one bar before fig. 42. Strings and wind sound out bare F-C-F 5ths against an organ dissonance, whilst a defiant theme is heard in the brass and percussion. The bare 5th, particularly in the "home" key of a movement or symphony, is usually a signal in Brian's music that the end has arrived. In this case, however, Brian makes it perfectly clear that he has no intention of ending matters at this point. Twice the organ, wind and brass crash out the 5ths and twice their challenge is met by a contradictory upthrust in the strings centered on G:

Ex. 8

After the second dramatic gesture, the tension collapses like a pricked balloon. The strings' defence strategy seems to have worked and music of a gentle, consolatory nature ensues. However, all is not plain sailing by any means. A rich climax results in a further F-C-F chord accompanied by a funereal roll of muffled side-drums. The C is held over in a clarinet and bassoon which in turn slither grotesquely down the scale:

Ex. 9

A scurrying string passage ensues marked Allegro Moderato ma Deciso. Heroic gestures abound and, following a brief moment of respite, the strings begin a swirling figuration which passes to the wind. A dance-like section follows, energetic, but not altogether free from menace. A solo violin ushers in a tender passage based loosely around F minor (ex. 10), which in turn gives way to a carefree interlude for wind and percussion.

Ex. 10

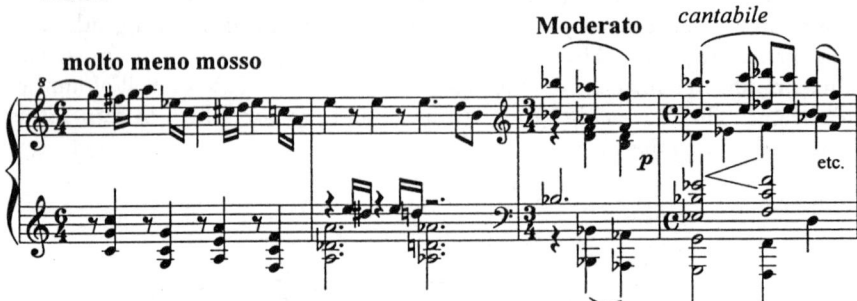

The swirling figuration returns, this time with added brass - the trombones leaping around with the triplet dance figure previously heard in the strings. Four big cadential chords usher us into the coda of the symphony. This begins solemnly in F minor, but one soon becomes aware that all is not well. Paced out in steady crotchets, the music takes leave of F and moves uneasily through G major, to A minor, and to C major, the dominant of the home key. Jack-booted side-drums urge us unexpectedly into G♭ major - the key which caused the original tension at the outset of the symphony. The key is emphasized by the addition of the organ whilst brass and low strings and wind stride sternly downwards. The effect is grimly triumphant - as of an enemy pompously striding around the capital city of a conquered nation. Suddenly, we are jerked by sheer brute force down a semitone to a great chord of F minor. Two plagal cadences - still emphasizing minor tonality and both ending on a blazing "tierce de Picardie" - lead to the final chord heavy with F-C-F 5ths. Victory, it would seem, has been achieved at the 11th hour - but only just!

Ex. 11

It will be noticed that I have avoided describing Brian's Fourteenth Symphony in the kind of terms usually found in symphonic analysis. It is almost impossible, in my view, to refer to Brian's highly unorthodox structures in terms of conventional exposition, development and recapitulation. Brian is what is known as an "intuitive" composer - that is to say the governing factor in his music is not a pre-conceived form or structure, but the initial inspiration, usually set down at furious pace in a pencil sketch. It has become a matter of common knowledge that Brian could not bear to be disturbed whilst engaged on the preliminary sketches of a new symphony - all the other stages he referred to as "purely mechanical".

Thus, I feel it is a mistake to look for conventional structures in the Brian symphonies - although some of them do occur from time to time. What is more apparent is the way in which Brian's muse leads him to engage in continuous variations on his material. I believe the Symphony No. 14 to be an excellent example of Brian's skill in that direction. Consider exx. 12, 13 and 14:

Ex. 12

Ex. 13

Ex. 14

None of these could be described as a symphonic "subject", but all of them play a vital role as the "building blocks" from which extended sections are constructed. Sometimes the intervals of these phrases are altered almost out of recognition, but the general line is maintained, giving a feeling of great cohesion and unification. Remarkable too is the way in which Brian controls the emotional tension in this work. Each great outburst, each relaxation of mood, seems to develop from the foregoing material in a completely natural manner (to this listener at least) - the final coda arriving with the same kind of inevitability one finds in the symphonies of Mahler, and yet we are caught out right at the end with that unexpected victorious coup.

I firmly believe - and the study required for this article has confirmed that belief - that the work under consideration will ultimately prove to be one of Brian's most effective symphonic essays. This statement, however, can only be demonstrated by adequately prepared performances. The only one the symphony has had to date was a studio performance (together with No. 21) by the London Symphony Orchestra under Edward Downes which, although excellent in many ways, fell short of an ideal account by reason of an orchestra somewhat unfamiliar with Brian's idiom and a conductor wrestling with a highly individual (and partly illegible) score. This is not to denigrate the remarkably powerful reading from Downes and the LSO, but today we are in the happier state of having at least one orchestra conversant with Brian's style (the Philharmonia) and a number of conductors who have now had ample opportunity of achieving a rapport with the music (Sir Charles Mackerras and James Blair between them have been responsible for six of Brian's major works being heard in London over just four months, to name but two conductors!). The constant editorial work done by Graham Hatton has also helped to clear up ambiguities and has paved the way for clear thinking. It is, then, my sincere hope that those concerned with projecting performances and executing them will be encouraged to investigate the Symphony No. 14 in F minor and to give the work at least another airing, so that a fairer assessment be made and the work reveal what I believe to be its true significance. I am a firm believer in letting music speak for itself. Let us hope that, in this case, it will be allowed to do so.

Myer Fredman/Robert Simpson: Preparing Brian's scores for performance[1]

At the time of my first involvement in the preparation of some of Havergal Brian's symphonies for performance I had very little previous knowledge (in real musical sound) of his style. Naturally one used one's aural imagination as in any other study but normally one usually has an unconscious recollection of other performances, or at least other works. With Havergal Brian, at that time, these were few. Generally speaking, Brian's style seems to be one of incredibly condensed thought and yet there is a large inner 'melos' running through. The works, however, take some time to live with in order that both aspects become apparent.

The scores themselves tended to hinder this search for the overall shape as Brian's handwriting deteriorated considerably with age; one seemed to spend so much of the time with a sort of magnifying glass trying to determine the correctness of the dots on the page. This, coupled with a need to clarify the texture, tended to make one lose sight of the wood for the trees - or was it the other way round? If Havergal Brian had been able to hear more of his music in the flesh earlier on I do not think his style would have altered, but it would have been stated with a greater textual clarity. This may sound like heresy, but it is not.

---

[1] Myer Fredman's note is an especially commissioned letter to the Editor from *Newsletter* 13 (IX-X 1977), p. 5. Myer Fredman has recorded with the London Philharmonic the *Sinfonia Tragica* (No. 6) and Symphony No. 16 for Lyrita (Lyrita SRCS. 67, now deleted). Robert Simpson's *Textual accuracy in the "Gothic"* is a letter to the Editor from *Newsletter* 21 (I-II 1979), p. 7.

I feel now that, thanks of course to the crusades of Robert Simpson and the early Brian enthusiasts, the first stage in comprehension of his work has been well and truly consolidated and the problems mentioned above recede into normality. I myself would love an opportunity to re-study and perform again those works with which I was involved. I know that the performances would be remarkably different.

Harold Truscott, in his fascinating and characteristically observant analysis of the *Gothic* Symphony, remarks that in the last chord of the scherzo the fifth horn's printed B was changed in Sir Adrian Boult's performance to an A, converting the chord into plain D major. He rightly remarks that the B anticipates the opening of the *Te Deum*, and notes that the harp parts (containing it in an arpeggio) were not altered. I can shed some light on this; the composer requested the change. He felt that the added 6th on a horn produced a disconcertingly cheap effect, and that the discreet presence of this note in the harps was sufficient. I agreed with him, and also felt that the clear D major chord in the orchestra had a touch of grandeur that was completely spoiled by the sustained added 6th; the fleeting traces of the B in the harp parts made the point without overdoing it. Brian was entirely satisfied by the result in rehearsal and asked me to make sure that the correction was made. If ever a really accurate score of the *Gothic* Symphony is prepared, this small but significant change must be included.

One curious point is the omission of the harp arpeggi from the chord at the beginning of the *Te Deum*, so that the fifth horn's B becomes the only one in the whole orchestra. The fact that just one player is adding a 6th inevitably sounds dangerously like a wrong note, and the obvious answer is to use the harp parts which the composer may have forgotten to write in the score at this point. I can see none but over-ingenious explanations of their absence when the chord is repeated on paper though not in performance (if there is no interval). The manuscript of Part II is lost, so we can't at present check what he actually wrote down; when Brian gave me the manuscript score of Part I he said he didn't know where the *Te Deum* was. The omission of the harps from the first chord of Part II was a perhaps not untypical small slip - the printed score (presumably proof-read by the composer) teems with mistakes. There is in *The Gothic* one magnificently comprehensive omission - when I asked him why the contralto soloist had no solo, he said "I forgot about her!" It's possible, of course, that he was treating me as Beethoven treated Schindler, but somehow he never struck me as having that kind of humour. If you tried to pull *his* leg he rarely saw it - as when, after he'd given me his twenty-oddth symphony (he was getting on for 90), I said "Now you've just got through your middle period, why don't you write some late quartets?" He considered this gravely and said "Well, maybe - but no, I don't really want to write quartets; I need the orchestra".

Barry Cronin: Arcadia v. Elysium: some thoughts on Symphony No. 27[1]

Following my request for tape copies of some of Brian's works, I received a number of replies - for which I am naturally very grateful. One member kindly sent me a tape of four of the late symphonies; I decided to listen to these works in a way different from usual. I chose one - Symphony No. 27 - played it a few times, listening with open ears and jotting down any thoughts that occurred to me, and then I compared the impressions made on me by the music with the impressions it made on Malcolm MacDonald (who, after all, is still the writer one turns to first if one wants to know anything about a work of Brian's). And interestingly enough it seems that on this occasion we differ, around the main points.

At about the time of composition of this 27th Symphony, towards the end of 1966 (Brian actually marked it "10 Dec 1966"), an important external event was taking shape in Brian's life: the first performance of his Seventh Symphony, of 1948. "There are wonderful things in that 7th Symphony", he wrote afterwards to Robert Simpson. The Seventh is one of Brian's masterworks, whereas No. 26, completed late that spring and most of it before the recording of No. 7, Malcolm MacDonald for one rates as the weakest of all his symphonies. It is perhaps no surprise to find Brian, in No. 27, bracing himself and setting to, fired with the joy of hearing his great No. 7, and trying his damndest to write as good again. Despite the fact that he was approaching the end of his 91st year, he did.

In a Radio 3 conversation between Brian and Robert Simpson - 22 February 1967 - Brian remarked: "... if you speak of the *Dramatis Personae* of a play ... somehow the flute... may be considered the principal character ...". A solo flute begins and ends this work; Debussy wrote *Syrinx* for a solo flute, and Syrinx was the name Pan gave to the pipes he fashioned from the reeds. Pan's domain was Arcadia, where I believe Brian's symphony has its home.

The first movement opens Lento, moving to Allegro giocoso e marcato sempre. As Brian has told us, the solo flute begins the work: a different and surprising move right at the start, for he is fond of jolting the listener to attention (perhaps a trick learned from Haydn?). The flute has a lonely sound to it - the lower woodwinds punctuating its discursive style. (This very beginning has a strange, other-world feel about it; it is as if the music had already been in progress, but had only just been made audible to us; has someone else said that, somewhere?) The strings usurp the flute's dominance for the briefest of moments, but not to be outdone it silences all with an agile and gentle solo passage ... perhaps this is Syrinx the nymph being awakened in the morning by a butterfly flitting round her scented face. The flute has hardly died before the timpani jauntily shove us into the Allegro: a bustling, open-air tune, not without good humour (Malcolm MacDonald says "jauntily enough", which I think is begrudging the music its naturalness). There is a profound confidence here - no dark

---

[1] From *Newsletter* 75 (I-II 1988), pp. 5-6.

shades that I can see. A typical Brian passage soon arrives, a climax for warring brass, that seem to vie for dominance but retreat with none having lost. This is succeeded by solo violin, oboes, clarinet and horn passing a single phrase between them; but the impatient flute cavorts happily once more. Is this Syrinx nervously looking about her, as the flute's melody finds darker keys?

The sun breaks through as the strings lead a call for more urgency, more seriousness. The brass and percussion return to disturb the scene even more. This is complex writing: rhythmically exciting, orchestrally challenging and intellectually stimulating, all in a few pages. Following these hard-fought few minutes the strings sing out alone an impassioned cry which could so easily be described as "essentially English" or "decidedly pastoral", and this leads me to the second movement and the music in general of the "English Musical Renaissance".

Why is so much English music of this century described as "unmistakably English" or "in a pastoral vein"? Why is the music of the English Musical Renaissance (an excellent term) almost synonymous with a pastoral mood? Warlock's remark of Vaughan Williams' *Pastoral* Symphony, that it reminded him of a cow looking over a hedge, never fails to make me smile, and yet there is an element of truth here: a tranquility, a calmness with blue skies and rich fields is conveyed. But too often the word "pastoral" is left glibly hanging in the air, some naïve label that is supposed to conjure up all sorts of paradisal images, but all too often forces many people to cringe and turn off their receptive faculties. Does the pastoral idiom stem from the Romantic poets of the 1790s and a little later? Goethe, Wordsworth, Byron, Keats, Shelley and others who were (if I may be forgiven the paraphrase!) charged with the grandeur of Nature:

> .. For Nature then ...
> To me was all in all ..
> (Wordsworth: *Lines Composed a few miles above Tintern Abbey*)

The ideas and ideals of these poets have survived and even increased their meaning over the intervening years, inspiring many artists since, and many English composers have been proud of such a fruitful literary heritage and utilized it unsparingly - in many different ways. Perhaps their obsession with Nature in all its grand forms has much in it of the earlier poets' obsession. We know that Brian was very fond of Shelley's poetry, if only from his setting of the first two huge Acts of *Prometheus Unbound*. This great poem is the antithesis of Byron's very famous and (at the time) enormously popular *Manfred*. Byron's "Dramatic Poem" concerns a world-weary, sensitive and doomed young man who shakes his fist at the Heavens (i.e. God) and defies death, while yet longing for it; and who believes himself to be unable to escape the clutches of his destiny. Manfred speaks for Mankind when he says:

> ... I have known
> The fulness of humiliation, for
> I sunk before my vain despair, and knelt
> To my own desolation.
> (Byron: *Manfred* Act II)

Manfred is a defeatist; he believes man, and from man the world, to be bad; or to quote a current colloquial saying "Life's a bitch and then you die".

Sharply opposed to this is Shelley's "Lyrical Drama" - the work I think Brian felt closest to him - which sets forth the optimistic aspect of early Romanticism (with Shelley and Blake at its head); the ideals that are here embraced are that man is essentially good (see Rousseau), and that he is a deep well of untapped potential. Prometheus, the fire-bringer, sacrifices his liberty to serve man, in the hope that man will make for himself a better world without the help of the Gods.

> Beyond the glassy gulfs we flee
> Of shadow-peopled Infancy,
> Through Death and Birth, to a diviner day;
> A paradise of vaulted bowers...
> (Shelley: *Prometheus Unbound* Act II)

I will now try to draw these two strands together, as I see them in Brian. Without doubt he was a Romantic - not Romantic from an extravagant outworn Mahlerian grandeur (outworn, that is, if anyone but Mahler is being extravagant); the *Gothic* Symphony is powerful but anachronistic: it should have been written as a collaboration between a dozen or so evil, debauched monks in the 15th century, and filled the air of the great cities of Europe as they were then. No, Brian was a Romantic from a love of Nature. (He didn't write five English Suites *just* for fun.) A love of Nature in a Romantic inspires sublimity. Not only did Brian set the important half of *Prometheus Unbound*, he also set the same poet's *The Cenci*, where Romanticism meets Gothic sensibilities and fierce passions run wild; he set Goethe's *Faust*, the archetypal Romantic figure along with, perhaps, his *Werther* (incidentally, Shelley translated parts of *Faust* - very well, too); Brian also set *Agamemnon* and it was to contrast (not to follow) Aeschylus' *Prometheus Bound* that Shelley wrote his play/poem. There are in Brian Romantic titles like *Wine of Summer* and *Sinfonia Tragica*. Does "pastoral" in the great British music of this century signify a sense of religious and divine beauty, but without the deity? Does, perhaps, this great slow movement of Symphony No. 27 portray a man, an old man who has seen and known so much, stumbling across a ruined church in the country, which breathes fragrant peace? And does he turn from this and from God, to seeing and knowing the wisdom in nature and natural things?

The music of this slow movement - marked Lento ma non troppo is of an integrity and passionate strength that strike one immediately as being a personal outpouring rather than something merely created. The main phrase - stated almost at the start and passed around from instrument to instrument - seems to me, on every hearing, infinitely beautiful. Despite being marked *forte* (after the trumpet's entry), there is yet a gentle breathing about the phrasing, and the scoring is that of an experienced master: it has a light feel but does not sound anywhere thin. This first key phrase is developed for some time, mainly between strings and woodwind. Brian shows a delight with his material by putting the melody in the bass and playfully experimenting above that with motifs for piccolo, oboe, xylophone and glockenspiel. For much of the movement's central section the tone is restrained, the scoring relatively lightweight, but a solo horn soon leads us to a more tense and harmonically dense section: sombre but powerful. We should remember that Pan - for all his good-natured antics and healthy revelries - was believed to be the instigator of sudden, unreasoning fear that overcame people (or animals) in dark, brooding, lonely places, and instilled in them a sense of Pan-ic. As the violins take us away from the twilight world of the solo horn, there is a momentary sense of oppression, and this is the movement's climax, for from here muted strings play out the remaining bars in a half-light, beautiful and still. It was here that I felt the performance I heard - from Sir Charles Mackerras and the Philharmonia Orchestra - didn't quite come off: the strings were not rapt enough, but perhaps that was the recording's fault!

Brian's lifetime of submission to the creative impulse may well have shown him that a sublimity (albeit temporal and often insubstantial) could only come from living to the fullest extent possible; i.e. testing one's latent powers; and that peace can never come from serving anything but oneself. The end of this slow movement, with its high strings and delicate celesta, sees a wise man in knowledge, for Pan can also mean "All" or the "Pasturer", a spirit as ancient and enduring as man himself. This music will endure.

The finale - Allegro con anima - is full of energy, yet has its darker moments. Malcolm MacDonald asserts that the movement's elegiac mood triumphs. This cannot be, for an elegy is a song, a lament for the passing of something loved, and hence cannot triumph, for however great was the thing we are mourning, it is now no longer and only time is triumphant.

The movement begins in a lively, buoyant manner that suddenly drops away to leave the woodwind almost floundering, though the violins soon lend a hand. As the Allegro fades, the flutes, oboe and bassoons weave its melody around one another; this is succeeded by a brief calm passage - violins and harp, with violins almost immediately becoming agitated; the speed increases, only to stop as suddenly with a held chord on violins and an appealing ascending figure on bassoons, this allowing the trumpet time to announce a furious, rhythmically adventurous and exciting few bars that recall some of the first movement's more impassioned moments. This is followed by a quieter, but nonetheless equally busy, section, from which the strings make increasingly dissonant pleas for some sort of return to more tranquil times.

The opening fanfare on horns now returns, with a surer feel to its high spirits than earlier, and where at the beginning the woodwind seemed taken by surprise with the fanfare, here they are not caught off guard and give us, with the high strings, a bouncy, almost cheeky little tune. After some jarring exchanges the oboe takes us into a curiously beautiful short section, and it is at this point in the movement that Malcolm MacDonald suggests an intentional quote from the most famous C minor symphony - Beethoven's Fifth. What are perhaps the most beautiful bars in the symphony follow, with blazoning brass and soaring strings, but it is quickly over and magically the solo flute, the main protagonist - emerges unscathed - remember Syrinx was not caught or raped by Pan - he simply grasped the reeds that she left behind, and she escaped while he fashioned the flute that still survives today. And Brian's flute allows the strings to return, though subdued, and the symphony eases to silence: resigned but stoically undefeated. This music, sad and perhaps sounding a little lost in places, is no memorial to death. It breathes an air of survival against great odds.

Rodney Stephen Newton: Some thoughts on the 30th[1]

Of the works performed at the 1976 Havergal Brian Centenary concerts at the Alexandra Palace, few others seemed to provoke as much controversy as Symphony No. 30. This astonishing product of Brian's extreme old age has been commented on and debated - sometimes quite vehemently - in the pages of the *Newsletter*. However, I decided to withhold my personal judgement until an opportunity presented itself of studying the full score, since I knew that there had been a number of accidents during the Alexandra Palace performance, and that the acoustic of that hall often played tricks upon the hearer. Upon obtaining a copy of the score - very kindly loaned by the indefatigable Graham Hatton - I realized that what came over the radio of the first performance of the work was indeed only a partial account of what was in the score. The "Ally Pally" acoustic did its usual job of submerging much of the detail of the first movement under a general mud of excessive reverberation, and in the second movement things went badly awry with the orchestra.[2] Whole sections of instruments missed their entries, the strings crept in nervously at one point hopelessly out of place, and the only section free from accident was the percussion (and please do not accuse me of nepotism!). The powerful coda began uncertainly and the ultimate dénouement seemed to fail to make its true impact. I do not intend to discuss the reasons for these mishaps as I never see the point of such post-mortems, but I think I have made it clear that the Alexandra Palace performance did not present a completely true picture of the work. I think it fruitless to argue for and against this piece solely on the grounds of the performance, and feel the symphony will only make its full impact in an accurate professional performance in a more sympathetic acoustic.

---

[1] From *Newsletter* 16 (III-IV 1978), pp. 5-7.
[2] Harry Newstone writes in a letter to the Editor from *Newsletter* 17 (V-VI 1978), p. 3: "In his article Rodney Stephen Newton refers to the things that 'went badly awry with the orchestra' in the second movement of Brian's 30th Symphony during its first performance at the Alexandra Palace in September 1976. He forbears to discuss the reasons for the mishap and most charitably does not mention that I was the conductor on that occasion. While I much appreciate his sensitivity in this, I am concerned that, as a result, some blame may be imputed to the (then) New Philharmonia Orchestra. To be sure, the conditions of preparation for this concert were less than ideal, but in the last analysis it must be said that throughout our difficulties the New Philharmonia Orchestra was patient, fully co-operative and immensely skilful, and that the fault for things going wrong was entirely mine. I shall hope that the future will bring me an opportunity to redeem the flawed presentation that this fascinating work received at its première."

Brian completed his 30th Symphony on 13 November 1967 - a year of outstanding activity for the veteran composer. He had put the finishing touches to Symphony No. 27, written Nos 28 and 29, then in just three months after the completion of the 29th Symphony, the 30th appeared. As Brian generally sketched out a work in pencil before making a short score, then a full score, it is reasonable to suppose that the music of No. 30 was already firmly in his mind even before he began to work on it. Furthermore this symphony is so drastically unlike its predecessors - gone is the neo-classicism of No. 29 - that one searches for a parallel. To obtain an idea of what might have inspired "Brian 30", we must go back to 1963. It is believed that in this year, the year of the 21st Symphony, Brian began to make plans for an opera on the subject of Sophocles' *Oedipus at Colonus*. He shelved the idea for a while before starting work in earnest in the fecund year of 1967. During this time he also envisaged a further opera on Sophocles' *Antigone* to make a double bill with *Oedipus*. Brian eventually ceased his labours on the *Oedipus* project, believing that the English translation he was using as a libretto was still in copyright - his adventures with *Deirdre of the Sorrows* had taught him all about that kind of problem! He declared, however, that the music contained some "fine stuff" and that he would use it in an orchestral work. The next one to appear was Symphony No. 30.

Searching back further, one comes across the Symphony No. 22 of 1964-65. This was written within a year or so of Brian's first ideas about *Oedipus*, and the similarities between this work and Symphony No. 30 are, I believe, more than coincidental. Both are two movement symphonies; both share the same dark mood; both are constructed in a similar, highly compressed manner. To add to these likenesses, the opening motive of the 22nd Symphony is quoted no less than three times in the second movement of Symphony No. 30. Thus, it is not unreasonable to suppose that Symphonies Nos 22 and 30 are in fact companion pieces and that No. 30 is a further development of the events in No. 22.

Brian calls the 30th Symphony "Sinfonia in B flat minor", although this key is studiously avoided until the climax of the first movement. Even the opening phrase twists like a snake around the B♭ tonal centre:

Ex. 1

This is followed by string and wind phrases which blossom into a warm cadence in F - the opening eight-note motive being ever-present in the bass line:

Ex. 2

There then follows a development of the opening material with increased chromaticism resulting from Brian's multi-layered counterpoint. The mood soon darkens and Brian begins moving in chords built on 4ths (rather than his beloved parallel 5ths). This gives the resultant harmony a misty feeling (a mist which the Alexandra Palace acoustic obligingly turned into a dense fog!). A number of episodes appear - some reflective:

Ex. 3

Some fantastic and bizarre:

Ex. 4

Some wild and warlike:

With the probable dramatic basis of this work in mind, it is perfectly possible to imagine that one is listening to the prelude to a stage tragedy. Perhaps that is what this first movement was intended to be in the first place.

Ex. 6

The wildness is answered by a melancholy passage for strings remarkably like one in Symphony No. 22 (exx. 6 and 7).

Ex. 7

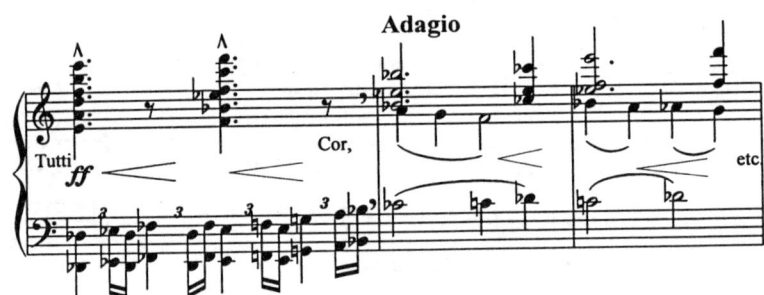

A further strong episode leads to a *calmato* passage in which we suddenly find ourselves listening to a string quartet. In just five bars Brian has moved from the power of the full orchestra to the intimacy of the quartet. A strong passage in the "home" key of B♭ minor brings us to the final climax of the movement which is abruptly truncated and answered by a calmer coda in which the opening theme appears in the bass once more. The final cadence is one of resignation, leading to the inevitable bare 5ths by means of a shortened statement of the "theme". There is a tiny bridge of a single *pizzicato* crotchet in F before the curtain rises on what is obviously the second movement - although Brian does not place any double bar line before it nor does he designate it in the full score as a separate movement.

The process here is so similar to the 22nd Symphony as to deserve comment. In both cases the second movement begins with a kind of march episode. The mood is similar although in the 30th the textures are tenuous and melancholy. Perhaps we have here two different treatments of the same operatic scene (exx. 8 and 9).

Ex. 8

Tempo di marcia e ritmico ♩= 90

Ex. 9

Moderato comodo e leggiero

The sparse writing continues until a short passage for wind quartet leads to an *allegro* in which 3/4 time is juxtaposed with 4/4 time. From here on the mood becomes increasingly darker and the textures appreciably thicken. Without warning, and in one single bar, Brian plunges us into a *maestoso e marcato* quote from Symphony No. 22 (see exx. 10 and 11).

Ex. 10

Ex. 11

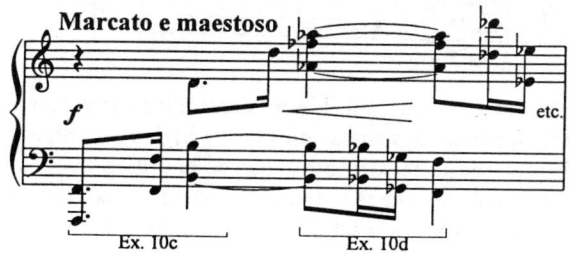

This is repeated a little further along by the brass and strings and leads to a powerful climax. There then follows a curious passage in 3/4 time in which the soft, marching percussion returns, over which the strings and wind play melancholy phrases. Strange visions seem to pass before us as weird figurations are heard (ex. 12).

Ex. 12

Solemn bells ring out, supported by heavy string chords, and with a roar from angry timpani we pass straight into the coda. This is announced by the opening motive of Symphony No. 22 once more - as clear a quote as one could wish for - and one is tempted to wonder whether this was not intended to represent Oedipus himself in the opera, as the upsurging theme in the opera *The Cenci* represents the evil Count Cenci (see exx. 13 and 14).

Ex. 13

Ex. 14

The coda is broad and powerful. Heavy descending figures stride through the bass line with the upper strings and wind soaring higher and higher, whilst trumpets and side-drums (the usual trio are required and used to great effect) sound out martially. The final cadence is as harsh a discord as may be imagined. Before the final B♭ and F open 5ths are reached there is a penultimate cry of despair with the trombones and tuba holding C♭ and G♭ against the B♭ and F of the rest (ex. 15). Perhaps this may have been a cry from the throat of the blinded Oedipus. The unsettled end of Symphony No. 22 has here found its grim resolution.

Ex. 15

I do not intend this article to be an analytical study of Brian's 30th Symphony. There is much that I have not mentioned and discussed for the reaction that I prefer to leave such things to the more able pen of Malcolm MacDonald. My aim here has been to stir up interest in this powerful work in the hope that one day it will take its place as one of Brian's most significant symphonies, and that further performances will reveal it to be the powerful experience for its hearers that I believe it to be.

Harold Truscott: Havergal Brian and the single-movement symphony[1]

For the next half hour or so I want to talk to you about a subject that interests me greatly, and which should, I think, interest anyone whose love of Havergal Brian's music goes beneath the surface. This is his strong inclination to the single-movement, or single-design, symphony. In half an hour I cannot say a great deal and certainly at the end I shall not have come to any world-shaking conclusion; but, then, this is not only not possible, it is hardly desirable. Thought on such a subject, if it is of value at all, should simply stimulate further thought in those who hear it.

In order to consider Brian fruitfully in this connection we must first consider the symphony of the past: what we call the "classical" symphony, although its composers did not, what many call the romantic symphony, but which I prefer to call simply 19th century symphony, and the 20th century; in the last category I am unashamedly selective and include only those works which show some respect for the symphony's past. And, so far as I come to any conclusion at all, it will be this: that the classical, 19th and 20th century composers, when they wrote one-movement symphonies, did so as an exception, even an abnormality, and

---

[1] This talk, given at the Havergal Brian Society/British Music Society "*Gothic* Day" meeting held at the London Penta Hotel on 25 May, was first published in *Newsletter* 31 (X-XI 1980), pp. 4-7.

largely by accident, whereas for Brian it became more and more clear that this was his natural expression. He is the one composer of symphonies, of whatever type, for whom the single-movement design was an essential.

Many composers have considered that they were writing a one-movement symphony when they had four miniature sections roughly corresponding to first movement, slow movement, scherzo and finale, all joined together. Some have, indeed, proudly drawn attention, in the remarks they made about the particular work, to this arrangement. But this sort of thing is not at all what I am referring to in the phrase "single-movement symphony". In fact, no matter what the quality of the music thus produced, these composers have succeeded only in writing a tabloid form of normal symphony; a normal symphony reduced in size, like a photographic reduction. What I specify as a single-movement design is a piece which encompasses the essential elements of a normal symphony, no matter how arranged, absolutely naturally within one unbroken design; in which there are no sudden switches to elements, tonal or thematic, which do not grow from what has preceded them, or, if the switch seems sudden, where the relevance in growth is displayed later if not sooner. It will be best here to give an actual example. The work is what I privately think of as Brahms' actual third symphony; it is the *Tragic Overture*. If any of you do not know this work, although I imagine most of you do, you would be well advised to study it on the score of its structure. In fact, even if you do know it, such study would not do any harm. You'd be surprised what you can still learn about it. Here we have not only a complete piece - that is, something that does not require anything else to complete the sense - but a complete symphonic design. We have a vigorous exposition of two groups, the second growing out of the first through a transition passage equally connected with each, backward and forward; the whole is one of Brahms' finest mature pieces of writing. There is an equally fine recapitulation and coda. In between is a development - a half-speed development; Brahms actually asks for half speed by indicating that crotchets shall now equal the previous minims, or quarter-notes equal half-notes. In other words we have, not a tabloid symphony but a complete symphonic or sonata design which includes, as a natural part of its progress, a definite slow movement; there is also the large coda, growing out of the previous music as the second group grew out of the transition passage, which itself grew out of the first group. The entire design is self-contained, and it has all the necessary elements, if we remember the three-movement classical symphony which persisted for so long. It is a genuine one-movement symphony, the first of which I am aware, for the only classical instance, Mozart's Symphony [in G major] No. 32, K. 318, scarcely qualifies, since it was written as what it manifestly is, a characteristic Mozart overture, for the unfinished opera *Zaide*.

As to whether Brahms was aware of what he had done in this piece I cannot say. He was the reverse of an inattentive artist but, as with anybody else, he could be taken by surprise. It could be that he was so unused to the idea of the concept he had produced that he called it overture, as something he was accustomed to, especially as a concert overture was what he had set out to write.

Certainly, when two years later he wrote the F major symphony he called it his Third. And this leads me to believe that what we have in the *Tragic Overture* was, in a sense, accidental. It was not planned as a one-movement symphony, but that is what resulted. And I believe that such things must largely be, with one big exception, to a certain extent accidental.

There are other designs which fulfil the same conditions, although not, of course, necessarily in the manner of Brahms' overture, but I must be content with listing a few of them. One is the *Symphonic Prologue to a Tragedy*, by Max Reger. Reger is often said to have written no symphonies; but, as is frequently the case with things that are often said, this is not true. He wrote a Symphony in E minor, somewhat influenced by Brahms, in 1890, when he was 17. Reger wrote another in 1896, in B minor, which he suppressed and which may even have been destroyed. In his main orchestral period, which produced, among other things, the Serenade and the *Hiller* and *Mozart Variations*, there are no works called "symphony". But there is the *Sinfonietta*, which is a large four-movement work lasting some 45-50 minutes, a symphony if ever there was one and Reger was not being coy in calling it sinfonietta; in his maturity he was a very modest man and just would not compare himself with the great symphonists by calling it a symphony. And there is the *Symphonic Prologue*.

The next work is not a symphony, but a piano sonata; the one in G minor, op. 22, by Nikolay Medtner, the Russian composer of German origin. This was composed in 1912, and, while it is a very different work, it does have, like the *Tragic Overture*, a genuine slow movement development; as with the Brahms, too, it is one long growth, everything, as it comes, growing or evolving out of what has preceded it. It is one of the most tightly-knit compositions in my experience, which is not small. Medtner's sonata also uses, quite naturally, the keys which have, as tonic, six out of the seven degrees of the G minor scale; and it, too, was arrived at accidentally. Medtner originally planned a normal three-movement sonata, but realized when he had completed this movement that he had also completed the work.

Sibelius must be mentioned; not, so far as I am concerned, so much for his Seventh Symphony, as for another work. The Seventh, magnificent though it is, has never convinced me of its single-movement status; and when I discovered that it was composed as a symphonic fantasia, and that it still had this title when it was first performed, and only gained the title Symphony No. 7, in one movement, between that performance and its publication, it only confirmed the impression I had already formed. I believe that Sibelius was right to begin with, and that this was a case where second thoughts were not best. On the other hand, he wrote another work which he also called symphonic fantasia (and did not change the name for publication), and this is a genuine single-movement symphony. It is the symphonic fantasia *Pohjola's Daughter*.

Then there is Roy Harris' Third Symphony. Strangely, on paper this work, which is not predominantly a sonata work, although it has elements, shows a fair amount of kinship with what I have called the tabloid symphony. But this is only to the eye. In fact, in performance it has no such suggestion. It is a genuine one-movement symphony, complete in every detail. I suspect that this work, too, achieved its single-movement status by accident. Some years ago I wrote to Harris asking him about this matter and also about some peculiar cuts which turn up in every performance but which are not in the printed score. I had, after an interval, a postcard from him, thanking me for my letter and saying that a full answer to my questions would follow. But it never did, and now he is dead.

My last example is fairly recent: it is Edmund Rubbra's Tenth Symphony, which interestingly reverses the usual process, since it consists of two outer slow-moving portions enclosing a much faster middle part, which, while Rubbra is not here fully using sonata style, but only what he wants, does have the function of a development. So far as I know this was planned as a single-movement work. It is worth noting that all these works, except Sibelius' doubtful Seventh Symphony, are isolated works in their composer's output.

I have spoken of the single-movement symphony, or sonata, design as an abnormality. My reason for this is in the nature of music. Writers have sometimes, as a convenient analogy, likened the three or four movements of a symphony or sonata to the three or four acts of a play. It sounds so obvious that it can seem reasonably convincing; but it is a visual comparison only. In fact, there is no connection. In my experience, convenient analogies where music is concerned are usually highly inconvenient stumbling-blocks to any accurate assessment because they are both visual (instead of aural, as they should be) and wrong, because they are reasoned from visual terms, and are the result of either laziness on the part of the writer or his inability to assess music, or a combination of the two. And the field of music criticism, unfortunately, contains many such irresponsible and incompetent people. The division into acts exists largely to build up subsidiary climaxes, allow for scene changes, and give the audience breathing space, to say nothing of the actors. But this is not the reason for the division into movements of a symphony or a sonata. Unlike a play or novel, music is, in normal circumstances, single-minded. So, in a way, is the novel or the play; a writer can only deal with one situation at a time; but he can, and does, intersperse situations of different character as the play or the novel progresses. Music cannot successfully do this, except in very rare circumstances: the Brahms-type portmanteau movements, as in the middle movements of the A major Violin and Piano Sonata and the F major String Quintet, are rare examples of this amalgamation. I could even quote one from a piano sonata by Clementi, in E♭, op. 5, as early as 1780. But they are very, very rare. I suppose I could also mention the third movement of Brian's Seventh Symphony, but that has such continual growth from scherzo to adagio that it scarcely fits the case. Occasionally one can find such extreme contrasts of mood and pace in very relaxed rondos. But can one imagine the scherzo suddenly popping up in the middle of the first movement of Beethoven's Ninth Symphony, or in the course of the Adagio? It is normal for music, and especially dramatic music, to deal with one thing at a time. The real reason for the division into movements is so that the composer may have space to show those other aspects of life for which his first movement drama gave him no opportunity, aspects which the novelist or playwright accomodates as he goes along.

I've spoken of dramatic music, and this, of course, is what sonata (and symphony, in these terms), in the sense in which classical and most later composers have used it, is concerned with. As drama it is vastly different from the drama of the theatre; its time-scale, for instance, is utterly different, a lesson Beethoven had to learn the hard way when he wrote his great but crippled opera *Fidelio*. An unsurpassed master of the dramatic time-scale of instrumental music, his very mastery in this field led him into quagmires when he tackled opera. Compare *Leonora* No. 3, for instance, with the opera proper and you will get an impression of speed in the overture similar to the old advertisement "That's Shell - that was!", which leaves the opera standing; and this is not the only way in which the overture annihilates the opera.

Now, because of this dramatic and single-minded nature of the normal first movement of a symphony or a sonata, coupled with the need to incorporate other aspects in other movements, there is a dual sense in this type of music, of compression on the one hand and expansion on the other. And since the main drama occupies only one out of three or, more often, four movements, in the majority of such works, the dominant impression is of expansion: expansion that would not be possible, or have the same effect even if it were, without the single-minded compression of the first movement.

The difficulty which comes from describing any music not of the theatre as dramatic is that the term generally conjures up in the listener's mind the idea of programme music as it is usually understood - what is often, naïvely, called "music which tells a story"; and this is not at all what I mean. In the sense in which this phrase is meant music cannot tell a story; it cannot illustrate extraneous objects or situations; it can only underline them when they are visible and audible, as in opera. It is doubtful if music can illustrate anything extraneous to itself that is not either a sound or a state of mind. And if you are a Wagnerian (as, indeed, am I) and believe that the *leitmotif* system as displayed in the *Ring*, for instance, contradicts what I have just said, remember that the themes which make up that system can only be known to indicate the characters or objects with which they are associated by first learning that they do. There is nothing about the sword motif to tell you that it is the sword it represents unless you first learn that it represents the sword. If the music could really project the image of the sword you would not need to learn the connection in the first place.

It would take far too much space here for me to explore this subject as it deserves, but I will say this: take any piece with a programmatic foundation, Berlioz's *Harold en Italie* or *Symphonie fantastique*, a tone poem by Richard Strauss or a prelude by Debussy (*Hommage à Mr Pickwick* is a good one) or any one of numbers of others, play it to half a dozen or a dozen, if you like, people who are accustomed to listening seriously to music, and who do *not* know the particular piece or anything about it, and see what suggestions you get as to what it concerns. I'll guarantee you will get half a dozen or a dozen different ones, and I doubt if any *one* will be the composer's.

The most important thing to learn about music, if one is going to understand it at any depth, is that music means what music is - and it means nothing else. Sir

Donald Tovey once said that, apart from technical terms, there are never any words in which to describe music, except where music is set to words; and then there are only its own words. He was right. The only words that can tell us anything specific about a piece of music are technical words, and *they* must be the right words. They often are not, and so people distrust them. But they are the only verbal guide; they are the only words that will help us at this moment.

I said that music cannot tell a story, and this is true, so long as it is extraneous suggestion that is looked for, as it is in most of what is called programme music. But on its own terms, using *only* its own terms, music can tell a story - of drama, of conflict, of all the things that go to make up most of the world's great fictional literature. On its own terms, using only its own terms - this is the thing that matters. By its own terms I mean the use of varying pace, themes (or tunes), of course, although these do not bulk so large as many people imagine, tonality and harmony, and the tensions brought about by the interaction of these elements. A superb example of this, worth anyone's while to study on these lines, is Schubert's so-called *Death and the Maiden* Quartet - a complete story told in purely musical terms; a story largely of frustration; not frustration felt in the composition of the music but expressed in the tonality and harmony of the music as a study of character, and it has nothing to do with "Death and the Maiden". In other words, in the kind of programme music of which I am speaking, themes, tonalities, harmonies, do not represent this or that character or object. They *are* the characters, the objects. This, of course, means that you must follow every tonal and harmonic twist and turn, every thematic development in its repercussions backwards and forwards, and this is not easy. Comparatively few people visualize listening in this way, but it is far from impossible, and certainly Schubert and the others expected it; no doubt they expected more than they will ever get, but it can be done. (And the more you listen in this intense way, purely to the music, the more you will get from it, often from works you thought you knew thoroughly. If you have never listened to them in this way you have scarcely begun to know their surface.)

It is, then, purely musical elements which convey the drama of instrumental music, of symphonic and sonata music; they all count, but more than any it is tonality and harmony, coupled with pace and dynamics, which are all-important. Obviously, I cannot go into great detail on this point, but I will give you one instance. In the coda of the first movement of Beethoven's Ninth Symphony there is a moment when everything is hushed, and a horn softly and clearly plays part of the movement's main theme, against sustained chords. Sir Donald Tovey likened this passage to the irony of Greek tragedy - the false calm and consolation before the final catastrophe. And what is it that produces this effect? You may be principally aware of the theme, but if you contrive to listen to the whole of the music at this point you will find that it is the hushed dynamic and the harmony that produces the effect, more than anything - the key, in fact, for it is the major tonic chord of D that predominates throughout this passage, in the inconclusive second inversion. This is only one of numbers of such tonal points in the movement, of which I suppose the best known is the huge mysterious simplicity of the beginning, with all its tonal consequences.

The history of the symphony, then, up to the beginning of Brian's work as a symphonist, is largely one of gradual expansion, in spite of the accent on compression in the first movement, and with expansion size, too, increases - not, however, as a matter of things blown up out of proportion, the views expressed in most histories of music notwithstanding. If you attempt to view a work such as Bruckner's Seventh Symphony from the standpoint of Beethoven's Third - provided you have got that right to begin with, which is not necessarily to be taken for granted - the Bruckner will inevitably seem to be out of proportion. On the other hand, viewed from Bruckner's standpoint the Beethoven work will seem to be just as much out of proportion. Concision is not only a matter of expressing what needs to be said in the shortest space, it also requires the use of the right means to achieve that end; and I will maintain that symphonies such as those of Felix Draeseke, the bulk of Bruckner's and Mahler's, or those of Franz Schmidt or Julius Bittner (this is not by any means the end of the list) are as concise as Mozart's Symphony No. 28.

And here Havergal Brian comes in as a rare creative spirit, going his own way, who, within his own symphonic output, virtually reverses the history of the symphony. Discounting the so-called *Fantastic Symphony*, which at one time he thought of as his first, and which was later broken up, he begins, as a symphonist, with his own brand of large-scale symphony and gradually, through the long line of 32, becomes briefer and briefer. Note, not smaller and smaller. More compressed, if you like. This has nothing to do with duration by the clock. Symphony No. 11, for example, is certainly a large work in thought and treatment, and lasts nearly half an hour, but in its lack of padding it is compressed indeed. No. 11, in my opinion, is a single-design symphony. Its various divisions, all based, in one way or another, on the initial figure, are each as necessary to the others as is each of what are usually called the first two movements of Beethoven's C♯ minor quartet necessary to the other; these are not two movements but one - one design, the fugue needing the 6/8 *Allegro*, the *Allegro* needing the fugue, to complete the sense. And this is true of almost every one of Brian's later symphonies - indeed, almost anything after No. 8, even though there are small divisions between "movements" in many of them. These are, or should be, no more than momentary breathing spaces. The sense is, in almost every case, one arching design and continuous. The thought is continuous in that, no matter how the tempo and mood may change and vary (and I know of very little other music of a like stature where such changes are so frequent, for the most part inherent, and kaleidoscopic in effect), it is constantly derived from the initial theme or themes (sometimes one only, scarcely ever more than two short ones).

By the time Brian comes to so cryptic and condensed a work as No. 12 one has all the substance with which works like *The Gothic* and Nos 2 to 4 filled their dimensions compressed into an incredibly small space. Cecil Gray once compared Sibelius' Fourth Symphony with a type of star called a White Dwarf. I know practically nothing about astronomy but I gather that a White Dwarf is a star practically on its last legs, with a mass resembling that of the sun, but with a radius more nearly like that of Earth - in other words, it's pretty dense. I think its density is reckoned as about 1,000,000 times that of water. One gets the point. The point here is that I think the comparison will do for Brian as well. I think I could make out a fair case, given time, for considering Symphony No. 22, *Symphonia Brevis*, as one of the weightiest and, in this sense only, densest of all Brian's symphonies.

I think that some of them (Nos 13 and 18 are two I have in mind, but there are others) are *too* compressed. No. 20, totalling 26 minutes, is an example. The material is different, of course, and the expressive direction, but it is very Brianesque - the Brian of the later stages, which is, perhaps, only different in style and character from the earlier by being more spasmodic and kaleidoscopic. I get the feeling sometimes that some of these works are being deliberately truncated - kept short of their full development. I don't mean that this was necessarily a conscious decision on Brian's part, although, if I am right about this, it may have been. In so far as I *am* right about this, if I am, it is a point against him. Understatement misses the mark as much as overstatement, in spite of the fact that the word "understatement" is frequently used as praise of a composer's work. The same is true, in my opinion, of Chopin, in such things as some of the preludes, for instance, which stop just as they need to continue and develop. Chopin was not, I believe, naturally a miniaturist, although he is so often described as one; he needed space in which to work out his ideas, in large-scale shapes that are his own. However, this is a digression. I have this same feeling about some of Brian's shorter symphonies.

Expansion, or, better, expansiveness, *can* be found in Brian's music. It is in a good deal of the music written before he embarked on the *Gothic* Symphony and its successors. It is in *Doctor Merryheart* and *In Memoriam*, it is in the First English Suite. It can be found also in the Third Symphony; for instance, at the point where he expands in the manner of an Austrian Ländler. But it becomes less and less an attribute of his music - and maybe this is one of the things that those who, as yet, are not convinced of the quality of his work find lacking in a good deal of it. Not that expansiveness is a hallmark of a good deal of today's music that is acclaimed. Brian can be jovial, but often even his joviality seems somewhat cryptic. This is music one has to live with and understand - and that takes time: more time than some are prepared to give.

Now, I've said that the drama of the symphony is dependent primarily on tonality and harmony, and this is true of Brian, too. But Brian's drama is rarely that of the sonata. He does at times use the sonata structure, or adaptations of it, very much in his own way, often seeming almost to parody it; and sometimes he writes an appearance of sonata form which, in fact, remains nothing but an appearance - visual, in other words, not aural. The first movement of the *Gothic* Symphony is an instance. At every point in that movement the things that seem to support sonata drama in fact negative it. And yet Brian's symphonic writing is full of real drama which, as with the earlier symphony, is derived from his use of tonality. His own use of tonality - no one else's.

On paper the first movement of *The Gothic* seems to display a sonata shape - but it is a purely visual image. There is apparently a division into first and second groups for an exposition, a large development and - recapitulation? A recapitulation you will not find. What is there is continuous development. Themes never reappear as they did before; they may start as usual, develop a new middle or hang out a new tail; or they emerge, in part, from a new beginning. Always they initiate new processes. The point of the exposition, so far as one can separate it from the rest of the movement, is not the dramatic one of the normal symphony, of a clash and conflict of keys. Brian gets his conflict in other ways. The basic key is the same throughout, sometimes D minor, sometimes D major, and visiting all sorts of other harmonies which continually receive a kick in the pants from D, who tolerates no lasting interference with his kingship in this movement. Brian, in fact, found a new way of using tonality dramatically. Perhaps I should say "new ways", for he rarely repeats methods. Nonetheless, his methods have a common basis - they all derive from his own musical personality, which pursues its own way, going so far along a line of thought, as suddenly appearing to abandon it to come in from another angle with new matter; but, in fact, constantly pursuing a steady path - a path, the steadiness and straightness of which become clearer with deepening experience of the music.

And always his tendency in his symphonies is to compress. It is ironic that the *Gothic* Symphony should have gained notoriety as the largest symphony ever written; but this sort of nonsense is difficult to lose. It is the more ironic in Brian's case, in that *The Gothic* was the first step towards his producing some of the most compressed and shortest works in the history of the symphony. It had to begin with something like this, feeling all the possibilities in full before he began to compress them. But the compression is already to be felt in this work. One of the most telling things about *The Gothic* is in something Havergal Brian once said to me about it. He told me that his vision of the symphony as he wrote it was so vivid and intense that he wanted to get it all into about 20 bars. As we know, he did not get it all into 20 bars; and that is not important. What is important is his mental conception, and the drive behind it. It was a drive which worked its way gradually through his entire symphonic output, and brought things, ideas, development, drama, everything, gradually closer and closer together. So that the real view of the *Gothic* Symphony is almost the opposite of that which sees it as the world's largest symphony. I hope that this latest performance will have put one more nail in the coffin of that particular lunacy.

On the score of its size, too, there is an interesting comparison with another work, with regard to number of bars. This is not a calculation I make as a rule - arithmetic does not prove much where art is concerned. But there is a point here. The comparison is with the first movement of Brahms' Third Symphony. This movement is one of the shortest first movements of any great symphony, outside the early classical, and the first movement of Brian's *Gothic* Symphony would appear to be one of the largest. But there are 35 bars from the beginning to the arrival of the second group in Brahms' movement, and 224 bars in the whole movement. There are 29 from the beginning to the arrival of the second group in

Brian's first movement, and only 60 bars more in the whole movement - a total of 284, if one counts the final chord, with its reverberation, as a bar.

My own impression of *The Gothic* - one of them, at least, for I have many - one of my strongest impressions of this work is that it is like a roll of paper, or a long rolled up photograph. Try to unroll that paper and, unless you put a weight on one end, it rolls up again after you, as you unroll the rest. *The Gothic* is, for me, like that. As the work progresses, the beginning chases you through it, the music gathers more and more weight, until with each hearing it is shorter and more compressed. And this is the real cause of its size - in spite of all the publicity ballyhoo - *not* the length and the huge forces used, but precisely this rolled-up compression. The work is a big step toward the compression which, in later works, produced the single-design symphony as a natural thing and, for Brian, the ultimate thing, that every part of his instrumental music had been leading to. It was done on his own terms, of course - but, then, as a composer everything that strange man did was done on his own terms. I come back to Brian's own remark as perhaps the most pertinent ever made about the *Gothic* Symphony, that his instinct was to try to get it all into about 20 bars. Hardly the attitude of a man setting out to write the world's largest symphony!

Miscellany

Neil Starling: Havergal Brian's large-scale choral works before 1914 - a preliminary investigation. With comments on Psalm 23 by Larry Alexander and Malcolm MacDonald[1]

PSALM 23 *THE LORD IS MY SHEPHERD*

The exact date of composition of Psalm 23 is not certain, varying sources suggesting dates between 1901 and 1905. In a catalogue of Brian's works compiled by Lewis Foreman and revised by Malcolm MacDonald,[2] the date suggested is 1904. Kenneth Eastaugh (p. 319) dates the work as 1904-5, but also suggests 1901 as a possibility. This was not Brian's first attempt at large-scale choral composition. Before the turn of the century he had written a *Requiem* for baritone solo, chorus and orchestra, with the text taken from the New Testament and Hymns Ancient and Modern. This is, however, lost - perhaps discarded or destroyed. If so, we can assume that Brian did not consider the work to be of a particularly high standard. The only other works composed before Psalm 23, of which we have any evidence, are a few solo songs, an anthem, and a few orchestral works. We can therefore assume that *The Lord is my Shepherd* is the earliest example of Brian's choral writing that still exists, unless it was preceded by the two part-songs *Shall I Compare Thee to a Summer's Day?* (SATB) and *Stars of the Summer Night* (SSAATTBB).

The version of Psalm 23 which now exists is not the original. Brian lost the full score at Lewes, Sussex, in 1920. He was left with just the vocal score, from which he made a new orchestral version in 1945, during a lull in composition following the completion of his vast cantata *Prometheus Unbound*. The orchestration is very much in keeping with that of the music written around the same time as Psalm 23, so Brian must have attempted to recreate the original version as far as possible, rather than bring it up to date with the style of his music of the 1940s.

Although Psalm 23 was composed so early in Brian's life, it had to wait until after his death for its first performance. This took place on 10 March 1973 at All Saints Church, Hove, Sussex, as part of a Havergal Brian Memorial Concert (the performers were the Brighton Festival Chorus, the University of Sussex Choir, and the Leicestershire Schools Symphony Orchestra, conducted by László Hel-

---

[1] This article is drawn from chapters of a thesis submitted as part requirement for the degree of M. A. at the University of Wales, Aberystwyth in 1983, and was first published in *Newsletters* 52 (III-IV 1984), pp. 2-4, 53 (V-VI 1984), pp. 2-3, 54 (VII-VIII 1984), pp. 3-4, 55 (IX-X 1984), pp. 2-3, 56 (XI-XII 1984), pp. 5-7, 57 (I-II 1985), pp. 6-8, 58 (III-IV 1985), pp. 3-4 and 59 (V-VI 1985), pp. 7-9. Larry Alexander's comment is a letter to the Editor in *Newsletter* 55, pp. 1-2, Malcolm MacDonald's comment an article entitled *Psalm 23 - early Brian or late?* in *Newsletter* 57, pp. 4-6, with the postscript being a letter to the Editor in *Newsletter* 72 (VII-VIII 1987), pp. 2-3.
[2] Lewis Foreman/Malcolm MacDonald: *Catalogue of works by Havergal Brian*, in *Newsletter* 37 (IX-X 1981), p. 6. A revised catalogue can be found on pp. 405-411.

tay, with Stuart Holland as the tenor soloist). It was the first and for a long time the only one of Brian's large-scale choral works to have been commercially recorded.

Despite the lack of performances in Brian's lifetime, the work did have its admirers when it was first written. When Brian met Elgar for the first time he showed him the setting. Elgar greatly praised the work, calling Brian a "modernist, a singer and original" (Eastaugh, p. 60). Bantock and John Coates (1865-1941, an operatic and concert tenor of high repute) both tried unsuccessfully to get it performed at the 1907 Gloucester Festival.

The version of the psalm used in this setting is Miles Coverdale's translation of 1535, as found in the Anglican Book of Common Prayer. As Brian was a church organist but, presumably even then, not an orthodox Christian, he may well have had in his possession a Book of Common Prayer but no King James Bible, which would explain his choice of version. It does not, however, explain why he chose to set the psalm in the first place. Obviously, as he was not a conventionally religious man, the text would not have contained any special personal belief. Nor would he have been asked to set the psalm by the church where he was organist, as this is obviously a concert setting, not intended for church use at all. Nor is the psalm particularly dramatic, unlike the others which he set, numbers 137 and 68. Whereas the latter are full of vivid pictorialism, offering great scope for musical invention, Psalm 23 is much less promising, though Brian does give it a dramatic treatment which seeks to emphasize every nuance of mood and feeling in the text. Psalm 23 has, of course, always been one of the best-loved of all the psalms, and it was probably this fact which caused him to choose it in particular. His musical heroes at the time were Strauss, Berlioz and of course Elgar, so it was inevitable that he should have chosen to set it on such a grand scale.

The orchestra used is large, including double woodwind (with the second flute and second oboe doubling piccolo and cor anglais respectively), four horns in F, four trumpets in C, three tenor trombones, tuba, timpani, percussion, harp, organ and strings. Brian frequently chose trumpets in C instead of the more usual transposition of B$\flat$.[3] The percussion is typical of Brian, ideally using five players, and including cymbals, bass drum, glockenspiel and three side drums played together throughout (almost certainly an orchestral feature which *was* new to the 1945 version). Organ sometimes featured in Brian's orchestra, and in this case he may have felt that it enhanced the religious tone required by the text. It does, however, appear in some of the symphonies: the Eighth serves as an example, where it is used for just three and a half bars, and only the pedals, in order to add weight to the bass of the texture.

Peter J. Pirie stated in a review of the first performance of Psalm 23 (*Reports - Hove, Musical Times*, London May 1973, p. 514) that: "I have been troubled ... by

---

[3] The B$\flat$ transposition was the most widely used by the time of the rewritten version of 1945, although at the time of the work's composition, at the beginning of the century, trumpets in various transpositions were widely used.

the lack of any definite personality ... I have failed so far to find any characteristic Brian style beside the massive constructional power." This comment is firstly a little unfair because Psalm 23 is such an early work, composed before Brian had had very much time to develop his own personal voice. Nevertheless, a person who is familiar with some of Brian's music would instantly recognize this as being his work, because of a number of quite distinctive stylistic features which are present. Certainly, it is flavoured with Wagnerian traits and, to an even greater extent, the music of his beloved Elgar, but the end result could not really be mistaken for the work of any other composer.

It falls into three basic sections, all of which are thematically linked. The two outer sections are choral, while the central section is for tenor solo. On no occasion do soloist and chorus sing together. The soloist plays a relatively small part, having only 33 bars in a composition 336 bars long, beginning at the words "Thou shalt prepare a table ..." and ending on "and my cup shall be full".

As with a great deal of Brian's music, the setting of Psalm 23 exploits the full range of emotions, from the serenity of the first vocal entry on the words "The Lord is my Shepherd", to the dark, sinister tones of "Yea, though I walk through the valley of the shadow of death", and the unrestrained joyousness of "for ever" at the *Sempre Poco Più Allegro* section beginning at bar 307. Often the change of mood is quite abrupt, as in bar 280. This tendency to switch suddenly from one mood to another quite different one was a life-long feature of Brian's compositional career.

The choral writing, though lacking the refinement of Elgar's vocal style, is always effective. The vocal lines are rarely contrapuntal in origin, the notable exceptions being the fugal passage which follows the tenor solo (commencing at bar 251), and the previously mentioned section beginning at bar 307. Brian often treats the four voices as two pairs, to produce antiphonal effects. They are usually paired Soprano/Alto and Tenor/Bass (ex. 1).

Often Brian feels the need to divide the parts in these passages, in order to fill out the harmony. At bar 28 there is one of the most beautiful passages in the entire work, where the female voices sing in four parts, unaccompanied, to the words "The Lord is my Shepherd", with a dynamic marking of *ppp*. The writing here cannot really be described as contrapuntal or imitative, but certain motives of thematic importance can be found in the various parts.

Ex. 1

One of the main criticisms which one could make is of the extreme amount of word repetition. After the initial statement of the words "The Lord is my Shepherd, therefore can I lack nothing", the first five words are repeated another four times in the unaccompanied section for female voices previously mentioned. After continuing the text as far as "... beside the waters of comfort", at bar 69 he repeats the words "The Lord is my Shepherd, therefore can I lack nothing". The work closes with a recapitulation of the introduction, and the titular phrase is again repeated. Here Brian is, to a large extent, making the text subservient to the structure, whereas normally in a choral work such as this one would expect the text to dictate the form of the work.

This composition is clearly the work of a symphonist. It is thematically integrated to a far greater extent than the vast majority of choral music of the time. It was composed very soon after Elgar's *The Dream of Gerontius*, a work which had itself been a revolution in oratorio composition because of its integrated symphonic nature. Many composers would have been tempted to divide the work into several movements, with very little thematic connection. Brian, however, made the music continuous, though it does fall into three clear sections, and is given its unity by the use of motives in a symphonic manner.

Brian introduces almost all the important motives in the opening 16-bar introduction, and those which appear later can be seen to have their origins in the material presented in the introduction. Furthermore, the three motivic ideas in the introduction are closely related by a four-note germinal unit. It is therefore apparent that all the material forming the entire work is interrelated.

The first ten bars of the introduction are shown in ex. 2, in which can be seen the opening three motives. The first is the falling figure F-E of bars 1-2, repeated in sequence in bars 3-4 as A-G. The rising bass figure A-B-C of the first two bars may also be seen to be of secondary importance.

Ex. 2

The second important motif appears in bar 5, and provides a contrast to the march-like first four bars, with its *pianissimo* string scoring. The third motif, and the only one which can really be described as a melody, appears in bars 7-8, and is repeated sequentially in bars 9-10. The four-note figure F-E-A-G which is presented in the first four bars also constitutes the first four notes of the third motif. It is significant that the first four notes of the second motif are phrased together, as these can be interpreted as a transposed and inverted version of the original four-note figure. The connection of these three motives is summarized in ex. 3, with the four-note figure marked "X". These three motives can be found throughout the music both in their original forms and in developed versions.

Ex. 3

The first choral entry, to the words "The Lord is my Shepherd", is accompanied in the bass by the second motif from the introduction. Immediately after this choral entry a new figure presents itself, accompanied in the bass by a variant of the second motif from the introduction (ex. 4 a). Ex. 4 b shows how this apparently new theme is in fact derived from the second bar of the third motif from the introduction.

Ex. 4 a

Ex. 4 b

The syncopated figure at the end of ex. 4 a will also be seen to be of thematic importance later in the work, and its rocking motion between adjacent notes suggests that it may be derived from the opening four bars of the introduction.

This is immediately followed by the next choral entry (see ex. 1), and this is accompanied in the orchestra by a restatement of the opening four bars, now in F major instead of the original C major. The female voices, in four parts, enter with the words "The Lord is my Shepherd", and though the material here appears at first sight to be new, a figure appears several times which is derived from the introduction's second motif, at original pitch (ex. 5).

Ex. 5

At bar 38 another new melody appears in the orchestra, and the main idea here is a falling semitone and a falling perfect 5th. If the third note of this figure is raised an octave, it becomes a falling semitone and a rising perfect 4th, which is identical in shape to the first three notes of figure X. At bar 42 the syncopated idea from the end of ex. 4 a appears, with the main melody of ex. 4 a in the bass. From this point until bar 69 all of the material is quite clearly derived from the themes which have already been presented, in virtually their original forms.

At bar 69 the voices return to the words "The Lord is my Shepherd", and here the orchestra takes up the melody which the female voices sang unaccompanied to the same words at bar 28. A repeat of the material from bar 38 in the orchestra is followed at bar 82 by the words "Therefore can I lack nothing", accompanied in the orchestra by ex. 4 a, and the section closes with two versions of the third motif from the introduction, the second being played *tremolando* in the bass, while above it an altered version of the X figure is played, with the intervals reduced, so the notes are F♯, F, A♭, G. It is probably coincidence that these four notes form a transposition of the famous B-A-C-H motif, used by many composers, including Liszt, Schumann, Schoenberg and Bach himself.

The music from bars 53 to 89 repeats the themes of bars 11-52 in the same order, although always varied to some extent, so this first section may be described as being loosely in binary form, with a short introduction.

The next section, marked *Andante Grazioso*, begins in F♯ major, a tritone from the original key of C major. It introduces a new theme on the cor anglais (ex. 6 a), which is shown to be derived from the third motif from the introduction (ex. 6 b).

Ex. 6 a

Ex. 6 b

This rising four-note figure will be seen to be of importance later in the work. The female voices, in four parts, vary this melody to the words "He shall convert my soul", and at "and bring me forth" the music moves into D major (bar 105), and, through the chords of C major and B♭ major (this progression reminding the listener of the very first choral entry), into F major. Here a new figure is introduced, the rhythm of which appeared 11 bars previously, and which is based on a retrograde of the four-note figure previously mentioned.

The cor anglais melody returns, and at bar 130 an *Allegro* section commences, introducing an idea which is derived from the three-note rising bass motif of the first bar of the work. This new idea has in its bass a figure similar to the second motif from the introduction (ex. 7).

Ex. 7

This instrumental section is 20 bars long, and the bass maintains the quaver running motion throughout. The chorus enters with the words "Yea, though I walk through the valley of the shadow of death". The orchestral material here is based entirely on the 20 bars which introduced the *Allegro* section, except that at bar 163 the second motif from the work's introduction appears. The choral writing here is sinister, rising up to a climax on the word "death", and falling away immediately to *pianissimo*. The chorus continues with "for thou art with me", with antiphonal exchanges between male and female voices. The orchestral material is still based on what immediately precedes it. At bar 186 the chorus continues with "Thy rod and Thy staff", passing through the key of B minor, although the music was in F major only a few bars previously. The vocal writing here is

274 Miscellany

contrapuntal, and is derived from the second motif from the introduction. The four bracketed notes should be compared with ex. 3 b (ex. 8).

Ex. 8

The words "comfort me" are accompanied by a variation on ex. 4 a with the syncopated quaver figure above it. This first main choral section is brought to a close by the return of the third motif from the introduction, and above it is a horn call on F and B♭.

The tenor solo is introduced with a five bar passage based on the horn call, now in crotchets instead of quavers. The tenor enters with "Thou shalt prepare a table before me against them that trouble me". At bar 216 the motifs from ex. 7 appear, with the quaver running figure on top. The soloist is almost drowned in a great orchestral climax, complete with loud cymbal clashes, depicting "them that trouble me". A five-bar orchestral interlude follows, based on the crotchet version of the horn call, ornamented with elaborate runs. This builds up to a massive climax (marked *fff*), and breaks off suddenly, to resume *pianissimo*, a Brian fingerprint. The tenor solo continues with "Thou hast anointed my head with oil", accompanied in the orchestra by the material which previously appeared at bar 195. The solo concludes with "and my cup shall be full", accompanied by the introduction's third motif. The music breaks off again, and the horn call returns to form a sort of postlude to the solo.

It can be seen that the themes in the tenor solo are those which occurred in the section before, and in the same order, so the bars 216-250 form a varied recapitulation of bars 130-206, in the same manner as bars 11-52 and 53-89.

At bar 251 a gentle fugal section begins, in G major, with the subject first presented by the tenors (ex. 9). The first four notes of the subject are the rising figure of ex. 6 b, while the little figure G-E-F♯ may be derived from the introduction's second motif.

Ex. 9

The music gradually increases in intensity until it reaches a huge climax at bar 279, where it breaks off, although the break is this time made less abrupt by a *rallentando* and a pause on the final B major chord. The music resumes, marked *Tranquillo*, and a series of patterns being on the words "for ever". The first consists of three bars of antiphonal exchanges between male and female voices. Then the divided sopranos sing a flowing descending figure which is passed in turn to the basses, altos and tenors. Each presentation of this figure is in the dominant key of the last, so D major is eventually reached. A new setting of " for ever" then appears, with the words being passed through the voices, from lowest to highest, on simple crotchet arpeggios of added 6th chords of D major, B♭ major and G♭ major. Another new figure appears, first in divided basses, then divided altos, of a highly chromatic and tonally unstable nature (ex. 10).

Ex. 10

An eerie chromatic ascent, with a *crescendo*, leads into a joyous passage in B major, with a contrapuntal texture, making use of the two figures from the fugue subject (ex. 11). The extreme amount of repetition of the phrase "for ever" is, we must assume, intended to give the impression of eternity suggested in the words.

Ex. 11

At bar 315 the chorus repeat the words "And I will dwell in the house of the Lord for ever", in octaves until the final word, where it splits into eight parts. This passage is accompanied by two ideas, the second bracketed motif from ex. 11, and a march rhythm, one of Brian's favourite rhythms, consisting of a dotted quaver and two demisemiquavers, repeated. This rhythm can be found in many of Brian's works, such as the opening of the Eighth Symphony, and also in the Twelfth Symphony.

As the chorus finishes, the first ten bars of the work are recalled, and the chorus sings, unaccompanied, "The Lord is my Shepherd" with the same harmonic progression as when they first sang those words. The orchestra brings the work to a gentle close with softly reiterated chords of C major, A minor, E minor and C major, a rather unusual concluding cadence.

PSALM 137 *BY THE WATERS OF BABYLON*

Soon after the completion of Psalm 23 Brian composed his next psalm setting, *By the Waters of Babylon*. He also wrote a number of orchestral works around this time, for which he gained a certain amount of recognition, both locally and in London. The First English Suite and the Concert Overture *For Valour* were both performed in the 1907 Henry Wood Promenade Concerts (Eastaugh, p. 79). The symphonic poem *Hero and Leander* also received a successful London performance around this time. Although Brian seemed to be a promising young composer destined for great things, 1907 was to prove the pinnacle of his career in terms of public acclaim.

By the Waters of Babylon was composed in 1905, and received its first performance in the Victoria Hall, Hanley. It was through this performance that Brian was able to meet Granville Bantock for the first time. Brian had been present at the first performance of Part I of Bantock's *Omar Khayyam* and he was so overwhelmed by the music that he was determined to meet the composer. Brian requested that *Omar Khayyam* be given at the same concert as the first performance of his own *By the Waters of Babylon*, and so when this was agreed to, Brian wrote to Bantock. The two composers became close friends, and remained so until the time of Bantock's death in 1946 (Nettel, *Havergal Brian*, pp. 41-42).

Brian composed *Babylon* at a time when he was working for a timber merchant, and he frequently took time off work in order to go to Manchester to attend Richter's Hallé rehearsals or to stay at home to compose. It was under such conditions that Brian produced what he considered one of his finest compositions up to that time. It was composed in just six weeks of spare and stolen time, and the full score was completed on 7 December 1905.

Just before the completion of the full score, Brian played through the work on the piano to some colleagues. They were in general impressed with the setting, despite Brian's indifferent piano skills (Eastaugh, p. 81). After Elgar, on another occasion, saw the work, he wrote Brian a very complimentary letter, saying "I find it very striking and original ... the 'Daughter of Babylon' section is beautiful. From here to the end is prophetic ... I congratulate you on the work and I hope I may hear it some day." (This was not sufficient praise for Brian who considered it his best work to date and was almost certainly hoping that Elgar would recommend it for performance. After this, Brian considered Elgar much less able to recognize original music.)

The first performance attracted favourable comment from the Press. *The Musical Standard* (Ernest Austin, *Queen's Hall Promenade Concerts - a composer from the North, Musical Standard*, London 21 September 1907) stated that "even the piano score revealed a unique sense of mysticism and vigour, two apparently opposite characteristics. Mr Havergal Brian ... is well equipped, and let us hope, ambitious." The same journal (W. H. Caunt, *Bantock's Omar Khayyam and Brian's Babylon, Musical Standard*, London 4 May 1907) had stated four months previously that "It is perfectly obvious that the composer thinks for himself and in what he says there is a determinative quality which, coupled to a yet greater felicity of style, will mark him out as an artist who is serious and yet sincere and well worthy of attention."

As stated above, the first performance took place in the Victoria Hall, Hanley, with the North Staffordshire and District Choral Society. The date of the concert was 18 April 1907, a month later than originally planned, and the consequence of this was that the Hallé Orchestra was unable to perform. Jean Sibelius (a close friend of Bantock) was due to attend the concert, but failed to appear, so Brian lost the opportunity of performing one of his works in front of one of the great contemporary composers (Caunt, *ibid.*). (Sibelius' *Finlandia* was performed at the concert.)

In 1908 the Musical League was created with the aim of promoting British music. Its leading organizers included Bantock and Delius. The first of the League's festivals took place on 24-25 September 1909, and consisted of three concerts, the last of which included the second performance of *By the Waters of Babylon*. This took place in the Philharmonic Hall, Liverpool, on the evening of Saturday 25 September. The concert also included Bax's *Fatherland*, Vaughan Williams' *Willow Wood*, two songs by Ethel Smyth, and Bach's cantata *Praise Jehovah* (Trevor Ian Bray, *Bantock*, London 1973, p. 17).

The festival attracted a considerable amount of publicity, not a small amount of which concerned the performance of *Babylon*. Critics varied considerably in their opinions of the work, ranging from the unreserved enthusiasm of the *Liverpool Courier*, to the singularly unimpressed attitude of *The Times*. The former said of the setting "... Havergal Brian furnishes us with a remarkably fine work of noble and elevated feeling, with a strong dramatic basis, and with every evidence of artistic unity. Mr Brian is a writer of great expressive power, and the vivid and unusually rich colouring of his orchestration enabled him to picture realistically, yet always appropriately, the scenes ... The work breathes a deep pathos, which is expressed in music of surpassing beauty, whilst the masterly way in which the voice parts are dealt with, often times independently from the matter in the orchestral score, does not escape attention."

The Times, however, was hardly able to find anything complimentary to say about the work, stating that "The orchestral introduction is the best part of the work. Once the voices have entered and he has to deal with the words, the composer seems quite unable to decide whether they are to be treated dramatically or reflectively ... 'O daughter of Babylon, wasted with misery' is set to no fewer than four musical themes, which are all more or less worked out as separate movements, and which gives an absurdly experimental effect, as though the composer were trying which would fit best. Finally, a fatal mistake from the dramatic point of view is made when, instead of ending when the psalm ends, a conventional repetition of the first words is added." (Both reviews, and several others of this performance, are reprinted in Foreman, pp. 28-31.)

Between the two performances of the work, the scoring was revised. The original version was scored for double woodwind, but for the Liverpool performance the scoring was expanded to triple woodwind. Tragically, like so many of Brian's works, the full scores of both versions (assuming there was once a full score of the second version) are now lost. In a letter to Reginald Nettel written just before Brian's death, the composer stated that he was contemplating re-orchestrating *Babylon*.[4]

---

[4] David J. Brown: *Editorial: Stop press*, in *Newsletter* 39 (I-II 1982), p. 2: "We were rather concerned that, following the sad deaths of Reginald Nettel and his wife in 1980, any Brian letters and other Brian memorabilia which might have been in Reg's possession could have been lost, destroyed or sold; Mr and Mrs Nettel left no immediate family. However, we are delighted to report that their nephew John Nettel and his sister have very kindly offered Reg's collection to

The vocal score was published by Breitkopf and Härtel in 1907, and this date means that it must have been taken from the original score for double woodwind. There are several indications of instrumentation on the vocal score, and these include cor anglais and bass clarinet, so one may assume that these instruments were played by the second oboist and second clarinetist respectively. It may therefore be possible that in the rescoring for triple woodwind Brian simply allocated these instruments (and presumably also piccolo and double bassoon) to separate players, instead of giving all of the work to the second player of each section.

The two performances of 1907 and 1909 were the only ones to take place before the disappearance of the full score(s). When, in 1945, Brian came to revise some early music, he re-scored Psalm 23, and not Psalm 137, which, we are led to believe, he considered the better work. This suggests either that Brian was still hoping for a first performance of Psalm 23 (which Psalm 137 had already had), or that the full score of *Babylon* was still in his possession, or at least, that he knew of its whereabouts.

In 1974 Gilliam Ward Russell made an arrangement of the setting with an organ accompaniment, and it was performed in this arrangement on 31 March 1982 by the Chelmsley Wood Choral Society at St Leonard's Church, Marston Green, Birmingham. (The performance was mounted and conducted by Philip Litchfield, with David Hill as the baritone soloist and Colin Druce as the organist.) Although this performance provided an opportunity for a new generation to be able to hear the work, it must be said that the organ is really a most unsatisfactory medium for the setting, in which the textures are quite clearly orchestrally conceived. The accompaniment is so idiomatically written that one can usually judge from the style of writing what instruments were intended. Also, as mentioned above there are several instrumental indications on the vocal score. A successful reconstruction of the full score is necessary before another truly satisfactory performance of the work can be given.

The formal construction of Brian's setting of Psalm 137 is very similar to that of Psalm 23. In both works an orchestral introduction presents most of the work's important themes, and this is followed by two long choral sections separated by a passage for a solo male voice. Even nearly 30 years later, when Brian came to set Psalm 68 in his three-movement Fourth Symphony, he wrote two choral movements, with one for solo soprano as the centrepiece. The settings of Psalms 23 and 137 both conclude with a recapitulation of the opening

---

us on indefinite loan, and the first batch, consisting of 61 letters to Reg from Brian as well as many other fascinating documents, have now arrived. The Brian letters prove to be of the greatest possible interest, dating as they do from 1944 when Reg Nettel was working on *Ordeal by Music*, right through to only a few days before Brian's death in 1972. In the very last letter, a six-page missive giving a great deal of information on the original full score of *By the Waters of Babylon* (but not, unfortunately, any real new leads on its present whereabouts - or indeed, whether it has survived at all) Brian astonishingly reveals that at the very end of his life he was contemplating re-orchestrating *Babylon*. In a much earlier letter of the '40s, the even more amazing fact is revealed of a hitherto undocumented Brian work. It seems that as a 'thankyou' for a gift of £20, Brian sent to Lord Howard de Walden what he describes as a 'long *Legend* for cello (or bass clarinet) and piano', some time in the late 1930s."

line of the text repeated to music from the beginning of the work. The only important difference is the placing of the fugal section. Whereas in Psalm 23 it immediately followed the tenor solo, in the later work it immediately precedes the baritone solo. Almost every large-scale choral work composed in Britain around this time contained a fugal section. The public expected to hear such a passage, and the composer felt obliged to include one to prove his worth as a composer, no matter how high a standard the rest of the music was. Even Elgar's *The Dream of Gerontius*, one of the finest choral works ever produced by an English composer, contains several fugal passages, notably at the words "Holy Mary, pray for him" in Part I (fig. 30, Novello score), and also in the "Demons' Chorus" in Part II (fig. 35).

By the Waters of Babylon begins in a sombre E♭ minor. The 38-bar orchestral introduction presents many of the work's most important themes. Two of them appear in the first six bars (ex. 12).

Ex. 12

The repeated-note triplets appear in various guises throughout the music, and the chord progression which accompanies them also appears later. The second theme is the most important in the whole work (ex. 12, bars 4-6), and is used as a sort of "idée fixe" to represent "Zion". In only two places in the score is the theme actually sung, and on both occasions it is to the words "When we remember thee, O Zion". Of the two occasions when the theme occurs purely orchestrally (apart from during the introduction), one follows a plea from the chorus "Sing us one of the songs of Zion", and the other appears in the middle of the baritone solo, after he has asked that curses should be poured upon him lest he should forget Jerusalem.

After the first two themes of the introduction have been heard, they are repeated exactly, but a tone higher, in F minor. Then, at the end of bar 12, a third theme is introduced (ex. 13).

Ex. 13

This is repeated sequentially, and then it becomes the bass of a new motif which has a triplet figure derived from the opening bars of the work. This motif plays an important part as a cadential figure (ex. 14).

Ex. 14

This is once again repeated in sequence, in the keys of G♭ major, B♭ minor and D♭ major, each key a 3rd higher than the last. A downward sequence is then used, consisting of descending chords of C♭ major (the chromatic equivalent of B major), A, G, F and E♭ majors. Each of these chords, except the last, is accompanied in the bass by the repeated triplet figure, and each chord is also converted into a dominant 7th in the first inversion, with a flattened 5th. The bass therefore follows the pattern of rising a minor 3rd and falling a tritone. Through these chords a huge climax is reached two bars before fig. 3 and, as was typical of Brian, the climax is suddenly cut off, and the music resumes very softly, making use of the triplet figure again. The chord of E♭ minor (the tonic chord) is reached, and for five bars the orchestra climbs the tonic arpeggio to prepare for the first choral entry. This occurs in bar 39, and is marked *misterioso*. The basses provide the melody (not heard in the orchestral introduction), accompanied by divided tenors. This is imitated exactly by the female voices in precisely the same manner as is found in Psalm 23 (see ex. 1) (ex. 15).

Ex. 15

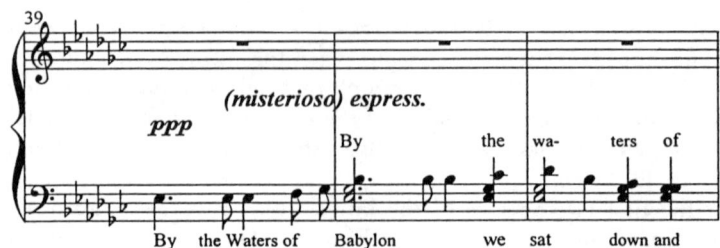

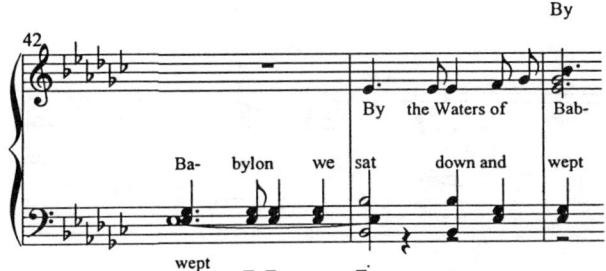

Placing the basses above the tenors was no mistake on Brian's part. He realized that the basses, singing so much higher in their range, would by necessity sing louder than the tenors, who are in a fairly low part of their range, so the melody would be clearly heard above the accompaniment.

The accompaniment throughout this passage is very light and thin in texture, consisting basically of a descending melodic minor scale on E♭, with the tonic being heard in six octaves. The *misterioso* effect of the voices is greatly enhanced by the accompaniment. The harmony suggested throughout the passage is tonic-based. The shape of the melody and the complete absence of a leading note give the impression of modality. It may be possible to consider the whole passage to be in the Dorian mode on E♭. Brian was completely unaffected by the English Folk revival of the time, and the modality which sprung from it, so we must consider this to be purely an instance of "local colour", designed to illustrate the lamenting of the Jews.

At the end of this section (bar 49) the opening of the introduction returns, in almost its original form. The triplet figure is announced as before, but this time the "Zion" theme is also sung in unison by the altos and tenors, to the words "When we remember thee, O Zion". The music is repeated in F minor, as in the introduction, but this time the "Zion" theme is sung by the sopranos and basses two octaves apart, while the altos and tenors sing the crotchet accompaniment found in ex. 12. This is a very unusual texture, though a similar one can be found in the "Benedictus" of Haydn's *St Cecilia* Mass where the bassoon, providing the bass of the texture, plays in octaves with the soprano solo, while the alto and tenor soloists provide the inner parts. There are, however, important differences. Brian's bass voice is not the real bass of the texture. This is provided by the orchestra, and is in fact an octave doubling of the alto part. There is also a problem of vocal range, which does not occur in the Haydn. While the sopranos are right at the top of their range, going up to A♭, and the altos and tenors are also fairly high in their range, the basses are quite low in theirs, and so they are not clearly heard although they share the melody with the sopranos. The effect of octave doubling is therefore to a large extent lost.

At bar 61 the words "O Zion" are sung by the choir in a very fragmentary manner (ex. 16), while the orchestral accompaniment suggests the melody of ex. 13.

Ex. 16

The bass figure which is set in motion here (a rising 3rd consisting of a quaver and a crotchet) is carried over into the next section, "As for our harps". Here the melody is sung by the basses, and is then passed over to the altos, the melody then being repeated a minor 3rd higher by the tenors and sopranos. The harmony over these 13 bars is most unusual, the progression being as shown in ex. 17.

Ex. 17

A large proportion of the next 70 bars of the setting makes use of a new melody, to the words "For they that led us away captive required of us a song and melody". Usually just the first phrase is heard. The entire melody is heard only once (bars 130-138), and is given in ex. 18 in its entire form.

Ex. 18

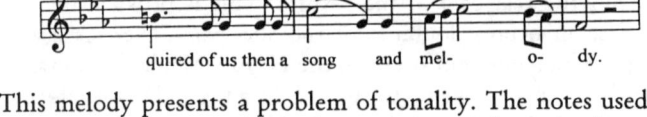

This melody presents a problem of tonality. The notes used are those of the C harmonic minor scale (with the exception of the B♭ in the penultimate bar), and the accompaniment would appear to confirm this key, as it is the music of bars 12-16 of the introduction (ex. 13). To further strengthen this view, the first appearance of the first half of this theme is accompanied in the orchestra by a bass pedal on C. Despite all these factors, the melody itself quite clearly has F as its tonic, so that the augmented 2nd, which in C minor would occur between the submediant and the leading note, now occurs between the third and fourth degrees of the scale. This would make the pedal on C a dominant pedal, rather than a tonic pedal.

This use of the augmented 2nd is quite clearly an attempt at "Eastern" colouring. Many of Brian's British contemporaries were interested in Eastern subjects, notably Bantock. These composers did not, however, attempt very often to colour their music in this way. The harmonic language of Bantock's *Omar Khayyam* is basically derived from Wagner and Strauss (though an exception will be noted in the section of this study dealing with *The Vision of Cleopatra*).

This interval of the augmented 2nd between the third and fourth degrees of the scale may be found in some Arabic music, and also, more significantly, in a great deal of Jewish music which has come under an Arabic influence. The melody shown in ex. 19 should be compared with ex. 18.

Ex. 19

This melody, *Hammawdil*, a religious song for the end of Sabbath, comes from Baghdad, which was the home of one of the earliest Jewish colonies outside Palestine, so, as *By the Waters of Babylon* is the song of the Jews in exile, there is an added significance in the connection between Brian's melody and the type of Jewish melody shown in ex. 19.

It is interesting to note that Brian's "Jewish" melody is normally sung by the choir simply in octaves, or two voices singing in octaves while the other two parts sing an extremely simple accompaniment, which could not possibly obscure the melody. At no time does the orchestra play the melody. This may be an attempt to suggest the way in which the Jews would have sung a song or chant. It would have been in unison, and either unaccompanied or simply accompanied by percussion (a drum or gong).

As was mentioned earlier, the orchestral accompaniment to the "Jewish" melody consists of the theme given in ex. 13 and, as in the introduction, it is followed by the cadential figure ex. 14. In bars 111-126 it is in a new form, the fall of a semitone and the return of the original note now being in the form of a lower chromatic auxiliary figure. However, after the final statement of the "Jewish" melody it appears in its original form, with the choir singing "in our heaviness" above it. The chord sequence which followed this in the introduction reappears, while the choir sing the impassioned phrase, "Sing us one of the Songs of Zion". Brian indicates that this line should be sung "ironically".

As in the introduction, the chord sequence mentioned above is followed by a restatement of the repeated triplet figure, so we see here the same process that was found in Psalm 23, with the music of the orchestral introduction being expanded in the first choral section, with the themes occurring in the same order.

A restatement of the "Zion" theme leads into the work's only fugal section. This has the unusual time signature of 5/2, which seems appropriate for the choir, who sing despairingly "How shall we sing the Lord's song in a strange land?". The section begins instrumentally in the key of A♭ major, but goes into F major for the entry of the voices. The basses are the first to present the subject of this section which takes the form of a fugal exposition (ex. 20).

Ex. 20

The voices enter in the order bass - tenor - alto - soprano, the tenors and sopranos having a "real" answer. When all four voices have entered the basses take up the subject, now in G major, with the other three voices in counterpoint above it. The music again moves into the dominant of the preceding key, for an orchestral interlude in D major. This consists of a truncated form of the subject, but with an elaborated ending. According to an indication on the vocal score, this passage was scored for brass and drums. According to a contemporary critic (Caunt, *op. cit.*) present at the first performance in 1907, this passage was not as powerful as it might have been, the scoring requiring a little more "fattening out".

The altos and basses enter in octaves, with a new melodic line, working in counterpoint with the subject and countersubject of the fugal exposition in the orchestra, but after singing as far as "How shall we sing the Lord's song" to the new material, they are cut off by the sopranos and tenors singing a variant on this new melody, a perfect 5th higher. The altos and basses are then allowed to complete their melody with "in a strange land", with the sopranos and tenors taking over once again, this time a 10th higher.

The full choir then enter in block harmony, with the impassioned cry "How shall we sing the Lord's song", with repeated chords hammered out by the orchestra. This comes to rest on a pause chord, after a *crescendo* from the dynamic marking of *fff*, and, in typical Brian style, the music cuts off, to resume after a pause chord, now with the dynamic marking of *pp*. After the tonal instability of the music since the voices entered in block harmony, the key of E minor is asserted on the final chord of the section. The voices sing a perfect bare 5th (another Brian "fingerprint"), tailing off one part after another to produce a *diminuendo* effect. Against this bare 5th the bass clarinet plays the fugue subject for the last time. It begins on G, so in the context of the fugal passage it would be considered to be in G major, but here it appears to be in E minor.

At this point the central section for baritone solo begins. An E is held on from the preceding chord, and, with syncopated rhythm, builds up into an E minor triad, which proves to be the submediant triad in the key of G major. A falling figure is set in motion, which is closely related to the opening motif of the work (ex. 21).

Ex. 21

Like the opening motif (ex. 12, bars 1-2), it consists of two elements; a repeated-note idea, now with a more elaborate rhythm, and an appoggiatura-like movement between two chords, which also bears some similarity with the opening figure in Psalm 23 (ex. 2, bars 1-4). This falling figure becomes more hurried over the next three bars, until it appears in semiquavers. Then three bars before fig. 23 a new, more passionate theme is presented (ex. 22).

Ex. 22

This theme dissolves into a repeated octave E, off the beat, and derived from the repeated G of ex. 21, and therefore ultimately derived from the repeated E♭ of the beginning of the work. The succeeding bars are full of motivic derivation. The first four bars of the section are given in ex. 23.

Ex. 23

The semiquaver run in the bass clearly stems from the bass of ex. 22, while the chord progression from the second half of the second bar to the first beat of the third bar is identical to that which opens the work, but now in E minor instead of E♭ minor. It also maintains its repeated-note accompaniment. The first four notes of the baritone solo may be seen to be identical to those of the opening choral entry (ex. 15), though again a semitone higher. The appearance of the minor 3rd and augmented 4th in the melody suggests the "Jewish" melody (ex. 18), though it is more likely that these characteristic intervals occur as a result of the accompanying harmonic progression, rather than a conscious attempt to use the scale which was used in the melody in ex. 18.

The phrase "If I forget thee, O Jerusalem" is repeated a tone higher, so the link with the work's opening is strengthened. The falling figure at the beginning of ex. 21 returns in the orchestra, now accompanied by a repeated octave A in triplets. The falling figure dominates the texture until the soloist reaches the words "let my right hand forget her cunning". At this point the orchestra takes over, and at bar 253 the theme presented in ex. 22 returns for just three bars. There then follows a series of tonally unstable brass chords, giving solemnity to a passage of recitative for the soloist. This section concludes with the words "If I prefer not Jerusalem in my mirth", and this prompts the appearance of the "Zion" theme. As this occurs in the middle of the solo section, the "Zion" theme becomes the focal point of the whole work.

At bar 267 the orchestra returns to the music which commenced with ex. 23, and the succeeding music is an exact repetition up to the point where the brass chords had begun in the first statement of the material. The baritone soloist, however, has a completely new melodic line, which concludes with an example of word-painting, as the words "Down with it, down with it, even to the ground", is set to a plunging melodic line, spanning a major 10th.

The use of the same material for the beginning and end of the solo section gives this portion of the work a ternary form, with the recitative passage and the "Zion" theme making up the central section. The choir returns in bar 288, with the female voices in four parts, answered by the male voices, in a manner typical of Brian's choral style. An example of similar writing in Psalm 23 has already been given (ex. 1). This passage only lasts for five bars, and appears at first sight to be totally unrelated to anything either before or after it. The melodic shape does, however, have a precedent in the baritone solo at the words "Remember the children of Edom" (ex. 24).

Ex. 24

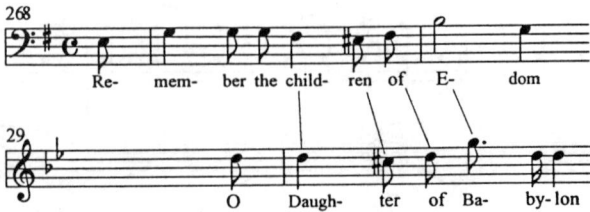

Then commences the section which Elgar described as "beautiful" (letter from Elgar to Brian, Hereford, 27 March 1906, quoted in part in Eastaugh, p. 73). It begins with a passage for semi-chorus, which may be assumed to be a part of the main chorus, as it has only this one short section, and is never required to sing at the same time as the main chorus. The section commences with tenors and basses divided into four parts, with a lamenting melody to the words "Daughter of Babylon, wasted with misery". Both the melody and the accompanying figure are related to the figure which normally accompanies the "Zion" theme. In ex. 25 the third bar of the melody, and the two bass parts, should be compared with the bass in bars 4-6 of ex. 12.

Ex. 25

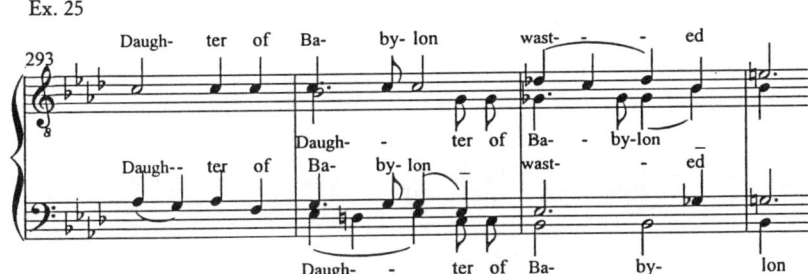

Soon divided altos take over from the tenors, as the same phrase is repeated, now in B♭ minor, instead of the original F minor. As the music heads towards a climax the sopranos and tenors join in at the words "Yea, happy shall he be that rewardeth thee as thou hast served us". All voices are now divided into two parts, although there is much doubling of parts, both at the unison and the octave. The phrase ends on an E♭ major chord, and woodwind cascades bring the music back to F minor, and the previous choral section is repeated intact, though now with full chorus. When the E♭ chord is again reached, at bar 330, the altos and basses set the same words to a new, though related, theme. This has much more urgency about it, due both to the tempo indication *molto stringendo*, and to the new rhythmic figure hammered out by the orchestra (ex. 26).

Ex. 26

The chromatically ascending motion is complemented in the next phrase, "Yea, happy shall he be", where a chromatically falling idea is taken up in all four parts. The doubling between male and female voices continues throughout this passage, and into the next, where the urgency is reinforced by the tempo indication *Più stringendo*. The words "O Daughter of Babylon, wasted with misery" are again taken up, but now the voices take up the rhythmic figure used by the orchestra in ex. 26. This is brought to a climax at bar 356, where the voices present the words "Blessed shall he be" in octaves, and through which a new version of the triplet figure emerges (ex. 27).

Ex. 27

The chorus divides into two parts again for a violent outburst at the words "and throweth them against the stones". After a five-bar orchestral interlude, the chorus, still in two parts with octave doubling, takes up the material presented by the orchestra in ex. 27, to the words "That throweth them against the stones". This is treated imitatively, accompanied simply by chords hammered out on the first and third beats of each bar. At bar 377 the music of ex. 27 returns, and again reaches a violent climax at "and throweth them against the stones". The psalm is now complete, but as with Psalm 23, Brian adds a postlude by reminding us of the work's beginning. As the final chord on the word "stones" is cut off, an E♭ string *tremolo* remains, leading the music back to the original key of E♭ minor, and the opening choral passage (see ex. 15). As in the first appearance of this material, it is immediately followed by the work's opening triplet figure, and the composition ends, appropriately, with an appearance of the "Zion" theme, with modified ending, to bring the work to a peaceful close.

Brian's setting of Psalm 137 makes full dramatic use of the text, something which was only partly achieved with the previous choral work, Psalm 23. According to Reginald Nettel (*Havergal Brian*, p. 35), Brian's setting of *Babylon* is a precursor in spirit of Walton's *Belshazzar's Feast*, which makes use of a modified version of the same psalm. It is interesting to note that there are certain parallels between the two works. In both instances the composer uses a baritone soloist at the point where the text turns to the first person singular, at the words "If I forget thee, O Jerusalem", and both revert to chorus at "O Daughter of Babylon". Although Brian must have been well aware of the logical appearance of a soloist at the point where the word "I" is introduced into the text, his use of soloist and chorus at certain points is quite obviously a formal device. Unlike many choral composers, Brian is careful not to allow the form to become the slave of the text. Both Brian's *Babylon* and Walton's *Belshazzar's Feast* are symphonic in nature, and therefore rely heavily on formal construction: Walton's approach is far less rigid, allowing more scope for the expression of the text, particularly in the use of the soloist.

An increase in dramatic impact from *The Lord is my Shepherd* to *By the Waters of Babylon* is accompanied by a richer harmonic language, as well as an increase in vivid pictorialism in the choice of psalm. In all these aspects, Brian paved the way for his final, violent psalm setting in the Fourth Symphony, *Das Siegeslied*. Even here, however, there is little relaxation in the formal construction. The symphony still maintains the principle of two choral sections separated by a soloist. Brian's full-blooded dramatic approach to the psalm bears little resemblance to the gentle, reverent type of setting which many composers have considered to be appropriate for a sacred work. His attitude to the Psalm is clearly that of a man who may have no Christian conviction, but who possesses a keen sense of drama and passion.

THE VISION OF CLEOPATRA

Much of Brian's output immediately after the composition of *By the Waters of Babylon* consisted of solo songs and part-songs. 1906 saw the appearance of his next large-scale work, *Carmilhan*. The score of this work is now lost, and the only information about it which is now available is that it was a setting of a poem by Longfellow, and that it was scored for contralto solo, chorus and orchestra (Eastaugh, p. 319). Brian called the work a dramatic ballad and, in a list of his works which he produced in 1907, *Carmilhan* was listed as Opus 14. If the first setting of Psalm 68, *Let God Arise*, was ever written, it must have appeared very soon after *Carmilhan*, as it is listed as Opus 15. Later, *The Vision of Cleopatra* appeared in its place as Opus 15 (Eastaugh, p. 80).

Brian's setting of *The Vision of Cleopatra* began life as an entry for a competition for composers as part of the Norwich Festival of 1908. The festival of the previous year included a competition for a cantata libretto on the subject of *Antony and Cleopatra*. The winning entry was that of Gerald Cumberland, a critic and poet, and was entitled *The Vision of Cleopatra*. The competition for composers in the following year was to set Cumberland's libretto.

By coincidence, the subject of Cleopatra had already been on Brian's mind for some time. In the spring of 1906 he had become captivated by an English translation of a book by Théophile Gautier entitled *Nuits de Cléopâtre*. Brian contacted Arnold Bennett, the novelist from the Potteries, with regard to the origins of this book, and in the ensuing correspondence on the subject, Bennett said that he had written a libretto for an opera, based on Shakespeare's *Antony and Cleopatra*, originally intended for a French composer (Nettel, p. 62). He suggested that Brian might like to use the libretto himself. This suggestion came to nothing, however, and Brian's attention was soon diverted by the Norwich Festival competition.

Work did not go smoothly on the composition, due to domestic difficulties which caused him to have to work during the night (Nettel, p. 63). The finished score reached the secretary of the Norwich Committee on the closing date (1 December 1907) of the competition. Brian's setting was one of 70 (there were 70 entries according to Nettel, p. 63, Eastaugh, p. 91, puts the number at only 33), and the works (with the MSS. not bearing the composers' names) were judged by a panel consisting of Bantock, Delius and Ernest Walker. Bantock withdrew from the panel, however, to be replaced by Coleridge-Taylor. The reasons for Bantock's withdrawal are not clear. Eastaugh (p. 91) states that it was simply because he knew too many of the entrants. Nettel (p. 63), however, claims that Bantock retired after a dispute with Delius over Brian's setting, and adds that Delius later stated that had he known that the setting was by Brian, he would have been in agreement with Bantock.

The competition's first prize was won by Julius Harrison, for which he received a cheque for 50 guineas. Brian also received a cheque, however, for which Henry Wood was a generous contributor. The publishing firm of Bosworth paid Brian £40 for the right of publication, and the vocal score subsequently appeared in print. In the following year, 1909, the work received its first and only performance. This took place at the Southport Triennial Music Festival, to which event the work is inscribed. The conductor was Landon Ronald, who, at around that time, began to gain recognition as an important interpreter of Elgar's music. The soloists included some of the leading singers of the day, the main role of Cleopatra being sung by the contralto Phillis Lett. The part of Antony was sung by John Coates (tenor), with Maud Phillips (soprano) as Iris and Lillie Whiteside (mezzo-soprano) as Charmion (Nettel, p. 65).

Rehearsals did not go smoothly, and the conductor was not satisfied with the amount of rehearsal time made available, and threatened to give up the attempt to conduct the work. He did go ahead, however, and the subsequent performance left both the critics and the audience a little bewildered. It was around this time that Continental audiences were hearing for the first time works such as Mahler's *Das Lied von der Erde* and Strauss' *Elektra*, so it is little wonder that the rather conservative British public should be somewhat baffled by a work which has a similar harmonic language to these two Teutonic masterpieces.

The critic for the *Daily Mail* did his best to grasp the meaning of the music, stating that: "He naturally enough favours the ultra-modern school, and *The Vision of Cleopatra* is perhaps one of the most intricate pieces of choral writing in existence. The setting is frankly oriental in texture, but Mr Havergal Brian has not contented himself entirely with the production of strange noises from uncouth percussion instruments. There is, of course, a good deal of this, and some of his discords can only be described as ear-splitting, but at the same time the composer has been wonderfully successful in attaining the true atmosphere surrounding Mr Gerald Cumberland's libretto, and the chorus 'Great Silence is o'er everything' is amazingly clear in conception." (Nettel, p. 65)

The *Musical Times* critic saw in the work much hope for the future, with his claim that: "... no one can deny that the composer has constructed a very clever superstructure upon a foundation that demands dramatic treatment. In listening to the music, one has a feeling that Mr Brian has yet to come into his own; and if 'his own' should prove to be a better seeking after melody, a greater regard to form, and a less strenuous use of the orchestra, he should in due time arrive at that goal which has immortalized the great masters." (Nettel, p. 65)

Arnold Bennett, the novelist from the Potteries, was fully aware of the degree to which both text and music were flavoured by a sensual element. He said of the performance: "If the good people of Southport only realize what they are listening to, they will assuredly walk out, pained and shocked." (Eastaugh, p. 92)

Bennett must have taken a particular interest in Brian's music, and in *The Vision of Cleopatra* in particular, because one of his short stories, *Why the Clock Stopped*, included a discussion of this work. Although Bennett frequently put real people around him into his novels and stories, it was usually with a fictitious name, but here Brian's own name was used. The story illustrates the difficulties which the work presented even to choirs as accomplished as those in the Potteries. The following two extracts from the story illustrate the point:

> He began to talk about certain difficulties in the choral parts of Havergal Brian's *The Vision of Cleopatra*, a work which he meant the Bursley Glee and Madrigal Club to perform, though it should perish in the attempt.
>
> He opened the score for Eva's inspection, and began to hum, and they hummed in concert, at intervals exclaiming against the wantonness with which Havergal Brian had invented difficulties. (Arnold Bennett, *Why the Clock Stopped*, from *The Matador of the Five Towns, and Other Stories*, London 1972)

A certain amount of controversy arose in the Press concerning the poem by Gerald Cumberland. Although by today's standards the poem is rather tame and inoffensive, the critics of the day were shocked by the sensual nature of certain passages which rendered the poem "not likely to engender music that would carry on the tradition of Mendelssohn's *Elijah*" (Gerald Cumberland, *Set down in Malice - A Book of Reminiscences*, Edinburgh 1918, p. 193). This was exactly Cumberland's intention, as he had grown tired of that tradition, and wanted to help to change the fashion. Sir Henry Wood was required by the Norwich Festival Committee to write to Cumberland, asking him to alter the poem so that a more acceptable version may be performed. Part of the letter read as follows: "Very much against my will, I am writing to ask you on behalf of the Committee of the Norfolk and Norwich Festival if it is possible for you to make any alternative version of the 'two objectionable lines' (I fail to find them myself) in your libretto *Cleopatra* ... from my point of view, the whole thing is absurd and ridiculous." (Cumberland, p. 193)

Like Wood, Cumberland was unable to detect the offending lines, but was eventually informed by Julius Harrison, the composer whose setting was to be performed, that the Committee did not approve of the lines "her white breasts gleamed" and also of "Her lips, tired of tame kisses, parted with the expectancy of proud assault". Cumberland altered these lines respectively to "her proud eyes gleamed" and "Her lips, curved into beauty, parted with expectancy of love's quick pain". A further passage was altered; where the original read "she was as one who lives for a last carnival of love, in which she may be stabbed and torn by large excesses of passion", the censored version became "she was as one who walks, with dreams for company, such dreams as madden one with longing, fear and dread that love be vanquished".

In the performance of Brian's setting of the poem the original lines were reinstated, and, as Cumberland records (Cumberland, p. 194): "the members of the audience did not leave their seats when the 'objectionable' lines occurred; rather did they seem to lean forward a little and listen more intently". In the score the altered version is present.

The Vision of Cleopatra is yet another of Brian's works which has become the victim of the loss of scores. The full score came into the possession of the publishing firm of Bosworth in London, and they published the vocal score. The full score was in Bosworth's hands until the Second World War, when, in 1940, an incendiary bomb hit the store room where the score was housed, gutting the room and destroying its contents. The firm has since stated that the orchestral material was almost certainly never published, and added that all of their printing plates were destroyed during the War (Wilfrid Chadwick, *Investigations Officers' Reports: 1, Newsletter* 39, I-II 1982, p. 4).

The vocal score lists the instruments which Brian used in the orchestration of the work. The orchestra is large, consisting of the following: piccolo, two flutes, two oboes, cor anglais, two clarinets, bass clarinet, two bassoons, double bassoon, four horns (5th and 6th *ad lib.*), three trumpets (4th *ad lib.*), three trombones, bass tuba, harp, glockenspiel, timpani, bass drum, side drum, triangle, castanets, Indian drum, gong, large cymbals and small cymbals. Although Brian omits them from the list, we can safely assume that the orchestra included the normal string section. There are a few markings of instrumentation in the score, mainly for trumpet fanfares, such as at fig. 21 and five bars after fig. 26. Two important glockenspiel passages are also marked, at two bars after fig. 14 and seven bars after fig. 49. Both passages include crotchet motion over the tonic and dominant of the respective keys, and both passages occur at the end of a choral section. An important horn melody is also marked (one bar after fig. 21), and the cor anglais has a lament over a timpani roll (four bars after fig. 25), to introduce Cleopatra's tragic solo "Now all is finished, all is done, my world is dead".

The choral forces required for the work are a small chorus, which Brian states should be "seated in the orchestra or behind the scenes", and a large chorus, which, one may assume, would be seated on stage as normal. The small chorus has the greater proportion of the choral passages, with several very short sections, while the main chorus is reserved for just two sections, the long chorus "Great silence is o'er everything" (which precedes Cleopatra's lament "Now all is finished") and the final section of the work, a *Marche Funèbre* which begins with the words "The sun has gone away to sleep". Of these, the former contains a central section for the small chorus. In the libretto, the passages which Brian designated for the small chorus (with the exception of the central section of "Great silence is o'er everything") are marked by Cumberland as "in the distance", which explains Brian's unusual placing of the small chorus.

The direct contrast in style between the psalms and the contents of this libretto required an equally direct change in style and form. One of the most obvious changes is in the move away from choral dominance. In the two psalm settings already discussed, the chorus has been the most important medium for the presentation of the text, with the soloists taking on a secondary role, providing a moment of contrast of timbre. The chorus was involved in the text in an active sense, whereas in *The Vision of Cleopatra* it takes on a passive role, commenting upon the events around it, but taking no part in them.

A further change of style is apparent in Brian's harmonic idiom. Although the two psalm settings have a harmonic language derived from Elgar and Wagner, and a thematic unity which gives the works a symphonic style, neither is so clearly flavoured by the chromaticism and motivic technique of Wagner's *Tristan* as is evident in *The Vision of Cleopatra*. Whereas *By the Waters of Babylon* has one theme which is identifiable with an extra-musical idea, *Cleopatra* extends this to something approaching a Wagnerian "leitmotiv" technique, with themes associated with the characters of the poem, especially Cleopatra and Antony. The use of these motives tends to make the music more contrapuntal than the previous works, with the vocal line usually quite independent from the melodic strands of the orchestra.

Malcolm MacDonald (*Perspective*, p. 15) draws attention to the "oriental" nature of much of the music. It is much more closely related to the "Eastern" elements of Bantock's *Omar Khayyam* than to the "Jewish" melody of *By the Waters of Babylon*. In fact, the opening passage of *The Vision of Cleopatra*, which is probably the most clearly "oriental" passage in the work, has a direct parallel in Part I of *Omar Khayyam*.

Ex. 28 a

Ex. 28 b

It can be seen that in both passages there is a tonic/dominant pedal throughout, though whereas in the Bantock example both the dominant and the tonic are present in the rhythmic figure which occurs in the bass, in the example by Brian only the tonic is in the bass, while both tonic and dominant are held throughout the passage in the upper part of the texture. In both cases the harmonic progression is from the tonic of the key to the minor chord based on the flattened 7th, and back to the tonic. In the case of the example by Bantock the tonic chord is always lacking a 3rd, until bar 131, where the major 3rd (C♯) is added. In the passage by Brian the tonic chord is always in the minor form, though the bare 5th is always prominent, being held throughout the section. The "oriental" flavour of this and other passages, coupled with intense chromaticism give this work a unique quality among Brian's works, and was to date the most tonally ambitious piece, looking forward to his symphonies of many years later.

The Vision of Cleopatra can be divided into five main sections, the first being an orchestral prelude entitled "Slave Dance", and the divisions of the other four sections being dictated by the text. Each of these sections can, however, be subdivided into scenes, each of which has its own thematic unity which makes it distinct from those before and after it. There is, nevertheless, a thematic thread which runs through the whole of the vocal part of the work, though the opening Slave Dance does not contain this motivic link.

The Slave Dance begins with a 12-bar introduction based on the material presented in ex. 28 b. The opening bars contain just the bare 5th (like the opening of so many of Brian's works), the C♯ and G♯ as shown on the third stave of ex. 28 b, then in the third bar the bass quaver figure joins in (the fourth stave of ex. 28 b). At bar 13 the dance itself commences, still with the quaver bass figure. The D of the preceding 12 bars persists, continuing the "oriental" flavour (ex. 29).

Ex. 29

The dance begins very softly and at a moderate tempo, but over the eighth bar Brian adds the marking "stately - gradually grow wild and riotous". The music at this point is in fact a "wild" version of ex. 29 (ex. 30).

Ex. 30

The quaver figure in the bass has now become a triplet figure, while the melody has become more decorated. The alternation between C♯ minor and B minor chords returns, still over a tonic pedal. As the music intensifies with an increase in tempo and louder dynamic markings, there is also an increase in rhythmic complexity, with triplets and quintuplets appearing more and more frequently. The chromaticism becomes more intense as the music swells to a climax. At bar 56, ex. 30 returns, now with the marking "wild and uneven". At bar 70 the music begins to subside, returning at bar 73 to the music of ex. 29, now with the tempo indication of *Lento*. As the dance draws to a close the bass quaver figure becomes fragmented, leaving the bare 5th (C♯ and G♯) as at the beginning.

The first vocal section, a solo for Iris (soprano), begins in E major, though the tonic chord contains an added 6th (C♯), so the feeling of C♯ minor is still strong. In the first six bars of the solo there are two ideas present which are associated with Iris. The first is a dotted rhythm in the bass, fluctuating between the tonic and dominant, and the other is a more impassioned melodic fragment (ex. 31).

Ex. 31

Six bars after fig. 8, at the words "She blooms with passionate ardour", the work's most important theme is presented. This is the motif which is connected with Cleopatra, and it first appears as a long melody, with a *tremolando* accompaniment above it, as Iris gives a description of her queen (ex. 32).

Ex. 32

This is the only time the melody is heard in full. The first five notes of ex. 32 are the most important, creating a Tristanesque motif which appears in various guises throughout the work. There are two important elements in the motif; firstly the upward leap of a 4th then a 5th, and secondly the appoggiatura movement of the fourth and fifth notes. The motif appears on several occasions either without (X^1) or with (X^2) the resolution of the appoggiatura (ex. 33).

Ex. 33

The last line of Iris's aria is preceded by a version of X^2 in one of its more recognizable forms (ex. 34). Usually the connection between a version of X and the original presentation of the theme is less obvious.

Ex. 34

Lento

The aria closes with a recapitulation of the two ideas associated with Iris, the dotted figure, and the melodic fragment given in ex. 31. As Charmion begins her aria (bar 115), new thematic material is presented, but after five bars the theme from the Slave Dance reappears, and, although it only lasts one bar, its presence continues to be felt, both in the repeated C♯ pedal of the work's opening, and in the appearance of D in a C♯ minor context. The appearance of music associated with slaves gives us an idea of Charmion's position in Cleopatra's palace. While the elements of the Slave Dance continue, X^1 makes an appearance, with the F𝄪 not resolving upwards as an appoggiatura, but falling to C♯, then to B♯. As with Iris's aria, this section closes with the same material with which it opened.

At bar 136 the small chorus makes its first appearance. It has a very short passage of only nine bars, and the texture is completely homophonic. There is very little accompaniment, mainly consisting of the C♯ pedal from the Slave Dance. The choral passage is closely related to the work's opening orchestral movement, having the falling movement through G♯, F𝄪 and F♯ which characterized ex. 29. The section ends with the glockenspiel playing C♯ and G♯ quavers over a span of two octaves, suggesting the first three notes of X.

The section for small chorus is followed by another aria for Iris, and this is based on the same two motives as her previous passage. The central part of the solo contains a canonic treatment of X^2, now in C major, and with the first note an octave higher. The solo ends with a new presentation of X^2, this in an almost unrecognizable form, though it contains all the notes of X^2.

Ex. 35

Allegro con fuoco

The first three notes of X^2 are in the opening tonic chord of ex. 35, while the appoggiatura (D♯ - E) is contained in the following two chords. The rising semiquaver line suggests the semiquaver arpeggio of bars 4 and 6 of ex. 32. The end of Iris's solo overlaps with the next section for small chorus, which is also introduced by ex. 35. The accompaniment of the chorus consists of arpeggio figuration (probably on violins) on A and D, clearly derived from the first three notes of X. The opening of the choral material itself also consists of upward movement through A, D and A, again suggesting the first three notes of X. The appoggiatura movement is also implied, but instead of the fall to E♭ which would be required for an accurate presentation of X^2, there is instead a fall of a 7th to B.

The choral writing is again very straightforward. Except for some independence of parts between altos and basses in the last three bars, the section consists entirely of soprano/tenor and alto/bass doubling. Even when individual parts divide there is still the doubling between male and female voices. This vocal style which uses much octave doubling may be a result of Brian's work as an organist. On this instrument it is normal for parts to be constantly doubled because of the use of the varying stops, and Brian may have transferred this technique, either consciously or subconsciously, to the chorus.

The imitative opening of the chorus soon changes to a homophonic texture during the mere eight bars of the section, and the voices end on a bare 5th, in typical Brian style. During the last two bars of the chorus the orchestra announces X^2 in the bass, with the figuration on the violins continuing. This leads to Charmion's second and final solo. The first six bars are characterized by statements of X^2 in semiquaver triplets and descending chromatic runs. At bar 191 the material of ex. 35 returns, but this is short-lived, because at bar 198 the music turns to the theme from the Slave Dance, as in Charmion's previous aria. This is immediately followed by a mysterious passage where X^2 is presented under a *tremolando* on the added 6th chord of E (with the 3rd missing), evoking the atmosphere of the words "But in tonight's cold moon she burns and glows" (ex. 36). The last five notes in the bass of ex. 36 can be seen to outline X (ignoring the D), and seven bars later Charmion's aria draws to a close.

Ex. 36

Another section for small chorus follows, this time only four bars long. The texture is again in two parts, with octave doubling between male and female voices. The chorus is accompanied by a memorable horn melody over a G♭ pedal (ex. 37):

Ex. 37

This melody is immediately repeated in canon, to begin Iris's final aria, where it accompanies the words "The day has gone, and soon they'll drink the heady wine which sparkles in each other's eyes". At this point there is an orchestral interlude of 17 bars, and both X^1 and X^2 are prominent. This material continues until the end of Iris's solo, which is followed by another section for small chorus. This is again only eight bars long, and is, until the last three bars, in two parts with octave doubling. These two parts are imitative, becoming homophonic when the texture splits into four, then eight parts. As with the second chorus, the bass of the orchestra enters with a version of X at the end of the passage. This marks the end of the first vocal section of the work.

The second section consists of a duet between Antony and Cleopatra. Antony's entrance is marked by a bold trumpet fanfare, and Antony is instructed to sing his first line "with great earnestness and enthusiasm". A theme is then presented which comes to be associated with Antony, although it contains in its inner parts an allusion to X^2 (ex. 38).

Ex. 38

Cleopatra's next entry again clearly states X in its first five notes, this time over a C and G bare 5th, reminding us of the work's opening. In the fifth bar of Cleopatra's solo the theme associated with her appears in its most complete form since its first appearance at bar 87. Here it corresponds to bars 3-7 of ex. 32. This is the only occasion in the work, after its first appearance, that the theme appears in a more complete state than its first five notes.

By contrast, Antony's next verse in the duet presents X in its most truncated form, as two chords, the first consisting of the first three notes of X (B, E, B), and the second containing the "appoggiatura" note (F♯), which remains unresolved. His next verse restates ex. 38.

Most of Cleopatra's vocal lines throughout the duet tend to be shaped by X, either in the five-note X^2 version, or just the first three notes of X. The truncated two-chord form of X makes several subsequent appearances, and the *Allegro con fuoco* version (ex. 35) also reappears. At the climax of the duet both voices sing simultaneously, beginning with independent parts, but soon singing in octaves. This is accompanied by a grandiose version of Antony's theme (ex. 38), more complex in its texture than on any other presentation. The duet ends with repeated chords hammered out in semiquavers, while X is again presented in the bass. In typical Brian style the music works up to a great *crescendo*, and is cut off suddenly, to resume very softly as the beginning of the next main section of the work. Cleopatra's aria "Far back within the womb of time" is introduced by two versions of X^1 (ex. 39).

Ex. 39

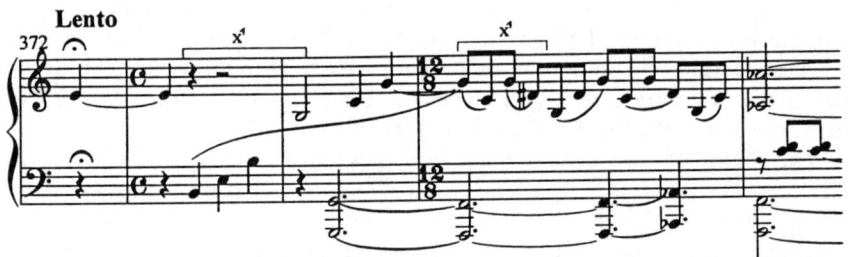

The first half of the solo is based mainly on the quaver rocking motion of ex. 39, along with syncopated repeated chords. The second half of the solo, beginning with the words "Whence slowly crept upon dreams" (bar 410), is introduced by a distant, subdued version of the fanfare which introduced Antony, preparing us for Cleopatra's lament upon the death of her lover. Again, the vocal lines are shaped by the first three notes of X, and the truncated, two-chord form of X is also present. The solo ends with the orchestra restating X^2 followed by the horn melody of ex. 37.

At this point the full chorus makes its first appearance, with the words "Great silence is o'er everything". The tranquility of silence is very well portrayed by the pure diatonicism of the passage, in direct contrast to the extreme chromaticism of everything that has gone before. The orchestral texture of this opening part of the chorus consists of arpeggios on the tonic added-6th chord with semiquaver running motion underneath, and a tonic pedal in the bass to make the tonality of the passage even more definite. The music returns to chromaticism when Brian feels that the words demand it, at the words "In our blood there is a sting, urging to love, both slave and king". The reappearance of chromaticism is accompanied by an increase in the complexity of the vocal texture. The chorus opens very softly with the altos and basses in unison, with the sopranos and tenors entering in canon. For the first 17 bars the voices are never in more than two parts, but at this point all four voices enter, though with Brian's customary octave doubling. At bar 486 the texture divides into eight parts, but there is some octave doubling. At bar 491 the small chorus provides a contrast at the words "Oh, for the secrecy of night". As with all of the other sections for the small chorus, this is very short, lasting only seven bars. A short passage with the glockenspiel playing an arpeggio figure derived from the first three notes of X leads to the next section for full chorus, where the words "For we are feverish with the thirst" are depicted by *staccato* quavers in four parts of the divided chorus, while the sopranos and first tenors sing the melody. The chorus ends on a great climax, and the music subsides for the beginning of the final main section of the work. This begins with a lament for cor anglais, which introduces Cleopatra's despairing solo "Now all is finished, all is done, my world is dead", which is accompanied by the truncated two-chord form of X^1 (ex. 40).

Ex. 40

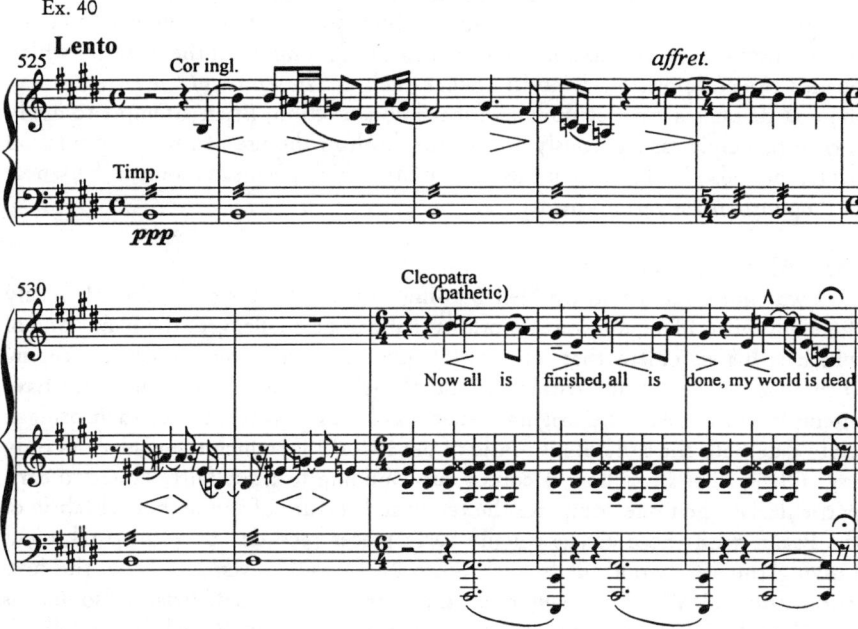

This section of the work is the most melodious and rewarding passage for a soloist, with arching melodic curves, instead of the angular lines of the previous sections, which even the most accomplished singers would find taxing. The first part of the solo introduces the truncated form of X, and also at bar 547 the theme of the Slave Dance appears. At the point where Cleopatra sings of Antony "His eyes have tears they cannot shed, his tale is told", the theme which is associated with Antony appears, and, in counterpoint with it, elements of the cor anglais lament (ex. 40, bars 1-4) can be found. At bar 570 both the words and the music of "Now all is finished, all is done" are repeated. At the words "Whence springs neither love nor bitterness" the vocal material is new, but it is accompanied in the orchestra by statements of X^2, and this forms a coda to the solo, so the whole aria is in the form A-B-A-Coda.

The work closes with a *Marche Funèbre* for the main chorus, with a very short passage for the basses of the small chorus. The music for this funeral march is based on the Slave Dance, and is therefore in 6/4 time, a rather unusual metre for a march. Apart from the first five bars where there is only one vocal part singing at a time, the choral textures are almost completely homophonic. A short recitative by the basses of the chorus leads to a 12-bar orchestral interlude, which is followed by the final choral entry, "Two suns have gone away to sleep", to the same material which had previously presented the words "The sun has gone away to sleep". This builds up to a great climax which subsides in the orchestra in the final bar, where the closing cadence comprises the two chords which were a feature of the work's opening, with the D sounding against the $C^!$ pedal. As at the beginning of the composition, the final tonic chord has no 3rd.

Like the two psalm settings previously discussed, Brian feels the need to close the work with a recapitulation, or at least, a brief reminder of the material which opened the composition. Even in a work such as *The Vision of Cleopatra*, where the text dictates a freer attitude to formal construction, Brian attempts to apply formal principles as rigorously as possible, both in the use of this recapitulation device, and also in the constant use of a motif which permeates almost the whole of the music in its various forms.

Larry Alexander comments:

I was quite fascinated by Neil Starling's thesis chapter on Psalm 23, nicely done but with, I feel, a few assumptions that can be challenged, the major one of which is his statement that "the (1945) orchestration is very much in keeping with that of the music written around the same time ..., so Brian must have attempted to recreate the original version as far as possible, rather than bring it up to date with the style of his music of the 1940s". To which the reader can only say "Oh?". That's not how it comes out sounding to these fairly educated ears, particularly when one compares the tenor and texture of the orchestral fabric of the Psalm with those of the equally early pieces recorded on Cameo Classics.[5] Leaving the very youthful English Suite No. 1 aside, even as late as the just-prior-to-World War I *In Memoriam* and *Doctor Merryheart*, Brian's "sound" is considerably different in these works than it is, say, in his (shall we call it?) "middle period" - *The Tigers* right up to and including Symphony No. 5 - and it is a much farther cry from the work that appeared post the unknown *Prometheus Unbound* when the composer's struggle to utter originality was finally achieved.

---

[5] Cameo Classics released English Suite No. 1, *Doctor Merryheart, Fantastic Variations on an Old Rhyme, In Memoriam, For Valour, Festal Dance, Burlesque Variations* and *Two Herrick Songs* in 1979-81 on three LPs (GOCLP 9010, 9012 and 9014), now reissued by Campion on 2 CDs (RR2CD 1331/1332). All works were played by the City of Hull Youth Symphony Orchestra, conducted by Geoffrey Heald Smith, the *Herrick Songs* were sung by the Saint Nicholas Singers.

Psalm 23 was one of the first of Brian's works that I became familiar with, the CBS Classics disc fortunately being available when I first fell head over heels in love with this man's music; it is still among my "top ten" Havergal Brian. The reason for this instant rapport between me and the Psalm is the same as for my equally instant rapport with the Eighth, Tenth, Thirteenth ... it is quintessential *late-period* Brian, at least in its sound. This is not to take anything away from the man who composed the line of the music as far back as the turn of the century. Quite the opposite. That he was that good that early is spectacular. Shocking - I recall that my first impression was an astonished "My God: he actually wrote that in 190*1*?" (as per the CBS liner notes). *N*obody wrote like that in 1901! Nobody!

Well, the truth is, I think, that that's right. Nobody did write like that in 1901, not even Havergal Brian. What he wrote in that first true decade of his career was excellent stuff, more than merely "promising". The extracted *Fantastic Variations on an Old Rhyme* from that first symphonic attempt is also among my all-time Brian favourites. But I cannot see that the orchestral sound of it, or any of its "brothers" of the era, has more than a remote resemblance to what the man was putting down in those staves post-*Prometheus*. The Psalm rightfully belongs at the head of the composer's incredibly productive penultimate period. Extrapolating, perhaps, I am convinced that it was the final trigger that produced the likes of the *Tragica* and on, an opportunity for Brian to examine the methods and conceptions of the scoring he was doing without having to worry about the melodic lines *per se*. It is perfectly plain that the experience taught him much in terms of coalescing that utterly individual style and, more than anything else, is what we have to thank for the wonders of the 8th, 16th, 22nd, 23rd and 24th (inclusive).

Of course, the orchestration of the Psalm did not come out of nowhere, and it makes one more frustrated than ever that the cantata preceding is lost. Because in the light of this theory of mine it is the ultimate transition, the piece in which Brian *had* to have gone from middle period to "first late". Traces of the coming transition are apparent in the 1937 *Wine of Summer* - the tense little high violin figures that open the piece come immediately to mind - but this is pre-echo, if you will. Not yet the real thing. The real thing as far as it is currently possible for *us* to hear it, blossoms with the reworked 1901 Psalm 23. And that is the major importance of this work. Early Brian and late in one single entity. The result is not an amalgam at all, but an incredibly integrated symphonic whole that looks forward a lot more than back. One can point to chords and orchestrations as much as one wants, but that does not change the basics: Psalm 23 is such a forward-looking piece that if we regard it as essentially a 1901 creation Brian would have had to have cringed back from it and returned to that post-Tchaikovskian idiom he was quite naturally and logically working in in the Edwardian age, saving his creativity for 40 years, knowing that he was too ahead of his time.

No. Impossible. The piece must have been rewritten totally in 1945. The shape of the melodies, the harmonies, may have remained the same, but the lucidity of the orchestration, the handling of the choirs and the relationships between the instruments: Brian didn't start doing that until around that time of his life, not before. Never before. Perhaps Malcolm MacDonald can call on example after example to prove me wrong; I wonder what Robert Simpson might have to say on the subject. I wonder what other Society members might have to say?

Malcolm MacDonald replies:

Larry Alexander's letter touches on one of the many "Brian enigmas" that we can't simply resolve in any decisive fashion because we have no hard evidence on which to base a conclusion; in a sense his letter reflects this because his points are couched so much in the form of general assertions ("how it comes out sounding to this pair of ears") that they are difficult to discuss in specific terms. In his last paragraph he seems to be claiming Psalm 23 as "late Brian" through and through, in form as well as orchestration, even if founded on material which originally goes back to the early years of the century. I have grave doubts about this; but there's no way anyone can firmly gainsay him.

It has become clear to me over the past few years - for a number of reasons which would take far too long to elucidate here - that the "received dating" of most of Brian's early scores (as promulgated by Reginald Nettel in *Ordeal by Music*, but ultimately relying on information supplied to him by Brian) tends to be three or four years too early, and this affects Psalm 23 as much as other pieces. The 1901 date, which I adhered to in my sleeve-note for the CBS disc, should probably be revised to "about 1904", as it is in the work-list published in *Newsletter* 37 [cf. pp. 405-411 in the present book]. A minor point in context, but it serves to highlight the fact that we have no contemporary scrap of paper dealing with the original version of the work that would help to tie it down more precisely: no score, no sketch, no letter (there is a story of Brian's having shown it to Elgar, which can hardly be earlier than 1905).

All extant manuscript material is of the second, 1945 version. At the end of the full score, Brian notes: "Original full score lost at Lewes, 1920. New full score completed at 25 South Way, North Harrow, March 7 1945". Of the *circumstances* of the full score's loss we know nothing whatever. Brian may in fact have destroyed it, and indeed there are several missing works from the Great War period (and immediate pre-War years) which would seem to have faded from view at the same time; maybe it got mislaid in moving house; or what? Equally important, we don't know what it was that *survived* 1920 - i.e., what Brian based his 1945 score upon. There is indeed a manuscript vocal score, with no date upon it, but the handwriting and paper are identical with the full score, and strikingly unlike the earliest surviving Brian MSS. (such as the 1903 *Burlesque Variations*). However, since Brian's note only refers to the loss of the original *full* score, it seems reasonable to surmise that the original vocal score, or at least a short-score sketch, was still available to him in 1945. (The vocal score is in fact in short-score form, which is why the Musica Viva publication is of a specially commissioned piano reduction.) Otherwise Brian would surely have signalled the fact of necessary recomposition from memory, as he did in his prefatory note to the Violin Concerto. There could have been many reasons for his then replacing this original source with a fresh vocal score - ranging from actual (but not necessarily major) revisions to the musical substance, to the sheer physical circumstance that the old vocal score could well have been in fragile condition, and not up to his current standards of legibility.

So we have simply no means of comparing the 1945 version with the original in any respect. But we can and should compare it with various pieces of relevant "parallel" evidence: for character and structure with the vocal score of *By the Waters of Babylon*, an authentic production of a couple of years later; and for orchestral style both with the other extant early works, *and* with the one available case of a work that Brian rescored in the absence of a full score that has subsequently been recovered: namely the first 120 bars of *The Tigers*, of which he produced a new version in 1969.

Form, etc.

As far as character and structure are concerned, I find myself very much in agreement with Neil Starling's conclusions, as suggested in his on-going series: that *By the Waters of Babylon* duplicates many of the processes found in Psalm 23, but extends them in scale and complexity, while introducing more original features. Of course we could try to stand this argument on its head: to say, for instance, that the 5/2 fugal section in *Babylon* ("How shall we sing the Lord's Song") is rather diffuse, and on an awkward subject - whereas the "But Thy loving kindness" fugue in Psalm 23, by its relative concision and simplicity, shows the hand of a mature and experienced composer. But that approach doesn't convince me. The very presence of a comparatively straightforward fugal section limited to "real" answers (compared to the much more involved sequence in *Babylon*) tends to identify Psalm 23 as an early work: and it seems more commonsensical to assume that the young composer essayed a small-scale fugue on a straightforward subject first, before going on vastly to expand and vary this feature in *Babylon*. The large amount of fairly literal repetition of thematic elements points to an early date too, though the thematic organization in itself is impressive. Harmonically, also, the musical language identifies itself as "early" Brian, not least through its saturation with triadic sonorities - triads which are commonly heard in full, with their 3rds, in root position. The characteristic "later Brian" bare 5th has little to do in Psalm 23 (and not much more in *Babylon*).

This is not to deny that the Psalm, even if written around 1904, is in many respects a highly individual piece; that it sounds unmistakably like Havergal Brian (it has become clear that there was *no* stage of his career at which he didn't sound like himself); that it constitutes a considerable advance on the 1903 *Burlesque Variations*; and that it contains things that are strikingly prophetic of his later work. (The most "prophetic" section, to my mind, is the *Tranquillo*, bars 280-300, on "for ever", with its aerated textures, disembodied treatment of tonality, and rapt, mystic, vein of meditation. If Larry wants to maintain that this was actually *composed* in 1945, I can't disprove it; but I don't hear anything inconsistent with *circa* 1904 in the chromaticism of the immediately following bars, nor in the climactic cadence at bars 306-7.)

But in general the personal voice is not yet particularly highly developed: it's music "of its time", displaying certain turns of phrase that seem to echo Elgar and other contemporaries ("But thy loving kindness", a wonderful tune, is positively Parryesque); and the influence of Wagner, *Das Rheingold* especially, is obtrusive and not wholly assimilated - though capitalized upon with skill and expressive point. An inchoate late-Romanticism is especially noticeable in the orchestral accompaniment of (for me) the least successful section, the big tenor solo ("Thou hast prepared a table before me"). And the vocal line here - though it starts (bars 212-3) with that most characteristic Brian shape which I traced throughout the symphonies on pp. 170-1 of my Volume 3 basically displays the asymmetrical, "negative" type of word-setting which Mike Smith (*Newsletter* 50 [pp. 342-349 in the present book]) has identified as a trademark of the early songs. (The word-setting in *Wine of Summer* and *Prometheus* is often cantankerous, but not in *this* way.) I have no difficulty, therefore, in accepting that Brian in 1945 may have revised Psalm 23 in many of its details: but I feel strongly that the work he has transmitted to us is essentially the one he wrote in or around 1904.

Orchestration

It is illuminating to compare the orchestra of Psalm 23 as listed in the 1945 score with that of the first version of *Babylon*. This latter valuable piece of information appeared in the pre-première report in the *Staffordshire Sentinel* and it seems not to have been known to Neil Starling: I give it here in the form of a direct quote, and have put the Psalm's instrumentation in the same order for purposes of easy comparison:

Babylon
  strings ... 3 flutes and piccolo, 2 oboes, 1 cor anglais, 2 clarinets, 1 bass clarinet, 2 bassoons, 1 double bassoon, 4 horns (6 horns *ad lib.*), 3 trumpets, 3 trombones and bass tuba, harp, 3 tympani, bass drum, side drum, cymbals, tambourine and large gong[6]

Psalm 23
  strings, 2 flutes (2nd takes piccolo), 2 oboes (2nd takes cor anglais), 2 clarinets, 2 bassoons, 4 horns, 4 trumpets, 3 trombones, tuba, harp, timpani, bass drum, side drum, cymbals, glockenspiel and organ.

On the face of it the *Babylon* list appears to contradict the statement that this work was originally scored for *double* woodwind - but since it is reporting a *total* instrumentation only it gives no indication of doublings, and the basic woodwind line-up could still have been 3.2.2.2, only one player more than the Psalm. If we accept that, the two orchestral constitutions are very closely matched: *Babylon* has slightly greater range of colour and flexibility in the wind, plus two notionally "Oriental" instruments in gong and tambourine; the Psalm being

---

[6] *Mr Havergal Brian's* Babylon / *Sir Edward Elgar's Opinion of the Work* - unsigned preview article in *The Staffordshire Sentinel*, 16 April 1907. "3 tympani" (*sic*) of course means 3 *drums*, not 3 sets; and though Brian late in life demanded "1-3" side-drums for the Psalm, the score itself indicates one only.

slightly more austere, with the "ecclesiastical" element of the organ, and one pitched percussion instrument, the glockenspiel (but this occurs in several of Brian's pre-1914 scores, whereas post-1914 he invariably complements it with a xylophone). The 1945 version of the Psalm, therefore, uses an orchestra that is quite consistent with his practice *circa* 1904.

When we turn to the *use* of that orchestra, however, we find that Larry Alexander is undoubtedly correct in his contention that the "sound" which Brian obtains is, in general, strikingly different from that of the early works for orchestra alone. Though it would be an extremely lengthy process to enumerate the differences in detail, I think they may be summed up broadly and simply: the orchestral works are much more concerned with instrumental colour "for its own sake". They are full of attention-demanding and -holding devices of timbre, texture, and execution, and they show Brian exploring and extending the full gamut of sonority made available to him by the various examples of Strauss, Debussy, and Rimsky-Korsakov. We see this in his taxing use of woodwind and brass ensembles, his experimentation with percussion effects, his frequent complex, multi-divided textures for strings. Orchestral virtuosity *as such* is one of his prime expressive aims during the early period. We do well to note, also, that he approached it through the forms to which it was most appropriate - character-suite, bravura variation-sets, and more or less programmatic tone poems. This brand of virtuosity is immensely developed, but with special structural significances, in the early symphonies between the wars.

The 1945 score of Psalm 23 approaches the orchestra from an entirely different viewpoint. Though extremely sensitive in its use of the instruments, colour as such is rarely employed even for illustrative purposes, and even then is used in a straightforward and traditional way: the pastoral oboe for pastures green, the insistent drumbeat in the Valley of the Shadow of Death. From first bar to last, the orchestra's role is conceived as *functional*, in that it exists to reinforce the music's thematic and polyphonic essence.

Now this is indeed the standpoint from which Brian views the orchestra in the first works which he wrote after 1945 (Symphonies Nos 6 and 7 and *The Tinker's Wedding*): and Larry is right, it is a "symphonic" standpoint. But we cannot assume that it wasn't his standpoint for *choral* works from the beginning. First, Psalm 23 and *Babylon* are vastly different in their *musical* character from the more extrovert orchestral works, and would seem to demand a more restrained use of the orchestral resources.[7] Second, it's obvious that the orchestra's overriding *raison d'être* in these psalm-settings is to accompany the chorus, and thereby to reinforce the *chorus's* thematic and polyphonic essence. (A relevant comparison here - so long as we remember that the use of the orchestra is more extreme in every way - would be that between Symphonies Nos 2, 3, 4 (second movement), and 5 on the one hand and the choral movements of No. 4

---

[7] If any of the purely orchestral pieces shares something of the expressive character of the Psalms, it is (intermittently) *In Memoriam*: the handling of the orchestra in this work is not impossibly different from *Psalm 23*, and in some features - the use of the organ, for instance (very different from its employment in the symphonies), the resemblance seems very close.

on the other. Again, in the choral music, the orchestration, though massive, is much less keyed to colouristic and virtuosic effect.)

The orchestral style of Psalm 23 therefore, seems to me no more inconsistent with "early Brian" than the constitution of the orchestra itself. Not that I suppose it was Brian's intention to attempt a detailed historical reconstruction of the lost full score. He would naturally have brought to bear all the garnered experience of the intervening 40 years. If that lost score were to turn up we'd undoubtedly find a myriad divergence in detail, representing a gain in professionalism, and in most, probably all, of those details we'd consider the 1945 score preferable. But his approach may well have been to provide a generalized "early Brian" orchestration in accord with the work's "early Brian" material, while avoiding anything that his current standards of orchestral technique could no longer accept.

The Prometheus connection?

Larry Alexander has nevertheless raised a very interesting point in getting us to think about how Psalm 23 (1945 version) might relate to *Prometheus Unbound* (completed 1944) and the series of symphonic works that resumed in the winter of 1947-8.

Prometheus, the most crucial work in Brian's oeuvre after *The Gothic* and *The Tigers*, remains a yawning gap in our knowledge; and even in the absence of the full score, the vocal score deserves a whole series of articles to make a preliminary assessment of its place and significance. I hope to attempt that before we are all very much older; but at the moment I will confine myself to a couple of observations.

The two-act form of *Prometheus* divides it neatly into two halves, each dominated by a principal protagonist - Prometheus in Act I, Asia in Act II - and on the musical level, too, the two acts constitute a kind of "masculine/feminine" dualism. The dramatic Act I, in its extended solos and choruses, demonstrably inherits and develops aspects of the Fourth and Fifth Symphonies. These are further developed in Act II, but in the direction of greater lyricism; and this tendency leads to an increased simplicity and directness in the material itself. That *may* to some extent lend the material resemblances to some of Brian's early music. It certainly, in my opinion, has some bearing on the relative directness of expression in the succeeding symphonic works. Also, for many reasons (better laid out in an article on *Prometheus* than here), Brian seems, during its composition, to have been glancing back over his life and reviving old memories - which would include the works of his earliest period. But - independently of that - the score gives off something else, very strongly: in some ways *Prometheus* is Brian's most "Wagnerian" creation.

I don't want that statement to be misunderstood. The work isn't derivative from or cannibalistic upon Wagner. But it is Brian's own great confrontation with an absolutely crucial Wagnerian theme - Redemption through the Love of Woman (Asia representing in Brian's scheme what Goethe calls "das Ewig-Weibliche") - and Brian was most certainly aware of the Wagnerian resonances of what he was doing. (Indeed, at some points he appears to challenge Wagner directly and deliberately on his own ground: the superb "Dawn" Prelude to Act II looks like a conscious re-thinking, wholly in Brian's own terms, of the opening of *Das Rheingold*.) I think it's *possible*, therefore, that this personal assimilation of Wagnerian concepts recalled to Brian's mind the work in which, as far as we know, he had first tried to make a creative, though far more simplistic, use of Wagner - Psalm 23, whose marchlike main idea evokes the Entrance of the Gods into Valhalla, and thus draws an ambiguous parallel between the House of the Gods and the House of the Lord. Perhaps, if he was unsure what direction to take after *Prometheus* (and the exalted super-lyricism of its final sections remains unparalleled in his entire output), this may well have struck him as the first reasonable moment to revivify the *Psalm*: marking time on a not wholly unrelated creation while his artistic impulses adjusted to the significance of what he had actually achieved.

The complete gap in composition from 1945 to the end of 1947, however, suggests that the Psalm's re-scoring stands as an appendix to Brian's "Middle Period" (of which *Prometheus* is the final climax as well as "final transition" - Larry is right here, though I don't think in quite the way he expects) rather than "at the head of the penultimate period". The most I can say is that its clear-cut structure and thematic economy may have helped to turn Brian back towards those features, which are certainly on display in the works of 1948.

The Tigers re-scoring

Finally, the joker in the pack. Once again, a detailed article is really needed to compare the 1969 re-scoring of the first 120 bars of *The Tigers* with its 1929 original, but the result of such a comparison can be very simply stated; the two versions are entirely different. The 1969 score is definitely in Brian's latest style, and there is no sign of any attempt to recall the original, apart from a couple of places where the material practically specifies its own instrumentation. One should be cautious of generalizing from this one instance, of course: *The Tigers* is a very different kind of work from Psalm 23, and Brian's attitude to re-scoring (to say nothing of his aural memory) may have been very different in 1969 from what it was in 1945.

On the other hand - Larry Alexander could reasonably claim that *The Tigers* fragment is the only piece of hard evidence on how Brian *re*-orchestrated that we have, and as far as it goes it supports his case. But I can't take that as conclusive proof on the matter. Which is where I came in ...

Postscript

I would like to add a footnote to my article which concerned itself with the relationship of the existing (1945) version of that work to its original (c. 1904) form, which according to Brian's own testimony was "lost at Lewes, 1920". I stated then "we don't know what it was that *survived* 1920 - i.e. what Brian based his 1945 score upon", but went on: "... it seems reasonable to surmise that the original vocal score, or at least a short-score sketch, was still available to him in 1945". A couple of pieces of evidence which have been staring me in the face for years have finally made me certain that the original vocal score did indeed survive until 1945.

In fact, one of these pieces is in the original *Ordeal by Music*, which concludes with a list of Brian's works up to 1944 that states (p. 140) that Psalm 23 was with Cranz, though "not yet issued". Having gone through a period of many years when it seemed safest to doubt practically every published statement about Havergal Brian that couldn't be independently corroborated, this must have been a detail that I suppressed. But the corroboration has been there for a long while.

Brian made some typescript lists, all slightly different in detail, of his own works and their distribution between publishers. These lists seem to date from the 1930s or '40s, and one of them was undoubtedly the basis for Reginald Nettel's catalogue in *Ordeal by Music*. As long ago as 1973, Brian's daughter Jean Furnivall very kindly supplied me with copies of two of these typescript lists which Brian had continued to annotate, one into the 1950s and the other into the '60s. The former, which ends with the annotation "complete list verified Saturday Dec. 20th 1957" includes "The 23 Psalm" under the heading "Cranz Edition", but this is one of a whole group of titles that has been crossed out in ink and annotated "withdrawn from Cranz now with H.B.". Together, therefore, Nettel and Brian clearly indicate that Cranz at some period held material for Psalm 23.

And if we turn to Cranz's 1932 Havergal Brian brochure - handily reproduced in Lewis Foreman's *Havergal Brian and the Performance of his Orchestral Music* (pp. 50-51) - we receive a very precise confirmation. There, among "IN PREPARATION ... VOCAL WORKS", is the final entry:

TENOR SOLO - WITH CHORUS AND PIANOFORTE:
The 23rd Psalm

The interpretation of this evidence seems to me pretty obvious. Even when he "lost" the full score of Psalm 23 (and we still don't know how that happened), Havergal Brian retained the vocal score, and he was content to assign it to Cranz as a work that could be performed with piano accompaniment (though there is no evidence that any such performance ever took place). When Cranz were forced to stop trading during World War II, the vocal score was returned to him along with a large number of other small works, and clearly this must have been the basis on which he constructed the new full score in 1945: or rather, 1944-45, as is confirmed by references in two contemporary letters that he wrote to Nettel (references I had read, but failed to remember when writing my article). On 15 December 1944 he told Nettel: "Did I tell you that Cranz cancelled the contracts *for the unpublished works*. So I have a number of things including ... the setting of the 23rd Psalm. The score was lost and, as it now appears to me a little masterpiece I am rescoring it for its original orchestra". On 18 February 1945 he again briefly mentioned "... this Psalm 23 - which lies before me as written at Hartshill".

The phrases "its original orchestra" and "as written at Hartshill" should be treated with reserve, of course. But they certainly indicate that Brian's intention was a "restoration" rather than a "new realization" of the orchestration; and this perhaps provides a partial answer to Larry Alexander's letter, which sparked off my article.

However, as I pointed out, the vocal score which is now extant appears to be contemporary with the 1945 full score! So Havergal Brian must have destroyed the original and made a new one - perhaps because it was now very fragile, perhaps because he no longer tolerated his early standard of calligraphy (some of his early manuscripts are very spidery indeed), or perhaps because he had introduced revisions into the substance of the music while re-orchestrating it.

Reginald Nettel: *Cleopatra*'s librettist[1]

The year 1908 saw something of a stir around the Cathedral Music Festival of Norwich. The committee had offered two prizes for a new composition to be performed there. One prize of £25 was offered for a libretto for a cantata, and a further prize of £50 for a musical setting of the winning poem.

The prize for the libretto was won by the Manchester journalist Gerald Cumberland, for a poem in blank verse on the subject of *The Vision of Cleopatra*. A sample of Cumberland's "poetry" may be gauged from this passage:

<pre>
Iris.   And when with regal, arrogant step she passed
             Across the portico, her white breasts gleamed;
             Her neck seemed conscious of its loveliness;
             Her lips, tired of tame kisses, parted with
             The expectancy of proud assault; she was
             As one who lives for a last carnival
             Of love, in which she may be stabbed and torn
             By large excess of passion.
Charmion.   Oh! Our Queen
             Has wine for blood; her tears are heavy drops
             Of water stolen from some brackish sea
             Or murderous waves; her heart now leaps with life
             And now lies sleeping like a coiled snake,
             But in tonight's cold moon she burns and glows;
             Her heart is housing many a mad desire,
             And she is sick for Antony.
Iris.   The day
             Has gone, and soon they'll drink the heady wine
             That sparkles in each other's eyes. Once more
             Venus and Bacchus meet, and all the world
             Stands still to watch the bliss of living gods.
</pre>

---

[1] From *Newsletters* 18 (VII-VIII 1978), pp. 3-4 and 19 (IX-X 1978), pp. 5-6.

Gerald Cumberland quoted this in a best-seller he wrote while on active service in the First World War (*Set down in Malice*, Edinburgh, November 1918; second edition, March 1919), and went on: "There was a little more to the same effect, and when I wrote the stuff I thought it very fine and still think it rather pretty. But a section of the musical press attacked it violently, and for a couple of months I was quite a notorious person. I gathered from the articles and letters that appeared that my dramatic poem was not likely to engender music that would carry on the tradition of Mendelssohn's *Elijah*. That had been my object [however] in writing it. I was sick of that tradition. I wished to help to break it."

While this storm was still raging Cumberland received a letter from Sir Henry J. Wood, who was to conduct the festival. He wrote:

> Very much against my will, I am writing to ask you on behalf of the Committee of the Norfolk and Norwich Festival if it is possible for you to make an alternative version of the 'two objectionable lines' (I fail to find them myself) in your libretto *Cleopatra* .... From my point of view, the whole thing is absurd and ridiculous.

But Sir Henry had not mentioned which lines were being found "objectionable" and Cumberland could not find them, so he showed them to "the most maiden aunt" and watched for her blushes. But she let him down. She read it and said "Oh, Gerald, how nice! I do think you have such pretty thoughts!"

Meanwhile the prize for composition of the music had gone to Julius Harrison, who identified the offending lines. The committee objected to "Her white breasts gleamed" and also to "Her lips, tired of tame kisses, parted with The expectancy of proud assault". Well, Cumberland never described himself as a genius with God-given authority. He wanted the lolly and he altered the lines. In this form *The Vision of Cleopatra* was given with Julius Harrison's music at Norwich and at Queen's Hall, London, but never again. The runner-up in the contest was Havergal Brian. His version, not having had the honour of a cathedral festival performance, was left unshriven; in Cumberland's original version, therefore, it appeared in the published edition of Bosworth, and was performed at Southport in 1909. This is the version with which we are here concerned. Brian was one of 70 composers led by the lure of *Cleopatra* and £50 to try his luck with a cantata on Cumberland's *Vision*.

He, Brian, has told us how he had to work under difficulties, for he was then living in the terraced house at 11 Gordon Street, Hartshill, Stoke-on-Trent. In such houses privacy is difficult beyond a certain point, and music next door was tolerated to a greater extent then than now. The man next door decided on a course of scale practice on the piano - mostly *glissandos* - and Brian had to try to compose a *Vision of Cleopatra* against this noise. Of course he couldn't. Brian was, in fact, more in need of silence than some other composers have been. Have you ever thought why one of his songs was composed sitting in the reading room at Stoke Public Library? Because there was a large notice on the wall commanding SILENCE, and this was strictly enforced. Such bliss could not be guaranteed in Hartshill with children in the house. Besides, at the time he was composing the *Vision* his wife was in hospital awaiting an operation. Brian therefore had to work through the night at his score, and it was finished only just in time to reach the Norwich Committee on the last day fixed for the receipt of entries.

The committee in their wisdom had arranged with three independent judges - Granville Bantock, Frederick Delius and Dr Ernest Walker. Then, in order to rule out favouritism among these distinguished men, they required that all entries should be identified by a pseudonym. Brian chose a rather phony Eastern name for himself - "Holy Pabrun".

The correspondence between Bantock and Delius at this time shows light on the way these things worked out. On 16 December, 1907, Delius wrote: "By the way there are remarkably few gifted musicians in England, if I am to judge from the scores that Wood has sent me for the prize cantata. Ye Gods! My lowest estimation seems to be considerably above their standard. Well! you will see for yourself when you get them ... yesterday and today I have been occupied with the cantatas and have sifted two big piles down to 3 or 4. I am awaiting another packet from Wood and also the full Orchestral scores." This was followed on 2 January 1908 by "I want you to look at the Cantatas and choose the 3 or 4 you think the best & I will tell you which ones I have chosen & then we can pick the prize one". A further letter of 2 February continues: "Has the prize cantata been decided yet - I am afraid they will give it to a mug. If they give it to any other than the 3 I picked out I shall protest as there is no question of the others."

The three quotations given above are taken from Lewis Foreman's book *Havergal Brian and the Performance of his Orchestral Music*, but I have seen in the Bantock-Delius correspondence (which I have not got by me at the moment) that Delius was troubled most by the fact that some of the candidates were well-trained but devoid of originality, while others had originality but lacked training. He mentioned that such a situation would not have occurred abroad (Delius was a dedicated Anglophobe at this time) but that in case of doubt he would probably plump for one with ideas which were not too badly expressed.

There is nothing in the correspondence to show on what point the two men disagreed, but Bantock could be as firm as Delius when his judgement was questioned, and the two men differed. As a result, Bantock withdrew from the panel of judges and Samuel Coleridge-Taylor was appointed in his stead. Brian told me that they disagreed about the composition he had submitted, and I have no doubt this could be so. One must be very naïve to believe that Bantock would not recognize the handwriting of some of his pupils and friends in the manuscripts submitted. Julius Harrison was a pupil of his and Havergal Brian a friend. Apart from that, the pseudonym "Holy Pabrun" must have hinted that here was someone having ideas like his own on Eastern lore. One can exonerate Bantock from favouritism, however, since he knew both the composers whose works were at the top of the list, but he did not tell Delius. Delius and he differed on the value of Brian's work and that was the end. Coleridge-Taylor, according to Cumberland, recognized Harrison's writing on his MS., and was in favour of this, but again, there is no need to suggest bias. Harrison got the prize.

A sequel came when the identity of the pseudonyms was revealed in the press, for Brian had done a lot to get decent performances of the music of Delius, and it is to the credit of Delius that he, who could be a difficult man, felt gratitude, for he wrote to Bantock: "To my astonishment I see from a paper cutting that the 'Holy Pabrun' was Havergal Brian's. I am very sorry he did not get the prize - if Coleridge-Taylor had only mentioned the 'Holy Pabrun' he would have tied with the other & they would have been obliged to play them both and divide the prize." Delius added that they would have to put a piece of Brian's in the programme of the Musical League Festival to be given in 1909.

This they did. It was Brian's rescored setting of *By the Waters of Babylon*. You will find that this is reported in some quarters as the first performance, but this is not strictly so. A performance of this same work scored for an orchestra with double wind had taken place in Hanley in 1907; the Musical League performance in Liverpool in 1909 was only the first performance of the rescored version for triple wind. Brian told me this himself; the full scores of both the double and triple wind versions of *Babylon* have long been lost.

It would seem that Sir Henry Wood took a hand in the competition affair confidentially, for Brian received a cheque for £50 from the Norwich Festival Committee in appreciation of his setting of *Cleopatra*, and they mentioned that Wood had subscribed handsomely towards this sum. That was not all. Bosworth's paid Brian £40 for the right of publication, and their vocal score can still be found in libraries. (It is virtually impossible now to tell what happened to the scores of *Cleopatra* and the two versions of *Babylon* after their performances. They could have been among the manuscripts given by the first Mrs Brian to the local butcher after Brian left her in 1913, or they might have been with the publishers. Bosworth's premises were bombed in World War II and it seems likely that *Cleopatra* was destroyed at that time.) Brian thus got as much as Harrison in cash, and he had a performance too - not at the Norwich Festival but at Southport in 1909. Landon Ronald conducted, Phillis Lett sang the name-part, John Coates that of Antony, Maud Phillips that of Iris, and Lillie Whiteside that of Charmion.

The reputation of this work was one of amazing difficulty in performance and intense passion in the audible effect. We can only tell now from the vocal score, but the work looks to me to be rather inclined towards Bantockery. Bantock, it should not be forgotten, was at the height of his fame in 1907, and he had influence. Julius Harrison later tried to throw off the influence of Bantock on his compositions, including *The Vision of Cleopatra*. It was a necessary move. Brian may have wanted with *Cleopatra* to please Bantock in particular, but one has to admit that he was not much good at it. I have often wondered at those who profess to see evidences of Elgar's style in the early Brian works. No doubt Brian worshipped Elgar, but when he put pen to paper the result came out quite otherwise. It is one of the advantages of being awkward.

Some of the press notices that followed hearings of *The Vision of Cleopatra* are to be found in Lewis Foreman's *Havergal Brian and the Performance of his Orchestral Music*, my own *Ordeal by Music* and *Havergal Brian and his Music*, so there is no need to repeat them here. Arnold Bennett's *When the clock stopped* in the *Matador of the Five Towns* volume can also be read with interest. He too said that the cantata had the reputation of being extremely diffficult.

What is the bearing of all this on the development of Havergal Brian's musical life?

It happened at a crucial point. As we have seen, Brian was working under difficulties at Hartshill. It was in consideration of this, and of his merits as a composer, that a director of the famous potting firm of Minton's came forward with the money to enable him to live a free life, devoting himself entirely to his music.

But let us look for a moment at the influence of the Church. Brian had been brought up under the influence of the Church of England, had been educated in its schools, served as choirboy and organist, and accepted its principles and social environment, but he had written nothing for its ritual. What he had written to Biblical texts were the settings of Psalm 23 and Psalm 137, but both of these compositions, although based on the form of the Anglican Church anthem, were on too big a scale to be used in church. They could have been performed at a cathedral festival, but were not.

Brian's first experience of a cathedral festival (as distinct from the Diocesan Festival he had attended in Lichfield as a choirboy) was at the Three Choirs Festival of 1905, where he went on the invitation of Elgar. He conformed to the custom of the times by appearing in Worcester in top hat and morning coat, only to find that Elgar, alone among the elect of Worcester, wore loose tweeds. Elgar's reputation in Worcester was so firmly established that he could get away with this. His native city honoured him that year by making him a Freeman, at a ceremony which Brian attended with some awe. There he saw that a prophet might, after all, be honoured in his own city and among his own people.

But Elgar's tweeds were a protest. In the opinion of many of his musical friends, the cathedral festivals were too stuffy. Among these was Gerald Cumberland, who wrote: "They hate (or else they are afraid of?) every emotion that is not a religious emotion. They think that God made our souls and the devil our bodies. They may be right; if they are, it is clear that the devil is not lacking in consideration."

The censoring of the "objectionable" lines in Cumberland's libretto for *The Vision of Cleopatra* was what might have been expected. Indeed, the whole work was such as the Deans and Chapters of the Three Choirs and Norwich might object to. Cumberland knew this. His protest against the stuffiness of Deans and Chapters was one with Elgar's tweed suit: "Music, an unwilling handmaid of charity, was 'indulged' in. One did not have music every day, for that would have been frivolous; but one had it in great lumps every twelve months, and had it, not because one cannot live fully and vividly without art, but because it made a good excuse for a social 'occasion'. The music itself was excused - for in the minds of these people it required an excuse - by the fact that the whole festival was organized for charity, the vice that causes so many sins."

True, not everything was suitable for performance in a "sacred edifice", but that was taken into account. There was always a secular concert in the Town

Hall, followed by a ball which was the social highlight of the week. It was for the secular concert that *The Vision of Cleopatra* was intended. But Deans and Chapters were all the time inching into the secular programmes until they were treated almost as if they were cathedral performances. In fact, as Cumberland said: "Their 'secular' concerts are echoes of the concerts given in the cathedral", and, as Cumberland wrote in a passage already quoted, he was sick of that tradition and, with *Cleopatra*, he was helping to break it. He must have expected some objection to be made to his libretto, and one feels that his use of a maiden aunt to test it was not so innocent as it seemed.

Cumberland admired Brian's music enormously, but was cool towards Elgar's. When he called Elgar "aristocratic" to his face, he thought of it as a French revolutionary might have done; but at the word "Elgar rose like a fat trout eager to swallow a floating fly". It was Elgar's loyalty (at that time) to the oratorio tradition which annoyed Cumberland, who followed Ernest Newman in believing that the English oratorio was played out. Brian was in the midst of these conflicts, and he was edging away from the Church tradition.

But it was not easy. Handel's *Messiah* was annually gorged upon in Stoke-on-Trent, and Brian said nothing against it, but he was not led that way. Nor was Arnold Bennett. Brian, described by Cumberland as "a young fire-eating genius from the Potteries", planned a meeting between Bennett and Cumberland in the interval of a Strauss concert, and Brian stood aside in amusement while Bennett cut Cumberland down to size. "I see", said Cumberland, "that you continue writing for *The New Age* in spite of their violent attacks on you." "Yes", he (Bennett) answered laconically.

Bennett, one of the highest paid writers in the world, wrote regularly for *The New Age* without payment. It was an honour. The editor, A. R. Orage, set the highest standard of journalism in the country and never lowered his sights. (He refused everything that Cumberland sent to him.) Lord Alfred Douglas, on the other hand, who edited *The Academy*, printed several of Cumberland's poems, and it was probably through Cumberland that Brian began to take an interest in Lord Alfred Douglas' own poetry. It was many years, however, before Brian's admiration for Douglas' poetry led him to his Fifth Symphony, with Douglas' *Wine of Summer* for its theme.

There is in the Bantock correspondence a letter from Brian expressing his puzzlement at the contrast between Lord Alfred Douglas' sensitive mind, as shown by his poetry, and the reputation by which Brian had formerly heard of him as the partner of Oscar Wilde in the offence for which Wilde went to prison. Amongst the working classes homosexuality is rare. It is a problem mainly for intellectuals. Brian knew the word "Oscarwilding" as smut, and smut alone, but now that he was among highly sensitive men (the "aristocrats" of culture), he was in a better position to understand the nature of sex in its various ramifications. (It should be remembered that although we are familiar with the work of the Viennese psychologists today, their writings were little known before the end of the First World War.) An English translation of Richard Le Gallienne's *Little Sleeper*, set to music by Brian, had been heard in concerts sung by John Coates without benefit of copyright. It was when the chance came for publication that Brian began to think of this, and got Cumberland to make a lyric that went with the music. This was published under the title of *Soliloquy on a Dead Child*, and had its origin in a poem by the Persian poet Hafiz, who lost his favourite boy at the age of ten, and each spring, on the boy's birthday, visited his grave to pray. Could paederasty inspire so great a love? Brian was to learn that the working class outlook was not all. After Brian's fall into disrepute in the Potteries, Arnold Bennett dropped him, but Lord Alfred Douglas - who had the reputation of being a very difficult man to get along with - became Brian's pen-friend. I have in my possession a letter dated 15 February, 1937, from Douglas to Brian, in which he says: "Arnold Bennett always was one of my *bêtes noires*, although I never spoke to him in my life. Had you written to me, I would have been pleased, and would have responded at once".

No greater contrast in men can be found than between Brian and Cumberland. Both left for London in the same year. Brian burned his boats in the Midlands; Cumberland left his Manchester editor on excellent terms and continued to send London reports to him after the move. He earned £650 in his first London year, and could have made more, but would not make a slave of himself. Later he earned over £1,000 a year - easily.

It was no surprise to Cumberland that Brian was not able to earn a living from his work as a composer. There was money to be made in this way, but everybody knew that Brian would not do it. There is a paragraph in Cumberland's *Set down in Malice* which reports a conversation with the conductor Landon Ronald at Blackpool where Brian and Cumberland were in attendance. Ronald was a popular composer whose song, *Down in the forest*, was sung everywhere. "I sometimes feel a pig", said Ronald, "making money by my trifles when so many men with much greater gifts can only rarely get their work performed and still more rarely get it published. You told us just now", he said, turning to Brian, "that you would like to make money by your compositions. Who wouldn't? Well, it would be foolish of me to advise you to try to write more simply, with less originality, on a smaller scale. It would be foolish, because you simply couldn't do it. No; you must work out your own salvation: it is only a matter of waiting: success will come." As we all know, Brian worked out his own salvation and success came, but only after a very long wait.

And what of Cumberland? Would he be surprised to learn that in due course the only people to know anything of his lyrics would be those who listened to Brian's settings of them?

I think not. Cumberland was a realist. He never pretended that his poetry was for ever.

Granville Bantock: Havergal Brian and *The Tigers*[1]

Fifty years ago we were drawing near to a Golden Age, though at the time we seem to have been unaware of the fact. For a long period we had been living in a fool's paradise, and on a starvation diet. Our grandparents knew and cared little for the art of Music, unless it was presented to them in four-part vertical harmony, and dressed up as a hymn-tune, or as a respectable oratorio. Students and would-be Bachelors of Music were not allowed to write consecutive 5ths, and were forbidden - in my own student days at the R.A.M. - to listen to the sinful progressions of a Richard Wagner, or to the "circus-music"(?) of Franz Liszt. Under such irrational prohibitions the Muse came near to suffocation and a comatose condition. She might have packed up her baggage, and departed for a more hospitable land. Indeed, I am inclined to believe that she did actually escape, and take up her residence in Russia, where she gave birth to a progeny of world-famous composers such as Rubinstein, Balakirev, Borodin, Taneiev, Mussorgsky, Rimsky-Korsakov, Glazunov, Tchaikovsky, Scriabin, and Stravinsky. She succeeded, however, in founding a distinctly national school, which is more than likely to survive and influence the future development of Music.

The outlook in this country was well-nigh desperate before the "Nineties", but the situation improved, and salvation seemed to be at hand, heralding the advent of Sullivan with the *Golden Legend*, Parry with *Judith*, Stanford with *Shamus O'Brien*, Mackenzie with the *Dream of Jubal*, and Cowen with *Thorgrim*. Although performances were few and far between, it was a welcome change from the sterility of former years. But the time was not yet, though the finger of fate seemed to be pointing the way. Most of these works deserve revival, and should not be allowed to sink into neglect and oblivion, though they may never gain the popularity of *Hiawatha*, by Coleridge-Taylor, which is still a favourite among choral societies.

Of course it will be argued that the present time is not suitable on account of the War. Agreed. But not so very long ago the B.B.C. must have expended quite a large sum in giving a performance of Schoenberg's *Gurrelieder*, in which few people could have been interested then, or now. However, the new century was at hand, and we were yet to hear of Elgar, Delius, and Sibelius. Fortunately aid was forthcoming, and the opportunity for a more liberal policy was inaugurated and developed by three native-born conductors - Sir Henry Wood, Sir Thomas Beecham, and the late Dan Godfrey - who possessed the necessary faith, courage, enthusiasm, and enterprise. The remarkable and epoch-making record established

---

[1] From *Newsletter* 46 (III-IV 1983), pp. 3-7. The article was written in 1944 and seems never to have been published before (cf. references in this book on pp. 5-6), it was published in connection with the BBC recording of the opera from 2 to 8 January 1983 (first broadcast on 3 May 1983). Longer *verbatim* quotes from the opera libretto are omitted in this version, as in the *Newsletter* edition, because of the availability of the vocal score and the libretto of the opera.

by Wood, of conducting an unbroken series of Promenade Concerts during 50 consecutive seasons culminated in the Jubilee Celebration during the present year of 1944 - a wonderful achievement, worthy of the generous public acknowledgement it evoked. While Beecham gave considerable attention to making known the music of Delius, and Richard Strauss, Wood showed a more eclectic spirit, and not only opened wide the door to Elgar, and Sibelius, but to a host of other composers, whose works were given a first performance and a public hearing. Godfrey at Bournemouth followed the same path, and showed a similar spirit of enterprise and encouragement by inviting British composers to conduct performances of their own works.

It did really seem as if the renascence of a Golden Age for Music was dawning in England, until the outbreak of the War in 1914 dashed all our hopes to the ground. During this period (1900-14) we had frequent visits from Sibelius, and Richard Strauss, to conduct their own works. The influence of Debussy, and the Russian Ballet was making itself felt. Choral and Orchestral Societies were active, and making good progress. Nor should we omit to mention the stimulating effect of the great Triennial Festivals at Birmingham, and Leeds, the Three-Choir Festivals at Gloucester, Worcester and Hereford Cathedrals, the annual Welsh National Eisteddfod, the Scottish Môd, the Irish Feis, and all the local provincial Competition Festivals scattered throughout the British Isles. The organizers, adjudicators, and competitors reminded one of backwoods-men, engaged in clearing away the accumulated lumber and undergrowth of years, and blazing the trail into a new and more fertile region. The Elizabethan nest of singing birds was once more a reality, to be heard, seen, and enjoyed. Musical pilgrims journeyed to Edinburgh, and sat at the feet of Donald Tovey, the Erasmus of this renascence. In the sixth and final volume of his *Essays in Musical Analysis*, published as recently as 1939, Tovey, who possessed the keenest, widest, and soundest musical knowledge of his age, or any other age, wrote an appreciation of Brian's *Fantastic Variations on an Old Rhyme* in the following words - words that will be remembered as prophetic, and likely to be endorsed by a future and more enlightened generation. He writes:

> I hope that performances of such works as this may draw attention to a composer who has achieved things on a vast scale which may have to wait as long for recognition as usual. This composer will achieve more; but even for the recognition of his smaller works he is being made to wait longer than is good for any composer; and far longer than is good for any country whose musical reputation is worth praying for.

When Richard Strauss acknowledged the dedication and full score of Brian's gigantic *Gothic* Symphony, he described the work as "großartig". Higher praise by so great a Master could not be given.[2]

---

[2] Editor's note: Correctly, Strauss wrote, "wie es scheint großartig"; the proper translation of this is "as it seems, great" - which means that it is not necessarily sincerely felt.

The district known as "The Potteries" lies in the heart of England. Here Havergal Brian was born at Dresden, in the parish of Trentham, R. D. Stone, Staffordshire on 29 January in the year 1876. It is perhaps a wise dispensation of Providence that a particular seed should occasionally be allowed to fall, and sow itself in some sheltered spot, where it can germinate in safety, and develop into a sturdy plant; rather than to undergo a precarious existence and possible extinction in the open and more dangerous public highway. The forgotten seedling may in time become a lofty landmark and prove a beacon to guide the footsteps of a future generation. Neglect may be an advantage to the artist, who is willing and able to detach himself from the log-rolling fraternity, and who scorns to avail himself of Press publicity and notoriety. Mozart was buried in an unknown pauper's grave. Schubert and Mussorgsky achieved posthumous fame after a life of neglect, poverty, and disappointment. However fickle the general public (the great G. P.) is known to be, we cannot blame the poor blind monster, who allows himself to be rationed in regard to his taste, and to be fed by the self-appointed guardians of his captivity. On the other hand we ought to congratulate, without envy, the child of good fortune, who enjoys the respect, friendship, and affection of his contemporary peers and fellow-workers in similar fields of art and culture. This is a compensation of real value, and such recognition far outweighs the ephemeral favour of popularity acquired by the costly efforts of a publicity agent. The all-important thing, however, is to produce the actual work. For this purpose a satisfactory environment of tranquility, favourable for meditation and concentration of thought, is needed. "Work while it is called Today; for the Night cometh, wherein no man can work". These words of Carlyle still ring in our ears, and will inspire all generations to be up and doing.

On several occasions Brian generously exerted himself to create a local interest in the music of his contemporaries, and his enthusiasm for the choral works of Elgar, Delius, and others, bore a rich harvest of fruit. Mainly due to his personal efforts, the North Staffordshire Choral Society, then at its zenith, gave inspiring performances of their major works. I well remember the rare occasion on which Delius conducted at Hanley his *Appalachia* in a somewhat uncertain and disconcerting manner, probably due to nervousness. Beecham would bring down his London Orchestra an hour or so before the actual performance, and I am not likely to forget an extraordinary first performance of Brian's Overture *Hero and Leander*, from which the horn parts had been omitted by the copyist, and the players, responding to urgent signs from Beecham, who was conducting, repaired the deficiency by improvising a *ff tutti ensemble* counterpoint of "Life on the Ocean Wave". Brian's astonishment and inner feelings must have been inexpressible. At any rate they remain unutterable. Those were great days. After the musical banquet we would adjourn to the lounge of the North Staffs Hotel at Stoke, and talk and argue indefinitely until the dawn, in spite of the protests of the veteran night-porter. On these occasions the Symposium was often enlivened by the company of Ernest Newman, Gerald Cumberland, Sammy Langford, Frank Mullings, and other welcomed visitors.

But we have delayed too long, and the audience is growing impatient. The tigers are ravenous, and the public is already assembled to see them fed. The auditorium is full of expected listeners, including a few dilettante spectators, a cadaverous looking critic with his note-book in hand, a bevy of beautiful ladies wearing gossamer evening-gowns in the Grand Circle and Box-tiers, officers in uniform, ATS, WAAFS, WRENS, RAFS, a Lord-Bishop in gaiters, an Anglican clergyman, etc., etc. The singers are ready. The lights are dimmed. The orchestral players have ceased their interminable tuning. The conductor, Herr von Teufelsdröckh, appears from somewhere beneath the stage, bows to the audience, is received with fantastic applause, turns and faces the curtain, raises his baton, and ...

PROLOGUE

Scene 1

Hampstead Heath. Bank Holiday Carnival.[3] Background of Hobby Horses, Stage roundabouts, Aunt Sallys. Happy holiday crowd. Costers and their children. Conversational opening between Toy-seller (soprano), Sweetmeat-seller (contralto), Old-Clothes-seller (tenor), Fruit-seller (bass), while various Stall-holders are attending to their exhibits. The Fruit-seller pats his dog, and gives a carrot to a donkey. The minute stage directions are worthy of attention, and deserve to be quoted in full. The action is interrupted by the arrival of a Bill-poster. He puts down a short ladder and, mounting to the platform near by, takes a big bill from his bag, and unfolds it carefully. Reading it to himself, he shakes his head, and rubs the board with his paste-brush to the accompaniment of descriptive and pantomimic music from the orchestra.

A Costermonger enquires - "What's it about?"

---

[3] Vivian Moses writes in a letter to the Editor in *Newsletter* 48 (VII-VIII 1983), p. 7: "Your Editorial in *Newsletter* 47 prompted me to ask a friend in the offices of the *Hampstead and Highgate Express* to look up the issue in 1914 which might have reported the August Bank Holiday fair on Hampstead Heath. The relevant date is 8 August 1914, and a copy of the original is to be found in the Local History Library at the Swiss Cottage branch of the Camden Public Libraries. In 1914, the Bank Holiday fell on 3 August, the day before the outbreak of war. The 'Ham & High' noted that many thousands of people spent the Bank Holiday on Hampstead Heath but, while children and young people were boisterously happy, the holiday spirit was not strong and the crowds were less dense than usual. People were reading editions of the various newspapers, gravely wondering what the future might hold for them. It was a beautiful day and the distant views from the Heath were lovely. Some 74 children were taken to the Lost Children's Tent and by nightfall all but two had been claimed by their parents or guardians. There were 14 accidents and numerous cases of drunkenness but no serious misdemeanours. Indeed, only five charges were brought at the police court on Tuesday. Unfortunately there is no specific mention of a fair either in that issue or in the preceding or following ones. However, other local events did take place more or less as usual. Alexandra Palace, for example, was visited by 25,000 people and there was a comprehensive series of continuous amusements. The only alteration to the published programme was the abandonment of a balloon ascent from the south front. It is probably safe to conclude that activities on the Heath also pursued their normal course and that the usual collection of stalls and side shows were in place."

The Bill-poster replies - "Read it, I'm off."

There follows an amusing dialogue in slang dialect among the Costers, who regard the poster with perplexity, being unable to read it. However, one of the Costers, Henry, offers his assistance. He mounts the platform, and peers at the poster gravely through a pair of large tortoise-shell-rimmed glasses. He falls back in a state of collapse, slowly recovers, and in reply to the anxious enquiry of the Crowd - "Anything serious, Henry?" announces with a stifled yawn - "There's a war, and this paper says that every man is wanted" - (general consternation) - "under seventy-five". To an anxious Costerwoman, who asks - "Whose war is it, Henry?" he can only reply - "The paper doesn't tell yer that. It only says - 'Everybody (in falsetto) under seventy-five'". After this portentous announcement Henry descends the ladder, and disappears in the crowd. The news is received with laughter and merry-making, and ironic shouts of - "War! Under seventy-five! Every man!"

Two policemen now enter, while the orchestra begins to play, *pp*, a series of fantastic variations on the well-known tune, "Has anybody here seen Kelly?" There is immediate silence. Each constable takes from his pocket a photo, and scrutinizes the faces of the Costers, and Stall-holders. The fun grows fast and furious as the search proves unavailing, and many comic incidents will be noted. The police are kept busy taking their own notes, while the orchestra develops the theme with much ingenuity. A sudden interruption is caused by the entrance of an enormous elephant with large tusks, and ornamental bells. A ruffianly-looking keeper, tall and swarthy, with cheap showy ear-rings, carries a long whip and a megaphone. On top of the elephant is a chubby-faced young man, roguish, elegantly dressed, and wearing a silk hat. The tempo changes to *pomposo e grave* as the keeper through the megaphone shouts over and over again - "Make way! Make way!" The police call upon him to "Stop!" but the Man on the elephant exclaims - "Go on. Take no heed. This is my animal." The crowd joins in with hilarious laughter and further exclamations of mirth, adding to the increasing uproar.

Police (growing impatient) - "Tell your man that he is wanted".

Keeper - "Oh, what for? Please understand that he is not *my* man. I am *his* man, and this is *his* elephant."

The "Kelly" tune asserts itself in the orchestra, *mp*, *f*, and *pp*, as the dialogue becomes more heated and insistent. There is another interruption, when a Town-Crier, wearing old-fashioned gorgeously brocaded robes, knee-breeches, silk-stockings, buckle shoes, and Dick Turpin hat, enters ringing his bell, and accompanied by Assistants similarly attired. The Town-Crier unfolds a long roll, pulls out a big handkerchief, and blows his nose. He cries out - "Lost from his home" - but the Assistants excitedly pull his sleeve, and whisper in his ear. The Town-Crier corrects his mistake, and continues: "Lost in the park one young man, age twenty-three, and (to the Assistants' "Yes Yes!") age twenty-one, short and stout, morning-dress, wears a silk hat, easily gets excited. Name unknown. Bring him to me if you find him" (adding to the Police, and throwing the roll at them) "This matter is now out of your hands, Constables!"

The Police depart amid the cheers and jeers of the crowd. The Man on the elephant exhorts the Keeper to "Move on. We are wasting time", and after strenuous efforts to escape from the surrounding onlookers the elephant and his two companions slowly make their way across the stage, and depart. A sprinkling of holiday-makers remain around the stalls, gossiping and laughing. The Artist-Photographer, described as a queer-looking man, is seen coming down stage followed by a party of two good-looking ladies, carrying open green parasols, and accompanied by two gents, young and fashionably dressed in morning clothes, and grey top hats. The Artist-Photographer has a long beard and moustache, age fifty, vivacious and loquacious. He has a camera and easel, and looks like the Doll-maker in *La Poupée*. He poses the group in front of the Old-Clothes stall, much to the amusement of the spectators. The following conversation ensues:

Artist-Photographer: "I think this will suit very well" (to the Old-Clothes-Seller) "shall you mind if I pitch my party here?"

Old-Clothes-Seller: "Not at all. Yet, I would make but one condition. You shall photograph me with your party."

Artist-Photographer: "Yes, that is not a difficult matter, I am sure."

He places the two gents with crossed legs on the ground, with the two ladies standing behind, and the Old-Clothes-Seller between them.

Artist-Photographer: "Please come here. Take your stand beside this Lady, and smile like the rest of the party." He gets behind the black cloth, and asks for "Silence", becoming very fussy with excessive gesture and exaggerated respect. He shuffles the party about, indicating what he wants. Members of the crowd amusedly mock his gestures, and repeat his directions. The scene makes capital fun of a situation with which we are all too familiar.

The Artist-Photographer continues: "Many thanks! Very pleased! Please reform as you were before. (To the Ladies) It is unfortunate we have wasted time. Please wear your usual charming smile. Gentlemen, as you were before. Still. And with a natural expression, one - two - three (pressing button). It is over."

Old-Clothes-Seller: "Many thanks. Here is my card, and my address." The Artist-Photographer, accompanied by the Ladies and Gentlemen, departs.

A Young Man, answering to the description of the Town-Crier, now enters followed by another crowd. He applies to the Old-Clothes-Seller for the costume of a Pantalon, and appears to be very satisfied when it is handed to him. He conceals himself in the crowd from the Town-Crier and his Assistants, who have returned in search of him, and the curtain falls abruptly upon this unconventional, yet exhilarating opening Scene, so unexpected, so original, and so full of incident. There is not a dull moment anywhere. The music provides a bright and descriptive accompaniment throughout, and develops the "Kelly" theme with facile invention and true ingenuity.

Scene 2

It is now Night. The Scene is the same as in 1, but nearer the Hobby Horses - in white and gold - and away from the stalls. The Carnival is in full swing. The stage is thronged with dancers in fancy attire, with Pantalon and Columbine as principal dancers. Gaudily coloured decorations and brilliant lights. The Hobby Horses move slowly at first, gradually increasing pace until they suggest galloping across stage. An orchestral movement (*Allegro vivace*) entitled "Wild Horsemen" (running to 16 pages of the vocal score), with its vital energy, thematic development, and brilliantly effective orchestration, provides a clever parody of the "Walkürenritt" and forms a fitting prelude to the action that follows. A police Constable enters, vigorously blowing his whistle in an authoritative menner, and orders the crowd - "You crazy people! It is quite time to go to bed" - who slowly and unwillingly depart. Pantalon and Columbine remain behind, while the music continues with hints and reminders of the "Wild Horsemen", and prepares the way for the diverting scene that follows. Pantalon unfolds his love for Columbine, who declares that she has had enough of love. She repulses his advances with increasing warmth and passion. But her anger is shortlived, and the Scene ends with Columbine exclaiming - "I will go with you, Pantalon! Our life is love! Come, my Pantalon!" The two grotesques embrace, and run away laughing as the Curtain falls, bringing the Prologue to a satirical climax.

ACT ONE

Scene 1

The drop-curtain suggests a row of houses in a street. Military music is in the air. Excitement is afoot, and groups of people hasten across the stage. Three Clergymen enter from Left, walk to the centre of stage and listen. They are followed by three other Clergymen, who enter from Right, and stand listening with the firstcomers. All are elderly gentlemen with grey beards, and vary in size. They exclaim: "Listen. Soldiers marching. Let us go and see them."

Hearing a distant trumpet call, they hasten away. A Lady enters with a perambulator, followed by two overdressed Dudes, complete with monocle, and silver-headed cane. They soon depart, and an Organ-grinder appears, accompanied by his monkey. He stands before a door with his back to the audience, and grinds away, until he is interrupted by a police Constable, who tells him to "Move on, and take that thing away." The Constable ushers the Organ-grinder off the stage. Three over-dressed Ladies make a short appearance before they also vanish, and the stage is then occupied by a crowd of Labourers, smoking short clay pipes, City-Men in silk hats, poor, and fashionably attired women.

Scene 2

The drop-curtain now rises, disclosing the approach to a large railway station. The crowd, as before, acting as Chorus, assisted by the Clergymen, Ladies, etc., and Police trying to maintain order. (The Chorus is here divided into six separate sections with 21 vocal parts.) Excitement grows as the crowd, welcoming the approach of the famous regiment of the "Tigers", utters enthusiastic acclamations, and comments on their smartness. The Colonel (Sir John Stout) rides on a stage horse, leading the battalion, and takes up his position by the entrance to the Station archway. Meanwhile the "Tigers" stand at attention facing him on the opposite side. The regimental Sergeant-Major, a very fussy person with a huge walrus-like moustache, rushes forward and salutes the Colonel, who forthwith addresses his men, and compliments them on their fine appearance and military bearing.

He then proceeds (*quasi Recit.*): "I can see that many of you have left home, who never left home before. Many of you have left wives weeping, whilst some wives may be glad you have left." His concluding words: "My lads, don't forget what I have told you. Work hard, with a keen sense of duty, and you will be rewarded.", are hailed by all with shouts of approval and enthusiastic applause - "Long live the Tigers!"

The Act closes abruptly with a triumphant "Hurrah!" as the Curtain falls.

ACT TWO

Scene 1

Midnight. Interior of a small room, sparsely furnished with a camp-bed on which the Colonel, with head just above the bed-clothes, is asleep. His military uniform is suspended from hooks in the wall, and his hat is on a chair, while his jack-boots occupy a conspicuous place near the stage curtain. To judge from the strange sounds that emanate from the orchestra in an extended and descriptive introduction, we may assume that the Colonel's slumbers are far from peaceful, and evidently disturbed by discordant and unusually fearsome nightmares. Occasional *sforzatos* interrupt with grunts the prevailing *pianissimo*, and indicate a restlessness of mind and body. Ghostly apparitions succeed each other in the following order: a Red Indian in full war-dress, the ghost of Alexander the Great, and Napoleon. They utter a few admonitory words such as "Sir John! Sir John! I shall remember thee in the day of battles. We shall meet again in the happy hunting-ground. Farewell!", and then as suddenly vanish.

The last apparition is that of a tall excitable woman, dressed in black. She points to the bed as though warning him. The following dialogue ensues:

Lady: "Sir John! Sir John!"

Colonel (raising himself in bed): "Oh! my god!"

Lady: "I am always thinking about you ... Do you think of me busy with the laundry, mending your socks and shirts, darning your pants, etc. ... Like me you are not young, Sir John, and the temptations are very great, ... Never forget you are an English Knight and a Grandpa. Your great age shall save you from the ladies. Beware of scandal, Sir John! ... Whilst you are away, I shall be quite happy, knowing that the high sense of honour and dignity of an English Knight will protect and save you. Farewell, Sir John!"

A brief descriptive orchestral *Allegro* brings this Scene to an effective and dramatic close.

Scene 2

A military parade ground. A summer day with bright sunlight. The Battalion is at early morning parade awaiting arrival of the Colonel. A short orchestral introduction (*Andante moderato*) precedes the rise of the curtain. As the clock strikes nine the Colonel walks down from the barracks, accompanied by his Adjutant, and greets his men with the spoken words - "Sorry I'm late, boys".

It appears that the forthcoming manoeuvres will include a sham battle with a companion regiment, known as the "Hornets", acting as the enemy.

Colonel (addressing his men): "If my dreams come true, I am sure we shall win. Now about the enemy. Don't under-rate him. For some reason or other he wears trousers - I can't explain it. Don't be afraid of them. For the honour of the ancient Tigers, be alert and attentive. In the field pay attention to your N.C.O.s."

The curtain falls as the troops march off. Strains of "Yankee Doodle" are heard from time to time in the Interlude that is played during the change of Scene. Below a high sustained E, a clearly defined march rhythm in the basses asserts itself with artful significance.

Scene 3

A wooded landscape in sunshine. Time - noon. A Bishop, accompanied by fashionably dressed ladies and gentlemen, has come to view the scene of action between the "Tigers" and "Hornets".

Bishop: "When I was a curate in the East End I belonged to the 'Tigers'." (Musing to himself) "What fine times we had to be sure."

A lady interrupts as she sees the troops deploying, and exclaims "Look, look, look!" - but the Bishop continues - "I am a great believer in hard work. My grandfather was a great upholder of the maxim that 'A man shall not eat his breakfast until he has earned it'. He would often quote another when he suspected I was dreaming or browsing - 'My boy, the devil will find some dirty work for idle hands to do.'" The ladies withdraw shocked, but the Bishop goes on: "Ladies, ladies! I beg your pardon. I was merely quoting my grandfather. My grandfather was a most strange man, yet very righteous and godly. Do you know, he had such peculiarities. He would not suffer a duck to be killed and cooked for the table, because he once saw a duck swallow a frog. He could never forget that frog. How its two eyes seemed to stand out pleading for help, whilst it was slowly but surely sucked down the juicy throat of the duck."

The ladies again withdraw shocked.

Bishop (continues): "Ladies, you surprise me. I'm afraid you are too sensitive. Speaking of idleness, from what I know of Sir John, the Colonel of the 'Tigers', he will not allow the boys much time for idleness."

Lady: "I hear he allows no drink stronger than lemonade in the regimental canteen."

Bishop: "The regiment is famous for its sobriety", and so on, with ironical, witty, and sparkling dialogue occasionally in Recitative, until the entry of Colonel Sir John Stout, who now approaches the group with dignity. Meanwhile

Mrs Freebody, described as gorgeously overdressed, most distinctive and talkative, has stood out conspicuously from the rest of the group since the rise of the curtain. Accidentally she knocks off the Bishop's hat with her large parasol, and apologises profusely. The Bishop appears somewhat abashed, but recovers his *sang-froid*, and introduces the lady to the Colonel.

Bishop: "Sir John, this is a great friend of mine, Mrs Freebody." (A pause) "I want you to know her, for she is keenly interested in all moral and social work, anything which will tend to uplift the sorrows of the great poor, the decline of the National Birthrate. She is especially devoted to the Missions to the Heathen."

Mrs Freebody (pensively): "How I do love soldiers! I think they are awfully nice. How is the battle going, Sir John?"

Colonel: "Very well so far, but it is much too early to say."

First Lady: "I do hope the 'Tigers' win."

Colonel: "Yes, it will be a great honour if we do win. We have worked so hard."

(A loud noise like a ship's siren is heard.)

Colonel: "That is a signal that I am wanted."

Mrs Freebody: "I am so sorry, Colonel. I would like to talk to you about the dear 'Tigers'."

Colonel: "Well! Come and see the boys. Our quarters are not far from here, at Mont Duresco."

Mrs Freebody: "Thank you very much, I shall be delighted."

Colonel: "I am sorry to go, but I am wanted." (Exit Colonel)

Bishop (calling to Sir John): "Good luck, Sir John!" (to the ladies) "I suppose he is wanted to solve some important tactical problem. Perhaps a mere 'Yes' or 'No' from Sir John will decide today's battle." They go in the direction following the Colonel's retreating figure.

Scene 4

The scene is now enlivened by a Chorus of Haymakers (SSCC), bronzed, young and healthy, in white sun-bonnets, who rush forward to watch the battle from a safe distance. Attention may here be drawn to an effective parody of the battle section from Strauss' *Heldenleben*. In short ejaculatory phrases, such as "The 'Tigers' are charging the 'Hornets'" (contraltos), followed by "The 'Hornets' are charging the 'Tigers'" (sopranos), we may gather that the spectators are watching, and taking a lively interest in the battle that is now raging in the distance (off stage). The excitement grows intense as the fortunes of war fluctuate on either side. Presently, the "Tigers" enter running, evidently in flight from the "Hornets", and the maidens come forward to their assistance. The action develops hilariously into a Promenade and Dance. The enthusiasm of the merrymakers, however, is damped and interrupted by the unexpected appearance of the Sergeant-Major in a towering rage.

Sergeant-Major: "What in the name of Adam and Eve are you doing here? Oh, this is treachery most foul, sneaking away to petticoats from the din and roar of battle. You renegades! So soon forgetting what the dear old Colonel said

328 *Miscellany*

on conduct and discipline. To think that Tigers can spring so high, and fall so low. Fall in! Dress by your right! Right turn! By your right, Quick March!"

And so the "Tigers" are marched away back to their barracks, accompanied by the lamentations of their late festive partners.

Scene 5

The scene now changes, and we are back on the military Parade Ground of Scene 2, where the battalion is drawn up at attention, awaiting dismissal. The Bishop, and his ladies, Mrs Freebody, and the Haymakers, are among the spectators. The Colonel enters, and addresses the men.

Colonel: "My lads! I am very sorry to say you have done badly. I never saw Tigers run so fast ... If you behave like this in a sham battle, what will you do in a real battle? ... Remember, they who fight and run away, live to fight again."

The Sergeant-Major salutes the Colonel. And so, observing that the men must be hungry, the Colonel gives the order of "Rapid Fire", and dismisses them. They respond with a mighty "Hipppppppppppppp Hip hurrah!" as the Curtain quickly falls.

ACT THREE

During the interval preceding the final Act, and the continuation of the story, it would seem as if Brian sought for some relief and change of mood from satirical humour to a more serious vein of the imagination and an expressive sympathetic pity for the follies of humanity. He therefore introduces two orchestral interludes in the form of Ballet, thus conforming to the customary tradition of Opera, and public expectation. The Ballet is presented in two movements, entitled respectively (1) "Gargoyles" and (2) "Lacryma".

The reader will understand their symbolic significance more clearly if the action of each Ballet is described in the composer's own words. The orchestra, as in the Introduction to the third Act of *Die Meistersinger*, opens *Lento* with an exposition in fugal style. The description that follows is quoted literally from the vocal score.

"Gargoyles" (on a Cathedral Tower)

The curtain rises showing the interior of a Police Station. The policemen are fast asleep. It is gloomy, and not much is discernible. The stage becomes totally dark, and by very imperceptible degrees represents the Tower of a Cathedral, surrounded by fantastic grinning gargoyles, whose visages vary, suggesting sometimes a less malicious grin, or even an expression of kindness. This is but an illusion cast by the slowly enveloping light, which is gradually showing up the complete outlines of the fantastic battalion. From the centre rises a gargoyle more fantastic than the rest. He is apparently the leader in the nightly midnight march of the gargoyles around the Cathedral Tower. He leaps down from his position, the heads of the other gargoyles watching him as though waiting for a signal. Slowly he moves around the Tower. His steps are elastic, airy, and light.

He raises his hand, and signals to the gargoyles. One by one they join him, until all the gargoyles have left their stations in the stonework, and, with the Griffin at their head, the gargoyles continue their nightly and ghostly march. The march gradually becomes intensified as the gargoyles, headed by the Griffin, appear to be filled with a fiery glow, which grows and grows in fierceness and intensity, until huge tongues of fire rush from the mouths of the gargoyles. These flames subside, and the stage grows dark again. From the dark shadows the outline of the gargoyles is seen again as at the commencement. (Curtain)

"Lacryma" (Tears of Sorrow)

A striking contrast is provided by this second interlude. The curtain rises on a darkened stage - and the author resumes his description of the action.

Moonlight shadows, - showing the second Tower of the Cathedral with groups of flying angels. The Virgin is in the centre, to whom the angels turn their faces. Only their hands and faces are seen. They are weeping. The Virgin turns to the East, and puts out her hands as though appealing to some one in the distance. The others do as she does. By imperceptible degrees the light becomes fainter, and the stage is dark again. The moonlight gradually returns. The Virgin and flying angels are seen again looking towards the East. They slowly turn their heads, fold their hands on their breasts, and bow their heads. The music ends, *ppp*, with a sorrowful phrase borrowed from the opening bar of this movement. Like an iterated sob, it fades away into silence.

It should not be forgotten that the action of these two *scènes de ballet* takes place inside a Police Station, and we are therefore entitled to assume that these visions may in some mysterious way indicate the dreams enjoyed by the sleeping constables. Be this as it may, the situation is undeniably grotesque and ludicrous, in spite of the air of gravity with which the details are elaborated. The symbolic meaning of these two Ballets will be interpreted according to the mood or imagination of the listener. The music affords a welcome contrast with its sad and unexpected changes, its fleeting air of mystery, and poetic suggestion from the boisterous energy, vitality, and satire of the first two Acts, to which attributes we now return in a more chastened spirit, as the action of the third and final Act is now to be unfolded. We are back again in this mad old world, while Brian, chuckling like *Till Eulenspiegel*, overturns our baskets, and makes further fun of our foibles and proprieties. The policeman, in sombre uniform, with his slow and heavy-footed tread, his good-natured and courteous manner, and serene urbanity is always a ridiculous figure on the English stage, especially as he was portayed in the old-time Harlequinade. He seems to exercise a peculiar fascination upon, and makes an immediate appeal to Brian's imagination and sense of humour. We need not therefore be surprised to find the "Bobbies" in this Act claiming our attention, and enjoying a monopoly of the stage.

Scene 1

Interior of a Police Station. The Sergeant and his Clerk are at their desks looking very busy. A telephone bell rings. The Sergeant goes to the 'phone, and picks up the receiver. Sergeant: "What did you say? - Yes! - I'll take it down. Half a minute - Go on, please - Forty five did you say? - Fifty miles inland? - Oh I have it all right - I will ring up the 'Tigers' at once - It is most exciting - Thank you! 5.2.4. - Please, are you the 'Tigers'? - Is the Battalion in or out? - Are your lights out?" - from which we gather that an air-raid is expected. He continues: "But why are your lights on, if the battalion is out? Is the Colonel there? - Where is Sir John? - Who am I speaking to? - As you are the orderly room clerk, you had better take a message - to this effect, - '*that forty-five Zeppelins are on their way, fifty miles from the coast, and that all lights must be put out. The "Tigers" are required to guard the river bridge.*'" The sergeant bangs the telephone receiver and blows his whistle. Twelve policemen enter, and stand to attention.

Sergeant (addressing his men): "You are going to be very busy. Forty-five Zeppelins are coming. I don't think they have arrived yet, so it won't be any use putting out the lights. You must go on special duty. Tell everybody it is the 'Tigers' birthday." He then gives the policemen their orders, and in chorus (tenors and basses) they recite their duties: "No light may shine. All clocks must stop. No trains may run. No bells may ring. No dogs may bark. None may drink. It is the 'Tigers' birthday!" The Sergeant orders - "Constables, to your duties", and the men march out, followed by the Sergeant. (Curtain)

The next scene suggests by its witty antithesis a subtle reminder of the Third Act of *Tristan*, with its somewhat strained, yet romantic emotionalism.

Scene 2

Approach to a stone river bridge with outlines of an old-fashioned inn at one end of the bridge. A Constable is on patrol duty near a large red pillar-box. Stage quite dark. Lights appear in the inn, and bass voices are heard, *pp*, from within, singing with alcoholic expression followed by shouts of "Throw them out". Whereupon the Constable bangs on the door, and orders the roisterers as they emerge to "move away quietly". They disperse muttering to themselves "What a dreadful night." Mrs Pamela Freebody, wrapped in furs, enters and enquires of the Constable - "Will you be good enough to direct me to Mont Duresco".

Constable: "Yes, Madam. May I enquire what you want there tonight?"

Mrs Freebody: "I wish to make a call upon the Colonel."

(At this moment the Colonel enters, and is saluted by the Constable.)

Constable: "Sir, here is a lady - wishes to see you."

Colonel: "Why, it is Mrs Freebody." (Shaking hands) "How do you do? Your visit tonight surprises me."

A car, sounding its motor-horn, comes along with powerful headlights, and the exasperated Constable orders - "Put out those lights."

Female (in car, with rasping voice): "What's up?"

Constable: "Zeppelins, man. Do as you are told."

The lights are put out, and the Constable moves away, leaving the stage to the Colonel and Mrs Freebody. (...)

After a while it commences to snow, and continues until everything is covered with a pall. Lights appear at various windows right and left. During the amusing Trio, into which we are now led, the Constable, in the distance, is heard shouting the reiterated order "Put out that light", and the Colonel vainly expostulates "No, no, no no!" to Mrs Freebody's advances. The stage and houses are now covered with snow. The Colonel shakes the snow from him, and Pamela does the same. The Constable, who has come to the centre of the stage covered with snow also, disappears. The Colonel, somewhat ruffled, shakes his cloak and shouts: "No, no, no! - Yes!" He draws himself up to a great height, and proceeds, Lohengrin-like, with his narration.

Presently, far away in the distance appears the outline of an ancient castle (Mont Duresco), shown up by numerous small lights. The Tattoo sounds. Pamela tries to dissuade him from leaving her, but in vain. The Colonel puts up his sword. After making an assignation for the following night in the same place, the Colonel walks away. Pamela remains looking at his retreating figure. The Constable reappears, and slowly walks across the stage, as the curtain falls for the change to the last scene.

Scene 3

Mont Duresco in the background. In the foreground is a long one-storey building with a clock-tower in the centre. Everything is covered with snow. Two cooks, disguised, appear in foreground carrying ropes, with the object of removing the bell-clappers from the tower. The comedy is Shakespearian as the two characters prevaricate, and mishandle the entire business of getting the job done. However, after a good deal of much ado about nothing, all's well that ends well; the work is accomplished at last, and with a loud crash the clappers fall to the ground.

It is now midnight, the scene as before, and as the composer indicates, the design of the Finale is an approach from dead silence to mad tumult, from darkness to Mont Duresco in flames. There is a sound of fire-bells. Firemen enter, and wheel round into the centre of the stage, looking anxiously about them.

Firemen (sniffing and blowing out their enormous moustaches): "Fire! Fire! Where is the fire? Who rings the bells? Where can it be? Where is the fire? Is there a fire? We can't smell it. Where are the Police?"

The Firemen hurry off, as the Police enter excitedly from the opposite direction. Police: "What noisy bells! Why do they ring? Zeppelins they cannot be. We must see what is the matter. Let us go and call the Firemen. Haloo! Haloo!"

The Police hurry off as a group of Bargemen (basses), followed by Villagers (sopranos, contraltos and tenors) rush forward from all sides shouting "What can this mean? Never was there such a racket, Firemen! Peelers! Zeppelins! Where are the Tigers?"

Presently the "Tigers" are seen running from Mont Duresco, which is now on fire with flames mounting higher and higher, reminding us of the fate of Valhalla, in *The Twilight of the Gods*. With the return to the stage of the Firemen, and Police, there is ample material for the entire ensemble to build up a mighty choral and orchestral climax, and Brian rolls up his sleeves for the undertaking.

The Firemen, Tigers, Villagers, Bargemen and Police are distributed among 15 separate vocal parts.

The Colonel enters clad in pyjamas looking scared. The regimental Sergeant-Major comes forward in his night-shirt. He salutes the Colonel, and in a recitative explains how all the confusion came about. After a final choral outburst there is a long silent bar. The lights very slowly disappear, and the stage gradually becomes empty, as the Police indicate, and superintend the general dismissal. Only Sir John Stout remains in the centre of the stage deep in his thoughts. It grows quite dark, except for a small red light in the direction of Mont Duresco.

A long drum-roll (*ppp*) on D adds to a short, far-distant wail of voices behind the scene. Mrs Freebody suddenly steps forward. Sir John, awakening from his reverie, and in spoken words, exclaims "Dear Pamela!", to which she responds, also in spoken words, "Dear Sir John!", and the curtain falls quickly as the orchestra sustains (*ppp*) the common chord of D major.

The ending is abrupt, wholly unexpected, yet naïvely significant. Our sides are sore with much laughter, or we have been utterly bored. Opinions, of course, will differ. They have always done so, especially when estimating the value of Opera as a form of art. Personally, I find it unconvincing; musically, I can enjoy the great moments; dramatically, it is improbable and impossible, for the action is resolved into a series of unnatural situations, that do not happen in real life. The public does not like to see itself ridiculed, or to be discovered taking part in a Bacchanalian orgy. Hence, how refreshing it is to meet with an opera so alive with wit and fancy, that is able to reveal so much of the hollowness of the world in which we live. Some people are only too ready to act like tigers in search of prey. Others will be rudely shocked to recognize a familiar form among those tigers, who are ever hungry to devour their human victims, yet it cannot be denied that these Tigers have sprung from a rich and fertile imagination, indicating uncommon patience and perseverance, originality, and vital spirit, devoted industry, and achievement.

In spite of the complacent innuendos and fatuous platitudes of our musical scribes and pharisees, the fact remains that the English are entirely indifferent to, and ignorant of the work of their living writers and composers. Only by means of propaganda and large poster advertisement is it possible to stimulate any interest in Albert Hall concerts, and Exhibitions. The modern and quickest method is to employ a publicity agent. The public, as usual, misinformed, has already and long ago forgotten the favourable reception it gave to Brian's early activities before 1914, when he led the van in creating a local interest in the "Potteries" for the choral works of Elgar and Delius, while he modestly stood aside in regard to the performance of his own works. However, there did occur a few isolated performances of the distinctive choral and orchestral work *By the Waters of Babylon*, also a Symphonic Poem *Doctor Merryheart*, an English Suite, and a *Festal Dance*, all of which were published by the enterprising firm of Breitkopf and Härtel at Leipzig, and in the early decade of the present century. A remarkable one-act opera, *Cleopatra*, the libretto by Gerald Cumberland, was awarded the second prize by adjudicators appointed for the occasion, and so far, I believe, has only had one concert performance, though the vocal score has been published, and has been available during the last 30 years. Attention has already been drawn to the *Gothic* Symphony, dedicated to Richard Strauss, and to his generous acknowledgement. It is hoped that the need may soon arise for an analysis and discussion of this important work.

It was entirely owing to the enterprise and foresight of a foreign publisher, Dr Cranz, that the vocal score of *The Tigers* was engraved and published in 1932. But, save for solitary performances of two short instrumental extracts by the B.B.C., the music still awaits recognition, sympathetic consideration, and an adequate performance. If Brian had only been a comrade of the U.S.S.R., the name of Briansky, or Brianovsky might have been as familiar to the world, and to England in particular, as that of Tchaikovsky. The heart of Swinburne must have been heavy when he sang:

> England, what of the night? -
> Night is for slumber and sleep,
> Warm, no season to weep.
> Let me alone till the day.
> Sleep would I still if I might,
> Who have slept for two hundred years.
> Once I had honour, they say;
> But slumber is sweeter than tears.

And yet, why despair? The present crisis of this great world War is upon us, and the people of our land have risen to the call with an awakening, and a courage beyond belief, inspiring one and all with the united will to conquer, or to die. This is sufficient to give a good reason for hope, and to dispel the gloomiest doubts. Though the present may be dark, the future is bright with promise. Let us re-find, and bring to the light our hidden treasures of Art, Literature, and Music. We have the Theatre, if not an Opera House. We have the artists, the singers, and the best orchestral players in the world. Impatiently, yet not without confidence, perhaps we may be permitted to ask - "How long is this work to remain without a hearing, or adequate representation? How long, O Lord, how long?"

Malcolm MacDonald: Let the Roar of the *Tigers* be Heard in the Land ...[1]

No other work of Brian's than *The Tigers* (not even the massive cantata *Prometheus Unbound* - though that, perhaps, is the next in importance) will so radically enlarge our awareness of the composer's range, and our understanding of him as

---

[1] From *Newsletter* 31 (X 1980), pp. 3-4.

an artist. The later music-dramas - *Turandot, The Cenci, Faust, Agamemnon* - are straight adaptations of stage plays (or at least poems in dramatic form) by great writers of the past: Brian's literary efforts were limited here to judicious compression, and the musical language has much in common, both in style and quality, with his symphonies of the late 1940s and early 1950s. That's to say, these works conform to a fairly orthodox conception of opera, and their music is compounded, however superbly, of elements with which we are already familiar.

The Tigers is, in every sense, a very different story. First, the libretto is entirely his own invention, the largest piece of imaginative literature to have survived from his pen: and its sureness of touch, mastery of stagecraft, eldritch wackiness and psychological depth were hardly to be expected. Sir Donald Tovey's verdict, that it showed Brian "to be a satirist of very wide range", is entirely valid, but only indicates one of the many levels on which the libretto operates. For, second, the entire conception is staggeringly original for mid-Great War England: a response to the Somme and the Home Front equally far removed from the stoicism of Wilfred Owen or the civilized rearguard action at Garsington. If we had to guess the writer of this mixture of broad farce, satires on the military and authority generally, sheer fantasy, dream symbolism, melodrama, absurdist theatre and Marx Brothers anarchy played out against a background of world catastrophe (all the more compellingly present for being almost entirely ignored by the characters themselves), we might hazard that it was a brilliantly idiomatic English translation from the Viennese dialect of Karl Kraus, with interpolations from the more surrealist writings of Mikhail Bulgakov, edited for the stage by Bertolt Brecht - certainly not the work of an obscure clerk in a Birmingham munitions factory, contemplating the ruins of a once-promising composing career.

Much of the libretto, nevertheless, boils down to the venerable and incalculably precious comic occupation of deflating pomposity and showing up the ridiculousness of stock attitudes - especially the attitudes of the military and all those who think that there is really something rather splendid about war. For its time, therefore, it was a damned unpatriotic thing to write: nowadays, the fundamental common sense that powers the fantasy is more likely to excite our admiration.

We can point to many things which might have given Brian some of his ideas: his personal experiences of military bungling and bull in the Honourable Artillery Company; images from his own early works (the English Suite No. 1 stands far behind the opera's Prologue; *Doctor Merryheart* even further but no less significantly behind the later Acts); the Music Hall; the works of Samuel Butler (an acknowledged influence on the libretto); a Wagner-parody opera like Strauss' *Feuersnot*; Offenbach (Mrs Pamela Freebody, who does so love soldiers, is plainly a daughter of the Grand Duchess of Gerolstein); possibly Stravinsky's *Rossignol* (whose fantastic aspect Brian deeply admired); and, of course, Gilbert & Sullivan operetta. Equally, we can point to many seeming echoes of its methods and attitudes in places as diverse as Bernard Shaw's *Heartbreak House* (which has more than just a Zeppelin-raid in common with Brian's vision), *Oh! What a Lovely*

War, and Spike Milligan's *Goon Show* scripts. But the totality is like nothing else in English literature, and like no other opera libretto anyone has written; the "seeming echoes" are illusory, for the work has remained virtually unknown, and these spiritual kinships simply prove how far Brian was ahead of his time.

Musically, *The Tigers* is the work in which Brian finally seems to find himself (a fact which makes the loss of the two major scores preceding it, *Kevlaar* and English Suite No. 2, all the more regrettable). The opera does indeed sum up and capitalize upon the satirical orchestral works of the pre-War years - but just as the humour is far more complex (and has a far more serious *point*), so is the music incomparably richer and capable of far greater emotional depth. (Any one of the several "symphonic dances" which punctuate the action would have counted as a major achievement in his pre-1914 *oeuvre*.) It anticipates, and goes far beyond, anything that Bliss, Walton, Lambert or Berners were to produce in the way of musical humour in the 1920s. The presence in the Prologue of a complete set of *Symphonic Variations on "Has Anybody here seen Kelly?"* seems to parody, before the event, Berg's use of self-sufficient instrumental forms in *Wozzeck*; just as the extensive use of vibraphones in Act II anticipates by years their official "first appearance" in serious music in *Lulu*; while the counter-marching bands in the same passage seem to have strayed in from Ives' *Putnam's Camp*. There are, too, intentional parodies - of *Walküre*, *Tristan* and even the Battle Scene from *Ein Heldenleben* - but they are always gloriously relevant to what happens on stage.

More important, however, is the fact that here, for the first time, Brian seems to be making the fully creative use of his unconscious mind that is a hallmark of his mature compositions. Not only is the humour (both literary and musical) predominantly associative, sparking off spontaneously (and "laterally" - cf. John Aldridge's article in *Newsletter* 29 [p. 81ff. in the present book]) along unexpected trains of thought; but the whole opera, with its non-sequiturs and nonsense which nevertheless have such disturbing power, begins to look like a metaphor for the processes of the unconscious. Its logic is dream-logic - Colonel Stout (a dreamer in at least two senses) tells us as much at the end, as he stands popeyed in his nightshirt: "This is the worst of all nightmares". We, and Brian, are the dreamers, and part of the fascination is that nightmare is never far away. The Tigers, that regiment "of ancient glory", fights only sham battles, the only Zeppelin raid is a false alarm - but these are inversions of the fact that, somewhere off-stage, people really are suffering and dying in their thousands. The opera lets us know this inescapably in the symbolic ballet around a cathedral tower that begins Act III - a weird vision of demons and weeping angels, apparently dreamt by a dozing policeman. Here everything that the "conscious" action (the parade-ground pomposities, the shambolic drill, the casual flirtations) has tried to suppress comes boiling to the surface. Here is the heart of the opera, and doubtless it was in Brian's mind when he later averred that *The Tigers* was no simple burlesque but "just as serious as *Die Meistersinger*".

Composed between 1917 and 1919, *The Tigers* was the first fruit of the most traumatic, and perhaps most crucially formative, period of Brian's life. The second main fruit was, of course, *The Gothic*. But the opera seems to have been revised (both in libretto and therefore, presumably, in music) at various times in the years that *The Gothic* was in the making; and it was only after *The Gothic* reached completion that *The Tigers* was fully scored. The orchestra isn't quite so large, but it is very different in constitution, highly flexible, and the style of scoring is unique - it looks forward, indeed, to the Second and (especially) the Third Symphonies, but stakes out its own entirely individual, iridescent sound-world to intensify the dreamlike aura.

The Gothic and *The Tigers* are poles apart. They have a few points of contact: the grand miscellaneousness of inspiration, the compulsive march-rhythms, so differently treated. Most significant is the fact that what "boils to the surface" in the cathedral-tower ballet is the most substantial *musical* pre-vision of *The Gothic* in Brian's *oeuvre* so far: the symphony's tremendous slow movement and fantastic scherzo are adumbrated in the two finest of the symphonic dances, "Lacryma" and "Gargoyles". But in general *The Tigers* inverts all *The Gothic*'s values - it is the last thing one would anticipate from the composer of that vast, deeply serious, choral symphony. Which is why it is so significant to our understanding of Brian. They are the opposite sides of the same coin: the obverse knows nothing of the reverse, yet both are graven into the same piece of metal. We must know them both to begin to grasp the toughness and flexibility of Brian's metal (and mettle!). Without doubt, *The Tigers* is a queer, idiosyncratic creation - as eccentric to operatic history (and especially to the unhappy, often lacklustre story of British opera) as *The Gothic* is ultimately central to the traditions of the European symphony. But it is also, just possibly, the greatest comic opera in the English language. It is high time we all had a chance to hear it![2]

---

[2] A number of members of the Havergal Brian Society were present at the BBC recording sessions of the opera. Godfrey Berry writes in *Newsletter* 45 (I-II 1983), p. 5: "To hear *The Tigers* in performance has been a rewarding and revealing experience. Like the very different *Das Siegeslied*, *The Tigers* is a work of much greater subtlety and sophistication than a superficial acquaintance might lead one to suppose. It is cast in a series of 'dream' sequences - the main action developing a single thread of dream logic, the Prologue preparing the way with a different treatment of the same basic subjects (war, love, and the relationship between dreams and reality). Let the fact that the opera is continuously entertaining and frequently very funny fool nobody: at the deeper levels of understanding this is an intensely serious work dealing with some of the issues most fundamental to human existence. On one level at least *The Tigers* can be seen as belonging to the same creative tradition as those other great English works 'in the verisimilitude of a dream', *The Pilgrim's Progress* and *Alice in Wonderland*. In operatic terms its closest relative is probably Martinů's *Julietta*, although Brian's hero (whoever he may really be!) is as patently sane as Martinů's is insane. I have no doubt that *The Tigers* would go well on the stage, although possibly a small amount of tactful editing would be necessary to make staging it a practical proposition." Rodney Stephen Newton writes (p. 6): "The first thing that struck me, as it did when I first perused the full scores, was the remarkable transparency of the orchestral texture. Brian has used an outsize orchestra for his opera (indeed, the problems of housing such an ensemble even in our largest opera pits would be considerable), but he uses it for the most part with discretion. Many passages are very lightly scored and often only small sections of the orchestra are used. The next surprise was the remarkable modernity of the orchestral sound. Brian's orchestration in the opera is full of imaginative touches with some splendid brass writing, innovative use of what were then very unusual tuned percussion instruments (the two vibraphones and the tubaphone - a sort of tubular glockenspiel) and the daring harmonic

procedures which almost belie the true dates of composition for the work." The complete recording was extensively praised, the most voluminous item being a letter to the Editor in *Newsletter* 48 (VII-VIII 1983), pp. 5-6, by Larry Alexander: "After several hearings of *The Tigers*, the upshot is that I have never heard a more schizophrenic work of art in my whole life, one which left me gasping, simultaneously awed and confused. It's got all of Brian's mature virtues (as they were at the time of *The Gothic*) and magnifies all the flaws. It veers, or should I say careens, from mind-boggling brilliance to mind-boggling incompetence - I can't think of another word - within the space of bars, and then ricochets back like the steel dumdum in a pinball machine. What is especially striking is how closely it does parallel *The Gothic*: the interlude with the compliant ladies during the battle, for instance, is right out of the last moment of the symphony, and the penultimate section of 'Wild Horsemen' could almost be considered a first draft for the xylophone-infested nightmare in the third movement. But whereas everything *flows* naturally and creatively in *The Gothic*, building and building a huge and imposing edifice, that sadly doesn't seem to be the case with *The Tigers* (not, at least, on the basis of these first hearings). What's missing is *structure*. Inner logic. Consistency. That may be due to the fact that this is so personal a work to Brian, coming as it does out of his dreadful First World War experiences, everything going mixed-up and upside down and coming out untranslatable in terms of anyone else's experiences. What had attracted me to the best that this amazing composer was capable of was the fact that his 'quirky' individuality was, when considered whole, utterly universal in appeal. *The Tigers* just isn't that ... although, to come down in agreement with Andrew Clements in *The Financial Times*, it is indeed 'in the purely orchestral music that the most memorable moments occur'. In my opinion, the reason for this is the fact that Brian was a creative genius who was at his very best when he was at his most abstract, dealing with pure rather than specific drama and emotion. Theatrical performance with its concrete images and physical limitations was just too confining to the scope of that incredibly unencumbered brain. The logic of plot and character (development) were too tedious to waste time over: nit-picking. Whereas he could build to the imposing and utterly devastating climax which crowns *The Gothic*, it is just nowhere near the case with the opera. And the music, monumental though it most surely is, suffers as a result. Oddly enough (and I know I am a heretic for this), I have always considered *most* opera to contain lesser music than that which is written directly for the orchestra, leaving out the usual Mozart masterpieces, the occasional Puccini and Mussorgsky, not to mention *Peter Grimes*. Verdi to me is a 'nice' composer, only rising to greatness at the very end of his life and then more because of having all that preceding practice (it falls into the category of 'he finally got it right, thank God'). But at least those composers had some decent libretti to set their music to, words with as nice a logic as the music. I understand that Brian was eager to throw away the rules and I am hardly against that: when it comes to art the rules have to be expendable - as long as you first let your audience in on what you are up to. For example, *A Funny Thing Happened on the Way to the Forum* when it first opened pre-Broadway in Washington D.C. began with a charming little duet called 'Love is in the Air'. The rest of the musical was a raucous piece of slapstick hysteria but it opened with 'Love is in the Air' and after that audiences weren't sure that it was 'all right' for them to laugh! Only after Stephen Sondheim was induced to replace the song with 'Comedy Tonight!' did (a) the audiences feel they had licence to laugh and (b) the show became a hit. Brian's Hampstead Heath opening is quite lovely and even makes a kind of way-out sense in relation to the rest of the opera just on the strength of the 'War is declared' announcement (although it does take a bit of a stretch to shoehorn the 'Pantalon and Columbine' love duet into the point). But, strict old constructionalist that I am, it really would have pleased me a whole lot more had the Prologue been used to sow a few seeds which later in the piece could grow into wonderful flowers. As for the other little odds and ends, wandering through the minefield Brian has left us, the first thing which comes to mind is the difference in creative level one gets when one considers, say, the character of Sir John. Take his lectures to his regiment. All I have been able to think of was that other lecturer to the troops, George C. Scott at the commencement of the film *Patton*. Imagine if you will how a Havergal Brian could have set such imagistic words as 'let some other sonafabitch die for his country'. That's the kind of real acid *The Tigers* seems to be crying out for, the kind that the elder Brian would have revelled in, the old curmudgeon. What I am really flailing about to say here is that my objection isn't really to the lack of any conflict whatever in the piece, but to the lack of anything being at *stake*. We aren't even given the impression that these boys are going to be cannon fodder 'over there', because we don't have any idea who they are. To offer another example, the Tigers as a regiment aren't in any danger of being disbanded, so that's not at stake either. The illicit 'affair' between Sir John and Mrs Freebody not only goes nowhere, but causes nothing else to go anywhere. If death is not a consequence, how about dishonour? Wasn't it Ibsen who said that if the stage directions at the beginning of a play describe a gun over a mantlepiece, then by golly by the end of Act III that gun had damned well better go off? Where is Lady Stout when we need her? Or the man on the elephant? Or the Wild Horses? A practical joke and its reverberations just cannot be where it all ends, not if we are to care for the people and their circumstances, comic or otherwise. Effect and unbridled imagination are just not sufficient, not now, nor in 1918. What it leaves this listener with is a feeling not of modernity, nor even of surrealism - it leaves me with a feeling of unprofessionalism. It makes a writer drool, though, in a way. 'Now let's see - I could take this score note for note and still change the storyline *so* and the characters *so*, making it all one lovely, coherent and *funny* piece ...' Anything to make it not look as though Brian took all his twigs and threw them up in the air, writing them down wherever they landed, never minding the fact that a few fell down a curbside grate and were never missed. For all that, I have to reiterate: musically speaking, the opera is an ear-opener from beginning to end, never for a moment dull or tedious even when it is at its most outrageously unstructured. Every opera (as far as I am concerned) has highs and lows; the good ones have more highs, and *The Tigers* is on that level very good indeed. What amazes me most is how much the music relates in its own Brianesque way to what Britten only got around to doing a quarter of a century later in *Peter Grimes*. That Havergal Brian was writing a score on that level, as 'modern' as that, I find nothing short of astounding. However, what ultimately makes *Peter Grimes* more of a total achievement than *The Tigers* is its dramatic impact, the fact that its narrative is inexorable and incontestable, a latter-day Greek tragedy existing to give its audience catharsis. On one hand this seems to be a non-musical aspect of the two works but in an opera (speaking utopianly) the essence of the drama is the essence of the music, the latter expressing the former and vice versa. To discuss a libretto without the music attached might be a real exercise in futility. Does one discuss a blueprint once the building is up? That some believe this work to be as great an achievement as *The Gothic* is not un-understandable to me. It is in its way a great work, flaws and all, and I can see many people reacting to it with immense enthusiasm. There isn't the least bit of musical incompetence in it anywhere, and I hope no-one gets the impression that I am suggesting there is. What Brian created he created deliberately and, like *The Gothic*, it will have to be dealt with as a sin of commission, rather than a sin of omission. One man's lack of coherence is another man's deliberate fragmentation: the breaking of the mirror and the replacing of its shards in a mosaic pattern which might even have no need of all the pieces that fell in the first place ... thus explaining the 'loose ends'. My complaint is that the mosaic Brian constructed lacks the cumulative power that any ... any ... work of art I think ought to boast. Whether that comes from making us, the audience, really care about the people on the stage, or making our jaws drop open at the sheer inventiveness of what has been written down, or whatever, that last line between brilliance and greatness is toed, but not crossed. On mulling it over, I have to conclude that perhaps *The Tigers* is in its own way as 'abstract' as *The Gothic*. Perhaps my problem is that I accept abstractions on a concert stage and I am just not as comfortable with them in the opera house, when I am watching and hearing real live people in *roles*. Roles just aren't abstract to this mind of mine. They must live and breathe and act according to the constraints of their own characterizations; they can be parody but only if they are at the same time honest and real. I feel somewhat cheated when I am presented with something the creator chooses to lose, or to not follow through. Why? Did he lose interest? If so, why keep them in the first place? Or, conversely, if they serve a function,

Martyn Becker: Brian's impatient *Tigers*[1]

Life for Havergal Brian around the start of the Great War was a time of great stress, and his response to it is evident in the stuff of his comic opera *The Tigers*. Brian's mental turmoil around this time is well documented, and even though the country was at war when he penned his first sketches in 1916, his sense of the absurd was such that the work which took shape was a comic opera apparently on the folly of war. Or was it? This opera and the Third English Suite were more or less the only major works to come from his pen from the time of *Pilgrimage to Kevlaar* to the turn of the decade, and a great deal of mental energy went into the creation of *The Tigers*, taking it beyond the comic, although there is much in it which is genuinely funny.

What does "beyond the comic" mean? Well, I'll explain by analogy. Anyone who has ever seen the recent film *An American Werewolf in London* wouldn't, I'm sure, call it a comedy because of its subject matter and the efforts made by the film's producers to create a genuinely chilling, atmospheric effect. Yet it is a very funny film, and the comedy juxtaposed directly with the horror creates a distinct sense of unease. The effect is similar in *The Tigers* because here the comic is spliced with a series of fantastic, nightmarish scenes which leaves the listener (certainly *this* listener) slightly unnerved at the end. There appears to be almost genuine paranoia present: the "Wild Horsemen" interlude in Scene 2 of the Prologue; the Act II appearances of the Red Indian, Alexander the Great, Napoleon and Sir John's wife (berating him for being "heavy on your underthings"!); the Act III nightmare of "Gargoyles". There are even shades of *Götterdämmerung* in the burning of Mont Duresco in the closing pages.

This brings me to the "impatient" of the title. Once Brian had his ideas in order, it almost appears that he was in some impatience to get the plot onto paper, and wasted no time in getting his characters into play. Indeed, so keen is he to get it all moving that the Fruitseller starts the ball rolling after less than three seconds of orchestral introduction (surely quite a stumbling block in an actual staging, unless there is somebody *very* quick on the curtain)! There is the vexed question of what the Prologue is actually about, as it appears to have little connection with the body of the opera, save the fact that a poster announces that "there is a war" and everybody under the age of 75 is required to enlist (more on this later). The Prologue, to me, is Brian venting his satirical fury on his vision of the impotence of war without actually making overt reference to it.

Two episodes in the Prologue lead me to this way of thinking, and the first of these bursts straight in on us. The Fruitseller whose "Don't you think it's very hot?" opens the opera has a dog and a donkey which immediately become rowdy

---

wouldn't it be only fair play to give us a hint as to what that function is? And yet, through all of it, the bits and pieces, the shards, are just so incredibly Brian. As I felt when the Forlane set came out, this is the first music which *sounds* like Havergal Brian wrote it, he and no other. And that alone, finally, makes *The Tigers* as a whole important and special."

[1] From *Newsletter* 65 (V-VI 1986), pp. 6-7.

(and even fight?) for no apparent reason. Could these animals allegorically represent the sides in the Great War being fought at the time of the work's composition? Especially as it subsequently transpires in the *tutti* passage for the costermongers that the dog's name is Jerry ("Quiet, Jerry!"). The second is Scene II where Pantalon tries (and succeeds) to woo Columbine.[2] This short scene on its own appears to be entirely divorced from the action and even the spirit of *The Tigers*, except that Brian may also be venting here his mental fury at war itself, and his own circumstances at the time. "What about these arms?" asks Pantalon, obviously meaning his own two, outstretched. Columbine's answer, "I am tired of arms and faces. I want life", is semantically different from the type of dialogue surrounding it in that it is a little unusual to express disillusionment with people in that way. Is it Brian expressing his tiredness with military arms, and the disinterested faces that appeared to surround him? Perhaps this is an instance of "cutting out the military iron" that Adrian Ure and Ted Heaton have commented on in these pages.[3]

---

[2] David Perrins writes in a letter to the Editor in *Newsletter* 76 (III-IV 1988), p. 6: "I have to cast my mind back nearly 30 years, when I wrote an article on the subject for the Christmas issue of a magazine. Godfrey Berry is, of course, quite right in stating that the English pantomime started from the Italian Commedia dell'Arte and was then a mime, with no dialogue. Without going into unnecessary detail, the two main events that created the Victorian pantomime were the genius of Joe Grimaldi, which raised the part of the clown to one of prime importance, and a change in the law regarding censorship in 1843. As a consequence, the two-part pantomime developed, with the Harlequinade and the more modern story linked by a spectacular transformation scene. Harlequin was the leading part, and his name appeared in all the titles; some on familiar subjects, such as 'Dick Whittington or Harlequin Lord Mayor of London', others less so, such as 'Jack in the Box or Harlequin and the Princess of the Hidden Isles'. These were most popular in the 1860s and 1870s and the last pantomime in London with Harlequin in the title was in 1888 at the Theatre Royal, Drury Lane, though the tradition lingered on for some time out of London. It would seem that Brian must either have seen one of these pantomimes, or heard about them from a friend or relative, as he used two of the principal Commedia dell'Arte characters, Columbine and Pantalon, in his early orchestral piece later incorporated in his First English Suite. Certainly, this relationship between *The Tigers* and the Victorian pantomime does help to explain its structure, and accounts for the otherwise inexplicable appearance of the two Commedia dell'Arte characters late at night on Hampstead Heath on August Bank Holiday! Perhaps this is another case of those later Brian irrelevancies, that turn out to be not irrelevant at all if one can 'tune in' to the elliptical workings of his mind." Adrian Ure writes in *Newsletter* 53 (V-VI 1984), p. 6: "The relevance of the Prologue to the main action is of course not narrative but thematic. (By this I mean not *musical* links, though there are a few of those, but *dramatic* ones). It never occurred to me at the time to consider that other opera where Harlequin makes an appearance in a basically serious context - I mean *Ariadne auf Naxos*. Granted that the subject of that opera is nowhere near that of *The Tigers*, it could still have given Brian a hint or two. Had he seen it when he came to compose *The Tigers*, I wonder? I should imagine that *The Tigers* would perplex a first-night audience in much the same way as *Ariadne* did - the mixture of serious and comic elements. Strauss and Hofmannsthal obviously felt constrained to add a prologue 'explaining' how the mixture came about so the plebs in the audience could understand it better! Just imagine an audience coping with *The Tigers* - that leap from Act II to Act III (partly aided by the interval, of course), then to the quasi-*Fledermaus* Policemen's scene."

[3] In this connection Adrian Ure wrote in his article Investigating *The Tigers* (due to its incompleteness not reprinted in this book) in *Newsletter* 62 (XI-XII 1985), p. 4: "In January 1925,

Perhaps the opera's attitude towards authority in the form of police, the army itself and even some of the supposedly upper class characters are all forms of Brian's sniping at the sort of people who'd been making his life miserable. The faceless authority of the police, the buffoon-like soldiers who didn't think they were capable of scaring the milkmaids in the "Green Pastures" scene, the dudes who make a quick appearance in Act I Scene 1; perhaps they are symbols of the alienation that Brian felt was happening to him.

A couple of other matters raise themselves in my mind, one to do with the opera itself, and the second with the Prologue in particular. Firstly, Adrian Ure in his admirable series of articles says that the date of the action is probably August 1914, at the outbreak of the First World War.[4] Why? Almost deliberately, I feel, no specific dates are mentioned, so why should we feel obliged to invest the action with a date? Why couldn't the carnival be fictitious, and indeed the war itself? Was Brian writing specifically about the First World War? Perhaps the war of *The Tigers isn't* the Great War but a parallel war in a parallel, or fictitious England where buffoonery and suspect enlistment ages are commonplace. After all, the "Tigers" themselves are a fictitious regiment.

Is this too fanciful? I think not; science fiction deals with this sort of thing on a regular basis, so why shouldn't Brian invent a fictitious war and people it with

---

looking at his libretto for the first time in six years, Brian announced, 'I intend rewriting the whole thing, with a brand new second act and cutting out every scrap of military iron in the work'. Perhaps fortunately this rather radical impulse seems to have faded before the proposal could be implemented. It is interesting as being illustrative of a change in attitude and creative response to the fact of global war, but Brian no doubt wisely realized that with the suggested changes *The Tigers* would have been not an altered work but an entirely different one. The 'military iron' remained; I should think that any changes carried out at this time amounted to tinkering with details, rather than outright revision." Ted Heaton replies in a letter to the Editor in *Newsletter* 63 (I-II 1986), pp. 1-2: "Adrian Ure's reference ... in his article on *The Tigers* called to mind my reaction on first reading this passage in Eastaugh's book, i.e. ... 'cutting out every scrap of military iron in the work' (p. 253). Brian's use of the word 'iron' jarred. This is a noun and there is not much reference to military hardware on the opera. What is there - and plenty of it - is military *irony*, which causes those who see the jokes such hilarity. These range from the muddled orders given on the two parades which feature in the opera to the apology given by Colonel Sir John Stout to the 'boys' for being late on parade. In addition, there are many scenes and episodes which, as has been pointed out many times, are pure Goon Show material, but often based on this mythical body of 'militarily trained' personnel, 'The Tigers'. It should be remembered that this was being written with the 'horror and futility' of the First World War not only in Brian's mind but also in the mind of every serving soldier. Had the opera been produced in the '30s, a good proportion of the audiences would have been ex-servicemen, on whom these jokes would not have been lost, nor the many others throughout the opera. So the question remains: Did Brian mean 'iron' or did he mean 'irony'? Is it possible to have clarification by reference to the original correspondence? Has the 'y' faded with age and not photocopied accurately? In the meantime, let us be glad that Brian did not delete anything from his original conception. The advice 'always trust your first instinctive reaction' is advice Brian may or may not have been given, but in the fulness of time, followed. And to the benefit of the opera and its many present-day admirers; without the portrayal of mad militarism and gross incompetence, the work loses much of its humour and impact."

[4] Adrian Ure: Investigating *The Tigers*, in *Newsletter* 63, (I-II 1986), p. 2.

folks that he can identify with; with military hardware from within his own frame of reference - the technology of the day?

The other matter is of the young man on the elephant, and the missing person being sought by the two policemen in the Prologue. Who is he? we ask ourselves. What is his importance, his significance to the plot? Could it not just be that the orchestra happens to be playing the variations on *Has anybody here seen Kelly?* at the time, and it's a little Brian joke to have Kelly up on the stage while he (the composer) spends most of the rest of the Prologue varying the tune? It's certainly a possibility.

Moving to the music itself, there are many striking features, not least the introduction to the whole work, which as mentioned is very short indeed. In fact, in terms of duration and variety of fantastic scoring, it reminds me of *Das Rheingold*, even to a theme echo in the Prologue. Nobody could accuse Wagner's opera of being comic, and he takes far longer than Brian in mood-painting at the outset. The point about the Wagner reminiscence in the Prologue is an interesting one, and commentators have mentioned the "Ride of the Valkyries" in connection with "Wild Horsemen", and indeed the apparent reference to the *Heldenleben* battle music of Richard Strauss. As a layman, I must ask - is it all intentional, or has Brian worked them in subconsciously because of his regard for these composers? Could it perhaps be that we, the listeners, make the connections ourselves by being superanalytical? I'm thinking of things like the fact that Andrew Lloyd Webber's "Don't cry for me Argentina" appears to haunt the opening theme of Bruckner's Seventh Symphony, and falling and rising 5ths in Bruckner's Fourth sound very similar to John Williams's *Superman* film music (as my four-year-old son spotted the other week!). Set against deliberate quotations, e.g. the finale of Beethoven's Ninth in Tippett's Third Symphony, then it certainly provides food for thought.

Ultimately, regardless of what interpretations we may care to put on the philosophical aspects of *The Tigers*, it is the music which will win or lose it friends. Personally (and a lot of people think this way, I'm sure), the score is littered with delights, and a stage performance might not do justice to the imaginary vision that elephants and gargoyles summon up. Maybe it is better to lie back with one's eyes shut, listen to the music, and let one's imagination run riot ...

Mike Smith: Brian's word-setting[1]

The thoughts which follow were stimulated by Brian Rayner Cook's and Roger Vignoles' recording of Brian songs and by the broadcast of *The Tigers*. I have also drawn on *The Vision of Cleopatra*, some published songs not on the Cook/Vignoles record,[2] and *The Gothic*, which is the latest piece I consider. I have confined

---

[1] From *Newsletter* 50 (XI-XII 1983), pp. 5-7.
[2] The record, containing 17 songs, was issued by Auracle in 1982 (AUC 1003).

myself almost entirely to solo setting; the forthcoming Altarus disc will provide an opportunity to ponder the very different question of Brian's ensemble writing.

Words-and-music is acknowledged to be a difficult subject. In fact it is even more difficult than it is supposed to be; most writers on song never get to grips with it at all (though they may think they have). They talk about words, or about music, and they may even compare them; but very rarely do they discuss the two together, as they interact and as we hear them. Yet word-setting, apart from its intrinsic interest, can be very revealing of a composer's style and general musical makeup. His treatment of words may make explicit attitudes which are implicit elsewhere in his work, and allow us to describe these more precisely.

Word-setting can also tell us a lot about a composer's development. It is a truism that in the "partnership" of words and music the music is usually dominant: the words have only that meaning which is permitted them by the music. Even so, music does not impose its will automatically. It has to convince, by its own power and interest, that its "reading" of the text is a possible one. The greater the consistency and distinctiveness of a musical style, the more convincingly it will project a poetic text. On the other hand, a style which is unsure of itself, one which is not fully consistent or individualized, will sound inadequate if the text has any character about it. Word-setting is thus a sensitive indicator of stylistic maturity; and this may apply to the idiom of a period as well as to the style of a particular composer.

In Brian's music, word-setting shows up one important trait to particular advantage. This I must rather clumsily call his *negativity*. Harold Truscott says: "Brian's conceptions often begin with agreement and, by intent, gradually fall apart", and he refers to Brian's "tendency to self-destruction" in the symphonies (Truscott in *Two Studies*, p. 11). I would see this as just one manifestation of something I feel in most of Brian's music. I am conscious of the absence of tunes, the avoidance of patently coherent structure, the frustration of harmonic expectations. Brian's champions have argued, often correctly, that he usually puts something different, but equally valid, in its place. All the same I believe that this sense of something denied, this "negativity", is *in itself* an important, even a crucial, principle in his music.

Brian's denials come from the same source as his eccentricities (in many cases they are one and the same). They spring from a distrust of easy solutions, of the obvious, the tried and tested, the conventional. Of course, Brian shared this underlying attitude with most of his contemporaries: music in the 50 years after Wagner, and to a large extent since, is one long attempt to avoid the obvious. With some composers (Britten, Stravinsky) one feels that this is largely a matter of taste and Brian had enough of the supercilious intellectual about him to make this a consideration. But mostly it is a matter of *conviction*. To lapse into the comfortable is not permitted, because it belies experience. This is a kind of puritanism: it underlies most modern developments in the arts, and no doubt it was particularly strong in Brian through background and inheritance. Its straightforward, more affirmative side appears in the famous Goethean epigraph to *The Gothic*: "Whoever strives with all his might, that man we can redeem". But it has to be admitted that the negative side is often stronger in Brian - rejection, exasperation, cynicism, and a characteristically puritan penchant for cutting off one's ears to spite one's face.

This attitude is most clearly revealed in vocal music. Musical puritanism originated in the Reformation controversy over music in church and its effect on words, or The Word. It has since affected many composers and almost all critics (the puritan party in music, like its religious and political counterparts, is the party of the politically aware and voluble). It has become almost an axiom of song-criticism that music should strive to preserve the *sense* of a poetic text, and that changes in the original meaning of the words, as a result of musical setting, are to be regarded as distortions. (This, one would think, is in direct opposition to the fact already referred to, and just as generally accepted, that music in song dominates words. As I said, words-and-music is a difficult subject.) Under this dispensation lyrical dilation on the one hand, and formal restriction on the other, have been particularly suspect. This appears clearly in Brian's models, Wagner and Elgar. Wagner's campaign against Italian opera was the expression of his outrage at the distortion of poetic sense by musical form. Elgar abandoned the lyric mode of *Gerontius* for the declamatory style of *The Apostles* and *The Kingdom*.

Brian does not apply this principle consistently (he does nothing consistently). But it is there, in various guises, throughout the earlier vocal music. Sometimes his "puritan" word-setting may simply be a result, or side-effect, of characteristic "negative" musical procedures. But often enough it seems to be deliberate; and in a composer like Brian, restlessly intellectual and deeply interested in literature, this is hardly surprising. Brian seems to have thought that words, like life, should not be sentimentally distorted.

Word-setting, as I've already suggested, may be a useful guide to a composer's development, since any uncertainty of style will immediately be shown up against a poetic text. This is certainly true for Brian, who is at a double disadvantage in the early vocal works: his own style is unformed, and he is working within a musical culture which is itself unstable. But there is a third problem: Brian's "negative" stance, with its concomitant "puritan" concern for words, actually reduces the effectiveness of his settings. Brian's impatience with conventional forms and styles is evident; but he is forced to work within them, because he has not yet evolved a personal alternative. He is therefore working against himself, and his "readings" are that much less convincing.

I can most conveniently illustrate and elaborate these points by taking a few well-known features of Brian's symphonic writing and describing their approximate equivalents in (chiefly) the songs.

The symphonies are notable for their highly contrapuntal texture, with particular prominence given to the bass. The songs often create a similar effect: the piano's "accompaniment figures" are often motifs in their own right, and the voice is sometimes no more than one strand - and not always the most interesting - in a musical argument carried mainly by the piano. There are good examples in *On Parting, Take, o take, The Message,* and *When the Sun Goes Down* (not on the Auracle record, but published with *On Parting* and *Love is a merry game*). Bass motifs are particularly important in *Why dost thou wound*, *When the Sun Goes Down*, *The Birds* (another Blake song, contemporary with *The Land of Dreams*), and even the "lighter" *Lady Ellayne*. *The Vision of Cleopatra* had lots of contrapuntal activity in the orchestra - especially the lower parts - (this is quite clear from the extant published vocal score) in which the vocal line seems often to be subsumed (anticipating *The Tigers*). Short rhythmic figures are of great importance in the songs as well as the symphonies, as in *When icicles*, *Why dost thou wound*, and *Care-charmer sleep*. Indeed, one realizes with some surprise (these being *songs*) that, as in the symphonies, rhythm is at least as important a structural element as melody.

What Brian's procedure amounts to is an attempted denial of lyricism. "Attempted" only, because the overall shape of the songs suggests a conventional lyric style. It sounds as though the tunes ought to be there. The medium is the wrong one for what Brian is trying to do. Furthermore, he has bravely rejected the obvious aid of melody, but as yet has nothing very distinctive to offer instead. The settings sound unconvinced and (to me) often unconvincing.

Despite the difference in scale, there are structural parallels with the symphonies too. Naturally there is little opportunity for Brian's favourite technique of continuous development; but there is the same fondness for contrast and fragmentation and the same distrust of neat forms. This last becomes almost an obsession when Brian has to deal with one particular kind of form - the couplet. Present him with a couplet and he will do all he can to destroy its fearful symmetry (exx. 1 a & b).

Ex. 1

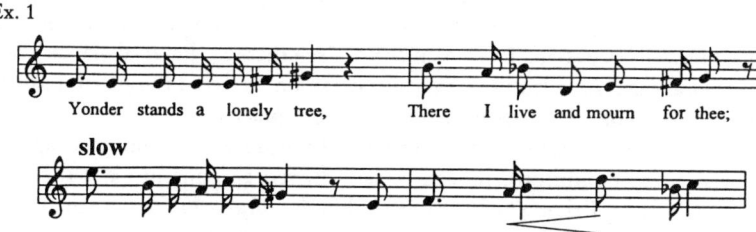

The short rhymed lines of *The Vision of Cleopatra* are treated similarly. Through contrast, rhythmic alteration, and other means, Brian distorts and expands the forms of many of his texts. The aim is to bring out the sense of the words by dramatic emphasis - a hallmark of the "puritan" style from early opera onwards. *Why dost thou wound* and *Love is a merry game* are structured on changes in style, whilst *The Soul of Steel* and *The Defiled Sanctuary* proceed by a series of stops and starts, and Brian's versions of all these are more dramatic than the originals. In *When the Sun Goes Down* the basic triple metre of the poem is wrested to something much more declamatory (ex. 2).

Ex. 2

But the most obvious indication of Brian's concern for "sense" is his use of enjambment. Where the sense goes across the line-end, so does Brian, as in *Why dost thou wound*:

Ex. 3

An extreme example is *The Message* (exx. 4 a & b).

Ex. 4

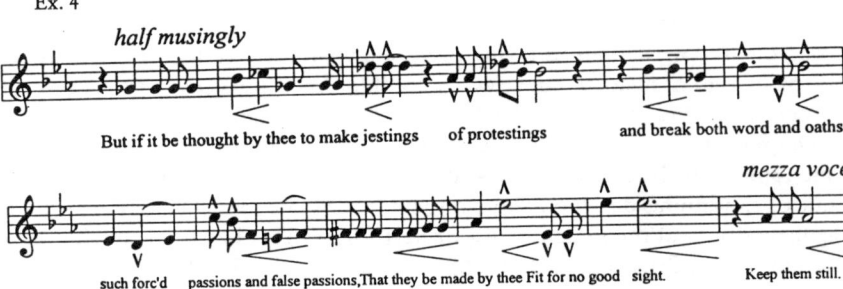

And here again, it seems to me, the result is often unsatisfactory. As with lyricism, Brian goes only part way. The texts are distorted, but still recognizable. *The Message*, for instance, starts off as if it were going to match the poem's form, then veers away, as above. The poem is not "re-created" (Peter Warlock's word), just messed about.[3] As with lyricism, too, Brian has rejected the natural assistance of the poem's shape, but gives us insufficient to replace it.

There is an ironic twist here. "Puritan" composers seem rarely to appreciate that poetic form conditions, indeed is part of, sense. Thus in ex. 4 the pairs of short lines, which Brian partly observes but largely overrides, seem to me to make their point much better than his "dramatic" accents and dynamics; whilst in ex. 5, from *Sorrow Song*, his repetition and rephrasing actually obscure the idea. The "puritan" approach is here self-defeating. Of course, if the musical idiom were sufficiently self-assured, we shouldn't notice; but we do.

Ex. 5

The effect of Brian's harmonic style is less easy to demonstrate by particular examples, but the same general points can be made. As has often been noticed, it is

---

[3] This is quite apart from changes in the words themselves. Brian's text differs considerably from any other I have seen, and though I have not checked all the editions Brian might have used, I am sure some of the changes must be his.

an amalgam of the various alternatives available in the early years of the century. Each of these separately has its own effect in relation to words. Diatonic writing has a definiteness and finality which rubs off on verbal statements. Wagnerian chromaticism, by contrast, deprives its text of finality but lends it both urgency and subtlety. Thoroughgoing atonality imposes an emotional extremism which carries its own authority. Brian uses all these but commits himself to none for long enough to benefit from these positive effects. Doubtless he scorned to do anything so easy. Later on the elements became fused, so that the whole carries conviction. But in the songs this is not really the case.

Brian's impatience with the conventional was more than just that. The conventional was bad because it was wrong; and he had the genuine puritan urge to get it right. He must have realized, and been mortified to realize, that his attempts to do so had often been counterproductive. He found two ways out of the impasse. The first is parody - a very modern mode, and highly characteristic of Brian. He had failed to "get it right"; in parody he could disclaim any attempt at doing so, and (when necessary) show his contempt for the efforts of others. This is most obvious in *The Tigers*, but can also be seen, in a much more refined form, in the Blake settings for children's voices. Here the musical setting is simplified to something superficially like a nursery rhyme, with the strong and unvarying rhythms of that form. Brian's characteristic rhythmic distortions of the text thus acquire a kind of traditional justification, as at the beginning of *The Chimney Sweeper*, a marvellous song (ex. 6).

Ex. 6

The effect is of conscious simplification and is capable of ironic interpretation, as at the end of the same song where Brian's characteristic unbalancing of the couplet produces a grim emphasis (ex. 7).

Ex. 7

In *The Tigers*, parody is more overt, even flamboyant. Beethoven, Debussy, Wagner, Elgar, even Holst and Stravinsky are victims. But parody is present even when no particular model can be detected. Passion, drama, solemnity, lyricism are all exaggerated to the point of absurdity. And the word-setting itself, from the underlay to the shape of the phrases, often sounds pointless or perverse. Brian's "negativity" has a field day here.

Parody - and especially the heady, irresponsible orgy of it in *The Tigers* - was one way out of Brian's problem with words. The other way was more direct, and Brian found it also in *The Tigers*. His rejection of the lyrical, the formal, the harmonically conventional was abortive in the songs because the medium was predisposed towards these qualities. *The Tigers* at last provided him with an appropriate vehicle: its normal style (at least in the solo writing) is freely declamatory, unconstrained in form, and harmonically adventurous. No wonder one constantly hears in it pre-echoes of Brian's mature orchestral writing. It is the work in which he found himself; and he did so, in part, by winning the battle with word-setting.

The Gothic is indebted to *The Tigers* in many ways, not least in its treatment of words, which is equally extreme. Both solo and choral writing are distinguished by persistent and clearly deliberate false accent and outlandish phrasing; of the choral sections Harold Truscott writes "words criss-cross and syllables are drawn out, the result being that with the clearest enunciation possible the words are at times barely, and at other, more frequent times, not at all discernible". He concludes "the music is not so much denying as destroying the meaning of the words ... the spirit behind this setting of the 'Te Deum laudamus' is, no doubt unknown consciously to the composer, nihilistic" (Truscott in *Two Studies*, pp. 28-29). Now "nihilistic" will do excellently for *The Tigers*, but I can't accept it for *The Gothic*, largely because I'm sure that the end of the symphony (from "In te domine speravi") is sincerely, indeed desperately, meant and felt. The "negativity" of *The Gothic*, which is certainly present, lies rather in the underlying trait with which I began: Brian's contempt for the easy and obvious.

Brian's models in *The Gothic* were the pre-Reformation composers, for whom a liturgical text and the truth behind it were taken for granted, so that they were free to elaborate and fragment as they pleased. The elaboration was a measure of their devotion. The famous epigraph represents Brian's distinctively post-Reformation application of this principle, personal and agonized with its implication of "Unless you strive with all your might, you *won't* be redeemed". To set the text in a less complicated and difficult manner, to make it more accessible, would have been to insult both it and him. I am reminded of Thomas Mann's Adrian Leverkühn and his great oratorio *Apocalypsis cum figuris*: "in it dissonance stands for the expression of everything lofty, solemn, pious, everything of the spirit; while consonance and firm tonality are reserved for the world of hell, in this context a world of banality and commonplace".

There may be further resonances: Brian, the religious sceptic, may at the same time be testing the *Te Deum* and what it affirms - saying, in effect, "stand up to *that* if you can". (This again recalls Leverkühn and his "atrocious competition with the goodness above".)

The Tigers and *The Gothic* were both liberating works for Brian, in that they allowed him to be unrestrained, absolute - in a word, extreme. They were a necessary stage. However, one cannot be perpetually at extremes. The direction his word-setting, as such, subsequently took in *Wine of Summer*, *Prometheus Unbound* and the late operas remains to be explored. As regards word-setting, to my mind Brian's most successful work in the early period is to be found in the Blake songs contemporary with *The Tigers*.[4] Here, and particularly in *The Land of*

---

[4] *Pace* Malcolm MacDonald's sleeve note, which assigns them to January 1919, the published scores of *The Birds* and *The Land of Dreams* are marked "Erdington. 1917 Winter" and "Erdington. Winter 1917" respectively.

Dreams, he seems to have found a truly personal idiom. Harmonically and melodically it is as free as *The Tigers*. It is still "negative": one is still conscious of things being withheld; but because the idiom is consistent and individual the things no longer seem necessary, and the withholding sounds deliberate. Hence the reading of the words is convincing; and Brian has relaxed enough to respect and so profit from the poetic form to some degree.

Blake said "If the fool would persist in his folly, he would become wise". The motto of the puritan might be "to thine own self be true". Brian persisted in his eccentricities until they became individuality; in his "negativity" until it changed from a disruptive element to a necessary principle. The early vocal music embodies this process. If even in the later Brian "negativity" still carries a suggestion of self-protective defiance, that is hardly surprising. But what it mostly conveys to me is stoicism and unsentimentality. This music of "self-destruction" is the most inspiring and strengthening I know.

Rodney Stephen Newton: Havergal Brian and the bare 5th. With a comment by Ted Heaton[1]

Over the period of a composer's creative life certain mannerisms appear which may be identified as representing the essence of that composer's personal style - musical fingerprints, if you like. One might draw attention to the spikiness of Stravinsky, the fragmentary austerity of Webern, the lush, modal melodies of Puccini, and so on. With Havergal Brian there are a number of these fingerprints which pervade the vast majority of his scores, from early days right through to the late symphonies, and tell us as we listen "yes, that's Havergal Brian all right" - even if the work we are hearing is unfamiliar. One of the most commonly occurring of these is Brian's use of the bare 5th - that is, the root of a chord together with the note five steps above it (counting the root as one) but with no 3rd. Brian employs this interval as we employ commas and full stops in written English - to close sections of a work, a movement or a piece as a whole. The 5th obviously held a special significance for Brian and, in order to attempt to understand this, we should first of all consider his interest in early music.

To composers of mediaeval days (and right through to the Baroque era) the interval of a 5th represented perfect balance. Music of early times frequently comes to rest on a bare 5th or an octave, thus signifying that balance has been achieved. Listening to music by Dufay, Dijon, Gesualdo, Josquin des Prés and Lassus will provide many examples of this, and also of other devices that Brian admired and, in some cases, adopted. Thus, the appearance of the interval of a 5th at cadential points in Brian's music seems to imply pretty much the same sort of

---

[1] From *Newsletter* 18 (VII-VIII 1978), pp. 5-6. Ted Heaton's comment was a letter to the Editor (*The Physics of the bare 5th*) in *Newsletter* 23 (V-VI 1979), pp. 2-3.

thing as it did in the music of his beloved Gothic era - that equilibrium has been achieved.

The psychological implications of this practice are also worth considering. Take, for example, the closing pages of the Tenth Symphony of Brian. After storms, angry disjointed marches and searches after peace, the music dissolves into an anxious, questioning phrase for a solo violin supported by softly shuddering strings. The answer to this question is really a non-answer:

Ex. 1

Slow moving bass instruments move into place like the cogs of some vast engine to reply to the violin with a twice-stated final cadence, each time ending on a bare 5th. Thus the work ends neither hopefully nor tragically, but with a feeling of "what will be - will be" - a cold, impersonal, impassive comment on all that has gone before, but one perfectly in accordance with Brian's personal philosophy. (In this particular example I beg leave to differ with my good friend Malcolm MacDonald, who in his first volume on the symphonies, p. 182, seems to hear an implied C major in these closing bars.)

Brian does not always approach his closing bars in the same way. Sometimes the final 5ths appear as the summit of a great progression, as at the conclusions of Symphonies Nos 16 and 24:

Ex. 2

Sometimes they appear abruptly, as if to halt the music in a head-on collision, as in Symphony No. 17:

Ex. 3

In a few instances, the 5ths arrive as a soft answer or shout of protest, as in Symphony No. 28:

Ex. 4

Frequently, an ordinary perfect cadence is given a peculiarly "Brianesque" flavour by the absence of the 3rd of the chord, as at the end of the opera *Turandot*:

Ex. 5

With characteristic perversity, Brian sometimes ends on a major chord, but often the major 3rd is restricted to a couple of instruments, the rest sounding out the 5th so strongly that, at first hearing, the piece still sounds as if it has come to rest on a bare 5th, as at the end of Symphony No. 20. This also illustrates a favourite harmonic twist of Brian's, whereby the final bars of 5ths are wrested from the preceding harmonies by sheer force of will - dropping down a semitone. It seems that, whatever the foregoing argument, Brian always intends a balanced ending - albeit sometimes rather grudgingly.

A further feature of Havergal Brian's music is the manner in which he employs movement in parallel 5ths. Many composers use movement in consecutive 5ths - another device springing from the Middle Ages - and I would imagine most readers will have come into contact with such composers as Vaughan Williams, Holst, Bax - or even the film composers Franz Reizenstein and Miklós Rósza. All these are fond of parallel 5ths in their music, but Brian never seems to sound like any of them. With true independence he creates a distinctive sound-world of his own, involving almost an obsession with movement in 5ths. This imparts to the music much of its rugged character, but steers clear of the tone colours of the other composers mentioned above by virtue of the fact that Brian uses his 5ths in a *contrapuntal* manner, whilst Holst, Bax and Co. tend to use parallel 5ths as a *harmonic* device, often underlying a melody:

Ex. 6

Ex. 7

Paul Hindemith is one of the few composers resembling Brian in his contrapuntal use of parallel 5ths, but once more the resultant sound is totally different.

The stark sound of a bare 5th seems to sum up the character of Havergal Brian perfectly - unyielding, tough, uncompromising and with that touch of fatalism that was inherent in Brian's nature. Many examples of similar uses of the 5th may be quoted from the works of other composers (readers may like to investigate the Brian-like endings of the first movements of Liszt's *Dante* Symphony and Respighi's *Church Windows* as well as the astonishingly modern-sounding Prelude to Haydn's *The Seasons*), but none using the interval quite as distinctively or with such unfailing regularity as Havergal Brian.

Ted Heaton comments:

On re-reading Rodney Newton's article on Brian's use of the bare 5th, together with the comments in my contribution on HMV ASD 3486 (Symphonies Nos 8 & 9, recorded by the Royal Liverpool Philharmonic Orchestra under Sir Charles Groves - cf. *Newsletter* 18) on orchestral timbre in the bass regions, I have been giving some more thought to both. In almost all of Brian's works there are prominent roles given to bass instruments such as the tuba, euphonium, bass trombone, bass clarinet, and contra-bassoon. The organ, with its possibilities of very deep bass tone in the pedals, is used in Symphonies Nos 1, 2, 3, 4, 8, 9 and 14. The use of the interval of the 5th is familiar to us all, but I would like to restrict the comments here to Brian's use of the 5th in the bass regions, where it can be of great importance from the acoustic point of view.

When two simple harmonic tones are combined, differing in frequency by a few Hz (1 Hz = 1 cycle/sec.), then if the two tones are of equal intensity, the resultant combination produces audible "beats". As the two tones swing in and out of phase, they produce increases or decreases in loudness, hence the beats. This is most readily heard on a piano where one of the treble strings is very slightly out of tune with the other two; apart from the unpleasentness, careful listening will detect the beats. The reduction of the beats to zero is achieved by the intervention of a skilled piano tuner. Reference to books on acoustics theory will show that the mathematical treatment of the effect is rather formidable, and this is clearly not the place to explore the details.

All musical intervals, then, produce this effect to some degree but we are, in general, unconscious of the physical manifestations. But the interval of the 5th has a different property. In this case, when the tones are combined, the swings in and out of phase produce beats which occur at half the frequency of the fundamental note or, in musical terms, one octave lower than the fundamental.

Ex. 8

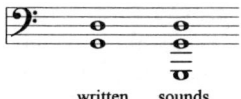

This effect is utilized by some organ builders who provide a "Quint" (10²/₃ ft) stop in the pedal organ, which when combined with a 16 ft stop produces a tone equivalent to a 32 ft stop at much reduced cost. Terminology varies, but the Quint may be combined with the 16 ft stop in one marked "Resultant Bass". In order for the effect to be fully realized, the notes must be sustained at steady intensities without vibrato - hence their use in organs where the wind pressures are mechanically maintained. The effect is almost impossible to reproduce on the piano, although a favourite trick of pianists who accompany hymn singing is to play the bass in octaves one octave lower than written and to include a 5th; the richness of tone produced is dependent upon the size and quality of the pianoforte being used, the acoustic quality of the hall and the degree of vigour of the participants.

Extending this concept to Brian's use of the 5th in the bass instruments of the orchestra, the combination tone produced will have the elements of the fundamental an octave lower. For example, when Brian writes for two tubas playing a 5th apart in the first of the last four bars of the first movement of *The Gothic*, this will produce a note an octave lower than that played by the second tuba to reinforce the aural effect the three *fortissimo* chords in this bar have on the listener. The pedal registration here is interesting; Brian calls for the 8, 16, 32 and 64 ft stops to be drawn, which sound the notes as written and one, two and three octaves lower respectively. The last chord of the movement is, of course, a bare 5th, and look at the organ pedal: a bare 5th, *ff*, which, if played with a 64 ft stop drawn, would produce a note *four* octaves lower than that written, three octaves below bottom D on the pianoforte. Such a note would be felt rather than heard; the frequency is approaching the regions of infra-sound. (The 64 ft stop on the organ pedal is, in any case, extremely rare. The organ at Liverpool Anglican Cathedral, the largest Gothic cathedral in the world, has one, and it would be of interest to learn of any others.) We may never know if Brian appreciated the physics of the use of this chord, and it might be an aspect of the unconscious Brian yet to be explored in depth, an instinctive act to produce musical sounds lower than the instruments producing them.

But another consideration comes to mind. Whether a musical sound is heard or felt depends upon the frequency of the vibrations and whether these frequencies develop their full wavelengths. And this is where the problem of the very deep bass lies. For a low note of, say, 20 Hz, the wavelength of this tone is $1120/20 = 56$ ft, 1120 being the speed of sound in air in ft/sec. In other words, for a note of that frequency to be heard, there must be a distance of at least 56 ft between the sound source and the listener for the full wavelength to develop. Although there will always be a controversy about this among hi-fi "experts", it is generally considered to be impossible to reproduce such low notes in the domestic environment because there is, in general, not sufficient room available for the wavelength to develop, no matter how sophisticated the speaker system. In any case, most amplifiers are provided with a filter circuit to prevent such very low frequencies ever reaching the speakers, where subsonic oscillations could cause severe physical distortion and damage to the speaker cone. In the concert hall, these very low notes *will* be heard (or felt) and we will never be conscious of the full frequency range (sorry, Decca!) of Brian's music on records or tapes. We must have more live performances. The sheer physical impact of much of Brian's music, so alive in the memories of those of us who have heard live studio and concert performances, can never be adequately reproduced electronically because these lower regions are governed by immutable physical laws. There is much that we can do; we all hope that a wide dissemination of the recorded repertoire to date (and whatever may come in the future) will stimulate the concert producers to be more adventurous, and we can all "learn the notes" from our records and tapes and derive enormous pleasure from so doing, but the real thing ... ah, there is nothing quite like it![2]

---

[2] Editorial note: It is not astonishing that Brian's real renaissance was dated in the digital era.

Harold Truscott/Peter Hill: Havergal Brian's solo piano music[1]

1. The *Three Illuminations* and *Four Miniatures*

Havergal Brian, prolifically creative though he was, put most of his energies as a composer into the orchestra, with the voice or voices a close second. In his youth he was a church organist and, automatically, a pianist, as well as playing the violin and the cello to a certain extent. Orchestral instruments fascinated him, and so especially did the sound of an orchestra. But, considering his ability as a pianist, he wrote remarkably little for this instrument.

I have always thought it a great pity that he did not put his mastery of the piano to the production of some large-scale works for that instrument, particularly piano sonatas which, no doubt, would have been as individual in their approach as are the symphonies. As it is, the only large-scale piano work is the *Double Fugue*. However, he did not produce any piano sonatas; his ideas were always orchestral or vocal, or both - or almost always. Even as it is, he did write a few notable works for the piano, more than he did in the field of chamber music, where only one surviving work can possibly qualify: the *Legend* for violin and piano, written between 1918 and 1920. He did, apparently, write a string quartet and a piece for cello and piano at the beginning of the century, not to mention the mysterious "long *Legend* for cello (or bass clarinet) and piano" apparently dating from much later, and mentioned in a letter to Reginald Nettel, but these are all lost.

First, there is the group of pieces published as *Three Illuminations*, composed in 1916. They were followed by *Four Miniatures*; as with the *Legend* these were written between 1918 and 1920. Both of these sets are the result of his sense of humour, if we except the two miniatures that were drawn from two Blake settings. The expression of humour, of one kind or another, in the sense of the comic, is an aspect of Brian's character much in evidence in his earlier work, although it changed its expression with the passage of time. He early had an ear for the songs of Music Hall artists such as Albert Chevalier, Marie Lloyd, Vesta Tilley and others, and in one way or another, usually without direct quotation, their rhythm and spirit affected his own ideas - especially the spirit, which was often that of sheer cheek, of the street urchin, the thumbing of one's nose to imposed and often unjustified and misplaced authority, and the hatred of all pomposity. The American counterpart is in the work of the brilliant silent film comedians, especially those who worked in the Mack Sennett studio. As late as

---

[1] From *Newsletters* 42 (VII-VIII 1982), pp. 4-6, 43 (IX-X 1982), pp. 4-6, 44 (XI-XII 1982), pp. 5-7, and 47 (V-VI 1983), pp. 3-4, Peter Hill's notes on the fugues are from *Newsletter* 34 (III-IV 1981), pp. 2-3. Peter Hill has recorded the complete piano music, together with Malcolm MacDonald and Ronald Stevenson's arrangement of the funeral march from *Turandot*. The speaker in the *Three Illuminations* is Christopher Kay (Cameo GOCLP 9016 D).

February 1958 Brian wrote to me that when he listened to Sir Adrian Boult's broadcast of "Wild Horsemen" from *The Tigers*, he fancied he heard bagpipe tunes, and Chevalier's *Laugh, laugh, I thought I should have died* and *Knocked 'em in the Old Kent Road*. Somewhere deep in Brian's musical soul there was a strong affinity with the music of the Music Hall, and the element of racy and, at times, outrageous humour these often represented. It was as likely to pop up in the later symphonies as in the works written before he started *The Gothic*; and there are many such traces in the later symphonies. Brian was never attracted to folksong, and once told me he had never been moved by one; there is no trace of any or their effect in his music, and yet he is as English in his expression as a composer could be. Some of that Englishness, though by no means all of it, comes from his deep attraction to the Music Hall songs; and, if we are honest, we must admit that these, which, with the whole tradition that called them into being, are a purely English phenomenon, are far more redolent of the English character than many so-called English folksongs which actually had their origins abroad.

This type of humour turns up in such an early work as the First English Suite, composed about 1904. This has, among other things, a presentation of *God Save the Queen* that is grotesque - far more so than Debussy's half-unrecognizable lopsided version in *Hommage à Mr Pickwick*; Brian's makes sure of being recognized, even, in its repeated wallops from the bass drum, being quite prepared to bludgeon one into recognition. Not subtle, but effective - just as a sock filled with wet sand is effective. Elsewhere in the same suite there is music which could well have been designed to go with the antics of Ben Turpin, or Billy Bevan, or Andy Clyde, or Snub Pollard or many others of the Sennett company of clowns.

During the next decade Brian's humour, or his musical expression of it, changed a good deal. From Mack Sennett he seems to have veered round to a sort of Buster Keaton outlook. Put another way, his humour became sarcastic, or satirical - so far as music can be satirical or sarcastic. How far that is, I am not sure. I *am* sure that sounds suggestive of the sarcastic can be musically produced, as I believe Mahler produced them in a piece such as the Ländler second movement of the Ninth Symphony.[2] Why snarling trills on the clarinets, for instance,

---

[2] Malcolm MacDonald writes in a letter to the Editor in *Newsletter* 65 (V-VI 1986), p. 5: "I outlined Brian's knowledge of Mahler in Volume 3 of my study of the symphonies (pp. 138-9), but I will expand a bit. Briefly to recapitulate, the first Mahler symphony he got to know was No. 8, in 1930, under Henry Wood, followed by Nos 9 and 4 (in that order) under Boult. During the 1930s he borrowed the scores of 'all' of them from an unknown source - whether this included *Das Lied von der Erde* and the then-available movements of No. 10 I don't know - as well as acquiring 78rpm discs of No. 4 under Walter. He also owned Paul Bekker's book of analyses of the symphonies (published in German in 1921). Considering that until the late 1950s Mahler's music was generally cold-shouldered by the British critical establishment, these facts indicate an unusual degree of interest on Brian's part. Brian was certainly maintaining this interest in Mahler in the late 1940s. Specifically, he wrote a fairly long review-article in the May 1946 *Musical Opinion* (pp. 229-30) prompted by the appearance of the first English translation of Alma Mahler's *Gustav Mahler: Memories and Letters*. And in November 1947 he listened to a BBC broadcast - almost certainly the first British performance - of Mahler's Third Symphony,

should suggest sarcasm, I do not know; I know that in certain conditions, conditions which Mahler had produced in that movement, they do, for me. It *is* possible to be satirical in music - music alone, that is, without the aid of words or, in opera, actions as well. Two composers who certainly produced it are Dussek and Alkan; the former perhaps most obviously (there are subtler examples in his work) in his one-movement piano sonata, *La Chasse*, which is like nothing so much as a musical expression of a Walt Disney cartoon depicting a fox hunt set at sixes and sevens by the intrusion of a lolloping carthorse. Far more subtle are the superb piano rondo, *To, to Carabo*, and the finale of the *Sonata in D major* op. 13 No. 2.

Satire I think there is in some of Brian's music of this period, roughly from 1910-20, although elements of it persist throughout his work; and it is perhaps suggestive that this period of roughly ten years includes the composition of most

conducted by Sir Adrian Boult. Brian was moved to write to Boult (his letter is in the BBC Written Archives Centre at Caversham) to record his thanks for such a fine performance of a work which he had given up hope of ever hearing. In the course of his letter he states that 'some months ago' he had been sufficiently interested in this symphony to translate for himself a long critique of an early performance under Mahler himself, written by the Austrian composer Wilhelm Kienzl (1857-1941; Brian was interested in Kienzl too, and wrote an article about him which I intend to include in Volume 2 of *Havergal Brian on Music*). So yes, there is good evidence that Mahler No. 3 was much in Brian's thoughts not all that long before he began work on his own Eighth Symphony. (Before his Seventh Symphony too: would anyone like to consider parallels between the march-music in the first movement of Mahler No. 3 - originally entitled 'Spring marches in' and that in the second movement of Brian No. 7?) As for other connections: Brian himself stated (I think in a letter to Robert Simpson, but I can't lay my hand on the exact reference as I write this) that the opening of his Eleventh Symphony's second movement is intended as an allusion to the beginning of Mahler No. 4. But I've never found any comments by him on Mahler's Fifth. Mr Pike's view - that the opening of Brian No. 10 is a 'Brianic reworking' of the start of that symphony - is by no means 'musically illiterate': there are strong similarities of rhythm and gesture. But 'influence' whether consciously accepted or unconsciously exploited - is a far more complex matter than we allow in most of the frames of reference we set up to discuss it; and in viewing this passage of Brian we must take into account the whole Austro-German tradition of 'symphonic funeral march' to which Mahler and Brian both contributed so richly. The passage could equally well be seen as a vast harmonic, textural, and rhythmic expansion of the basic gesture at the start of Brian No. 8, and was more likely so intended." David Lambourn adds, in a letter to the Editor in *Newsletter* 66 (VII-VIII 1986), p. 7: "Malcolm MacDonald suggests that Havergal Brian did not become acquainted with Mahler's music until 1930. However, I think there is a fair chance that Brian may have seen or heard a Mahler score before this date. There were, on my count, at least eight Mahler performances in Britain before 1914, one of them being a concert given by the Hallé Orchestra in January 1913, in which the Symphony No. 1 was given. During the 1920s the Fourth Symphony was played in Liverpool, Birmingham, Newcastle, Manchester and London, two of the performances being broadcast live. Mahler's music was not, therefore, as infrequently played as we imagine today. I have seen the letter to Adrian Boult of November 1947 which Malcolm MacDonald mentions. In it, Brian writes that he had not seen a Mahler score for 20 years, when they were all lent to him for a short time (he particularly mentions No. 4 and No. 8). If interpreted literally this would be about the time that he was completing the *Gothic* Symphony. Mahler's Fifth Symphony, to which Steven Pike refers (letter to the Editor in *Newsletter* 64, III-IV 1986, pp. 2-3), was first performed in Britain by Heinz Unger and the London Philharmonic Orchestra in 1945. However, as Malcolm MacDonald suggests, it seems more likely that Brian was reworking his own music at the opening of his Tenth Symphony, than that of another composer."

358 Miscellany

of the sketches, although not the full completion of the work or the orchestration, of *The Grotesques*, which was the original title, up to publication, of what became *The Tigers*; for grotesquerie is, I think, an even more accurate name than satire for this quality in much of Brian's music which most displays it.

The *Three Illuminations* for piano are, whether or not Brian designed them for this purpose, in the nature of studies for *The Tigers* - just as earlier Busoni had written orchestral pieces, such as *Nocturne symphonique*, which proved to be studies for *Doktor Faust*. Brian certainly drew upon these pieces for many aspects of the music of the opera. They were written in 1916, and it was shortly after that Brian began to work on *The Tigers*. They are programmatic pieces; each has a brief story written by Brian and printed before each piece - but, like a good deal of programme music, they make better musical sense without the programme. It is true that without the programmatic clue two of them, Nos 1 and 3, would be a rather peculiar collection of odds and ends which interfere with each other and get in each other's way, and yet these somehow (a word one often needs in describing the logic in sound of Brian's music, which is frequently not apparent to the eye) manage to make musical sense.

The first piece is called "The Boys and the Pastille", with a brief story concerning two boys who clatter into church one Sunday and cough, whereupon an old lady gives then a pastille to suck, which they divide. They tell their friends and the following Sunday they all troop into church and produce a chorus of coughs, only to find that the old lady has forgotten to bring her pastilles. An abbreviated version of this is printed above the music - very abbreviated, since it deals only with the arrival of all the boys and their disappointment. There is an organist who is sure of only two pedals, and a distorted version of "There is a Happy Land" as the preacher enters, etc. The piece is full of things which make perfect musical sense, in spite of cutting across each other, but which can in no way, unless one reads the programme, suggest what the words tell us. In fact there is no mention of the organist or the preacher in the story; they are only mentioned in what is printed above the music.

In the second piece, "The Butterfly's Waltz", we meet with one aspect of Brian's wry musical humour in that the waltz, which is there in rhythm in the bass, is combined with perky music of a quite different character, and the three beats of the waltz are spread across basic two-beat bars (ex. 1).

Ex. 1

We also meet in this one a figure of four semiquavers, usually, though not always, the first three repeating the same note or chord, the fourth dipping down a step, which becomes a notable feature of Brian's style, being used expressively in a variety of ways (ex. 2). It crops up in *The Tigers* and can be heard, *not* humorously, at the end of the second bar of the *Gothic* Symphony. The story is a whimsy about a butterfly chased by a wasp and looking for a place to lay her eggs.

Ex. 2

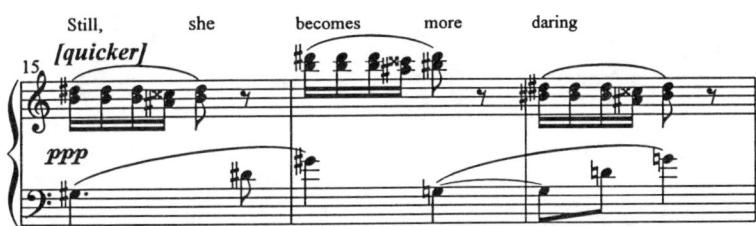

The third and final piece is the most ridiculous in its story and the most determinedly illustrative of the three. "Venus and a Bobby" is its title, and its story concerns a constable gazing up at night at a lighted window in which occasionally he sees a lady, whom he has heard singing as Venus at the opera (Brian's humour almost guffaws here). He feels love-sick, but at last sees his sergeant emerge from the house. The end is a little too slick (in words) for my liking. The constable says to the sergeant "Kiss me, sergeant", to which the latter replies "As you like it".

Many facets of Brian's musical imagination haunt these pieces: his love of organum-like moving chords of octaves and 5ths (ex. 3), his use of common chords in a manner in which they contradict each other (ex. 4), his individual use of augmented triads (ex. 5), and triplet repeated chords as they appear later in, for instance, the slow movement of *The Gothic* (ex. 6). In many ways the pieces were a try-out, and particularly point to *The Tigers*, which, incidentally, features a music-hall song, "Has Anybody here seen Kelly?", as the theme of the symphonic variations and in other parts of the opera, in which again the four semiquaver figure is prominent, being the musical, or rhythmical, representation of the word "anybody".

360 *Miscellany*

Ex. 3

The bobby stands in the silent night . . . . he hears a noise above - looks up. Says he - "What's a 'Zepp'?"   Still and

Very slow

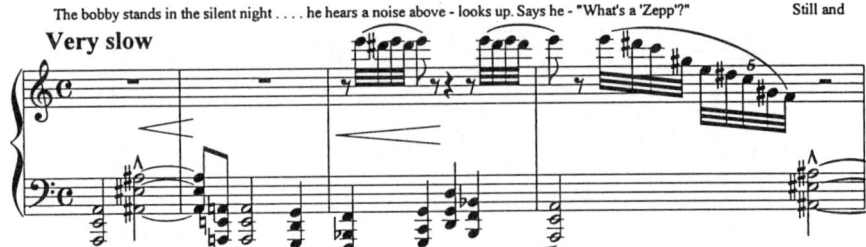

The left hand must always be played with great mystery because it nearly always represents the bobby.

Ex. 4

Ex. 5

he swoons . . . .   leaning against a

Ex. 6

Bobby is all excitement, he hears footsteps coming downstairs . . . . .   and rushes to the

door . . . .   *(footsteps)*   it does not open

What matters here is the music, exactly as with *Doctor Merryheart*, written four years earlier, which also has a whimsical programme description, of the Doctor, attached to it; this is funny but it tells us nothing about the music, which is no more humorous than is the music which accompanies the "joke" at the end of Haydn's *Farewell* Symphony. Perhaps it would be more accurate to say that the music of *Merryheart* has nothing to tell us about the description of the Doctor. However, if such starting-points helped Brian to produce the music they were worth their weight in gold. The three pieces reveal a style unusual, as might be expected, already showing signs of the habit of starting ideas, breaking off, and coming in from a different direction which, with quite different music, informs so much of his late symphonic writing. But, although cast in an unusual mould, they are eminently pianistic, with a use of the keyboard new but natural - which is not to say they are easy to play. In fact what these pieces and the *Four Miniatures* show us is how easily some of his earlier orchestral music could have slid on to the piano if he had so willed - with a somewhat different treatment, but essentially the same music.

The *Miniatures* include, in the second and fourth, transfers from two songs written about the same time. They are simply the piano parts of settings of Blake's *The Land of Dreams* and *The Birds*, without their vocal parts. But here, as so often in connection with Brian, mystery raises its head. Reginald Nettel, in his *Havergal Brian and his Music*, tells us that the publishers (Augener) "pointed out to Brian that the accompaniments to *The Land of Dreams* and *The Birds* would stand on their own merits as pianoforte compositions. They offered to publish them as such"; and, in fact, with the addition of two more, untitled, they did so, in 1921. But this argues that Augener had already seen the songs; why, then, did they delay publishing them, as they did, for 11 years, until 1932?

It is possible that someone at Augener was acute enough to perceive that in the two songs the piano part and the vocal part are somewhat at loggerheads. In character, and in tonality, they often pursue their separate ways - and yet together they manage to make a reasonable whole, of a somewhat acid type. Nonetheless, separating one from the other does far less damage than would be the case in the majority of outstanding songs. (There is, however, one place in *The Land of Dreams* (ex. 7) where the overlapping chords of the piano part alone lose something by the omission of the voice recitative part.) At times the piano seems to set out to contradict the voice, and what it is singing about. In short, we have in the songs an example of the dichotomy of thought, the contradictoriness, which came to the fore so much in the *Gothic* Symphony. Perhaps, on second thoughts, Augener were not acute enough to perceive this, but merely realized that the piano parts were full and satisfying by themselves. After all, they did eventually publish the songs.

Ex. 7

The style of the four pieces is so continuous from the *Three Illuminations* that they could well have been published all together as either "Seven Illuminations" or, better, "Seven Miniatures". The *Miniatures* have no programmatic associations, except the original connection of Nos 2 and 4 with Blake's poems. No. 3 is not unlike "The Butterfly's Waltz", sharing a suggestion of the overlapping of a three-crotchet rhythm with a predominant two-crotchet time, although in this case there is a plain three-four passage in the middle. There is, also, again the four-semiquaver figure almost as it appears at times in *The Tigers*.

The seven pieces are not especially difficult, but they do need imaginative technique. Brian's intervals and, indeed, his melodic lines as a whole, do not always move in obvious directions, although once one is used to the music they seem natural, and they are essentially pianistic. Obviously, Brian was able to think according to his medium for, in spite of the likeness of much of this music to that of *The Tigers*, which I have stressed, the writing generally and the climaxes in the opera are quite characteristically orchestral, whereas what is presented in the piano pieces never asks for orchestral sound, but only that of the piano, even though that quality is used in an unusual manner.

There remains the question of the descriptive programmes. Presumably, these were to be printed in the concert programmes; but what of the pointers printed above the music, which illustratively are more revealing concerning the music than the descriptions printed before the music? Were these to be called out as the pieces were played, as on the recent recording, and as was done on the radio recently in a broadcast of Dussek's *The Sufferings of the Queen of France*? Or were they, I wonder, only for the consumption of those who bought and played the pieces privately?

2. The *Prelude and Fugue in C minor*

By 1921, Brian was immersed in work on the *Gothic* Symphony, his prime concern for many years. His approach to counterpoint was no more conventional than was his attitude to anything else musical, although he had studied traditional counterpoint (no one but a fool, wishing to be a composer, would avoid it), and put himself through the mill with it. There is no doubt whatever that he could, if he so desired, write a fine traditional fugue with the best of them. Mostly, he chose not to. Musically, he was capable of subjecting himself to stringent discipline. While working on the symphony he wrote some contrapuntal studies for aspects of the larger work. Later, in 1924, he reworked some of these to produce the two *Preludes and Fugues*, in *C minor* and *D minor and major*, and the *E♭ Double Fugue*, all for piano.

The *C minor Prelude* is an interesting example of Brian's short thinking at this time, with a fully resonant use of the keyboard. But I find it the less interesting of the two Preludes. For me, three points stand out about it: the almost persistent semiquaver arpeggios, which move with characteristically unexpected, and unexplained, changes of harmonic direction; the piece being too short, not as a prelude to the Fugue that follows, but as a structure using the material on which it is based; and the final chordal passage, impressive in its use of keyboard sonority, losing power by its constant repetition of the same rhythm - three bars of minim and two crotchets, two bars of two minims each; this four times, only modified by the final cadence. It is true, too, that that chordal passage is the final result of a theme growing gradually throughout the piece, and that it had gained in this way a certain strength, which is dissipated and weakened by this final four-fold statement.

The Fugue is a different matter. Like the *D major Fugue*, and unlike the *Double Fugue*, this one has a fairly long subject, occupying four bars. And yet, for all practical purposes, it is a two-bar subject, for only in a short episode near the beginning of the Fugue are the third and fourth bars used for development. The rest is concerned only with the first two bars. Why, then, a four-bar subject? I think there is no question that the third and fourth bars are there to complete a natural rhythm started by the first two bars; they fulfil a rhythmic need which governs the whole piece. I quote the first nine bars as ex. 8.

Ex. 8

364 Miscellany

Ex. 8 contains the subject, its answer and the first bar of the third entry. I include this to show a curious movement from supertonic to tonic, as the last chord in the eighth bar consists only of D and A, the D arrived at from a C♯. It works, nonetheless, crude as it looks on paper. But Brian's music is full of visual crudities which are aurally convincing, even compelling.

At the end of the exposition the D major chord resolves onto G and begins a series of sequential rises, utilizing, for the only occasion in the Fugue, the fourth bar of the subject for development in tenor and bass, the fourth step arriving at C♯ minor harmony and full-blooded use of that same fourth bar in soprano and bass (ex. 9).

Ex. 9

The last two bars of ex. 9 are taken up a further step to D minor, where the sequences cease; the second D minor bar begins the subject in the bass under a widespread climax to a top A, tenor takes the truncated subject a 5th higher on A, against whole bar triplet minim chords not the easiest of rhythms to bring off accurately (ex. 10).

Ex. 10

The figure of triplet minim chords in the right hand makes a four-bar phrase rising to a top A♭, but underneath the tenor subject, after two bars, gives way to another beginning on F, which brings the first bar of the subject with its dotted rhythm continuation extended to lead to a new episode lasting for nine bars, built on a new melodic shape (ex. 11).

Ex. 11

The strength of this Fugue is more than once shown to be apparent perversity turning to creativity - a phrase that would be a good summing-up of many aspects of Brian's work; one could almost say that other people's perversity is Brian's creativity; in this Fugue we have it on a small scale. The apparent perversity at present consists of this nine-bar episode, based on a theme different from the subject but connected to it by having the same rhythm as that subject's first two bars, remaining throughout, except for a momentary unexplained G♭, on F minor, and at the 10th bar moving up quite nonchalantly to G minor, just as the answer in the exposition moved from D to C. And what it moves to appears at first to be further treatment of the real subject, all four bars of it, in proper fugal style. Nothing so normal; it is the beginning of a two-part canon, the theme beginning in the bass and imitated at the same pitch a bar later. I say the *beginning* of a canon, for that is all it is. After five bars it gives up and leads to a development of the first bar of the subject in fairly full-blooded tones (ex. 12).

Ex. 12

Notice that the bass figure in the second and other alternate bars of ex. 12 is almost the same as the first bar of ex. 11 - almost the same. That bar was a diminished triad; this one occupies a full perfect 5th; but the relationship is clear. And as the top part moves up and dies out on an extreme octave A♭ the bass figure descends into the depths, its last three bars having the rhythm, but not the thematic shape, of the second, third and fourth bars of the original subject.

What the bass leads to is a quaver pedal point on the tonic chord of C minor, emphasizing the dominant, which persists for some bars before disappearing; another aspect of Brian's perversity. Again and again in these fugues he appears for a moment to be doing the normal (or customary) thing, only to show that the normal, for him, is merely the prelude (whether misleading or not depends on our attitude) to the unexpected - or unusual, or abnormal, or whatever one likes to call it. The thing that matters is that when music is right it is automatically normal, and Brian's Fugue sounds right. One can see now one reason why he studied traditional fugue: one has to know what one is flouting in order to do so to any creative purpose.

In any traditional fugue the pedal point would almost certainly indicate the beginning of the final stage, perhaps with a piling up of *stretto* (overlapping) entries of the subject; and this stage of Brian's Fugue begins as if that is the only object it has. After four bars (three bars of *stretto* entries) the pedal bass dies out, giving way to a tenor entry starting on G, the upper harmony somewhat at odds (ex. 13).

Ex. 13

But the point here is not so much the slightly distorted harmony; it is the cessation of the quaver bass, to give way to the comparative lack of rhythmic movement in that tenor entry (fourth bar of ex. 13), which is a little like a slap in the face. With all the apparently normal ingredients going strong, Brian can deliver these slaps - it is no wonder that his music has aroused critical hostility. But one thing which gives life to the music here, and prevents it from sounding simply perverse, is the D♭ in the alto part (bar three of ex. 13), immediately contradicted by the soprano D in the next bar.

However, the new departure proves to be a development of the second bar of the fugue subject, moving in a *crescendo* to a further development of a figure related to that in the first bar of ex. 11, again with the same rhythm; but it is extended this time, and built up, on overlapping entries, to a climax from which the music descends, in pitch and volume, to the real concluding stage of the Fugue. Once more Brian begins his *stretti*, once more things are not what they might have been had the music been pursuing a more normal course. This time the bass starts, with only a bar's lead; again the subject gets no further than the first two bars, with two interesting bars following (ex. 14).

Ex. 14

As ex. 14 shows, the third bar in the bass is a figure of quavers, which is maintained with the third entry (entries are in the order of bass, tenor, alto, soprano), the broken 3rds extended through the fourth bar; these become important. Ex. 14 also shows a different third bar in the tenor, also maintained by the soprano. The four entries complete, the extended broken 3rds and the new tenor and soprano third bar are combined against subject overlaps in bass and tenor, growing in volume to a *ff* climax on a very much blunted D minor, where internal dissonances bring a touch of acid to the music (ex. 15). Notice the two pairs of notes I have bracketed, which give the acid touch.

Ex. 15

So once again Brian has done the right thing in the wrong way. The closing portion of a fugue should produce (or be able to produce) *stretti*, according to all the most correct manuals on the subject. Brian's closing portion produces *stretti* - but not precisely according to the most correct manuals. On the other hand, they are certainly according to the living nature and common sense of this remarkable music, so perhaps it is as well that the correct manuals did not have their way.

From here the music builds up to a final climax, counterpoint forgotten. The subject is thundered out in *ff* chords, against an imperious bass figure (ex. 16), and the fourth bar is drawn out against a rapid rising scale in octaves. It gives place to a *Lento* cadential final statement of the subject with yet new harmony, and dies out to practically nothing.

The scope of this short four-page Fugue is tremendous, and the vivid life of the music is all drawn from Brian's doing the right things in the wrong way - or the wrong things at the right time. In other words, although it is different from his other music, it is thoroughly characteristic of him.

Ex. 16

3. Prelude and Fugue in D minor/major

With the *D minor Prelude* we are in a quite different world from the rather four-square one of the C minor. The music moves, in its six-eight rhythm which at first seems to be languid but gradually reveals more and more of the energy coiled up in it, at times in an aura of reflection from the first movement of *The Gothic*, and with an ease and fluency which speak volumes for the contrapuntal mastery expressed in its rich two-part writing. Its expressive power is immense, and grows as the music proceeds. The Fugue, in D major, is simply superb, one of the finest things of its kind in this century's music; one would have to go to some of Reger's or Franz Schmidt's fugues, or the best of Hindemith's, for its equals. Its calm, almost methodical, progress continually reveals new facets of the resources contained in its subject, until its final abandonment of counterpoint, in the brass-like fanfares which reinforce the end of the piece, comes as the natural climax to the rich, rolling polyphony which precedes it.

Marked *Andante moderato*, with *e rubato* as a safeguard against the Olympean calm with which it opens being spoiled by unnecessary hurry, the Fugue moves, for roughly its first half, as on a sparkling sea, a stately galleon. There could scarcely be a greater contrast with the *C minor Fugue*. Part of the difference lies in the nature of the subject (ex. 17), which moves in longer bars than the C minor subject, with a fair proportion of longer notes.

Ex. 17

Also, the counterpoint flows largely on diatonic notes of D major (or notes on the D major scale), in a sort of happy serenity, without the jerky chromaticism that is a feature of the C minor almost from the start. Except for the occasional G♯, gently corrected to G, there is, in fact, only one abnormality in the exposition - and it is a curious one, although it is fully explained by the preceding counterpoint. Although composers use a codetta in a fugal exposition (that is, an extension of the subject in an answer entry, to meet the next entry at tonic pitch) for a variety of reasons, the main one concerns the use of a real answer (an exact transposition of the subject) in order to restore the tonic for the next entry at tonic pitch. Brian's is a real answer for the first two bars, but a tonal answer for the third and fourth; notice that the interval D-C♯ in the third bar of the subject has become A-F♯ in the third bar of the answer: a minor 3rd instead of a minor 2nd: and this keeps the music on D, ready for third entry, at tonic pitch. So far, so good. But Brian uses a codetta of a single bar in an unusual place in his exposition, and for none of the usual reasons. Ex. 17 shows the subject, with the answer following immediately. But the third entry, in the soprano, at the original tonic pitch, has an extra bar inserted before the second appearance of the answer (ex. 18).

Ex. 18

The D major also uses a countersubject (so does the C minor, for the length of the exposition, but not beyond); that is to say, the continuation of the subject voice against the answer, a continuation which is then maintained, often for the length of the Fugue; where the subject appears, so does the countersubject, so that at times such pieces almost become a kind of double fugue - the type with two subjects announced simultaneously. Some of Handel's finest "double" fugues are of the type that maintains a countersubject. Brian maintains his countersubject (it can be seen in the tenor in the last four bars of ex. 17) for roughly half of the Fugue; for so long, indeed, that it appears as though he is going to be a good boy and maintain it throughout. However, this he does not do.

Again, for very nearly half the Fugue, Brian's harmony is very restrained; it circles round and about the diatonic harmonies of D major. Apart from one bar interposed between one statement of the subject and another, which is suddenly highly chromatic, nothing disturbs the diatonic movement of the music except the occasional G♯, quickly naturalized. But at last the music begins to sink, away from D, apparently, introducing a C , B♭, E♭, and making a cadence on to the dominant 7th of B♭, just as though the music is moving into that key; there is no indicated retarding of tempo. But the reaction is not B♭, but D minor, with an increased pace, *Poco più Allegro*.

Ex. 19

Brian now begins a very closely argued development of the first two bars of the subject, with counterpoint derived from, but not the same as, the countersubject (ex. 19). Notice that the crotchet rests which until now have begun the first and third bars of the subject have disappeared; the theme starts now with three emphatic minims. A tiny point, perhaps, but one that makes a good deal of difference in character. Most of the 19 bars that start with ex. 19 have the effect of close *stretto* entries of the first two bars of the subject, although some of the entries are deceptive, having only the three opening minims and then going their own way. Occasionally, too, the whole four-bar subject makes itself heard. Harmonically, the music dithers between D minor and, with inserted E♭s, the B♭ that was avoided when this episode started.

Ex. 20

Suddenly all this is cancelled and the music opens out to a climax on B major (ex. 20), only to relapse beautifully on to A, leading back to D minor, and a further increase of speed. Fresh counterpoint introduces the subject one bar later, and an interesting point about it. The two supporting parts are highly chromatic, but mainly they hover between D minor and B♭ major; but the subject, taken on its own, is the clearest F major (ex. 21).

Ex. 21

Harmonic suggestion remains ambiguous, C major vying with A minor at one point, as the Fugue becomes more excited, with more and widespread movement (ex. 22). This leads eventually to a passage fully on D marked *Grandioso*. Here the *stretti* cluster in three layers at first, with characteristic C major against D major, and both against A major (ex. 23).

372 Miscellany

Ex. 22

Ex. 23

They lead to B major once more and a cessation of counterpoint. With a pressing on of speed we hear three fanfares (Brian writes "with forced, brassy tone"), the initial chords moving up each time, from B to C♯ minor, to C major, with an E at the top. A final relapse to D ends the piece with a flourish.

As to the standing of the Fugue as piano music, I have some doubts. It seems to me to have organ written all over it, not only because of its longish sustained pedal points, and it also presents some of the problems for the fingers that one might encounter in trying to play an organ work on the piano, from the organ score (ex. 24).

Ex. 24

It would be interesting to hear it on the organ; it reminds me, at times, in its thought, though not in its sound, of Reger's great *Organ Fugue on BACH*, and even of the final one of Schumann's six *Fugues* on the same subject. But the Prelude is as much redolent of the piano as the fugue is, to me, of the organ. The *Prelude and Fugue* together form a masterpiece of musical thought, as necessary to a complete view of its composer as any of the larger works.

4. The *Double Fugue* and *John Dowland's Fancy*

The *Double Fugue* is the largest of Havergal Brian's piano works, almost the length of a symphonic movement not of Brucknerian or Mahlerian proportions; in fact, it is larger than some of Brian's later ones. Not that there is anything in the least symphonic about it. It is pure contrapuntal keyboard music; the argument or discussion produces clashes, as discussions will, but there is nowhere the kind of dramatic conflict with which a symphony is concerned. Unlike the *D minor Prelude* and *D major Fugue*, which are suggestive, the one of the piano, the other of the organ, the *Double Fugue* can live comfortably on either, with very little adaptation, although I believe the piano to be its true home.

Brian has called it a *double* fugue, and in the main it is. It is of the type which states a theme, develops it, states a second, develops that, and combines the two in a final climactic passage. Bach used this scheme at times, in the great *St Anne* Fugue, for instance; Reger almost always when he wrote a double fugue. But Brian's handling of this basic shape is his own, as one might expect. Usually, in a fugue of this kind, the second subject is introduced roughly halfway through the piece, or even later; in other words, the initial subject has at least half the length of the Fugue in which to develop its argument before the second subject appears. Brian's two-bar first subject has 24 bars' development, including the exposition, out of a total for the piece of 257 bars, before the second subject, also two-bar, is announced and developed for 33 bars, whereupon a slow three-bar link, again using second subject, leads to the first combination of the two subjects. So that only 60 of the 257 bars have gone by when Brian reaches what is usually the final stage of a fugue of this type. In other words, the Fugue would seem to have a tail almost four times as long as its body. Obviously, there must be more to his plan - and there is, a lot more. There are certainly hints at the rhythm of the first subject during his development of the second, but they are no more than hints and do not deflect the course of the music in the slightest. Having got the normal course of such a double fugue out of the way in double quick time, Brian begins to expand.

And this brings us to the nature of his subjects. Both are short - two bars; the first, fairly fast, perky and with a strongly marked rhythm.

Ex. 25

It is the kind of subject Reger might have written, though his would almost certainly have been longer; and, indeed, a good deal of the music associated with Brian's theme has the look of Regerian counterpoint, though not the sound, which is the important thing. But, also, that first subject does not suggest that it is capable of producing a piece of the dimensions of this *Double Fugue*. Up to the beginning of the combination of the two subjects, the proportions seem right for a fugue of which this combination is the beginning of a short final phase, whereas little more than a fifth of the actual ground covered has been traversed. It is not too much to say that the real business of the fugue begins now, with the return of the first subject and the beginning of the combination of the two, so that the initial development of the first subject, and that of the second, are by way of being a prelude to the real piece.

One of the reasons why I believe that the first subject does not suggest that it is the starting-point of a large work is that, apart from being short - which would not be reason enough in itself, although it adds weight - it is self-contained melodically; that is, it ends on a long note, in the rhythm of the theme, a whole beat, which stops the flow momentarily. Generally speaking, a composer leaves some leeway at the end of a fugue subject, so that it glides into its own continuation. Bach almost invariably does; and, of course, he is not above slightly altering the end of his subject if it suits him. Brian maintains this rhythmic stop at the end of the first subject almost throughout the piece, only once, near the beginning, splitting the final beat into two quavers. Otherwise, he depends upon movement in other parts to carry the music on, which it does very well. Nonetheless, the rather short-breathed first subject, with its deadstop ending, would have had a hard time projecting a piece the actual size of the *Double Fugue* if it were not for three things. One is the second subject which, in contrast to the first, is smooth and evenly flowing, although the same length, and has provision for easy continuation (ex. 26).

Ex. 26

376 Miscellany

But even this would not have smoothed the growth and progress of a piece this size alone; it is helped by two other items. The first sign that the music is not moving true to form - the form shown in the proportions of the two subjects and their development - is that the "final" stage carries on for far longer than would have been the case if it really were the final stage. There is, in other words, a considerable development of the combined subjects, in which the music moves easily into distant harmonic regions and back again, as should be possible in any good fugue, where clash of actual tonalities is not the object. What this leads to, in its own good time, is a passage of 25 bars marked *Andante*, the first of these two items (ex. 27). Here there are many things to remind us of the first subject, but no statement of it; it is done through likeness of figure and textural growth from this. Brian has drawn out all its inwardness here, largely through the use of the semiquaver groups of the second bar of the subject, projected with smoother writing that grows out of the tied connections used at the end of statements of the subject. In other words, Brian is subtly developing the subject without stating it.

Ex. 27

This leads to an even larger and slower passage of 52 bars (ex. 28), again suggestively using bits of the first subject, starting in E♭ minor, coupled with something that has played no part at all since it was first heard - a bar of descending crotchets which linked the answer (the second statement of the subject, on the dominant) at the outset of the piece to the third appearance of the subject: the fifth bar of the Fugue, in other words.

Ex. 28

Gradually, we get hints of the second subject, and there is also the first subject in inversion, still in E♭ minor. The passage moves and mounts in a calm that is almost awestruck, and the whole 52 bars is one of the greatest imaginative conceptions in the whole of Brian's output.

These two passages lift the whole piece on to an altogether higher plane than the music could have inhabited if it had kept only to the dimensions suggested by its first 60 bars. Eventually, we reach the final stage at the original tempo, and one of Brian's great triumphal conclusions. Music of this kind you will not find in the later symphonies, but there is plenty of evidence that it is the same mind that conceived and carried both to a conclusion. There will never be a surfeit of music of this calibre from any composer.

Chronologically, Brian completed his contribution to solo piano music in 1934, with a delightful lightweight piece, *John Dowland's Fancy*. This was intended to be the first movement of a four-movement suite, but pressure of other work deflected his attention and the rest of the suite was never written down. What prompted this music I do not know; presumably he had an interest in music of the Renaissance and the Golden Age, abroad and in England. He never talked to me much of any music of the past, except Beethoven and Schubert at times; once or twice of Brahms. Otherwise, composers we discussed were either contemporary or of the very recent past: Strauss, Holbrooke, Bantock, Reger and, once, Pfitzner. There is an interesting letter quoted in Reginald Nettel's book, dated March 1924, which includes this sentence concerning the *Gothic* Symphony: "Structurally, it belongs more to Palestrina and our own William Byrd - well, quite as much as the *Tristan* Prelude is a development of a germ or an idea[,] as are the Palestrina and Byrd works". And in another letter, to Walter Allum: "I am not so sure that I don't derive equally as much pleasure *reading* the works of the great Flemish master Josquin de[s] Prés for instance as listening to a Beethoven symphony under Toscanini". I must say that I am not sure what the sentence in the first quotation is meant to say. How the *structure* of works by Palestrina and Byrd could have affected the first three movements, for instance, of *The Gothic* is beyond my comprehension; they could and probably did affect the handling of some of the choral writing, but the sentence as it stands is too sweeping. And I would have thought that any piece of music is the development, in some degree, of an idea. Brian's sentence seems a little incoherent, as though something essential had been omitted; a misprint, even. However, the important thing here is the reference to Palestrina and Byrd; also, to Josquin des Prés. Obviously, Brian was used to reading music of both 15th and 16th centuries, and had, presumably, heard some of it, and no doubt Dowland was one who had caught his interest. I cannot find any actual quotation from Dowland, but certainly, without deserting a style which is definitely his own, however lightweight, Brian has managed to convey a good deal of the atmosphere of this 16th and 17th century composer, rather as Pfitzner, in the wonderful prelude to his opera *Palestrina*, managed to evoke the general atmosphere of the 16th century without writing a bar that was not characteristic of his own musical personality. As the Brian piece gathers weight and moves into more personal writing, after a quiet and restrained beginning, it is not difficult to detect that certain harmonic qualities deeply embedded in Brian's personal style of musical thought may well have been partly shaped by study of 16th century music. The connection may be difficult to hear between, for instance, a late symphony and the music of Dowland or Byrd, Palestrina or Victoria, but this delightful piece provides a clue that is more than slender.

I cannot help regretting that in the years that followed, as Brian's other operas and the later symphonies unrolled themselves, he did not return to the piano to express himself; but the small, in number of items, body of music he left for the piano is still matter for gratitude, including as it does two undoubted masterpieces, and any number of glimpses of the way that extraordinary mind worked.

Piano music forms only a tiny proportion of Brian's output. Yet within this handful of works is one of his most ambitious compositions in any medium - the *Double Fugue in E♭* - together with two substantial *Preludes and Fugues* (in C minor and D minor/major).[3] The unusual choice (for Brian) of piano, together with the presence of a number of impractical passages (particularly in the *Double Fugue*) in which the lines are allowed to diverge well beyond the stretch of normal hands, suggest that these fugues were "paper" compositions, essays in contrapuntal technique for which the piano was used merely for convenience. This view is endorsed by Brian's own explanation that these fugues, along with several small choral pieces in strictly canonic style,[4] were originally conceived without a specific instrument in mind and that they were written "with many similar works (since destroyed) as preliminary studies to my writing the finale of my *Gothic* Symphony" (letter to Robert Keys, 28 January 1946[5]).

---

[3] All these works were published by Augener in 1948 and carry the inscription "Moulsecoomb Sussex 1924".

[4] The surviving pieces from this group are an *Introit* setting of the word "Amen", three canons to words by the 18th century poetess and playwright Hannah More, and a setting of Alexander Pope's *The Dying Christian to his Soul* to which Brian gave a title from the poem's first line, *Vital Spark of Heavenly Flame*. All are strict four-voice canons. The first of the Hannah More canons was published in a musical supplement in *The Musical Times*, June 1969. The remaining works are published by Musica Viva. Although more limited in expression, their closeness to the fugues in time and intent is underlined by the extensive use of canon in the *Double Fugue*.

[5] Robert Keys writes in a letter to the Editor in *Newsletter* 36 (VII-VIII 1981), p. 6: "Just to clarify a little: it was in 1944 that I was in Leamington and the task of running the local music club was thrust upon me for lack of anyone else, whereupon I set to work to try to put together a few more interesting and unorthodox programmes than had previously been the case. I wanted to feature William Baines, whose music I already knew through my piano professor, Frederick Dawson: but what to go with them? At this point, Reginald Nettel's book *Ordeal by Music* came out, and here were two points of contact - I had met Nettel in Leek once in the 1930s and Havergal Brian was a name always of interest since my father had sung in a choir under him, and talked of this 'great musician' - and so it seemed an ideal twinning for the programme. Of necessity it had to be a concert with piano only and Brian was known, if at all then, by

As Malcolm MacDonald has pointed out, Brian's explanation is curious for two reasons. The *Te Deum* finale of *The Gothic* does indeed contain a number of strict *a capella* canonic passages, but no substantial fugal writing as such, unless one counts the imitative treatment of "In te, Domine speravi", which may best be described as a double fugue exposition. Moreover it is far from clear why Brian should have felt the need for preliminary exercises given the small but significant part which fugal style plays in works written before *The Gothic*.[6]

Whatever their workshop origin, there is nothing remotely academic or tentative about the feel of these fugues. Brian's approach to fugue is fervently dramatic, and although the common devices of fugal writing - *stretto*, inversion, augmentation, etc. - are used with assurance and vitality, their role is always subservient to a formal idea which owes nothing to traditional fugal design and which Brian pursues with characteristic single-mindedness.

The individuality of Brian's approach is illustrated by the way he handles his fugue subjects. Instead of building his form around a series of middle entries, he prefers to explore the subject through various kinds of development, often twisting its basic shape and altering its mood almost beyond recognition. The subject is not a source of stability but rather of purposeful insecurity, undergoing during the course of the fugue a transformation which adds to its personality and stature. The triumphant entries which conclude the *D major* and *C minor Fugues* avoid any sense of bombast because they provide a genuine climax to the subject's progress.

This sort of architecture is seen at its clearest in the *D major Fugue* which moves by degrees from clarity and restraint towards an extravagant climax. At first the mood and tonality of the subject and answer remain calm, unfolding undisturbed against a harmonious tracery of counterpoints. The two sections that follow, each marked by an increase in tempo, become progressively more hard-edged and turbulent, the subject distorted in rhythm and finally almost overwhelmed by the accumulating tensions. Significantly the Fugue ends not with a return to the mood of the opening nor with a comfortable re-affirmation

---

orchestral and choral works: so I set to work to find out about any piano music. I finally got in touch with the man himself, receiving a letter from him on 28 January 1946. He must have investigated the Preludes and Fugues - then, as he wrote - still in manuscript and decided to let me use them. They went into my programme on 9 May 1946. I guess the knowledge of my father and conversations with Nettel and Leonard Furnivall must have decided him to trust me with their performance. Further thought brought him to the decision (with a performance, even thought only mine, to back it) to try to get them published. Somewhere in the midst of this I finally got round to paying my first visit to Harrow and played them and other things to him. They were already in process of publication, and it was at this point that he said that whichever came from the publishers first should be dedicated to me. This proved to be the Prelude and Fugue in D. Afterwards we tried to get the BBC to take them on and for this purpose the publishers Augener sent me proof copies to have on hand for the project, but nothing came of it. We lacked Bob Simpson! I only send all this to clear up the one corner about the dedication which may or may not have any bearing on why the Double Fugue was dedicated to Elfreda."

[6] See, for example, the early *Psalm 23* and *By the Waters of Babylon* (both for chorus and orchestra), the fugal middle-section of the *Festal Dance* for orchestra (1908), the fugal coda of *Doctor Merryheart* (1912) and, especially impressive, the opening and closing sections of the "symphonic dance" *Gargoyles* from the Opera *The Tigers* (1917-29).

but with a blazing *Grandioso* which underlines the subject's newly acquired character at the same time as restoring its original shape.

The *C minor Fugue* makes an interesting comparison. Once again the overall movement is from a quiet opening to a vast climax. Here, however, the progression is less obviously linear, the intervening stages being filled out not by a cumulative development of material but by a series of episodes which give an oddly static impression.

As with the *D major Fugue*, the exposition itself gives no hint of the violence to follow, unfolding with quiet authority into an "orthodox"-sounding, four-part texture. Neither mood nor texture have any future however; rising chromaticisms lead swiftly to a series of wrenching shifts of tonality and the music judders towards a crisis. The tensions of this passage are reflected in the following episodes which test out the subject in various guises, juxtaposing straightforward diatonic versions with weird distortions which blur the subject's tonal solidity. For all their sharp dissonances, and the vehemence of the expression marks, these episodes strike one as curiously clinical in effect. It is difficult to know whether their lack of direction was a deliberate feature of Brian's design, or whether he was simply uncertain how to explore the middle ground between the extremes of contrast in the opening statement. The music finally establishes a momentum as the two forces - diatonic and disruptively chromatic - collide in a *stretto* of searing intensity which convincingly "earns" the huge climactic entry of the subject. In contrast to the *D major Fugue*, Brian ends by softening the severity of his design, allowing the music to die away with a gentle reminiscence of the subject.

Taking the Fugue as a whole, it is difficult to say how well this fragmented structure works; certainly there is a temptation for the pianist to impose a sense of forward-motion which I am not convinced was intended. Whatever its problems, however, they pale beside those of the *Double Fugue* which makes enormous demands on the player not only in terms of virtuosity and stamina, but also in the sheer difficulty of making its enormous proportions cohere. At first sight, the work bristles with inconsistencies - expositions unaccountably cut short, *stretti* that lose their way, apparently unmotivated switches of tonality, and in general passages of unmistakable authority alongside much that appears inconsequential.

Once again it is Brian's attitude to his subjects which is the key to the architecture. As before, Brian is at his most conventional and least characteristic in the exposition, a particularly tame affair in the *Double Fugue*. No sooner has the fourth voice entered, however, than Brian kicks over the music's confines - its narrow range of interval and harmony - as if to make fun of the exposition's timid orthodoxy. A subsequent attempt at a "triumphant" clinching of the subject is likewise instantly deflated.

The second subject fares no better. It has hardly been stated before Brian seizes on its potential for imitative development and the music slithers towards a stridently cacophonous version with the subject, in *fortissimo* octaves, in *stretto* and augmentation. A tiny flashback to its original form, *mistico e più lento*, slyly underlines the joke.

Thus far, the piece is not so much a fugue as an anti-fugue, more anarchic than constructive. This instability finds balance, however, at the centre of the work in the two lengthy slow sections in which the music achieves a seamless, beautifully sustained continuity and a mood of profound and passionate seriousness. The link between this music and the outer sections is easier to feel than to define, although one can hear specific similarities in melodic and rhythmic contour. More concrete connections are made by the appearance of the two subjects, combined and inverted, which, chameleon-like, take on the melancholy colour of their surroundings.

With the return of the *Allegro* tempo it is clear that transformation of the Fugue's subjects is taking place. The final development of the first subject takes the form of a thrilling series of *stretti*, a far cry from the note-spinning of some of its earlier manifestations. The end is brilliantly resourceful. Brian avoids either bombast or cliché, rapidly juggling the two subjects through a series of clashing tonalities in a final exuberant display.

What makes Brian's brief flirtation with fugue so fascinating is that one can sense the tensions arising from the self-imposed discipline of fugal composition. Conventionally, fugue suggests qualities of economy and close-knit logic largely alien to Brian's musical personality, with its great virtues of explosive energy and an almost wastefully fertile imagination. In view of this, it is characteristic that Brian's response to the challenge of fugue should have been so uncompromisingly original, and typical that the most interesting and rewarding of the three works - the *Double Fugue* - should also be the most problematical.[7] It is a provoking, perverse sort of piece, always likely to convince some listeners more than others; but whatever its failings, it remains something a great deal more valuable than a mere curiosity.

Rodney Stephen Newton: Havergal Brian and the percussion section: a broad survey[1]

"I suppose you like Havergal Brian's music because of all that percussion!" So said an orchestral player to me recently - and one who had taken part in the 1976 Brian Centenary concerts. My enthusiasm for Brian is certainly not founded on his percussion writing alone, although I must confess that at times he appears somewhat generous with respect to that department. Although by present-day standards his percussion writing is generally conventional, Brian certainly manages in places to put his own individual stamp on his percussion parts.

---

[7] Malcolm MacDonald has conjectured that the dedication of the Double Fugue to Elfreda Brian, the composer's youngest and favourite daughter, may well indicate that Brian had a particular affection and regard for the piece.
[1] From *Newsletters* 13 (IX-X 1977), pp. 2-5 and 14 (XI-XII 1977), pp. 4-5.

Brian's percussion department is basically that of the romantic orchestra of the first half of this century, the orchestra used by Elgar, Strauss, Mahler and to a large extent Shostakovitch. The instruments principally employed are glockenspiel, xylophone, tubular bells, side drum(s), cymbals, castanets, triangle, tambourine, tam-tam, with occasional use of vibraphone, wind and thunder machines and the Indian tabla. In the main, only one set of timpani is used, although that requirement is occasionally raised to two or even three sets. In the operas there are a few passages needing more than one timpanist, but in general these spots could be covered by the percussionists who are resting at these points.

It is with a consideration of Brian's timpani writing that I would like to begin this short study. The instruments in use during the first period of Brian's creative life (i.e. that up to and including the *Gothic* Symphony) were somewhat less sophisticated than those in use today. Pedal-tuned timpani certainly were in use, as were timpani tuned by means of a master screw (and still used by the Vienna Philharmonic), but in this country the preference was generally for timpani tuned by means of five, six or eight hand screws. This ruled out any sudden changes of tuning on each drum, and a lack of standardization in both drum sizes and quality of heads meant that each set had virtually its own individual characteristics. Thus, throughout Brian's work, we find an eminently practical approach to timpani tuning. There is nearly always time to change notes comfortably, and the notes chosen fit, in the main, well within the best working range of each drum. Only in an isolated passage in the *Gothic* Symphony do we find notes crowded in a manner that would work best on pedal timpani.

There are a few instances of notes in the upper register of the timpani being used (top A in Symphony No. 2, top G in the Prelude to *The Cenci* and Part II of *The Gothic*) but nothing like the stratospheric writing of Janáček, for example, is found. At the other end, however, we find Brian frequently employing the low register of the timpani to great effect. In the first half of this century timpani heads were exclusively made from animal hide - calf and goat being the most common - and a distinctive feature of animal heads as against the plastic heads in general use today is a great richness of sound in the lower range of any given drum. Thus composers from Wagner onwards showed great interest in the sombre, funereal qualities of low timpani notes (listen to the low D and E♭ entries in Mahler's Ninth Symphony and observe the way they colour the music with dark thunder-clouds). Brian was obviously acutely aware of this potential and frequently makes use of low notes to give an effect of foreboding. However, with characteristic independence Brian does something quite different from anyone else at the very outset of the *Gothic* Symphony. After a couple of bars of introduction, two timpanists crash out a rhythmic motto - in octaves! (ex. 1)

Ex. 1

This type of writing is quite unique in my experience, and I should be most interested to hear from anyone who can quote a parallel example from any other composer. The effect is of elemental power and force, grasping the listener by the scruff of the neck, as it were. Similarly, the following arpeggio passage seems quite peculiar to Brian, although it may have its origins in Richard Strauss' timpani writing in *Salome* (ex. 2).

Ex. 2

Brian's disposition of notes between his timpanists is sensible and practical - although there are places in Symphony No. 2 where, from my examination of the score, there seems to be some confusion as to which timpanist plays which notes. Perhaps someone involved in the performance of this work might let me know how these problems were resolved. Havergal Brian's admiration of Berlioz caused him not only to emulate the French master in the use of large choral and orchestral forces, but also in the use of timpani as harmonic instruments. The opening of Symphony No. 2 recalls the Berlioz of the *Symphonie fantastique* (exx. 3 & 4).

Ex. 3

Ex. 4

In *The Cenci* there are two entries involving four timpanists (one drum per player). These spots may be played on one set of timpani by the principal timpanist and three other percussionists who are *tacet*. In the first case, however, the players must take up their positions as Beatrice sings 'Am I, or am I not, a parricide?', involving a bit of a scramble over a couple of bars of very quiet music. This, however, is not beyond the bounds of practicality and has a parallel in Ginastera's opera *Bomarzo* - also in a passage involving four timpanists.

Ex. 5

The most striking example of Brian's multiple timpani writing is to be found in Part II of the *Gothic* Symphony. Here the writing (for two orchestral timpanists and four in the additional brass groups) is so individual as to almost call for a separate study. In ex. 5 the low range of the timpani is again exploited together with some showy stick work in the playing of the grace notes. Such writing is quite unique to Brian.

During the period encompassing Brian's later works, pedal timpani complete with plastic heads (affording a wider upper range from standard-sized drums), fine tuning devices and note gauges (ensuring accurate intonation in rapid changes of pitch) established their pre-eminence over the hand-screw models. However, we find Brian ignoring the *glissandi* and scales that were now becoming commonplace in contemporary music. On the contrary, his timpani writing still remained basically simple, showing no desire to return to the flamboyant style of the *Gothic* Symphony. In the main, only one set of timpani is required in the later symphonies - with the exceptions of Nos 22 and 25 which both require two players, the parts still being conservatively written.

The xylophone and glockenspiel appear in all Brian's major works, often in unison, giving a diamond-hard glint to the music. Often the instruments pick out little phrases in the upper lines of the orchestra and sometimes they augment the wind in scale passages (a mannerism found in many of Brian's symphonies).

In addition to these typical ways, for Brian, of using these instruments, the glockenspiel and xylophone are also given many solo passages containing elements of both virtuosity and atmosphere. For instance, the glockenspiel is featured in Symphony No. 8 (ex. 6) and at the opening of Symphony No. 12 (ex. 7), as well as in the highly imaginative music preceding the "storm" in Symphony No. 10 (ex. 8). One could go on for pages giving examples from his *oeuvre*, but I think the above cases give an adequate impression of Brian's feeling for colour in his writing for the glockenspiel.

Ex. 6

Ex. 7

Ex. 8

Brian's xylophonist is frequently allowed to demonstrate his technique in passages demanding the utmost ingenuity in sticking. The following examples illustrate that point, I think:

Ex. 9

Ex. 10

Ex. 11

Such moments - particularly the *Gothic* Symphony extract - have already ensconced themselves in the percussionists' rogues gallery of tricky solos!

Brian's use of the vibraphone, on the other hand, is extremely sparing. A couple of "guest appearances" in Symphonies Nos 21 and 28 are the only appearances of this beautiful instrument in Brian's output as far as I can discover. I find it somewhat remarkable that a composer with such an acute sense of orchestral colour and timbre should have almost ignored an instrument of which he must have been aware for some years. It is a matter for personal regret that no place was found for the vibraphone in passages such as that in Symphony No. 14 where Brian evokes an icy, shimmering atmosphere over a darkly gliding bass line.

Brian uses tubular bells in a number of his works. *The Gothic* has a part in the *Te Deum* for a standard set of chimes, but more often Brian uses just one or two bells. These can be in the normal range (middle C to the F above) or, as in the Seventh Symphony, low bells. In this instance Brian conjures up an image of Strasbourg Cathedral in one of the many works inspired by Goethe. Sometimes, however, Brian's bells can sound like spectres at the banquet, as in Symphonies Nos 25 and 30, where they enter without any warning as if sounding some strange death-knell.

We shall now turn our attention to the untuned percussion instruments - the chief of these being the side-drum. Brian's side-drum parts are, again, of a basically simple nature, relying on elementary rudiments for any ornamentation, but once more he puts his own stamp on his writing for the instrument. It is frequently used in a solo role and also to underline the main instrumental lines, giving fierce rhythmic impetus at times. The peculiarity lies in the fact that Brian insisted that *three* side-drums be used for his works, as against the usual one. Although the effect is often exciting, it does lead to certain problems of balance in performance.

Malcolm MacDonald has described the sound of three side-drums in unison as "heavy" and "penetrating" - and this is so. However, the final result is sometimes so heavy and penetrating that the music is all but obscured. It is perfectly possible to obtain a heavy, threatening sound from a large, deep shell side-drum tuned carefully (an instrument with calf or goat heads and gut snares would be especially suitable) - and a single instrument of this nature might prove perfectly acceptable in symphonies like Nos 20, 21 and 22, where no undue prominence is given to the side-drum. However, I don't think this is the ultimate answer by any means.

There are plenty of Brian works such as the Sixth, Seventh and Eighth Symphonies in which any reduction in the number of side-drums would considerably weaken the overall effect (ex. 12).

Ex. 12

Here, for example, much of the bizarre, funereal atmosphere would be lost with only one side-drum in action. Notice also that Brian is fully aware of the differences in tonal colour obtained by releasing the snare mechanism. This can be done fairly quietly on most modern instruments - although on older models with only a screw to tension the snare, it was necessary to muffle the instrument by placing a handkerchief between the snare and the snare head.

Returning to the "à 3 or not à 3" problem. I think the only satisfactory solution is for both conductor and principal percussionist to use their discretion and musicianship in deciding just when three drums are essential to the overall effect, and when one drum may do. In addition a close ear must be kept on the balance of the drums. From an examination of the scores, it is clear that Brian wrote his side-drum parts with one composite sound in mind - that is, when a *fortissimo* passage occurs, the *resultant* dynamic of the drums must be *fortissimo* - not the *individual* dynamic of each player! Observing this point in future Brian performances may greatly assist in clarifying the general orchestral texture, and allow the principal lines to emerge instead of being submerged under a barrage of sound.

Brian's handling of the other untuned percussion instruments is fairly conventional, although once again *The Gothic* provides a wealth of curious examples of highly original writing, the like of which Brian never repeated, as far as I can ascertain. Chains are prescribed in Part II, as are a thunder machine (Brian did *not* want the tinny thunder sheet that so often occurs and is so ineffectual) and a "bird scare" (i.e. a football rattle - called "scare crow" on p. 184 of the published score!). However, for the vast majority of his works, Brian employs a normal section in the usual manner. Wind and thunder machines turn up in Symphony No. 10, and an Indian tabla in English Suite No. 4, but these are exceptions.

Brian's use of the tam-tam has led me to the conclusion that the instruments in common use today do not quite give the sound that Brian seems to have had in mind. Most of our orchestras use large tam-tams manufactured in Switzerland which give a piercing sound when struck heavily, have considerable sustaining power, but are generally lacking in low harmonics - a deficiency that becomes plain when these instruments are struck softly. From a study of his scores, it would seem that Brian had the darker-toned tam-tams of Eastern manufacture in mind. These instruments (happily still fairly easy to obtain) have less sustaining power than their Swiss counterparts, but give a deep sinister sound when struck softly and produce a far more distinct sound on immediate impact in *fortissimo* passages. This quotation from Symphony No. 9 will serve to illustrate the sort of writing that has led me to this conclusion (ex. 13).

Ex. 13

Brian's treatment of the percussion section as a whole is essentially dramatic. He builds, in places, great blocks of sound with his multiple side-drums, bass drum and tam-tam all rolling togther. His use of the instruments in this manner is reminiscent of Shostakovitch who also favours great waves of sound from his percussion section. This is not to say that Brian is insensitive in his percussion writing - far from it. There are many examples of his use of percussion ensemble passages in the *pianissimo* range. Two good examples are the third movement of Symphony No. 21 (ex. 14) and the second movement of No. 30. In both cases the percussion whirr and click away like some fantastic machine.

Ex. 14

Returning to Brian's louder passages, we come once again across the problem of balance. Over the last 20 years or so the dynamic ranges of most major orchestras have become wider and, with the increase in the size of timpani, drums, cymbals and gongs, it is very easy for the percussion to swamp in passages like the coda to Symphony No. 16. In the recording studio these moments are no problem, but in the concert hall great care must be taken to ensure a correct balance while preserving the dramatic impact.

In the course of this article I have only scratched the surface of the subject under consideration. However, I hope I have at least provided an insight into a significant aspect of Brian's work and perhaps provoked discussion over a few points. Increased public performance will help to bring the problems into focus and provide answers in future years - until then there are so many areas of this fascinating and important composer to study, and I hope this article may encourage other instrumentalists to make a study of Brian from their own standpoint.

The exciting discovery of the manuscript full score of *The Tigers* causes me to amend some of the statements I made in my article. The most astonishing feature regarding the percussion score of *The Tigers* is the use in Act 2 of the vibraphone - two vibraphones to be exact! Previously I made mention of the fact that Brian uses the vibraphone only in a couple of brief instances in his later symphonies - but here we have him employing the instrument only a few years after its introduction.

The vibraphone was invented by a certain Hermann Winterhof of the Leedy Drum Company of America in 1916, and by 1921 the original instrument had been developed into more or less the instrument we know today. However, the vibraphone was not exported to this country much before the 1930s and then was only to be found in the dance band. However, we now have the evidence of Brian's own hand that the opera was completed in July 1929. Moreover, Alban Berg is generally credited with the introduction of the vibraphone into serious music in his opera *Lulu* - but this was not until 1934! How, then, did Brian come across what was at that time a very obscure instrument? I think the answer lies in the fact that much of the early work on *The Tigers* was done in Birmingham where the firm of E. A. Parsons - then one of the world's foremost percussion instrument manufacturers - had its premises. At that time they were in serious competition with Messrs Leedy and would have wasted no time in obtaining details of the latest developments and possibly even constructing their own prototypes. Furthermore, as Ernest Parsons Snr. and his sons, Ernest Jnr. (under whom I studied) and Albert, were all distinguished timpanists and percussionists and close friends of Sir Granville Bantock, they would doubtless have known Brian well in those days.

The part in the opera is given to two players on one line each (one consistently bass and the other treble) and combined with the tubaphone - an instrument consisting of a series of slim metal tubes laid horizontally after the manner of the glockenspiel. It is clear that Brian fully understood the *vibrato* effect and the possibilities of phrasing by using the damper pedal.

In addition to this, my good friend Graham Hatton observes that I omitted to mention Brian's use of the jingles (sleigh bells) in my article. Brian uses this instrument sparingly to give the occasional splash of colour to a passage (again, it is present in the Prologue of *The Tigers*). Readers familiar with the LPO/Fredman recording of *Sinfonia Tragica* will know the arresting sound of the jingles towards the middle of the big "battle" sequence. Brian actually asked for "small un-tuned bells" - but I think the large sleigh bells used on the recording give a pretty fair account of what he meant. Mr Hatton also draws my attention to the ruthe (a switch made of birch twigs used on the bass drum in German military bands, and also by Haydn, Mozart and Mahler) in Brian's *Faust*. I am properly ashamed of this omission, considering my work on Brian's operas. The ruthe (pronounced "roota") is used very briefly but its inclusion is remarkable since it is a peculiarly German device and *Faust* is the most authentically "German" of Brian's stage works.

Christopher J. Kettle: Brian, Mahler, Shostakovitch and Schoenberg: some idle thoughts. With comments by Larry Alexander and Malcolm MacDonald[1]

Martin O'Leary's interesting comparison of some symphonies by Brian and Mahler (*Newsletter* 38 [pp. 224-226 in the present book]) reminded me of a remark I heard seven years ago. In January 1975, still reeling from *Das Siegeslied* at the Alexandra Palace three months earlier, I went to hear Dr Robert Simpson give an illustrated lecture about Brian to the London Symphony Orchestra Club. I was eager to find out as much about Brian as I could, and I was not disappointed; it was fascinating, and Dr Simpson left nobody in any doubt as to the utterly individual character of Brian's music. I was surprised, then, that the chairman, in thanking Dr Simpson, said that he had enjoyed what he had heard of Brian's music because it reminded him of two of his favourite composers, Mahler and Shostakovitch.

This seemed a puzzling remark; it is easy to understand someone finding both Mahler and Shostakovitch congenial, but Brian didn't seem remotely comparable to either. The only superficial similarities I can think of are the commonness in all three of march rhythms and fanfare figures, often highly inventively scored; and the use of (some would say reliance on) the sheer might of the orchestra to overpower rather than to enchant the listener. Mahler liked to use a much expanded orchestra, capable of a weight of sound which he used more sparingly and subtly than Brian, despite his fondness for dramatic gestures; Shostakovitch's orchestra usually sounds enormous, but actually is so only in the Fourth and Seventh Symphonies.[2] All three composers make use prominently of a large per-

---

[1] From *Newsletters* 39 (I-II 1982), pp. 6-7 and 93 (I-II 1991), p. 3. Alexander's comment was first published in *Newsletter* 40 (III-IV 1982), pp. 3-5, MacDonald's is extracted from his article *Symphonia brevis* at the Royal Festival Hall, from *Newsletter* 50 (XI-XII 1983), pp. 2-3.

[2] Martin Anderson writes in a letter to the Editor in *Newsletter* 72 (VII-VIII 1987), p. 2: "Shostakovitch's Seventh Symphony was the subject of much propagandising effort during the Second World War: front cover of *Time*, performances and broadcasts, and so on, all to revive the fighting spirit. The three side drums in its first movement may well have been something new then, and would have been unlikely to escape the attention of Havergal Brian of all people (Vol. 1 of his writings suggests that he had ears as sharp and open as anyone's). When do the oft-noted three side drums enter *his* work? In the Sixth Symphony, written just under 7 years after

cussion section; although the martial, battering sound of Shostakovitch's percussion is closer to Brian, several of Mahler's dramatic or atmospheric percussion effects remind me of Brian: the famous *crescendo* in the Finale of the Second; the brief outburst which ushers in the coda of the first movement of the Sixth; the retreat beaten by "several side drums" in the first movement of the Third; and the fugitive passage in the same movement (a few bars before fig. 13) in which the first attempt to establish the march of Summer fizzles out. The percussion writing of the Fifth Symphony's funeral march also sounds to me quite Brianian; and there are many other instances to my musically inexpert ears - but I probably already deserve to be drummed off this particular field by Rodney Stephen Newton!

All three composers have a mordant and highly individual sense of humour. There may be some similarity between the prankish irreverence of some of Brian's early music and the satirical Shostakovitch of *The Nose*; and there is something Brianish about a man who can produce a deliberately unportentous Ninth Symphony. But the comparison cannot be pressed. We know that Mahler and Shostakovitch were both men in whom high good humour could mask an essential introspectiveness; and in their music we sometimes sense that laughter and anguish travel along the same nerve. Mahler's ironic humour, or "hectic gaiety", often seem conditioned by the question which he posed in the opening movement of the Second Symphony: "Is it all a huge joke?" Laughter can distort; see, for example, a picture contemporary with Mahler's last phase - the *Laughing Self-Portrait* by Richard Gerstl (whose brief but violent impact on Schoenberg is made clear in Malcolm MacDonald's *Master Musicians* book), painted shortly before his suicide at the age of 25.

I have come across none of this in Brian. His humour seems closer to that described by Robert Simpson of Nielsen: "The Sanguine man cares not a fig for the world; difficulties do not deter him, for he has never heard of difficulties; he is full of rude vigour and gusty laughter." Dr Simpson goes on to comment: "There have been very few genuine expressions of the Sanguine in music since Beethoven's 'unbuttoned' mood ... Mahler occasionally tries but is too nervous." Brian is not always convincing when he adopts this tone; but there is a splendidly characteristic sturdiness about his laughter, even when he seems to be laughing things off.

The intriguing thing about Brian and Shostakovitch is, for me, the fact that they were faced with diametrically opposed situations as 20th century artists. Brian, after an auspicious start, had to contend with almost lifelong obscurity; Shostakovitch was dogged by the problems of his public role as composer under a regime which never left him alone to write as he wished. He was too famous; and one wonders how Brian would have fared in his position, and how Zhdanov and his henchmen would have coped with the "awkward cuss". I imagine he would have given them no end of trouble; some symphonies - Nos 4 and 15 for example - might well have earned him the judgement suggested by the critic Felix

---

the composition of the Shostakovitch, with the retro-active instruction that three side drums be used in all his earlier works with a part for one. Coincidence?"

Salten after the first Vienna performance of Mahler's Third - "For that, the man deserves to be locked up for a few years". It is difficult to imagine Brian writing in the required vein of po-faced patriotism to reinstate himself in official favour.

It is probably no accident that the Shostakovitch symphonies which I find most moving and powerful fit no traditional symphonic mould (and have in some cases been dismissed as formal failures), and are characterized by an emotional ambivalence or complexity which is irreducible to a simple statement: the Fourth, Eighth, Thirteenth and Fifteenth. These works show a very different personality from Brian's reacting to the world in which they both lived, and have a Mahlerian intensity of feeling whether the "subject" is war, injustice or personal tragedy - Shostakovitch never seemed quite to shake off Mahler as Brian, early in his career, shook off Strauss. It is quite interesting that the Shostakovitch Fourth was written at the same time as the Brian Fourth and the Vaughan Williams Fourth; all three are violent and disturbing works in a deeper way than the also contemporary Walton First, where the orchestra is required to perform with the agility and ferocity of a Muhammad Ali in his prime. The Shostakovitch, especially the long first movement, is a vast and explosive melting-pot in which the ideas seethe in barely-controlled fury; the Brian delivers its blows with lethal accuracy and crushing force. Of course, there was plenty of violent music about in the '30s, and earlier - Prokofiev, Varèse (whose possible influence on Brian has been noted, especially in the bombardment which shatters *The Gothic*), and so on back to *The Rite of Spring*; but the Brian is uniquely powerful. The dancing of Brian's Jews in the blood of their enemies is far more chilling, for example, than the *allegro giocoso* triumph of Walton's in *Belshazzar's Feast*; and whereas Shostakovitch's war symphonies are graphic - especially the first movement of the *Leningrad* and the two scherzos of the Eighth, which remind me of *The Tigers* and *Das Siegeslied* respectively - Brian's is prophetic. It is risky to tie music to events, unless the connection is obvious (as in the *Leningrad*); imagine trying to make something of the fact that *The Rite of Spring* anticipated the First World War by a year! But *Das Siegeslied* seems to me to be a uniquely momentous work, delivering a message as timeless as it was timely.

We are all sick of statistics to show how extraordinary Brian was, but here are two more for the pile: had Brian died at Mahler's age, he would just have had time to finish *The Gothic*, and had he died at Shostakovitch's age, he would just have finished *Prometheus Unbound*, having written no symphony since *Wine of Summer* (a symphonic tally one-third the size of Shostakovitch's!). What a loss would have been there, and what might Mahler have been writing in the 1940s, or Shostakovitch now?

Martin O'Leary pointed out the extreme contrast in the length of Brian and Mahler symphonies: most of Brian's are no longer than Haydn's or Mozart's, whereas Mahler's are nearly as long (and as eventful) as a film or a football match. Yet length can be an illusion. I can remember feeling a sense of satisfaction and full nourishment after curtain-raiser performances of Haydn 44 or 102; I would have been happy to miss the more "substantial" items which followed on each occasion. Brian is so demanding, and occasionally indigestible, that I can't imagine wanting to hear anything after one of his symphonies, except an immediate repeat performance. The natural analogy for a Mahler symphony is a journey - usually a long and absorbing one; Brian's are more like wrestling with a complex and knotty problem, where different approaches have to be tried, varied or abruptly dropped, and a solution is not always possible - at any rate, not a convincing one. There is an extraordinary density-in-economy: if Schoenberg felt "air from another planet" transforming his music, Brian seems to be trying to deal with matter from another planet. If, as Harold Truscott has memorably suggested, Brian's music went through a Black Hole in the third movement of *The Gothic*, this is perhaps a result: like matter on Jupiter, his later symphonies have a density which gives them weight utterly disproportionate to their size.

The Gothic invites comparison to Mahler by its scale and heroic aspiration. Cardus, taking account of the imperfections of Mahler's Third, quoted Browning - "Ah, but a man's reach should exceed his grasp!" The same might be said in defence of *The Gothic*, if defence is needed. Brian takes as his motto famous words from that key Romantic work, Goethe's *Faust* (a copy of which was always in Mahler's pocket toward the end of his life): their sentiment is more starkly expressed by Louis MacNiece (a translator of *Faust*) in *The Dark Tower*:

> A man lives on a sliding staircase -
> Sliding downwards, remember: to be a man
> He has to climb against it, keeping level
> Or even ascending slightly: he will not reach
> The top - if there is a top - and when he dies
> He will slump and go down regardless. All the same
> While he lives he must climb.

No redemption is offered here. "Immer strebend" - "ever striving" - has become a grimmer business since the death of Romanticism and the new respectability of disillusionment and despair. Romanticism's death-throes come, if anywhere, in that grinding chord near the end of *The Gothic*. But not for Brian the late Mahlerian music of resignation, haunted by a sense of loss: rather a re-engagement of the enemy on new ground. For MacNiece, striving is still noble (though pointless); where Brian goes far beyond Mahler is his ability to gaze, Beckett-like, clear-eyed into the void, and write what he sees. At times in Brian I am powerfully reminded of the loneliness of the two tramps on the road in a terrifying and unfathomable universe in *Waiting for Godot*, or the suffocating darkness which encloses Hamm in *Endgame*, or Winnie buried up to her neck in earth in *Happy Days*. "They give birth astride of a grave, the light gleams an instant, then it's night once more." The only course open to Beckett's characters is to "keep going" as long as possible - not to succumb: that phrase constantly recurs in Beckett's *The Unnamable*, which Berio married to the music of the scherzo of Mahler's Second in the central movemant of his *Sinfonia*. That movement is about the closest Mahler came to what we would call "the absurd", the contemplation of existence as meaningless; and he turned from it with a "cry of disgust" towards his Romantic, quasi-religious apotheosis. Mahler had a horror of this kind of vision, which surfaces in several of his scherzos and culminates in the mocking laughter of the ape among the tombstones in the moonlight in the first song of *Das Lied von der Erde*; he struggled, sometimes frantically, to overcome or suppress it. Brian, in some memorable passages, seems able to confront it.

In the end we are left with the struggle. In Mahler's Sixth, the closest to Brian, it doesn't matter that "nought availeth", and no apotheosis is pasted on. The life-affirming energy with which it is waged survives its own extinction: the negative forces which appear to triumph are somehow neutralized; they lose their sting. For me, the best of Brian's symphonies, from *The Gothic* onwards, provide a similar exhilaration; which is one reason why, in spite of my own quite different standpoint as a committed Christian, they retain their power to absorb utterly, and to move.

One of the things I have been looking forward to reading in the second volume of *Havergal Brian on Music* is Brian's reputedly substantial journalism on Schoenberg. My curiosity was again whetted recently while I was listening to Christoph von Dohnanyi's performance of *Die Jakobsleiter* (part of the "Schoenberg: the Reluctant Revolutionary" festival on the South Bank a little over two years ago). A phrase of The Dying One's vocalize suddenly brought to mind the corresponding passage in the "Judex" movement of *The Gothic*. I say "corresponding", but of course in their contexts these similar dramatic devices function as almost exact opposites. Schoenberg's Dying One breaks into a "purgatorial judgement scene" (MacDonald), and her abandonment of words signals the point at which the Soul soars ecstatically free of the constraints of the body. Schoenberg's Ladder leads upwards - the close of his unfinished cantata quieter transfiguration than Mahler's "Alles Vergängliche" (I am still recovering from one of Tennstedt's recent performances!), but it is at least as moving and effective. Brian's similarly other-worldly soprano, however, breaking into the chorus' anxious mutterings, brings a chill to the music; the sound may emanate from remote regions comparable to those into which Schoenberg's Soul finally journeys, but this cold voice is the spirit of denial, or at least of detachment and distance, instilling fear that the fast-fading splendours of "Te Deum Laudamus" are not to be regained at the work's end. The ensuing march begins the headlong descent to judgement which forms the movement's climax: the direction is exactly contrary to Schoenberg's.

More generally, there are odd parallels and contrasts between Schoenberg's work (1917-22) and Brian's (1919-27). *The Gothic* may well have derived crucial impetus from the Great War; Schoenberg's call-up on the other side, however, prevented him from fulfilling his vision for *Die Jakobsleiter*. Both men proved physically unfit for active service. After the War, Brian was slaving at *The Gothic* while Schoenberg was finding it impossible to complete his work. Schoenberg's original 1917 conception for a "vast religious choral symphony" (MacDonald) would have made the scale and forces of *The Gothic* look almost puny, and would certainly have displaced it in the notorious Guinness publication. After completion, *The Gothic* languished for decades; *Die Jakobsleiter* was never finished, and Zillig's performing version was only made after Schoenberg's death. Both works were eventually first performed in the same year, 1961, in London and Vienna respectively; the first London performance of the Schoenberg followed the year before Boult's *Gothic*.

Malcolm MacDonald, as so often, has put his finger on the really important similarity in his summing-up of *The Gothic* (Volume 1, p. 55): "As Brian's boldest stride into the unknown, it profoundly moves the hearer by its sense of risking all for the realization of a personal vision. This heaven-storming, all-or-nothing quality is shared by very few works of this century: one might mention, for the nearest comparison, Schoenberg's *Jacob's Ladder* and Tippett's *The Vision of St Augustine*. In such works as these, formal perfection is beside the point: it is the intensity of the vision that matters."

I would only add one other odd correspondence. The archangel Gabriel opens *Die Jakobsleiter* with the words: "Whether to right or left, forward or backward, uphill or downhill - you must go on, without asking what lies before you." Dika Newlin *(Bruckner Mahler Schoenberg*, p. 259) describes Gabriel as "the spokesman of the author's own ideas", and his opening command as "a telling statement which has been quoted by Wellesz as typical of Schoenberg's attitude towards life". Eastaugh quotes the following (p. 248; unfortunately without giving any source) as Brian's philosophy during the *Gothic* years, when he was at perhaps his lowest ebb, dogged by failure - the years in which Schoenberg was struggling fruitlessly with *Die Jakobsleiter*: "Go straight on, neither look right, nor left, nor behind. Don't care a damn!"

Speaking of Schoenberg, I went to a splendid BBC Symphony Orchestra Festival Hall concert last October which culminated in a performance of *Erwartung*, and in one of the intervals I made so bold as to approach John Drummond on the subject of programming Brian at the Proms. He was very gracious, but assumed, as so many do, that I meant *The Gothic* (one of those moments when the piece really does seem like an albatross round Brian's neck), dismissing it with the remark "I don't believe in it". He also said that when the BBC put on such pieces, "only people like yourself come to it". I wasn't quite sure how to take that! He was, as I say, very pleasant, but I left him with the distinct feeling that no headway had been made.

Larry Alexander comments:

Christopher Kettle's article on Brian, Mahler and Shostakovitch, which was fascinating, intriguing stuff, calls for comment. To begin with, Kettle's initial reminiscence about the chairman's remarks at the Simpson lecture, Brian's music having reminded him of his favourites, Mahler and Shostakovitch: hardly the first time I've heard similar comparisons from certain music-lovers I've introduced Brian's work to. One friend, for example, immediately classified what I played of the pre-'48 Brian as "heavy into a Mahler trip" and what I played of the post-'48 Brian as "very Shostakovitch". Nor was he alone ... but, I have to say, I found that sort of reaction on the superficial side, similar to what those who dislike, for example, rock music say when they say it all "sounds alike". Kettle is absolutely right when he indicates Shostakovitch's extreme debt to Mahler on a stylistic level: his example of the Russian's Fourth Symphony is about as on-target as they come. Equally I could cite the second movement of Shostakovitch's Fifth. Many times I have by accident found that scherzo playing on my car radio and, even though I know it backwards and forwards as Shostakovitch, leapt to the immediate and ignorant conclusion that it was something by Mahler which had slipped my sieve-like mind.

But I am not sure that Kettle, obviously an appreciator of Shostakovitch's scores, gives him his full stylistic due when it comes to the later work, especially the post-heart attack stuff (mid-'60s to 1975). It has to do, I think, with Shostakovitch's relationship to the commissars throughout his career, with or without the testimony of *Testimony* which if anyone has not read it, they should. Kettle wonders how Brian would have fared with the Zhdanovs, speculating that he'd have given them "no end of trouble" ... as Shostakovitch did, albeit gingerly, with great trepidation, pushing, retreating, pushing, retreating. Until that heart attack freed him, freed him to write whatever he felt: what could they do to him, then?

Up till that point, however, Shostakovitch always fell back into what I call his Mahler mode whenever he went "too far". We have to remember that the composer withdrew his Fourth Symphony not because it was too messy or modern for Stalin's tastes (to be honest, I'm not so sure the great dictator would have liked the piece but I don't think he'd have taken as much umbrage as he did, over it alone), but because of the *Lady Macbeth of Mtsensk* debacle. If anything in Shostakovitch's *oeuvre* is non-Mahlerian, it is the original score to *Lady Macbeth* - maybe I'm crazy, but I hear more Bartók in it, more Stravinsky: it is almost, *almost*, a mainstream Parisian-school work. The proof of the contention is, of course, the Fifth Symphony, Shostakovitch's apology to the "proletariat" for being too "modern" and anti-socialist. As I said, there are times when I can't tell it from Mahler at all!

Later, the same thing. Shostakovitch gets into trouble in 1948 with the "depressing" Eighth Symphony. So: no wonder the Ninth is deliberately lightweight ... and no wonder the Tenth is so Mahlerian (I won't even discuss the Eleventh and Twelfth, which make the programmatic Second and Third sound like the Beethoven Ninth). It's Shostakovitch's gesture to the powers-that-be: so sorry, I got carried away, but I'll go back to being a good boy, you don't have to hit me. While the result may be to make the Shostakovitch Ninth unportentous in a Brianesque way, the motivation doesn't seem to me to be at all the same, and that is a good example of the difference between these contemporaries. Brian in his obscurity had the freedom to thumb his nose at convention precisely because no one knew he was there. Who could he insult or distress? The man didn't, as far as the musical establishment was concerned, exist. That which doesn't exist doesn't make waves. Perhaps if Brian were Shostakovitch he would have made those waves, or perhaps he would have made just so many and then backed off, preferring, as Shostakovitch preferred, to "keep going" in his own guerilla-type way, hitting and running.

Conversely, incidentally, had Shostakovitch been Brian, not too much would have turned out different in terms of attitude. Proof: what Shostakovitch wrote in the last decade or so of his life, when his health gave him the same freedom Brian enjoyed from World War I on, whether Brian wanted to "enjoy" that "freedom" or not. Now the Russian could be bitter, snide, sardonic, acid ... and honest. The Mahler influence is gone. I beg to differ with Mr Kettle on his Fifteenth Symphony. While I agree with him that it is an utter masterpiece, that it has Mahler's intensity of feeling, it is not at all Mahlerian; not in the slightest, quotes from Wagner notwithstanding. What it is is the kind of individual statement that of all other composers only Havergal Brian was capable of making, a kind of detached emotionalism that only comes from the rejected ... or the dying. Mahler's emotionality was of a different sort, I feel: the Austrian was never resigned to anything, especially not the inevitability of his own mortality. Not even in the Cooke-completed Tenth does he ever rise above the battle to give an objective comment. Shostakovitch does in his last quartets and in that Fifteenth Symphony (the first movement is a "toy store" indeed!). Brian does from his Sixth Symphony on. And maybe that's what the people who sense the kinship between Brian and Shostakovitch hear, an extra-musical affinity as opposed to two composers who "sound alike".

Interestingly, one could more effectively trace Mahler's influence to almost the same Shostakovitchian independence in another British composer, namely, Benjamin Britten who, like the Russian, goes from a heavy Mahler sound to a more aesthetic modernism not far removed from Shostakovitch's. Compare the Shostakovitch Fourteenth, say, with Britten's Cello Symphony. I like an awful lot of Britten's work, although not nearly as much as I like Brian's - and I think it comes down to the fact that recognizing Britten's work on the basis of sound alone is not always a possibility, whereas it most certainly is in the case of Brian ... and Dmitri Shostakovitch.

Kettle touches on yet another influence on northern European music of the 20th century outside of the Stravinsky-Schoenberg circles: Denmark's Carl Nielsen. There is Nielsen in Brian, considerable Nielsen, in fact: the opening of the Sixth, much of the Eighth and Tenth, *Elegy* - just around the time of Robert Simpson's discovery of Brian, the latter was taking what Nielsen had done and synthesizing it into his own sound, just as in Sweden Allan Pettersson was in his own special way (talk about composers and their influences: the neurotic Mr Pettersson is one hell of an example! There's Mahler and Nielsen and Shostakovitch and ... on and on. Pettersson, too, has a distinctive style, grating though it might be, overstaying its welcome as it often does - and evolved like the others into something utterly personal, losing the influences along the way). I often wonder what Brian would have thought of Pettersson's gargantuan effusions: I'm not sure he would have reacted well to them and yet he might have come to a grudging sort of acceptance: "I might not like what he says but, well, he says it well enough ...".

Going back from Mr Kettle's article to the editorial "diatribe" on recordings, the fact is that a large measure of the problem is not even the record companies but the public itself - and when I say "the public" I mean the knowledgeable, concert-going segment of society, that minority as compared to the population as a whole, just of Western civilization. A recent review of a Philharmonic concert in New York put the whole thing in a nutshell when it remarked that almost half the audience fled a fairly new 14-minute piece which was not dodecaphonic or atonal: they simply did not wish to experience that which was unfamiliar - it might bite them. Last year a Los Angeles audience hooted at the "Madam, Look!" movement of Shostakovitch's Fourteenth Symphony, walking out in droves because the sound of Russian-language laughter was so alien to them. A large number did it this year with the same composer's Tenth Symphony even before Simon Rattle brought his baton down, not even wishing to try it on for size. Tonal works, both. Beautiful. Original. What we are fighting are closed ears, a goodly portion of the concert-going, record-buying public unwilling to listen to anything after Mahler; not because it can't be hummed but because to learn to like it requires a bit of effort.

Part of the problem stands with the music critics, all of whom were, I'd say, academically trained to the point of brainwashing. In large measure they are all of a certain age and outlook on both sides of the Atlantic. Stravinsky is good, Shostakovitch is not so good, Oliver Knussen is terrific, Havergal Brian is unknown. "Unknown" is its own reward as far as these taste-makers are concerned: there has to be a "reason" a composer is unknown, and that reason can only be that he has nothing to offer, nothing to say, no originality (that they can hear!) and even to sit through one piece is a time-waster. Well, you keep reading stuff like that week in and year out and you foster an attitude in the attendees. Unknown is no good, period. It goes with the feeling that most people have on the worth of any sort of material, be it music, art, or writing: if it isn't bought it isn't anything. If a large professional concert organization or a large professional record company is not willing to do it it isn't of consequence ... and even if they do make a tentative step does it matter if nobody wants it anyway? Thus the proverbial vicious circle.

I wish I knew a way to break the ring, but I don't. The letters I write seem to get me no real progress, only a kind of grudging acknowledgement. Yes, yes, but no thanks. Can't afford it. We'll talk to our guest conductors. What do they know? Have any of them ever sat down and listened to a tape or a record (if any) or asked for a score? Last January after a Pettersson concert in New York I conversed briefly with Sergiu Comissiona on the possibility of the American or Baltimore Symphony Orchestras performing any Brian. "Ah" he said. "Brian. *The Gothic*, yes!" But Comissiona isn't going to do *The Gothic* in Baltimore, or even in New York - and he also isn't going to do any other Brian work either. He's got his composer to champion in Pettersson ... who had the great good fortune late in his unfortunate life to get himself the backing of no less than the management of the ABBA soft rock group in Stockholm.

This is what Brian needs: one conductor, one backer. An angel, to use the Broadway term, to publicize, to perform, to raise money and use his influence. Sir Charles Mackerras might have been that person, but I think he's too engrossed in Janáček at the present to really devote the time and commitment. Look among the young up-and-coming conductors, then: find the Levine or the Rattle or whoever who is attached to an orchestra and who has the programming clout, someone who doesn't just give Brian's music lip-service, but who really adores it and wants to promulgate it. All I know is that very few people in America, at least, were prepared to sit through a symphony by that post-Wagnerian derivative, Mahler, until Leonard Bernstein (no less) got up one hour on *network* television and lectured and played excerpts. All of a sudden everyone involved with music wanted to hear more - having not given Mahler their attention, no, but Leonard Bernstein. That was the draw. Mahler was incidental ... until Bernstein opened their ears.

I cannot believe that, within a reasonable period of time, a well-known conductor won't come along to be Brian's champion, to do for Brian what Bernstein did (in America) for Mahler. On the other hand, the fact is that I can believe it all too well. Life is not fair, and Brian isn't the only good composer out there that no one of "importance" has heard.

Malcolm MacDonald comments:

(...) Arnold Schoenberg, whom one might have expected to be a fanatic for exactitude in these matters, actually went so far as to propose that there should be such a thing as a "first performance tempo" for most contemporary music, including his own. This tempo might be considerably slower than the composer's metronomic ideal, but should be chosen to enable the players to get the largest possible proportion of the notes right, and the conductor to obtain correct balance and maximum clarity of texture. Only when these paramount objectives had been achieved could the performers gradually work up the speed in subsequent performances, as familiarity with the music bred greater confidence and dexterity. He himself demonstrated the effectiveness of this concept in Vienna in June 1918 with a historic series of ten public rehearsals of his First Chamber Symphony - not an "atonal" or serial or even particularly new score but, like Brian No. 22 [*Symphonia Brevis*], a tonal work of considerable contrapuntal density which had yet to receive a completely satisfactory performance. (...)

It's generally realized by now - even by professional music-critics - that Schoenberg's music, be it tonal or "atonal", demands to be listened to with the most exacting attention, for the reasons outlined in Berg's classic essay *Why is Schoenberg's Music so Difficult to Understand?* (1924), which takes as its example ten bars of the securely tonal but rigorously polyphonic First String Quartet. This degree of attention needs to be extended equally to Havergal Brian, whose artistic aim was never merely to comfort our ears with Elgarian opulence, RVW-style pastoral, Delian chromatic languor or Baxian Celtic twilight. Those content to let music "wash over them" will always find Brian dissatisfying, for his purpose is to engage the mind.

Interestingly enough, the *Symphonia Brevis* displays to me some strong (and presumably wholly coincidental) affinities with the aforementioned Schoenberg Chamber Symphony,[3] not only in its polyphonic elaboration but in the nature

---

[3] Brian knew much Schoenberg (cf. Vol. 3, ch. 25), very likely including the Chamber Symphony, although I have found no specific reference to it in his writings. But the similarities I mention here are of a piece with Brian's other music, and do not to my mind suggest any direct "influence". The Schoenberg was originally composed for 15 solo players not only for maximum

and fluidity of its materials. Both works are dominated by a boldly rising figure, Schoenberg's being his famous chain of perfect 4ths (ex. 1 a), while 4ths both perfect and augmented are the chief intervals of Brian's figure (ex. 1 b). Brian, though, is far readier to alter his theme's intervallic content at many junctures throughout the symphony.

Ex. 1 a

Ex. 1 b

One of Schoenberg's contrasting themes is closely paralleled by the main contrasting idea of Brian's first movement (exx. 2 a & b), which is also capable of being radically reworked (ex. 2 c).

Ex. 2 a

Ex. 2 b

Ex. 2 c

In both works, the "seamless" contrapuntal flow is partly counterbalanced by less "active" passages in which chordal ideas are built up note by note, the emerging harmony keeping the tonal argument on the move (ex. 3 a: Schoenberg; ex. 3 b: Brian - and cf. also the wonderful example of this between figs 12 and 13).

---

clarity but as another practical concession to the limitations of the average orchestral player of its time (1906). However, the fact that he *twice* made alternative versions for full symphony orchestra shows that he thought its level of polyphonic involvement quite appropriate for any large orchestra good enough to handle it; and of course his later orchestral compositions are clearly based on the same assumption.

Ex. 3 a

Ex. 3 b

There are, of course, certain further parallels in the highly compressed portmanteau-forms of the two works: but all this is merely to reinforce my point that Brian's music demands concentration as complete as that customarily afforded by listeners to Schoenberg; and that until newspaper critics are prepared to listen with their ears and brains rather than their prejudices, we need not be unduly surprised by the sights that greet our eyes on the review pages. Some of them - and, if you'll excuse a personal remark, some of *you* - still don't really think much of Schoenberg, after all. Whereas Brian, as far back as 1931, thought him "probably the most accomplished musician living".

Robert Simpson: The Brian revival[1]

In the early 1950s Havergal Brian, if he was thought of at all, was supposed to be some kind of megalomaniac eccentric, largely due to the mythical *Gothic* Symphony, which few had seen but many had reproached at their prompting. Some of the few had looked at the score and made crushing reports for the BBC. When I joined this majestic organization in 1951 it was in innocence of this that I thought to take advantage of the facilities to investigate a number of "neglected" composers of whom I had heard but with whose work I was largely unfamiliar. Some were foreign, some British; among them was Brian. The Eighth Symphony

---

[1] From *Newsletter* 52 (III-IV 1984), p. 2.

was the first thing of his to reach my desk; it was so impressively original that I at once sent for the reports on any other Brian works that had been submitted to the BBC, going back as many years as possible. These included some of the earlier symphonies, among them *Wine of Summer*. The reports proved consistently negative and sometimes derisory, especially about the comically saurian *Gothic* Symphony. This work I had seen once some years before, but only briefly, and I now wondered if the composer of the Eighth Symphony could ever have perpetrated so grotesque a folly. A proper study of the giant score made it clear that some of my most respected colleagues had missed something (it should be added that these were mostly not BBC colleagues - the reading panel in those days consisted entirely of distinguished "outside" musicians). So I set about trying to get the matter put right.

The first thing to do was to get No. 8 played; Adrian Boult as always was willing, and did it characteristically better than most first performances. It attracted serious attention, and so began the long process. At that time Brian was composing his Tenth Symphony, so the process in part consisted of trying to catch up with him. Making up the backlog tended to come afterwards, since the later works, being on the whole smaller, were easier to get into programmes. It was also (and still is) my feeling that the symphonies between *The Gothic* and *Das Siegeslied* were transitional, that their inconsistencies would prove more interesting in the light of later developments. *Das Siegeslied* would have to wait until its enormous difficulties and cost could be broached. Since no one else would volunteer, I had to make the decisions - and to cajole funds for the projects.

The purpose of looking at all these "neglected" composers was not to find causes to champion; it was to improve my education and largely to find out, so far as my own judgement permitted, if injustices had been done. In all cases except Brian's I had to agree with the neglect; as Tovey said, time is not wall-space. You can exhibit fifth-rate painters without too much waste, but time, which music must illuminate, cannot be wasted, and only a small proportion of music is worthwhile; in this field we are the more compelled to discriminate. There is a danger in thinking that if a composer is neglected he is likely to be something special! Even so, we must find out - both advocacy and rejection should come from knowledge, not hearsay, and it is in any case the duty of a public body like the BBC to give the listener, within obvious limits, the chance to judge for himself; most listeners can't read scores and their only means of judging is through the ear. And it's the listener's right to ask for it and to receive a sensible, fair reason for non-compliance.

Even for a professional, score-reading can be difficult, especially if the music is complex and, as in Brian's case, original. Complexity itself is hard to auralize from the paper; no one but a sight-reader with a phenomenal technique could cope with, say, Sorabji's *Opus Clavicembalisticum*. I pored for years over this music, only gradually synthesizing the sounds in my head. Even then it was impossible to gauge whether the music, as a whole, possessed the power of suggestion that makes all great music look beyond itself, signify dimensions greater than its physical size. This is something you can perceive only after the sound itself can long be taken for granted. Eventually hearing it (admittedly in a performance littered with wrong notes and seriously wanting in considered observant faithfulness, recorded unwisely at a public recital when it should have been carefully done with a good microphone balance in studio conditions to allow accuracy in the playing as well as clarity in the musical meaning) it so happened that I was disappointed but not altogether surprised to find that far from suggesting more than itself, the vast work seems obsessively ingrowing. Even so, this impression could be dispelled by a better performance in better conditions - though the Devil knows how difficult it is!

What has this to do with Brian? It underlines the fact that his orchestral scores are notoriously difficult to read, and that their performance is equally so. In fact, orchestral first performances are nearly always bad, as many composers have reason to rue. Economics brutally limit rehearsal and an orchestra normally sees an unfamiliar work for the first time a day or two before the performance, which becomes a tightrope act of more or less success, a purely physical, not an artistic, achievement. Only when a composer's idiom is rooted in the minds of musicians can they perform him properly, putting technical problems in their place and adding the essential spark that comes from their own considered and spontaneous responses to the music itself. So there is still a long way to go before Brian's best work is assimilated; in the meantime it has been satisfying to find his cause adopted by so many fine champions, notably Malcolm MacDonald with his remarkable volumes on the symphonies, written with the kind of insight and enthusiasm that make the reader want to hear the music. Like all pioneers in such fields he will find disputants and will no doubt change his own mind on some things - but I am certain that Havergal Brian himself would have been both fascinated and delighted to have evoked such advocacy. It has also been a pleasure to watch the growth and activities of the Havergal Brian Society, with its remarkable achievements - it is lucky to possess so lively and imaginative a nucleus, the secret of all successful movements. There's still a long way to go, and it's possible that Brian will never be a "popular" composer; but at his best he is durable. That is better than becoming the centre of a vogue, the sure sign of eventual collapse, and steady, discriminating support for his music will make sure that Brian is always there. In the long run the occasional good performance is better than a rush of bad ones, which can do untold damage. There are some formidable composers who rarely stand in the limelight but who will always be returned to - Busoni, Reger, Pfitzner, Alkan and some more - Brian I think will belong to this perennial band.

Catalogue of works by Havergal Brian*

Dates are those of composition, quoted from the manuscripts when these were available, otherwise deduced from printed scores, from Havergal Brian himself, or from his letters. Location of MSS., first performances and a discography have consciously been omitted due to the following reasons: several manuscripts are on loan at the Royal College of Music, this may change at any time; a current discography can be found on the Havergal Brian Society internet website, and for the first performances one needs not only thorough research (on the orchestral music already done by Lewis Foreman) but there would still be immense gaps in knowledge.

c. 1892
Canadian Boat Song, song (Anon.=David Macbeth Moir?) (lost)

?1895-6
Anthem, for chorus (text unknown) (lost)

c. 1899
Songs:
   I Shot an Arrow (Longfellow) (lost)
   Wanderer's Night Song (Goethe, trs. Henry Morley) (lost)
   Today and Tomorrow (Gunby Hadath) (lost)
   A second Gunby Hadath song, title unknown (lost)
Requiem for baritone, chorus and orchestra (lost)

1900-2
Tragic Prelude, for orchestra (lost)

c. 1902
Pantalon and Columbine, for small orchestra (original version) (lost)
   later incorporated in English Suite No. 1 as mvts. II and III

1903
Burlesque Variations on an Original Theme, for orchestra   (dur. 28'30")
   Theme and Variations I-VII
   Hartshill, Stoke-on-Trent, 'composed Spring and Summer 1903, completed September 1903'

?1903-4
Legende, for orchestra (lost)
Shall I Compare Thee to a Summer's Day? part-song for SATB (Shakespeare)
(Movements of a) *String Quartet* (lost)
English Suite No. 1, for orchestra   (dur. 25'30")
   I. Characteristic March. II. Valse. III. Under the Beech Tree. IV. Interlude. V. Hymn. VI. Carnival

1904
For Valour, concert overture for orchestra (first version lost, revised 1906)   (dur. 12'30")

Psalm 23 for tenor, SATB chorus and orchestra
   full score lost, reconstructed 1945 (dur. 15'30")

1905
By the Waters of Babylon, for baritone, SATB chorus and orchestra   (dur. c.25')
   revised 1908-09; vocal score published, full score lost; available in arrangement by Gillian Ward Russell (1974) with organ accompaniment
Stars of the Summer Night, part-song for SSAA TTBB (Longfellow)

1904-6
Three songs for contralto or baritone and piano:
   Sorrow Song (Daniel)
   The Message (Donne) (perf. 1905)
   Farewell (Heber) (perf. 1905)
Hero and Leander, symphonic poem for orchestra (score lost by Sir Thomas Beecham)

1906
(Four) Songs for tenor and piano (Cumberland):
   Day and Night
   When I lie Ill
   If I could Speak
   Another song (lost)
   Stoke-on-Trent, Jan. 1906
Songs:
   Soliloquy upon a Dead Child (Cumberland)
   Stoke-on-Trent, 6 Feb. 1906; rev. 1972 as *Little Sleeper* (Hafiz, trs. Richard Le Gallienne), for tenor or soprano and piano
   A Faery Song, for mezzo-soprano and piano (Yeats)
   Stoke-on-Trent, 3 July 1906
Part-songs:
   Soul Star, lullaby for SATB (Helen Bantock)
   earlier version to text by Philip Marston, lost
   Lullaby of an Infant Chief, for SATB (Scott)
   Come o'er the Sea, for SATB (Moore)
   Cradle Song, for SATB (Yeats)
   In a Fairy Boat, rondel for SSAA (Weller)
   Tell me, thou Soul of Her I Love, for SATB (Thomson)

---

* From *Newsletter* 37 (IX-X 1981), pp. 6-9. Prepared by Lewis Foreman in 1974, revised by Adrian Ure (*Newsletter* 93, I-II 1991, p. 5-6) and Malcolm MacDonald, 30 September 1981 and 15 May 1990 (*Newsletters* 35, V-VI 1981, p. 2, 43, IX-X 1982, p. 2, 51, I-II 1984, p. 3, 94, III-IV 1991, p. 7-9 and 100, III-IV 1992, p. 3) and by Lewis Foreman, Malcolm MacDonald and Jürgen Schaarwächter for the present edition. Wilfrid Chadwick gives additional information in his Investigations Officers' Reports, as does David J. Brown concerning the *The Tigers* rediscovery, in *Newsletter* 14 (XI-XII 1977), pp. 1-3 (with a reply by Harold Truscott in *Newsletter* 15, I-II 1978, p. 2). For published scores, cf. Reginald Nettel, *Havergal Brian and his Music*, pp. 205-214 (work-list by Lewis Foreman).

Twilight, for SATB (Longfellow) (lost)
Carmilhan, dramatic ballad for soli, chorus and orchestra (Longfellow) (lost)

c. 1906-7
Let God Arise (Psalm 68), for soli, chorus and orchestra (lost)

1907
Work for cello and piano (perf. Hanley and London, 1907) (lost)
Fantastic Variations on an Old Rhyme, for orchestra (originally first movement of *A Fantastic Symphony*) (dur. 11'30")
Stoke-on-Trent, Aug.1907, rev. 1912
Scherzo and Slow Movement, for orchestra (middle movements of *A Fantastic Symphony*) (lost)
The Vision of Cleopatra, tragic poem for SMsAT soli, SATB chorus, SATB semi-chorus and orchestra (Cumberland) (dur. c. 50')
Stoke-on-Trent, 7 July 1907; vocal score published, full score lost

1908
Festal Dance, for orchestra (originally fourth movement of *A Fantastic Symphony*) (dur. 6'30")
Stoke-on-Trent, Aug. 1908
Fairies' Song, part-song for SSAA (Cumberland) earlier version to text by Philip Marston, lost

1908-9
Humorous Legend on Three Blind Mice, for orchestra (rev. in three movements of *A Fantastic Symphony*) (lost)
Work for chorus and orchestra (Scott) (lost)
The Soldier's Dream (Campbell), for orchestra or voices and orchestra (lost)

1910
In Memoriam, tone poem for orchestra (dur. 20')
Trentham, 27 October 1910
Songs:
   Why dost thou wound and break my heart? for tenor and piano (Herrick)
   Stoke-on-Trent, 3 Jan 1910
   The Night Piece, for tenor and piano or orchestra
   Stoke-on-Trent, 6 Jan 1910; orchestral score lost
Daybreak, part-song for SATB (Longfellow)

?1910
The Mad Maid's Song, for mezzo-soprano and piano or orchestra (Herrick)
Stoke-on-Trent, 3 Jan. 1910; orchestra score lost

1911-2
Doctor Merryheart, Comedy Overture No. 1
Trentham, 1911-12 (dur. 17'30")
Three Herrick Pieces, for SSAA and orchestra:
   Go, Happy Rose (lost, probably destroyed by composer)
   Requiem for the Rose (dur. 9'30")
   The Hag (dur. 2'30")

1912-3
Pilgrimage to Kevlaar, ballad for chorus and orchestra (Heine, trs. Todhunter) (lost)

1914
The Maiden and the Flower Garden, children's operetta for voices and piano (Cumberland) (lost)
Three Dances, for small orchestra, arranged from *The Maiden and the Flower Garden* (lost)
Songs: (unison songs incl. piano):
   The Blossom, for voice and piano (Blake)
   The Mountain and the Squirrel, unison song for children (Emerson)
   The Little Black Boy, unison song (Blake)
   The Chimney Sweeper, unison song (Blake)
   Piping Down the Valleys Wild, unison song (Blake)
   The Lost Doll, for voice and piano (Kingsley)
   What does Little Birdie Say? for voice and piano (Tennyson)
   The Fly, unison song (Blake)
   Robin Redbreast, unison song (lost)
Part-songs:
   Grace for a Child, for SA and piano (Herrick)
   Ye Spotted Snakes, for SSAA (Shakespeare)
   He was a Rat, for SATB (Anon.)
   Summer has come, Little Children, for SA and piano (Cumberland)
   Goodbye to Summer, for SA (Allingham)
   The Lamb, for SSA and piano (Blake)
   And will he not come again? for SSAA and piano (Shakespeare)
   The Moon, for SA and piano (Cumberland)
   The River, for SA and piano (Cumberland)
   The Little Boy Lost, for SA and piano (Blake)
   The Little Boy Found, for SA and piano (Blake)
   If I had but two Little Wings, for SA and piano (Coleridge)
   A Song of Willow, for SSA and piano (Shakespeare)
   The White Lily, for SSAA and piano (McDonald)
   Violets, for SSAA and piano (Herrick)
   Laughing Song, for SSAA and piano (Blake)
   Infant Joy, for SSAA and piano (Blake)
   Pastoral: the Shepherd, for SSA and piano (Blake)
   Spring - Sound the Flute, for SSA and piano (Blake) (also arranged for SA and piano)
   The Dream, for SSA and piano (Blake)
   The Echoing Green, for SSA and piano (Blake)
   A Child's Prayer, for SA and piano (M. Betham-Edwards)
   The Knight's Leap (part-song?) (lost)
   A Gipsy Song, for SSAA (Ben Jonson) (lost)
   Clown's Song (Shakespeare) (lost)
   The Legend of Altenahr, for male voices (lost)
   Marching Along (part-song?) (lost)
   The Sweetest Dream (lost)
   The Owl, for female voices (lost)
   Will You Buy any Rope? (lost)
   Sympathy (part-song?) (lost)

Hie upon Hielands, for male voices (trad. Ballad) (lost)
The Sands of Dee, for SATB (trad.) (lost)
Love's Remorse (part-song?) (lost)
Meg Merrilies, for male voices (Keats) (lost)
The Curate and the Mulberry Tree (part-song?) (lost)
Red May, military march for orchestra (lost)

1915
English Suite No. 2, *Night Portraits*, for orchestra (lost)
  I. Processional. II. Carnival. III. Requiem. IV. Witch Dance. V. Passing of Night. VI. Recessional
Part-songs:
  The Fairy Palace, for SSA and piano (Drayton)
  O Mistress Mine (part-song?) (Shakespeare) (lost)
Legend, for orchestra (lost)
Short orchestral work, title unknown (companion piece to *Legend*) (lost)

1916
Razamoff, symphonic drama for orchestra (unfinished, lost)
Three Illuminations, for piano
  I. The Boys and the Pastille. II. The Butterfly's Waltz. III. Venus and a Bobby
  arrangement for orchestra: *Three Comedy Dances*, for orchestra (lost)

1917-29
The Tigers, burlesque opera in prologue and three acts (libretto by the composer) (dur. c. 180')
Prologue: Scene I, Hampstead Heath. Scene II, Wild Horsemen (leading to Pantalon and Columbine). Act I: Scene I, "Drop curtain suggesting row of houses in a street". Scene II, "Approach to a large Railway Station". Act II: Scene I, Midnight. Scene II, Military Parade Ground. Scene III, Woodland scenery; time - noonsunshine. Scene IV, Promenade and Dance. Scene V, Military Parade Ground. Act III: Ballet (on a Cathedral Tower): I Gargoyles II Lacryma (Tears of Sorrow). Scene I, Night. Interior of a Police Station. Scene II, Approach to a Stone River Bridge. Scene III, Mont Duresco in background. Clock tower in foreground (leading to Finale) scene as before. Time - Midnight. "The design of this Finale is an approach from dead silence to mad tumult."
Composed 1917-19, orchestrated 1928-29. Originally known as *The Grotesques*. Vocal score published 1932. New orchestration of part of Prologue 1969
Subsidiary works (for concert performance):
Symphonic variations on "Has Anybody here seen Kelly?" (from Prologue, Scene I)
Symphonic dance *Wild Horsemen* (from Prologue, Scene II)
Symphonic dance *Green Pastures* (from Act II, Scene IV)

Symphonic dance *Gargoyles* (from Act III, Ballet)
Symphonic dance *Lacryma* (from Act III, Ballet)
Shadow Dance (from Act III, Scene III)
These six items (total dur. 55') are all slightly reworked from the opera, and were arranged in 1921-22 before the rest of the opera was orchestrated.
Fanfare from *The Grotesques*, piano score only, published in *Fanfare*, 1 (5) (1921), p. 91

1918
When the Sun Goes Down, three songs (Temple Keble)
  I. When the Sun goes down. II. On Parting. III. Love is a merry game
The Soul of Steel, song for voice and piano (Blake)
The Phantom Wooer, part-song for SATB (Beddoes)
Two Scenas, for baritone and piano or orchestra (C. R. Barber) (lost)

1918-9
Songs:
  Renunciation, for medium voice and piano (Temple Keble)
  Lady Ellayne, for medium voice and piano (Keble)
  The Defiled Sanctuary, for medium voice and piano (Blake)

1918-20
Four miniatures, for piano   (dur. 9'30")

1919
Tales of Olden Times, three pieces for small orchestra
  I. The Evicted Tenant. II. The Blind Girl. III. The Old Coach
  lost, probably destroyed by composer
Songs:
  The Land of Dreams, for voice and piano (Blake)
  The Birds, for voice and piano (Blake)
  When icicles hang by the wall, for voice and piano (Shakespeare)
  Care-charmer sleep, for voice and piano (Daniel)
  Ah! County Guy! serenade for equal voices (Scott)
  The Poet's Dream, for voice and piano (lost)
  On a Poet's Lips I Slept (Shelley) (lost)
  Music when Soft Voices Die (Shelley) (lost)
  Call for the Robin Redbreast (Webster) (lost)
  Sonnet: My Lute, for voice and piano (Drummond) (lost)
  Hymn to Diana, for voice and piano (Ben Jonson) (lost)
Part-songs:
  Pack Clouds Away, for SSA and piano (Heywood)
  Absence, for SSAA (Anon.)

Under the Greenwood Tree, for SSA (Shakespeare)
Spring, the Sweet Spring, for SA (Nash)
It was a Lover and his Lass, for SSA (Shakespeare)
Fear no more the Heat of the Sun, for SATB (Shakespeare)
Mine be a Cot Beside the Hill, for SA and piano (Rogers) (lost)
Fair Pledges of a Fruitful Tree, for SA and piano (Herrick)
To Daffodils, for SA and piano (Herrick)

?1919
Legend, for violin and piano (dur. 6'30")

1919-21
English Suite No. 3, for orchestra (dur. 18')
   I. Ancient Village. II. Epithalamium. III. Postillions. IV. The Stonebreaker. V. Merry Peasant (completed 5 May 1921)
   Also piano version (lost)
A Wish, for two voices and piano (lost)

?Early 1920s
Buster Keaton Overture, for orchestra
   sketched, unfinished, material incorporated in other, undetermined, works

1921
Full Fathom Five, part-song for SSAA and piano (Shakespeare)

1922
Songs:
   Since Love is Dead (Bowles)
   I Know, and You! (Bowles) (lost)
   Go Happy Rose, for voice and piano (Herrick) (lost)
   A proposal (lost)
   The Twilight House (Bowles) (lost)
   Far from Thee (Taylor) (lost)
   Stars of Destiny (lost)
   Where Shadows Flee (lost)

1924
Introit Amen (sic.), for SATB
Choral canons:
   O Happiness, Celestial Fair, for SATB (Hannah More)
   Sweet Solitude, for SATB (More)
   Shall I then be Spared?, for SATB (More)
   Vital Spark of Heavenly Flame, for SATB (Pope)
Double Fugue in E♭, for piano (dur. 15')
   "Moulsecoomb, Sussex, 1924"
Prelude and Fugue in C minor, for piano (dur. 8'30")
   "Moulsecoomb, Sussex, 1924"
Prelude and Fugue in D minor and major, for piano
   "Moulsecoomb, Sussex, 1924" (dur. 9'30")

?1924
English Suite No. 4, *Kindergarten*, for orchestra
   I. Thank You. II. Where is he? III. Something or Nothing. IV. The Man with a Gun. V. Jingle. VI. The Lame Duck. VII. Gentle Bunny. VIII. Death of Bunny. IX. Ashanti Battle Song (dur. 14')

1925
Take, Oh Take those Lips Away, song for voice and piano (Shakespeare)
Part-songs:
   Blow, Blow thou Winter Wind, for SATB (Shakespeare)
   Come Away, Death, for TBarB and piano (Shakespeare)
   Mine be a Cot Beside the Hill, for SA and piano (Rogers)

c. 1926
Songs:
   At Candlelight (Gunby Hadath) (lost)
   Without You (Hadath) (lost)
   Song of Betrayal (Hadath) (lost)

1919-27
Symphony No. 1 (formerly No. 2) in D minor, *The Gothic*, for SATB soli, SATB choirs, children's chorus, four brass groups, and large orchestra (*Te Deum* text) (dur. 105')
   Part I: I. *Allegro assai*. II. *Lento espressivo e solenne*. III. *Vivace*. Part II: IV. *Allegro moderato* ("Te Deum Laudamus"). V. *Adagio molto solenne e religioso* ("Judex Crederis"). VI. *Moderato e molto sostenuto* ("Te Ergo Quaesumus")

1930-1
Symphony No. 2 (formerly No. 3) in E minor, for large orchestra
   I. *Adagio solenne - allegro assai*. II. *Andante sostenuto e molto espressivo*. III. *Allegro assai*. IV. *Lento maestoso e mesto* (dur. 48')
   completed 6 April 1931
The Battle Song, symphonic poem (short score), evidently for brass band
'1930-31'

1931-2
Symphony No. 3 (formerly No. 4) in C♯ minor, for large orchestra
   I. *Andante moderato e sempre sostenuto e marcato*. II. *Lento sempre marcato e rubato*. III. *Allegro vivace*. IV. *Lento solenne* (dur. 53'30")
   completed 28 May 1932

1932-3
Symphony No. 4 (formerly No. 5) in C major, *Das Siegeslied*, for soprano solo, SATB choruses, and large orchestra (Psalm 68) (dur. 48')
   I. *Maestoso*. II. *Lento*. III. *Allegro (bewegt)*
   completed 10 December 1933

?1933
Prelude, for soprano and double chorus
   lost; almost certainly a creation of typographical error

1934
Concerto for violin and orchestra (short score only) (lost)

John Dowland's Fancy, prelude for piano(dur. 3'30")
   First mvt. of projected, unfinished *John Dowland Suite*. The three further mvts. were never written down

1935
Concerto in C major for violin and orchestra
   I. *Allegro moderato*. II. *Lento*. III. *Allegro fuoco*
   A new work, completed 8 June 1935, based on some of the same themes as the lost *Concerto* of 1934 (dur. 38')

?1935
Work for organ, title unknown (lost)

1937
Symphony No. 5 (formerly No. 6), *Wine of Summer*, in one movement, for baritone solo and orchestra (Lord Alfred Douglas) (dur. 21') completed 18 June 1937

1937-44
Prometheus Unbound, lyric drama for SSSSSSSMs MsMsAAAAATTTTTBarBarBBB soli, SATB choirs, SATB semi-chorus, SSAA semi-chorus, and very large (?) orchestra (Shelley, Act I and Act II only, uncut) (dur. c. 240')
Act I vocal score begun 10 Nov. 1937, completed 22 March 1939. Act II vocal score begun 31 March 1939, completed 24 June 1942 (composition suspended between 26 Aug. 1939 and 27 Nov. 1941). Full score, now lost, completed Sept. 1944.

c. 1944
Legend, for cello or bass clarinet and piano (lost)

c. 1946
"Celtic Choral Poem", for female voices
   existence doubtful

?1947
Adagio e dolente, for a bass instrument and piano (fragment only)
Deirdre of the Sorrows, opera (Synge) (unfinished, destroyed)

1948
Symphony No. 6 (formerly unnumbered), *Sinfonia Tragica*, in one movement, for orchestra
   Allegro ma non troppo - Lento - Allegro vivace
   21 Feb. 1948. Intended as Vorspiel to a proposed opera *Deirdre of the Sorrows* (dur. 19')
Symphony No. 7 in C major, for orchestra
   I. *Allegro moderato*. II. *Allegro moderato ma maestoso*. III. *Adagio - allegro moderato - adagio*. IV. *Moderato* (dur. 40'30")
   'Mar. - Sept. 1948'; completed 14 Sept. 1948
The Tinker's Wedding: Comedy Overture No. 2, for orchestra (dur. 7'30")
   6 March 1948

1949
Symphony No. 8 in B♭ minor, in one movement, for orchestra (dur. 23')
   17 May 1949

1950-1
Turandot, Prinzessin von China, music-drama in three acts. ("Ein tragikomisches Märchen nach Gozzi von Schiller": abridged by the composer, set in German) (dur. c. 150')
   Act I: Prelude. Scene I, The environs of Pekin. Scene II, The environs of Pekin. Act II: Prelude. Scene I, Great Hall of the Divan. Act III: Scene I, A magnificent room. Scene II, Great Hall of the Divan.
   Vocal score: "pencil sketches 2nd week April 1950, pencil sketches complete June 7 1950". Ink copy completed 13 Sept. 1950. Full score dated "Friday May 18 1951"
   Subsidiary works:
   Three Pieces from *Turandot*, for orchestra (1962). This comprises the Prelude to Act I of the music-drama and reworkings of two sections of the same Act

1951
Symphony No. 9 in A minor, for orchestra
   I. *Adagio - allegro vivo*. II. *Adagio*. III. *Allegro moderato* (dur. 27')
   "July-Nov. 1951"

1951-2
The Cenci, music-drama in eight scenes (dur. c. 120')
   Preludio Tragico. Scene I, An Apartment in the Cenci Palace. Scene II, A Garden in the Cenci Palace. Scene III, A Magnificent Hall in the Cenci Palace - a Banquet. Scene IV, An Apartment in the Castle of Petrella. Scene V, Before the Castle of Petrella. Scene VI, An Apartment in Orsino's Palace. Scene VII, A Hall of Justice. Scene VIII, A Hall of the Prison.
   (Shelley, abridged by the composer from Acts I, IV and V of the play, set in English)
   Vocal score: "pencil sketches completed May 29 1952, ink copy completed July 24 1952". Full score dated: 1 Sept. 1952 (Overture), 29 Sept. 1952 (Scene I), 11 Oct. 1952 (Scene II), 4 Dec. 1952 (Scene IV).
   Subsidiary works:
   Preludio Tragico, for orchestra
   Flourish, for four trumpets

1953
English Suite No. 5, *Rustic Scenes*, for orchestra
   I. Trotting to Market. II. Reverie (for strings). III. The Restless Stream (for wind and percussion). IV. Rustic Revels (dur. 22')
   12-27 June, 1953

1953-4
Symphony No. 10 in C minor, in one movement, for orchestra (dur. 20')
   "16 Jan. 1954"

1954
Symphony No. 11, for orchestra (dur. 29')
   I. *Adagio*. II. *Allegro giocoso*. III. *Maestoso e pesante - allegro marcia*
   "29 April, 1954"

Elegy, symphonic poem, for orchestra (dur. 14')
7 June 1954

1955-6
Faust, music-drama in a prologue and four acts (Goethe, abridged by the composer from Part I, set in German) (dur. c. 150')
Prologue in Heaven. Act I: Scene I, Faust's Room. Scene II, Faust's Room. Act II: Prelude - Through the Air. Scene I, The Street. Scene II, Evening - Gretchen's Room. Scene III, Gretchen's Room. Scene IV, Gretchen's Room. Act III: Scene I, Night - The Street before Gretchen's Door. Scene II, Cathedral (Dom). Act IV: Scene I Gloomy day - country. Scene II, Night Ride of Faust and Mephistopheles. Scene III, Dungeon.
Vocal score composed between April and Aug. 1955 (completed 19 Aug.). Full score completed 11 May 1956.
Subsidiary works:
Prologue in Heaven,
Prelude to Act II, for orchestra
Gretchen Songs from Act II, for soprano and orchestra
Cathedral Scene from Act III, for soprano, bass, SATB chorus, organ and orchestra
Abend, for orchestra (Prelude to Act II, Scene II)
Night Ride of Faust and Mephistopheles, for orchestra (Act IV, Scene II)

1957
Symphony No. 12, in one movement, for orchestra
"Feb. 4, 1957" (dur. 12')
Agamemnon, music-drama in one act (Aeschylus, abridged and adapted by the composer from Blackie's "Everyman" translation, set in English) (dur. 39')
Full score dated April 1957

1959
Symphony No. 13 in C major, in one movement, for orchestra (dur. 18')
"Nov.-Dec. 1959"

1959-60
Symphony No. 14 in F major, in one movement, for orchestra (dur. 21'30")
"Feb. 10, 1960"

1960
Symphony No. 15 in A major, in one movement, for orchestra (dur. 20'30")
Symphony No. 16, in one movement, for orchestra (dur. 17'30")

1960-1
Symphony No. 17, in one movement, for orchestra
"Sketches Nov. 26, 1960, Full score Jan. 8, 1961" (dur. 14')

1961
Symphony No. 18, for orchestra (dur. 15'30")
I. *Allegro moderato.* II. *Adagio.* III. *Allegro e marcato sempre*
"Feb.-May, 1961"

Symphony No. 19 in E minor, for orchestra
I. *Allegro spiritoso e con anima e leggiero.* II. *Adagio allegretto.* III. *Con anima e giocoso*
"Nov. 5, 1961" (dur. 19')

1962
Symphony No. 20 in C$^\sharp$ minor, for orchestra
I. *Adagio - allegro agitato.* II. *Adagio ma non troppo, cantabile e sostenuto.* III. *Allegro vivo*
"May 31, 1962" (dur. 25'30")
The Jolly Miller, Comedy Overture No. 3
"April 13, 1962" (dur. 4'30")

1963
Symphony No. 21 in E$^\flat$ major, for orchestra
I. *Adagio - allegro e con anima.* II. *Adagio cantabile e sostenuto.* III. *Vivace.* IV. *Andante - maestoso - allegro con fuoco* (dur. 28')

1964
Concerto for cello and orchestra (dur. 20'30")
I. *Allegro.* II. *Andante.* III. *Allegro moderato*
"April 13 1964"
Concerto for Orchestra, in one movement (dur. 15')
June 1964
Symphonic movement
unfinished, destroyed

1964-5
Symphony No. 22, *Symphonia Brevis*, for orchestra
I. *Maestoso e ritmico.* II. *Tempo di marcia e ritmico adagio* (dur. 9'30")
First movement "22 Dec. 1964"; Second movement "Jan.8 1965"

1965
Symphony No. 23, for orchestra (dur. 13'30")
I. *Moderato - allegro con anima.* II. *Adagio non troppo e pesante*
Symphony No. 24 in D major, in one movement, for orchestra (dur. 17')

1965-6
Symphony No. 25 in A minor, for orchestra
I *Allegro risoluto.* II. *Andante cantabile.* III. *Allegro ma non tanto* (dur. 25')
"10 Jan. 1966"

1966
Symphony No. 26, for orchestra (dur. 16'30")
I. *Allegro risoluto.* II. *Allegro moderato e grazioso - giocoso - allegro assai*
Symphony No. 27 in C major, for orchestra
I. *Lento - allegro giocoso e marcato sempre - Moderato.* II. *Lento ma non troppo.* III. *Allegro con anima* (dur. 22')
"10 Dec. 1966"

1967
Symphony No. 28 in C minor, for orchestra
I. *Moderato.* II. *Grazioso e leggiero.* III. *Andante espressivo.* IV. *Allegro vivo* (dur. 15')
"April 1967"
Symphony No. 29 in E major, for orchestra
I. *Adagio - allegro.* II. *Lento cantabile sempre.* III. *Allegretto grazioso.* IV. *Adagio - allegro molto - adagio*
"July 31 1967" (dur. 19'30")

Oedipus Coloneus, opera after Sophocles (Sir George Young translation) unfinished; lost, probably destroyed?
Symphony No. 30 in B♭ minor, for orchestra
   I. *Lento*. II. *Moderato comodo e leggiero*
   "Nov. 13 1967" (dur. 15'30")
Festival Fanfare, for brass (originally *Fanfare for the orchestral brass*) (dur. 1'30")
"Christmas 1967"

1968
Symphony No. 31, in one movement, for orchestra (dur. 13')
Legend for Orchestra, *Ave Atque Vale* (dur. 7')
"May 31 1968"
Symphony No. 32 in A♭ major, for orchestra
   I. *Allegretto*. II. *Adagio*. III. *Allegro ma non troppo*. IV. *Allegro moderato* (dur. 22'30")
"June-Oct. 1968"

Arrangements by Havergal Brian of other music

c. 1909
Johann Sebastian Bach: Aria from Cantata No. 34 *O ewiges Feuer*, arranged for tenor and piano (lost)

c. 1920
Piano transcription of an unidentified work by Elgar (whereabouts unknown)

1925
Ralph Vaughan Williams: *Sancta Civitas*, vocal score

undated (probably early 1930s)
15 transcriptions (short scores):
   Thomas Augustine Arne: Overture from *Judith*
   Johann Christian Bach: Overture from *Amadis de Gaule*
   Johann Christian Bach: Overture from *La Clemenza di Scipione*
   Johann Sebastian Bach: Chorus "Friede über Israel" from Cantata No. 34 *O ewiges Feuer*
   Hector Berlioz: *March to the Scaffold* from the *Symphonie fantastique*
   Michail Glinka: Overture from *Ruslan and Ludmila*
   Christoph Willibald Gluck: Overture from *Alceste*
   Christoph Willibald Gluck: Overture from *Iphigenie in Aulis (Iphigénie en Aulide)*
   George Frideric Handel: Overture from *Aelius (Ezio)*
   George Frideric Handel: Overture from *Rodelinda*
   Gasparo Spontini: Overture from *Olympia (Olimpie)*
   Gasparo Spontini: Pas de Cinq 1 and Pas de Cinq 2 from *Olimpie*
   Gasparo Spontini: Marche Triomphale from *Olimpie*
   Richard Wagner: *Huldigungsmarsch*
   Richard Wagner: *Kaisermarsch*

?1930s
Basil Maine: *Te Deum*, arrangement for chorus and orchestra (whereabouts unknown)

1937
George Frideric Handel: Two songs from *Venus and Adonis* ("Dear Adonis" and "Transporting Joy"), arranged for voice and piano

Index

Aeschylus 19, 56, 246, 410
Aldridge, John xi, 61, 80, 89, 335
Alexander, Larry 130, 146, 267, 302, 304-305, 307-309, 311, 337, 395
Ali, Muhammad 392
Alkan, Valentin 357, 403
   piano rondo, *To, to Carabo* 357
   piano sonata, *La Chasse* 357
   Sonata in D major op. 13/2 357
Allen, J. 34
Allingham, William 406
Allum, Walter 19, 46, 53, 59, 377
Alt, Greenhouse 5
Anderson, Jeffrey 105, 107-113, 115-117, 120
Anderson, John 9-11
Anderson, Martin J. 390
Anderton, Howard Orsmond 38
Aristophanes 56
Arne, Thomas Augustine
   Judith 411
   Rule Britannia 234
Arnold, Matthew 152, 158
Atterberg, Kurt 110
Auden, Wystan Hugh 151, 160
Austin, Ernest 276

Bach, Johann Christian 5
   Amadis de Gaule 411
   La clemenza di Scipione 411
Bach, Johann Sebastian 14, 16, 25-26, 56-57, 67, 69, 132, 142-144, 272, 374-375
   B minor Mass 26
   Fantasia and Fugue in G minor 97
   Lobet Gott in seinen Reichen 277
   O ewiges Feuer, O Ursprung der Liebe 411
   (ed. Busoni): Prelude and Fugue in D 14
   (orch. Respighi): Prelude and Fugue in D 14
   'St Anne' Fugue 374
   St Matthew Passion 26
   (ed. Busoni): Toccata in C major 12-14
   (ed. Busoni): Toccata in D minor 14
   (ed. Busoni): The Well-Tempered Piano 14
Bacon, Francis 139
Baïf, Jean-Antoine 142
Bailey, Arthur 35, 61
Baines, William 378
Balakirev, Mily 318
Bantock, Granville 5-6, 10, 32, 37-47, 49-53, 57, 108, 110-111, 115, 122-123, 128, 130, 140, 144-145, 172, 268, 276-277, 283, 290, 293-294, 313-314, 316, 318, 377, 389
   Ferishta's Fancies 57
   Helena Variations 57
   Omar Khayyam 57, 276, 283, 293
   Pagan Symphony 32
   The Great God Pan 57
   Vanity of Vanities 32
Bantock, Helen 32, 38, 405
Bantock, Raymond 38, 40
Barber, C. R. 407
Barlow, Harry 119
Bartók, Béla 187, 190-191, 200, 396
Bax, Arnold 113-114, 352, 399
   Fatherland 277
   Mater Ora Filium 30
   Symphony No. 1 113
Bax, Clifford 114
Baxter, James Reid vii, ix
Becker, Martyn xi, 93, 101, 173, 175, 193, 339
Beckett, Samuel 160, 393
Beddoes, Thomas Lovell 407
Beecham, Thomas 7-8, 10, 36, 58, 73, 169, 318-320, 405
Beethoven, Ludwig van 13, 55, 59, 65, 79, 88, 103, 119-120, 132, 141-144, 148, 154, 162-166, 202, 226, 243, 259, 261, 347, 377, 391
   Choral Fantasia in C minor, Op. 80 104
   Egmont, Op. 84 29
   Fidelio, Op. 72 259
   Leonore, Overture No. 3, Op. 72 259
   Missa Solemnis in D major, Op. 123 154, 159
   Piano Concerto No. 5 in E♭ major, Op. 73 *Emperor* 104
   (orch. Weingartner): Piano sonata in B♭ major, Op. 106 13
   Rondo a capriccio in G major, Op. 129 *Rage Over a Lost Penny* 104
   String Quartet in C♯ minor, Op. 131 261
   Symphony No. 1 in C major, Op. 21 174
   Symphony No. 3 in E♭ major, Op. 55 *Eroica* 104, 151, 261
   Symphony No. 4 in B♭ major, Op. 60 202-203
   Symphony No. 5 in C minor, Op. 67 29, 148, 157, 247
   Symphony No. 6 in F major, Op. 68 *Pastoral* 65
   Symphony No. 7 in A major, Op. 92 174
   Symphony No. 8 in F major, Op. 93 65
   Symphony No. 9 in D minor, Op. 125 133, 142, 144, 146, 148, 154, 157, 159, 162-166, 174, 226, 258, 260, 342, 396
Belloc, Hilaire 25, 28
Bennett, Arnold 73, 122, 171, 289, 291, 315-317

414 Index

Berg, Alban 150, 335, 389, 399
   Lulu 335, 389
   Wozzeck 335
Bergson, Henri 70
Berio, Luciano 393
   Sinfonia 393
Berkeley, Lennox 9
Berlichingen, Götz von 79, 107, 175, 191-192
Berlioz, Hector 7, 19, 26, 56, 142-144, 155, 167-168, 268, 383
   Béatrice et Bénédict 216
   Harold en Italie 259
   La damnation de Faust 121
   Requiem 154-157
   Symphonie fantastique 224, 259, 383, 411
   Te Deum 132-133, 155
Berners, Gerald Tyrwhitt-Wilson Lord 73, 335
Bernstein, Leonard 399
Berry, Godfrey 61, 84, 88, 91, 336, 340
Betham-Edwards, Matilda 406
Bevan, Billy 356
Birtwistle, Harrison 101
Bismarck, Otto von 72
Bittner, Julius 261
Bizet, Georges 195
Blackie, John Stuart 410
Blair, James 242
Blake, William 46-47, 56, 58, 62, 140, 145, 154, 156, 159, 246, 345, 347-349, 355, 361-362, 406-407
Blesh, Rudi 172
   Shining Trumpets 172
Bliss, Arthur 56, 335
Böhm, Georg 14
Böhm, Jacob 140
Böhm, Karl 116
Borodin, Alexander 318
Boughton, Rutland 198
   Symphony No. 2 198
Boulez, Pierre 150-151
   Rituel 151
Boult, Adrian 10, 17, 25, 116, 148-149, 168, 170, 243, 356-357, 395, 402
Bowles, William Lisle 408
Brahms, Johannes 16, 69, 88, 109, 111, 152, 162, 256-258, 377
   String Quintet in F major, Op. 88 258
   Symphony No. 1 in C minor, Op. 68 162, 169
   Symphony No. 3 in F major, Op. 90 16, 263
   Tragic Overture, Op. 81 256-257
   Violin sonata in A major, Op. 100 258
Bray, Trevor Ian 37, 277
Brecht, Bertolt 334
Brian, Elfreda 59, 379, 381
Brian, Hilda 21-22, 46, 57
Brian, Isobel 33-34, 57
Brian, William Havergal
   Absence 407
   Adagio e dolente 409
   Agamemnon 19, 30, 56, 79, 106, 227, 246, 334, 410
   Ah! County Guy! 407
   And will he not come again? 406
   Anthem 35, 267, 405
   At Candlelight 408
   Ave Atque Vale 411
   The Battle Song 408
   The Birds 345, 348, 361, 407
   The Blossom 406
   Blow, Blow thou Winter Wind 408
   Burlesque Variations on an Original Theme 302, 304-305, 405
   Buster Keaton Overture 24-25, 219, 356, 408
   By the Waters of Babylon 36, 54, 57, 61-62, 71-72, 112, 275-289, 293, 305-307, 314-315, 332, 379, 405
   Call for the Robin Redbreast 407
   Canadian Boat Song 405
   Care-charmer sleep 345, 407
   Carmilhan 128, 289, 406
   'Celtic Choral Poem' 409
   The Cenci 19, 105-106, 246, 254, 334, 382-383, 409
   A Child's Prayer 406
   The Chimney Sweeper 347, 406
   Clown's Song 406
   Come Away, Death 408
   Come o'er the Sea 405
   Concerto for cello and orchestra 105, 199, 410
   Concerto for Orchestra xi, 105, 199-200, 410
   Concerto for violin and orchestra 45, 408
   Concerto in C major for violin and orchestra 45, 304, 409
   The Curate and the Mulberry Tree 407
   Day and Night 405
   Daybreak 406
   The Defiled Sanctuary 78, 345, 407
   Deirdre of the Sorrows 22, 198, 206-207, 212, 249, 409
   Doctor Merryheart 11-12, 14, 25, 36, 49-54, 63, 119, 216, 262, 302, 332, 334, 361, 379, 406
   Double Fugue in E♭ 13, 26, 123-124, 355, 363, 374-376, 378-381, 408
   The Dream 406
   The Echoing Green 406
   Elegy xi, 22, 199-200, 397, 410

Index   415

English Suite No. 1   36, 43, 54, 64, 112, 262, 275, 302, 334, 340, 356, 405
English Suite No. 2, *Night Portraits*   42, 54, 78, 335, 407
English Suite No. 3   12, 41, 339, 408
English Suite No. 4, *Kindergarten*   xi, 387, 408
English Suite No. 5, *Rustic Scenes*   234, 409
A Faery Song   405
Fair Pledges of a Fruitful Tree   408
Fairies' Song   406
The Fairy Palace   407
A Fantastic Symphony   12, 49, 51, 64, 72, 127-130, 198, 216, 261, 302-303, 319, 332, 379, 406
Fantastic Variations on an Old Rhyme   12, 51, 64, 72, 127-130, 302-303, 319, 406
Far from Thee   408
Farewell   405
Faust   19, 105-106, 120, 198, 334, 390, 410
Fear no more the Heat of the the Sun   408
Festal Dance   49, 51, 64, 127-128, 130, 302, 332, 379, 406
Festival Fanfare   411
The Fly   406
For Valour   50, 108, 275, 302, 405
Four miniatures   41, 355, 361-362, 407
Full Fathom Five   408
A Gipsy Song   406
Go Happy Rose   406, 408
Goodbye to Summer   406
Grace for a Child   406
The Hag   302, 406
He was a Rat   406
Hero and Leander   275, 320, 405
Hie upon Hielands   407
Hymn to Diana   407
I Know, and You!   408
I Shot an Arrow   405
If I could Speak   405
If I had but two Little Wings   406
Three Illuminations   54, 355-360, 362, 407
In a Fairy Boat   405
In Memoriam   36, 51-52, 54, 94-95, 130, 262, 302, 307, 406
Infant Joy   406
Introit Amen   378, 408
It was a Lover and his Lass   408
John Dowland Suite   409
John Dowland's Fancy   122, 374, 377-378, 409
The Jolly Miller   24, 83, 410
The Knight's Leap   406
Lady Ellayne   345, 407
The Lamb   159, 406
The Land of Dreams   345, 348-349, 361, 407
Laughing Song   406

Legend, for cello or bass clarinet   278, 355, 409
Legend, for violin   355, 408
Legende   405, 407
The Legend of Altenahr   406
Let God Arise   62, 107, 289, 406
The Little Black Boy   406
The Little Boy Found   406
The Little Boy Lost   406
Little Sleeper   316, 405
The Lost Doll   406
Love's Remorse   407
Lullaby of an Infant Chief   405
The Mad Maid's Song   406
The Maiden and the Flower Garden   42, 406
Marching Along   406
Meg Merrilies   407
The Message   344, 346, 405
Mine be a Cot Beside the Hill   408
The Moon   406
The Mountain and the Squirrel   406
Music when Soft Voices Die   407
The Night Piece   406
Oedipus Coloneus   79, 249, 254-255, 411
O Happiness, Celestial Fair   408
O Mistress Mine   407
On a Poet's Lips I Slept   407
The Owl   406
Pack Clouds Away   407
Pantalon and Columbine   323-324, 337, 340, 405, 407
Pastoral: the Shepherd   406
The Phantom Wooer   407
Pilgrimage to Kevlaar   42, 47, 335, 339, 406
Piping Down the Valleys Wild   406
The Poet's Dream   407
Prelude and Fugue in C minor   26, 123, 362-368, 378-380, 408
Prelude and Fugue in D minor and major   25-26, 123, 363, 368-374, 378-380, 408
Prelude   408
Prometheus Unbound   71, 198, 245-246, 267, 302-303, 306, 308-309, 333, 348, 392, 409
A proposal   408
Psalm 23   114, 128, 130, 267-275, 278-280, 283, 285-286, 288-289, 302-310, 315, 379, 405
Razamoff   40, 407
Red May   42, 47, 407
Renunciation   407
Requiem   68, 267, 405
Requiem for the Rose   302, 406
The River   406
Robin Redbreast   406
The Sands of Dee   407

Brian (contd.)
Shall I Compare Thee to a Summer's Day? 35, 267, 405
Shall I then be Spared? 408
Since Love is Dead 408
The Soldier's Dream 128-130, 406
Soliloquy upon a Dead Child 317, 405
A song, title unknown 405
Song of Betrayal 408
A Song of Willow 406
Sonnet: My Lute 407
Sorrow Song 346, 405
The Soul of Steel 345, 407
Soul Star 405
Spring - Sound the Flute 406
Spring, the Sweet Spring 408
Stars of Destiny 408
Stars of the Summer Night 72, 267, 405
String Quartet 355, 405
Summer has come, Little Children 406
Sweet Solitude 408
The Sweetest Dream 406
Sympathy 406
Symphonic movement 199, 410
Symphony No. 1 in D minor, *The Gothic* vii, xiii, 3-6, 10-11, 19, 26, 30, 40-42, 56, 70, 77-79, 81, 90, 93, 98, 102, 104-105, 107, 110, 113-119, 123, 130-176, 180, 185, 187, 194, 196, 198, 223, 226, 242-243, 246, 255, 261-264, 308, 319, 333, 335-338, 342-343, 348, 350, 353-354, 356-359, 361-362, 368, 377-379, 382, 384, 386-387, 392-395, 398, 401-402, 408
Symphony No. 2 in E minor xi, 25, 70, 79, 83, 95, 106-107, 170-193, 201, 261, 307, 336, 353, 382-383, 408
Symphony No. 3 in C♯ minor xi, 25, 102, 104, 173, 175, 193-197, 200, 202, 261-262, 307, 336, 353, 358, 408
Symphony No. 4 in C major, *Das Siegeslied* 62, 104, 107, 145, 150, 155-156, 227, 261, 278, 289, 307-308, 336, 353, 390-392, 402, 408
Symphony No. 5, *Wine of Summer* 246, 302-303, 306-308, 316, 348, 392, 402, 409
Symphony No. 6, *Sinfonia Tragica* 22, 54, 104, 176, 198-199, 200-216, 242, 246, 303, 307, 387, 389-390, 397, 409
Symphony No. 7 in C major 17, 22, 79, 93, 98, 103-104, 173, 216-224, 244, 257-258, 307, 357, 386-387, 409
Symphony No. 8 in B♭ minor ix, 19, 22, 96-98, 104, 206, 216, 224, 226, 229, 261, 268, 275, 303, 353, 357, 384, 387, 397, 401-402, 409
Symphony No. 9 in A minor ix, 17, 19-20, 22, 36, 82, 104, 224-226, 353, 388, 409

Symphony No. 10 in C minor 20, 22, 26, 99, 104, 161, 303, 350, 357, 384, 387, 397, 409
Symphony No. 11 20, 22, 104, 198, 216, 261, 357, 409
Symphony No. 12 22, 30, 79, 106, 149, 216, 227, 229-230, 234, 261, 275, 384, 410
Symphony No. 13 in C major 84, 227-234, 262, 303, 410
Symphony No. 14 in F major 82, 84, 106-107, 233-242, 353, 386, 410
Symphony No. 15 in A major 104, 234, 391, 410
Symphony No. 16 99, 101, 104, 242, 303, 350, 388, 410
Symphony No. 17 101, 103-104, 350-351, 410
Symphony No. 18 99, 104, 200, 262, 410
Symphony No. 19 in E minor 104, 199, 410
Symphony No. 20 in C♯ minor 83, 199, 262, 351, 386, 410
Symphony No. 21 in E♭ major 36, 82, 106, 118, 121, 199, 242, 249, 386, 388, 410
Symphony No. 22, *Symphonia Brevis* 104, 199, 201, 230, 249, 252, 254-255, 262, 384, 386, 390, 399, 410
Symphony No. 23 104, 303, 410
Symphony No. 24 in D major 104, 303, 350, 410
Symphony No. 25 in A minor 104, 384, 386, 410
Symphony No. 26 124, 244, 410
Symphony No. 27 in C major 104, 124, 244-249, 410
Symphony No. 28 in C minor 104, 249, 351, 386, 410
Symphony No. 29 in E major 104, 249, 410
Symphony No. 30 in B♭ minor xi, 79, 104, 149, 248-255, 386, 388, 411
Symphony No. 31 93, 103-104, 411
Symphony No. 32 in A♭ major 58, 117, 411
Take, Oh Take those Lips Away 344, 408
Tales of Olden Times 407
Tell me, thou Soul of Her I Love 405
The Tigers xi, 3, 5-12, 17, 19, 42, 47, 58, 64-65, 78, 120-121, 129, 134, 148, 161, 180, 193, 196, 198, 302, 305, 308-309, 318-342, 345, 347-349, 356, 358-359, 362, 379, 389, 392, 405, 407
The Tinker's Wedding 3, 24, 65, 198, 307, 409
To Daffodils 408
Today and Tomorrow 405
Tragic Prelude 405
Turandot, Prinzessin von China xi, 19, 105-106, 334, 351, 355, 409

Twilight 406
The Twilight House 408
Two Scenas 407
Under the Greenwood Tree 408
Violets 406
The Vision of Cleopatra 43, 54, 107-109, 122, 127, 283, 289-302, 311-317, 332, 342, 345, 406
Vital Spark of Heavenly Flame 378, 408
Wanderer's Night Song 405
What does Little Birdie Say? 406
When I lie Ill 405
When icicles hang by the wall 345, 407
When the Sun Goes Down 344-345, 407
Where Shadows Flee 408
The White Lily 406
Why dost thou wound and break my heart? 345-346, 406
Will You Buy any Rope? 406
A Wish 408
Without You 408
Work for cello and piano 406
Work for chorus and orchestra 406
Work for organ 409
Ye Spotted Snakes 406
Bridge, Frank 169
Briggs, P. Stanley 61-62
Britten, Benjamin 9, 59, 68, 92, 115, 127, 157, 338, 343, 397
  Cello Symphony, Op. 68 397
  Peter Grimes, Op. 33 9, 337-338
  War Requiem, Op. 66 157
Brown, Clarence 138
Brown, David ix
Brown, David J. viii-x, 91, 102, 104, 149, 193, 234, 277, 405
Browning, Robert 393
Bruckner, Anton 28-29, 97-98, 102-103, 116, 132, 144, 151-153, 167, 173-174, 196, 231, 261, 374, 395
  Symphony No. 1 in C minor 28
  Symphony No. 2 in C minor 28, 152
  Symphony No. 3 in D minor 103
  Symphony No. 4 in E♭ major 28-29, 103, 116, 342
  Symphony No. 5 in B♭ major 28-30, 116
  Symphony No. 6 in A major 116
  Symphony No. 7 in E major 28, 98, 261, 342
  Symphony No. 8 in C minor 28, 98, 103, 152
  Symphony No. 9 in D minor 28, 132, 152
  Te Deum in C major 132, 153, 157
Bruno, Giordano 139
Bulgakov, Mikhail 334
Busch, Adolf 31

Busoni, Ferruccio (see also Bach) 12, 14, 79, 358, 403
  Doktor Faust 79, 358
  Nocturne symphonique 358
Butler, Samuel 69, 334
Buxtehude, Dietrich 14
Byrd, William 144, 377-378
Byron, George Gordon Noel 245

Cairns, David 155
Campbell, Thomas 129-130, 406
Cardus, Neville 112, 393
Carlyle, Thomas 320
Caruso, Enrico 127, 129
Casaubon, Isaac 139
Caunt, W. H. 276-277, 284
Chadwick, Wilfrid 32, 292, 405
Challinor, F. A. 34
Chaplin, Charles 24, 65
Chevalier, Albert 17, 355-356
Chopin, Frédéric 14, 56, 59, 143, 262
  Piano Concerto in E minor, Op. 11 13-14
Clare, John 49
Clark, Edward 116
Clementi, Muzio 88
  Piano sonata in E♭, op. 5 258
Clements, Andrew 337
Clyde, Andy 356
Coates, John 108, 114, 268, 290, 314, 316
Cobbett, William 217
Cocteau, Jean 155
Coleridge, Samuel Taylor 406
Coleridge-Taylor, Samuel 108-109, 290, 313-314
  Clarinet Quintet in F♯ minor, Op. 10 109
  Meg Blane, Op. 48 109
  Scenes from the Song of Hiawatha, Op. 30 109, 318
Comissiona, Sergiu 398
Conrad, Joseph 88
Cook, Brian Rayner 342
Cooke, Deryck 118, 397
Copernicus, Nicolaus 139
Cornelius, Peter 111
  Der Tod, das ist die kühle Nacht Op. 11/1 111
Counsell, Bernard G. xi, 40, 134
Courtauld, Samuel 10, 14
Coverdale, Miles 268
Cowen, Frederic Hymen 123, 318
  Thorgrim 318
Cromwell, Oliver 107
Cronin, Barry 244
Cumberland, Gerald 54, 289-293, 311-313, 315-317, 320, 332, 405-406

Dagg, Norman V.   5
Daniel, Samuel   405, 407
Dante Alighieri   160, 352
Darwin, Charles   69
Dawson, Frederick   378
De Bono, Edward   81-82
Debussy, Claude   72, 172, 181, 190, 244, 259, 307, 319, 347, 356
   Hommage à Mr. Pickwick   259, 356
   Images for orchestra   181
   Syrinx   244
Dee, John   139-140
Delius, Frederick   45, 108, 122, 142-143, 277, 290, 313-314, 318-320, 332, 399
   Appalachia   320
   Brigg Fair   123
Descartes, René   140
Diaghilev, Sergey   73
Dickinson, Emily   48
Disney, Walt   357
Dohnanyi, Christoph von   394
Donne, John   56, 156, 405
Douglas, Alfred   316-317, 409
Dowland, John   56, 122, 374, 377-378, 409
Downes, Edward   106, 242
Draeseke, Felix   261
Drayton, Michael   407
Druce, Colin   278
Drummond, John   395
Drummond of Hawthornden, William   407
Dufay, Guillaume   349
Duke of Sutherland   34
Duke, Brian   67
Dupré, Marcel
   Prelude and Fugue in G minor   135
Dussek, Johann Ludwig   88, 357
   The Sufferings of the Queen of France, Op. 23   362
Dvořák, Antonín   17-18, 115
   Carnival Overture, Op. 92   18
   Piano Trio in E minor, Op. 90 *Dumky*   18
   The Spectre's Bride, Op. 69   115
   String Quartet in F major, Op. 96 *American*   18
   Symphony No. 3 in E♭ major, Op. 10   18
   Symphony No. 4 in D minor, Op. 13   18
   Symphony No. 7 in D minor, Op. 70   18
   Symphony No. 8 in G major, Op. 88   17
   Symphony No. 9 in E minor, Op. 95   17

Eastaugh, Kenneth   xiii, 33, 37, 40-51, 78, 91, 128, 130, 267-268, 275-276, 287, 289-291, 341, 395
Eckermann, Johann Peter   27, 137
Edwards, Philip   105
Ekman, Karl   29

Elgar, Alice   57, 63, 114
Elgar, Edward   32, 34-38, 43, 45, 55-59, 62-64, 68-69, 72, 95, 109, 111-112, 114-115, 121-123, 132, 144, 151, 169, 171-172, 177-178, 189-190, 196-197, 234, 268-269, 276, 287, 290, 293, 304, 306, 314-316, 318-320, 332, 344, 347, 382, 411
   The Apostles, Op. 49   344
   The Dream of Gerontius, Op. 38   35, 61, 114, 270, 279, 344
   Falstaff, Op. 68   191
   The Kingdom, Op. 51   344
   The Light of Life, Op. 29   115
   Pomp and Circumstance, Op. 39   196
   Scenes from the Saga of King Olaf, Op. 30   35, 62, 115
   The Spirit of England, Op. 80   134
   Stars of the Summer Night   72
   Symphony No. 1 in A♭ major, Op. 55   36, 197
   Symphony No. 2 in E♭ major, Op. 63   36, 95, 180, 193, 197
   Variations on an Original Theme, Op. 36 *Enigma*   62-64
Eliot, Thomas Stearns   158-160
Emerson, Ralph Waldo   406
Erasmus, Desiderius   139, 319
Euripides   56

Fairbairn   9-11
Fairfax, Bryan   105, 119, 123, 169
Fauré, Gabriel   154
   Requiem   154
Faust, Johannes   79, 120, 130-131, 133, 136, 140-147, 152, 154
Fenney, William J.   45
   In Early Spring   45
   Rhapsody   45
Ffrangcon-Davies, David   114
Ficino, Marsilio   139, 144
Fields, Gracie   65
Fletcher, Dr   73
Ford, Ford Madox   26-27
Foreman, Ronald Lewis Edmund   xiii, 12, 52, 91, 102, 127, 267, 277, 310, 313-314, 405
Forster, Edward Morgan   157
Foster, Muriel   114
Franck, César   46
Fredman, Myer   242, 389
Freud, Sigmund   66, 69-71, 74-78
Fricker, Herbert Austin   112
Furnivall, Jean (née Brian)   21-22, 43, 310
Furnivall, Leonard   379
Furtwängler, Wilhelm   116

Galilei, Galileo   139
Gautier, Théophile   289

Index 419

Gay, John 65
George V Rex 108
George, Stefan 116
Gerstl, Richard 391
Gesualdo, Carlo 132, 349
Gibbon, Edward 27
Gibbs, Cecil Armstrong viii
Gilbert, William Schwenck 334
Ginastera, Alberto 383
  Bomarzo 383
Gissing, George Robert 122
Glazunov, Alexander 110, 318
Glinka, Mikhail 411
  Ruslan and Ludmila 411
Gluck, Christoph Willibald 411
  Alceste 411
  Iphigénie en Aulide 411
Godfrey, Dan 10-12, 52-53, 318-319
Goethe, Johann Wolfgang von 19, 26-28, 56, 62, 70, 79, 106-107, 120, 130-133, 136-137, 140-144, 154, 170, 175, 191-192, 222, 245-246, 308, 343, 386, 393, 405, 410
Goodsell, Don ix, 91
Goossens, Eugene 5, 56, 73, 169
Gounod, Charles 120
  Faust 120
Gozzi, Carlo 409
Graham, Leonard 33
Graham, Martha (née Brian) 33-34
Gray, Cecil 261
Greef, Arthur de 55
Grieg, Edvard 55, 143
Grimaldi, Joe 340
Grimm, Jakob 222
Grimm, Wilhelm 222
Grossel, Martin C. vii, ix
Grove, George 67
Groves, Charles 224, 353

Haas, Robert 28, 103
Hadath, Gunby 405, 408
Hafiz 317, 405
Hager, Leopold 10
Handel, George Frideric 67, 144, 370, 411
  Ezio 411
  Messiah 316
  Rodelinda 411
  Venus and Adonis 411
Hardy, Thomas 122, 150
Harris, Roy 258
  Symphony No. 3 257
Harrison, Julius 49-51, 108, 128, 290-291, 312-314
  The Vision of Cleopatra 108, 290-291, 312-314
Harrison, Sidney 135

Hartmann, Karl Amadeus 106
Harty, Hamilton 116, 169
Hatton, Graham xi, 199, 242, 248, 389
Havergal, W. H. 67
Haydn, Joseph 67, 88, 216, 244, 281, 390, 392
  The Seasons 352
  St Cecilia Mass 281
  Symphony No. 44 in E minor 392
  Symphony No. 45 in F♯ minor 361
  Symphony No. 102 in B♭ major 392
Heald Smith, Geoffrey 302
Heaton, Ted 73, 172, 340-341, 349, 353
Heber, Reginald 405
Hegar, Friedrich 111
  Phantom Host 111
Heine, Heinrich 56, 111, 406
Heltay, László 267-268
Hemmings, Theophilus 34, 63, 67-69
Herrick, Robert 56, 302, 308, 406
Heseltine, Philip 245, 346
Heywood, John 407
Hill, David 278
Hill, Peter 355
Hindemith, Paul 106, 191, 200, 352, 368
Hitler, Adolf 75
Hofmannsthal, Hugo von 340
Holbrooke, Josef 28, 32, 38-39, 44-45, 48, 72, 123, 172, 370
  Bronwen 48
  Variations on Three Blind Mice 72
Holland, Stuart 268
Holst, Gustav 113, 347, 352
  First Choral Symphony, Op. 41 203
Horenstein, Jascha 28
Hornby, David 173
Horowitz, Vladimir 14
Hughes, Frank 34
Humperdinck, Engelbert 47
  Die Wallfahrt nach Kevlaar 47
Hynais, Cyrill 28

Ives, Charles E. 171, 174, 191
  The Unanswered Question 157
  Three Places in New England 335

Jaeger, August Johannes 109
James, Henry 88
Janáček, Leoš 154, 170, 382, 398
  Glagolitic Mass 154-155
Jesus 140, 159
Johnson, Edward 118
Johnson, Stephen 167-170
Jones, Inigo 139
Jonson, Ben 406-407
Josquin des Prés 43, 55, 349, 377

420   Index

Jung, Carl Gustav   74, 76-80, 83-84, 139-140, 144-145

Kay, Christopher   355
Keaton, Buster   24-25, 219, 356, 408
Keble, John   67
Keble, Temple   407
Kennedy, Michael   132
Kenner, Hugh   160
Kepler, Johannes   139
Kettle, Christopher J.   xi, 148, 175, 194, 390, 395-397
Kettle, Paul   xi
Keys, Robert   26, 378
Kienzl, Wilhelm   357
Kingsley, Charles   406
Klindworth, Karl   14
Kling, Otto M.   51
Klopstock, Friedrich Gottlieb   154
Knussen, Oliver   398
König, Johann Balthasar   67
Kraus, Karl   334

Lambert, Constant   335
Lambourn, David   132, 357
Landon, Howard Chandler Robbins   216
Langford, Sammy   112, 320
Lassus, Orlande de   349
Le Gallienne, Richard   316, 405
Le Jeune, Claude   142
Lett, Phillis   290, 314
Levine, James   398
Lewis, Matthew Gregory   136
Lill, John   122, 124
Liszt, Franz   143, 272, 318
   Dante Symphony   352
   Faust Symphony   173
Litchfield, Philip   278
Lloyd Webber, Andrew
   Evita   342
Lloyd, Marie   355
Longfellow, Henry Wadsworth   289, 405-406
Löwe, Ferdinand   28
Luker, A. J.   135
Luther, Martin   155
Lutosławski, Witold   200
Lyell Tayler, Henry   128

MacDonald, Malcolm   viii, x-xi, xiii, 20, 22, 37, 54, 61, 74-75, 80-84, 94, 98, 100, 102, 104-106, 109, 127, 130, 132, 146-150, 157, 160-161, 171, 173, 175-176, 188, 194, 202, 216, 219, 222, 233-234, 244, 247, 255, 267, 293, 303-304, 333, 348, 350, 355-357, 379, 381, 386, 390-391, 394-395, 399, 403, 405
Mackenzie, Alexander Campbell   18, 318
   Scottish Concerto for piano, Op. 55   18

The Dream of Jubal, Op. 41   318
Mackerras, Charles   98, 104, 176, 242, 247, 398
MacNiece, Louis   393
Maderna, Bruno   151
Mahler, Alma   356
Mahler, Gustav   37, 68, 74, 103, 116-117, 132, 146-147, 149-150, 152, 154-156, 160-161, 167, 171, 175, 187, 190, 202-203, 224-226, 241, 246, 261, 356-357, 374, 382, 390-393, 395-399
   Das Lied von der Erde   234, 290, 356, 394
   Symphony No. 1 in D major   357
   Symphony No. 2   150, 152, 154, 160-161, 175, 190, 203, 391, 393
   Symphony No. 3 in D   149, 203, 356-357, 391-393
   Symphony No. 4   116, 356-357
   Symphony No. 5 in C♯ minor   153, 357, 391
   Symphony No. 6 in A minor   188, 224-226, 391, 394
   Symphony No. 7   173, 224-226, 357
   Symphony No. 8 in E♭ major   79, 102, 150, 155-156, 160, 167, 356-357, 394
   Symphony No. 9   175, 178, 356-357, 382
   Symphony No. 10 in F♯   356, 397
Maine, Basil   411
   Te Deum   411
Major, Miss   61
Malipiero, Gian Francesco   56
Mallol, Clarinda   55
Malory, Thomas   191
Mandelstam, Osip   137-138, 149
Mandry, Kevin   ix
Mann, Thomas   79, 135, 146-147, 158, 348
Marcus Aurelius   140
Markevitch, Igor   106
Marlowe, Christopher   79, 140
Marshall, Alan   ix, 167
Marston, Philip Bourke   405-406
Martinů, Bohuslaw   336
   Julietta   336
Marx, Brothers   334
Marx, Karl   69
McDonald   406
Medtner, Nikolay   16, 257
   Piano sonata in G minor, Op. 22   257
Mendelssohn Bartholdy, Felix   102, 112
   A Midsummer Night's Dream, Op. 21 & 61   221
   Elijah, Op. 70   291, 312
Meredith, George   122
Messiaen, Olivier   151
   Et Expecto Resurrectionem Mortuorum   151
Milligan, Spike   81-82, 89, 335, 341
Milton, John   150, 157
Mirandola, Pico della   139

Moir, David Macbeth 405
Montaigne, Michel de 139-140
Moore, Thomas 405
More, Hannah 378, 408
Morley, Henry 405
Moses 139
Moses, Vivian 321
Mozart, Wolfgang Amadé 67, 69, 88, 119, 122, 193, 256-257, 320, 337, 390, 392
   Piano Concerto in D major, K. 451 216
   Symphony in C major, K. 189k 261
   Symphony in G major, K. 318 256
   Symphony in C major, K. 551 *Jupiter* 97
   Zaide, K. 336b 256
Mullings, Frank 320
Mussorgsky, Modest 26, 318, 320, 337
   Boris Godunov 337
   Pictures at an Exhibition 26

Nash, Ogden 408
Nettel, Reginald xi, xiii, 3, 5, 17, 19-21, 24-26, 30, 36-37, 44, 47-49, 53, 58, 61, 75, 77, 79-80, 91, 106, 128, 161, 171, 276-278, 288-291, 304, 310-311, 355, 361, 377-378
Newman, Ernest 45, 53, 106-107, 112, 122, 316, 320
Newstone, Harry 31, 104, 216, 248
Newton, Isaac 139, 190
Newton, Rodney Stephen 233, 248, 336, 349, 353, 381, 391
Nielsen, Carl 110, 116-118, 173, 391, 397
   Symphony No. 3, Op. 27 *Espansiva* 117
   Symphony No. 5, Op. 50 116
Nietzsche, Friedrich 69
Nowak, Leopold 103

Offenbach, Jacques 334
   La Grande-duchesse de Gérolstein 334
Ogdon, John 14, 17
O'Leary, Martin 198, 224, 390, 392
Orage, A. R. 316
Orff, Carl 106
Orwell, George 84, 158
Ottaway, Hugh 93, 100
Ouseley, Frederick Arthur Gore 63
Overton, Bill 168
Owen, Wilfred 157-158, 334

Palestrina, Gian Pierluigi da 31-32, 144, 174, 377-378
Paracelsus 139-140, 140, 194
Parry, Charles Hubert Hastings 127, 306, 318
   Judith 318
Parsons, Albert 389
Parsons, Ernest Jnr 389
Parsons, Ernest Snr 389
Passage, Charles 191

Payne, Anthony 93
Peake, Mervyn 152
Pearce, A. L. 66
Penny, Alfred 62-63
Penny, Dora 62-63
Perrins, David 340
Petrassi, Goffredo 200
Pettersson, Allan 397-398
Pfitzner, Hans 31-32, 174, 377, 403
   Käthchen von Heilbronn, Op. 17 31
   Palestrina 31-32, 174, 377
   Piano Quintet in C major, Op. 23 31
Phillips, Maud 290, 314
Pickard, John 93, 101-103, 173
Pike, Lionel J. 148, 157
Pike, Steven 357
Pirie, Peter J. 268
Plaistow, Stephen 151
Platon 137, 139
Pollard, Snub 356
Pope, Alexander 378, 408
Pope, Stanley 197
Porter, Andrew 93
Previn, André 115
Prince Albert
   Te Deum 61, 136-137
Prokofiev, Sergey 392
Puccini, Giacomo 337, 349
Pursey, Miss 6
Pythagoras 137

Rakhmaninov, Sergey 59
Rankl, Karl 198
Rapoport, Paul xiii, 37, 40, 44, 49, 79, 131, 137, 142, 144, 146, 148, 159, 162
Rattle, Simon 398
Ravel, Maurice
   La Valse 175
Raybould, Clarence 17-18, 53
Reeves, William 28
Reger, Max 12-14, 25-26, 30-31, 173, 257, 368, 374-375, 377, 403
   Fantasia and Fugue on BACH, Op. 46 374
   Hiller Variations, Op. 100 257
   Mozart Variations, Op. 132 257
   Piano Quintet in C minor, Op. 64 13
   Preludes and Fugues, Op. 99 13
   Serenade in G major, Op. 95 257
   Sinfonietta in A major, Op. 90 257
   String Quartet in D minor, Op. 74 13
   String Quartet in E♭ major, Op. 109 13, 31
   Symphonic Fantasy and Fugue for organ, Op. 57 13-14, 25
   Symphonic Prologue to a Tragedy, Op. 108 257
   Symphony in B minor 257

Symphony in E minor   257
Vater Unser   30
Reizenstein, Franz   352
Respighi, Ottorino (see also Bach)   14
   Vetrate di chiesa   352
Richter, Hans   6, 26, 72-73, 112-113, 116, 119, 276
Richter, Jean Paul Friedrich   26-28
Rimbault, Edward Francis   33
Rimsky-Korsakov, Nicolay   307, 318
Robinson, Herbert Minton 39, 43-44, 49-50, 130
Rodewald, A. E.   123
Rogers, Mr.   121
Rogers, Samuel   408
Ronald, Landon   52, 107, 290, 314, 317
Rósza, Miklós   352
Rubbra, Edmund   viii, 116, 258
   Symphony No. 10, Op. 145   258
Rubinstein, Anton   318
Rudkin, David   151
Russell, Bertrand   38
Russell, Gilliam Ward   278, 405

Sadie, Stanley   93
Salten, Felix   391-392
Sand, George   56
Sargent, Malcolm   14, 115
Satie, Erik   54
Saxby, Graham   170
Schiller, Friedrich von   142, 144, 154, 166, 409
Schmidt, Franz   173, 196, 203, 261, 368
   Symphony No. 4 in C major   203
Schmidt, Ole   75, 148-149
Schoenberg, Arnold   56, 80, 90, 102, 106, 116, 132, 146-147, 167, 172, 174, 178, 181, 190-191, 203, 227, 272, 318, 390-391, 393-395, 397, 399-401
   Chamber Symphony No. 1, Op. 9   203, 399-401
   Das Buch der Hängenden Gärten, Op. 15 116
   Die Jakobsleiter   394-395
   Erwartung, Op. 17   395
   Gurrelieder   116, 318
   Pierrot Lunaire, Op. 21   116, 172
   String Quartet No. 1 in D minor, Op. 7 399
   String Trio, Op. 45   80
Schubert, Franz   7, 29, 56, 88, 110, 194, 196, 260, 320, 377
   Alfonso und Estrella, D. 732   110
   Fierrabras, D. 796   110
   Rosamunde, D. 797   110
   Symphony No. 4 in C minor Tragic, D. 417   110
   Symphony in B minor Unfinished, D. 759   29, 110
   String Quartet in D minor, D. 810   260

Schumann, Clara   57
Schumann, Robert   57, 79, 109, 151, 272, 374
   Six Fugues on BACH, Op. 60   374
   Scenen aus Göthe's Faust   79
   Symphony No. 3 in E♭ major, Op. 97   151
Schütz, Heinrich   144
Schwarz, Rudolf   116
Scott, George C.   337
Scott, Giles Gilbert   61
Scott, Walter   112, 127, 129-130, 405-407
Scowcroft, Philip L.   34
Scriabin, Alexander N.   318
Sennett, Mack   355-356
Shakespeare, William   35, 56, 60, 62, 90, 114, 122-123, 139-141, 143, 157, 192, 222, 289, 331, 405-408
Shaw, George Bernard   69-70, 334
Shawe-Taylor, Desmond   93
Shelley, Percy Bysshe   56, 62, 71, 145, 198, 245-246, 407, 409
Shostakovitch, Dmitri   99, 153, 194, 342, 388, 390-392, 395-398
   Lady Macbeth of Mtsensk, Op. 29   396
   The Nose, Op. 15   391
   Symphony No. 2 in B major, Op. 14   396
   Symphony No. 3 in E♭ major, Op. 20 The First of May   396
   Symphony No. 4, Op. 43   390, 392, 396
   Symphony No. 5 in D minor, Op. 47   396
   Symphony No. 7 in C major, Op. 60 Leningrad   390, 392
   Symphony No. 8 in C minor, Op. 65   392, 396
   Symphony No. 9 in E♭ major, Op. 70   391, 396
   Symphony No. 10 in E minor, Op. 93   99, 153, 396, 398
   Symphony No. 11 in G minor, Op. 103 The Year 1905   396
   Symphony No. 12 in D minor, Op. 112 The Year 1917   396
   Symphony No. 13 in B♭ minor, Op. 113   392
   Symphony No. 14, Op. 135   397-398
   Symphony No. 15 in A major, Op. 141   392, 397
Shuker, Tim   227
Sibelius, Jean   29-30, 88, 103, 116-117, 148, 171, 175, 191, 217-218, 257-258, 261, 276-277, 318-319
   Finlandia, Op. 26   277
   Pohjola's Daughter, Op. 49   257
   Symphony No. 1 in E minor, Op. 39   116
   Symphony No. 2 in D major, Op. 43   116
   Symphony No. 3 in C major, Op. 52   116

Symphony No. 4 in A minor, Op. 63   148, 261
Symphony No. 5 in E♭ major, Op. 82   116
Symphony No. 6 in D minor, Op. 104   217-218
Symphony No. 7 in C major, Op. 105   203, 217, 257-258
Violin Concerto in D minor, Op. 47   116
Simpson, Robert   vii, 17, 21, 60, 96, 103, 105-107, 109-124, 137, 148, 165, 167-170, 173-174, 198, 234, 242-244, 304, 357, 379, 390-391, 395, 397, 401
Smetana, Bedřich   112
Smith, Mike   306, 342
Smyth, Ethel   277
Sondheim, Stephen   337
  A Funny Thing Happened on the Way to the Forum   337
Sophocles   155, 247, 411
Sorabji, Kaikhosru Shapurji   402
  Opus Clavicembalisticum   402
Spontini, Gasparo   411
  Olimpie   411
St Ambrose of Milan   133
St Augustine   133, 395
St Francis of Assisi   140
Stalin, Yosif   396
Stamer, Lovelace   63
Stanford, Charles Villiers   109, 318
  Shamus O'Brien, Op. 61   318
Starling, Neil   267, 302, 305-306
Stevenson, Ronald   91, 355
Stewart, Charlotte   38, 40, 49
Stockhausen, Karlheinz   137, 150
  Gruppen   150
Stokowski, Leopold   104
Storr, Anthony   77
Stradal, August   28
Strauß, Johann
  Die Fledermaus   340
Strauss, Richard   30-32, 37, 56, 63-64, 72, 115, 117, 132, 140, 143-144, 156, 168, 171, 173, 181, 190, 196, 259, 268, 283, 307, 316, 319, 333, 340, 342, 377, 382-383, 392
  Eine Alpensinfonie, Op. 64   161
  Ariadne auf Naxos, Op. 60   340
  Eine Deutsche Motette, Op. 62   30
  Elektra, Op. 58   30, 290
  Feuersnot, Op. 50   334
  Die Frau ohne Schatten, Op. 65   72, 140
  Ein Heldenleben, Op. 40   156, 175, 192, 327, 335, 342
  Metamorphosen   30
  Don Quixote, Op. 35   63-64
  Der Rosenkavalier, Op. 59   30, 196
  Salome, Op. 54   383

Stravinsky, Igor   56, 106, 155, 188, 190, 318, 343, 347, 349, 396-398
  Oedipus Rex   155
  Le Rossignol   334
  Symphony of Psalms   151
  The Rite of Spring   392
Strecker, Ludwig   106
Strecker, Willy   106
Sullivan, Arthur   110, 334
  Overture *Di Ballo*   110
  Overture *In Memoriam*   110
  The Golden Legend   318
Swedenborg, Emanuel von   140
Synge, John Millington   3, 22, 24, 65, 198, 206-207, 212, 249, 307, 409

Tallis, Thomas   187, 190
  Spem in Alium   132
Taneiev, Alexander   318
Tarshish, Bennett   14
Taverner, John   132
Taylor, P. J.   101, 103-104, 173
Taylor, Paul   408
Tchaikovsky, Pyotr Ilyich   46, 59, 102, 175, 303, 318, 333
  1812, Op. 49   82
  Fatum, Op. 77   104
  Romeo and Juliet Fantasy Overture   104
  Symphony No. 6 in B minor, Op. 74 *Pathétique*   173, 203
Tennstedt, Klaus   394
Tennyson, Alfred   43, 153, 406
Thomas Aquinas   136
Thompson, Herbert   127-128, 130
Thomson, James   405
Tilley, Vesta   355
Timlin, Robert   61, 83
Tippett, Michael   101, 115, 133, 154, 159, 189, 200
  A Child of Our Time   159
  Symphony No. 1   115
  Symphony No. 2   115
  Symphony No. 3   133, 154, 159, 342
  The Vision of St Augustine   395
Todhunter   406
Toller, Owen   101, 103, 173
Toscanini, Arturo   377
Tovey, Donald Francis   5, 13, 110, 260, 319, 334, 402
Trismegistus, Hermes   139, 146
Truscott, Harold   viii, xi, xiii, 3-33, 52, 77, 84, 88-89, 146, 148, 161, 173, 216, 243, 255, 343, 348, 355, 393, 405
  Piano Sonata No. 3 in G♯ minor   15
  Piano Sonata No. 5 in B minor   16
  Piano Sonata No. 7 in C   14-17

Piano Sonata No. 10   17
Truscott, Margaret   3-4, 15, 23
Turpin, Ben   356

Unger, Heinz   357
Ure, Adrian   xi, 340-341, 405

Valentine, Mrs   53-55
Varèse, Edgard   133, 167, 194, 392
   Amériques   133
   Arcana   194
Vaughan Williams, Ralph   xi, 9, 55, 73, 113, 116, 187, 191, 197, 223, 352, 392, 399, 411
   Hugh the Drover   113
   A *Pastoral* Symphony (Symphony No. 3)   245
   Sancta Civitas   113, 411
   A *Sea* Symphony (Symphony No. 1)   116, 203
   Symphony No. 4 in F minor   116, 392
   Willow Wood   277
Velikovsky, Immanuel   139
Verdi, Giuseppe   133, 154, 337
   Requiem   154
Victoria Regina   21, 43, 61, 85, 136, 340
Victoria, Tomás Luis de   378
Vignoles, Roger   342

Wagner, Richard   56, 64, 69, 73, 83, 104, 132, 140, 143-144, 150, 152, 174, 190, 206, 259, 269, 283, 293, 296, 306, 308-309, 318, 334, 342-344, 347, 382, 397, 399, 411
   Der Fliegende Holländer   206
   Der Ring des Nibelungen   64, 83, 174, 188-190, 192, 259, 306, 309, 331, 324, 334-335, 339, 342
   Die Meistersinger von Nürnberg   9, 174, 328, 335
   Huldigungsmarsch   411
   Kaisermarsch   411
   Tristan und Isolde   132, 293, 296, 330, 335, 377

Waine, Elijah   33
Walden, Howard de   278
Walker, Bertram B.   33
Walker, Ernest   55, 108, 290, 313
Wallace, William   43, 123
Walpole, Hugh   28
Walter, Bruno   149, 356
Walton, William   62, 115, 193, 288-289, 335, 392
   Belshazzar's Feast   62, 115, 288-289, 392
   Concerto for Viola   115
   Symphony No. 1   115, 193, 197, 392
Warlock, Peter, see Heseltine
Warr, Eric   17, 198
Webern, Anton   90, 227, 349
Webster, John   407
Weill, Kurt   106
Weingartner, Felix von (see also Beethoven)   13
Weller   405
Whiteside, Lillie   290, 314
Wilbraham   61
Wilde, Oscar   71, 316
Wilhelm II, emperor of Prussia   73
Williams, John   342
   Superman   342
Wilson, Colin   194
Wilson, Flip   147
Winterhof, Hermann   389
Wodehouse, Pelham G.   28
Wolfrum, Philipp   13
   Weihnachtsmysterium   13
Wood, Henry J.   312
Wordsworth, William   245

Yates, Frances   139-141
Yeats, William Butler   56, 153, 405
Young, George   411
Yule, David   194

Zhdanov, Andrey   391, 396
Zillig, Winfried   395